Handbook of Demonstrations and Activities in the Teaching of Psychology

Volume III

Personality, Abnormal, Clinical-Counseling, and Social

edited by

Mark E. Ware
Creighton University

David E. Johnson
John Brown University

D1560926

LEA LAWRENCE ERLBAUM ASSOCIATES, PUBLISHERS
1996 Mahwah, New Jersey

Lawrence Erlbaum Associates, Inc., Publishers
10 Industrial Avenue
Mahwah, New Jersey 07430

Library of Congress Cataloging-in-Publication Data

Handbook of demonstrations and activities in the teaching of psychology /
  edited by Mark E. Ware, David E. Johnson.
     p.   cm.
  Includes bibliographical references and index.
  Contents: v. 1. Introductory, statistics, research methods, and
history -- v. 2. Physiological-comparative, perception, learning, cognitive,
and developmental -- v. 3. Personality, abnormal, clinical-counseling, and social.
  ISBN 0-8058-1793-X (set : alk. paper). -- ISBN 0-8058-1790-5 (v. 1
: paper : alk paper). -- ISBN 0-8058-1791-3 (v. 2 : paper : alk.
paper). -- ISBN 0-8058-1792-1 (v. 3 : paper : alk. paper)
  1. Psychology--Study and teaching (Higher) 2. Psychology--Study
and teaching--Activity programs. 3. Psychology--Study and teaching-
-Simulation methods. 4. Psychology--Study and teaching--Audio
-visual methods. I. Ware, Mark E. II. Johnson, David E., 1953-
. III. Teaching of psychology (Columbia, MO)
BF77.H265 1996
150'.71'1--dc20   95-42447
                                                                      CIP

Printed in the United States of America

10 9 8 7 6 5 4 3 2 1

Dedicated to

Charles L. Brewer

teacher, colleague, and friend

Table of Contents

Preface

The history of teaching psychology is as old and as new as psychology in the United States. G. Stanley Hall, one of modern psychology's promoters, devoted considerable attention to the teaching-learning processes including the founding of the journal, *Pedagogical Seminary*, in 1891. In addition Hall (1905) examined the meaning of pedagogy and concluded that pedagogy aimed to "unfold all the powers of the individual to their maximal maturity and strength" (p. 375). In earlier writing about pedagogy, Hall (1881) commented that "reverence of knowledge for its own sake is superstitious. Ignorance is preferable to knowledge which does not affect life, and the object of discipline is to make it practical" (p. 321).

More recently, one committee at the National Conference on Enhancing the Quality of Undergraduate Education in Psychology discussed the use of pedagogical techniques authorities refer to as active learning. The committee's observation (Mathie, 1993) that pedagogy should "include strategies that foster critical thinking and problem-solving skills" (p. 184) seemed to reiterate and operationalize Hall's conclusion. Members of the committee also observed that "there is too much information being offered to students and too little attention being paid to the strategies for learning, inquiry, and problem solving" (p. 184). Thus for over 100 years, psychologists have recognized that effective teaching and learning consist of developing and applying students' skills. Because effective teaching strategies are never out of vogue, this book consists of a collection of tried and tested teaching demonstrations and activities.

Teaching of Psychology (ToP), the official journal of Division Two of the American Psychological Association, previously published all of the articles in this book. Since its inception in 1974, *ToP* has become increasingly respected as a journal devoted to improving teaching and learning at all educational levels. An article (Weimer, 1993) in an issue of *Change* featured three from among almost 50 pedagogical journals; *ToP* was one of those three. The year 1993 also marked the completion of two decades of publishing *ToP*. Those interested in a history of the journal will find the founding editor's (Daniel, 1992) personal account both stimulating and informative.

We organized 291 articles into three volumes. Volume 1 consists of 91 articles about teaching strategies for courses that make up the core of most psychology curricula; introductory psychology, statistics, research methods, and history of psychology. The topical headings in Volumes 2 and 3 reflect the order of topics in many introductory psychology texts. Volume 2 consists of 104 articles about teaching physiological-comparative, perception, learning, cognitive, and developmental psychology. Volume 3 consists of 96 articles about teaching personality, abnormal, clinical-counseling, and social psychology.

In general we assigned articles to courses in which authors developed the demonstration or activity. A table at the end of each volume identifies the primary course in which readers can use each demonstration. In many instances, we also identified other, secondary, courses in which readers might use demonstrations.

The percent of articles representing each of the 13 topical areas was about evenly distributed. Noteworthy exceptions with more than 10% of the total number of articles were developmental (14%), research methods (13%), and social (12%).

Curious readers might speculate about trends in publishing demonstrations and activities during each of *ToP*'s two decades. Inspection revealed that 62% of the total number of articles appeared during the second decade. The number of articles for developmental and social psychology showed the most dramatic increases. History and statistics were the only topics that showed a decrease in the number of articles. We can offer no unequivocal explanation for such trends.

We would like to acknowledge the assistance of several individuals who contributed to this book. Marianne Haindfield, Sergio deLourenco, and Paul Marchio from Creighton University and Beth Magallon and Blaine Hubbard from John Brown University provided dedicated and persistent assistance.

Mark E. Ware
David E. Johnson

References

Daniel, R. S. (1992). *Teaching of Psychology*, the journal. In A. E. Puente, J. R. Matthews, & C. L. Brewer (Eds.), *Teaching psychology in America: A history* (pp. 433-452). Washington, DC: American Psychological Association.

Hall, G. S. (1881). American and German methods of teaching. *The Harvard Register*, *3*, 319-321.

Hall, G. S. (1905). What is pedagogy? *Pedagogical Seminary*, *12*, 375-383.

Mathie, V. A. (with Beins, B., Benjamin, Jr., L. T., Ewing, M. M., Hall, C. C. I., Henderson, B., McAdam, D. W., & Smith, R A.). (1993). Promoting active learning in psychology courses. In T. V. McGovern (Ed.). *Handbook for enhancing undergraduate education in psychology* (pp. 183-214). Washington, DC: American Psychological Association.

Weimer, M. (1993, November-December). The disciplinary journals on pedagogy. *Change*, 44-51.

SECTION I:
PERSONALITY

Emphasizing Writing Assignments

Susan Mueller (née Susan Cloninger) described a method in which students wrote papers using different theories of personality to understand the published biography or autobiography of a real person. The instructor provided questions to guide discussion and written assignments that related text material to the term paper. According to the author, advantages of this method were its intrinsic interest to students, its breadth of scope within a liberal arts framework, and its effectiveness in fostering critical thinking and classroom discussion.

James Polyson had students write papers explaining the behavior of their favorite TV characters in terms of the theories covered in the course. Students interpretations included brief descriptions of the characters' specific words or actions that exemplified the concept from one or more theorist. The author described students' favorable reaction to the assignment and listed a sample of the programs and themes that students chose.

Janet Carlson's students wrote four short papers, each interpreting the personality of a fictional character from a comic strip or children's story by using a specific theoretical orientation; psychoanalytic, dispositional, phenomenological, and behavioral. The author discussed advantages of this technique as well as student evaluations.

Susan Beers developed an exercise in asking questions as preparation for writing essays. The goal of the exercise was to encourage students to analyze and evaluate personality theories. Students wrote questions that they discussed and classified according to Bloom's taxonomy. Twice during the term students chose questions to develop into essays and students discussed rough drafts of the essays in small groups. The proportion of evaluative questions that students wrote increased during the term. A questionnaire administered at the end of the term indicated that 90% of the students viewed the exercise positively.

To help them understand Maslow's construct of peak experiences, James Polyson directed students to write about their own experiences. An additional goal was to help students develop their writing skills. Although the author used this exercise in introductory psychology, it has direct application in personality classes. Student evaluations confirmed the activity was successful and pointed out some potential problems.

Instigating Miscellaneous Techniques

With the goal of increasing students' awareness of their own implicit theories of personality, Marlowe Embree had them complete an 18-item questionnaire about various issues in personality. The instructor completed the questionnaire four times, each time taking the role of a prototypical figure in personality theory (Skinner, Freud, Rogers, and Glasser). In class, the instructor compared student responses to the prototypes and discussed the class's perspectives on the issues.

Richard Logan described how he used "Three Approaches to Psychotherapy" as a case study for interpreting each client's personality from various theoretical perspectives. The author reported that students sensed that they participated in a dialectical process involving competing approaches to personality.

To encourage students to examine several basic issues of personality and to avoid confounding them with the wealth of theoretical and research details, Gene Bauer and Dale Wachowiak developed a debate format. The issues included questions such as (a) whether personality should focus on data-gathering or theory-building, (b) humans as homeostatic organisms or self-actualizers, (c) whether genetic or environmental determinants were more critical, and the like. Each author accompanied by one student argued opposing sides of the issues. The results from pre- and post-debate attitudinal measures on the issues revealed a complex three factor interaction. Students' evaluation of the debate format was uniformly favorable. The authors recommended several format changes.

Jane Einhorn designed an activity in which students used their own experience to develop a distinction between self and personality; the author characterized the former as more central and the latter as more peripheral. The instructor had students identify their favorite color, song, flower, smell, scene, person, and food. She then instructed students to identify whether each item reflected self or personality. Almost all students identified the scene as a reflection of self and the other a reflection of personality. The instructor also had students discuss which answers their best friends had known and which they had not. The results led to some interesting revelations.

Using a component of Kelly's theory of personal constructs, dichotomous templates, Mitchell Handelsman developed an exercise to increase students' abstract and relational thinking skills. The instructor identified personality concepts (e.g., id, ego, superego) and asked students to construe them, that is to identify how two of the concepts were similar to each other and different from the third, using some important dimension. Working in small groups, students construed several sets of three or more concepts. The author pointed out that such an exercise encouraged students to familiarize themselves more thoroughly with definitions of terms because of the exercise's challenge.

Allen Hess developed a "parts party" activity to promote student participation in his personality class. The instructor assigned each student to a different construct for a given personality theory. The students role played their constructs and interacted with one another. Afterward students discussed their interactions and associated feelings.

To facilitate the learning of theoretical principles associated with a psychoanalytic perspective on personality, Janet Carlson devised a board game called *Psychosexual Pursuit*. Student teams competed against each other to complete their psychosexual development while retaining considerable psychic energy to invest in adult concerns. The author described the rules governing play and special advantages of this learning experience. The article contains a reproduction of the game board.

Gordon Bear described a humorous slip of the tongue incident that afforded a vivid introduction to personality theories. Interpretations consisted of classic Freudian thinking, a contemporary psychodynamic perspective, and two cognitive models that view the slip as unmotivated.

Despite shortcomings in Sheldon's personality theory, William Davidson used the theory to assess a classroom exercise designed to increase students' understanding of Sheldon's theory. After the instructor described the three types of physiques, he had students identify friends who fit the physiques. Students read a list of adjectives describing each of three temperaments and assigned one of the temperaments to each friend. The instructor tallied the results and listed them on the chalkboard. Students who participated in the demonstration achieved a higher test score on Sheldon's theory than students who had not participated. The author described limitations of and alternative uses for the exercise.

Ludy Benjamin described a two part activity involving personality and psychological assessment. The instructor directed the class to identify 25-30 terms they associated with the construct of personality. The class limited the number of terms to the eight that were major components of personality. Working in eight small groups, one for each construct, students prepared two items to measure their construct. The instructor compiled the items and had each student administer the inventory to two students who were not members of the class. Subsequently, the instructor tabulated responses to the items. Discussion focused on gender differences, items that were supposed to measure the same thing, and items that failed to discriminate. Additional discussion items included reliability, validity, test construction, and the like. This exercise's original use in introductory psychology has particular utility in personality classes.

1. EMPHASIZING WRITING ASSIGNMENTS

Persons in the Personality Theory Course: Student Papers Based on Biographies

Susan C. Mueller
Russell Sage College

A method is described for incorporating student papers based on published biographies or autobiographies into an upperdivision undergraduate personality theory course. Questions are offered for the purpose of guiding discussion and written assignments, relating text material to the biography term paper. The advantages of this method are its intrinsic student interest, its breadth of scope within a liberal arts framework, and its fostering of student critical thinking and classroom discussion.

In teaching an upper-level undergraduate course in personality theory, I have wrestled with the discrepancy between the excitement I felt about theories and the insights they offered about myself and people in my life, on the one hand, and the much more abstract and lifeless version of the field that students seemed to be getting from the textbook. I tried to revitalize the course with supplementary readings, and although sometimes they worked and sometimes not, even the successes were too limited in scope to convey to students the transformation in understanding people, which I deemed the aim of studying personality theory. Of course, it is possible that my vision was not realistic for undergraduates in a first personality course; but I knew some of these students in other contexts and felt that they were capable of sharing more of my vision. The route must be at fault.

An experiential component was needed—an intellectual laboratory. Textbook abstractions are only a convenient summary of the concepts of a discipline whose value and truth cannot be established except in application. A variety of techniques exist for applying personality concepts to people, but I dismissed many of them as impractical or undesirable. The simplest technique would be selfexamination. After all, being a person oneself is an implicit course prerequisite, so that material is readily at hand. Introspective exercises and journals were a possibility—and I had used them with success in an elective course on "The Self." But such introspective devices are less suitable for a personality theory course, because many personality theories are centrally concerned with the issue of maladjustment, and self-diagnosis in the context of the class-room raises ethical dilemmas. What are we to do with the student who, rightly or wrongly, makes the self-diagnosis of, for example, an anally fixated, non-self-actualized neurotic? Teachers typically do not have the time or training to deal with the kinds of situations such assignments are likely to elicit.

An alternative, offered by many text writers, is to illustrate each theory with its originator's biography. Freud's oedipal conflict, Adler's conquest over rickets, and Skinner's disciplined life make fascinating topics for discussion. But this approach conveys the impression that a theory lacks consensual scientific validity. This intimation, repeated throughout the term, probably outlasts attempted antidotal lectures on experimental validation.

Another option is to require students to apply theories to standard case materials. One supplementary text available for this purpose is written by White, Riggs, and Gilbert (1976). While this approach avoids the worst pitfalls of the self-analysis and theorist biography methods, it risks the limitation that students may not readily relate to the particular biographical materials selected by the instructor. Without interest in the case materials themselves, the student experiences a dry academic exercise.

Another method, which I shall describe, retains the objective and integrative strengths of the case materials approach, yet avoids its tendency toward academic artificiality by giving students greater latitude to explore directions suggested by their own interests. My students write a term paper using various theories of personality to understand the biography (or autobiography) of a real person, living or dead. Theories become less abstract-tools for understanding, rather than dry conceptual schemes to be memorized. And because the target person is selected by the student, rather than assigned by the instructor, there is room for self-exploration in a manner less threatening, and less invasive of privacy, than straightforward self-analysis.

A wealth of material is available for this purpose, and the variety is enormous—from historical figures to current rock stars, from heroes and heroines to tragic and demagogic villains. In three class sections (from 1981 to 1983), 71 students have written on 58 different target persons. (See Table 1 for a summary of persons whom students have analyzed.) Though nearly all of my students at this women's college have been female, many (45%) have written about men.

THE ASSIGNMENT

Students are required to submit a term paper analyzing their selected target person, using concepts from a variety of theories presented in the course. The assignment has an explicit and focused aim of applying theoretical material to the understanding of specific individual lives. This concern with application, which I think of as highlighting "correspondence rules" for relating theory to observables, influences both the selection of material to be covered in lecture and the kinds of assignments made throughout the term. For example, in lecture, rather than simply explaining the concept of Freudian psychosexual stages and fixations, soldiers metaphor and all, I am compelled to describe traits commonly thought to be derived from various psychosexual stages. (The list provided by Engler, 1979, p. 55, is good for this purpose.)

I provide several directive questions throughout the term to facilitate the task of applying theories to biographies (see Table 2). Students write brief (one page) answers, and class discussions build on these interim reports. Because these reports constitute preliminary conceptualizations of sections of the term paper, students are obligated to work on the term paper throughout the course, and they receive feedback about their ideas from fellow students as well as from the instructor. This structure eases the student's burden at the end of the term and has substantially improved the papers submitted, compared with earlier terms in which no interim reports were required.

The course is organized around five paradigms: the trait paradigm, the learning paradigm, the psychoanalytic paradigm, the sociocultural paradigm, and the existentialhumanistic paradigm. Each paradigm is introduced with a lecture describing and evaluating the perspective. The text I currently use is Hergenhahn's *(1984) An Introduction to Theories of Personality*, which provides students with a highly readable and concise description of each theory, thus freeing class time for supplementary topics and discussion. I do not follow the order of the text because the modified progression described here seems more appropriate for the course as it is constituted.

Trait Paradigm

The course begins with trait theory, both because the concept of individual differences is a central issue in personality theory, and because the trait approach is more descriptive and less dynamic than other material, making it easier for students to apply without extensive background. I point out the historical logic of beginning here in honor of Allport's first personality course in this country. Students consider the relevance of this approach to the biographies they have selected by identifying two or three salient traits of their target persons, illustrating each trait with supportive details. Class discussion of the process of inferring traits as underlying dispositions from behavioral observations is enriched by the wealth of detail that students bring to the course from their diverse biographies.

Learning Paradigm

The next perspective, learning, follows logically since some of the behavioral observations considered by students in the trait perspective do not seem to them to be sufficient evidence to infer a general personality trait. Learning principles provide an alternative conceptual scheme, emphasizing current and environmental determinants. Social learning theory profits from a fairly thorough discussion of modeling, including reasons for the choice of a particular model.

Table 1. Persons Selected for Analysis by Students

Louisa May Alcott	Jill Kinmont
Lauren Bacall	G. Gordon Liddy
Elizabeth Blackwell	Anne Lindberg
Louise Bryant	Charles "Lucky" Luciano
Barbara Cartland	Helen Keller
Joan Crawford	John F. Kennedy
Salvador Dali	Henry Kissinger
Dorothy Day	Douglas MacArthur
Emily Dickinson (2)	Malcolm X
Babe Didrikson (2)	Margaret Mead
Walt Disney	Jim Morrison (2)
Eleanor of Aquitaine	Wolfgang Amadeus Mozart
Frances Farmer	Richard Nixon
Albert Fish	Lee Harvey Oswald
F. Scott Fitzgerald	Elvis Presley
Jane Fonda	James Earl Ray
Betty Ford	Carl Rogers
Anne Frank	Eleanor Roosevelt (7)
Sigmund Freud (2)	Franklin D. Roosevelt
Mahatma Gandhi	Lillian Roth
Judy Garland	Russell Sage
Kahlil Gibran	Edie Sedgwick
Barry Goldwater	B. F. Skinner
Patricia Hearst	Captain Slocum
Lillian Hellman	Elizabeth Cady Stanton
Katherine Hepburn	Harry Truman
Adolf Hitler (4)	Gloria Vanderbilt
Alice James	Maria Von Trapp
Janis Joplin	Shelley Winters

Note: Numbers in parentheses indicate number of students reporting on a given person (if more than one).

Psychoanalytic Paradigm

The psychoanalytic perspective as it is portrayed in most personality theory texts offers much abstract theory but little systematic help at a level that enables undergraduates to relate these concepts to observable manifestations. As mentioned above, I supplement text material with descriptions of traits characteristic of oral, anal, and phallic personalities, in order to provide continuity with the trait approach previously covered, and to show the relevance of psychoanalytic theory to normal personality. The biographical method provides a ready opportunity for students to seek evidence of trauma at the appropriate psychosexual stage in order to explain the adult personality traits they have observed. Several kinds of additional supplementary presentations are helpful and can be used as time permits. Dream interpretation is generally a high-interest topic for students, and provides an opportunity to consider symbolism and the language of the unconscious. Frequently, though, students report that no dreams are discussed in the biographical material they are reading. When students report on persons in the arts-for example, van Gogh—or persons who are or seem to be psychotic, there is an opportunity to use these materials as illustrations of the effect of id processes on overt behavior. Other biographies provide ready evidence of sexual inhibition or sublimation.

Table 2. Questions Assigned for Brief Written and Oral Reports

1. *Trait Paradigm:* Identify one trait that characterizes the personality you are studying. Argue either side of the "generality-specificity" issue, that is, the trait is *general* and enduring, or it is *specific* to a particular set of environmental stimuli and reinforcements. Give details from the biography to support your point.
2. *Learning Paradigm:* Describe some aspect of the personality that has been influenced by environmental reinforcements or conditioning. Explain this influence, and speculate how the personality might have been different if the environment had been different.
3. *Psychoanalytic Paradigm:* Describe the unconscious conflicts and contents of the personality. Give supporting evidence.
4. *Sociocultural Paradigm:* Identify the one most significant other (e.g., mother, father, sibling) in the childhood experience of the personality that you are studying. Describe the effects of this relationship.
5. *Humanistic Paradigm:* Evaluate whether or not the personality you have investigated can be characterized as self-actualized. Give reasons.

Sociocultural Paradigm

In the next course unit, dealing with the sociocultural paradigm, students consider significant others in the childhood experience of the individual. This issue is one that students find easy to address, and one they frequently raise on their own, even when I have omitted this question. An alternative discussion could focus on the cultural context as it influences personality, an issue that sometimes emerges, particularly in biographies of 19th-century women, where students clearly see the culturally limited options available to their selected persons. Within this paradigm, Erikson's developmental theory (which I have been sometimes tempted to omit because it is covered in developmental courses) is greeted enthusiastically by students, whose papers effectively use this approach, perhaps because Erikson's naming of basic virtues is concrete

and because the developmental perspective is well-suited to biographical material.

Humanistic Paradigm

Humanistic theories invite interpretations of whether or not the figure was self-actualized. The concept of "selfactualization" can be detailed with Maslow's (1971) oftquoted list of characteristics of self-actualized persons. But, because so few persons are self-actualized, a more thorough description of the earlier stages seems warranted. The biographical data often suggest particular obstacles to selfactualization that emerge from the cultural context or the particular environment, and this is an insight that has implications beyond the academic assignment. Students may also consider whether, and how, persons are able to transcend potentially limiting environments. The question raised by Anderson (1975), whether "self-actualization" is a purely scientific judgment, or a value judgment, is readily understood by students grappling with the task of judging whether their target person is self-actualized. (Student decisions sometimes surprise me; always, the discussion is lively.) This experience of separating the issue "Do I like the person?" from the question, "How psychologically developed is this person?" is also a potentially important learning experience for real life.

DISCUSSION

Significant amounts of history can be learned through biographical selections, and this helps break down the artificial walls created in academia among various disciplines. Students readily see that a particular trait manifestation must be considered in an historical context. They readily acknowledge the effects of economic depression, war, and cultural values as they attempt to understand their chosen target person.

I do not formally discuss in class the thesis that target persons are chosen for various psychologically determined reasons. That seems to me to violate the trust created by the assignment, taken (as it generally is) at face value. But clearly target persons are not chosen at random, as insightful students occasionally proclaim with excitement.

Because each student is an "expert" on the biography selected for intensive investigation, the passivity that is fostered by the model of teaching in which the teacher is the expert (cf. Mann et al., 1970) is avoided. Students have an opportunity to truly be the one in the room who knows the most about a particular topic, a strength similar to Aronson's (1978) concept of the jigsaw classroom, which encourages a climate of mutual respect. Brilliant scholars and mediocre students alike can contribute to the unusual community effort to glean interesting tidbits about "real people"—that Adolf Hitler was a vegetarian and a chocolate freak, that Joan Crawford cleaned what her maids overlooked, and so forth. The instructor is also a learner in this process. I have learned much from students about popular heroes and heroines, as well as traditional literary and historical figures, and the excitement that comes from mutual learning and teaching has energized all of us.

There is an important difference between the expertise a student feels through this assignment and the inflated overconfidence of a pedant. In my experience, students are humble in their interpretations and do not consider themselves to be expert personality analysts, either in this course or beyond. Perhaps the underlying theme of the course, that all theories have some merit but also significant shortfalls—a theme frequently repeated by allusion to the metaphor of several blind men each confronting part of an elephant—offers some protection. In addition, the incompleteness of any particular viewpoint is emphasized by the requirement that projects be comprehensive, including all perspectives. To some measure, humility may emerge naturally from the inevitable complexity of the task, in which biographical materials offer much of interest that defies definitive explanation by any theory, particularly when several biographies with similar apparent causes produce divergent outcomes.

The same complexity that protects from overconfidence, however, introduces another danger. The comprehensibility and applicability of theories may be too readily taken as evidence of the theory's validity (although lack of class consensus about which theories are useful mitigates this risk). A thorough discussion of scientific validation through empirical research seems particularly needed as protection against this danger. Perhaps an ambitious class could even frame hypotheses (or obtain them from lecture or research) based on various theories, and then test them, using their selected biographies as a database. (That might make a creative final exam question!) Obvious methodological difficulties would have to be acknowledged, but the exercise would be a way of stressing empirical validation, not simply comprehensibility, as a test of a theory's value.

One of the main benefits of this exercise is that it encourages students to talk about people, helping to restore the "person" to the field (cf. Carlson, 1971). It seems to me that this is a major strength of the per-

sonality theory course, as opposed to a course in personality research. The assignment is one that can be discussed with others outside the class—other students, parents (whether highly educated or not)—and thus it confirms an image of education as an enterprise that develops persons, rather than simply filling them with some foreign matter called knowledge. Although the course as I teach it maintains a rather traditional format, rather than a structurally innovative one (cf. Rogers, 1969), it does encourage students to spend much time and effort examining material of their own selection, and provides a forum for interchange of ideas with other learners. Most importantly, the major aim of a course in personality theory—to learn to view people with an educated vision—is extensively practiced throughout the term.

References

Anderson, W. (1975). The self-actualization of Richard M. Nixon. *Journal of Humanistic Psychology, 15,* 27-34.

Aronson, E. (1978). *The jigsaw classroom.* Beverly Hills, CA: Sage.

Carlson, R. (1971). Where is the person in personality research? *Psychological Bulletin, 75,* 203-219.

Engler, B. (1979). *Personality theories: An introduction.* Boston: Houghton Mifflin.

Hergenhahn, B. R. (1984). *An introduction to theories of personality* (2nd ed.). Englewood Cliffs, NJ: Prentice-Hall.

Mann, R., Arnold, S. M. Binder, J. L., Cytrynbaum, S., Newman, B. M., Ringwald, B. E., Ringwald, J. W., & Rosenwein, R. (1970). *The college classroom: Conflict, change, and teaming.* New York: Wiley.

Maslow, A. M. (1971). *The farther reaches of human nature.* New York: Viking.

Rogers, C. R. (1969). *Freedom to team: A view of what education might become.* Columbus, OH: Merrill.

White, R. W., Riggs, M. M., & Gilbert, D. C. (1976). *Case workbook in personality.* Prospect Heights, IL: Waveland Press.

Student Essays About TV Characters:
A Tool for Understanding Personality Theories

James A. Polyson
Indiana State University Terre Haute

Several studies have supported the idea that undergraduate instruction is more effective when the course content is relevant to the students' real-world needs and interests (e.g., Menges & Trumpeter, 1972; Solomon, 1979). One means of accomplishing that goal has been to use popular media presentations to illustrate concepts used in psychology courses. For example, Nissim-Sabat (1979) found the use of popular films such as *One Flew Over the Cuckoo's Nest* to be quite effective in helping students grasp basic concepts in abnormal psychology. Similarly, Maas & Toivanen (1978) used clips from the *Candid Camera* television show to demonstrate psychological and interpersonal phenomena in an introductory course. Psychology instructors also have employed media-related materials in participatory exercises. Riger (1978) described a useful exercise in which students conducted content analyses of sex role portrayals in various media. Solomon (1979) facilitated the learning of experimental methods by having students replicate the experiments used to sell products in TV commercials. It appears that students respond enthusiastically to the use of popular media in the psychology classroom.

The present paper describes an exercise in which students in Theories of Personality wrote brief essays explaining the behavior of their favorite TV characters in terms of the theories covered in the course. I had observed in prior semesters that students seemed to respond to my own use of TV characters as examples in lectures and the decision to assign the paper was based on that observation.

Method. The exercise was assigned in two consecutive semesters. In the first semester it was offered as an extracredit assignment. I chose not to require the paper at first because I was not sure how worthwhile it would be as a learning experience or how difficult it would be. The stated purpose of the assignment was to give the students a chance to apply the theories we had covered in the course up to that point (Freud, Adler, Horney, Reich, Erikson, Rogers, and Maslow). The maximum length was two typed pages. Students were told that the brief length would enable them to concentrate on the quality of their writing. They were instructed to focus on a specific episode of a TV show, to use the first paragraph or two to describe briefly the circumstances and plot of the episode, and then to explain in terms of a personality theory why one character behaved the way he or she did.

It was pointed out that all interpretations should include a brief description of the character's specific words or actions which exemplified that concept. Students could use more than one theorist if necessary. Finally, they were informed that after the papers were graded I would describe to the entire class the basic ideas contained in each paper and read excerpts from the best ones (unless the student requested that I not do so). Of the 38 students in the first semester, 20 completed the assignment and earned extra credit. No one requested that their paper be exempted from presentation in class. At the end of the semester participants were asked to complete an anonymous questionnaire that assessed whether the assignment had been worthwhile, interesting, and consistent with their personal goals for the course. An open-ended item inquired about any aspect(s) of the assignment the student liked and/or disliked most. In the second semester, the procedure was identical except that the paper was required. Of the 36 students in that class, two requested alternate assignments because they never watched what one of them termed the "boob tube.:"

Results. Student evaluations of the assignment were extremely favorable for both semesters. Of the 54 participants, 78% found the assignment "quite worthwhile" and 22% judged it "somewhat worthwhile." Not a single student in either semester judged it "not very worthwhile" or "totally worthless." Eighty-one percent found it "quite interesting," 19% found it "somewhat interesting," and again not a single individual marked that it was "not very interesting" or "downright dull." Almost all of the students indicated, that the assignment was consistent with their personal goals for the course. Results also show that 100% of all participants responded ayes" to an item asking whether the assignment should be repeated in future semesters.

An additional questionnaire item assessed whether the assignment had a negative or positive impact on the student's enjoyment of the program itself. I had been concerned that writing about a TV character might detract from what is undoubtedly a major source of recreation and entertainment for many students (Cosmetic, Chafe, Katzman, McCombs, & Roberts, 1979, p. 178). However, a majority (65%) of the present sample indicated that the assignment enhanced their enjoyment of the TV program, 6% said it detracted, and 30% reported that the assignment had no effect on their enjoyment.

Reactions to the exercise were slightly more favorable during the first semester. Ninety per cent of the students who wrote the essay for extra credit found it both "quite worthwhile" and "quite interesting" compared to 71% and 76% respectively when the essay was required. Again, however, the response was quite favorable in both semesters. It appears that some of the second semester students who might not have participated had the exercise been optional found it to be enjoyable and beneficial.

Discussion. Every student who participated in the exercise was able to find a TV character whose behavior in one episode could be understood through the application of personality theories. Twenty-eight different shows were represented among the 54 essays, with characters from *MASH* (7 essays) and *The Guiding Light* (6 essays) being the most popular. Other shows which were selected by two or more students were: *Archie Bunker's Place, The Odd Couple, Dallas, The Andy Griffith Show, Mary Tyler Moore Show, General Hospital, Dynasty, Too Close for Comfort, Happy Days, Little House on the Prairie, All My Children, Taxi, Benson, One Life to Live,* and *Alice.*

Almost all the essays seemed to be carefully written and every single paper contained at least one or two interesting, original ideas. Most of the students wrote about the maladaptive tendencies or defenses exhibited by characters like Archie Bunker, Felix Unger of *The Odd Couple,* Barney Fife of *The Andy Griffith Show,* J. R. Ewing of *Dallas,* and Nola Riordan of *The Guiding Light.* The students found no shortage of TV characters who evidence neurotic trends, psychosexual fixations, overcompensatory striving, defense mechanisms, or character armor. Characters from soap operas and evening dramas such as *Flamingo Road* seemed to offer particularly salient examples of psychopathology-related constructs. Examples of family conflicts also were available as students used Freud or Adler to explain the sibling rivalries on *Too Close for Comfort,* the pampering of Mrs. Ohlsen's/s adopted daughter Nancy on *Little House on the Prairie,* and the Oedipal overtones in one *All in the Family* rerun.

But there were also a number of papers which focused on the psychologically healthy behaviors of various characters. For example, one student argued quite effectively that Andy Griffith is an example of Maslow's self-actualized person and another discussed how the *MASH* character Hawkeye uses humor to sublimate his fear and rage about the war. One essay explained Private Judy Benjamin's enlistment in the Army as an attempt to break out of her neurotic trend of helplessness (Horney) and another excellent essay discussed how Mary Tyler Moore's organismic valuing process (Rogers) helped her decide between her job and her boyfriend. Even Archie Bunker, the subject of two essays about his underdeveloped social interest and projective defenses, was described in a third essay as exhibiting healthy rather than neurotic striving when he purchased Kelsey's Bar against the advice of friends and family. In addition, several essays contrasted a characters healthy versus neurotic behaviors.

Students' written comments indicated that one of the things they liked best about the assignment was simply having an opportunity to write about their own favorite TV character. This is consistent with a study by McKeachie, Lin, Moffett, and Daugherty (1978) who found that teaching is more effective when it allows students to express their own views and interests. Sharing their ideas with classmates also seemed to be an enjoyable experience. The class discussions were quite lively and several students wrote that the prospect of having excerpts from their paper read and discussed in class made them put more work into the assignment (which, in turn, probably made it a better learning experience for them).

The questionnaire data indicate that students did judge the exercise to be a valuable learning experience. An article by Vande Kemp (1980) argued that the use of case studies is an effective method for teaching psychological concepts. Case examples may be particularly useful for understanding the highly abstract constructs in many personality theories. Although I did not objectively measure the learning which resulted from this assignment, a number of written comments corroborated my impression that it stimulated their thinking and helped them learn the theories. Some students wrote that the assignment helped them prepare for the final exam because they had to review each theorist in order to decide which one best explained their particular character. Also, and perhaps most important, many students viewed the essay as an opportunity to apply what they had learned in class. The exercise was therefore consistent with a major theme of the course: Personality theories can be useful as well as theoretical.

For 65% of the students, writing the essay was not just a useful tool for understanding personality theories; it also enhanced their enjoyment of the TV program. Consistent with the findings of Riger (1978), it appears that television can be a more rewarding experience when students become active, thoughtful consumers rather than passive recipients. Considering the maladaptive functioning modeled by many TV characters, the benefits to students who apply an understanding of psychology to their TV viewing may involve more than enhanced enjoyment. Although research on the behavioral effects of TV has focused on children/s modeling of aggression (Comstock et al., 1979), there is growing evidence that uncritical TV viewing may have other possible detrimental influences on adolescents and young adults. For example, Corder-Bolz and Cox (Note 1) found that adolescent girls who accepted as realistic the romanticized love relationships on TV were far more likely to become pregnant. Although their study did not prove a causal relationship, there is cause for concern. One way of addressing that type of concern is to help our students learn to watch TV intelligently by applying the knowledge they learn in the classroom.

In summary, this was a very rewarding exercise for the students and for me, as well. I think that perhaps the basic reason for its success was the fun involved in writing, reading, and discussing essays which applied some of the classic theories of psychology to the popular characters of TV.

References

Comstock, G., Chaffee, S., Katzman, N., McCombs, M., & Roberts, D. *Television and human behavior.* New York: Columbia University Press, 1979.

Maas, J. B., & Toivanen, K. M. Candid Camera and the behavioral sciences. *Teaching of Psychology,* 1978, 5, 226-228.

McKeachie, W. J., Lin, Y. G., Moffett, M. M., & Daugherty, M. Effective teaching: Facilitative vs. directive style. *Teaching of Psychology,* 1978, 5, 193-194.

Menges, R. J., & Trumpeter, P. W. Toward an empirical definition of relevance in undergraduate instruction. *American Psychologist,* 1972, 27, 213-217.

Nissim-Sabat, D. The teaching of abnormal psychology through the cinema. *Teaching of Psychology,* 1979, 6, 121-123.

Riger, S. A technique for teaching the psychology of women: Content analysis. *Teaching of Psychology,* 1978, 5, 221 -222.

Solomon, P. R. Science and television commercials: Adding relevance to the research methodology course. *Teaching of Psychology,* 1979, 6, 26-30.

Vande Kemp, H. Teaching psychology through the case study method. *Teaching of Psychology,* 1980, 7, 38-41.

Notes

1. Corder-Bolz, C., & Cox, C. *Impact of television upon adolescent girls' sexual attitudes and behavior.* Paper presented at the annual meeting of the American Psychological Association, Montreal, Canada, 1980.
2. The author gratefully acknowledges Geoffrey Buck for his assistance in the preparation of this manuscript.

From Metropolis to Never-neverland: Analyzing Fictional Characters in a Personality Theory Course

Janet F. Carlson
Graduate School of Education and Allied Professions
Fairfield University

To enhance learning in a course on personality theories, students Write four short papers, each interpreting the personality of a fictional character from a comic strip or children's story by using a specific theoretical orientation: psychoanalytic, dispositional, phenomenological, and behavioral. Advantages and other aspects of this technique are discussed, as are student evaluations.

In structuring an entry-level graduate course in personality, I believe it important to provide fairly complete, balanced coverage of a range of theories. This approach exposes students to the broad conceptual strategies that constitute the field as well as to individual theorists within these perspectives. Several textbooks are organized by four or five such perspectives (e.g., Carver & Scheier, 1988; Liebert & Spiegler, 1990; Ryckman, 1989), making the task of providing balanced exposure somewhat easier.

Many students enter the course with a favorite theoretical perspective. Vyse (1990) noted that senior psychology majors and those who have completed courses in personality or abnormal psychology were "most likely to have adopted a theory" (p. 227), as 59% of the respondents in his study reported having done so. The entry-level graduate students who are the subjects of this article are similar to the psychology majors sampled by Vyse. They have chosen psychology as their academic focus and have had some coursework in related areas. Thus, it is not surprising that many of them declare theoretical preferences early in the course. Developing a particular orientation may be helpful in some areas of practice, but students in a course in personality theory are not yet deeply involved in service delivery. They should consider alternative theories to broaden their own horizons or, at least, to develop an appreciation of theories favored by professionals who may not share their perspective. Thus although textbooks offer broad coverage of personality theories, many students appear to need encouragement and direct experience with other theories to get out of their psychoanalytic, humanistic, behavioral, or other theoretical ruts.

To provide an experiential component to the personality theory course, Mueller (1985) assigned a term paper that applied one theory of personality to published biographies of real people. Mueller noted that this assignment made the theories less abstract. Logan (1988) described the use of a well-known, though somewhat dated, film series, *Three Approaches to Psychotherapy* (Shostrom, 1965), as a case study illustration of a variety of perspectives on personality. Similarly, Polyson (1983) suggested studying a television character's behavior as an effective method of increasing the relevance of the personality course's content.

Although these techniques have merit, they are limited in several ways. A single paper, such as Mueller (1985) and Polyson (1983) assigned on a biographical or television character, does not push the theoretically entrenched student beyond the comfort of the preferred orientation. The biographical assignment relies on secondhand accounts of an individual's life, unless the selected person has written an autobiography. Polyson's assignment is also limited by its dependence on a relatively brief portion of a character's behavior. Shostrom's (1965) film series illustrates the differences in therapeutic approaches stemming from theoretical differences, but observing the film does not require students to apply theoretical principles actively.

To address these shortcomings, I require a series of four papers, in each of which students analyze a character's behavior over time according to a specific theoretical orientation. The technique allows students to use firsthand information without eliciting the undesirable aspects of conducting a self-examination (Mueller, 1985) or an analysis of a family member or friend.

At the beginning of the semester, students select a fictional character from a comic strip or a well-known children's story as the subject. They are advised to select a character based primarily on their familiarity with and liking for the character, as they will spend considerable time analyzing the character's personality according to each of the four theoretical orientations covered in the course: psychoanalytic, dispositional, phenomenological, and behavioral. Without citing examples, I inform students that they may select people or animals who may be superheroes (e.g., Batman, Spiderman, and Superman), fictional but realistic characters (e.g., Tom Sawyer), fantasy figures (e.g., Alice-in-Wonderland, Peter Pan, Pinnochio, and Winnie-the-Pooh), or comic strip characters (e.g., Calvin, Cathy, Dagwood, Garfield, and Snoopy). Two or 3 weeks into the semester, I ask for confirmation of each student's character to be sure the characters are appropriate. Characters should appear in print, and the source should provide enough information for a credible analysis. Characters who say or do very little (e.g., Woodstock from the comic strip *Peanuts*) are difficult to use. Although the choice of character is left as open as possible, I do require that students choose characters with whom I am already familiar. Otherwise, evaluating the papers becomes difficult and prohibitively time consuming.

Students may apply a specific theory from the family of theories under study, or they may use concepts common to all the members of a particular orientation. The five- to seven-page papers are due at the end of each unit of lectures and readings on each orientation.

Students have been quite creative in their approaches to the assignment, both in selecting characters and in choosing a topic. Some have written excerpts from hypothetical therapy or testing sessions with the character. One student applied the dispositional perspective to Dagwood Bumstead, assembling a CIA dossier to assess his appropriateness for a job involving extensive travel and international espionage.

Evaluation

To evaluate the activity, I mailed a survey to all students who completed the course the previous semester. Directions indicated that the survey was intended to provide feedback to the instructor about the personality course and that respondents should not put their names on the forms. Preaddressed and prestamped envelopes were provided. Two follow-up letters were sent about 4 and 8 weeks after the first mailing. One survey was returned undelivered; of the remaining 18 surveys, 13 (72%) were completed and returned.

The survey included 10 questions that asked students to endorse or rank their preference for components of the course. Students rated these items on a 5-point scale ranging from *not at all helpful* (1) to *very substantially helpful* (5). On the two questions specifically addressing the papers, 10 respondents (77%) indicated that the assignments helped them quite a bit or very substantially in understanding the strategies covered in the course, and 11 (85%) indicated that the assignments helped them quite a bit or very substantially in developing a more comprehensive appreciation of the approaches used to conceptualize personality. In response to a question asking them to endorse those aspects of the course that had helped broaden their perspectives on personality, 12 (92%) students indicated that the papers had contributed to this development, and half of these respondents ranked the papers as the "single most important influence."

In addition, two open-ended questions asked about the best feature of the course and course improvements. In response, 6 (46%) listed the paper assignments as the best feature. Although no one suggested elimination of the papers or major modifications to the assignment, suggested improvements included requiring fewer assignments, grading less strictly, doing a sample character analysis as a class activity, and incorporating historical figures as potential subjects.

In previous classes, informal feedback indicated that students found the assignment appealing, as it provided an interesting challenge that contained elements of choice and creativity. The variety of characters has kept me interested and challenged as well. Students have said such things as, "This is the best way to teach this course" and "It's a lot of work, but you really do learn the material." Students also indicated that other components of the course were important in their learning. One survey item listed eight aspects of the course, and students indicated which ones contributed to their learning. All respondents checked three or more items. Thus, although the assignment contributes substantially to broadening students' understanding, it is just one component of a successful course.

Advantages

One advantage of this technique is that the experience begins early in the semester and extends throughout the course. Students apply knowledge of personality theories several times, and they must be fluent in more than one theory in order to do well in the course. Furthermore, students directly encounter the strengths and limitations of each perspective. For example, many students create fictitious therapy sessions to illustrate how a therapist with a given orientation would view the character's personality. Students discover this format works well for some orientations (e.g., psychoanalytic) but not for others (e.g., trait approaches).

Each paper requires a fairly complete analysis of the character's personality. Because I am familiar with the characters, I can readily note when some salient feature of a personality is overlooked. The focus of each paper shifts with the emphasis of the particular perspective under review. For example, for the psychoanalytic perspective the papers invariably center on intrapsychic events, whereas many of the behavioral papers emphasize observed actions. The assignment permits a deeper exploration of single theorists if the student is so inclined. Most students, however, have not found it necessary to go beyond the textbook, supplementary readings from a list I provide, and class lectures.

Limitations

If students are to profit from the feedback, it must be specific and returned promptly. I generally provide detailed written comments within 1 week for a class of about 20 students. Beyond this modest number, it may be difficult to give such timely feedback. The feedback should include how well the student applied the theory to the character and how well the character's behaviors illustrate this application. A modification of the technique may be feasible for larger classes, such as creating a single term paper with four subsections corresponding to each of the conceptual strategies covered in the course or altering the length of each paper.

References

Carver, C. S., & Scheier, M. F. (1988). *Perspectives on personality.* Needham Heights, MA: Allyn & Bacon.

Liebert, R. M., & Spiegler, M. D. (1990). *Personality: Strategies and issues* (6th ed.). Chicago: Dorsey Press.

Logan, R. D. (1988). Using a film as a personality case study. *Teaching of Psychology, 15,* 103-104.

Mueller, S. C. (1985). Persons in the personality theory course: Student papers based on biographies. *Teaching of Psychology, 12,* 74-78.

Polyson, J. A. (1983). Student essays about TV characters: A tool for understanding personality theories. *Teaching of Psychology, 10,* 103-105.

Ryckman, R. M. (1989). *Theories of personality* (4th ed.). Belmont, CA: Brooks/Cole.

Shostrom, E. L. (Producer & Director). (1965). *Three approaches to psychotherapy* (Film). Santa Ana, CA: Psychological Films.

Vyse, S. A. (1990). Adopting a viewpoint: Psychology majors and psychological theory. *Teaching of Psychology, 17,* 227-230.

Questioning and Peer Collaboration as Techniques for Thinking and Writing About Personality

Susan E. Beers
Sweet Briar College

An exercise in asking questions as preparation for writing essays was developed to encourage students to analyze and evaluate personality theories. Students wrote questions that were then discussed and classified according to Bloom's taxonomy. Twice in the term students chose questions to develop into essays. Rough drafts of the essays were discussed in small groups. The proportion of evaluative questions that students wrote increased during the course of the term. A questionnaire administered at the end of the term indicated that 90% of the students viewed the exercise positively. Having copies of others' questions and discussing rough drafts were rated as particularly useful.

One of the first decisions teachers of personality make is which of the many theories should be covered in a course. However, most of us would be sorely disappointed if, at the end of the term, students had only memorized the handful of theories we had chosen. The value of studying personality theories lies in the comparison and evaluation of alternative viewpoints, not in memorizing them. Because such reasoning involves complex skills, many students require support as they approach course material. I have attempted to offer such support by integrating questioning and the writing of essays into my course in personality.

Although many teachers encourage students to raise questions, question asking is not often formally taught. In the typical classroom, it is the teacher who asks the questions and the students who respond (see Dillon, 1984). Although a good deal of research has been conducted on the types of questions teachers ask and the types of responses questions elicit from students (e.g., Carin & Sund, 1971; Groisser, 1964; Sanders, 1966; Wilen, 1984), little work has been done on ways to help students themselves raise interesting questions. This is a pity as creative work invariably involves exploring the parameters of a question (Csikszentmihalyi & Getzels, 1970; Moore, 1985).

A variety of schemes have been proposed for understanding questioning (cf. Christenbury & Kelly, 1983). This exercise, and some others (e.g., Carin & Sund, 1971; Hunkins, 1976), relied on Bloom's (1956) taxonomy of educational objectives. Bloom's taxonomy includes six cognitive objectives: knowledge, comprehension, application, analysis, synthesis, and evaluation. Awareness of the taxonomy, it is argued, helps students raise thoughtful questions by making them familiar with the various levels at which questions may be asked.

Creative thinking may begin with a question and is often sustained through the act of writing. Current literature on the writing process emphasizes that writing does more than simply record thought. Writing is a powerful tool for learning: for discovering and developing one's thoughts as well as communicating them to others (Elbow, 1981; Flower & Hayes, 1981; Newell, 1984).

As interest in the writing process has increased, a variety of strategies for integrating writing with other classroom activities have emerged. One of the more popular is peer group collaboration, in which groups of students assist each other as they engage in writing projects. Although peer collaboration may not always be an effective substitute for teacher commentary (Newkirk, 1984), it does have the advantage of providing students with a known, rather than ambiguous, audience for their writing, and it encourages students to focus on the essentially communicative aspects of the writing process (George, 1984).

In the spring of 1984 I attempted to support students' efforts in thinking and writing by making question asking and peer collaboration in writing central activities in my course in personality. The exercise was designed to serve three purposes: to encourage students to raise questions, to help students become aware of different levels of questioning, and to encourage students to see writing as an integral part of the inquiry process. The course enrolled 28 students, most of whom were sophomore or junior psychology majors.

Description of the Exercise

Students were assigned to write three questions derived from class discussion, readings, or their independent thinking each week of the term, except for those weeks that essays were due or exams were taken. Each week, copies of all the questions were made available to each student.

During the first week, students received little guidance concerning the nature of the questions that might be written. They were simply told to write questions that would be appropriate for a good essay exam. Copies of that week's questions were returned to the students with a handout (Stano, 1984) listing Bloom's taxonomy and key words that might be found in questions in each of Bloom's six categories. Two key words for each category were as follows: knowledge—*state, list;* comprehension—*explain, identify;* application—*apply, demonstrate;* analysis—*compare, differentiate;* synthesis—*create, hypothesize;* evaluation—*judge, revise.*

Each student was assigned two questions (at random, without replacement) to classify according to the taxonomy. Class discussion focused on the utility of the taxonomy and the function of various types of questions. Students were quick to note that questions at the level of knowledge and comprehension might be appropriate when material was new or difficult to understand. They seemed to appreciate, however, that questions at the higher levels were more interesting. Students were encouraged to consider the questions that they had written and try to write questions one step higher in the taxonomy for the subsequent week.

Questions were categorized by the students four times during the course of the term. Their questions also served as the foci for lectures and were included on the exams.

The writing of three- to five-page essays served as the culminating activity for the question-asking exercise. Twice the class was divided into small groups to "look for interesting essay topics" in the questions that had been written for that week. Class discussion focused on what makes an essay topic interesting, and how one might begin to organize essays addressing the questions that the groups had chosen.

The essays also were discussed. Students chose topics and then brought copies of rough drafts of their essays to class. In that class meeting, students worked in small groups to read and discuss each other's work. The essays were to be revised on the basis of these discussions before being submitted to the instructor.

The process of question writing, categorization, discussion of rough drafts, and revision was repeated as students wrote a second essay. Participation in the question-writing activities accounted for 15% of a student's grade, as did each of the essays. The remaining 55% of the grade was determined by the student's performance on two in-class exams and a take-home final.

Evaluation

The proportion of questions classified in each of Bloom's categories during the four times students engaged in the classification exercise is presented in

Table 1. Proportion of Questions Classified at Each Level of Bloom's Taxonomy

Cognitive Level	Week 1	Week 2	Week 4	Week 9
Knowledge	.00	.00	.02	.05
Comprehension	.45	.31	.26	.45
Application	.00	.14	.00	.00
Analysis	.33	.33	.26	.19
Synthesis	.05	.05	.07	.02
Evaluation	.05	.12	.28	.22
Unclassifiable	.12	.05	.12	.07

Table 2. Student Ratings of the Usefulness of the Question Asking and Essay Writing Exercise

Component	Usefulness						
	1	2	3	4	5	6	7
Writing Questions	.05	.11	.05	.11	.16	.37	.16
Categorizing Questions	.05	.00	.10	.25	.25	.15	.20
Copies of Questions	.00	.05	.10	.05	.30	.25	.25
Discussion of Drafts	.06	.06	.00	.00	.28	.28	.33
Overall Utility	.00	.00	.10	.00	.25	.35	.30

Note. Based on a 7-point scale ranging from *not at all useful* (1) to *very useful* (7).

Table 1. These data should be interpreted with caution. Although questions were often discussed in class, no formal attempt was made to assess the reliability of their categorization. To the extent that the data may be trusted, they indicate that students wrote more questions at the evaluation level as the term progressed. Questions at the level of comprehension decreased early in the term, but may have increased later in the term.

At the end of the term students completed a questionnaire to rate the utility of each component of the exercise and the exercise as a whole. The proportion of students rating each component at each point of a 7-point scale ranging from *not at all useful* (1) to *very useful* (7) is presented in Table 2. Students' written comments were also solicited.

Table 2 indicates that the majority of students rated writing and categorizing questions as above average in usefulness (69% and 60%, respectively). However, a sizable minority rated these components as average or below average in usefulness. In the written comments, several students mentioned that they found writing questions useful because it encouraged them to keep up with the reading. Others mentioned that, over time, writing questions became routine. Although some students may have become bored with writing questions, 80% indicated that they found having copies of others' questions above average in usefulness.

It is my impression that the question-writing and categorization tasks had a number of positive effects. Question writing made for a livelier class than might have occurred otherwise. The majority of students clearly had at least skimmed the readings prior to class, and were "primed" to attend and to participate in discussion. In their written evaluations, several students categorized the class as a whole using Bloom's taxonomy, and one student mentioned that she categorized exam questions in another course before answering them. Although I have no way of knowing how many students transferred their knowledge of questioning from this course to others, it does seem that the categorization task helped at least some students to think about the nature of knowledge and learning more explicitly than they had previously.

Although I would not eliminate writing or categorizing questions from this exercise in the future, I am concerned about the students who found the exercise, over time, tedious. In the future, tedium might be reduced if fewer than three questions were required each week. Fewer questions would also allow time for more questions to be explicitly addressed in class meetings.

As indicated in Table 2, 89% of the students found the small group discussions of rough drafts to be above average in utility. The quality of their writing was probably facilitated by this component of the exercise, as it ensured that rough drafts would be written at least 2 weeks before an essay was due, increasing the probability of revision. Importantly, involvement in the writing of others seemed to increase students' interest in both course content and writing. Several students mentioned that they wished there had been the opportunity to read others' essays after they had been revised. Although students write essays or longer papers in all courses I teach, never before have students indicated an interest in learning from the writing of their peers.

Overall, 90% of the students indicated that this exercise was above average in utility. I also believe that, on the whole, the exercise was a success. Although I was a bit disappointed that the level of student questions did not consistently increase as the term progressed, it seemed most important to encourage students to become sensitive to questioning at a level appropriate to their understanding of specific course material. I think that this goal was accomplished.

In addition, reading students' questions allowed me to plan classes that would both interest and inform students. Although it was a bit disconcerting to be told often that I "wasn't needed" as I dropped in on the small discussion groups, it was delightful to see students actively engaged in writing and talking with each other about course material. And, most important, I read few dull essays. Rather, I read essays on "George Kelly's Unconscious Desire to be Sigmund Freud," "A Defense of Radical Behaviorism," and "Similarities Where One Least Expects Them: Freud and Rogers." Many were essays that made me think in new ways about theories I have taught for 10 years.

Moore argues that "the productive question is more important and often a greater achievement than the solution" (1985, p. 85). The exercise described here did not ensure that only productive questions would be raised, but it did encourage students to seek out interesting questions. Although the exercise seems particularly well suited to the topic of personality, it could be adapted to other courses that require students to address complex theoretical material.

References

Bloom, B. S., Jr. (1956). *Taxonomy of educational objectives: Handbook 1. The cognitive domain.* New York: D. McKay.

Carin, A. A., & Sund, R. B. (1971). *Developing questioning techniques: A self-concept approach.* Columbus, OH: Charles E. Merrill.

Christenbury, L., & Kelly, P. P. (1983). *Questioning: A path to critical thinking.* Urbana, IL: National Council of Teachers of English.

Csikszentmihalyi, M., & Getzels, J. W. (1970). Concern for discovery: An attitudinal component of creative production. *Journal of Personality, 38,* 91-105.

Dillon, J. T. (1984). Research on questioning and discussion. *Educational Leadership, 42,* 50-56.

Elbow, P. (1981). Writing *with power.* New York: Oxford University Press.

Flower, L., & Hayes, J. R. (1981). Plans that guide the composing process. In C. H. Frederiksen & J. F. Dominic (Eds.), *Writing: The nature, development, and teaching of written communication: Vol. 2. Writing: Process, development and communication* (pp. 39-58). Hillsdale, NJ: Lawrence Erlbaum Associates, Inc.

George, D. (1984). Working with peer groups in the composition classroom. *College Composition and Communication, 35,* 320-326.

Groisser, P. (1964). *How to use the fine art of questioning.* Englewood Cliffs, NJ: Prentice-Hall.

Hunkins, F. P. (1976). *Involving students in questioning.* Boston: Allyn & Bacon.

Moore, M. T. (1985). The relationship between the originality of essays and variables in the problem-discovery process. *Research in the Teaching of English, 19,* 84-95.

Newell, G. E. (1984). Learning from writing in two content areas: A case study/protocol analysis. *Research in the Teaching of English, 18,* 265-287.

Newkirk, T. (1984). Direction and misdirection in peer response. *College Composition and Communication, 35,* 305-311.

Sanders, N. M. (1966). *Classroom questions: What kinds?* New York: Harper & Row.

Stano, S. S. (1984). *Critical thinking handout.* Unpublished manuscript, Catholic Schools Office, Diocese of Erie, Erie, PA.

Wilen, W. W. (1984). Implications of research on questioning for the teacher educator. *Journal of Research and Development in Education, 17,* 31-35.

Notes

1. The preparation of this paper was funded by a Cabell Faculty Enrichment Grant.
2. I thank the students in Pyschology 218 (Spring, 1984) for their enthusiasm and support.

Students' Peak Experiences: A Written Exercise

James Polyson
University of Richmond

In an exercise described in this paper, undergraduate psychology students wrote about peak experiences they have had as a way of helping them understand Maslow's theoretical construct by relating it to meaningful events in their own lives. An additional goal of the exercise was to help students develop their writing skills. At the end of the semester, students completed an anonymous questionnaire assessing whether the assignment had been a worthwhile learning experience consistent with their personal goals for the course. Student evaluations confirmed that this was a successful activity; the course facilitated their understanding of Maslow's theories and provided an enjoyable learning experience. The exercise also encouraged students to integrate affect and intellect, consistent with Carl Rogers's views on the exploration of feelings as an important part of academic learning.

One of the methods Abraham Maslow (1962) used to understand what happens during a peak experience was to develop a composite picture of this phenomenon based on the written comments of college students. Maslow's procedure suggested the possibility of having undergraduate psychology students write essays about peak experiences they have had as a way of helping them understand the theoretical construct by relating it to meaningful events in their own lives. An additional goal of this exercise was to help students develop their writing skills.

THE WRITTEN ASSIGNMENT

After a brief lecture on peak experiences, students in three introductory psychology classes ($N = 122$) and one personality class ($N = 40$) were asked to describe a peak experience as vividly and accurately as possible. That is, they were to write an essay describing where they were at the time of the peak experience, what they were doing, how they felt during and after the experience, and what the experience meant to them then and now. Just as Maslow asked his psychology students over 20 years ago, the present students were asked to "think of the most wonderful experience of your life: the happiest moments, ecstatic moments, moments of rapture, perhaps from being in love, or from listening to music or suddenly 'being hit'

by a book or painting, or from some creative moment" (1962, p. 67). They were referred to Maslow's characteristics of a peak experience, which had been covered in the lecture, but were reminded that one peak experience is not likely to involve all the physical, cognitive, and emotional characteristics of Maslow's "composite."

The maximum length of the paper was two typed pages. Three grading criteria were announced:

1. demonstrated ability to apply Maslow's theoretical construct while describing and explaining a personal experience;
2. adherence to requirements such as length, and turning it in on time;
3. quality of the writing: Students were given a handout summarizing some of the major criteria for good writing in psychology such as conciseness, clarity, smooth flow of ideas, spelling, and grammar. In grading papers, I made brief notations, to point out writing problems and strengths.

Students were told that the brief length would allow them to concentrate on the quality of their writing; therefore, content and style would be weighted equally in the grading procedure. They were also informed that after the papers were graded I would read aloud some excerpts from the best papers, unless the student requested that I not do so. Perhaps due to the personal nature of the exercise, 28 of the 162 participants (17%) requested that their papers be exempted from presentation. Students were also given the opportunity to choose an alternate assignment of similar length and difficulty, but no one pursued that option.

At the end of the semester, students completed an anonymous questionnaire assessing whether the assignment had been a worthwhile learning experience consistent with their personal goals for the course. An open-ended item inquired about any aspect(s) of the assignment the student liked and/or disliked most.

STUDENT EVALUATIONS

Student evaluations corroborated my subjective impression that this was a very successful activity. When asked "How worthwhile was this assignment?," 65% marked "quite worthwhile," and 33% marked "somewhat worthwhile." Only 2% indicated that the assignment was "not very worthwhile" and no one checked "totally worthless." The students were also nearly unanimous in their approval ratings on the item "How interesting was the assignment?" In addition, a vast majority (93%) of the students responded "yes" to the item "Was this assignment consistent with your personal goals for the course?" and 96% marked "yes" to the question "Should this assignment be repeated next semester?" Perhaps the key item on the questionnaire from an instructional standpoint was "Did this assignment facilitate your learning of Maslow's theories concerning peak experiences?" Ninety-five percent responded "yes." Chi-square tests suggest that the exercise was equally effective in both courses.

DISCUSSION

The thoughtfulness and enthusiasm students showed during this assignment were impressive. Every student was able to write about a peak experience that demonstrated at least a few of the characteristics of Maslow's construct-the intrinsically good feelings; the total attentiveness in the here and now; the effortless functioning; the spontaneity and harmony with the environment; and/or the freedom from blocks, fears, and doubts. Most of the peak experiences had occurred during athletic, artistic, religious, or nature experiences, or during intimate moments with a friend or family member. There were a number of peak experiences in which the student achieved an important personal or collective goal. There were also peak experiences in which the student overcame some adversity or danger or helped someone in need.

In short, these essays presented a wide variety of happy, fulfilling experiences. That was a primary reason for the success of the exercise, according to students' comments. They enjoyed reminiscing about a joyful event and learning about others' happy experiences. Many students also liked the fact that the exercise involved creative expression in conjunction with scientific theory and they liked the opportunity to apply what they had learned. Several students remarked that this was the first time they had actually looked forward to writing a paper in college.

These written comments along with the questionnaire data show that writing about an important personal experience in order to understand a major theoretical construct was a very good learning experience. That is consistent with the finding by McKeachie, Lin, Moffett, and Daugherty (1978) that teaching is more effective when it allows students to express their own views and interests. Similarly, I found that this exercise enhanced my own interest in peak experiences. I became aware of how important these events are in the lives of my students, and I began to appreciate the richness of Maslow's construct. I decided to learn more about empirical research and practical applications involving peak experiences, especially in

the field of sports psychology (e.g., Ravizza, 1977). And I truly enjoyed focusing on such an optimistic topic in courses that frequently emphasize psychopathology and human problems.

Despite the overall success of the assignment, students' comments pointed out a few potential problems. A few students found it embarrassing to hear feelings being discussed in the classroom, and there were a few suggestions that the writer's name should not be mentioned during the presentation. These concerns emphasize the need for sensitivity and respect when discussing students' peak experiences. Not giving the names is a reasonable option; however, it might detract from the learning experience if the authors were unable to answer questions or discuss the experience from their unique perspectives. Furthermore, identifying the authors seems consistent with the principle of taking responsibility for one's views and feelings. In my opinion, the option of not having one's paper presented in class is a sufficient precaution.

A few students did not like being graded on this paper, even though I emphasized that it was the paper and not the peak experience that was being graded (by definition the latter would receive an A+). And there were some complaints about the emphasis I placed on writing as a grading criterion. I believe that effective writing is an important component of this exercise. I am comfortable grading and providing feedback to students about their written communication and it appears that a growing number of psychology teachers feel likewise (Calhoun & Selby, 1979; Klugh, 1983; Spiegel, Cameron, Evans, & Nodine, 1980).

As with any good educational exercise, there were some students who found this one difficult. Apparently there was little difficulty in choosing a peak experience but, as several students noted, it was hard to write about feelings. In fact, that is what I liked best about the assignment: It encouraged students to integrate affect and intellect, consistent with Carl Rogers's (1969) views on the exploration of feelings as an integral part of academic learning. In that respect, it may be possible to generalize the present technique to other topics and courses.

References

Calhoun, L. G., & Selby, J. W. (1979). Writing in psychology: A separate course? *Teaching of Psychology, 6*, 232.

Klugh, H. E. (1983). Writing and speaking skills can be taught in psychology classes. *Teaching of Psychology, 10*, 170-171.

Maslow, A. H. (1962). *Toward a psychology of being.* Princeton, NJ: Van Nostrand.

McKeachie, W. J., Lin, Y. G., Moffett, M. M., & Daugherty, M. (1978). Effective teaching: Facilitative vs. directive style. *Teaching of Psychology, 5*, 193-194.

Ravizza, K. (1977). Peak experiences in sport. *Journal of Humanistic Psychology, 17,* 35-40.

Rogers, C. R. (1969). *Freedom to learn.* Columbus, OH: Charles E. Merrill.

Spiegel, T. A., Cameron, S. M., Evans, R., & Nodine, B. F. (1980). Integrating writing into the teaching of psychology: An alternative to Calhoun and Selby. *Teaching of Psychology, 7,* 242-243.

Note

An earlier draft of this paper was presented at the Division Two Activities Exchange at the 1984 APA Convention. I wish to acknowledge the chair of that program, Joseph J. Palladino, for his helpful comments on that draft. I also thank Darlene Burbage for her assistance in the preparation of this report.

2. INSTIGATING MISCELLANEOUS TECHNIQUES

Implicit Personality Theory in the Classroom:
An Integrative Approach

Marlowe C. Embree
University of Wisconsin–Sheboygan County Center

In an attempt to increase students' awareness of their own implicit theories of personality, students in a Psychology of Personality course were asked to complete an 18-item questionnaire dealing with various issues in personality. The instructor completed the questionnaire four times, each time taking the role of a prototypical figure in personality theory (Skinner, Freud, Rogers, and Glasses). Student responses were compared to the prototypes as a vehicle for discussing the class's perspective on issues discussed in the course.

The notion of implicit personality theory (Bruner & Tagiuri, 1954) has played an important role in social psychology. However, it is largely ignored in many undergraduate-level treatments of personality. Perhaps one reason for this apparent discrepancy is the fact that, traditionally, implicit personality theories are thought to be very different from formal theories of personality. The former are thought to consist largely of expectations about interrelationships between traits (e.g., the expectations that a kind person will also be generous). These expectations form the basis of a theory of personality in the sense that they generate predictions about what people are like. However, the expectations are implicit in that they are not acquired through formal instruction and are not necessarily accessible to conscious awareness and analysis. In contrast, formal theories of personality consist largely of statements about wider issues in personality (e.g., processes of personality development). The statements and predictions of formal personality theories are articulated in precise terms, unlike those of implicit personality theory. Then, too, formal theories of personality are learned in the classroom, rather than being generated empirically in the process of social interaction.

Thus, it is difficult to integrate the notion of implicit personality theory into a course in personality, because the manner in which formal personality theories are usually treated in the classroom does not lend itself well to a study of implicit personality theory. In teaching the Psychology of Personality course, I have attempted to treat the notion of implicit personality theory in a manner that encourages students to evaluate what they think about the issues raised in the study of the formal theories, by structuring the course around a consideration of ways in which formal theories differ (based largely on the analysis of Hall & Lindzey, 1970). The demonstration discussed in this article represents one way of making these issues explicit.

Method

Subjects

Subjects were 10 students (those present on the day of testing, of 12 enrolled) in the spring, 1984 Psychology of Personality class. Although a sample of this size is of questionable value for research purposes, the results obtained were instructive and useful pedagogically.

Procedures

Students were asked to complete an 18-item Likert-type questionnaire. Each item consisted of a short statement about personality (e.g., "People frequently are not aware of the real reasons for their behavior"). Students were asked to rate the extent to which they agreed or disagreed with each item on a 7-point scale, high scores representing strong agreement.

As a basis for analyzing student responses, I completed the questionnaire four times, each time responding as if I were a key figure in the psychology of personality. The four individuals chosen, in an attempt to represent points of view prototypical of major theoretical orientations, were Skinner, Freud, Rogers, and William Glasser, the founder of reality therapy. This method enabled student responses to be compared with those of psychologists whose theories were presented in class. The 18 scale items, the four prototype ratings for each item, and the subjects' average ratings on the items are presented in Table 1.

Table 1. Prototype Ratings and Mean Student Ratings of the Questionnaire

Item Number	S	F	R	G	M
1. Because each person is a unique individual, there is really no point in trying to fit everyone into a single "theory."	1	4	7	4	5.5
2. It's more important to be concerned with what people do, not why they do it, if one is concerned with helping them to change.	7	1	1	7	2.2
3. Understanding how people view their own lives is very important in coming to an adequate understanding of personality.	1	4	7	7	6.1
4. People (e.g., children) really do go through "stages"; the stages are real, not just a way of speaking about behavior.	1	7	4	4	5.1
5. People frequently are not aware of the real reasons for their behavior.	4	7	4	4	4.5
6. A person must make a deliberate, conscious choice to change, or she or he cannot be helped.	1	4	7	7	6.0
7. If I wanted to know something about a person, I'd find it much more useful to have a personal interview with her or him than to look at some objective personality test results.	1	7	7	7	5.2
8. A person is the product of her or his environment.	7	4	1	1	5.2
9. If one understands adults, she or he will have no trouble understanding children.	7	4	4	4	3.1
10. The focus of therapy or counseling should be to change outward behavior, not inward thoughts or feelings.	7	1	1	7	2.0
11. People are usually quite consistent from one situation to another.	1	4	4	4	4.4
12. What people choose or decide is an important determinant of what they do.	1	1	7	7	5.7
13. Understanding people's motives and goals is an important part of helping them to change.	1	4	7	7	5.9
14. Formal psychological tests provide a complete, overall picture of personality.	4	1	1	4	3.2
15. Early childhood experience largely determines adult personality.	1	7	1	1	4.9
16. The current environment largely shapes what a person is and does.	7	1	1	1	4.3
17. The same general laws or principles apply to all people.	7	4	1	4	3.0
18. The notion of the "unconscious mind" is a very useful one in attempting to help people to change.	1	7	4	1	4.4

Note. S = ratings for Skinner, F = ratings for Freud, R = ratings for Rogers, G = ratings for Glasser.

Results

In order to assess student agreement with each of the four prototypes, "agreement scores" were calcu-

lated. Viewing each set of responses geometrically as a point in 18-dimensional space, a subject's agreement with a given prototype can be conceptualized in terms of the Euclidean distance between the two points (subject and prototype). From an extension of the Pythagorean theorem, this distance can be compared as follows:

1. Subtract the subject's score on each item from the prototype rating for that item, obtaining a difference score for each item.
2. Square each difference score.
3. Add them.
4. Take the square root of the sum.

To convert this distance to an index of agreement with the prototype, divide by MD (a number indicating the maximum possible distance between subject and prototype, as discussed later), subtract this value from 1, and multiply by 100. (MD differs for each prototype, being 24.372 for Skinner, 20.785 for Freud, 22.649 for Rogers, and 21.424 for Glasser.) The index of agreement can range from 0 (*minimal agreement with the prototype*) to 100 (*maximal agreement*). This technique, although less mathematically sophisticated, is somewhat akin to discriminant function analysis (Morrison, 1976).

Most students took a Rogerian point of view in the sense that eight of the students (80%) had a higher AR (agreement with Rogers) score than AS (agreement with Skinner), AF (agreement with Freud), or AG (agreement with Glasser) scores. The remaining two students could be classified as Freudian in orientation by the same criterion. Similarly, the mean AR score (56.7) was the highest of the four, followed by AF (49.3), AG (43.9), and AS (28.1). Looking at score ranges, one gets the impression that students took a dim view of behaviorism (AS scores ranged from 16 to 38), and they were fairly supportive of the other three positions (ranges from: 42-61 for AF, 48-67 for AR, and 31-62 for AG).

Another way in which these data can be analyzed is to look at the correlations between the scores. Two cautions are needed here. First, a sample size of 10 is inadequate for drawing firm conclusions from the correlation matrix. Second, because the scores are not statistically independent, to some extent a pattern of negative correlations between scores is unavoidable. Nonetheless, the pattern of correlations is interesting.

Given the fact that reality therapy was developed as an alternative to classical psychoanalysis (see Glasser, 1975), it is interesting to note that AG and AF scores are negatively correlated ($r = -.64$, $p < .05$). Conversely, AG and AR scores are positively correlated ($r = .66$, $p < .05$), a relationship that may reflect the fact that Glasser and Rogers would probably agree on many of the issues covered by the questionnaire (but not necessarily on other issues, e.g., the extent to which therapy should be directive). No other correlations were significant.

Discussion

These results were presented to the students in class. Two general points were made: first, the class as a whole had some definite points of view concerning the formal theories discussed in class (favoring phenomenology and largely discounting behaviorism); second, there was some internal consistency in student responses (endorsing one view necessitated rejecting others).

It would be of interest to use this or a similar questionnaire as a before-after tool to see if student responses are substantially modified as a result of exposure to course material. Of course, there is the danger that students would be unable to respond meaningfully to the questionnaire before taking the class. However, the questionnaire items deliberately avoid formal terminology, possibly circumventing this problem.

Perhaps the major pedagogical advantage of the questionnaire is that it alerts the students to the fact that they do have opinions—sometimes very decided ones—about the very issues that have traditionally divided personality theorists. From a theoretical perspective, it is significant that implicit personality theory is often viewed in a relatively narrow sense (in terms of perceived interrelationships between traits rather than unarticulated abstract propositions about personality). Schneider (1973) notes that "there has been an emphasis on the dimensional aspect of trait similarities to the relative exclusion of questions concerning the content and dynamic qualities of implicit personality theory" (p. 307). This may account for the fact that implicit personality theory is not widely incorporated into the classroom teaching of the psychology of personality. This study is a small step toward integrating a broader view of implicit personality theory into the classroom presentation of formal theories of personality.

References

Bruner, J. S., & Tagiuri, R. (1954). The perception of people. In G. Lindzey (Ed.), *Handbook of social psychology* (Vol. 2, pp. 634-654). Cambridge, MA: Addison-Wesley.

Glasser, W. (1975). *Reality therapy: A new approach to psychiatry.* New York: Harper & Row.

Hall, C. S., & Lindzey, G. (1970). *Theories of personality* (2nd ed.). New York: Wiley.

Morrison, D. F. (1976). *Multivariate statistical methods* (2nd ed.). New York: McGraw-Hill.

Schneider, D. J. (1973). Implicit personality theory: A review. *Psychological Bulletin, 79,* 294-309.

Using a Film as a Personality Case Study

Richard D. Logan
Development of Human Development
University of Wisconsin—Green Bay

This article describes how I use the well-known film series, Three Approaches to Psychotherapy, *which was created to demonstrate different approaches to psychotherapy, as a case study for interpreting the filmed client's personality from various theoretical perspectives.*

While taking a testing course in the 1960s, I learned how the Wechsler Adult Intelligence Scale can also serve as a diagnostic projective technique. Since then, I have tried to find psychological materials that can be used for purposes other than their original one. In particular, I am always looking for theoretically unbiased, case-study materials for students in my theories of personality course. The search is frustrating. For example, written case histories usually reflect the author's own theoretical inclination. Especially when they are used to illustrate different theoretical perspectives, such materials should not be biased toward or against any viewpoint.

The three-part film series *Three Approaches to Psychotherapy* (Shostrom, 1965), features Carl Rogers, Fritz Perls, and Albert Ellis giving demonstrations of their respective approaches to therapy with an actual client. The film series apparently saves its purpose of introducing different approaches to psychotherapy, judging by its long use in counseling, therapy, and adjustment courses. The purpose of the three films is to illustrate different versions of the therapeutic process. However, over the course of the sessions, the client (Gloria) provides a great deal of information about her life and character that invites interpretation for another purpose. This information is not filtered through constructs of a case-study author, although Rogers, Perls, and Ellis do exert some constraining influence. Therefore, these films lend themselves to an assignment in which students are asked to make and support different theoretical interpretations of Gloria's personality.

I use the film series in my course on theories of personality, the textbook for which is Rychlak's (1981) *Introduction to Personality and Psychotherapy.* I show the segment with Rogers counseling Gloria as we begin studying Rogers's theory and after we study Freud, Adler, Jung, Sullivan, Dollard and Miller, and Skinner, in that order. I divide the class into six small groups. Each group views the film and interprets the client's personality or behavior from a particular theoretical perspective. Each group then describes for the class the significant themes its members observed from their assigned theoretical viewpoint. The suitability of the film for this exercise is borne out by the fact that students are able to present thorough interpretations from each perspective. The Freudian group sees a panoply of traits characteristic of an unresolved Oedipus complex; the Adlerians see a neurotic overstriving for perfection; the Jungians see a wrestling with the unconscious shadow complex and faces of the anima and animus; the Sullivanians see indications of a dissociated sexual/angry self; and the Dollard and Miller group sees a powerful approach-avoidance conflict surrounding sex, men, and father. I ask the Skinnerian group to observe the interaction between client and therapist; they usually make some interesting observations about how Rogers may be shaping Gloria's behavior—and vice versa—with various social reinforcers, such as smiling, nodding, and saying "mm-hmm." If time permits, I show the entire series, including Perls and Ellis as well as Rogers, and all three sessions become the material for personality interpretation.

Because the film series portrays realistic therapeutic sessions, students feel that they are participating in a dialectical process involving competing approaches to personality theory. The exercise also serves as preparation for the take-home final exam, which requires students to write several extensive theoretical interpretations of a lengthy case study. The exercise also helps to emphasize the important point that there is no one path to the truth in the field of personality theory.

References

Rychlak, J. F. (1981). *Introduction to personality and psychotherapy.* New York: Houghton-Mifflin.

Shostrom, E. L. (Producer and Director). (1965). *Three approaches to psychotherapy* [Film]. Santa Ana, CA: Psychological Films.

The Home-Court Advantage:
A Debate Format for the Teaching of Personality

Gene Bauer and
Dale Wachowiak
University of North Carolina at Charlotte

Students given the opportunity to listen to formal debates between professors show high motivation and sharpened critical thinking

The teaching of Personality courses at an undergraduate level within colleges and universties typically follows one of two basic formats The professor may take a Hall and Lindsey approach to the task This smorgasbord or survey type of course involves introducing the student to ten to twelve major personality theorists, the important tenets of their theories and the research that has been generated in support of the various theories Another popular approach to the teaching of personal By is the "selected topics" approach This type of course structure involves focusing upon research developments bearing on topics such as anxiety, intelligence, aggression, sexual behaviom etc.

It was after having participated in such courses as both students and teachers for several semesters that both of us began to share frustrations with the traditional modes of Caching Atonality Foremost among these frustrations was the general difficulty involved in sensitizing the student to the relationships between theory, research and the establishment or acceptance of certain suppositions about human nature as fact or truth Related to this development was a desist as instructors to familiarize students with the central issues that confront personality theorists When both authors were assigned to teach a separate section of personality during the same semester, the time seemed ripe for some sort of collaborative effort. It is our intention in this paper to present an innovation that we have included in our introductory Personality courses at the University of North Carolina at Charlotte.

An Issue-Oriented Approach. All personality theories adopt a particular stance with regard to certain basic assumptions about the nature of man. Moreover, people in general, when dealing with themselves and others, assume a stance with regard to these same issues.

Hjelle and Ziegler (1976) see the following as the basic questions: (a) To what extent is man capable of free choice? (b) If man is not free, to what extent is he determined by constitutional factors versus environmental controls? (c) To what extent is man a rational (conscious) organism? (d) Is man basically are actor or does he act upon his environment in a proactive fashion? (e) Is man driven by homeostatic, drive-reduction principles or does he seek to grow in a self-actualizing manner? (f) Is man capable of being broken down into component elements or is the whole the only appropriate object of study? (g) Is man knowable through scientific study? (h) Can such studies remain objective or is man only to be understood from a subjective frame of reference? We felt that by organizing a course around such basic issues, students would be forced to examine, if not change, their implicit assumptions. They would also be forced to confront the ambiguity inherent in the study of man's nature. The question was what course design would prevent the issues from being clouded over by theoretical details?

The Debate Format. We concluded that the best vehicle for displaying the basic issues and for revealing the controversial nature of the field would be the formal debate. We, therefore, agreed that in each of our classes, throughout the semester, we would stage seven debates.

Our choice of debate topics represented a modification of the Hjelle and Ziegler list, in the direction of eliminating those issues which might prove too methodologically or philosophically esoteric for undergraduates, and incorporating several issues which might increase student interest.

The first debate topic dealt with the issue of whether the psychology of personality should focus upon data-gathering vs. theory-building. It was hoped that this initial debate would allow for a discussion of the roles theories play, the methods in which data and theories interact, and the radical behaviorist's opposition to theory construction. The second debate centered upon the controversy surrounding the existence of an unconscious. This debate allowed for an exposition of the Freudian position and the problems inherent in attempting to find empirical support for a theoretical construct. Man as a homeostatic organism vs. man the self-actualizer served as the topic of the third debate. This debate allowed for the introduction of certain humanistic objections to drive-reduction conceptions. The fourth and fifth debates focused upon classic issues: whether man is free or determined and whether genetic or environmental determinants are more critical. The last two topics selected, though not central issues to all personality theorists, were of interest to the authors and had stimulated much discussion among students in earlier classes. The sixth debate dealt with objective and normative vs. projective and idiographic methods of personality assessment. We felt these issues provided a pragmatic opportunity for getting at Allport's idiographic-nomothetic division. The final debate was concerned with the effectiveness of psychotherapy in producing personality change.

Prior to the first week of classes, we agreed upon the side of each debate each would present. In order to provide some sort of consistency, the first author agreed to support the "hard-headed" side of each debate topic: e.g., the psychology of personality should focus on data gathering, there is no unconscious, man is a homeostatic organism, etc. The second author presented the "soft-headed" side of the debate topics. In order to allow for student participation, each author recruited one student to assist in the preparation and presentation of his side of the debate. To reinforce student participation, an otherwise required paper or oral report was waived for the students who chose to become involved in the debates.

Each debate was presented once in Professor A's class and once in Professor B's class. The format of the debate hour was setup so that during the first ten minutes, student A, from the class of Professor A, would present arguments in support of thesis one of the issue being debated. This would be followed by student B's ten minute presentation of thesis two of the same issue. Professor A would then provide additional support for student A's thesis as well as rebut the arguments presented by student B. Professor B would follow with support of his student's arguments and attack the arguments espoused by Professor A and his student. The remaining ten minutes of each debate class period was set aside for a question and answer period. During the final minutes of the hour, the class was then asked to show their support by voting for one of the theses of the debate topic.

Outcome and Evaluation. First of all, anyone intending to become involved in such a debate format must be ready and willing to lose. There is a distinct home-court advantage! Of the six topics or 12 presentations completed (the idiographic-nomothetic argument was dropped for lack of time in the semester), only twice did one side win in front of the other professor's students. Fortunately, neither professor's self-esteem is highly dependent on his forensic abilities (although one did find a few of the other's debate tactics a bit irksome).

Table 1
Pre-Post Debate Means and Standard Deviations for the Six Issues

		Professor A's Class		Professor B's Class	
		Pre-	Post-	Pre-	Post-
Theory vs. Research	M	2.97	3.84	2.70	2.44
	SD	1.26	1.00	.97	1.03
	N	38	32	33	29
The Unconscious	M	1.42	1.41	1.40	2.03
	SD	.62	.97	.69	1.30
	N	38	31	33	29
Homeostasis vs. Heterostasis	M	4.02	4.16	3.63	3.16
	SD	1.09	1.07	1.43	1.17
	N	38	26	33	24
Heredity vs. Environment	M	3.89	3.60	4.15	3.96
	SD	.96	1.28	.78	.86
	N	38	30	33	31
Free Will vs. Determinism	M	2.36	1.85	2.85	3.03
	SD	1.04	.96	1.05	2.19
	N	38	27	33	30
Psychotherapy	M	2.05	1.96	2.45	2.44
	SD	.85	1.37	.81	1.22
	N	38	29	33	27

Attitude Assessment. To evaluate the debates beyond the voting to determine the winners, students were asked to assess attitudes toward each of the issues on a five-point rating scale. These ratings were made during the first and last weeks of class.

The pre-debate measures provided some indications of the classes' views on various theories of personality. At the outset, the classes tended toward a conception of people as self-actualizing, environmentally-determined, yet basically free organisms with an unconscious and the potential to be changed by psychotherapy. There was relatively little variation either between classes or within classes on these pre-debates ratings.

Did the debate-styled course have any effect on these basic assumptions? The pre- and post-debate mean ratings by class are presented in Table 1. It can be seen by examining the results that no *dramatic* shifts in opinion were produced. However, a 2 x 2 x 6 (Instructor X Pre-Post x Issues) analysis of variance performed on these ratings does indicate that the debate approach did produce statistically significant shifts in certain assumptions (See Table 2). The significant interaction effects would indicate that the degree of attitude change is dependent upon both the issues in question and the instructor to whom the student is regularly exposed. Professor A's students became significantly more theoretical and hereditarian, while Professor B's class became significantly more homeostatic in orientation and skeptical about the existence of an unconscious. These changes were all in the direction of the stances taken by their own professors.

Course Evaluation. On the assessment blanks obtained during the last week of c lass, the students were a also asked to indicate on a I-5 rating scale the extent to which the debates contributed to their understanding and enjoyment of the course. It can be seen from Table 3 that these ratings were uniformly high. The students were also asked to reflect upon the good and bad aspects of the debate format. On the positive side, most students found the debates fun and informative. They appreciated the opportunity to weigh the evidence simultaneously for both sides of each issue.

Table 2
Table of the Analysis of Variance For Teachers, Pre-Post Measures and Issues

Source	df	SS	MS	F
Teacher = A	1	5.2	5.2	5.31*
Pre-Post = B	1	73.62	73.62	75.12**
Issues = C	5	511.84	102.92	105.02**
A X B	1	7.37	7.37	7.52**
A X C	5	75.57	15.12	15.43**
B X C	5	39.49	7.90	8.06**
A X B X C	5	13.16	2.63	2.68*
Error	762.96	747.55	.98	

*$p < .05$
**$p < .01$

Table 3
Means and Standard Deviations for Course Evaluation Items

Item		Professor A	Professor B
Understanding	M	4.27	3.70
	SD	.86	.96
	N	33	33
Enjoyment	M	4.48	4.06
	SD	.74	.88
	N	33	33

Some reported that the debates forced them to make use of research tools while being involved in a process which brought out facts which would not normally be brought out in class. On the negative side, the most common complaint was that the debates were too rushed and that not enough time was available for questions and answers which might aid the assimilation of the knowledge presented. Some students also felt that the debaters resorted to too many emotional tactics. On the whole, however, most students felt that the debates were a distinctive and positive innovation.

Conclusions and Future Plans We found the debate format to be a productive learning device in an under-graduate personality course. It induced both students and professors to examine the issues underlying all theories and to synthesize research evidence into a coherent and convincing argument. This process forced the development of research and argumentation skills. Such a public examination of personal beliefs seems to facilitate attitude change besides contributing to course enjoyment and an understanding of the basic issues.

We plan to make several format changes in the coming semester: The course lectures and readings will be organized about the issues; students will be involved in either researching, writing, or presenting the debates through the use of a team approach. The evaluation of the debate presentations will be done by independent judges in accord with methods commonly found in formal debates. However, the entire debate process will not be turned over to the students. The professors will still be involved in the debate presentation. It was clear that the opportunity to watch their professors dodging the verbal slings and arrows of each other was a novelty which aroused student interest and sharpened critical thinking.

Reference

Hjelle, H. J., & Ziegler, D. J. *Personality theories: Basic assumptions, research, and applications.* New York: McGraw-Hill, 1976.

Note

This article is based upon a paper presented at the convention of the American Psychological Association. Washington, DC. 1976.

Teaching Personality: Discovering the Difference Between Self and Personality

Jane Einhorn
Union County College

In teaching a course in personality, it is often very difficult to convey to the students the key difference between the self and personality. The students' difficulties are mirrored by psychologists themselves, who also disagree about the distinction. My own conclusion is that the telling difference between the two concepts lies in the centrality of the characteristics. That is, the self presents itself as the central and (although growth is possible) practically immutable core, but the personality is more peripheral and fluctuating in its reaching out toward others.

My method of communicating this to students is by inductive, particularistic reasoning. In that way, I need not present them with a predigested distinction that they will readily forget. Instead, they were asked to draw out the difference between self and personality from their own experience. It was then easy to compare their several ways of looking at this for the class, and the principal difference of the centrality of the concepts could then be clearly seen. They were asked to write down their favorite color, song, flower, smell, scene, person, and food. After having completed the list, they were to go back and indicate for each choice whether it reflected their self or their personality.

I expected that of all seven terms, it would be "scene" that most reflected the self. This was true for most of my 25 students. A peaceful ocean scene was most frequently cited, as if in its peace and seclusion we are alone with our "selves."

According to the students, color is not always a reflection of our self because it sometimes is related to the way we relate to the world, as in our choice of color in clothing. Favorite food was selected as a key to personality rather than self. It expressed something about the individual. Favorite person seemed to reflect both personality and self, and the other items were evenly split between self and personality.

The stated purpose of this class exercise was to have each student discover the difference between self and personality, and it accomplished its purpose. Some of the students' definitions of self were, "true inner feelings," "my real sense of being," "me as an individual," "everything that is close and significant to me," "self is something that has been part of me as long as I can remember," "things that reflect an integral part of me," and the part of you that "doesn't change."

Personality, on the other hand, was defined as "something that changes with exposure," "aspects of my being . . . more directly influenced by my environment," "changes with time and moods," "how you act and what you reveal," "capable of change and more outward," "things a little further removed," and finally, "I don't have separate identity in my personality, I seem to try to fit the mold."

These definitions of self and personality were derived by the students after having compared those topics on which they answered "self" to those on which they answered "personality." As an additional step, the students were asked to go back to the list and indicate which answers their best friend knows about and which they don't know about. After appraising their own answers, I got such diverse responses as, on the one hand, "My personality can be picked up by an acquaintance, only your best friend knows the real you," and, on the other, "It seems that I have not even let my best friend in close enough to know. my deepest thoughts."

It should be noted that the students' excitement in participating in this exercise was reflected in one student's statement upon discovering for herself the difference between self and personality: "This is all very exciting; I actually got goose pimples."

Abstract and Relational Thinking via Personal Constructs

Mitchell M. Handelsman
University of Colorado at Denver

When concepts are taught in class, they are usually introduced with a definition and embellished with one or more examples. Often, however, the relationships among concepts are not pursued directly. Several problems result. First, students do not learn how to think abstractly and hence to relate concepts to each other. Second, students get concept definitions and examples confused. For example, they may define the superego as "when you feel guilty about having premarital sex." Third, students feel frustrated when they are asked to relate concepts on the test if they have not been shown how to do this during class periods.

The exercise described here is designed to address these concerns. It is based on Kelly's (1955) theory of personal constructs. Constructs, for Kelly, are dichotomous templates that people use to interpret and anticipate their experience. People abstract relevant features of events, objects, and people, and use these dimensions to "construe" similarities and differences among elements of experience. For example, the construct "tall versus short" can be used to appreciate the similarity, along that dimension, between Wilt Chamberlain and Ronald Reagan, and their difference from Willie Shoemaker.

In order to assess the idiosyncratic constructs people use, Kelly devised the Role Construct Repertory Test. The person taking the test is asked to construe sets of three significant people to determine how two are similar and different from the third along an important and relevant dimension. For example, an individual's mother and brother may be well-educated, but his or her father is not. The construct "educated versus not educated" may be an important tool in that person's hypothesizing about these people. This person can construe other significant persons with the same construct.

The adaptation of this approach for classroom use involves substituting important course concepts for people. For example, the concepts id, ego, and superego are written on the board. Students are then asked to construe them, that is, to state how two of the concepts are similar and different from the third along some important dimension. One such construct may be "innate versus acquired." The id would be construed as innate, while the superego and ego would be construed as forming after birth. Or, the id and superego could be construed as "not in touch with reality," in contrast to the ego, which would be construed under the opposite pole, "in contact with reality." Once these constructs are developed, they can be used to construe other concepts to be studied later. For example, the construct "active versus passive" may be used to relate the concept of "ego" as postulated by Freud, Hartmann, and White. Later, Jung's and Adler's conceptions of ego may be construed along the same dimension.

One effective way to use this technique is to have students work in groups to construe several sets of three (or more) concepts. In the course of discussion, students will first need to become familiar with the concepts involved - if they haven't already. They will actively seek definitions and examples of concepts from books, notes, and each other. They will then share ideas about important features to be abstracted and constructs to be applied. In short, they will be actively learning and using course material.

Although development of abstract thinking is the primary goal of the exercise, it could be that students will learn the content more effectively. Students may be more motivated to learn the concepts in this exercise because they are doing so as a means to an end (i.e., accurate construction), rather than as a sterile and arbitrary end in itself.

Rather than move from the concepts to the concrete level of examples, this exercise compels students to move up a level of abstraction to features that refer to the relationships among concepts. For example, in addition to seeing the ego and superego as independent concepts, the student can now see them as similar in their lack of independent energy (in contrast to the id), and as differing in their contact with reality. In introducing this exercise to students, it is useful to talk about different levels of abstraction, and to attack directly the differences among examples, definitions, and higher-order abstractions.

Because Kelly's constructs imply contrast as well as similarity, students will have a new way to handle "compare and contrast" questions. They can do more than simply define each concept in turn. Although some students are able to answer such questions anyway, the present technique allows all students to learn-and practice-the skills involved.

The discrepancy between what is taught and what is tested can be reduced by having some test questions worded exactly as the exercise itself. Questions that tap students' ability to construe sets of concepts may also allow them to be more creative. The specific constructs used are less important than the skill of appropriately applying a construct to a group of concepts. Students may generate and correctly apply contructs that the instructor had not thought of. Consequently, students may not think that they have to read the instructor's mind in order to demonstrate mastery of material and skills.

At the extreme of allowing this skill to be content-free, the author has asked the following question on tests: "Choose three concepts we've studied, and tell me how two of them are similar and different from the third along some important dimension. Be creative." This allows students to demonstrate the skill they have learned at the same time as they demonstrate knowledge of course content. An added advantage is that it reduces the salience of the typical argument that students didn't excel on the test because the professor asked the wrong questions.

Rather than teach content and hope that students will somehow pick up abstract and relational thinking skills in an indirect fashion, this exercise facilitates the direct teaching of such skills. After the specific course content has been forgotten or become obsolete, students will be able to continue using the skills they have learned.

Reference

Kelly, G. A. (1955). *The psychology of personal constructs* (2 vols.). New York: Norton.

The "Parts Party" as a Method of Teaching Personality Theory and Dynamics

Allen K. Hess
Oakland University

The lecture format is frequently used in teaching large Psychology of Personality courses. However, drawbacks of the lecture format, notably student passivity and resulting boredom, and the experiential base of many personality concepts make the lecture format less than satisfactory. I have had success in involving the students using an active, experiential learning technique, the "parts party which provides students of varied interpersonal sophistication with a working knowledge of personality theory and dynamics.

The "parts party" is a therapeutic technique, used in Virginia Satir's training workshops, that involves a person assigning to individuals significant parts of himself (e.g., "sexiness," "need for status," "envy," etc.). The parts-people then interact with one another and afterwards discuss the various alliances, conflicts, feelings and relationships they formed. Insights into personality structure and dynamics of the individual are often achieved by the group with tremendous impact and clarity.

In a Personality course of 65 students I used the "parts party" when the students were having difficulty understanding some Jungian concepts. Eight groups were formed and each was assigned a Jungian construct. The individuals in each group milled about, role-playing his or her group's construct. After a period of 5 to 15 minutes the frequency with which the various parts came into contact with other parts and the nature of the contacts were explored by the class and gave vivid experiential evidence of how the theory works. The young adults playing "shadow" overwhelmed the "superego" while those playing "anima" and "animus" were confused. This provided material for discussion on the nature of the constructs as these students experienced them. Discussion focused on their controlling of impulses, integrating of society's goals with their own, and developing identity. In contrast, older adults playing "superego" were sure of their part and contested "shadow." Easily the "parts party" can be employed in Developmental Psychology courses to illustrate generational issues and conflict, using figures such as "James Dean," "Bernard Baruch" and the "middle-aged businessman."

In a Personal Dynamics module in an Applied Psychology course of 35 students the "parts party" was useful in illustrating the elicitation of behavior from others as a function of one's presentation of self and the ensuing constraints on one's behavior restricting a person to his role. People chose the most salient or stereotyped part of historical characters and milled about as that part, conversing with others in cocktail party manner. "Jesus Christ" aroused people to admire or attack him for his serene attitude. "Marilyn Monroe" as sexiness, "Sgt. Snorkel" (from "Beetle Bailey" comics) as brute power and aggression, and Mme. Curie as a bright and dedicated scientist elicited quite different reactions from others and, in response, the students found themselves locked into those roles.

Students have responded favorably, even enthusiastically, to the "parts party," with a number of "aha's" during lecturettes when concepts were understood cognitively and experientially. Discussions were lively, involving students who were otherwise quiet in class. Also students referred to the "parts party" session in subsequent class hours when asking questions or making comments.

When using the "parts party" the instructor should budget from 40 to 90 minutes for the exercise. For most effective use of the "parts party" the instructor should plan on interspersing lecturettes during the feedback period. The feedback usually takes about twice the time that the "party" period lasts. Familiarity with the main features of the theoretical concept role or part is essential for the student to begin to act the part.

In summing up, a therapeutic technique has been modified to serve as a didactic device in teaching personality theory and dynamics. Clearly techniques like this require skills and attitudes an instructor may not possess, and thus should be used by those with training in interpersonal dynamics. The "parts party" technique, originating in a therapy context and used as a large class teaching device, can serve in other settings. Such settings include inservice training in mental health agencies, at case conferences, in interpersonal skills seminars, or wherever "components of identity" (Levy, 1970) (that is, personality characteristics, traits, needs and the like) can be identified and understanding of their organization, structure and dynamics is sought.

Reference

Levy, L. *Conceptions of personality: Theories and research.* New York: Random House, 1970.

Psychosexual Pursuit: Enhancing Learning of Theoretical Psychoanalytic Constructs

Janet F. Carlson
Fairfield University

In order to facilitate the learning of theoretical principles associated with the psychoanalytic perspective on personality, I devised a board game called Psychosexual Pursuit. *The game is especially useful in classrooms with student teams competing against each other to complete their psychosexual development while retaining considerable psychic energy to invest in adult concerns. Rules governing play and special advantages of this learning experience are discussed, and the game board is reproduced.*

Courses in personality are taught in most undergraduate psychology programs. Course titles such as Theories of Personality document the substantial theoretical bases on which most such courses rely. Instructors who teach these theory-oriented classes are often confronted with the difficult task of vitalizing potentially dry material in an effort to sustain student interest and facilitate learning. The issue also faces textbook authors and publishers, as evidenced by the attempts of several authors to enliven the material with demonstrations (Liebert & Spiegler, 1987), exercises and experiments (Phares, 1988), or other mnemonic aids (Ewen, 1980). Although textbook selection and creative lectures may suffice to translate theoretical constructs into more hands-on learning experiences, this is not always the case.

Perhaps more than the other major personality strategies (Liebert & Spiegler, 1987; Millon, 1973; Pervin, 1975; Scheier & Carver, 1988), the psychoanalytic perspective is particularly difficult to present as class activities or demonstrations. Note, for example, the treatment of this strategy in Liebert and Spiegler (1987). The other strategies discussed by these authors (e.g., dispositional, phenomenological, and behavioral) have as many as seven demonstrations of the theories or parts thereof. The psychoanalytic strategy, however, has but one. To offset this lack, I developed a game called *Psychosexual Pursuit,* the details of which are summarized in this article.

Overview

The game is suitable for up to 50 players. A team approach works well when enrollment is too high (e.g., more than 10 students) to permit individual play. Each player or team requires a game piece (coins or checkers work well), two dice, $100 of play money (small denominations), and a copy of the game board (reproduced as Figure 1). The object of the game is to complete one's psychosexual development and "finish" as an adult, while retaining as much psychic energy (play money) as possible. The four sides of the game board correspond to four stages of psychosexual development—oral, anal, phallic, and genital. There are substages for the oral and anal stages and a period of latency separates the phallic and genital stages, in keeping with traditional psychoanalytic theory (Cameron & Rychlak, 1985; Phares, 1988).

How to Play

The player places the game piece on the open triangle space preceding the six square spaces at each stage of development. One die is rolled to determine the square to which the game piece is moved. The player must then pay the indicated amount of libido, represented by the play money. The higher the roll, the greater the expenditure of psychic energy consumed by the resolution of the crucial conflict associated with the stage. A percentage system is used, so bankruptcy is unlikely, although anything is possible—as in real life. Bankruptcy, therefore, represents a highly maladaptive adjustment, such as one might observe in

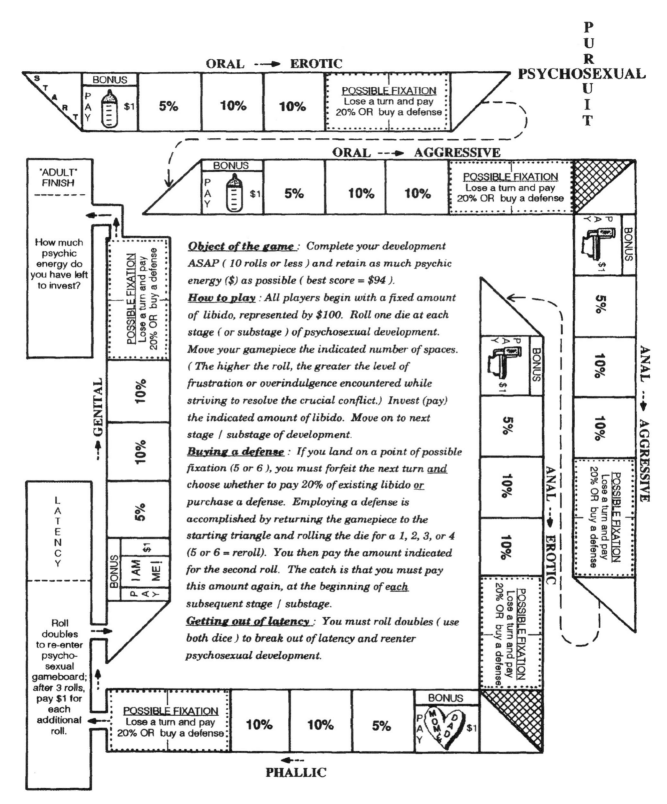

ORAL ---→ EROTIC

PSYCHOSEXUAL

P
U
R
S
U
I
T

BONUS

PAY $1

5%   10%   10%

POSSIBLE FIXATION
Lose a turn and pay
20% OR buy a defense

ORAL ---→ AGGRESSIVE

BONUS

PAY $1

5%   10%   10%

POSSIBLE FIXATION
Lose a turn and pay
20% OR buy a defense

BONUS PAY $1

5%

ANAL ---→ AGGRESSIVE

10%

10%

POSSIBLE FIXATION
Lose a turn and pay
20% OR buy a defense

BONUS PAY $1

5%

10%

10%

ANAL ---→ EROTIC

POSSIBLE FIXATION
Lose a turn and pay
20% OR buy a defense

"ADULT" FINISH

How much psychic energy do you have left to invest?

POSSIBLE FIXATION
Lose a turn and pay
20% OR buy a defense

GENITAL →

10%

10%

5%

BONUS PAY I AM ME! $1

LATENCY

Roll doubles to re-enter psycho-sexual gameboard; after 3 rolls, pay $1 for each additional roll.

POSSIBLE FIXATION
Lose a turn and pay
20% OR buy a defense

10%   10%   5%

BONUS PAY MOM♥DAD $1

PHALLIC

START

Object of the game : *Complete your development ASAP (10 rolls or less) and retain as much psychic energy ($) as possible (best score = $94).*

How to play : *All players begin with a fixed amount of libido, represented by $100. Roll one die at each stage (or substage) of psychosexual development. Move your gamepiece the indicated number of spaces. (The higher the roll, the greater the level of frustration or overindulgence encountered while striving to resolve the crucial conflict.) Invest (pay) the indicated amount of libido. Move on to next stage / substage of development.*

Buying a defense : *If you land on a point of possible fixation (5 or 6), you must forfeit the next turn and choose whether to pay 20% of existing libido or purchase a defense. Employing a defense is accomplished by returning the gamepiece to the starting triangle and rolling the die for a 1, 2, 3, or 4 (5 or 6 = reroll). You then pay the amount indicated for the second roll. The catch is that you must pay this amount again, at the beginning of each subsequent stage / substage.*

Getting out of latency : *You must roll doubles (use both dice) to break out of latency and reenter psychosexual development.*

Figure 1. The game board for Psychosexual Pursuit.

the psychotic individual (Vaillant, 1977). Very high rolls (5s or 6s) place the player at risk for fixation, and the player must decide whether to "gamble" by employing (i.e., buying) a defense or to pay 20% of the remaining assets. Upon choosing to buy and use a defense, a player returns the game piece to the appropriate starting triangle and rerolls one die to determine the mechanism's price ($1, 5%, or 10%). The second roll must be less than 5; otherwise, the player rolls until obtaining a 1, 2, 3, or 4. Although the defense must initially cost less than the 20% option, the player must pay the same fee at the starting point of each subsequent stage of development. This procedure is consistent with the psychoanalytic view that defenses require a continuing investment of psychic energy (Kendall & Norton-Ford, 1982), and that some defenses are more efficient and less costly than others (Vaillant, 1977).

Upon completing a given stage or substage, the player moves the game piece to the next open triangle at the subsequent developmental stage. Play then advances to the next player or team.

Latency corresponds to the period between the phallic and genital stages or roughly from Age 6 to Age 12 (Phares, 1988). During this time, the player is essentially suspended from psychosexual activity until rejoining the game as an adolescent by using both dice and rolling doubles. This procedure ensures that every player will spend at least some time in latency and will eventually reenter psychosexual development. If doubles do not turn up on three rolls, a player must pay $1 for each roll beyond the third. After traversing the genital stage, the player emerges as a young adult and tallies up the remaining assets to determine how much psychic energy is left to invest in the pursuits of adult life.

Advantages and Commentary

Perhaps the most compelling advantage of Psychosexual Pursuit as a teaching aid is its intrinsic appeal to students. It also uses materials that are readily available to most instructors, such as checkers, dice, and play money. More to the point, however, is the fact that students must rely on or learn several important psychoanalytic constructs in order to do well in the game. In reality, the students are likely to learn these things before playing the game. Knowing that they are about to play the game, they pay close attention to the instructor's explanation of the rules, which also consti-

tute the basics of the psychoanalytic theory. The directions reviewed before the game begins include an explanation of possible outcomes, such as bankruptcy, and can be used to relate the procedures to theoretical constructs more directly. During the game, students must apply knowledge about the operations of defense mechanisms, the nature of libido as a fixed energy system, the benefits of adequate conflict resolution, the disadvantages of becoming fixated, as well as the names and sequence of the various stages and substages of psychosexual development. By experiencing the consequences of these processes, the students' learning and interest are increased. For these reasons, the game is popular and exciting for students in my class and serves as a valuable learning tool as well.

References

Cameron, N., & Rychlak, J. F. (1985). *Personality development and psychopathology: A dynamic approach* (2nd ed.). Boston: Houghton Mifflin.

Ewen, R. B. (1980). *An introduction to theories of personality.* New York: Academic.

Kendall, P. C., & Norton-Ford, J. D. (1982). *Clinical psychology: Scientific and professional dimensions.* New York: Wiley.

Liebert, R. M., & Spiegler, M. D. (1987). *Personality: Strategies and issues* (5th ed.). Chicago: Dorsey.

Milton, T. (Ed.). (1973). *Theories of psychopathology and personality* (2nd ed.). Philadelphia: Saunders.

Pervin, L. A. (1975). *Personality theory, assessment, and research* (2nd ed.). New York: Wiley.

Phares, E. J. (1988). *Introduction to personality* (2nd ed.). Glenview, IL: Scott Foresman.

Scheier, M. F., & Carver, C. S. (1988) . *Perspectives on personality.* Needham Heights, MA: Allyn & Bacon.

Vaillant, G. E. (1977). Natural history of male psychological health: V. The relation of choice of ego mechanisms of defense to adult adjustment. *Archives of General Psychiatry, 33,* 535-545.

Note

I thank Kurt F. Geisinger for his careful reading of the manuscript and constructive comments.

A Freudian Slip?

Gordon Bear
Ramapo College of New Jersey

A humorous slip of the tongue affords a vivid introduction to theories of the mind. Interpretations offered here derive from classic Freudian thinking, a contemporary psychodynamic perspective, and two cognitive models that view the slip as unmotivated.

A college freshman is telling his roommates an anecdote about George Washington Carver (1864-1943), the scientist who discovered hundreds of uses for the peanut. According to a biography the student had read, Carver used to say of himself, "When I was young, I was intensely curious about everything and prayed, 'Lord, teach me the mysteries of the universe,' but God replied, 'I'm sorry, George, those mysteries are reserved for me alone.' So [Carver continued], I changed my prayer to 'Lord, teach me the mysteries of the peanut,' and God answered, 'All right, George, that's more your size.' "

From the student's mouth, the second prayer emerges as "Lord, teach me the mysteries of the penis." Embarrassed, the student corrects himself and finishes the anecdote. His roommates chuckle, perhaps at the mistake, and change the subject. The student ponders another mystery: Where had that word penis come from? He had been thinking about Carver's humility, not about sex, but he was largely lacking in sexual experience, and none was easily forthcoming at his all-male school. Perhaps, then, that slip of his tongue enunciated an unconscious wish.

I offer this incident as a possible example of a Freudian slip (Freud, 1901/1960). The classic psychodynamic interpretation posits an anxiety-provoking sexual impulse, operating independently of the conscious line of thought, that took advantage of the similarity between penis and peanut to press past the forces of repression and momentarily capture control of the vocal mechanism.

After discussing Freud's theory of parapraxes, the instructor can cite more recent psychodynamic theorizing and research. Weiss's (1990) observations of psychoanalysis suggest that repressed material becomes overt not through sudden victory in a struggle against censorship but through intelligent planning that eventuates in unopposed action at a carefully chosen moment. Weiss's theory of "unconscious control" raises the possibility that the student unconsciously had in-

tended for some time to introduce the topic of sexual experience and merely took advantage of an opportunity. In this interpretation, no mental conflict existed at the moment of the slip.

Cognitive psychology also recognizes the unconscious (Kihlstrom, 1987) and offers theories of parapraxes, from which one may construct interpretations of the slip as an unmotivated error. Motley's (1985) work suggests that extraneous sexual thoughts—not necessarily repressed, just operating in parallel with those to which the student was attending—caused activation to spread through associated items in the student's lexicon. The word penis was thus activated both by semantic associations to the sexual thoughts and by phonological association to the intended word peanut. Penis thereby became more strongly activated than peanut and reached the threshold for pronunciation first.

Norman's (1981) cognitive theory raises the possibility that the student was thinking ahead to speaking a word like genus or Venus (e.g., "Carver's crossbreeding produced new species within the genus of legumes"). In what Norman would call the faulty triggering of a schema for action, penis may have resulted from a simple mental combination of peanut and genus. (Heckhausen & Beckmann, 1990, offered an alternative to Norman's theory but do not consider slips of the tongue.)

The incident retold here has several pedagogical virtues. It is humorous and vivid and illustrates a larger lesson about the possibility of an unconscious mind. It allows a classic psychodynamic interpretation but also modern alternatives. Because it is amenable to those incompatible interpretations, it demonstrates a limitation of anecdotal evidence: inconclusiveness .

Moreover, it truly happened, as I can testify, for I was that embarrassed freshman in the fall of 1961.

References

Freud, S. (1960). The psychopathology of everyday life. In J. Strachey (Ed.), *The standard edition of the complete psychological works of Sigmund Freud* (Vol. 6). London: Hogarth. (Original work published 1901)

Heckhausen, H., & Beckmann, J. (1990). Intentional actions and action slips. *Psychological Review, 97,* 36-48.

Kihlstrom, J. (1987). The cognitive unconscious. *Science, 237,* 1445-1452.

Motley, M. T. (1985). Slips of the tongue. *Scientific American, 253,* 116-127.

Norman, D. *A.* (1981). Categorization of action slips. *Psychological Review, 88,* 1-15.

Weiss, J. (1990). Unconscious mental functioning. *Scientific American, 262,* 103-109.

Physique-Personality Relationships: Classroom Demonstration of Sheldon's "Constitutional" Psychology

William B. Davidson
University of South Carolina—Aiken

Undergraduate courses in introductory psychology, personality, and adjustment typically contain sections devoted to biological individuality. The search for dispositions that have a biological-genetic basis has a long history, one which has led to the current predominance of the "twin method." Twin studies compare the similarity of identical twins with that of fraternal twins for various personality characteristics. This method produces a strong case for the heritability of certain dispositions (Buss & Plomin, 1975). Prior to the advent of twin studies in modern personality literature the most convincing arguments for the biological basis of normal personality rested primarily in the work of William Sheldon (1942). His "constitutional" approach to psychology correlates types of physique with personality types. In spite of certain shortcomings in the methods he used, Sheldon's work is included in most psychology textbook discussions of biological individuality because of its thoroughness and interest value. This article presents a way of introducing students to Sheldon's ideas by having them use their own personal experience. A classroom demonstration using student observations is outlined, a summary of these observations is reported, and the pedagogical value of the demonstration is tested.

Sheldon identifies three basic components of physique and three basic components of temperament. His research supports the positive relationship between each component of physique with one, and only one, component of tempermanent. See Table 1 for how they are related.

Sheldon believed that the relationships revealed by his research might represent the common operation of biological factors. That is, the genetic messages which influence the physical structure of the body might also influence the growth and direction of personality. There are at least two central problems with

Table 1
Physique-Temperament Descriptions and Relationships

Physique	Temperament
(1) Endomorph (round, soft, heavy-set)	(1) Viscerotonia (relaxed, sociable, easy-going, good-natured)
(2) Mesomorph (hard, firm, muscular)	(2) Somatotonia (bold, assertive, active, adventurous)
(3) Ectomorph (thin, frail, delicate)	(3) Cerebrotonia (restrained, inhibited, cautious, private)

drawing such an inference from Sheldon's work, one involves *design* and the other *methods.* With regard to design, his research is correlational and thus cannot identify the cause of the observed relationships between physique and temperament. There are a number of alternative explanations for these relationships (for review see Hall & Lindsey, 1970). For examples, (a) individuals are pressured to conform to social expectations that are the product of individual differences in physical appearance, (b) personality-shaping reinforcers such as athletic prowess are selectively available on the basis of physical structure, and (c) certain personality characteristics such as activity level may influence physical development. A second major problem with Sheldon's research entails a deficiency in his methods. Specifically, the observers who rated people's physique also rated their personalities. The non-independence of these ratings probably artifactually inflated observed relationships due to preconceptions in the observers, a point which will be elaborated upon later. Nevertheless, Sheldon's ideas have been heuristic in stimulating research interest in biological determinism in personality development.

Nowhere is biological individuality *more visibly* apparent than in physique characteristics. Thus, Sheldon's use of physical structure as the manifest expression of underlying biological determinants lends itself readily to students' observations of their friends. The present study outlines a classroom demonstration which involves students' observations of friends' physiques and the personality characteristics which accompany these physiques. The similarity between these ratings and Sheldon's predictions is statistically tested and the pedagogical value of the demonstration is evaluated by using students' test performance. Limitations and potential elaborations of the demonstration are also discussed.

Method

Classroom Demonstration. Three undergraduate psychology courses (introductory, adjustment, and personality) were used to collect student observations. Prior to discussing Sheldon's ideas in each class, the instructor described three types of physique using the adjectives contained in Table 1. Students wrote the names of six friends or acquaintances who best fit the descriptions—a male and a female for each of the three types of physique. Students then read from a blackboard three sets of adjectives corresponding to each of the three temperament components listed in Table 1. The sets of adjectives were labeled with letters "A," "B" and "C" rather than with Sheldon's "viscerotonia," "somatotonia," and "cerebrotonia." Students rated their six friends by designating to the right of each name which set of adjectives best described each of them: A, B. or C.
For each class student ratings were summed using a hand count and presented on the blackboard in a form similar to that used in Table 2. The instructor then discussed Sheldon's theory and predictions, the degree to which student observations were consistent with the "constitutional" approach and the major design limitation of Sheldon's work (causal inference from correlational data).

Evaluation of Demonstration. Three sections of an introductory psychology courses were used to evaluate the Sheldon demonstration. In one section (*n* = 28) the demonstration was presented as discussed above; in another section (*n* = 28) Sheldon's research and its limitation is design were presented for an equivalent amount of class time but no demonstration was given; in a third section (*n* = 44) Sheldon was mentioned but not discussed. The same instructor taught all sections with the same textbook. Approximately two weeks after the material on Sheldon was

Table 2
Temperament Ratings for all Classes
(number of cases)

Physiques	Temperaments		
	Viscerotonia (A)	Somatotonia (B)	Cerebrotonia (C)
Endomorph			
(1) Male	39	11	6
(2) Female	31	19	6
Total	70	'30	12
Mesomorph			
(3) Male	10	41	5
(4) Female	10	42	4
Total	20	83	9
Ectomorph			
(5) Male	16	10	30
(6) Female	10	11	35
Total	26	21	65

presented (or mentioned) in class students were tested with 11 true-false questions. Three of the questions dealt with Sheldon and eight questions covered other course material. The three Sheldon items were:

> According to William Sheldon, physique is related to personality.
> Mesomorphy is the personality type.
> Ectomorphy and cerebrotonia are correlated.

The Sheldon questions could have been answered on the basis of material presented in the text. The primary purpose of the demonstration was to introduce students to Sheldon's work in a way that would capture their interest and familiarize them with Sheldon's ideas. Accordingly, the three Sheldon items which were used to evaluate the demonstration measured knowledge of Sheldon's theory; they did *not* assess students' understanding of the limitations of Sheldon's design or methods. This point will be elaborated further in the discussion section.

Results

Demonstration—Student Observations. Student ratings were placed in a 3x3 frequency table with three levels of physique and three levels of temperament. Table 2 presents the combined observations of the three classes in which the demonstration was conducted. Treating the ratings for males and females together for each physique, the resultant 3 x 3 chi-square analysis for the combined classes produced χ^2 = 160.4; *df* = 4, *p* < .0001. The individual chi-squares for each class were: χ^2 = 66.6, χ^2 = 47.9, χ^2 = 49.5, all with *p* < .0001. The relationships between physique and temperament were all in a direction which was consistent with Sheldon's predictions.

Evaluation of Demonstration. In order to determine whether the demonstration helped students learn and remember Sheldon's "constitutional" theory of psychology, test performance in the demonstration class was compared with test performance in the two no-demonstration classes. Table 3 presents the means for the Sheldon items (3) and the non-Sheldon items (8) for the three classes. Analysis of variance was used to compare classes on both types of items. For the Sheldon items, $F = 2.84$, $df = 2, 97$, $p = .06$. A planned comparison between the demonstration class and the two no-demonstration classes combined pro-

Table 3
Test Performance for Sheldon and Non-Sheldon Items in Three Classes

| Class | Mean Correct | |
	Sheldon Items (N=3)	Non-Sheldon Items (N=8)
1. (Demonstration presented)	2.18	5.64
2. (Sheldon discussed but no demonstration)	1.75	5.11
3. (Sheldon not discussed)	1.66	5.11

duced $F = 5.6$, $df = 1, 98$, $p = .02$. The demonstration class performed significantly better on the Sheldon items than did the two no-demonstration classes. For the non-Sheldon items, the three classes were not significantly different from each other $(F = .88, df = 2, 97, p = .42)$. Thus, the three classes were composed of students with roughly the same test-taking abilities. Yet teaching style influenced the test performance of students on the course material in which teaching style was systematically varied.

Discussion

The purpose of the present study was twofold: (a) to determine whether student observations tend to be consistent or inconsistent with Sheldon's theory of personality, and (b) to determine whether a classroom demonstration exploring this consistency (or inconsistency) is pedagogically valuable in familiarizing students with Sheldon's approach. With regard the first issue, the study presents strong evidence that Sheldon's ideas are congruent with students' experiences. Due to obvious shortcomings in method, this evidence does not confirm Sheldon's theory so much as it affords instructors an opportunity to use the demonstration as an educational aid. One such pedagogical value would be enhancing students' familiarity with Sheldon's ideas. The present study supports this contention. Students who were exposed to the demonstration learned relevant material better than did those students exposed to the material in another manner (lecture and/or reading the text). One possible explanation for such findings is that instruction techniques which force students to *actively* work with course material rather than *passively* receive it aids their understanding and memory. Such an explanation is consistent with the work of others who have observed the value of demonstration-discussion teaching formats as opposed to the lecture style (Arbes & Kitchener, 1974; Brender, 1974; Kirschenbaum & Riechman, 1975).

Another explanation is that material which corresponds to students' experience is more readily processed cognitively by them when they are made aware of this correspondence. This explanation is also supported by the observations of others (Hess, 1976; Grasha, 1974). The present study does not answer such possibilities so much as it raises them. Further research is needed to clarify the relative efficacy of teaching styles that emphasize active application of course material by students and teaching styles that expose the consistency between psychological theory and student experience.

There are other potential pedagogical uses for the demonstration that were not explored in the present study. For example, the demonstration technique contains a bias that was also present in Sheldon's research method: the same observers rated both physique and personality. These non-independent ratings introduce the possibility that a third factor could influence obtained physique-personality relationships: namely, the observers' preconceptions about how people with certain physiques typically behave. An instructor might explore this as a research issue by discussing some of the factors that influence "person-perception" (for review see Hastorf, Schneider, & Polefka, 1970): social stereotypes, prejudice, preconceived expectations, personal motivation, correspondent inferences, and cognitive consistency to name a few. The demonstration format used in the present study might be useful in enhancing students' ability to critically appraise research methods. Based on certain time constraints in the classes used to evaluate the demonstration, this particular endeavor was beyond the scope of the present study.

References

Arbes, B., & Kitchener, K. Faculty consultations: A study in support of education through student interaction. *Journal of Counseling Psychology*, 1974, *21*, 121-126.

Brender, N. Participation exercises in a psychology course. *New Directions for Community Colleges*, 1974, *2*, 17-22.

Buss, A., & Plomin, R. A *Temperament Theory of Personality Development*. New York: Wiley, 1975.

Grasha, A. "Giving psychology away": Some experiences teaching undergraduates practical psychology. *Teaching of Psychology*, 1974, *1*, 21-24.

Hall, C., & Lindzey, G. *Theories of personality.* New York: Wiley, 1 970.

Hastorf, A., Schneider, D., & Polefka, J. *Person perception.* Reading, MA: Addison-Wesley, 1970.

Hess, A The "Parts Party" as a method of teaching personality theory and dynamics. *Teaching of Psychology*, 1976, *3*, 32-33.

Kirschenbaum, D., & Riechman, S. Learning with gusto in introductory psychology. *Teaching of Psychology,* 1975, *2*, 72-76.

Sheldon, W. *The varieties of temperament: A psychology of constitutional differences.* New York: Harper, 1942.

A Class Exercise in Personality and Psychological Assessment

Ludy T. Benjamin, Jr.
Texas A&M University

Our course in introductory psychology provides two kinds of classes for the students: a large lecture section of approximately 240 students that meets twice a week and a small group class (20-30 students) that meets once a week for each student. Thus each large lecture class is subdivided into 8-12 smaller groups. Activities vary in these small groups but they have in common an attempt to take advantage of the small class size and thus to do things that could not be handled in the large lecture section. Some small group sessions involve demonstrations, others experiments, and still others are discussion oriented. This article describes a two-week exercise that focuses on personality and psychological assessment. That is, it is a two-part activity conducted in successive weeks in conjunction with lecture material on personality the first week and psychological assessment in the second week. These small groups are staffed by graduate students who have completed (or are currently enrolled in) a graduate course on the teaching of psychology.

Procedure. The personality activity begins with the instructor making some introductory remarks about the nature of personality as a construct and the difficulty psychologists have in defining it. The students are then asked to call out terms that they feel are part of the construct of personality. The instructor merely serves as a recorder at this time, writing each of the terms on the chalkboard. Usually in 5-10 minutes there are 25 to 30 terms on the board including such things as sense of humor, sociability, friendliness, honesty, sincerity, leadership, and so forth. At this point, the instructor tells the students that they are going to participate in the construction of a personality test. To do this they need to narrow their list of terms to the *eight* that they feel are major components of personality. (There is nothing magical about the number eight, more or fewer terms could be used.) In this part of the exercise the instructor takes a more active role in the process by encouraging students to eliminate most

terms from the list, otherwise the class will spend the entire hour in debate without reducing the number of terms. Some terms can be eliminated quickly because most students will agree that they are of lesser importance. In other it' cases terms can be combined, for example, sociability and; friendliness, or honesty and trustworthiness. We have found that the final list of eight terms is usually agreed upon by about 20-25 minutes after the start of class.

Quickly the instructor divides the class into eight groups, each composed of 2-4 students. This can be done easily by forming groups where students are created so that they do not have to move around. Next, one of the terms is assigned to each of the eight groups and each group informed that they have 10-15 minutes to jointly write two items that they believe will measure that particular characteristic of personality. In order to ensure uniformity in the format of the items, several examples are provided for the students, typically using one of the terms that was not included in their final eight. For example, suppose that leadership is a term that the class did not select. The instructor might give them sample items such as "when I join clubs, I like to assume one of the officer positions in the club" or "people usually seek my opinion when they are having problems." Students are made to understand that the questions need to be written so that they can be answered 'true" or "false."

If there is time at the end of the class, several of the groups are asked to read one or more of the items they have written. Someone in each group should have the responsibility of recording all the items on a single sheet. These sheets are collected and students are given instructions about the rest of the exercise. They are told that their items will be used to construct a personality test made up of 16 questions that is, the two items they generated for each of the eight terms the class selected. (Poorly written items may be included since the results they are likely to produce will lead to interesting discussion.) These questionnaires will be coded with a number corresponding to each class so that students will not use the questionnaire generated by some other class. The tests are typed and copies made available a day or so after the class meeting. They are placed in an envelope marked with the class number and can be picked up at the office of the graduate student in charge of that class section. Students are told to take one copy of their test and administer it to two students (preferably one male and one female) who are not enrolled in the introductory psychology classes. The test contains a disclaimer which indicates that it has no validity and is being used solely for instructional purposes. Answer sheets contain only the number code for the particular form of the test and the sex of the person answering the questions. Students in the small group classes are told to bring those responses to class with them the following week.

Analysis. The class session in the second week is begun by placing the numbers 1 through 16 on the chalkboard and listing the number of "true" responses for each item by sex. This tallying procedure is accomplished easily by having the students "vote" by a show of hands. The instructor might begin with responses from males, starting with item 1, by asking for a show of hands on "true" responses. Students who had not tested any males obviously would not vote at that time. Other students would hold up one hands both hands, or no hands, depending upon the responses of their male subjects. The response frequencies for female subjects are then recorded in the same manner. It is also important to note the total number of female and male subjects in the survey to provide a context for evaluating the data. Students in the class will need to have their copy of the survey in front of them so that the discussion that follows is meaningful. The recording of these responses on the board usually takes no more than 10 minutes.

We usually focus the discussion on three kinds of findings. First, are there any items that show major sex differences in terms of the frequency of responses? Typically one or two items will show such differences and the students are asked to speculate on the reasons for the different response patterns. Second, we look at the pairs of items (which are not adjacent in the test since the items are randomly distributed prior to typing) that are supposed to be measuring the same characteristic. It is common to find that one member of the pair of items will produce a response pattern that is quite different from the other member of the pair. Such a result makes for an interesting discussion about what the two items may be measuring. Third, we look at the items to see if any seem not to discriminate, that is, items which nearly everyone answered either true or false. In addition, we give the students a handout showing the various sets of eight terms generated by the other classes. This information is useful to show the lack of consensus in defining the most important characteristics of personality.

Values. There are a wealth of issues surrounding personality and psychological assessment that can be experienced and discussed in this exercise, e.g., issues of reliability and validity, difficulty in defining constructs, issues in item construction and test construction, and so forth. We have used the exercise in our course for the past two years and it has rated as a favorite activity for a number of students. We believe that the assets of the activity are as follows: (a) it teaches students about the complexity of psychological constructs, (b) it taps an area, personality, that is familiar to students and of great interest to them, (c) it gives them first-hand experience with the issue of face validity, (d) it gives them an opportunity for participation in some small group (2-4 students) activities, (e) it provides them with an opportunity to actually collect some data, (f) it gives them some experience in thinking about the meaning of questionnaire results, (g) it shows them some of the problems inherent in psychological assessment, (h) it gives students a closer look at some of the problems of the trait approach to personality, and (i) it provides an excellent vehicle for class discussion with minimal involvement from the instructor. The feedback we have received in written evaluations from students indicates that they view those two weeks as a significant learning experience.

Of course the activity that has been described here can be modified in a number of ways, even to fit larger classes. Instructors should make whatever modifications they desire to best fit their teaching situation.

SECTION II:
ABNORMAL

Teaching with Simulations

Students in Charles Fernald's abnormal and exceptional child classes took a bogus personality test and received false feedback about their performance; the false feedback indicated a high level of abnormality. Students discussed their discomfort with the feeling of being labeled deviant and were thoroughly debriefed. The author discussed the ethical and pedagogical implications of the exercise.

James Gardner encouraged students to consider thoughtfully the ways society categorizes mentally ill persons using the Myth of Mental Illness game. Student volunteers played roles of persons waiting for a bus as the class observed. None of the roles portrayed a person with a mental illness. A sixth student attempted to engage each of the other persons in conversation by asking questions. After the role-playing exercise the class attempted to identify the roles played by each student. Many students believed that they detected a person portraying a mental illness even though none were doing so. The activity pointed out ways that individuals can apply labels such as mental illness inappropriately.

Jerry Deffenbacher demonstrated the effects of cognitive processes on emotion by asking students to imagine the occurrence of a distressing event. Simultaneously, students experienced one of three cognitive scenarios designed to elicit feelings of anger, depression, or moderate sadness. Students noted their reactions and their evaluations showed that the scenarios produced different types and degrees of responses.

Kirby Gilliland gave extensive case studies to graduate-level drama students and asked them to develop a portrayal of a person described in the case studies. After rehearsals, the drama students attended an abnormal psychology class and either a mental health professional or a panel of students interviewed them. Students believed the portrayals improved their mastery of the course material.

Three computerized case simulations, originally developed for graduate training, were used as adjuncts in Matthew Lambert and Gerard Lenthall's undergraduate courses in Abnormal Psychology and Counseling Theories. The simulations presented clients with agoraphobia, chronic headache pain, and bulimia. Students took a therapist's role and assessed, diagnosed, and treated the simulated clients. The experience allowed them to practice many course-related concepts.

Michael Lyons and his colleagues gave pairs of students the opportunity to choose a psychiatric disorder and role-play it in a clinical interview. One student played the role of client while the other played the role of therapist during a videotaped session. The instructors showed the videos to the class and afterward encouraged discussion. Students enjoyed the assignment and believed that it promoted valuable discussion.

Timothy Osberg, in class and without warning, began a monologue that illustrated the disordered thought and speech of a schizophrenic. The monologue contained examples of the common disturbances in the content and form of thought characteristic of schizophrenia. After the monologue the instructor thoroughly debriefed the students. Both introductory and abnormal psychology classes found the demonstration engaging and useful.

In Frederic Rabinowitz's abnormal psychology class, three student volunteers played the role of an accused serial killer, and the instructor played the part of a court-appointed clinician to role-play conditions that might encourage the manifestation of a multiple personality. The exercise used methods similar to the interviewing procedures and context of the Hillside Strangler murder case (i.e., students acknowledged the presence of more than one personality). The author discussed the ethical considerations of using this procedure.

Leon Schofield and Matthew Klein conducted a simulation in which the instructor and students played various roles representing an in-patient psychiatric facility. The roles included patients, patients' parents, hospital administrators and staff, and legal staff. Part of the exercise involved a commitment hearing complete with judge, lawyers, and expert witnesses. The authors discussed several ways to implement the exercise with a minimum amount of time.

Using Field Experiences

Forrest Scogin and Henry Rickard provided the opportunity for students to fulfill a component of an abnormal psychology course by doing volunteer work in a hospital setting. Students spent 25 hr in their assigned facility. The program operated for many years, and student reactions were quite positive. The program supplemented the traditional course offerings and provided a service for the university and mental health facilities. The authors included guidelines for implementing and managing a volunteer program.

Some students in Geoffry White's abnormal psychology class chose to complete a term assignment that required them to do an extensive interview with either a mental health professional or a person who suffered with a psychiatric disorder. The students identified an interviewee, wrote a brief literature review related to the interview topic, and submitted an interview report at the end of the term. Students studied topics such as hyperactivity, child abuse, drug abuse, and pedophilia. Students believed this project facilitated their learning in comparison to more traditional term paper assignments.

Teaching with Case-Studies

David Perkins described an assignment in which students organized, prepared, and revised a case-study of abnormal behavior using a single theoretical perspective. Students chose persons of historical significance as their subjects. The assignment provided an excellent opportunity to integrate psychology with other liberal arts disciplines and received very positive evaluations from students.

Mary Procidano required her students to write a case-study reaction paper and a research proposal in an abnormal psychology course. Students chose the case-study from a list generated by the instructor and used selected journal articles as models for development of the research proposal. Students valued the research proposal because it provided an opportunity to be creative; they valued the case-study method because it gave an opportunity to read an interesting book.

Teaching about Suicide

George Domino described a technique he used to alter attitudes of students toward suicide. Small group activities and readings about suicide constituted the influence attempts. The instructor found that students' attitudes changed significantly in a postcourse assessment.

This article described a class activity using the Revised Facts on Suicide Quiz that focused on myths and misinformation about suicide. Richard Hubbard and John McIntosh administered the quiz to their students after lectures on depression. Subsequently the authors discussed the results in class. The activity can take 55 to 75 min but can be modified for shorter or longer time periods. The article also contained references to support correct quiz answers.

Instigating Miscellaneous Techniques

Dana Anderson developed a teaching exercise for an undergraduate abnormal psychology course to strengthen students' critical-thinking abilities. Students completed a term paper critiquing a book that questioned conventional wisdom in the field. The article listed several books representing a variety of unconventional perspectives. Students completed the paper in stages during which they read the book, took a position on the book's topic, and wrote two drafts of the paper. The exercise increased students' historical perspective and sensitized them to controversial issues. The exercise also required students to engage in an active dialogue with their instructor about an issue raised by the book.

Joan Chrisler assigned her students the task of writing a poem about the experience of mental illness. The instructions for the assignment were open-ended (i.e., students could write poems in any form). The author presented several examples of low and high quality poems along with tips for grading. Writing poetry promoted creative thinking and empathy for the mentally ill.

An adaptation of the television game show, Jeopardy ©, helped overcome some of the discomfort of studying for the final exam in Carolin Keutzer's abnormal psychology class. The game increased student interaction, encouraged the application of information, and added a light touch to a subject students sometimes find distressing.

Over a period of years, Arnold LeUnes organized numerous field trips to psychiatric and correctional facilities. In this article, he described the pedagogical significance of these trips and offered some tips for instructors who intend to incorporate field trips into their courses.

Michael Fleming and his colleagues described a course entitled Psychology and Film: Images of Madness, which a psychologist and a film historian taught. Feature films constituted the major elements of instruction. The films allowed students to investigate the relationship between art and psychology and the effects of the film medium on perceptions and attitudes. The authors listed the themes and films that they used.

1. TEACHING WITH SIMULATIONS

Feeling Abnormal: Simulation of Deviancy in Abnormal and Exceptionality Courses

Charles D. Fernald
University of North Carolina at Charlotte

Most courses and text books on abnormal psychology and psychology of exceptional children discuss research on the social and personal consequences of classifying and labeling individuals as abnormal, disturbed or exceptional. However, the mere reporting of research findings may have little personal impact upon students. This is unfortunate because many of these students will later become teachers and mental health paraprofessionals who will be involved in screening, referring and evaluating individuals, perhaps without careful consideration of the consequences of classifying people as deviant. I have incorporated an experiential activity into my abnormal and exceptional child courses to give students a personal glimpse of what it's like to be considered abnormal or exceptional. The rational for including this activity is that if students personally experience being judged abnormal, they will more likely (a) remember relevant research literature better; (b) become sensitized to the feelings of individuals who are classified as deviant; (c) use care and caution in classifying as abnormal, individuals they will later work with. Students who have participated in this procedure generally report that it did make them feel deviant and that it was a very worthwhile activity. The procedure is basically a replication of the study of the effects of experimentally induced deviancy by Freedman and Doob (1968) adapted for classroom use.

Because this procedure can induce mental stress and because deception is involved, an instructor should employ the technique only after careful consideration of the ethical issues involved. Although most students have felt that I was unduly concerned about possible negative side effects, students could become angered at being deceived or become distressed at being told they are poorly adjusted. Although the procedure is an instructional, not research technique, it is useful to review the APA Ethical Principles on Research (APA, 1973) especially the sections on mental stress, deception and obtaining informed consent. Consultation with colleagues, the department chairperson or an ethics committee would also be wise. When a decision is made to use this technique, care must be taken, as described below, to insure that participation is voluntary, to warn students before they begin that learning the results of the personality test may be stressful, to minimize stress by quickly revealing the deception, and to thoroughly debrief students so they understand the nature and rationale for the deception.

Method 1. Administer a "personality test" to students. During a class period early in the semester students are given test booklets called "Haley Breif Personal Adjustment Inventory," to complete on computer scored answer sheets. (This Inventory was constructed by selecting 50 items from several published personality tests.) Students are told that participation is entirely voluntary and that the purpose of the test is to expose them to personality testing similar to what will be discussed later in the course. They are told that test scores will be returned and they may enter their name or a private identification number to guarantee confidentiality of results. They are told that receiving results can be mentally stressful and for that reason they should feel free not to participate. It is emphasized that there are no penalties for not participating.

2. Low adjustment scores are recorded on each individual student feedback sheet. Each student's name or i.d. number is copied onto an individual test results form. A very low adjustment score is assigned to each sheet without regard to actual responses on the Inventory. If a control group is used, low and average scores can be randomly assigned to the two groups.

3. Prepare bogus summary of class results showing most students obtained good adjustment scores. A frequency distribution supposedly showing class test results is prepared and duplicated. The horizontal axis of the graph is labeled "Poor Prognosis" at the low end and "Excellent Prognosis" under the high scores. Two scores are located at the extreme low end, clearly away from the other scores which are rather normally distributed and clustered around the central, "good adjustment" portion of the graph.

4. Distribute bogus graph to class members and explain class results. Just before lecture material relevant to the effects of classification and labeling is discussed, I return the "results" of the test. I start by discussing the personality inventory to make the results appear credible. For example, I emphasize that the Haley Inventory is a well constructed psychometric device, highly reliable and empirically validated. I also

note that the test measures primarily long term personal adjustment (i.e., it has good predictive validity) so that even if the present test score indicates good adjustment, the student may currently be experiencing temporary stress, and conversely, the student may perceive himself well adjusted now, but receive a poor score, since the test shows eventual, not present status. The graph supposedly showing class results is then distributed and explained in detail, emphasizing that a few students received very poor scores but most were normal.

5. Return individual "adjustment scores" to students. Individual forms reporting their "scores" are returned to students after "computer analysis." They are told not to reveal scores to other students in order to "maintain confidentiality. " Students are told how to locate their scores on the class distribution. There are usually questions about the interpretation of very low scores and the explanation of poor prognosis is repeated along with statement about the empirical validity of the test.

6. Solicit reaction to adjustment scores and discuss. I have usually distributed a questionnaire concerning student responses to receiving poor scores, to determine whether the procedure induced a feeling of deviancy and then the nature of responses to this feeling. Student reactions are also discussed in class. If control, "good score" subjects are also included the reactions of the two groups can be compared in a class discussion as well as quantitatively from questionnaire results.

7. Debrief the students. After discussion and data collection, the deception is disclosed and much effort is spent in thoroughly debriefing the students. The procedure and rationale is explained in detail and a written debriefing explanation is also distributed. Students are questioned to insure they understand the deception. There will also be class discussion relating their personal reactions to induced deviancy with findings in the literature. During the subsequent class period the debriefing information is repeated and students are again questioned to clarify any misconceptions.

Results. Data were collected from 83 students during three recent semesters of my course, Psychology of Exceptional Children for advanced psychology undergraduates and master's level graduate students in education. Students in each class were randomly assigned either a poor adjustment score (N = 50) or a good adjustment score (N = 33). Subjects responded to the seven items of a 5-point Likert-type questionnaire concerning their reactions upon learning their adjustment scores.

Analysis of variance comparing total questionnaire scores revealed that the two groups responded with significant differences in the predicted direction, $F(1, 44) = 7.61$, $p < .008$. Significant differences appeared in a number of individual questions as well. The poor adjustment score subjects indicated they had more doubts about their normality, $F(1, 49) = 9.176$, $p < .004$, felt the test was less valid, $F(1, 81) = 8.011$, $p < .006$, and felt more angry and hostile about the test results, $F(1, 49) = 6.45$, $p < .01$, than did control subjects. These results are generally consistent with the research literature. There were no significant differences on other questions concerning desire to change aspects of oneself, or willingness to disclose results to class members.

Informal feedback from students has indicated that most were glad they had participated, most felt it had a powerful effect upon them and felt it sensitized them to the problems of people who are classified as deviant.

References

American Psychological Association. *Ethical principles in the conduct of research with human participants.* Washington, DC: Author, 1973.

Freedman, J. L., & Doob, A. N. *Deviancy: The psychology of being different.* New York: Academic Press, 1968.

The Myth of Mental Illness Game: Sick Is Just a Four Letter Word

James M. Gardner
University of Queensland

Though the medical model remains a potent force, in recent years alternative conceptions of human behavior have emerged. in regard to the issue of institutionalization, the major alternative conceptions (e.g., Szasz, Goffman, Scheff, Braginsky, Blatt) postulate that (a) there is no such thing as mental illness, and (b) the label "mentally ill" and the use of involuntary institutionalization are best viewed as socioeconomic/political instruments designed to repress various groups. Although this model gains increasing attention within the field, the general public remains shackled to the belief that "mental illness" is an illness like any other.

In the course of research on the attitudes of high school students, I developed an exercise which has proven very useful in illustrating the 'myth of mental illness" to the students. The exercise takes place during the third of six 40 minute sessions (an expanded version of 10 sessions at the college level is now being developed). In the first session the students are asked to name every possible synonym for mental illness. Students who come up with unusual names are asked to provide the etiology of the term.

In the second session the class is divided into small groups (4-5 each) and half are given the assignment of defining mental illness (without using any of the synonyms used in the first session)l and the other half try to define mentally healthy (without recourse to mental illness or any synonym). Group leaders are elected and then report back their definitions, and the rest of the session is spent pointing up the difficulties (impossibilities) in satisfactorily defining either term.

In the third session, the Mental Illness Game (MIG) is introduced, followed in subsequent sessions by a 30-minute videotape dramatization of Szasz's (1970) *The Manufacture of Madness,* then a review of local conditions in psychiatric institutions, and the final session is a 40-minute meeting with ex-inmates of institutions. Evaluation takes place pre- and post-course. To begin the MIG, six volunteers are selected and along with the author, they leave the room. Once outside they randomly choose role identifications from a group of six 3 x 5 in. index cards. The roles are:

1. An escaped convict, previously convicted of murder.

2. A successful business executive whose spouse has just announced the existence of a love affair, whose child is in the hospital, and whose car just broke down this morning.
3. An unemployed person married with two children, who desperately needs a job, and is on the way to an interview.
4. A person on the way to a sale.
5. A lonely person, who has few friends, is depressed, became bored watching TV, and is going somewhere just to have "something to do."
6. The sixth card reads as follows:

"You are waiting at the bus stop for the Valley bus. Your role is to try to engage each of the waiting passengers in conversation so that the class can observe how they act. Some of the helpful questions you might use are: Is this the bus to the Valley? Do you have the proper time? Does the bus usually run late? Do you have change for a dollar? etc."

While each student volunteer studies the role chosen, the class is instructed to watch and observe the behavior of each person. After sufficient time to study the roles, the catalyst student (sixth card) comes back to the classroom, followed one-by-one by each of the others (the identity of each student is unknown to everyone). Each student is given about one minute of interaction with the catalyst, with complete freedom to interpret the role in their own way. The entire skit takes approximately 10 minutes.

Once the skit is completed, each of the six cards is collected, the actors return to their seats, and the class is then informed of the purpose of the skit. Then the names of each student-actor are placed on the board in the left hand column of a seven by seven table and the class is invited to vote on which role they think each student played (the catalyst is listed last). The roles are listed sequentially (not simultaneously) at the top of each column and the class is polled to determine how many believe each participant could have played that role, then the next role is considered, and so on. The roles are presented in the order described earlier, except that the non-existent role "a mentally ill person" is inserted as the fourth role voted upon.

Once the voting is completed, the total picture is examined. The first step is to inspect the data across participants to see which students appeared to play several roles and which were identified with only one role. Next, we look at the roles to see which ones were clearly identified or which appeared to be played by many actors. Then, we ask the actors to inform us which role they played, and we discuss the accuracy of the decisions. When the last actor (the catalyst) describes his/her role, I note that I have "tricked" the class—i.e., the catalyst played him/her self, and therefore, does not appear in the six listed roles. We then focus on the fourth column headed "mentally ill" and count up the total number of responses here, and compare this with the other column totals (usually it is one of the highest totals). We note how easy it is for people to be labelled "mentally ill" even when there is no mental illness.

The high school course has been evaluated twice, each time with groups of similar students, and in each case it has been compared with a traditional medical model course which emphasized diagnostic nosology, assessment of psychiatric disorders, and methods of treatment and cure. Two measures were used to assess the impact of the different approaches: a composite 7-point opinion survey including items from established inventories (Altrocchi & Eisdorfer, 1961; Gilbert & Levinson, 1957; Rabkin, 1972; Cohen & Struening, 1962), and a request for volunteers to spend one-half day per week working with inmates of similar age and sex.

Though both courses resulted in reduced authoritarianism, the medical model course increased students' feelings that causal determinants of problems in living were rooted in childhood, whereas the MIG-centered course resulted in increased emphasis on psychosocial influences and in social tolerance. Moreover, the interaction with ex-inmates had no impact at all upon students completing the medical course, but students in the MIG-centered course continued to develop changes in attitudes (e.g., decreased authoritarianism, increased psychosocial orientation). The greatest difference between the two courses oc-

curred in the number of volunteers: only 64% of the students from the medical courses were willing to spend one-half day per week with inmates, whereas 94% of the MIG students volunteered.

Theoretical advances in recent years have offered a viable alternative to the traditional medical model explanation of problems of living. Despite this fact, practical applications have lagged behind, particularly in the area of teaching. The MIG-centered course described here offers one alternative teaching approach which appears not only to convey the theoretical implications, but is superior in some respects to the traditional medical orientation.

References

Altrocchi, J., & Eisdorfer, C. Changes in attitudes towards mental illness. *Mental Hygiene,* 1961, *45,* 563-570.

Cohen J., & Struening, E. L. Opinions about mental illness in the personnel of two large mental hospitals. *Journal of Abnormal and Social Psychology,* 1962, *64,* 349-360.

Gilbert, D. C., & Levinson, D. J "Custodialism" and "humanism" in staff ideology. In M. Greenblatt, D. J. Levinson, & R. H. Williams (Eds.). *The patient and the mental hospital.* Glencoe, Ill.: Free Press, 1957.

Rabkin, J. S. Opinions about mental illness: A review of the literature. *Psychological Bulletin,* 1972, *77,* 153-171.

Szasz, T. The manufacture of madness. New York: Harper & Row, 1970.

Note

The evaluation components in this report were completed as part of an honours thesis by Mrs. C. Schultz.

Demonstrating the Influence of Cognition on Emotion and Behavior

Jerry L. Deffenbacher
Colorado State University

An exercise demonstrating the influence of cognitive processes on emotion and behavior is described. Students visualize themselves as having recently experienced the termination of an important male-female relationship. While doing so, they are exposed to one of three cognitive scenarios designed to generate feelings of depression, anger, or moderate sadness with a sense of coping. After each visualization, the nature and extent of emotional reactions and behavioral tendencies are noted and later related to class goals. Evaluation indicated that the scenarios produced different types and degrees of reported affect, suggesting that the exercise produces the desired results. Common uses of the exercise are described.

Cognitive processes have long had an important place in psychology, and developments of the last 2 decades highlight the influence of cognition on many phenomena. Thus, exercises that demonstrate the influence of cognitive variables are very useful in psychology classes. This article describes such an exercise, along with an evaluation of its effectiveness and examples of its use.

Description of the Exercise

The exercise takes approximately 10 min, requires only a board or overhead, and uses an induced mood paradigm (e.g., Velten, 1969). The cognitive effects are not generated through repetition of affect-related words, but by having students visualize a life stressor while attending to selfdialogue provided by the instructor. The stressor involves the breakup of an important male-female relationship; it was chosen because of easy identification for most students and its relatively high rating on the Schedule of Recent Life Events (Holmes & Rahe, 1967).

Some instructors may begin the exercise with little introduction in order to reduce potential demand characteristics or because of other class goals. Other instructors may wish to introduce the topic of cognitive influences on emotion and behavior to set up the exercise. If an introduction is used, it will vary with the instructor, purposes, and topics, but generally will emphasize the influence of information processing on emotion and behavior. For example, in teaching ab-

normal psychology, I have introduced the topic as follows:

Many in class tend to think that life events "cause" us to feel and behave in certain ways. Our language strongly supports this notion. For example, "Psychology tests really depress me, " "Speeches make me very anxious," or "My dad drives me crazy when he treats me like a child" [examples were chosen because of ease of identification and common experience in class]. The external events (psychology tests, speeches, and dad) are seen as causing the feelings of stress (depression, anxiety, and anger) and associated reactions. It is true that some reactions are caused fairly directly by an external stimulus such as a startle reaction to a loud, unpredicted noise or pain to a physical injury. For many important human emotions and behaviors, however, this commonsense notion is not valid. Reactions are determined more by the beliefs we hold about the event than by the event itself. It is how we evaluate or cognitively appraise the situation that strongly influences our emotional and behavioral reactions.

If such materials were not desired before the exercise, they could be used as part of the debriefing and in linking the exercise to goals and objectives of the lecture.

Then the exercise is introduced. The initial goals are to outline the process and encourage student involvement. This introduction might be presented as follows:

In order to give you a personal sense of how attitudes or cognitions influence our experiences, I want to set up a brief experiment with you. In a minute I am going to ask you to close your eyes and imagine that you are a person who is facing a significant life stressor. As you imagine the situation, put yourself into that situation, like it is happening to you right now. As you do this, I am going to read you some thoughts you might be having. Let the thoughts sink in, and attend to the feelings and reactions they generate in you.

The stressor is then described. Students are asked to imagine that they are a 21-year-old whose boyfriend/girlfriend has just broken off an important, steady relationship of the last 2 years. Students are asked to close their eyes and be that person as they are read the first (depression) scenario (order of scenarios can be altered to fit class goals):

Ok, now get yourself comfortable, close your eyes, and imagine that you are that person . . . [give about 10 sec for this to be done]. . . . Remember, you are that 21-year-old whose boyfriend or girlfriend has just left you . . . [3 to 5 sec pause] . . . and you are thinking to yourself. . . [scenario is read in a slow manner using pacing and inflection to communicate a depressive tone]. . . . I gave him/her all my love, and he/she threw it all away. . . . My only real chance at love, and it's gone. . . . I'll never find anyone else. . . . But I must have his/her love, without it I'm nothing. . . . I can't live without him/her. . . . It's hopeless. . . . Life is empty, meaningless. . . . It's all my fault. . . . If only I had been able to love him/her more, this would not have happened. . . . But maybe he/she is better off without me. . . . Maybe, everyone is better off without me . . . [with the instructor's voice trailing off. . .

Visualization and experiencing continue for about 15 sec. and then students are asked to open their eyes and write down their reactions. After students write down their reactions, the instructor asks students to report the reactions aloud. Commonly reported elements include depression, despair, extreme sadness, hopelessness, lost and alone, rejected, suicidal, and occasionally anxiety or anger. These reactions are written on the board or overhead as they are mentioned. As reports dwindle, the instructor notes the clustering around a theme of depression.

Then the class is asked to repeat the process as the second (anger) scenario is introduced:

Ok, now let's repeat the process. Settle yourself and close your eyes . . . [10 sec for students to do this]. . . . Now imagine that situation again . . . your boyfriend or girlfriend has just left you . . . [5-sec pause] . . . and you are thinking to yourself. . . [the remainder of this scenario is read in a brusque, fast paced, angry tone]. . . . That creep! [instructor may fill in any negative label that feels comfortable]. . . . He/she can't do that to me! . . . . No one can do that to me and get away with it. . . . He/she can't leave me. . . . I'll show him/her. . . . By god, if I can't have him/her, no one can! . . .

Approximately 15 sec are given for visualization and development of reactions. Visualization is terminated by asking students to open their eyes and write down their experiences. After 20 to 30 sec. the students report their reactions to this scenario. Common reactions include anger, rage, revenge, vindictiveness, hostility, and homicidal feelings. The instructor writes these adjectives in an area separate from the descriptors of the prior scenario, and the theme of anger is pointed out. If desired, the instructor may note that some students appear to be trading the suicidal feelings of the prior example for homicidal feelings in this

example. It may also be noted that, although the situation has not changed (the same person lost the same important relationship), the reactions have changed dramatically.

The class is asked to repeat the process a third time, and the realistic, negative emotion scenario is introduced in a normal tone and pace:

Once again, close your eyes and let yourself be that person . . . [10sec]. . . . Remember, you are that 21-year-old, and your boyfriend or girlfriend has left you. . . and you are thinking to yourself. . . . I wish he/she hadn't broken off the relationship because I really love him/her. . . and I wish he/she felt the same about me as I feel about him/her . . . and wanted to work on our relationship. . . . I'm really sad that he/she is gone. . . . It's going to be very lonely without him/her. . . . While it hurts now, and probably will for some time to come, it's not the end of the world. . . . Maybe we'll work it out, and maybe we won't. . . . I sure hope we do, but if we don't, I'll survive. . . . In time, I'll probably find other important relationships . . .

Again, approximately 15 sec are allowed for visualization before the instructor tells students to open their eyes and write down their reactions. In 20 to 30 sec the instructor inquires about reactions and writes these responses on the board or overhead so that students can see all three lists at once. Simultaneous access to all three lists makes contrasts among experiences easier. Reactions to the third scenario tend to be a mixture of negative emotions (sadness, loneliness, hurt, and mild depression) with coping feelings and orientations (realistic, able to go on, able to cope, not overwhelmed, optimistic, and hopeful). The instructor may want to reflect on the mixture of emotional and behavioral characteristics and contrast it with the two previous lists. Again, pointing out different reactions to the same stressor will be instructive.

At this point, students rate the intensity of their negative emotions produced by each scenario on a scale ranging from *none of the reaction or calm* (0) to *maximum amount of negative emotion or overwhelmed* (100). Experiences with each scenario are rated and written down. Then, while the instructor points to the first list and refers to the first (depressive) scenario, students give aloud a rating from 0 to 100 for their experience. Several scores are written on the board, and a rough modal score is noted. This process is repeated for each scenario. The instructor can refer to the range of scores to demonstrate individual differences in reactions, whereas reference to the mode suggests some commonality in strength of reactions. The results may be summarized by noting that reactions vary widely in type and intensity as a function of cognitive processing because the situation was unchanged throughout. This summary prompts further discussion that usually covers the purposes of the exercise.

Table 1. Intensity of Negative Emotions From the Exercise in Four Psychology Classes

| Class | Cognitive Scenario | | | | | |
| | Depression | | Anger | | Realistic Negative | |
	M	SD	M	SD	M	SD
Introductory	75.72	13.98	75.74	15.40	28.69	16.08
Personality	74.41	16.02	70.83	17.46	32.00	18.19
Abnormal	72.78	16.99	71.43	18.42	26.65	15.38
Stress Management	83.61	13.78	82.37	15.97	37.13	14.65

Evaluation of the Exercise

The effectiveness of this exercise was evaluated in four undergraduate, summer-session classes (introductory psychology, theories of personality, abnormal psychology, and a seminar on stress management). The first three were taught by other faculty, and I taught the fourth. Instructors were given a draft of this article and asked to introduce the exercise at an appropriate point in their classes. They followed the instructions except that, prior to the exercise, students received a form on which to record their reactions and ratings (0 to 100) for each scenario. After each scenario was completed, students listed their reactions and recorded ratings before these were listed on the board. The anonymous recording sheets were turned in at the end of the exercise and discussion. Data from 5 students in introductory psychology, 3 each in personality and abnormal psychology, and 1 from stress management were discarded either because of the absence of a response to one scenario or a comment that reflected lack of involvement with the scenario (e.g., "That would never happen to me" or "I just couldn't get into that one"). Final sample sizes were 35 for introductory, 28 for personality, 37 for abnormal, and 38 for stress management.

Data are summarized in Table 1. Univariate, repeated measures analyses of variance (ANOVAs) revealed significant differences across scenarios in introductory psychology, $F(2, 68) = 103.25$; personality theory, $F(2, 56) = 74.53$; abnormal psychology, $F(2, 72) = 144.21$; and stress management, $F(2, 74) = 147.17$; all $ps < .001$. Newman-Keuls post hoc tests ($ps < .001$) showed that the depression and anger scenarios produced significantly more intense ratings than the realistic negative scenario in all classes, but did not differ from one another in any class.

Although some demand characteristics may be present in the use of this exercise, data were collected anonymously, which should have reduced the influence of demand factors. This evaluation suggests that the exercise generated significant differences in reported type and intensity of reactions in a variety of undergraduate psychology classes and may, therefore, be used successfully in the manner described. In addition, all instructors reported that the exercise generated many questions and comments, further supporting the notion that students were actively involved with it.

Uses of the Exercise

This exercise can be used to introduce the topic of cognitive influences. For example, in introductory psychology and the psychology of motivation and emotion, it might be used to introduce the influence of cognitive factors on emotion, motivation, and behavior. It can demonstrate person factors in Person x Situation interactions in personality and social psychology classes. The importance of person factors is shown by pointing out that situational factors (loss of relationship) remain constant across the scenarios, but that reactions change dramatically as person factors (self-dialogue) change. It can help outline the importance of cognitive processes in coping with stress, adjustment, and psychopathology for introductory, adjustment, and abnormal psychology classes. It also can be used in discussions of cognitive processes in counseling and psychotherapy (e.g., in introductory, abnormal, adjustment, and clinical or counseling psychology courses) and to introduce cognitively oriented psychotherapies, such as rational emotive therapy (Ellis, 1962) or cognitive therapy (Beck, 1976).

The technique introduces general topics in an experiential way and provides examples of specific psychological concepts. For example, notions such as absolutistic thinking (Beck, 1976) or irrational beliefs (Ellis, 1962) may be demonstrated in thoughts such as "I have to have her love" from the first scenario. Other cognitive constructs, such as catastrophizing (e.g., "I can't live without him/her") and over-generalization ("I'll never find anyone else" or "Life is empty, meaningless"), can be introduced. If contrasting examples are desired, they can be drawn from the third scenario (e.g., "I wish she wanted to work on our relationship" as a preferential statement; "It's not the end of the world" as a realistic negative, noncatastrophizing characterization; and "While it hurts now, and probably will for some time to come" as a temporally discriminant thought). The specificity hypothesis (Beck, 1976; Greenberg & Beck, 1989), which suggests that different emotions are related to different information-processing patterns (e.g., depression to cognitions about loss), can be demonstrated. An additional scenario demonstrating anxiety specificity could be constructed by having students imagine that their friend has mentioned relationship problems and is coming over to discuss them. The person could be depicted as worrying in anticipation of a relationship breakup and might be thinking thoughts such as "What's wrong? I just know that I'm going to be dumped. What will I do? I can't take it." Different types of attributions (Abramson, Seligman, & Teasdale, 1978) may be illustrated. For example, "It's hopeless. Life is empty, meaningless" (global, stable, external attribution), "it's all my fault" (global, stable, internal attribution), and "if we don't, I'll survive. In time, I'll probably find other important relationships" (more specific, unstable, internal attribution) can be contrasted. Examples such as these allow the instructor to use the exercise for introducing specific concepts as well as general topics.

References

Abramson, L. Y., Seligman, M. E. P., & Teasdale, J. (1978). Learned helplessness in humans: Critique and reformulation. *Journal of Abnormal Psychology, 87,* 32-48.

Beck, A. T. (1976). *Cognitive therapy and the emotional disorders.* New York: International Universities Press.

Ellis, A. (1962*). Reason and emotion in psychotherapy.* New York: Stuart.

Greenberg, M. S., & Beck, A. T. (1989). Depression versus anxiety: A test of the content-specificity hypothesis. *Journal of Abnormal Psychology, 98,* 9-13.

Holmes, T. H., & Rahe, R. H. (1967). The social readjustment rating scale. *Journal of Psychosomatic Medicine, 11,* 213-218.

Velten, E. A. (1969). A laboratory task for the induction of mood states. *Behavior Research and Therapy, 6,* 473-482.

Use of Drama Students as "Clients" in Teaching Abnormal Psychology

Kirby Gilliland
University of Oklahoma

One of the more difficult problems encountered in teaching abnormal psychology has been presenting course content in a manner which allows students to grasp the full meaning of the material in a factual sense and also be able to operationalize their knowledge in a "real world" setting. Bibace, Crider, Demick, and Freimuth (1979) noted that this problem is ". . . Related to the emphasis these courses placed on the memorization of what then seemed to be oddsounding labels for different types of people—people whom we never saw nor heard, but only read about." The important factor is that students need to observe and interact with people experiencing mental problems to better understand the full range and nature of specific clinical syndromes.

Several difficulties arise when one attempts to resolve this problem. Ethical considerations concerning the privacy of institutionalized patient populations may preclude the more meaningful aspects of class visits to mental hospitals. Logistical difficulties in managing exposure and supervision for as many as one hundred students (or more!) are self apparent. Some rather unique attempts which were designed to circumvent these problems and offer practical clinical experience to abnormal psychology students have been reported. Simulated mental hospital wards were designed both as comprehensive experiences (Claiborn & Lemberg, 1974), and as briefer simulation exercises (Schofield & Klein, 1975). Commercial films (Nissim-Sabat, 1979) and audio/video tapes (Bibace, Crider, Demick, & Freimuth, 1979) have also been utilized in presenting case study material. Although more general in their intent, structured game-like exercises (Gardner, 1976) and innovative, partially self-designed course formats (Ruble, 1975) have also been proposed. The purpose of this report is to present another innovative technique for presenting realistic clinical experience: The use of drama students trained to simulate psycho pathological case studies during an in-class standard clinical interview.

The Simulation. An agreement was made with the university drama department to have as one of the class projects in a graduate acting course the presentation of six representative case studies each from one of the major diagnostic categories. Six graduate drama students were originally assigned to the project. Each student was given a case study—the selection based partially upon interest in a specific syndrome, background and exposure to various syndromes, and obvious constitutional, demographic, and gender similarity to the actual cases (although these can usually be modified to fit a wide range of potential actors). The case study material was extensive, much as one would find in an exhaustive intake interview, and supporting technical material on their specific diagnostic category and syndrome from several abnormal psychology and psychiatry texts. The drama students would then construct a character from the case study, supporting material, and their unique backgrounds. As these characters evolved, I would have a conference with the actor to refine his or her understanding of the technical information, the specific case study, and the most efficient and g graphic way to present the case. Dress rehearsals of the presentation (clinical intake interview) were scheduled one week before the actual class presentation. These dress rehearsals were video-taped, and through discussion, analysis, and viewing of the video-tapes (as well as additional rehearsals, if needed) the presentations were refined to a surprising level of realism.

In some semesters the class in abnormal psychology was told that the presentations were by drama students. In other classes they were given a cover story to the effect that clients from a local community mental health clinic had volunteered to be interviewed concerning a mental problem from which they were recovering. Those classes who were deceived as to the nature of the "clients" they saw, were informed at the end of the first presentation that the "client" was really an actor. Thus, subsequent presentations did not involve the deception. It was judged from a technical teaching standpoint and from the response of students that the approach involving an initial deception was the most effective. Students who were initially deceived reported that they were more impressed and were able to attend to subsequent presentations with more realism in mind than if they knew from the start that the clients were actors.

The first in-class interview of a client/actor was done by the instructor or other trained mental health professional. This gave the students an opportunity to observe skilled interviewing practice and compare that to course content material on the subject. Subsequent interviews were often conducted by panels of three or four student volunteers from the class. The interviews were video-taped either by the instructor, instructional aides for the course, or by the university Instructional Service Center personnel. Following the interview, class discussion took the form of differentially diagnosing the disorder and suggesting possible treatment strategy. The importance of adequate information gathering technique (interviewing skill) and accurate diagnosis for the development of effective treatment plans were thus demonstrated.

The potential for instruction was found to be high using this technique. Aside from the obvious real-life aspect of the demonstrations, the class as a whole was given the opportunity to ask questions after the formal interview was completed. The interviews and case study material can be designed to highlight particular problems or interesting features of the specific syndromes, various interviewing techniques, or problems interviewers often face. The quality of classroom discussion following the presentation can be improved immeasurably by the ability of the drama students to slip in or out of their role for further questioning of the "clients if needed. A video or audio tape library can be developed for future use in teaching, supervisions or research. Finally, one unexpected result was that the drama students were highly enthusiastic and reported significant benefit from the challenge of learning a character from a psychological perspective and constructing a dialogue from a known character (case study) the opposite of what they usually are asked to do in their training.

Evaluation. This innovation was evaluated by comparing the course evaluations of two abnormal classes, one taught with the use of drama student clients (Spring semester) and one without (preceding Fall semester). The course content, text and instructor were held constant. Four questions from standard course evaluations were compared. There were no significant differences between the classes based on initial interest in the subject material $t(87) = 0.211$ or the course workload, $t(86) = 1.46$. However, the students in the course utilizing drama student clients did rate their course significantly higher in a rating of general course quality as compared to other university courses $t(87) = 2.631$ $p < .05$, and they felt they learned significantly more in the course $t(87) = 2.48$. $p < .05$ as compared to the students in the course without drama student clients.

On the basis of a survey concerning the quality and helpfulness of the drama student-client presentations 91% of the students surveyed felt the presentations were above average (46%) or excellent (45%) in quality (five point scale for all questions). Also, 94% of the students felt the presentations were helpful (51 %) or very helpful (43%) in understanding the course material, and 88% felt moderately assured (46%) or strongly assured (42%) that the presentations aided in their mastery of applying the course material.

Ninety-four percent of the students said they would definitely recommend (26%) or strongly recommend (68%) the class to other students .

Discussion. The use of drama students as "clients" in the teaching of abnormal psychology has provided a unique learning experience for those taking the course as well as for the drama students who participated; has produced a valuable resource in the form of a video-tape library; and has provided a powerful technique for conveying more realistic clinical experiences. This innovation is not without cost. Considerable time must be spent by a clinically trained and experienced person to construct adequate case studies, amass pertinent supporting literature and coach the drama students to produce believable and educationally useful case presentations. Video-tape capability is more demanding and not absolutely necessary but it adds significantly to the ability to coach the drama students and supplies one of the major by-products a video-tape library. Judging from the evaluation data and the enthusiastic response of those students exposed to the drama student client presentations as well as the drama students themselves, it appears that this innovation adds significantly to the effective teaching of abnormal psychology.

References

Bibace, R., Crider, C., Demick, J. & Freimuth, M. The clinician's "World of Action" as an approach to teaching abnormal psychology. *Teaching of Psychology,* 1979, *6,* 152-155.

Claiborn, W. L., & Lemberg, R. W. A simulated mental hospital as a undergraduate teaching device. *Teaching of Psychology,* 1974, *1,* 38-40.

Gardner, J. M. The myth of mental illness game: Sick is just a four letter word. *Teaching of Psychology,* 1976, *3,* 141-142

Nissim-Sabat, D. The teaching of abnormal psychology through the cinema. *Teaching of Psychology,* 1979, *6,* 121-123.

Ruble, R. Spicing up an abnormal psychology course *Teaching of Psychology,* 1975, *2,* 43-44.

Schofield, L. J. & Klein, M. J. Simulation of the mental hospital experience. *Teaching of Psychology,* 1975, *2,* 132-134.

Note

The author would like to thank Diane Puglisi, Jean Ann Nicks, Chuch Highfill, Lisa Kaighn, Michael Foley, Joey Sanchez, and Bart Ebbink for their outstanding efforts as actor/clients; Alan Langdon, drama coach, for his cooperation in developing this innovation; and Dara Andress and Lisa Portwood for their efforts in videotaping.

Using Computerized Case Simulations in Undergraduate Psychology Courses

Matthew E. Lambert
Department of Psychiatry
University of Missouri-Columbia at the
Missouri Institute of Psychiatry

Gerard Lenthall
Keene State College

Three computerized case simulations, originally developed for graduate training, were used as adjuncts to undergraduate courses in Abnormal Psychology and Counseling Theories. The simulations reflect problems of agoraphobia, chronic headache pain, and bulimia. In using the simulations, students took a therapist's role and were to assess, diagnose, and treat the simulated clients' problems. Students found the simulation task to be a valuable learning tool, enabling them to test many concepts covered in course material. Conclusions and implications are discussed.

Computer simulations for use in teaching undergraduate psychology courses have steadily increased over the past several years (Castellan, 1983). Among the programs that have found a receptive audience in undergraduate instructors are those simulating psychological experiments (e.g., Anderson, 1982; Castellan, 1983; Eamon, 1980; Eamon & Butler, 1985; Grant, 1983; King, King, & Williamson, 1984) and social research methodology (Fazio & Backler, 1983).

Despite the apparently successful use of simulations in research methodology-oriented courses, few simulations have been developed for other undergraduate psychology courses. Simulations for Abnormal Psychology or other specialized courses, such as Counseling Theories, could facilitate student understanding of course material. Simulations could also expose students to various aspects of psychology not available through textbooks; such exposure might affect a student's decision to pursue a psychologically related career.

This article describes three computerized simulations used in undergraduate Abnormal Psychology and Counseling Theories courses.

Therapy Case Simulations

The three computerized simulations were variations on a case simulation developed for graduate-level behavior therapy training and described by Lambert (1987a, 1987b). The cases, named *Mr. Howard, Mr. Kopf,* and *Ms. Barnes,* reflected problems of agoraphobia, chronic headache pain, and bulimia, respectively. These are relatively common problems seen in mental health facilities and often discussed in students' course materials. The goal of each simulation was for students to take on a therapist's role, diagnose, and then treat the simulated client using various psychological tools provided in the simulations. Those tools included psychological tests, consultations and referrals to other health professionals, interviews, and specialized behavioral assessments and treatments. Approximately 50 to 60 pieces of information could be gathered by using the various tools during the simulation process.

Content for each simulation was selected by reviewing the behavioral literature published between 1980 and 1987 for each of the problem behaviors simulated. Behavioral assessments were selected if at least two research studies used them as either initial screening or outcome measures. Similarly, treatments were selected if they had been found to have had some efficacy in at least one treatment study. Assessments and treatments that previous research had demonstrated to be ineffective or inefficient were also included. Such options provide students the opportunity to explore the types of case information generated by inappropriate assessment or treatment strategies. When the research literature was inconclusive about the validity of an assessment or treatment approach, I made decisions based on my previous experience working with the simulated problems. Traditional psy-

chological tests were also included so that students could see how the information elicited with these instruments differed from the more specialized behavioral techniques.

The simulations were programmed to run on any IBM or compatible personal computer equipped with a graphics adapter card and operating under PC/MS DOS Version 2.1 or later. The simulations could be enhanced by the use of a color monitor and a printer. Although not necessary for simulation use, a printer is desirable so that students may receive hard copies of the simulation summaries and personal records of their performance with the simulations. Each simulation takes approximately 45 to 60 min to complete.

Using the Simulations

Individual students sit in front of a microcomputer and proceed through the simulation, entering responses on the keyboard and receiving information from the computer screen. When starting the programs, users are presented an on-line orientation to the simulation task, describing their role in completing the simulations. After entering demographic data, to be stored by the computer along with simulation performance data, students are provided a statement of the client's presenting problem and told that the client is waiting to be seen. The following presenting problem statement appears at the start of the agoraphobia (Mr. Howard) simulation:

> Mr. Howard was referred to the mental health center because of increased feelings of tension and restlessness which are interfering with his ability to work. This tension and restlessness has been getting worse over the last 4 to 5 months. Mr. Howard is now in the waiting room ready to see you for his first appointment.

After the presenting problem statement, a menu (see Table 1) appears on the screen. Students choose various diagnostic assessment or treatment categories from the menu by pressing the keyboard number associated with that option. Selecting one of the main menu options leads to a submenu from which specific techniques may be chosen. After selecting a specific assessment or treatment from the submenu, the student is presented with a summary of the method's use and its outcome for that simulated client. Users may then select other assessments or treatments in the same category or branch directly to another assessment or treatment option. This branching strategy provides a more accurate reflection of an actual therapeutic process.

As an example of these procedures, selecting the Gather Assessment Information option from the main menu leads to a submenu (see Table 2) listing specific assessment areas available to the student. Similarly, selecting the Cognitive Behavior Assessment submenu option is followed by another menu listing specific cognitive assessment strategies. Choosing one of the specific assessment strategies is then followed by a description of the assessment technique, such as the description presented next for the cognitive assessment strategy of Self-Monitoring Level of Anxiety Over a 24-Hr Period.

Table 1. Main Menu Options for the Agoraphobia Simulation

1. Examine intake information
2. Gather assessment information
3. Conduct treatment
4. Consult with another health professional
5. Refer to another health professional

Table 2. Assessment Submenu Options for the Agoraphobia Simulation

1. Clinical behavioral interview
2. Psychophysiological behavior assessment
3. Cognitive behavior assessment
4. Motoric behavior assessment
5. Psychological testing
6. Behavioral inventories
7. Review *DSM-III* diagnostic criteria

Mr. Howard is asked to subjectively rate his level of anxiety at 1-hr intervals for a 24-hr period beginning at 7 00 a.m. On a Monday until 7:00 a.m. the following day. He is to use a 10-point scale for the ratings, with 1 being *not anxious* and 10 being *as anxious as he could be.*

After reading the description, the student is offered options of following through with the assessment and viewing the results, selecting other assessments, conducting treatment, or consulting/referring to other health professionals. Multiple branching paths programmed into the simulations enable students to move directly from one assessment strategy to another at any time. The procedure for selecting and implementing treatments is also structured in this way.

Students proceed through the simulations in this manner, selecting assessments and treatments, trying them out, and observing the results. Because of the multiple branching possibilities, no one assessment and treatment pattern is necessary to elicit successful case resolution. Students may explore as few or as many menu options as they desire in working through the case. The larger the number of menu options selected, the more opportunities students have to observe the range of behaviors that can be affected by having psychological problems.

On the other hand, students may also gain an understanding of how clients respond when treatment is drawn out due to the use of inappropriate or inefficient assessments and treatments. The simulations are programmed to recognize if the cumulative real-time duration of assessment and treatment strategies would

exceed 6 months without significant change in the client's symptoms. Upon this recognition, the computer flags certain client statements for presentation to the student following completion of any further treatment approaches. The statements presented next, which could follow selection of an excessive number of assessment or treatment options, were taken from the agoraphobia simulation:

Mr. Howard still reports not being able to go back to work for more than a day or two at a time. He informs you that he is in danger of losing his job if he can't return to work on a regular basis soon. He makes this statement to you: "How much longer will I have to suffer with this?"

Mr. Howard returns for his next session stating he suffered an "anxiety attack" while at the store with his wife. The people running the store thought he was ill and wanted to call an ambulance for him. He states, "this isn't working either, I want you to do something that's going to help me, not make me worse."

From this flagging component, students should come to understand that providing psychological treatment involves a balance between collecting sufficient information to understand a problem and providing efficient treatment to alleviate it.

Use in Undergraduate Courses

Two simulations, Mr. Howard and Mr. Kopf, were used with an Abnormal Psychology class ($N = 27$) during the fall semester of 1986. Seven students completed the Mr. Howard simulation and 20 students completed the Mr. Kopf simulation. The third simulation, Ms. Barnes, was used by 16 students in a Counseling Theories course during the spring semester of 1987.

Students in both courses were informed that completing one of the simulations was a course requirement, yet their performance would not be graded. They were told to view the simulation exercise as a learning experience to facilitate understanding the course material. Each student was required to write a one-page reaction paper upon completion of the simulation exercise.

Before working with the simulations, all students were given an orientation to microcomputer use by the faculty supervisor of the computer laboratory. Orientation sessions were given during regular class times and consisted of instruction in starting the computers and loading the simulation software. Students were also given an instruction sheet describing the simulation start-up process and were informed that a computer lab consultant would be available to assist them with any problems.

Because of high demand for computer use and a limited number of microcomputers, one microcomputer was reserved for several days during which students were to sign up for a simulation session outside of regular class time. Thirty-min sessions were established for the Abnormal Psychology students, but the class had difficulty completing the simulations in the allotted time. Therefore, the time period was expanded to 60 min for the Counseling Theories students.

Students' Reactions

The students' reaction papers indicated that they generally viewed the simulation exercise as a positive learning experience that should be continued and possibly expanded. The majority of students reported that the exercise helped them understand how material learned during the course is actually used when working with real people. However, many students indicated that the simulation exercise demonstrated limitations in their knowledge of psychology. This lack of knowledge led some students to view their simulation performance negatively.

Many students included statements supporting the use of microcomputers as teaching tools. Several students who stated that they were initially anxious about using a computer reported that the simulation exercise reduced their anxiety. It is uncertain if this perceived anxiety reduction generalized to other computer-related tasks.

Conclusions and Implications

Undoubtedly, student reactions to the simulations reflected a favorable Novelty effect"—all agreed that the simulations were an interesting change of pace. In addition, many students were pleasantly surprised to find that they enjoyed working with the computer. Those positive reactions are notable, but what appears especially relevant is that the majority found using the simulations to be a valuable learning experience.

Many students find it difficult to master abstract concepts, inherent in Abnormal Psychology and Counseling Theories, unless they have concrete examples, which such simulations provide. At the same time, the simulations acted as a motivator for learning the methods and strategies necessary to integrate course material. Moreover, the simulations not only spurred the students to make decisions, thus actively applying their knowledge, but in several instances, the process of doing so increased their knowledge. Having to make repeated decisions in a task such as this quickly elucidates unknown areas of ignorance. The simulations' detailed descriptions and explanations of assessment and treatment methods were a decided asset, filling in those areas that many students chose to explore. This advantage was most likely underutilized, however, because students only had access to the simulations once during the semester. An arrangement allowing the students to control when and for how long they use the simulations can probably facilitate learning even more.

Two caveats to further use of these simulations in undergraduate settings must be remembered; both are based on the original intended use with graduate-level education. First, because the simulations provide a context for increased student involvement and because younger students lack a coherent professional identity, some students may overreact to what they perceive as a poor (or good) performance. Instructors may need to provide some advance inoculation here. They should emphasize that the simulations are used only as supplements to the course and that a perceived good or poor performance implies neither good nor poor therapeutic skills.

Second, the simulations represent a very distinct theoretical perspective. Students may embrace the theoretical model portrayed in the simulations merely on the basis of its presentation via a computer. Accepting information as factual simply because it was presented by a computer has been a concern stemming from the use of other psychologically related software (Sampson, 1986). If courses are based on a generalist model seeking to make students aware of a range of theoretical orientations, efforts should be made to represent the programs as just one of several approaches to treating the problems portrayed.

Despite these potential concerns, the use of computer case simulations in undergraduate psychology courses offers significant potential. An ideal situation is one that includes computer simulations as part of a reasonably priced instructional package consisting of text, study guide, and material-oriented, computerized case simulations. Such a package could provide students with both theoretical and applied materials. With this package, students could get a "hands-on" feel for psychology.

References

Anderson, D. E. (1982). Computer simulations in the psychology laboratory. *Simulation & Games, 13,* 13-36.

Castellan, N. J. (1983). Strategies for instructional computing. *Behavior Research Methods & Instrumentation, 15,* 270-279.

Eamon, D. B. (1980). LABSIM: A data-driven simulation program for instruction in research design & statistics. *Behavior Research Methods & Instrumentation, 12,* 160-164.

Eamon, D. B., & Butler, D. L. (1985). Instructional programs for psychology: A review and analysis. *Behavior Research Methods, Instruments, & Computers, 17,* 345-351.

Fazio, R. H., & Backler, M. H. (1983). Computer lessons for a social psychology research methods course. *Behavior Research Methods & Instrumentation, 15,* 135-137.

Grant, M. J. (1983). Using computer simulation to teach attitude surveying. *Behavior Research Methods & Instrumentation, 15,* 574-576.

King, A. R., King, B. F., & Williamson, D. A. (1984). Computerized simulation of psychological research. *Journal of Computer Based Instruction, 11,* 121-124.

Lambert, M. E. (1987a). A computer simulation for behavior therapy training. *Journal of Behavior Therapy & Experimental Psychiatry, 18,* 245-248.

Lambert, M. E. (1987b). MR. HOWARD: A behavior therapy simulation. *The Behavior Therapist, 10,* 139-140.

Sampson, J. P., Jr. (1986). The use of computer-assisted instruction in support of psychotherapeutic processes. *Computers in Human Behavior, 2,* 1-19.

Note

A package of four (an additional case, Ms. Mayne [cocaine abuse], has been completed) simulations, software documentation materials, and related research materials are available on loan from the author to professionals wishing to use them in teaching graduate and undergraduate psychology courses. The programs are also available to researchers wishing to evaluate their usefulness in training mental health professionals. Information about how to construct and evaluate similar computerized case simulations may also be obtained from the author.

Video Taping and Abnormal Psychology: Dramatized Clinical Interviews

Michael J. Lyons
Columbia University
Carrie Bradley
Jeffrey White
University of North Carolina

Abnormal psychology is generally one of the most popular courses in most psychology departments. To a great extent this popularity is due to the intrinsic interest that the subject matter holds for many students. The subject matter is "real people" and every effort should be made to capitalize on the students' interest in people. Some institutions have video tapes of diagnostic interviews on file so that they may be used for educational and training purposes, but we did not have this resource available to us. Various approaches have been used to develop clinical material for use in abnormal psychology classes such as the use of drama students as "clients" (Gilliland, 1982). We decided to create our own tapes by having class members working in teams produce dramatizations of diagnostic interviews.

The first step was to circulate a list of disorders from which the students could select the one in which they were interested; this allowed the instructor to designate the disorders that would be covered while allowing the students to select topics of interest to them. The students signed up in pairs—some on the basis of an existing friendship, some on the basis of adjacent seats, and some with the informal matchmaking of the instructor. Following this the due date for each tape was assigned. Scheduling was arranged to allow students a minimum of two weeks to prepare their tapes.

One student from each team elected to play the role of the interviewing clinician and the other the role of the patient. Our class was a small honors section but a similar procedure could be utilized with sections of up to 30 or 40 students. The procedure might be modified for larger sections by including more than two students on each team. They were instructed to incorporate as many signs and symptoms of the disorder into their presentations as possible, consistent with a realistic interview. For certain disorders, such as anti-social and borderline personality disorders, this was best accomplished through the patient's history. For other disorders, such as schizophrenia, more emphasis was placed on the patient's current mental status, reflecting such phenomena as loose associations and delusions.

Each team of students met with the instructor for approximately one hour to learn how to operate the video taping equipment (although this could be done in class). They were also given information about interviewing, including an outline of a standard mental status examination. When possible, the instructor provided case history material and suggested the most salient characteristics of the disorder to incorporate into their presentation. Students were then left to their own devices to produce their tape. Offers by the instructor to remain present during the taping were always refused; most students seemed to feel less self-conscious working on their own. Various approaches were brought to bear on the project. For example, some students followed a script that they had prepared and used off-camera cue cards while others ad fibbed from a general outline.

The tapes were usually presented in class following an initial description of the disorder by the instructor and preceding the discussion of etiological theories. Students used various formats to present their tapes: some began with a "live" introduction to the case by the interviewer, others began the tape with an introduction, and others simply began with the interview. In some cases the tape was comprised of one interview, whereas in others, such as the tape on bi-polar disorder, segments of two interviews were included—one during a depressive episode and one during a hypomanic episode. The duration of most tapes was 20 to 30 minutes. Tape presentations were followed by class discussions during which other class members identified characteristics of the patient relevant to making a diagnosis. In general, the tape and the discussion following it took one hour of class time.

At the end of the semester the students completed an evaluation of their experience with the videotapes, both as producers and viewers. All of the students reported that the video tapes had increased their understanding of the various disorders; eight out of eleven responded "very much" or "quite a bit." All of the students found the presentations to be at least somewhat realistic and all indicated that they had learned more from the video tapes than from lectures or readings. All respondents indicated that it would be a good idea to incorporate this requirement into future abnormal psychology classes.

Students identified a number of positive aspects of this activity. Perhaps the most frequently mentioned was facilitation of class discussion. By being paired with a classmate the students came to know one another outside of class and became more comfortable with one another in class. The tape itself served as a stimulus for making observations and comments and this behavior generalized to other class activities. The presentations made the disorders more distinct and easier to conceptualize and remember; they were no longer just a list of signs and symptoms. Each student had an opportunity to learn about a particular disorder in depth as well as to see portrayals of a number of other disorders. One student wrote, "Putting yourself in the role forces you to gain an understanding of what you are portraying."

A general sentiment reported by students was that the project was fun and called upon their imagination and creativity. It also provided a break from the normal routine of lecture and discussion.

This procedure has several advantages over "lived in-class presentations. Use of the video tape format minimized "stage fright" and allowed students who are anxious about public speaking to enjoy presenting material to the class. It also allowed students to re-record as much as they felt was necessary to produce a quality finished product. The students were also quite interested in learning how to operate the video taping equipment, a skill which may be valuable for various purposes.

As with almost any course requirement, there were some criticisms and suggestions. Several students found it difficult to coordinate their schedules with those of classmates to arrange time to work together. Others disliked being dependent upon someone else's work for their grade, although this interdependency served to promote cohesiveness within the class. Some students were uncomfortable with the relatively unstructured nature of the task and would have preferred more specific direction and an initial example, presented in class, of a satisfactory tape.

Although there was an inevitable range of dramatic aptitude among the class members, the majority of finished tapes were, in our opinion, of excellent caliber. What had begun as a second choice to having tapes of actual patients developed into an activity with distinct advantages over "real" clinical interviews.

Reference

Gilliland, K. Use of drama students as "clients" in teaching abnormal psychology. *Teaching of Psychology,* 1982, *9,* 120-121.

The Disordered Monologue: A Classroom Demonstration of the Symptoms of Schizophrenia

Timothy M. Osberg
Niagara University

This article describes a demonstration that simulates a verbal encounter with a person experiencing symptoms of schizophrenia. Unannounced, the instructor launches into a monologue that illustrates the disordered thought and speech of a person with schizophrenia. The monologue contains examples of the most common schizophrenic disturbances in the content and form of thought described in the Diagnostic and Statistical Manual of Mental Disorders *(3rd ed., rev. [DSM-III-R]; American Psychiatric Association, 1987). Students in introductory and abnormal psychology classes find the demonstration engaging and useful.*

One of the challenges in teaching students about schizophrenia is to provide vivid descriptions of its symptoms. Recent films depicting case examples of people with schizophrenia have helped. For example, *Madness* (a segment from PBS's *The Brain* series) and *Into Madness* (from HBO's *America Undercover* series) contain some compelling case examples of this disorder. A more powerful demonstration of the bizarre symptoms experienced by people with schizophrenia would be for the instructor to model the typical outward presentation of schizophrenia to the class. This article describes a classroom demonstration that simulates a verbal encounter with a person experiencing symptoms of schizophrenia. My goal was to achieve a portrayal that was sensitive and accurate.

Procedure

Modeling schizophrenia does not require an instructor to learn all the bizarre behavioral nuances that may accompany it. Demonstrating the bizarre quality of language and thought that might be observed in a person with schizophrenia suffices. Before discussing schizophrenia and without any prior warning, I launch into the following monologue:

Okay class, we've finished our discussion of mood disorders. Before I go on I'd like to tell you about some personal experiences I've been having lately. You see I've [pause] been involved in highly abstract [pause] type of contract [pause] which I might try to distract [pausel from your gaze [pause] if it were a new craze [pause] but the sun god has put me into it [pause] the planet of the lost star [paused is before you now [pause] and so you'd better not try to be as if you were one with him [pause] because no one is one with him [pause] any one who tries to be one with him [pause] always fails because one and one makes three [pause] and that is the word for thee [pause] which must be like the tiger after his prey [pause] and the zommon is not common [pause] it is a zommon's zommon. [paused]. But really class, [holding your head and pausing] what do you think about what I'm thinking about right now? You can hear my thoughts can't you? I'm thinking I'm crazy and I know you [point to a student] put that thought in my mind. You put that thought there! Or could it be that the dentist did as I thought? She did! I thought she put that radio transmitter into my brain when I had the novocaine! She's making me think this way and she's stealing my thoughts!

You can read the monologue to students, but practicing it several times before class gives it a more spontaneous quality. Your affect during the monologue can also influence its impact. Persons with schizophrenia often show either inappropriate affect (e.g., laughing when talking about tragic things) or blunted affect (i.e., displaying no emotion at all). I suggest caution in how you modulate your affect during the monologue. Some instructors with a flair for the dramatic might want to heighten its impact by displaying the silly affect of the person with the disorganized subtype of schizophrenia. However, this runs the risk of offending students who may have a friend or family member who suffers from schizophrenia.

After the monologue and after students collect themselves (reactions range from laughter to incredulity), I explain that the speech was meant to demonstrate the language of a person with schizophrenia. I ask students to give their reactions to my speech. I ask them what they were thinking and if they felt uncomfortable. The answers to these questions prompt a discussion of how people with schizophrenia might feel about the way others react to them. The schizophrenic person might be sensitive to and hurt by the reactions of others. Other issues can also be examined. To what extent do the bizarre and seemingly meaningless ideas expressed have idiosyncratic meaning for the person? Might some of the delusions represent the person's primitive attempts to explain the symptoms he or she is beginning to experience? The monologue also helps to debunk the common misconception that schizophrenia means multiple personality.

While discussing the text's material on schizophrenia, I refer to the monologue because it contains simple examples of the more common disturbances in the content and form of thought as spelled out in the *DSM-III-R* (American Psychiatric Association, 1987). Disturbances in the form of thought include *loose associations* (jumping from topic to unrelated topic), *neologisms* (creating new words), *perseveration* (repeatedly returning to the same topic), and *clanging* (rhyming and punning). Disorders of thought content include *thought broadcasting* (believing others can hear one's thoughts), *thought insertion* (feeling people are inserting thoughts into one's mind), *thought withdrawal* (believing someone is removing one's thoughts), and *delusions of being controlled* (by some external force). Examples of these phenomena in the monologue include:

clanging—abstract/contract/distract; gaze/craze;
   makes three and that is the word for thee
perseveration—no one is one. . . and any one
   who tries to be one . . . fails because one and one
neologism—zommon
loose association—included throughout
thought broadcasting—You can hear my thoughts can't
   you?
thought insertion—You put that thought there!
thought withdrawal—she's stealing my thoughts
delusions of being controlled—she put a radio
   transmitter in my brain

I reproduce the foregoing list as an overhead (the monologue itself can also be reproduced as an overhead and presented before this) and review each example as I discuss the common symptoms of schizophrenia described in the *DSM-III-R*.

Evaluation

On the four occasions I have used this demonstration, the students have been very engaged by it. Their reactions are enthusiastic and generate lively discussion. Students evaluated the demonstration after I used it in an abnormal psychology class (*N* = 27). An open-ended question asked students to describe their thoughts as I spoke the monologue. Also, students rated the demonstration on a scale ranging from *not very useful* (1) to *very useful* (4) and indicated their recommendations concerning whether I should use the demonstration in future classes on a scale marked *No, Maybe,* and *Yes, definitely.*

Students' open-ended comments included: "I was confused"; "I thought you were crazy"; "It made me nervous"; "I couldn't understand what was going on. I looked around to see everyone else's reactions"; "I would have felt uncomfortable if someone I met on the street talked like that instead of a classroom professor"; and "I thought for [a schizophrenic] to do this must take some higher thought processes—the way he rhymed, etc." In light of some of these comments, one reviewer of this article pointed out the possibility that a student with a friend or family member diagnosed as schizophrenic might react strongly to the demonstration. However, to date no student has been upset after the demonstration. To the contrary, on one occasion, a student with a family member diagnosed as schizophrenic approached me after class to praise the demonstration. She confided that the demonstration and discussion had helped her gain a better understanding of her relative's disorder. Nevertheless, you might want to prepare yourself to handle any concerns raised by students during or after class by assembling referral information for a local mental health clinic or mental health organization.

The mean rating of the usefulness of the demonstration was 3.7 (*SD* = .49), indicating that students thought it had considerable merit. In addition, 100% indicated *Yes, definitely* in response to my question about whether I should use the demonstration in future classes. Thus, students consider the monologue an engaging and useful demonstration. It takes only 10 to 15 min. including discussion, and offers an alternative to lengthy video portrayals or field trips for introductory psychology or abnormal psychology classes.

References

American Psychiatric Association. (1987). *Diagnostic and statistical manual of mental disorders* (3rd ed., rev.). Washington, DC American Psychiatric Association.

Raymond, A., & Raymond, S. (Producers), & Raymond, S. (Director). (1989). *Into madness* [Film]. AR/SR Productions (HBO Presentation).

Sage, D. L., Jr. (Producer, Director). (1984). Brain, Part 7: Madness [Film]. New York: WNET.

Note

I thank Charles L. Brewer and three anonymous reviewers for their helpful comments on an earlier version of this article.

Creating the Multiple Personality: An Experiential Demonstration for an Undergraduate Abnormal Psychology Class

Fredric E. Rabinowitz
University of Redlands

The social psychological aspects of the multiple personality disorder were demonstrated to an Abnormal Psychology class through the use of role-playing procedures. Three student volunteers played the part of an accused serial killer, and the teacher played the part of a court-appointed clinician to reenact the conditions that might encourage the manifestation of a multiple personality. Following procedures that resembled the interviewing techniques and context of the Hillside Strangler murder case, volunteers acknowledged the presence of more than one personality. The pedagogical and ethical implications of creating the multiple personality in the classroom are discussed.

The multiple personality disorder has been recognized by the American Psychiatric Association (1987) and defined as a dissociative disorder that involves the existence within the individual of two or more distinct personalities, each of which is dominant at a particular time. The personality that is dominant at any particular time determines the individual's behavior. Each personality is complex and integrated with its own unique behavior patterns and social relationships.

It has been suggested that a disproportionate number of multiple personality cases have been diagnosed by a small group of clinicians (Spanos, Weekes, & Bertrand, 1985). Although only 13 cases were reported from 1934 to 1971 (Rosenbaum, 1980), the number of reported cases in psychiatric journals has increased exponentially since 1971, with some clinicians claiming to have seen 50 or more of these individuals (Allison, 1974; Bliss, 1980, 1984; Kluft, 1982). Although some investigators (e.g., Allison & Schwartz, 1980) believe that earlier cases had been misdiagnosed as schizophrenia or other personality disorders, others suggest that the increase in cases reported may be due to secondary gains achieved by playing the role of a multiple personality patient (Spanos et al., 1985; Thigpen & Cleckley, 1984).

The multiple personality phenomenon has been explained by psychodynamic theorists as well as social psychologists. The psychodynamic perspective suggests that individuals manifesting this disorder have experienced some severe childhood trauma that has resulted in an unconscious splitting defense mechanism to protect the ego from disintegration. When combined with psychological stressors in adulthood, this childhood predisposition toward splitting may result in an individual manifesting two or more distinct personalities, which have little knowledge of each other (Gruenewald, 1984; Herzog, 1984).

In contrast, the social psychological perspective suggests that individuals learn to enact the role of the multiple personality patient based on the widespread information about this disorder found in books and movies about multiple personality (Spanos et al., 1985; Sutcliff & Jones, 1962; Thigpen & Cleckley, 1984). The motivation to take on the multiple personality role may be rooted in a desire to avoid responsibility for ego-dystonic activities and to gain positive attention from the psychiatric community, which tends to perceive multiple personality cases as more interesting than most other disorders (Thigpen & Cleckley, 1984).

Sutcliff and Jones (1962) suggested that many manifestations of multiple personality occur following hypnotic procedures. Hypnosis is popularly believed to help tap into unconscious parts of the personality (Frankel, 1976), but it has also been described as a legitimate social context to allow for imagination and role demands to be manifested (Sarbin, 1976). A clinician who uses hypnotic procedures may actually legitimize the manifestation of a multiple personality by suggesting that another personality emerge and speak in the hypnotic state. During the trial of Kenneth Bianchi, the Hillside Strangler, hypnotic procedures were used to see if a hidden personality that knew about the murders existed (Schwarz, 1981). Bianchi described another identity that had actually committed the murders of several women in California.

Spanos et al. (1985) showed that individuals subjected to the same interviewing techniques and context as Bianchi would also manifest a multiple personality. Using these researchers' methodology, it was hypothesized that students asked to play the role of an accused murderer, subtly cued by an authority figure (e.g., the teacher), would show symptoms of the multiple personality disorder without advance knowledge of these symptoms.

The following demonstration was designed to show students: (a) the diagnostic characteristics of the multiple personality and how to distinguish it from other disorders, (b) how demand characteristics and contextual variables affect responses to the clinical interview, (c) the role of the courtroom psychiatrist in the legal system, and (d) how various theoretical models explain the existence of the multiple personality.

Procedure

The 27 students in the Abnormal Psychology course were asked to respond to an original questionnaire, the Imagination Potential Scale, at the beginning of the 90-min class. This questionnaire was designed after the Harvard Group Scale for Hypnotic Susceptibility (Shor & Orne, 1963) and based on data suggesting that a vivid imagination and deep involvement in the arts, reading, or religion are good indicators of suggestibility (Hilgard, 1965) . Three individuals, chosen from those who scored highest on the scale, were asked if they would take part in a classroom experiment. They were told that they did not have to participate and could withdraw if they were not comfortable with the procedures. After securing their permission, I took the three individuals outside the classroom and read them the following instructions based on the Spanos et al. (1985) study:

You are to play the role of an accused murderer, Harry (Betty) Michaels. He (she) has been accused of killing three women Ann, Louise, and Mary (three men: Andy, Larry, and Marty). Despite much evidence of guilt, a "not guilty" plea has been entered. The court has ordered a psychiatric evaluation. You will be asked to participate in a simulated psychiatric interview. You should play the role of Harry (Betty) throughout the interview, and use any knowledge you have about criminals and any information you can pick up from the setting to give a convincing performance. If I suggest the use of hypnosis, go along with role playing being hypnotized as well.

Each subject was brought into the classroom individually while the others waited in the hall, out of earshot of the class. The teacher identified himself as the court-appointed psychiatrist and asked the student to sit across from him. He requested the following information:

Tell my why you are here.
Tell me about Ann (Andy), Louise (Larry), and Mary (Marty).

Tell me about your childhood.
Tell me about your relationship with your parents.
Tell me about your girlfriends (boyfriends).

Following the answers to these questions, the teacher/psychiatrist says:

I believe it will be possible to find out more information under hypnosis. Is that O.K.? You will be hypnotized by the following procedure. Focus on the end of my pen; as I lower it to the floor, your eyes will become heavy and close. You will then be hypnotized.

After following these procedures, the subject will follow the suggestion to close his or her eyes. The next statements by the teacher/psychiatrist are directly from the Bianchi transcripts (Schwarz, 1981, pp. 139-143):

I've talked a bit to Harry (Betty) but I think that perhaps there might be another part of Harry (Betty) that I haven't talked to, another part that maybe feels somewhat differently from the part I talked to. I would like to communicate with that other part. When the different part is present, please raise your right hand.
Would you talk to me, part, by saying "I'm here?"
Part, are you the same thing as Harry (Betty) or are you different in any way?

The subject should respond to the questions and continue by answering the following:

Who are you?
Tell me about yourself.
Do you have a name I can call you?
Tell me about yourself, _____
What do you do?
Tell me about Ann (Andy), Louise (Larry), and Mary (Marty) .
Tell me about Harry (Betty). What is he (she) like?
When I count to 10 you will awaken from the hypnosis.
What do you remember from the hypnosis?

Results

The procedure was repeated for each subject as the class watched. At the end of the three performances, the three subjects were brought to the front of the room to be debriefed by the instructor and to answer questions from the class. The typical questions from the observers tended to focus on whether the subjects were really hypnotized and why they had described another personality during the interview.

All subjects acknowledged a second personality with another name. Although they initially denied guilt, they each admitted committing the crime when playing the part of the other personality. In each case, the second personality was described in diametrically opposed terms to the first (i.e., if Betty was nice and good, then Sarah was mean and vengeful). One of the subjects could not remember the name of her alternative personality when questioned following the demonstration. During the debriefing, which involved discussion about role playing and hypnotic suggestibility, the subjects agreed among each other that they were playing the role of being hypnotized and that the alternative personalities that emerged seemed to be easy explanations for their supposed deviant behavior.

The debriefing and question and answer session provided a lead-in to a discussion of multiple personality phenomena from various viewpoints. These included a definition of the disorder and its differential diagnosis, the specifics of the Bianchi case from which the demonstration was taken, theories about the etiology of multiple personality and its increased prevalence in recent years, the role of psychiatric and legal intervention, and clinical treatment considerations.

The results of this classroom demonstration coincided with those of Spanos et al. (1985). They found that when compared to a group of subjects exposed to less manipulative instructions and a no-hypnosis control group, the Bianchi treatment group subjects were more likely to choose a different name when asked about their other personality (81%), were likely to admit guilt of the crime when speaking as the second personality (61%), and were likely to have some amnesia of the hypnotic episode (61%).

Discussion

This demonstration suggests that the multiple personality can be created in the classroom situation; however, there are ethical and theoretical limitations to be considered. Because the instructor is using highly suggestive directions, it is possible that the subjects may actually become hypnotized during the demonstration. Knowledge of hypnotic procedures and trance states is highly recommended when performing this demonstration (e.g., Shor, 1969). Debriefing after the procedure should include information about the nature of hypnosis and suggestibility (e.g., Barber, 1972) as well as the role of demand characteristics and contextual cues (e.g., Orne, 1962).

It should also be emphasized that the Bianchi case appeared to be an example of a known sociopath manipulating the symptomatology of the multiple personality for secondary gain in his legal proceedings. Many researchers and clinicians believe that the multiple personality exists as a legitimate disorder and differentiate it from psychotic disorders, personality disorders, and malingering (e.g., Meyer & Osborne, 1987). Therefore, a discussion of various theoretical perspectives following the demonstration is essential to ensure that students do not assume that all multiple personality cases are always under the control of the identified individual, the result of creative imagination, or based on suggestive instructions from an authority figure.

References

Allison, R. B. (1974). A new treatment approach for multiple personalities. *American Journal of Clinical Hypnosis, 17,* 15-32.

Allison, R. B., & Schwartz, T. (1980). *Minds in many pieces: The making of a very special doctor.* New York: Rawson, Wade.

American Psychiatric Association. (1987) . *Diagnostic and statistical manual of mental disorders* (3rd ed., rev.). Washington, DC: Author.

Barber, T. (1972*). LSD, marihuana, yoga, and hypnosis.* Chicago: Aldine.

Bliss, E. L. (1980). Multiple personalities: A report of 14 cases with implications for schizophrenia and hysteria. *Archives of General Psychiatry, 37,* 1388-1397.

Bliss, E. L. (1984). A symptom profile of patients with multiple personalities, including MMPI results. *Journal of Nervous and Mental Disease, 171,* 197-202.

Franked F. (1976*). Hypnosis: Trance as a coping mechanism.* New York: Plenum.

Gruenewald, D. (1984). On the nature of multiple personality: Comparisons with hypnosis. *International Journal of Clinical and Experimental Hypnosis, 32,* 170- 190.

Herzog, A. (1984). On multiple personality: Comments on diagnosis, etiology, and treatment. International *Journal of Clinical and Experimental Hypnosis, 32,* 210-221.

Hilgard, E. (1965). *Hypnotic susceptibility.* New York: Harcourt, Brace & World.

Kluft, R. P. (1982). Varieties of hypnotic interventions in the treatment of multiple personality. *American Journal of Clinical Hypnosis, 24,* 230-240.

Meyer, R. G., & Osborne, Y. H. (1987). *Case studies in abnormal behavior.* Boston: Allyn & Bacon.

Orne, M. (1962). On the social psychology of the psychological experiment: With particular reference to demand characteristics and their implications. *American Psychologist, 17,* 776-783.

Rosenbaum, M. (1980). The role of the term schizophrenia in the decline of diagnoses of multiple personality. *Archives of General Psychiatry, 37,* 1383-1385.

Sarbin, T. (1976). Hypnosis as role enactment. In P. Sheehan & C. Perry (Eds.), *Methodologies of hypnosis* (pp. 123-152). New York: Wiley.

Schwarz, J. R. (1981). *The hillside strangler: A murderer's mind.* New York: New American Library.

Shor, R. (1969). Three dimensions of hypnotic depth. In C. Tart (Ed.), *Altered states of consciousness* (pp. 251-261). New York: Wiley.

Shor, R., & Orne, E. (1963). Norms on the Harvard Group Scale for Hypnotic Susceptibility, Form A. *International Journal of Clinical and Experimental Hypnosis, 11,* 39-48.

Spanos, N. P., Weekes, J. R., & Bertrand, L. D. (1985). Multiple personality: A social psychological perspective. *Journal of Abnormal Psychology, 94,* 362-376.

Sutcliff, J. P., & Jones, J. (1962). Personal identity, multiple personality, and hypnosis. *International Journal of Clinical and Experimental Hypnosis, 10,* 231 - 269.

Thigpen, C. H., & Cleckley, H. M. (1984). On the incidence of multiple personality disorder. *International Journal of Clinical and Experimental Hypnosis, 32,* 63-66.

Simulation of the Mental Hospital Experience

Leon J. Schofield, Jr.
and Matthew J. Klein
Hobart and William Smith Colleges

Role-assumption experiments have been conducted in real settings with students exposed to prison (Ringuette & Snyder, 1970) and mental hospital environments (Weitz, 1972). Brief simulation exercises have also been used successfully in training group psychotherapists (MacLennan, 1971), social workers (Bardill, 1971) and various mental hospital staff (France & McClure, 1972; Orlando, 1973). To our knowledge, however, only two studies have been reported in the literature using extended simulation as a teaching technique with undergraduates. Zimbardo (1972) has simulated a prison environment. The experiment was terminated prematurely because of serious traumatic effects upon participants. Claiborn and Lemberg (1974) have recently simulated a mental hospital environment, using more than 70 upper level students enrolled in a clinical psychology course. The simulation involved extensive planning over a two month period and role playing of the entire hospital staff as well as patients, nurses and psychiatrists. The actual "hospitalization" of the patients lasted 56 hours over a period of two consecutive weekends, including one overnight. the students responded in ways appropriate to their role; about a third of the patients expressed feelings of frustration, depression, powerlessness and helplessness.

The Simulation. In the spring of 1974, we initiated a simulation of a mental hospital environment as part of an abnormal psychology course. In contrast with the Claiborn and Lemberg (1974) study, the simulation: involved freshmen and sophomores; was not "a major portion" of the course; involved only the patients and some medical staff; did not result in extra financial expense (except $5 for a field trip); and was accomplished with few demands for space or equipment.

The patient volunteers were five females. Other class members participated as hospital staff (psychiatrist, psychologist, nurse, attendants), parents of one of the patients, and legal staff (lawyers, expert witnesses). Altogether 16 class members participated in some part of the experiment, while the remaining 69 observed in-class activities. One patient volunteered to be the "star patient" and she was given a pre-commitment interview (along with her "parents") and commitment hearing immediately following the simulation.

The senior author. the course instructor, participated as judge during the in-class commitment hearing. The second author, a senior psychology major earning independent study credit, participated as admitting psychiatrist and as the institution's psychologist. Both authors met frequently for planning purposes and maintained constant supervision of the experience. The second author met separately for about two hours with the group of patients, medical staff and legal staff. The participants' roles and duties were discussed; patients were not, however, given any details about their ward experience.

The intake interview, commitment hearing and in-class debriefing were conducted in a large classroom and the psychiatric ward was a large dormitory room.

Every effort was made to replicate the environment of a mental hospital ward. For example no books, pencils, pens, money, matches, cigarettes, etc. were allowed and permission had to be obtained from the attendants in order to obtain various items. Role-playing nurses and doctors took brief medical and psychological histories or conducted brief therapy sessions. Meals were brought onto the ward. A field trip was conducted to a local shopping center, with the attendants providing money for the patients to play pinball or purchase ice cream; conspicuous remarks were made by the attendants indicating that various patients had made progress in certain areas.

The "hospitalization" was to last 72 hours. However, it was ended after 48 hours by the instructor because of developing adverse psychological reactions, one brief escape and a few other escape attempts. It was followed by individual debriefing with the instructor, the in-class commitment hearing and an in-class discussion session.

The Results. As in Claibom and Lemberg's (1974) study and Zimbardo's (1972) study of prison simulation, the undergraduate students became involved in the extended role-playing to the point of exposing themselves to considerable discomfort. Initially there was general anxiety among the students over their confinement. However, after only five hours they began to feel bored and the psychiatric roles which each had planned for themselves were abandoned because they were too difficult to maintain . As the simulation progressed, the students experienced resentment over being told what to do by the staff members, as well as feelings of depression, apathy and helplessness.

During the pre-commitment interviews the "star patient" became genuinely concerned about what her "parents" were saying about her in an interview with the psychiatrist. The parents also expressed real concern and feelings of responsibility for their child and what they were getting her into. The mother, particularly, found it very difficult to give her up, even though she knew it was "a game." In a subsequent visit to the ward arranged on the parents' own initiative, the parents were very self-conscious and awkward, exchanging only superficial conversation with their "daughter. " After the visit, the star patient's "mother" rejected spontaneously her role instructions to support continued hospitalization for her daughter in testimony during the commitment hearing.

The attendants obviously felt awkward in their role and tried to make the patients feel comfortable. This was reflected in one attendant's willingness to be the object of tricks and teasing and in others taking them

for more walks than planned, allowing them to have a variety of things to pass the time, etc. The doctors, however, were more strict and quickly became rather authoritarian, distant and unemotional in their contacts with the patients.

Recommendations. The use of extended simulation experience in teaching undergraduate abnormal or clinical psychology courses can certainly improve student motivation and interest, while providing experiential learning about the roles, duties and pressures of patients and staff in mental hospital settings. Our study suggests that a meaningful simulation experience can be conducted with lower level college undergraduates, without its necessarily consuming the major portion of the semester's activities. It can also be carried out without extra expenditures and without unusual demands for space or equipment.

It should also be emphasized that simulation of the kind reported here and earlier by Zimbardo (1972) and Claiborn and Lemberg (1974) can be quite uncomfortable for the participants. The students' adoption of the suggested role plus their desire to make the project successful by continued participation—make it unlikely that they will withdraw from the stressful situation. It is the responsibility of the instructor, who hopefully has clinical experience. to closely supervise the simulation and end it before students experience tensions and conflicts which can not be easily reversed. In the present study, participants were carefully screened prior to the simulation and given at least a one hour individual debriefing session immediately following the simulation. These precautions should be followed in any simulation experience which is expected to be uncomfortable for the participants.

In spite of the difficulties involved in planning and supervising a simulated mental hospital setting, the exercise appears to be quite worthwhile as a teaching technique. The instructor may successfully simulate the entire hospital setting over an extended period of time as in the Claiborne and Lemberg (1974) study or focus primarily on a specific aspect of the hospital experience (e.g., patients' reactions) as in the present study.

References

Bardill, D. The ego ideal and clinical activity. *Social Work,* 1971, *16,* 75-80.

Claiborn, W., & Lemberg, R. A simulated mental hospital as an undergraduate teaching device. *Teaching of Psychology,* 1974, *1,* 38-40.

France, W., & McClure, J. Building a child care staff learning game. *Simulation and Games,* 1972, *3,* 189-202.

MacLennan, B. Simulated situations in group psychotherapy training. *International Journal of Group Psychotherapy,* 1971, *21,* 330-332.

Orlando, N. The mock ward: a study in simulation. In O. Milton and R. Wahler (Eds.). *Behavior Disorders: Perspectives and Trends* (3rd edition). Philadelphia: Lippincott 1973.

Ringuette, E., & Snyder, J. Role assumption as an aid in understanding criminal behavior. *Correctional Psychologist,* 1970, *4*, 119-121.

Weitz, W. Experiencing the role of a hospitalized psychiatric patient: a professional's view from the other side. *Professional Psychology,* 1972, *3*, 151-154.

Zimbardo, P. Pathology of imprisonment. *Society,* 1972, *9*, 4-8.

2. USING FIELD EXPERIENCES

A Volunteer Program for Abnormal Psychology Students: Eighteen Years and Still Going Strong

Forrest Scogin
Henry C. Rickard
University of Alabama

/

A volunteer experience in abnormal psychology is described. The program has been operating for 18 years, and student reactions have been quite positive. The program augments the traditional course offerings and provides reciprocal service for the university and mental health facilities. Guidelines for implementing a volunteer program are outlined, and suggestions for management are offered.

Abnormal Psychology is one of the most popular undergraduate psychology courses, and many students would undoubtedly report that it is one of the most interesting. Readings, lectures, and discussion are the usual fare, and the subject matter is amply suited for such instruction. At the University of Alabama, however, traditional abnormal psychology coursework has been augmented with volunteer work. This experiential component has been operating for 18 years, and merits attention for its longevity and its favorable reception by students. Similar programs in child development courses (e.g., Fox, Lopuch, & Fisher, 1984; Moffett, 1975; Stollak, 1975) and undergraduate internships (e.g., Shiverick, 1977) have been described, though apparently none are identical to the University of Alabama program. We would like to share the rationale and procedures for this program, as well as student feedback, so that other instructors may consider implementation.

Abnormal Psychology is an upper-level course. The two sections typically enroll between 80 and 100 students. A wide variety of majors take the course, with a preponderance of health-related majors enrolled (e.g., nursing, occupational therapy, and social work). Almost all of the students indicate that they have never worked or volunteered in a psychiatric setting, and a number of students enroll in the course primarily for the volunteer opportunity. Word of mouth and periodic media exposure in the student newspaper make prospective enrollees aware of this opportunity.

At the program's inception, Henry Rickard (the second author), impressed by the enthusiasm of a few students who had functioned as volunteers at the local state hospital, proposed making that experience available to all members of abnormal psychology classes. The department chair and the dean of Arts and Sciences supported the concept, and the innovation was launched in the fall of 1968. Fortunately, the major state psychiatric facility was located adjacent to the campus, and a large Veterans Administration neuropsychiatric hospital was nearby. The VA Hospital, in particular, had a well developed volunteer program that provided a ready vehicle through which students could receive orientation, legal protection, and general supervision. Consequently, the first class of 30 students was assigned to that facility for the semester. Approximately 25 hr of in-hospital experience was required. The occasional student who chose not to work in the hospital, because of personal concerns or time limitations, wrote a term paper or completed some other equivalent class assignment. Approximately 93% of the 30 students participating in the pilot program considered the experience worthwhile and advocated that it should be continued as part of abnormal psychology coursework.

The program has continued through a succession of instructors and mental health volunteer services coordinators. We estimate that over the years, more than 3,000 students have volunteered time, provided a valuable service to many patients, and enriched their educational experience. No major negative incidents (e.g., student injury or patient abuse) have occurred during this time, which suggests that potential concerns about negative outcomes are based on low-probability occurrences.

Full cooperation of mental health agencies is imperative for a successful volunteer program. First and foremost, agencies must be willing to have volunteers serve their facilities. Further, the volunteer services staff or contact person at the cooperating agency must be willing to take responsibility for placement, training, and record-keeping, otherwise the program will require inordinate faculty time. Fortunately, in our experience the volunteer services staffs of the two large psychiatric facilities have been willing to donate a considerable amount of time to such administrative tasks. In an early semester class session, representatives of the two major facilities present information pertinent to the volunteer experience. This session also serves as an orientadon that includes issues of confidentiality, appropriate dress and decorum, and patient rights.

Shortly after this presentation, students are informed of their volunteer assignments. An on-site supervisor is assigned Or each placement by the volunteer services coordinator, and students are given designated hours of attendance. Our students function more as companions to patients than as therapists, and accordingly, volunteer work has included transporting patients through the hospitals, assisting in recreational activities, leading educational classes, and most frequently, simply socializing. We believe that our students, as a group, may be superior volunteers in that they are bright, capable, and have a better than average background in psychology.

The minimum required hours of volunteer work have fluctuated over the years, but lately we have required about 20 hr per semester. Almost all of the students are able to meet this minimum requirement. The hours accumulated by the student are recorded by the volunteer services director and sent to the instructor at the end of the semester. Student progress is informally monitored by soliciting reports of interesting occurrences during their recent vises. More formal monitoring of progress by weekly conferences or written materials requires too much time in classes of 50 to 70 students. In institutions with smaller enrollments, such monitoring may be feasible, and undoubtedly would contribute to a richer learning experience. Students having difficulties with patients, stag or the course requirements are encouraged to meet individually with the instructor. The only other requirement for the volunteer component of the course is a brief typewritten narrative of the student's experiences as a volunteer. This paper is an effort to facilitate some closure on the student's exposure to psychopathology and the mental health delivery system. The assignment also allows the student to provide the instructor with informal feedback about the adequacy and relevance of the volunteer program.

Initially, students express some concerns about working in an inpatient psychiatric facility, and some discussion related to these concerns is advised before their first visits. Themes of personal safety, observer discomfort, contagious infection, and overidentification with patients have all been broached. A brief discussion of volunteer experiences precedes most classroom lectures during the semester, and serves to set an informal and interactive tone Or the material to Allow. Unfortunately, it is open hard Or the academic material presented in class to compete with the sometimes mysterious, tragicomic, and Fantastic behavior of long-term psychiatric inpatients. However, it is this sort of competition that is profitable.

Integration of lectures and readings with volunteer experiences is accomplished by continued discussion of students' reactions to their work during class time. We have observed that students are typically very at-tentive when their peers are discussing what has recently occurred at their volunteer site. Lectures on specific clinical problems and techniques are augmented by student descriptions of real-life observations of the syndromes and interventions. For example, presentation of symptoms of schizophrenia is greatly embelished by encouraging students to recount neologisms or clang associations they have heard patient produce.

There are several potentially negative aspects to the volunteer experience Or both students and instructors. For a variety of personal and logistical reasons, some students are unable to become involved in the volunteer program, therefore, alternative experiences must be arranged. In the past several years this alternative has consisted of preparing book reviews of biographical and autobiographical accounts of psychopathology. Students are discouraged from electing this option and few do.

Another potential negative aspect of volunteer work is the occasional student who experiences psychological conflict. For some, sustained contact with disturbed children and adults is distressing to the point of interfering with their own Functioning. In a class of approximately 60, an average of about 1 student will report such experiences to the instructor. One effort to minimize such negative reactions is to inform students that they will undoubtedly experience some naturally occurring discomfort in psychiatric settings. This is presented in the guise of the "medical student's syndrome," whereby identification with symptoms is a part of the learning process. Students are also encouraged to speak with the instructor if the volunteer work becomes problematic. As noted earlier, very few students find this necessary.

Before launching a volunteer program, the department or instructor should consult the university attorney to clarify individual and institutional liability. Likewise, the mental health facility must be willing to assume liability for volunteers. In this connection, we suggest that instructors refrain from advising ways in which students might best interact with patients. This is tempting in that students will often discuss problematic patient situations in class and will want guidance as to the most effective way to help (or not hurt) patients. Our practice has been to refer students to their facility supervisor for suggestions on how best to interact with their particular patient(s), including the processes of initiating and terminating the relationships.

We began a systematic evaluation of the volunteer experience in the spring semester of 1986. We devised a questionnaire, based in part on the instrument developed by Fox, Lopuch, and Fisher (1984), to assess students' reactions to the volunteer work. We also obtained demographic information about the students The results of this questionnaire are presented in Table 1.

Eighty-four students completed the questionnaire. Seventy-five percent of the respondents were women (which was the approximate percentage of women in the total class with an average age of 22.0 years. Seventy percent of the respondents were psychology majors or minors, with an average of 74.0 credit hours completed. Eighty-two percent of the students had no previous experience doing volunteer work in a mental health setting. To reduce evaluation apprehension, students completed the questionnaire anonymously and were informed that the results had no bearing on their grades.

The results of the survey suggest that students had a very positive overall reaction to the volunteer experience, became quite personally involved in the work, and reported a meaningful positive change in their attitudes toward psychiatric patients and mental health

Table 1. Means and Standard Deviations of Student Responses to a Volunteer Questionnaire

Question	M	SD
1. Please rate your overall reaction to the Abnormal Psychology volunteer experience.	7.79	1.58
2. How personally involved in the volunteer experience did you become?	7.29	1.70
3. Have your attitudes about psychiatric patients/mental health care changed as a result of your volunteer experience?	7.24	2.49
4. To what extent did the volunteeer experience increase your knowledge of abnormal psychology?	6.98	2.33
5. To what extent did the volunteer experience increase your motivation to study and understand material presented in the text and lectures?	6.73	2.37

Question	Positive/ Yes	Negative/ No
6. If there was a change in your attitudes, has this change been toward a more positive or more negative perception of psychiatric patients/mental health care?	91%	9%
7. Do you plan to continue your volunteer work after the semester ends?	29%	71%

Note. Eighty-four students completed the questionnaire. Questions 1 through 5 were fully-anchored, 11-point (0–10) Likert-type scales with higher values representing more positive responses.

care. A somewhat less positive impact on academic knowledge and motivation was reported. Interestingly, students generally did not intend to continue their volunteer work after the semester, despite their positive reactions. This disinclination to continue may be attributable to a number of factors, including graduation, summer vacation, employment, or simple disinterest. More clearly, it suggests that most students would not have sought out volunteer work in a mental health facility were it not a course requirement. However, the 29% of the students indicating an interest in continuation represents approximately 900 possible volunteers over the course of 18 years. The potential positive im-

pact of these persons on patient care and the community's perception of psychiatric treatment is enormous.

Another benefit of the volunteer program has been the decision or discovery by several students that a career in mental health or a related field is what they wish to pursue. Such sentiments have been revealed in the narratives students have written at the end of the semester. Conversely, some students have discovered that a career in mental health is not what they want to pursue. Whatever the case may be, exposure to the mental health care system is valuable "career guidance" for many of our students. In the students' written narratives of their volunteer experiences, the majority of the comments are positive. For example, one student commented, "It was a learning experience I will never forget," and another reported that "The volunteer work provided me with more insight into the material." Particularly gratifying were comments such as "I've not only found that I can work with people in mental institutions, but also that I have learned much and grown as a person by going there," and "Throughout my volunteer experiences, I felt I was making a difference." A few students did offer negative comments. For example, one reported straightforwardly that "I honestly did not enjoy my volunteer work" and another commented "I guess I felt like I was wasting my time." Among those who reported generally positive experiences, a frequent theme was the desire to exert greater beneficial effects on patients whom they contacted. For example, one student commented "The work frustrated me a little, because my goal would always be to get those people out of there, and with many of them, it is just impossible."

Implementation of a volunteer experience in abnormal psychology admittedly requires substantial planning and consultation. However, once the program is in place, our experience has been that little additional work is required. Thus, the initial efforts are rewarded by a continuing reciprocal service for the academic and mental health facilities. Students gain invaluable personal and professional experience, while the facilities experience an infusion of enthusiasm, intelligence, and welcome naiveté.

References

Fox, R. A., Lopuch, W. R., & Fisher, E. (1984). Using volunteer work to teach undergraduates about exceptional children. *Teaching of Psychology, 11,* 113-115.

Moffett, P. S. (1975). Inner-city field work in learning disabilities. *Teaching of Psychology, 2,* 119-122.

Shiverick, D. D. (1977). A full-time clinical practicum for undergraduates. *Teaching of Psychology, 4,* 188-190.

Stollak, G. E. (1975). Sensitivity to children Helping undergraduates acquire child care giving and mental health skills. *Teaching of Psychology, 2,* 8-11.

Note

We thank the volunteer staffs of Bryce Hospital and the Veterans Administration. Without their cooperation the program described here would have been impossible.

An Abnormal Psychology Community-Based Interview Assignment

Geoffry D. White
California State University, Fullerton

Activities and projects of various kinds have been suggested as important adjuncts to classroom teaching of Abnormal Psychology (e.g., Hansen, Hansen, D'Angelo & Smart, 1972; Price & Price, 1974). Instructors have struggled with new ways to make the subject matter interesting, involving, and more meaningful for their students. One hopes that students will make their own discoveries from an involving experience and that these will be remembered longer than material that is simply read.

The project described and evaluated in this report was offered as one of several options in the course. It involves students interviewing and observing the activities of individuals in the off-campus community who are concerned or involved with some topic in abnormal psychology(e.g., child abuse, transsexuals, drug abuse). The evaluation consists of anonymous student and interviewee ratings and comments concerning the project.

Method. At the beginning of the semester, students are informed that there are several term project options open to them. The interview project is presented as a way for students to combine two different kinds of sources of information on a topic of their choosing. First, they read from current books and journals in their area of interest. Secondly, students contact and interview an individual or group for a closer and more intimate look at the topic. The interviewees can either be mental health professionals or people who have or had any of the conditions described in the text (Davison & Neale, 1974). It is the students' responsibility to discover and meet with prospective interviewees. They are asked not to select someone they currently know, such as employers, coworkers, or family friends. An important part of the assignment is learning to be resourceful and assertive in interactions within the community. The process of locating interviewees, a brief literature review, and the interview report is submitted at the end of the course in a ten to twenty page paper.

Several steps are involved before the interview is conducted and observations made. First of all, students submit a one page proposal early in the semester which identifies their topic, their reasons for selecting it, how they plan to meet interviewees, and five literature references which must have been published after 1970. The latter requirement helps guarantee that current literature and theories are being explored and that students become familiar with publications i n major psychology journals. Students are encouraged to consult with the instructor and text for suggested sources of information.

This first step serves initial screening purposes. For example, students who select sensitive topics are asked to discuss them personally with the instructor. Projects which are too large, and are therefore unlikely to be covered adequately in an interview based paper, are given suggestions for narrowing their focus. Students are also given ideas and leads for finding someone interesting to interview.

The second step is that after the topic is approved students submit a five page paper with abstracts and discussion of at least ten journal articles and/or books related to the topic. Students can elect to make alterations in their proposal at this time. Also, at this time a one page outline of questions and issues to be discussed with the interviewee is attached to the review. This is returned with comments and suggestions from the instructor (e.g., students typically ask too many "closed-ended" questions requiring only a yes or no response). At this point students arrange an appointment with potential interviewees.

Finally, students are asked to submit the name, address, and phone number of the individuals they interview. They are also asked for at least a one page verbatim transcript of their interaction with the interviewee. Students are encouraged to audiotape their interview, if possible, and to erase the tape after submitting the final paper.

It is explained that the instructor may question the interviewees for further information, to arrange to have them as guest speakers, or to clarify some aspect of the interview. In some ways, this feature may have served to encourage accurate and honest reporting by students since it operates as a spot check procedure.

Subjects. Twenty-three out of 35 students taking Abnormal Psychology in the Fall 1976 semester selected and completed the interview project option. The remaining students in the course contracted for a variety of other term project options. Of the 23 students, 11 were Psychology majors. The remaining 12 were divided among other Humanities majors with a few students from Business and the Physical Sciences. This mix is fairly representative of the balance of psychology to non-psychology majors who take this course.

Twenty of the 23 (87%) interviewees responded by completing and returning the evaluation form mailed to them at the end of the semester. Only one of the respondents failed to include his or her name even though the form indicated that this was optional.

There were 11 male and eight female respondents. With the exception of two transsexuals, all respondents were providers of mental health services. The highest academic degrees obtained included: two MDs, three PhDs, seven Masters-level professionals, two BA degreed individuals, and five with two-year college degrees. The average age of the respondents was almost 41 years, with a range from 27 to 60 years.

Interview Topics. Topics concerned with children were the most numerous in this study, a result that is highly consistent over the four semesters that this project option has been used. Some of these topics included: hyperactivity, infantile autism, child abuse, the negative effects of divorce and of adoptions, and play therapy. Concern with adult topics usually ranks second among undergraduate students, which held up this semester as well. Topics here were: drug abuse, transsexualism, pedophilia, and the abuse of the aged in institutional settings.

It should be noted that over the last few years there has yet to be an instance where a student proposed to interview someone who was involved in a previous semester's projects. This may not be surprising considering that the Southern California area surrounding the instructor's university contains millions of people and hundreds of mental health facilities.

Results. The items and mean ratings for the students' evaluation of the assignment are presented in Table 1 along with the rating scale. A seven point rating scale was employed as shown in the Table. Only points 1, 4,

and 7 had labels and respondents were asked to evaluate the question or item by circling the appropriate numerical rating. As can be seen from these results, students felt that they had learned quite a bit compared to term projects in other courses. They enjoyed it, thought other courses could benefit from a similar assignment, but that it required more work than other projects. They thought the interviewees were interested in talking to them.

The items and mean ratings for the evaluations obtained from the interviewees are presented in the lower part of Table 1. The results indicate that the interviewees generally enjoyed being interviewed, would be happy to repeat the experience, and did not particularly find the interview an imposition on their time. They perceived the student interviewers as having prepared for the interview and very interested in the topic. On the other hand the interviewees reported that they themselves did not learn too much from the experience, which might have been expected.

Some representative comments made by several interviewees are the following:

"I would be glad to be the subject of an interview at any time. I think it's one of the best possible ways for students to learn 'straight from the horse's mouth'." "The student who interviewed me was very interested, polite, and seemed better prepared than some professionals have been who've interviewed me in the past." "A pleasant experience and a good assignment. Students find out that professionals don't know all the answers nor do they "win" all cases!"

Discussion. The small sample of data suggests that the interview project described in this paper was generally a successful experience as evaluated by students and their interview subjects. The discussion to follow focuses on important factors to be considered in assigning this or similar projects and several side benefits which occurred. The preparation required by students for the current project was greater than in previous semesters. For example, students were required to submit a five page literature review and an interview outline, both of which were edited and critiqued by the instructor. These assignments were aimed at producing students who were better organized and prepared to conduct the interview. It is suspected that lower ratings would have been obtained had the current evaluation procedures been carried out on previous semesters' projects. Indeed, in those cases where the interviewee commented that the student was not very well organized, the quality of the student's final papers was of lower overall quality than students receiving higher ratings on "preparation."

Instructors who plan to use these procedures should be prepared to spend more time than they may currently devote to reading and grading traditional projects and papers. in addition to reading the final papers, the instructor must screen the initial one-page

Table 1
Evaluations of the Interview Project

Rating Mean	Range	Item
		By Students
5.8	4 - 7	1. Compared to other term projects, how much time was devoted to this one?
6.3	5 - 7	2. Compared to other term projects, how much was learned from this one?
5.6	3 - 7	3. Compared to other term projects, how much did you enjoy this one?
5.6	4 - 6	4. To what extent do you think that other courses could benefit from this type of project?
4.3	1 - 7	5. How difficult did you find the role of interviewer?
5.6	3 - 7	6. How enjoyable did you find the role of interviewer?
3.6	1 - 7	7. How much difficulty did you have locating an interviewee?
5.3	4 - 7	8. How helpful was the interviewee in providing you with desired information?
6.2	5 - 7	9. Did the interviewee seem interested in talking to you?
		By Interviewee
5.3	4 - 7	1. How prepared was the interviewer?
5.8	3 - 7	2. How much did you enjoy being interviewed?
5.7	4 - 7	3. What kind of an impression did the interviewer make on you?
6.3	5 - 7	4. Did the interviewer seem interested in the topic?
3.2	1 - 7	5. How much did you learn from the interview?
5.7	4 - 7	6. Would you be willing to participate in another interview like this in the future?
3.1	1 - 7	7. To what extent was the interview an imposition on your time?

Rating scale:	1	2	3	4	5	6	7
	very poor/ very little			adequate/ average			very good/ very much

proposals and then the five-page reviews and interview outline. Finally, personal interviews must be made with those students selecting sensitive or difficult topic areas.

Greater time is also required for projects which raise certain ethical and logistical difficulties. That is, while innovative projects have greater possibilities they also have greater risks. Such projects require additional supervision by the instructor compared to the traditional library research review paper. Issues of confidentiality, invasion of privacy, being exposed to individuals with intense feelings about a particular project, and other potential hazards must be considered and discussed with students. In short, innovations in teaching. as in any area of psychology (e.g., clinical practice and testing), must be taken seriously for maximum benefit and minimum negative effects. The project described here was approved by the department's human subjects review committee. It is recommended that this procedure be used when nontraditional projects involve unsupervised students who have interviews with individuals who are not specifically provided by or known to the instructor.

It has been suggested that students might benefit from interviewing individuals whose socioeconomic status is considerably lower than that in the present sample. This experience would provide students with exposure to individuals who are not traditionally thought of as providing mental health services. For example, psychiatric technicians in hospital settings, members of minority groups hired as paraprofessionals in public mental health clinics, and low socioeconomic status volunteer workers in various community

psychology programs would all be available for interviews.

The additional time and energy required of the instructor was more than made up by several positive side effects of the project. It is gratifying to introduce students to a new form of term project which they enjoy and where learning occurs. In addition, several students have found employment as a result of the interview and observation of the interviewee's agency and activities.

Another tangible result is that the instructor has become much more familiar with the local community and its mental health resources. This information has been used to obtain interesting guest speakers for Abnormal Psychology and other courses. Knowledge about the variety of mental health services has also been helpful in directing graduate students in an applied psychology training program to potential fieldwork settings.

References

Hansen, P., Hansen, S., D'Angelo, B., & Smart, K. *Instructor's Resource Book for Coleman, Abnormal Psychology and Modern Life.* Glenview, IL: Scott Foreman, 1972.

Price, G. H., & Price, K. P. *Instructor's Manual and Resource Book for Davison & Neale, Abnormal Psychology: An Experimental Clinical Approach.* New York: Wiley, 1974.

3. TEACHING WITH CASE-STUDIES

A Case-Study Assignment to Teach Theoretical Perspectives in Abnormal Psychology

David V. Perkins
Ball State University

Teaching students to consider alternative theoretical paradigms helps them understand how psychologists think about behavior. This article describes an assignment in which students organize, prepare, and revise a case study of abnormal behavior using a single theoretical perspective. The assignment is personally meaningful for students, provides an excellent opportunity to integrate psychology with other liberal arts, and has received very positive evaluations from hundreds of students over the past 10 years.

Theoretical perspectives, or paradigms (Kuhn, 1970), have received increased attention in psychology courses at all levels over the past 20 years. This trend has been especially prominent in undergraduate courses in abnormal psychology (Sarason, 1983), for which most of the texts are organized explicitly in terms of theoretical perspectives (e.g., biological, psychodynamic, behavioral, cognitive, and humanistic). A key lesson of this approach is that data enlarge and shape our understanding of theories, which act as lenses, focusing our attention on certain types of empirical relations. However, it is difficult for many undergraduate students to appreciate the pervasive reciprocal influence of theory and data without an active, sustained effort.

A case-study assignment promotes active, self-directed learning by requiring students to teach themselves and the instructor about psychopathology and about relevant theoretical perspectives. Chrisler (1990) described an assignment in which the student selects a case from a predetermined list and then writes a paper summarizing the character's symptoms, diagnosis, and treatment. This article describes an alternative procedure that more explicitly emphasizes the role of theoretical perspectives in abnormal psychology.

Case-Study Assignment

An assignment I have required in Abnormal Psychology for the past 10 years involves the preparation and revision of a 10 page paper that examines an individual's life and behavior from a single theoretical perspective. Students are required to choose a figure from history, literature, the arts, or current events and must submit this choice for approval early in the term.

A representative list of about 150 individuals examined in previous papers is provided for illustration; however, students are encouraged to select an individual not on this list. Acceptable cases are those for which sufficient objective information about the individual's overt behavior patterns and circumstances (e.g., family living conditions, major life events, and milestones) is readily available. Fictional as well as real individuals are acceptable, and useful examples are Ernest Hemingway, Vincent Van Gogh, Betty Ford, Ivan Desinovitch, Holden Caulfield, Norman Bates, Theodore Bundy, and Marilyn Monroe. Although students rarely submit them, unacceptable cases would include a person known only to the student (e.g., a parent or friend), minor characters in literature, or other persons for whom little reliable information exists.

The 10 pages include three sections: (a) 2 to 3 pages summarizing the individual's behavior (details are presented in theory-free language, but are chosen primarily for their relevance to the given theoretical perspective), ending with a diagnosis using all five axes of the *Diagnostic and Statistical Manual of Mental Disorders* (3rd ed., rev. [DSM-III-R]; American Psychiatric Association, 1987); (b) 4 to 5 pages explaining the individual's behavior, using specific concepts from the chosen perspective (e.g., specific defense mechanisms, faulty cognitions, stigma, and social rejection); and (c) 2 to 3 pages outlining a hypothetical treatment regime based on the given perspective (e.g., psychoanalysis, systematic desensitization, or phenothiazines), including some prediction about the likely success or failure of this treatment.

One or more biographies of the individual are the primary sources most students use in summarizing the factual details. Most students also cite at least one source (e.g., the course text) for information about the theoretical perspective they use. Students are cautioned that a diagnosis stated or implied by an author or biographer may or may not be consistent with contemporary practice (i.e., *DSM-III-R*) and that they are responsible for providing a valid, defensible diagnosis.

The student's grade is based primarily on the accuracy, precision, and detail evident in applying the perspective to an analysis and treatment of abnormal behavior. The most frequent shortcoming is an etiological analysis that is insufficiently specific and detailed or includes concepts from more than one theoretical perspective.

This assignment is difficult for some students to do well. Therefore, I require students to submit both a rough draft and a revised final paper (only the latter is graded). It is also important to encourage steady work on this assignment throughout the course. In fact, the assignment may not be feasible in summer sessions or other intensive terms, although under these conditions I have had success substituting oral presentations of cases for written papers.

A few differences between this approach and that of Chrisler (1990) are worth noting. For example, instead of choosing from a predetermined list, each student takes full responsibility for finding a case to study, and the cases my students select tend not to be the classics (e.g., Dibs and Sybil) found on Chrisler's (1990) list. Chrisler seemed to focus more on the nature of therapy provided to the individual than on etiological explanation, whereas I reverse this emphasis. Finally, to provide for sufficient conceptual depth in a paper of 10 pages, my students are permitted to use only one theoretical perspective to structure the analysis, and the same perspective must be used in outlining the hypothetical treatment regime.

Discussion

This assignment is useful for a variety of reasons. It is helpful in evaluating a student's ability to think about behavior from an explicit theoretical perspective (i.e., as psychologists do) and to communicate these thoughts in writing. In addition, preparing a case study helps students see that any single perspective in psychology is incomplete and oversimplified (Mueller, 1985) and that a given perspective should be judged in terms of how useful it is, rather than whether it is true or false. Students also recognize that the usefulness of a given theory can be limited to a specific purpose. Psychoanalysis, for example, may produce interesting, heuristic insights into the origins of a case of obsessive-compulsive anxiety disorder, yet be of little value in facilitating the most effective treatment; on the other hand, a behavioral analysis of etiology in the same case may seem pedestrian, but lead to a relatively efficient and effective intervention.

This assignment also demonstrates the advantages and pitfalls of the case study as a method of research in abnormal psychology. For example, concrete illustrations of important psychological principles can be found in almost any interesting life, and the details of a particular case will sometimes stimulate further thinking by the student. As scientists, however, students also recognize the absence of systematic experimental controls in their case studies and how retrospectively fitting an imperfect theory to complex behavioral facts may bias the final conclusions.

A case-study assignment addresses the significant interest some students have in applying concepts from abnormal psychology to specific individuals. The diversity of individuals selected for study and the novelty of some cases that are presented convince me of the personal meaningfulness of this experience for most students. The almost unlimited number of potential cases provides an opportunity for undergraduate students to integrate abnormal psychology with material from literature, history, fine arts, or other fields, thus promoting a liberal education (Mueller, 1985; Williams & Kolupke, 1986).

Finally, from the instructor's vantage point, the high degree of structure makes this assignment relatively easy to grade objectively, even with a large class. Invariably, a few students perform much better on this assignment than they do on exams, and many students have told me that this case-study assignment was the single best element of the course.

References

American Psychiatric Association. (1987). *Diagnostic and statistical manual of mental disorders* (3rd ed., rev.). Washington, DC: Author.

Chrisler, J. C. (1990). Novels as case-study materials for psychology students. *Teaching of Psychology, 17,* 55-57.

Kuhn, T. S. (1970). *The structure of scientific revolutions* (2nd ed.). Chicago: University of Chicago Press.

Mueller, S. C. (1985). Persons in the personality theory course: Student papers based on biographies. *Teaching of Psychology, 12,* 74-78.

Sarason, I. G. (1983). Contemporary abnormal psychology: Developments and issues. In C. J. Scheirer & A. M. Rogers (Eds.), *G. Stanley Hall Lecture Series* (Vol. 3, pp. 75-115). Washington, DC: American Psychological Association.

Williams, K. G., & Kolupke, J. (1986). Psychology and literature: An interdisciplinary approach to the liberal curriculum. *Teaching of Psychology, 13,* 59-61.

Note

I thank Chris Lovejoy and two anonymous reviewers for helpful comments on earlier drafts of this article.

Students' Evaluation of Writing Assignments in an Abnormal Psychology Course

Mary E. Procidano
Fordham University

Students in an abnormal psychology class rated the usefulness of drafts for two writing assignments: a case-study reaction paper and a research proposal. Evaluative data indicated that the research proposal was more effective than the case study in develop ing students' interest in psychology. Students indicated that they valued the research proposal mostly for the opportunity to be creative; they valued the case study mostly for the opportunity to read an interesting book. Writing assignments and feedback to students should reflect important aspects of a discipline, and a clear rationale for the value of writing skills should be communicated to students.

Motivated by the writing-across-the-curriculum (WAC) movement, psychology professors have integrated a variety of writing assignments into their courses. However, there is little consensus regarding the relative value of different writing assignments, appropriate components of assignments, or criteria used to evaluate assignment effectiveness. I investigated the effectiveness of two types of writing assignments in an abnormal psychology course. Both assignments had reading and revision components, and their relative effectiveness was assessed by students' appraisal of the assignments' usefulness.

This project was guided by the assumption that assignments should reflect important themes or methods in a discipline. In abnormal psychology, for example, two salient and complementary approaches to collecting and interpreting data are idiographic and nomothetic. The idiographic approach, typified by case studies, is useful to explicate rare phenomena or procedures or to raise etiological hypotheses. In contrast, the nomothetic approach, typified by controlled empirical research, is used to generate general inferences about diagnostic or other groups (e.g., Davison & Neale, 1986). This project integrated both of these approaches into a writing assignment.

Blevins-Knabe (1987) suggested some appropriate outcome criteria for writing assignments by recommending that writing experiences should ameliorate students' writing deficiencies and promote their in volvement with course material. These criteria were used in evaluating the writing assignments described here.

The extent to which educational goals are achieved might be influenced by students' characteristics. For instance, more able students or those with more experience in a discipline may respond differently to some assignments than their less able or less experienced counterparts. However, the role of student characteristics has been neglected in the study of writing assignment outcomes.

Components of Assignments

Some perspectives are available in the current literature regarding assignment components that might improve students' writing skills. For instance, some authors have commented that the WAC movement has not attended adequately to students' serious difficulties in reading comprehension and higher order reasoning (e.g., Chamberlain & Burrough, 1985). In psychology, these limitations are evident when students accept the findings of empirical research in an unquestioning way (Anisfeld, 1987), skim research articles, or avoid the detail of method and results sections (Chamberlain & Burrough, 1985). Therefore, each assignment in this project included a reading component.

Descriptions of the WAC movement also have emphasized that good writing is a process and that feedback and revision should be integrated into writing assignments (e.g., Snodgrass, 1985). However, Mallonee and Breihen (1985) found that professors' written feedback is often used not for such educative purposes, but solely to justify the assigned grades. Sommers (1982) found that professors' written comments on students' papers were often characterized by "hostility and mean spiritedness" (pp. 148-149); such comments do not help students to revise papers or stimulate their motivation. My assignments incorporated reading, feedback, and revision. I provided constructive written feedback on the first drafts and allowed students to revise their papers.

This Study

This project evaluated case-study and research-proposal writing assignments in an abnormal psychology course. The assignments incorporated reading and feedback/revision components. The specific research questions were: Was it useful to require second drafts? What was the relative effectiveness of the two types of assignments? What role did student characteristics play in the obtained results? What was the nature of students' additional comments?

Method

Participants

The participants were 26 (19 women, 7 men) undergraduates (7 sophomores, 10 juniors, 9 seniors) enrolled in my abnormal psychology course. The class enrollment was 30; however, 2 students were not available for the assessment because they were exempt from the final exam, and 2 chose not to participate. Twenty-two students were psychology majors; the others were majoring in pre-med, sociology, and modern languages. All students had completed a prerequisite introductory psychology course. The number of previous psychology courses taken ranged from 1 to 10 (median = 3.5).

Procedure

For the case-study writing assignment, students read one book of their own choosing from a list of seven (Axline, 1969; Bruch, 1979; Clarke & Wardman, 1985; Freud, 1963; Levine, 1982; Sheehan, 1983; Vine, 1982). The books were chosen to reflect a range of disorders and etiological/theoretical perspectives. Based on information from the text and lectures, students presented their opinions about what they believed to be important issues in five-page reaction papers. One 50-min class period was devoted to explaining the purpose and nature of the paper, and ad hoc questions were entertained later.

For the research-proposal writing assignment, students wrote original research proposals, adhering to the guidelines of the *Publication Manual of the American Psychological Association* (American Psychological Association [APA], 1983). Fourteen published articles pertaining to a range of disorders were placed on library reserve for students to use as models. One class period was devoted to explaining the purpose and nature of the assignment and reviewing APA style. In addition, students were required to schedule individual appointments in which we discussed their topics and research designs; additional questions were entertained during and after class on an ad hoc basis.

Detailed written feedback was provided on the first drafts of both assignments. The feedback covered organization of the papers, clarity, correctness of the presentation, logic, research design, and grammatical points. Revisions were required on either or both papers if As were not achieved. (Each paper could be revised only once.) Moderately strict grading criteria were used. Each original draft counted for 10% of the final course grade, and each revision counted 5%, so that the writing assignments accounted for 30% of the final grade.

A graduate student administered the evaluation questionnaire after the final exam. The directions on the questionnaire indicated that it was intended to provide feedback to the instructor about the writing assignments. Students were directed to be honest in their answers and not to put their names on the forms. The first set of questions asked for background information (gender, year in school, and major). Students also were asked to indicate their grade point averages (GPAs) and the number of psychology courses taken previously as global indices of ability and prior experience, respectively. Then parallel sets of questions for each of the writing assignments were provided. Students rated the evaluative items on a 5-point scale ranging from *very useless and irrelevant* (1) *to very useful and relevant* (5).

The items were:

Overall, I found the assignment:
In terms of developing my writing skills, the assignment was:
In terms of developing my interest in psychology, the assignment was:
Overall, the comments provided on my first draft were:
For the purpose of revising my paper, the comments provided on my first draft were:
In terms of developing my writing skills, requiring a second draft of this paper was:
In terms of developing my interest in psychology, requiring a second draft of this paper was:

In addition, open-ended questions asked students to indicate what they liked most and least about each assignment. Responses were categorized and frequencies tabulated.

Results

The first set of analyses compared the relative usefulness of first and second drafts and of the case study versus research proposal. With one exception, the mean usefulness ratings ranged from 4.00 to 4.65 (i. e., between *somewhat useful and relevant* and *very useful and relevant*). Students evaluated the first and second drafts about equally. The one exception pertained to the case-study revision, which was judged to be less effective in developing interest in psychology, $t(17) = 4.57$, $p < .001$. (Two-tailed tests were used for all comparisons. The degrees of freedom term in analyses pertaining to revisions is smaller than that in other analyses, because students not required to revise papers could mark "not applicable" to questions about revisions.)

When case-study paper ratings were compared to research proposal ratings to assess the relative effectiveness of the two assignments, the one significant difference indicated that students perceived the research proposal to be more useful than the case study for developing their interest in psychology, $t(25) = 2.67$, $p = .01$.

Next, the roles of students' ability and prior experience were examined. GPA was related to some of the outcome criteria, including usefulness of the case study overall, $r(22) = .36$, $p = .04$, and with respect to developing students' interest in psychology, $r(22) = .48$, $p = .009$, and to usefulness of the research proposal with respect to developing writing skills, $r(22) = .53$, $p = .004$. The number of previous psychology courses was related to ratings of the usefulness of written comments provided on the first draft of the case study, $r(17) = .45$, $p = .03$, and marginally to the case study's usefulness in terms of developing writing skills, $r(23) = .29$, $p = .08$.

Finally, responses to the open-ended questions concerning what students liked most and least about the two assignments were categorized. Every student identified at least one positive aspect of the case-study assignment. The two most frequently reported responses were "learning about the subject matter" (14) and "reading the book" (11). Negative responses were less prevalent. For the research proposal, 19 students reported that they liked the challenge of "being creative" (11) and "designing [their] own experiments (8).

Discussion

Although students' ratings were generally favorable regarding both assignments and their revisions, the research proposal was more successful. Students found it more useful than the case study in developing their interest in psychology. Most of them enjoyed the opportunity to be creative by designing their own experiments. Requiring a second draft of the proposal also had demonstrable value.

Students may have perceived the nomothetic approach, and therefore the proposal, as more important than the idiographic approach in abnormal psychology. Such a perception is consistent with the emphasis in the lectures and textbook (Davison & Neale, 1986) as well as with the philosophy of the psychology department in which the course was offered (i.e., majors are required to complete four re search methods courses, including two semesters of statistics and research design and two of experimental psychology).

In contrast to the research proposal, the case-study paper may have seemed like a mere "writing exercise." In fact, the most positively evaluated aspect of the case-study assignment (learning about the subject, reading the book) seems attributable to the reading component of the assignment, rather than to writing.

Rewriting the case study was rated the least useful assignment. Perhaps this relatively low evaluation is attributable to the nature of the comments that were provided on the first draft, which may have lacked sufficient specificity to be helpful in rewriting. The most frequent problem that students had in writing the case-study paper was in relying heavily on presenting summaries of events in the books, rather than developing their own schemas of important issues and elaborating their own reactions.

Some of the most meaningful outcome criteria appear to have been influenced by students' ability (as reflected by GPA). More able students may be inclined to perceive assignments as more valuable.

This study was limited because it relied solely on students' opinions as outcome criteria. Future research should evaluate the effectiveness of these assignments in improving students' writing skills and comprehension. It also should be noted that the procedure used in this project was time-consuming and may be difficult to implement in large classes. Students did not need substantial prior experience with psychology to benefit from these assignments. Thus, the research proposal/revision combination appears to be generalizable to other types of psychology classes.

This exploratory study demonstrated the potential utility of writing assignments, particularly research proposals and revisions. The value of such assignments seems to depend on communicating to students a clear rationale for the value of writing skills and on integrating important aspects of a discipline into the assignments.

References

American Psychological Association. (1983). *Publication manual of the American Psychological Association* (3rd ed.). Washington, DC: Author.

Anisfeld, M. (1987). A course to develop competence in critical reading of empirical research in psychology. *Teaching of Psychology, 14*, 224-227.

Axline, V. (1969). *Dibs in search of self.* New York: Ballantine.

Blevins-Knabe, B. (1987). Writing to learn while learning to write. *Teaching of Psychology, 14*, 239-241.

Bruch, H. (1979). *The golden cage: The enigma of anorexia nervosa.* New York: Vintage.

Chamberlain, K., & Burrough, S. (1985). Techniques for teaching critical reading. *Teaching of Psychology, 12*, 213-215.

Clarke, J. C., & Wardman, W. (1985). *Agoraphobia: A clinical and personal account.* Elmsford, NY: Pergamon.

Davison, G. C., & Neale, J. M. (1986). *Abnormal psychology: An experimental clinical approach* (4th ed.). New York: Wiley.

Freud, S. (1963). *Dora: An analysis of a case of hysteria.* New York: Macmillan.

Levine, A. G. (1982). *Love Canal: Science, politics, and people.* Lexington, MA: Lexington Books.

Mallonee, B. C., & Breihen, J. R. (1985). Responding to students' drafts: Interdisciplinary consensus. *College Composition and Communication, 36,* 213-230.

Sheehan, S. (1983). *Is there no place on earth for me?* New York: Vintage.

Snodgrass, S. E. (1985). Writing as a tool for teaching social psychology. *Teaching of Psychology, 12,* 91-94.

Sommers, N. (1982). Responding to student writing. *College Composition and Communication, 33,* 148-156.

Vine, P. (1982). *Families in pain.* New York: Pantheon.

Notes

1. This research was supported by a Fordham College-Mellon Foundation Faculty Development Grant.

2. I thank Joseph Palladino, James Eison, Jane Halonen, and Barbara Nodine for their helpful conceptual suggestions and the anonymous reviewers for their valuable comments on an earlier draft of this article. Colleen Golden and Elisabeth Hennessey assisted in data analysis.

4. TEACHING ABOUT SUICIDE

Altering Attitudes Toward Suicide in an Abnormal Psychology Course

George Domino
University of Arizona

There is a prolific literature on virtually all aspects of suicide and suicide prevention, and it is generally agreed that suicide represents a serious and common concern both for clinical patients and more "normal" groups like college students. Surprisingly, little work has been done in the area of attitudes toward suicide and even less in attempts to systematically alter such attitudes, even though suicide is a basic topic in Abnormal Psychology courses.

The present report is one of a series of studies stemming from the development and application of a Suicide Opinion Questionnaire (SOQ), a 100 item attitudinal and factual instrument designed to cover a wide range of suicidal concerns. Prior studies have looked at the factorial complexity of attitudes toward suicide (Domino, et al., Note 1), at the attitudes of college students (Domino, et al., Note 2) and those of Jewish and Christian adults (Domino et al., Note 3). The focus of the present study is whether such attitudes can be altered within an academic context.

The subjects of the study were 17 college students, a random sample drawn from 89 students enrolled in a course in abnormal psychology. As part of the course, the 89 students met in smaller sections of approximately 20 students, formed on a random basis, once a week for 15 weeks, to investigate in depth a particular topic such as mental illness and creativity, cultural aspects of psychopathology, or suicide. As part of the suicide section, students were assigned readings and book reports on standard suicide texts (e.g., Alvarez, 1970; Farber, 1968; Lester, 1972), heard therapy transcriptions of suicidal patients, met with professional members involved in suicide prevention, as well as with suicide attempters. The focus of the section was both academic and experiential.

At the beginning of the semester, all students were assigned code numbers and were asked to complete the SOQ. Approximately 10 months after the completion of the course, the 22 students in the suicide section were contacted and again asked to complete the SOQ with code numbers supplied; three of the students could not be contacted, and two did not participate.

The SOQ questionnaires were scored on five areas based on the results of prior factor analyses: (a) Normality of suicide (22 items accounting for 16.8% of the variance, e.g., "Potentially, every one of us can be a suicide victim"); (b) Motivational aspects (18 items, 16.2% variance; e.g. , "Most suicide attempts are impulsive in nature"); (c) Religious-moral aspects (19 items, 13.9% variance,; e.g., "People who commit suicide lack solid religious convictions"); (d) Demographic dimensions (9 items: 8.7% variance; e.g., "The suicide rate is higher for blacks than for whites") and (e) Risk (8 items, 7.6% variance; e.g., "A person whose parent has committed suicide is a greater risk for suicide"). Scores on all questionnaires were changed to T scores using a normative sample of 400 college students, and were analyzed by a repeated measures ANOVA.

The results shown in Table 1 indicate that significant changes in attitude occurred on the first four

Table 1. Attitude Measures for Pre-Course and One Year Later on the Suicide Opinion Questionnaire

| Scale | T Score | | | | F | P |
| | Pre | | Post | | | |
	M	SD	M	SD		
Normality	52.1	10.17	55.2	8.52	8.35	<.025
Motivation	52.5	11.20	56.8	7.90	8.56	<.01
Religious	54.2	7.50	61.2	8.50	15.59	<.005
Demographic	54.7	8.00	57.7	7.70	12.32	<.005
Risk	53.6	9.00	56.9	6.90	2.57	ns

$df = 1,16$

areas, but not the fifth. Thus significant changes occurred in the students' attitudes toward suicide over a one year period of time. The time elapsed between the initial and subsequent testing was chosen purposely to eliminate any test-taking tendencies and to ensure an adequate follow up period. At the same time such a long period may dilute the effectiveness of the educational treatment in that such changes may have been caused by subsequent experiences: practical considerations did not permit the use of control groups at this time. These results may be viewed in the context of an initial study, which nevertheless suggests that attitudes toward suicide can indeed be altered in a more positive direction, and that the teaching of psychology can have measurable impact.

References

Alvarez, A. *The savage god.* New York: Random House, 1970.

Farber, M. L. *Theory of suicide.* New York: Funk & Wagnalls, 1968.

Lester, D. *Why people kill themselves.* Springfield, IL: Charles C Thomas, 1972.

Notes

1. Domino, G., Moore, D., Westlake, L, & Gibson, L. *Attitudes toward suicide: A factor analytic approach.* Manuscript submitted for publication, 1978.
2. Domino, G., Gibson, L., Poling, S., & Westlake, L. *Students' attitudes toward suicide.* Manuscript submitted for publication, 1 979.
3. Domino, G., Cohen, A., & Gonzalez, R. *Jews-Christians and suicide: A study of attitudes.* Manuscript submitted for publication, 1979.

Integrating Suicidology Into Abnormal Psychology Classes: The Revised Facts on Suicide Quiz

Richard W. Hubbard
John L. McIntosh
Indiana University at South Bend

Although most abnormal psychology textbooks and instructors give extensive coverage to topics such as depression, they cover suicide less consistently. This article describes a class activity using the Revised Facts on Suicide Quiz *(RFOS) that focuses on myths and misinformation students may have about suicide. The activity can take 55 to 75 min or can be modified for shorter or longer coverage. Suggestions for incorporating the RFOS in class discussion and references supporting correct quiz answers are provided.*

An informal review of standard textbooks and course syllabi in abnormal psychology reveals that although suicide is often mentioned, the degree of coverage is at best uneven. Suicide is an important topic for inclusion in abnormal psychology curricula for the following reasons:

1. There are more than 30,000 suicides annually, which ranks suicide eighth among the leading causes of death in the U. S. (National Center for Health Statistics [NCHS], 1992). Because a self-inflicted death occurs every 17 min, suicide represents an important area for prevention and intervention in the field of psychology.

2. Discussions of suicide can provide important illustrations of core concepts in abnormal psychology, such as depression, helplessness/hopelessness, cognitive distortions, and problems associated with alcoholism.

3. Suicide (especially among youth and the elderly) has received much media attention, and students are increasingly interested in the topic. One reason for this interest may be its personal relevance to some college students. Studies indicate that perhaps 40% to 50% of college students have suicidal thoughts and as many as 15% may have actually attempted suicide at some time (Slimak, 1990, p. 11). Student risk of suicide is estimated at about half that of nonstudents the same age (Schwartz, 1990). The overall suicide rate for those aged 15 to 24 is presently 13 per 100,000 population (NCHS, 1992). In addition, if conservative general estimates are applied, at least 1 of every 80 college students is the survivor of a loved one's suicide (McIntosh, 1989).

The Facts on Suicide Quiz

The original Facts on Suicide Quiz (FOS; McIntosh, Hubbard, & Santos, 1985) was developed as a research instrument to identify levels of knowledge and misconceptions about suicide. The original FOS consisted of 32 true-false items. Subsequently, 5 of the original questions were eliminated, 13 items that were

Table 1. Revised Facts on Suicide Quiz

Circle the answer you feel is most correct for each question.

"T" (true), "F" (false), or "?" (don't know)

T F ? 1. People who talk about suicide rarely commit suicide. [73%]

T F ? 2. The tendency toward suicide is not genetically (i.e., biologically) inherited and passed on from one generation to another. [46%]

T F ? 3. The suicidal person neither wants to die nor is fully intent on dying. [38%]

T F ? 4. If assessed by a psychiatrist, everyone who commits suicide would be diagnosed as depressed. [57%]

T F ? 5. If you ask someone directly "Do you feel like killing yourself?," it will likely lead that person to make a suicide attempt. [95%]

T F ? 6. A suicidal person will always be suicidal and entertain thoughts of suicide. [76%]

T F ? 7. Suicide rarely happens without warning. [63%]

T F ? 8. A person who commits suicide is mentally ill. [70%]

T F ? 9. A time of high suicide risk in depression is at the time when the person begins to improve. [47%]

T F ? 10. Nothing can be done to stop people from making the attempt once they have made up their minds to kill themselves. [92%]

T F ? 11. Motives and causes of suicide are readily established. [58%]

T F ? 12. A person who has made a past suicide attempt is more likely to attempt suicide again than someone who has never attempted. [80%]

T F ? 13. Suicide is among the top 10 causes of death in the U.S. [83%]

T F ? 14. Most people who attempt suicide fail to kill themselves. [74%]

T F ? 15. Those who attempt suicide do so only to manipulate others and attract attention to themselves. [64%]

T F ? 16. Oppressive weather (e.g., rain) has been found to be very closely related to suicidal behavior. [26%]

T F ? 17. There is a strong correlation between alcoholism and suicide. [68%]

T F ? 18. Suicide seems unrelated to moon phases. [49%]

19. What percentage of suicides leaves a suicide note? [40%]
   a. 15–25%   b. 40–50%   c. 65–75%

20. Suicide rates for the U.S. as a whole are _____ for the young. [8%]
   a. lower than   b. higher than   c. the same as

21. With respect to sex differences in suicide **attempts**: [65%]
   a. Males and females attempt at similar levels.
   b. Females attempt more often than males.
   c. Males attempt more often than females.

22. Suicide rates among the young are _____ those for the old. [7%]
   a. lower than   b. higher than   c. the same as

(continued)

Table 1. *(Continued)*

23. Men kill themselves in numbers _____ those for women. [67%]
   a. similar to   b. higher than   c. lower than

24. Suicide rates for the young since the 1950s have: [97%]
   a. increased   b. decreased   c. changed little

25. The **most** common method employed to kill oneself in the U.S. is: [28%]
   a. hanging   b. firearms   c. drugs and poison

26. The season of **highest** suicide risk is: [11%]
   a. winter   b. fall   c. spring

27. The day of the week on which **most** suicides occur is: [60%]
   a. Monday   b. Wednesday   c. Saturday

28. Suicide rates for non-whites are _____ those for Whites. [35%]
   a. higher than   b. similar to   c. lower than

29. Which marital status category has the **lowest** rates of suicide? [59%]
   a. married   b. widowed   c. single, never married

30. The ethnic/racial group with the **highest** suicide rate is: [15%]
   a. Whites   b. Blacks   c. Native Americans

31. The risk of death by suicide for a person who has attempted suicide in the past is _____ that for someone who has never attempted. [80%]
   a. lower than   b. similar to   c. higher than

32. Compared to other Western nations, the U.S. suicide rate is: [21%]
   a. among the highest   b. moderate   c. among the lowest

33. The most common method in **attempted** suicide is: [63%]
   a. firearms   b. drugs and poisons   c. cutting one's wrists

34. On the average, when young people make suicide attempts, they are _____ to die compared to elderly persons. [41%]
   a. less likely   b. just as likely   c. more likely

35. As a cause of death, suicide ranks _____ for the young when compared to the nation as a whole. [86%]
   a. the same   b. higher   c. lower

36. The region of the U.S. with the highest suicide rates is: [36%]
   a. east   b. midwest   c. west

Note. Answer key: true items—2, 3, 7, 9, 12, 13, 14, 17, and 18; false items—1, 4, 5, 6, 8, 10, 11, 15, and 16. Items for which the correct answer is "a": 19, 22, 24, 27, 29, and 34. Items for which the correct answer is "b": 21, 23, 25, 32, 33, and 35. Items for which the correct answer is "c": 20, 26, 28, 30, 31, and 36. For easier scoring in classroom settings, Questions 1 to 18 might be rearranged to alternate true and false items. Similarly, Items 19 to 36 may be rearranged to alternate a, b, and c answers. The percentages in brackets following each question refer to the proportion of 331 undergraduates enrolled in general psychology who correctly answered the item.

predominantly demographic in nature were rewritten as multiple-choice questions, and 9 new items were added (Questions 15, 20, 29, and 31 to 36 in Table 1). The modified quiz has a pool of 36 items: 18 true-false items focus on clinical issues and 18 multiple-choice questions assess primarily demographic information. The true-false and multiple-choice questions may be used singly or in combination; they are of sufficient length and include enough breadth of concepts for good pretest and posttest measurement as well. The authors recommended that instructors select at least half the items if they choose to create their own version. The items of the Revised Facts on Suicide Quiz (RFOS) appear in Table 1 (McIntosh, Kelly, & Arnett, 1992).

The RFOS has been a useful educational tool in our undergraduate abnormal psychology class. We typically use it in conjunction with lectures on depression or a full presentation on suicide. We accompany the quiz with a discussion of the clues or warning signs that would assist students in identifying those who might be depressed or suicidal (see, e.g., Shneidman, 1965). We also provide a list of the available resources for suicide prevention, intervention, and treatment both locally and on campus (see, e.g., Evans & Farberow, 1988, pp. 64-66). It is important to note that the topic of suicide can provoke strong emotions from prior attempters and friends and families of suicide completers. We acknowledge this fact at the onset and include resources for support and counseling among the list of local agencies.

We usually employ the RFOS in our abnormal psychology classes after a general lecture on depression, often by referring to a suicide that has been heavily reported in the media (e.g., celebrity suicides, such as Freddie Prinze or Marilyn Monroe, or the pact suicide of four high school students from New Jersey several years ago). After students have completed the quiz, either they are given an answer key and a discussion ensues or, when time permits, the instructor reviews each item and polls how many students answered items incorrectly.

In addition to using the RFOS in undergraduate abnormal psychology courses, we have also found it appropriate within the context of a lecture to undergraduates in a course on preventative community mental health and occasionally in other psychology courses (e.g., general psychology or psychology of aging). The RFOS (or FOS) has also been used as a pretest and posttest for in-service presentations for health care professionals (see McIntosh et al., 1985, for details and results) and crisis intervention trainees, as well as a discussion icebreaker with high school students and community groups. The quiz stimulates a great deal of discussion as it is scored immediately, and students have also indicated that it functions well as a handout or study guide for examinations.

Major benefits of the quiz have been that (a) it provides an organized structure for instruction in a field where research is scattered across several disciplines (e.g., psychiatry, psychology, sociology, nursing, public health, and social work), (b) it promotes discussion as students encounter their misconceptions regarding the topic, (c) the varied formats (true-false, multiple-choice) allow the material to be used in standard exams, (d) it covers a lot of material in a meaningful and interesting way, and (e) it includes questions that identify gaps in basic knowledge and misconceptions about the psychological processes associated with suicide.

Preliminary reliability and validity tests of the FOS have been conducted (McIntosh et al., 1992). These data suggest good psychometric qualities for each format. Factor analysis to determine specific clusters of questions (e. g., demographics, causes, signs, and clinical aspects) is underway. Unpublished data for 331 undergraduates enrolled in general psychology resulted in a mean score on the RFOS of 19.8 (SD = 2.7), or 55% correct for the 36 items, comparable to mean scores on the FOS of 59.1% (McIntosh et al., 1985). As in the study of the FOS, the RFOS performance was higher for the predominantly clinical items (M = 11.6, SD = 2.0; 64.4%) that comprised Questions 1 to 18, as compared to the largely demographic multiple-choice items (M = 8.2, SD = 1.7; 45.6%). However, note that the two categories of items represent different question formats (true-false vs. multiple-choice); the probability of answering a question

correctly by chance differs as well. Therefore, actual performance differences are minimal and not directly comparable. Performance by these 331 undergraduates (see Table 1) showed accurate knowledge about some items (e. g., 5, 10, 24, 35) and incorrect information about others (e.g., 16, 20, 22, 25, 26, 30,32). These findings regarding specific items were almost identical to those for the FOS.

Reference Guide for Answer Key

Full justification for each answer on the quiz is beyond the scope of this article. However, at least one source for each question is provided in Table 2. Further information for building a lecture around the questions and justifying the answers may be found in several core texts and articles (e.g., Evans & Farberow, 1988; McIntosh, 1985; Pokorny, 1968; Shneidman, 1985). Instructors should note that some of the answers are based on recent demographic data that will, of course, change over time. Although the quiz

Table 2. References Supporting the Answers of the RFOS

References	Items
Arana & Hyman (1989), p. 83; Kety (1990), p. 132	2
Buda & Tsuang (1990), pp. 27–28, 28–30	4, 17
Diekstra (1990), p. 540	32
Evans & Farberow (1988), pp. 120, 119, 244, 21, 254, 22, 244, 22	5, 10, 12, 14, 19, 21, 31, 33
Maltsberger (1991), p. 295	6
McIntosh (1991), pp. 61; 60–61; 58; 60; 65; 65; 65; 59; 63–65; 59–60; 63; 66–67	20, 22, 23, 24, 25, 26, 27, 28, 29, 30, 36
NCHS (1992), pp. 20, 20–21	13, 35
Pokorny (1968), pp. 57–58, 64–65, 71, 62, 66–70, 70–71	1, 8, 9, 11, 16, 18
Shneidman (1985), pp. 135, 143–144, 124–129	3, 7, 15
Shneidman & Farberow (1961/1970), p. 208	34

may need to be updated as new statistical trends in suicide become apparent, the need for this should be minimal, as the questions cover what appear to be stable relationships observed over the last several decades.

Questions in our classes that are frequently missed or that create much student interest include Items 2, 7, 8, 10, 15, 16, 19, 22, 26, and 30. Discussion usually focuses on explanations for high rates among the elderly and Native Americans, increases among the young, and theories related to motivations for suicide. Students also inquire about the influence of rock music lyrics and drug use on suicide rates and on "copy cat" or contagion observed in some high schools. Our class discussions always include social, cultural, and biological considerations, as well as psychological issues related to suicide. As discussions close, students are reminded that better outreach, assessment, and treatment are needed to reduce suicide rates and that eliminating myths about suicide can contribute to this goal.

References

Arana, G. W., & Hyman, S. (1989). Biological contributions to suicide. In D. Jacobs & H. N. Brown (Eds.), *Suicide: Understanding and responding: Harvard Medical School perspectives* (pp. 73-86). Madison, CT: International Universities Press.

Buda, M., & Tsuang, M. T. (1990). The epidemiology of suicide: Implications for clinical practice. In S. J. Blumenthal & D. J. Kupfer (Eds.), *Suicide over the life cycle: Risk factors, assessment, and treatment of suicidal patients* (pp. 17-37). Washington, DC: American Psychiatric Press.

Diekstra, R. F. W. (1990). An international perspective on the epidemiology and prevention of suicide. In S. J. Blumenthal & D. J. Kupfer (Eds.), *Suicide over the life cycle: Risk factors, assessment, and treatment of suicidal patients* (pp. 533-569). Washington, DC: American Psychiatric Press.

Evans, G., & Farberow, N. L. (1988). *The encyclopedia of suicide.* New York: Facts on File.

Kety, S. S. (1990). Genetic factors in suicide: Family, twin, and adoption studies. In S. J. Blumenthal & D. J. Kupfer (Eds.), *Suicide over the life cycle: Risk factors, assessment, and treatment of suicidal patients* (pp. 127-133). Washington, DC: American Psychiatric Press.

Maltsberger, J. T. (1991) . The prevention of suicide in adults. In A. A. Leenaars (Ed.), *Life-span perspectives of suicide: Time-lines in the suicide process* (pp. 295-307). New York: Plenum.

McIntosh, J. L. (1985). *Research on suicide: A bibliography.* Westport, CT: Greenwood.

McIntosh, J. L. (1989, Spring). How many survivors of suicide are there? *Surviving Suicide,* pp. 1, 4.

McIntosh, J. L. (1991). Epidemiology of suicide in the United States. In A. A. Leenaars (Ed.), *Life-span perspectives of suicide: Time-lines in the suicide process* (pp. 55-69). New York: Plenum.

McIntosh, J. L., Hubbard, R. W., & Santos, J. F. (1985). Suicide facts and myths: A study of prevalence. *Death Studies, 9,* 267-281.

McIntosh, J. L., Kelly, L., & Arnett, E. (1992). *The Revised Facts on Suicide Quiz: Reliability and validity tests.* Unpublished manuscript, Indiana University at South Bend, Department of Psychology.

National Center for Health Statistics. (1992). Advance report of final mortality statistics, 1989. *NCHS Monthly Vital Statistics Report, 40*(8, Suppl. 2).

Pokorny, A. D. (1968). Myths about suicide. In H. L. P. Resnik (Ed.), *Suicidal behaviors: Diagnosis and management* (pp. 57-72). Boston: Little, Brown.

Schwartz, A. J. (1990). The epidemiology of suicide among students at colleges and universities in the United States. In L. C. Whitaker & R. E. Slimak (Eds.) *College student suicide* (pp. 25-44). New York: Haworth.

Shneidman, E. S. (1965). Preventing suicide. *American Journal of Nursing, 65*(5), 111-116.

Shneidman, E. S. (1985). *Definition of suicide.* New York: Wiley.

Shneidman, E. S., & Farberow, N. L. (1970). Attempted and completed suicide. In E. S. Shneidman, N. L. Farberow, & R. E. Litman (Eds.), *The psychology of suicide* (pp. 199-225). New York: Science House. (Original work published 1961)

Slimak, R. E. (1990). Suicide and the American college and university: A review of the literature. In L. C. Whitaker & R. E. Slimak (Eds.), *College student suicide* (pp. 5-24). New York: Haworth.

5. INSTIGATING MISCELLANEOUS TECHNIQUES

Questioning the Conventional Wisdom and Critiquing Unconventional Perspectives in Abnormal Psychology: A Written Exercise

Dana D. Anderson
Pacific Lutheran University

This article describes a teaching exercise used in an undergraduate abnormal psychology course to strengthen students' critical-thinking abilities. Students complete a term paper critiquing a book that is itself a critique of the conventional wisdom in the field. Several books representing a variety of unconventional perspectives are available. The exercise aims at increasing students' historical perspective on the field and at confronting them with controversial issues. It also requires students to engage in an active dialogue with their instructor about an issue raised by the book. This dialogue culminates in the students defining a clear personal position on that issue. The exercise is consistent with an active approach to learning.

As Perkins (1991) noted, undergraduate abnormal psychology courses increasingly emphasize theoretical perspectives, usually the biological, psychodynamic, behavioral, cognitive, and humanistic viewpoints. It is important for students in such courses to understand these perspectives and to recognize, as Perkins's students did after completing a case study of abnormal behavior from a single theoretical perspective, that no one perspective constitutes an adequate account for all human deviance. Nevertheless, the risk remains that students will conclude that these usual five viewpoints exhaust the theoretical possibilities and that they constitute an adequate account for deviance. This risk seems exacerbated by the organization of most abnormal texts. The conventional five viewpoints are generally well integrated within the text, reappearing in each chapter to account for each category of disorder. Less conventional views are usually relegated to a single, early chapter and subsequently ignored.

Ironically, the chapter in which unconventional views are isolated is often the same chapter in which historical views are segregated. Costin (1982) noted that the latter type of segregation characterizes psychology tests and encourages students in their common misperception: The truth has always been and will always be whatever we currently hold it to be. Such text organization can deprive students of the historical awareness fundamental to critical thought. Furthermore, this organization avoids genuine engagement with some of the most controversial and sensitive ideas in the field. Costin (1985) suggested that genuine engagement with challenging ideas and an integrated historical perspective are necessary to our teaching if we are to meet our basic educational objective of training our students' intellects.

One exercise I use to counter these risks in my abnormal psychology course is a term paper assignment for which students must read and critique a book that takes an unconventional perspective on abnormal behavior. The list of books I use is attached to the course syllabus. It includes works from the antipsychiatry movement (e.g., Laing, 1967, 1969) and libertarian critiques of the mental health movement (e.g., Szasz, 1961, 1970) as well as Marxist (e.g., Brown, 1973; Foucault, 1965) and feminist (e.g., Chester, 1972; Ehrenreich & English, 1978) critiques of mental health professional practices. Labeling theory (e.g., Goffman, 1961; Scheff, 1984) is represented as is role theory (e.g., Sarbin, 1969; Sarbin & Allen, 1968). I include critiques by nonpsychologists of psychological testing (e.g., Gould, 1981; Green, 1981) as well as more general critiques of the social impact of psychology and its ideas (e.g., Gross, 1978, Wallach & Wallach, 1983). Works on the history of the mentally ill and their treatment (e.g., Porter, 1987; Valenstein, 1986) round out the list. The university library has copies of the books, and most are also available in paperback. Most of these works either document the history of the field of abnormal psychology or themselves influenced the field's history.

I instruct students to select one major theme from the book and to review critically the author's argument. Criteria for the review include the soundness of the author's reasoning, the quality of empirical evidence the author marshals to support the theme, and how well the author accounts for opposing points of view and rival interpretations of the evidence. Students must conclude their papers with a well defined and well supported position of their own on the theme critiqued. The position must be supported by both logical and empirical evidence, and it must be soundly reasoned and consistent with at least the research presented in class and the course text. I assist students in using these criteria because students are typically unfamiliar with them. Although Abnormal Psychology is a junior-level course for psychology majors, many non-majors enroll and introductory psychology is the sole prerequisite. Therefore, I spend the first day of class reviewing common research design flaws and logical fallacies.

Students select a book and theme by the third week of the semester. They then submit an opening paragraph stating their selections and outlining their preliminary evaluation of the author's argument. The early deadline discourages procrastination and allows corrective feedback for those students (few but inevitable) who are, despite instructions, writing a book report. The recommended length of the paper is 5 to 10 pages. The paper is completed in two drafts: one at midterm and one, incorporating response to my feedback, at semester's end. The first draft counts 20% of the course grade and the second draft counts 25%. This heavy contribution emphasizes the importance of students' critical thinking to course objectives. Grading, particularly on the first draft, takes into account students' typically low levels of logical and methodological sophistication. Grading emphasizes improvement beyond this baseline in the second draft. This draft-redraft approach is generally an effective way of teaching students to write (Baird & Anderson, 1990). The exercise creates a semester-long dialogue with each student. Such dialogue is vital for students to learn to communicate their thoughts effectively, and active involvement of students who must take a stand on an issue increases the quality of students' critical skills (Benjamin, 1991; Costin, 1985; Ferguson, 1986; Gorman, Law, & Lindegren, 1981).

In feedback to students, I address how closely their first draft matches the criteria for the paper and suggest areas for improvement. Almost always, improvement includes placing the work within its proper historical context and infer ring its relevance to contemporary concerns in the field. Despite my emphasis throughout the course on using a historical perspective, students rarely do so in their first drafts. For example, they often fail to realize that Szasz's (1961, 1970) works contributed to increased restrictiveness in involuntary commitment laws; they denigrate his critique of commitment procedures as outdated or as too idealistic to be practical. Students have difficulty understanding, in the abstract, what a historical perspective is. Most seem to require feedback on the particular relevance of history for their own paper's concern in order to appreciate the general benefits of a historical perspective. They do respond to the feedback; second drafts are better written and more historically informed. For example, students who, in their first drafts, dismiss as irrelevant Valenstein's (1986) criticisms of psychosurgery on the grounds that such surgery is rare today come to recognize by their second drafts the cautionary implications of his critique for other, more contemporary treatment. Several of these students recognized in their drafts that AIDS is as desperate a contemporary problem as schizophrenia was

in the 1940s and came to understand the currency of Valenstein's point that desperate problems encourage desperate, sometimes irresponsible, solutions. They viewed current medical and social responses to AIDS patients from a fresh, chastened viewpoint.

Besides being more historically informed, second drafts are generally better written, clearer, and more grammatical than initial drafts. Second drafts are better reasoned, showing fewer logical fallacies and internal contradictions, than first drafts. Assumptions are more clearly recognized as such; inferences are drawn with more awareness and care; and standards for judgments are articulated and defended where they were originally simple prejudices, left implicit or forwarded as self-evidently unimpeachable.

Student feedback generally supports the effectiveness of this exercise. Among 67 students completing three course sections during the past 4 years, the mean rating for the exercise on a scale ranging from *unsatisfactory* (1) to *exceptional quality, top 2%* (7) was 5.4. Student comments indicated they disliked the difficulty of the exercise and found it stressful but believed the exercise made them more reflective in their approach to deviance, clarified their ideas, and improved their critical abilities. Students were especially positive about the midterm feedback and the opportunity to respond in their second drafts.

This exercise requires students to confront with skepticism all the existing wisdom concerning human deviance. Such confrontation strengthens their critical abilities and provides the historical foundation on which they may someday construct new wisdoms of their own (Cole, 1982; Zachry, 1985).

References

Baird, B. N., & Anderson, D. D. (1990). Writing in psychology. *The Teaching Professor, 4,* 5-6.

Benjamin, L. T., Jr. (1991). Personalization and active learning in the large introductory psychology class. *Teaching of Psychology, 18,* 68-74.

Brown, P. (Ed.). (1973). *Radical psychology.* New York: Harper & Row.

Chesler, P. (1972). *Women & madness.* New York: Doubleday.

Cole, D. L. (1982). Psychology as a liberating art. *Teaching of Psychology, 9,* 23-26.

Costin, F. (1982). Some thoughts on general education and the teaching of undergraduate psychology. *Teaching of Psychology, 9,* 26-28.

Costin, F. (1985). Courage in the classroom. *Teaching of Psychology, 12,* 125-128.

Ehrenreich, B., & English, D. (1978). *For her own good: 150 years of the experts' advice on women.* Garden City, NY: Anchor.

Ferguson, N. B. L. (1986). Encouraging responsibility, active participation, and critical thinking in general psychology students. *Teaching of Psychology, 13,* 217-218.

Foucault, M. (1965). *Madness and civilization: A history of insanity in the age of reason.* New York: Random House.

Goffman, E. (1961). *Asylums: Essays on the social situation of mental patients and other inmates.* Garden City, NY: Doubleday.

Gorman, M. E., Law, A., & Lindegren, T. (1981). Making students take a stand: Active learning in introductory psychology. *Teaching of Psychology, 8,* 164-166.

Gould, S. J. (1981). *The mismeasure of man.* New York: Norton.

Green, P. (1981). *The pursuit of inequality.* New York: Pantheon.

Gross, M. L. (1978). *The psychological society.* New York: Simon & Schuster.

Laing, R. D. (1967). *The politics of experience.* New York: Pantheon.

Laing, R. D. (1969). *The divided self.* New York: Pantheon.

Perkins, D. V. (1991). A case-study assignment to teach theoretical perspectives in abnormal psychology. *Teaching of Psychology, 18,* 97-99.

Porter, R. (1987). *A social history of madness: The world through the eyes of the insane.* New York: Dutton.

Sarbin, T. R. (1969). The scientific status of the mental illness metaphor. In S. C. Plog & R. B. Edgerton (Eds.), *Changing perspectives in mental illness* (pp. 9-31). New York: Holt, Rinehart & Winston.

Sarbin, T. R., & Allen, V. L. (1968). Role theory. In G. Lindzey & E. Aronson (Eds.), *The handbook of social psychology* (Vol. 1, 2nd ed., pp. 488-567). Cambridge, MA: Addison-Wesley.

Scheff, T. J. (1984). *Being mentally ill: A sociological theory* (2nd ed.). New York: Aldine.

Szasz, T. S. (1961). *The myth of mental illness.* New York: Harper & Row.

Szasz, T. S. (1970). *The manufacture of madness: A comparative study of the Inquisition and the mental health movement.* New York: Harper & Row.

Valenstein, E. S. (1986). *Great and desperate cures.* New York: Basic Books.

Wallach, M. A., & Wallach, L. (1983). *Psychology's sanction for selfishness: The error of egoism in theory and therapy.* San Francisco: Freeman.

Zachry, W. H. (1985). How I kicked the lecture habit: Inquiry teaching in psychology. *Teaching of Psychology, 12,* 129-131.

Exploring Mental Illness Through a Poetry Writing Assignment

Joan C. Chrisler
Connecticut College

This article describes a poetry-writing assignment designed to encourage students to explore the experience of mental illness. No restrictions on format, length, or topic are given. This assignment promotes creative thinking and empathy for the mentally ill.

Encouraging creative thinking and enhancing writing skills are important goals of teachers at all levels. In recent years, *Teaching of Psychology* has published numerous articles on how to incorporate writing assignments into psychology courses (e.g., Beers, 1985; Bennett, 1985; Klugh, 1983; Nodine, 1990). This article illustrates an atypical and challenging writing assignment for courses in introductory or abnormal psychology.

The aim of this assignment is to increase students' understanding of mental illness and their empathy toward the mentally ill. Popular culture frequently presents the mentally ill as objects of humor or derision; textbooks, with their dry language and reliance on the medical model, are more likely to portray the mentally ill as collections of symptoms than as people. The idea for this assignment arose as I was trying to think of a way to encourage students to identify with those who have psychological problems. I wanted a short writing assignment that would encourage students to reflect on what it might be like to experience mental illness. Poetry, with its emotional base, vivid imagery, and often fragmented language, seemed ideal.

Writing Assignment

Students are told 2 weeks before the assignment is due that they are to write a poem about the experience of mental illness. The format, length, and topic are left entirely up to them. They may choose to be concrete or abstract, serious or humorous, or personal or theoretical, and they may describe the experience using first- or third-person pronouns. The poems need not be written in a rhyming format. Anything goes!

The class generally seems shocked when they are told about the assignment, but after being assured that they will be judged primarily on content, rather than format or poetic language, they rise to the challenge. Because length is unimportant, one can count on receiving several haiku. Someone will always hand in "Roses are red; violets are blue. I'm schizophrenic and so am 1." (This response is given a failing grade because, besides its lack of originality, it describes multiple personality and not schizophrenia.) However, most students take the assignment seriously and turn in work that shows that they have thought long and carefully about their topics. Most work is creative and interesting; some poems are so beautifully written that I refer them to the college literary magazine.

Students have responded to the assignment with varying degrees of enthusiasm. One student wrote about his negative emotional reaction to the assignment and titled it "Poemaphobia." (I gave him an A.) Many have told me that once they got over their amazement at being asked to write a poem for a psychology class they found the task to be both challenging and fun.

To earn an A, a poem must convey an excellent understanding (or be an excellent description) of anxiety, depression, psychosis, or some particular disorder (e.g., avoidant personality disorder). A B is given to a poem that conveys a good understanding or description of the experience of mental illness. Some latitude is available for the evaluation of writing ability. For example, an adequate description of avoidant personality would earn a grade of B; an adequate description that is also well written (e.g., the poem's lines contain the appropriate number of syllables for its rhyme scheme, and the poet's choice of words is good) would earn a B+. Oddly, despite the subjectivity involved in evaluating an assignment of this type, no students have ever complained about their grades.

For the past 2 years (after obtaining permission from the students—some give permission only if their work remains anonymous), I have posted the best work on a bulletin board in the psychology building. Much to the poets' delight, the display attracted students and faculty from all over campus.

I have used this assignment in three classes during the last few years and have been pleased with the results. I believe that the time students spend thinking about particular aspects of mental illness in preparation for this assignment results in better understanding and increased empathy for the mentally ill.

This is a versatile assignment for introductory and abnormal psychology classes. With a little ingenuity, it can be adapted for use in other courses. For example, students might write a poem about being elderly for a developmental psychology course, about the experience of chronic or terminal illness in a health psychology course, or about being the object of prejudice in a social psychology course. Readers are invited to try this assignment and judge its value for their classes.

References

Beers, S. E. (1985). Use of a portfolio writing assignment in a course on developmental psychology. *Teaching of Psychology, 12,* 94-96.

Bennett, S. M. (1985). Coordinated teaching of psychology and composition: A valuable strategy for students and instructors. *Teaching of Psychology, 12,* 26-27.

Klugh, H. E. (1983). Writing and speaking skills can be taught in psychology classes. *Teaching of Psychology, 10,* 170-171.

Nodine, B. F. (Ed.). (1990). Psychologists teach writing [Special issue]. *Teaching of Psychology, 17,* 4.

Note

An earlier version of this article was presented at the annual meeting of the American Psychological Association, Boston, August 1990.

Jeopardy© in Abnormal Psychology

Carolin S. Keutzer
University of Oregon

A version of the Jeopardy© game is described for use in an abnormal psychology course. This game can increase student interaction, encourage the application of information, and add a light touch to a subject that is sometimes distressing to students.

Abnormal psychology is an intrinsically interesting course, but at times a light touch is needed to compensate for the immersion in the more depressing topics. Using games in this class increases student interaction; encourages application of information to another arena, supplementing rote memorization; and militates against acquiring the proverbial "medical school syndrome." Games have been used in other psychology courses where they provided useful organization of the material for students (research methods; Gibson, 1991), enhanced learning of complex concepts (theories of personality; Carlson, 1989), and even provided comic relief from the anxiety-provoking task of preparing for the final exam (physiological psychology; Ackil, 1986). A favorite game with my students is the Jeopardy game.

This game is an adaptation of the television quiz show in which contestants select a category and give a response in the form of a question to the answer that comes up in the chosen category. Diagnostic "families" make excellent category topics. One set of six categories may include the following disorders: anxiety, dissociative, somatoform, psychosexual, personality, and mood. Five responses in order of increasing difficulty (as judged by the instructor or the game maker) are prepared for each category; their selection with the correct question is scored either 100, 200, 300, 400, or 500 points. For example, a 200-point answer may be, "a mood disorder involving mild, persistent depression over an extended period of time," and the correct question is "What is dysthymia?" If the category is continued to the 300-point level, the answer may be, "the period of time the symptoms must have been present to warrant the diagnosis of major depressive syndrome," and the correct question is "What is 6 months?"

If a player's response is correct, the player receives the points. If the player's response is incorrect, the player forfeits the point value. If the teacher indicates that the response to an answer is incorrect, then the first of the other players to signal has the opportunity to ask the question. That player responds and either wins or loses the same number of points. The player who asks the correct question chooses the next category and point value. If no player asks the correct question, the teacher reads the correct question aloud. The player who selected the previous category and point value then makes the next selection.

You can divide a class into three to six teams and designate a captain for each team. Extra people can be scorekeepers. Begin the game by having each captain roll a die. The player with the highest number goes first by choosing a category and the level of difficulty. Team leaders may each be given a small bell or clicker, or they may just raise their hands. The first one to signal the desire to respond is called on. Team members may whisper the correct response to their captains either before or after the captain has signaled.

The game continues until either a time limit or a point limit is reached. I use a time limit so that other tasks can be scheduled for the day. I often use this game at the beginning of the class period to provide stimulation for a later discussion and to get the students actively involved and enthusiastic about the subject. Twenty min seems about the optimal time to spend on the activity. Less time does not allow for the momentum to build and the class to become fully engaged; more time does not seem warranted for the benefits generated. A scorekeeper can keep score on the chalkboard so that the teacher and the students can follow the progress of each team.

There are many ways to vary the game. In a class of over 150 students, you may want to have 3 or 4 contestants and the rest act as the audience. Those in the audience may make a note of items that need clarification or further discussion. Members of the audience can also be called on when none of the contestants elects to respond or responds incorrectly. I have also used the game informally in a large class of 360 students as a warm-up during the first 5 or 6 min of class by asking students to raise their hands to give the correct question. Table 1 lists sample items for the dissociative disorder category.

In small classes where all members participate, I sometimes give prizes in the form of a bonus point on the next exam to the members of the winning team. In larger classes (100 to 300 students), bonus points for the top individual scores can be awarded. However, the game has an intrinsic appeal to most students and external incentives are not necessary.

At the end of each term, students evaluate the course on 15 items, such as "How satisfied were you with the teacher's knowledge of the subject?" and "Did the instructor use class time efficiently?" In addition, two optional, open-ended questions ask "What aspects of the course did you find valuable and would like to see retained or expanded?" and "What aspects of the course do you feel need improvement?" My last course had 144 students; 121 of them completed the survey. Of the students (*n* = 71) who wrote comments to the open-ended questions, none mentioned Jeopardy as something about the course that needed improvement. However, 23 of the 71 (32%) specifically

Table 1. Jeopardy Answers and Questions: Dissociative Disorders

100 points	Answer: Traveling amnesia
	Question: What is a psychogenic fugue?
200 points	Answer: A type of amnesia in which all events during a circumscribed period of time are blocked out.
	Question: What is localized amnesia?
300 points	Answer: A type of disorder most often associated with early childhood abuse.
	Question: What is multiple personality disorder?
400 points	Answer: A disorder dominated by a feeling of unreality and of estrangement from the self, body, or surroundings.
	Question: What is depersonalization disorder?
500 points	Answer: The type of accompanying amnesia in a true multiple personality.
	Question: What is asymmetrical? (Material learned by the primary personality is remembered by all of the secondary personalities, but material learned by a secondary personality is not known to the other secondary personalities or to the primary personality.)

mentioned the Jeopardy game as something valuable to be retained. My impression is that students greatly appreciate the opportunity to learn and have fun at the same time.

Although this game as described was devised for abnormal psychology, it can be adapted to suit almost any psychology course. I used a version of it in my theories of personality course once as a study aid for the midterm. The categories were famous theorists (e.g., Freud, Jung, Horney, and Adler), and the answers covered various concepts associated with each theorist. I allowed individuals to raise their hands to respond to the answer. The student who accumulated the most points had 1 point added to her midterm score (which turned out to be the highest score in the class before the addition). Gibson (1991) used the Jeopardy game in his research methods course, with categories ranging from general topics, such as the scientific method, to specific topics, such as reliability. My experience echoed his in that the game "stimulated enthusiasm for the topic and helped students identify where to focus their study for the exam" (p. 177)

References

Ackil, J. E. (1986). PhysioPursuit A trivia-type game for the classroom. *Teaching of Psychology, 13, 91.*

Carlson, J. F. (1989). Psychosexual pursuit: Enhancing learning of theoretical psychoanalytic constructs. *Teaching of Psychology, 16,* 82-84.

Gibson, B. (1991). Research methods Jeopardy: A tool for involving students and organizing the study session. *Teaching of Psychology, 18,* 176-177.

The Institutional Tour: Some Reflections

Arnold LeUnes
Texas A&M University

One of the most impressive learning experiences of my own undergraduate education was a field trip to Texas Department of Corrections facilities in Huntsville, Texas. I vowed at the time that I would incorporate such experiences into my own courses should I ever become a college professor, a dream far removed but vaguely aspired to at that time. Lo and behold, some 25 years later, I find myself to be a seasoned veteran of the teaching profession, having spent the past 17 years on the faculty at Texas A&M University.

My instructional duties have been largely in abnormal psychology, and as a part of the course I have arranged field trips to schools for mentally retarded persons, state mental hospitals, and correctional facilities for adults and youth. As of the end of 1982, I have arranged 79 tours of the aforementioned facilities, and 2367 of my students (almost entirely undergraduates) have taken part in the experiences.

My rationale for having the field trips is multifaceted. First, I profited so much from the previously mentioned TDC tour that I felt such experiences should become a vital part of the education process. Secondly, I believe that such exposure should allay anxieties, counter fears, and challenge fallacies and myths that exist with regard to mental patients, retarded people, and prison inmates, the facilities they reside in, and those who provide services for them. That this may be achieved is suggested by previous research I have conducted (LeUnes, Christensen, & Wilkerson, 1975). We found that attitudes held by students about mental retardation are significantly improved after a tour of a state school. We also subsequently found, however, that there are optimal ways to conduct a tour if you want the best response with regard to attitude change (Carsrud, Carsrud, Dodd, LeUnes, Rhine & Trout, in press). A third reason for having the tours generally centers around the concept of the informed citizen. Whether they go into the helping professions, the students will become voters and taxpayers. Some will become advocates for mental health issues. Being informed in any or all of these roles should translate into better understanding and care for those among us who have emotional or intellectual difficulties. Finally, the field trips provide a welcome break for all (professor included) from the day-to-day lecturing, note taking, and the like. Also it affords the opportunity for a more spontaneous and relaxed interchange between professor and students.

Despite the positives mentioned herein, all is not well with the field trip concept. In 1967, the first year I instituted tours in my classes, a total of 154 students went on 5 tours for an average of almost 31 each This popularity continued to a peak of 225 students on 5 tours in 1972, or over 45 per tour. Since then there has been a steady decline to the point that only 34 people went on 4 tours in 1981 and 1982 combined.

Yet another perspective from which the problem can be viewed is the number of students who take part in the field trips versus those who don't. In 1967, 58% of the students attended the tours. In 1979, the figure had dropped to 24% . In 1982, only 8% of my students took part in three field trips. From 1967 through 1974, 46% of the students went; from 1975 through 1982, only 31% attended. Again, we see a consistent and sizable decline in field trip participation.

One of my original suppositions was that tours should be of special interest to psychology majors. Their response, however, closely parallels that of the students from other majors. Over the past 16 years, 502 psychology majors attended a field trip whereas 592 did not. In 1967,57% of the psychology majors attended a trip; in 1982, only 14% took part.

What might cause this decline to happen has perplexed me for some time, and my speculations are merely that— speculations. One thing that comes to mind is the previously voluntary nature of the undertaking. I have always offered the trips as extra, never requiring participation. Initially, there seemed to be no reason to change the system; now I wonder.

Perhaps a tangible incentive is needed to bolster interest, though it bothers me philosophically to think that everything a student does in or out of the classroom must carry a tangible reward in order for it to be successful. Perhaps what is transpiring here is a manifestation of the pressures and conflicting pulls that currently permeate the educational scene nationally. The intense competition for jobs, graduate schools, and professional schools is well documented, and perhaps is so strong that the students see the time taken away from studies as unwarranted or even frivolous.

It is tempting, also, to think of the lessening of interest as symptomatic of our decreasing concern for the plight of people in need of help. An image of the so-called bystander apathy syndrome is easily conjured up here.

On a less pessimistic and more provincial level, it may be that the changing nature of the university itself is the culprit. In 1967, approximately 8000 students attended the university, previously all male and predominantly military. The university has now grown to 37,000; females are approaching parity in numbers, military students compose less than 10% of the student body, and the recent advent of fraternities and sororities has contributed to rapid change. It is conceivable that the division of time between studies and the newly-found social activities of a local nature have served to diminish time for and interest in such things as optional class field-trips.

A final speculation centers around, heaven forbid, characteristics of the instructor in question. Maybe I've gone downhill is a recurring thought. However, though I've aged from 28 to 44 in the process, student response of other kinds seems to have remained sufficiently constant over time so as to allow me to reject the hypothesis that I'm the main variable.

The solution as I see it is to either junk the project or shape it up. I refuse to throw out the field trips, so I'm left with the challenge of instilling some life into its barely breathing body. My plan at this time is to attack the problem from two sides. First, I shall weave the tour into the grading process, not from the perspective of coercion but rather as an extra credit; that is, the tours would substitute for a term paper, or as relief from an exam, say on the material covered by the tour itself. At the same time, setting the tours up in such a way as to maximize the desired effects seems mandatory. Securing cooperation from sponsoring facilities is increasingly important. The issues of right to privacy, right to treatment, and patient rights in general have created an air of suspicion and, at times, inhospitality that militate against further tours, particularly in the mental hospital sector.

The problems of visiting schools for mentally retarded persons are not quite as troublesome, and the quality of the tours has remained reasonably constant over the years. As for correctional facilities, they are only tangentially relevant to what I'm trying to accomplish and shall be discontinued.

When one considers the potential benefits of out-of-class educational experiences such as the institutional tour, it behooves all of us involved in the process to sell the idea, provide meaningful tours for our charges, and continue to research ways to demon-strate the validity of the process, thereby improving the quality of education for our students.

References

Carsrud, A., Carsrud, K., LeUnes, A, Dodd, B., Rhine, J., & Trout, S. The effects of institutional tours on attitudes toward the mentally retarded and their institutional settings. *Applied Research in Mental Retardation,* (in press).

LeUnes, A., Christensen, L, & Wilkerson, D. Institutional tour effects on attitudes related to mental retardation. *American Journal of Mental Deficiency,* 1975, 79, 732-735.

Images of Madness: Feature Films in Teaching Psychology

Michael Z. Fleming
Ralph L. Piedmont
C. Michael Hiam
Boston University

An interdisciplinary course, Psychology and Film: Images of Madness, has been taught at Boston University since 1979 by two instructors: a psychologist and a film historian. This course may be pedagogically unique because of its use of feature films (90 to 110 min) as a major element of instruction. The films allow students to explore the interaction between art and psychology and make them cognizant of the cinema's ability to reflect and affect our perceptions of madness and treatment. A student survey and course evaluation substantiated the effectiveness of this instructional program.

Educational films of under 60 min are widely accepted and appreciated by psychology instructors and students. Feature films (90 to 110 min) have not been used as frequently as educational films, although some instructors have employed such films with apparent success. Kinney (1975) found that the full-length commercial film, *The Wild Child* (1970), was rated very favorably by students in comparison to educational films on developmental psychology. Dorris and Ducey (1978) and Nissim-Sabat (1979) related their successes in teaching psychology courses that use feature films as an integral part of the instruction.

Feature films, even from the pre-1920s silent days, are particularly suitable for handling intimate psychological subjects. These films can offer students a unique opportunity to see realistic manifestations of psychiatric disorders, apply models of psychopathology, and suggest modes of treatment. Through the subtleties of editing and the juxtaposition of sound and image, a good feature film can also afford students a "firsthand" perspective on madness that is not easily imparted by lectures or textbooks.

The value of feature films in psychology courses, however, does not end with their power to render a convincing depiction of madness. Such films can also make students aware of an important interaction between art and psychology. This interaction involves the cinema's ability to reflect and affect popular perceptions of madness and treatment. *One Flew Over the Cuckoo's Nest* (1975), for example, perpetuated certain stereotypes about mental illness but created a national furor over the use of electroconvulsive therapy. A brief historical overview of film portrayals of madness will reveal to students that these popular perceptions, like psychiatric nosology itself, have changed over time.

Since 1979, Michael Z. Fleming (the first author) has been co-teaching an interdisciplinary undergraduate course, Psychology and Film: Images of Madness, with a film historian at Boston University. The average enrollment of 80 students is drawn about equally from the College of Liberal Arts and the College of Communications. The psychology faculty liked the idea of an interdisciplinary course, but thought that it should not count as one of seven courses required for the psychology major.

The course uses a series of modern and classic feature films to introduce students to the interaction between psychiatric and cinematic disciplines. We attempted to document the students' understanding of this dialectic process.

Course Format

The course is taught in 15 class sessions that meet for 4 hr once a week. The two instructors lecture at the beginning of class, a film is then screened, and class discussion follows. Class discussion after the film takes the following form:

1. Initially, students are encouraged to talk about how the film affected them, focusing on their subjective, affective responses. The film's power to present wrenching emotional struggles needs first to be reacted to on a feeling level, and students are encouraged to voice their feelings without worrying about grounding them in logic.

2. The second phase of discussion is to take the students' stated feelings and connect them to the specific visual and auditory stimuli in the film that elicited such feelings. Analysis concentrates on a careful process of consensual validation of what was actually shown as opposed to what we believe we saw (e. g., the specific images in the alcoholic hallucinosis in *The Lost Weekend,* 1948).

3. The final phase of discussion links the readings and lectures to the film. For example, readings and lecture material on posttraumatic stress disorder are linked to the major and seemingly minor stressors presented in *The Deer Hunter (1978)* and the characterological flaws of the three friends who go to war.

Much of the lecture material is centered on the various diagnostic categories from the American Psychiatric Association's *Mental Disorders: Diagnostic and Statistical Manual* (1st ed. [*DSM*], 1952) and the *Diagnostic and Statistical Manual of Mental Disorders* (2nd ed. [*DSM-II*], 3rd ed. [*DSM-III*], and 3rd ed. rev. [*DSM-III-R*], 1968, 1980, and 1987, respectively). Handouts are given on specific diagnostic categories from the edition of the *DSM* in effect when the film was released. (The *DSM* is presented as the official scientific description of psychopathology of a period.) The presentation is supplemented by brief excerpts from the *DSMs,* which are distributed at the beginning of class and include a short summary statement of the psychopathological entity presented in the film. The lectures emphasize the "scientific views" of a period and the historical context in which psychopathology must be placed. The succinctness of the *DSM is* especially helpful for those who are not psychology majors.

The film's interaction with the psychiatric community is documented by discussions of period psychiatric literature. Student discussion is encouraged and, because of students' enthusiasm, frequently lasts beyond the scheduled end of class. A budget of $1,500 covers the rental cost of the 12 films. Although there is a text for the course (Fleming & Manvell, 1985), students are expected to read outside sources on the topics discussed in class (see appendix). Grading is based on two 10-page papers and a midterm exam. Students are asked to choose from a series of paper topics on the cause-and-effect relation between a thematic motif in film and psychiatry. After selecting a topic, students are encouraged to meet with the instructor to formulate a specific question and to plan an appropriate method for investigating it. The instructor suggests pertinent references during these discussions.

Themes of Madness and Films Selected

The changing perceptions of madness are investigated by screening two feature films separated by at least 20 years. To be selected for the course, the film must have been popular and have generated literary criticism. Popularity is assessed by looking at the films' gross earnings published in *Variety* magazine. Films selected have also enjoyed coverage in the popular and academic press, and students are encouraged to use literary indexes to research this aspect.

The course has been offered 12 times; some of the film themes and representative films that have been incorporated are:

1. The family and madness: *Now, Voyager* (1942) and *Ordinary People* (1979).
2. Institutionalization of the mad: *The Snake Pit* (1948) and *One Flew Over the Cuckoo's Nest* (1975).
3. Possession as madness: *Dr. Jekyll and Mr. Hyde* (1931) and *The Exorcist* (1973).
4. Murder and madness: *White Heat* (1949) and *Halloween* (1976).
5. War and madness: *Twelve O'Clock High* (1949) and *The Deer Hunter* (1978).
6. Drugs and madness: *The Lost Weekend* (1948) and *The Rose* (1979).
7. Paranoia and madness: *Rope* (1948) and *Invasion of the Body Snatchers* (1978).
8. Sanity as madness, madness as sanity: You *Can't Take It With You* (1938) and *King of Hearts* (1966).
9. The psychiatrist and madness: *Spellbound* (1945) and *Face to Face* (1975).

The following analysis of *The Lost Weekend* is an example of the substantive issues that can be illustrated by film. When we present the film, we first set the historical context by describing the cinematic presentation of alcoholism before the release of *The Lost Weekend.* Previous film treatments lead into popular and clinical views of alcoholism and the evolution of these views as they affected and then came to be affected by *The Lost Weekend.* Students seldom appreciate the fact that Alcoholics Anonymous (AA) is a relatively recent movement which had to, and still has to, fight for the acceptance of alcoholism as a disease. The popular view that dominated the depiction of alcoholics in films up to 1945 was that of an anonymous, indigent derelict. The limited attention of the psychiatric community to alcoholism emphasized biological treatments with greatest interest given to the rest and isolation of such patients. Alcohol was ostensibly a weakness of the poor, and those who were not indigent and suffered from it were hurried away to sanitariums that treated those who needed a "rest."

Discussion of the film raises many points: (a) Students erroneously come to think of contemporary views as "enlightened" and as always existing or certainly existing since 1900. An exploration of the relatively recent advent of AA is, therefore, eye-opening and allows for discussion of the role of self-help groups in substance abuse. (b) The film serves as an introduction to the social and economic forces that influence diagnoses in terms of the perception that only the poor were alcoholics. (c) Biological psychiatry versus social psychiatry and the social political forces that influence the dominance of either a nature or nurture etiology are raised in discussion of the film. Students are encouraged to read the period professional and lay literature associated with the film. Although *The Lost Weekend* supports a social etiology for the protagonist's alcoholism, it avoids the issue of repressed homosexuality stressed in the popular book on which the screenplay is based. (d) The film graphically portrays both substance use disorders (maladaptive behavior that surrounds the taking of the drug) and substance-induced disorders as dramatically depicted in the formication hallucinations of delirium tremens.

Those who teach a course on film and mental illness have a number of formats from which to choose. Two of the most obvious are: (a) using specific films to portray particular abnormal states that reflect the DSM-III-R criteria, or (b) using film as both reflector and effector and doing so from a historical perspective. Using both to some degree is also possible.

Changes in Students' Knowledge and Opinions

Students in a recent class completed a 10-item questionnaire that focused on knowledge of mental illness and depiction of illness in the cinema. Students rated each question on a scale ranging from *very little* (1) to *very much* (5). The questionnaire was distributed to 35 students (23 women, 12 men) on the last day of class. These students were representative of those who have taken the course over the years. There were an almost equal number of communications, psychology, and other liberal arts majors. Questions were de-signed to determine if students believed their knowledge increased as a result of the course.

When asked how much they knew about the study of people with mental illness and the depiction of the mentally ill in the film media, students responded strongly in the affirmative (Ms = 3.8 and 3.9, respectively). Films were seen as providing very accurate depictions of posttraumatic stress syndromes (M = 4.1), substance abuse (M = 4.0), antisocial behaviors (M = 3.9), and depressive disorders (M = 3.7) . However, less well reflected in film were eating (M = 2.7) and sexual (M = 3.3) disorders. When asked the extent to which film influences individuals' perceptions of the mentally ill, students believed that the perceptions of the general public (M = 4.1), family members (M = 3.8), and nonmental health professionals (M = 3.6) were shaped by such images. Psychiatrists (M = 2.9) and the respondents themselves (M = 3.4), however, were rated as being less influenced by film.

University course evaluation forms were completed by all students (N = 35). Students felt that: (a) there were many opportunities for questions and discussion (M = 4.5), (b) the amount of work for the course was moderate (M = 3.3), and (c) the assigned readings were clear (M = 3.0) . Students considered the course germane to their education and careers (M = 3.9) and one they would definitely recommend to other students (M = 4.5). Overall, this course had a positive impact on the students. Not only was it effective in engaging the students in thought-provoking discussions and encounters, it was also a useful didactic vehicle for conveying a wide range of psychological information.

Conclusion

Courses like Psychology and Film: Images of Madness can help students who are going into mental health or communications fields to realize how each of their respective disciplines interacts with the other. Such courses can increase students' knowledge of psychopathology and their appreciation for how feature films influence our thinking about mental illness. From the students' perspective, the course provided information that they can take with them into their future careers in communication and psychology.

References

American Psychiatric Association (1952). *Mental disorders: Diagnostic and statistical manual* (1st ed.). Washington, DC: Author.

American Psychiatric Association. (1968) . *Diagnostic and statistical manual of mental disorders* (2nd ed.). Washington, DC: Author.

American Psychiatric Association. (1980) . *Diagnostic and statistical manual of mental disorders* (3rd ed.). Washington, DC: Author.

American Psychiatric Association. (1987). *Diagnostic and statistical manual of mental disorders* (3rd ed., rev.). Washington, DC: Author.

Dorris, W., & Ducey, R. (1978) . Social psychology and sex roles in films. *Teaching of Psychology, 5,* 168-169.

Fleming, M., & Manvell, R. (1985). *Images of madness: The portrayal of insanity in the feature film.* Cranbury, NH: Associated University Presses.

Kinney, D. K. (1975). Cinema thrillers: Reviews of films highly rated by psychology students. *Teaching of Psychology, 2,* 183.

Nissim-Sabat, D. (1979). The teaching of abnormal psychology through the cinema. *Teaching of Psychology, 6,* 121 - 123.

Appendix: Selected Bibliography on Film and Madness

A. General references

Fleming, M., & Manvell, R. (1985). *Images of madness: The portrayal of insanity in the feature film.* Cranbury, NH: Associated University Presses.

Munsterberg, H. (1970). *The photoplay: A psychological study.* New York: Dover.

Schneider, I. (1977). Images of the mind: Psychiatry in the commercial film. *American Journal of Psychiatry, 134,* 613-620.

Schneider, I. (1987). The theory and practice of movie psychiatry. *American Journal of Psychiatry, 144,* 996-1002.

B. Thematic references

1. Drugs and madness

Bacon, S. D. (1949). Current notes: A student of the problems of alcoholism views "The lost weekend." *Quarterly Journal of Studies on Alcoholism, 8,* 402-405.

Brower, D. (1948). An opinion poll on reactions to "The lost weekend." *Quarterly Journal of Studies on Alcoholism, 10,* 594-598.

2. War and madness

Grinker, R., & Spiegel, J. (1945). *Men under stress.* Philadelphia: Blakiston.

Renner, J. A. (1973). The changing patterns of psychiatric problems in Vietnam. *Comprehensive Psychiatry, 14*(2), 169-173.

Smith, J. (1973). Between Vermont and violence: Film portraits of Vietnam veterans. *Film Quarterly Studies, 26,* 24-33.

SECTION III:
CLINICAL-COUNSELING

Developing Skills Through Simulations and Role Playing Techniques

For the interviewing component of an undergraduate clinical psychology course, Kristi Lane trained undergraduate theater majors as clients. The actor created the character of a client after reading appropriate case studies. The instructor assisted by providing feedback, helping to create client history, background, and personality characteristics, and by monitoring the degree of pathology that the actor portrayed. The author concluded that the actors added a realistic component to the course.

To give students experience in an assessment interview, Bernard Balleweg developed The Interviewing Team. The team consisted of several students who interviewed the instructor who roleplayed a client. Each student on the team collected one type of information (e.g., behavioral or somatic symptoms). A debriefing session followed the interview in which students developed hypotheses for the causes of the clients problems.

Janet Matthews had her undergraduate students evaluate several adjuncts to the textbook in a clinical psychology course. Adjuncts included films, exercises, and professional literature. The exercises consisted of an introduction, similar to one of the ways of getting to know individuals in group therapy, a simulated intake interview, and a spin the bottle procedure in which the selected person role played an activity described on a card. Students' favorable responses to the exercises and the instructor's caveat about using the exercise were quite informative.

Andrea Weiss designed a method to teach verbal helping skills to students who did not have access to clinical populations. Students used open-ended interviews with volunteers as the primary training device; role-playing simulations and programmed instruction complemented this experience.

Kathryn Rickard and Robert Titley described an interviewing game used in a graduate-level, interviewing skills course. The goal of the game was to teach basic components of the interview process such as comfort with the interview, microcounseling skills, hypothesis generation, and hypothesis testing. The instructor played the part of a client and was interviewed by two teams of students. The article explained the students' role in the game and the game's procedure. Students gave favorable ratings to and positive feedback about the game.

To teach interviewing skills to first-year graduate students, John Sommers-Flanagan and John Means developed a four component exercise. First, the instructors told students that they should neither ask nor answer questions during their first two interviews. Second, students evaluated, orally and in writing, their own behavior during the interview. Third, peers, instructors, and analogue clients provided students with feedback regarding their interviewing skills and interpersonal styles. Fourth, the instructors evaluated the effects of the interview on the analogue clients because the graduate students acquired students from an introductory psychology research pool.

William Balch developed a role-playing exercise to demonstrate therapeutic techniques and processes more effectively. Volunteers played the roles of a client and the clients' father, mother, and friend. Each person offered direct advice to the client in a series of improvised, two-way dialogues. The instructor provided the participants with a hand-out explaining the situation and roles. The article contains a brief scenario for each role. A non-directive therapist concentrated on clarifying the clients' feelings. Although the author developed the exercise for an introductory psychology course, the technique also seemed particularly well suited for introductory counseling or clinical courses.

Jerome Ulman developed a game to help students synthesize elements of behavior modification techniques. The game consisted of groups to acquire synthesizing skills, team competition to encourage peer tutoring, and simulation games to increase students' motivation and learning. The author described several suggestions for game users, and he concluded that the game helped students better conceptualize behavior modification as a systematic approach to effective problem solving.

Donald Meck and John D. Ball evaluated a relaxation training program. One group of students received the training and one group did not. Both groups completed the Trait Anxiety Scale (TAS) before and after the program. The authors reported no difference between the groups prior to training. At the end of the program, those in the training program scored significantly lower on TAS than the controls. The relaxation experience illustrated one of the principles covered in the classroom and a scientific approach for evaluating a personal adjustment technique.

To communicate the experience of staffing and operations in a mental hospital, William Claiborn and Raymond Lemberg designed a 56 hr simulation for their students. The instructor and his teaching assistant selected a student to work as hospital director, who in turn hired other students for the next level of hospital management. With the final staff in place, participants prepared budgets, menus, treatment plans, and the like. Students also created a list of patients and developed roles for them. The authors concluded that the experience simulated many realistic aspects of professional mental heath roles.

Using Computers to Develop Clinical Skills

Students learned to analyze behaviors as examples of psychological defense using an interactive computerized teaching program that Roger Bibace and his associates developed. Students read a short paragraph describing a fictional situation illustrating a defensive behavior. Behaviors were analyzed in terms of actor-action-object propositions. The transformations in these three terms generated psychological defenses such as projection and reaction formation. Students' satisfaction with the program and their subsequent performance in identifying defense mechanisms indicated that the program helped to develop analytic skills.

John Suler used Eliza, a widely known computer program that reacts to the user by simulating the responses of a psychotherapist, as a teaching aid in undergraduate clinical psychology courses. The author pointed out that students' interaction with the program could enhance their understanding of interviewing and psychotherapy, the contrasts between clinical interactions controlled by humans and computers, and the role computers may play in the mental health field. The author also discussed methods for conducting the exercise, for integrating the program into the course syllabus, and for evaluating the exercise's impact on students.

Learning About Family Dynamics

J. Eugene Waters described a supplemental instructional method designed to address students' requests for concrete information about family communication and organization. The instructor administered two versions of the Family Environment Scale. One version assessed students' preferred family environment and the other students' real family environment. The instructor gave students national and class norms for the inventory. The author emphasized the importance of voluntary participation and ethical issues in the use of this technique.

To provide a meaningful service to a probation officer with an enormous caseload, Judith Kuppersmith and her associates developed a training model for 16 undergraduate students. The three instructors implemented a 10 week training program followed by eight weeks of close supervision in multi-family counseling groups. The authors also described the selection and training procedures as well as the benefits to the pro-

bation department, families, students, the college, and the community.

Louis Gardner described a method for promoting student interest and involvement in a marriage and family course. The method supplemented lectures with problem-solving sessions for small groups. The instructor used session outcomes to encourage critical evaluation by the entire class. Students' positive reactions to the course highlighted this interactive personal involvement.

Instigating Miscellaneous Techniques

Using the Adjective Generation Technique, Gene Smith summarized students' perceptions about psychologists. Students listed five traits they associated with a scientist and with a psychologist. Presentation and discussion of the two lists revealed that students viewed the two concepts quite differently. The author pointed out that instructors can use such an exercise to correct students' misconceptions about psychologists and reduce students' clinical bias toward psychology.

Students applied abstract research concepts to a concrete analogue of therapy evaluation using Richard Viken's classroom demonstration. Students rated their food consumption and mood before and after an absurd pseudotreatment. The instructor used the data to demonstrate that absolutely useless treatments may initially appear to be highly effective and that careful attention to research design is necessary for appropriate therapy evaluation. Student evaluations indicated that this experiment helped them understand and remember important issues in therapy outcome research.

Karl Schilling designed a library exercise for students in his introductory clinical psychology class to illustrate that ideas occurred in a context and to demonstrate the importance of cultural and professional context. For the first assignment, students found as much information as possible about the authors of their text. In class discussion, students identified the authors' interests and biases. The second assignment required students to prepare an annotated bibliography using at least 10 references cited in a "classic" article. With the latter exercise, students acquired a sense of the slow accumulation of information about ideas.

Gary George and his associates developed a series of videotapes and trained nine inmates to serve as peer counselors. Specifically, the program concentrated on using problem solving methods for personal, social, and educational issues. An observer rated counselors' practical skills recorded on the tapes and provided feedback. The authors described efforts to extend such training to prison staff. Applications to training students seems straightforward.

Gary Goldstein summarized a collaborative learning project for an upper-level undergraduate counseling course. Groups of students designed and presented a workshop on a therapeutic intervention for a specific patient population. Each student also wrote a paper on an individually selected topic. The article described examples of students' workshops, reactions to and evaluations of the assignment, and grading procedures. The author concluded that the assignment provided a model for the kind of collaborative work students may encounter in advanced study.

Dolores Hughes demonstrated the behavioral technique of participant modeling by introducing a snake into the classroom. Students expressed their level of fear of the snake and, through a series of progressive steps, approached and handled the snake. Several students in the moderate and high fear conditions eventually handled the snake. This activity could be used in a wide range of courses such as introductory, abnormal, or behavior modification.

Ray Hosford and his associates conducted a study to evaluate the effectiveness of two types of in-service training of correctional staff. Participants were case managers and correctional counselors who volunteered to receive training in behavioral counseling. One group received training sessions with the instructor present in the room; the other group received training using videotapes. Subsequently the authors evaluated members of both groups after they counseled an inmate whom the investigators had coached to behave in specific ways. The authors elaborate on the positive and equivocal outcomes of the study.

Henry Kaczkowski used a critical incident technique for five years in a graduate counseling course to help students develop group leadership skills. A critical incident consisted of a contextual framework, specific behaviors immediately preceding the choice point, surface and underlying issues forcing intervention, and implications of the intervention. The author developed videotapes depicting 30 scenes. The author described his assessment and modifications of the technique.

Dennis Klos gave his students the option of gathering personal data for a case study. Students had the tasks of designing a study, collecting interview data, writing a case narrative, and interpreting the material using two or more theories of development. The article included the author's criteria for evaluating the students' projects and his assessment of students' responses to the exercise as a teaching tool.

Mitchell Handelsman and Bobbin Friedlander developed an exercise for teaching about assertiveness. The exercise took place in the first of three fifty-minute periods devoted to assertiveness. The instructor came to the classroom and proceeded to write notes on a pad for the duration of the period. Only one out of 100 students asked the instructor to start class. At the beginning of the next class, the instructor asked students to complete a questionnaire that inquired about students' reactions to the previous class. Student responses to the questionnaire helped to initiate processing of the exercise. The author elaborated on the processing and highlighted some of the ethical and pedagogical issues associated with this exercise.

To demonstrate the potential influence of two Adlerian principles--earliest recollections and birth order--on personality, Les Parrott developed two exercises. In one exercise, students recorded and studied their earliest recollections. In another exercise, students discussed their position in their family constellation. Students in undergraduate and graduate introductory counseling courses rated both exercises highly; undergraduates valued the birth order exercise more, but graduate students valued the earliest recollections exercise more.

Douglas Chute and Barry Bank required about 30 advanced undergraduates in their clinical psychopharmacology course to prepare a major review paper and to summarize some aspect of their research for the class. Because the authors could not devote half of their class time to students' oral presentations, they organized a poster session, which was a noteworthy success.

1. DEVELOPING SKILLS THROUGH SIMULATIONS AND ROLE PLAYING TECHNIQUES

Using Actors as "Clients" for an Interviewing Simulation in an Undergraduate Clinical Psychology Course

Kristi Lane
Winona State University

Undergraduate theater majors are trained to be clients for the interviewing component of an undergraduate clinical psychology course. The actor creates the character of a client after reading appropriate case studies. The instructor assists by providing feedback, helping to create client history, background, and personality characteristics, and by monitoring the degree of pathology that the actor portrays. The actors add a realistic component to this course.

Finding "clients" is frequently a problem for instructors teaching an interviewing component of a clinical psychology course. Instructors in graduate programs are more likely to have access to new psychiatric inpatients who need intake interviews and can be used to train interviewing skills (Boice, Andrasik, & Simmons, 1984). Weiss (1986) noted that it is often difficult to find a clinical population for beginning students to interview. The problem of finding "clients" is most readily met by having trainees play the role. This practice presents the advantage of available clients but has the disadvantage of both client and interviewer knowing the techniques and purpose of the interview. The client may unknowingly assist the interviewer by giving answers that anticipate the interview procedure. Another solution to the client problem is to use subjects from the introductory psychology research pool who sign up to participate in a study called *interviewing experiences* (Sommers-Flanagan & Means, 1987). This practice was reported to be satisfactory, but the authors cautioned that emotional disturbances appeared in 15% to 25% of their introductory psychology clients. In response to this concern, Sommers-Flanagan and Means provided their graduate students with names of referral agencies and trained them to help make appointments at local agencies. Another potential problem results from ethical responsibilities if a serious personal problem and/or pathology (e.g., suicide ideation, chemical dependency, and relationship issues) is revealed. All these problems can be avoided by using a different source of clients. This article describes the unusual procedure of hiring and training theater majors to portray clients.

The actors are undergraduate theater majors who have had experience in improvisation. They are paid minimum wage from departmental funds. There is one actor for every 4 students, for a class size of 16 students. The instructor provides the actors with case-study dialogues (White, Riggs, & Gilbert, 1976) and case-study reports (Oltmanns, Neale, & Davison, 1986). The case studies are selected for an emphasis on adjustment disorders, anxiety disorders, mild or transitional depression, and identity issues. Major pathology is excluded from the case-study material because it is difficult to role-play and the students are inexperienced undergraduates. Each actor develops four clients with different presenting problems by using the case-study information and individual creativity.

The interviewing section is 40% of the class and lasts for 4 weeks of the academic quarter. In the first week, the class is taught the basic attending skills and listening sequence (Ivey, 1983). The actors do not participate in class because they are developing their clients and cross-checking that development with the instructor. The most frequent directives to the actors at this point are to reduce the pathology of the clients, to add background information and history, and to develop areas of normal functioning. Students practice the component skills by role playing in their groups. Ivey's (1983) sequence suggested short practice sessions of one skill at a time. I try to reduce the likelihood of student self-disclosure during roleplays by using a scenario in which the students have no personal experience and must improvise the role of a spouse coming to a therapist to discuss dissatisfaction with the marriage.

The actors participate as clients in Weeks 2 through 4. Students are aware of the function of the actors from the course syllabus and are excited about having a "real client." The actors rotate among the four student groups. This procedure works well because there are 4 hr of class each week, four student groups, and four actors. The actor spends 1 hr per week with each group. The hour is divided into 15-min sections so that each student has the opportunity to interview for 10 min while the other three students serve as observers who provide feedback to the interviewer for 5 min. When the next student becomes interviewer, the actor can either change clients or continue the role-play for up to two interviews. The students benefit from this rotation, by experiencing four actors and a minimum of eight role-plays, which provides opportunities to respond to varied problems and clients. This training element is readily available from the actor clients.

The actors are clients for the 10-min tape-recorded interview completed out of class at the end of Week 2. The clinical situation of responding to a new client is simulated by the instructor assigning actor clients for each interview. After students critique their tape recordings, they meet with the instructor to evaluate the interview.

During Weeks 3 and 4, the class hour has an initial period of 10 min in which the instructor discusses interviewing techniques (e.g., focusing on client problem and developing influencing skills) and provides general feedback based on observation of groups. Each group experiences two role-plays in each of the 4 class hours. The role-plays are 20 min long and focus on obtaining more extensive client information. The actor must continue to add depth to the character by developing the client's presenting problem such as describing the course and duration of symptoms, frequency of occurrence, and conditions under which the problem occurs. The most difficult acting task is for the actor to overcome the temptation to provide a monologue whenever the interviewer is silent. Actors have indicated that silence in improvisation needs to be filled, and they must fill it.

Each student interviewer is videotaped twice in an interview session with an actor client. After the first videotape, the students break into small groups to view and critique each member's videotape. The instructor meets with each group to review the tape, the critiques, and to provide evaluative comments. The second (and final) videotape measures the student's mastery of the interview skills and ability to critique those skills. The instructor meets with the actors to assist in deciding which role-plays to use in the final videotape. Students cannot request a specific actor, but they can request a specific "problem" to be role-played. The rare special requests usually involve particular interest in topics such as chemical dependency in women, stress due to disability from work injury, and abusive relationships. These are unique role-plays and more specialized than the actors would typically use. The practice simulates clinical settings that specialize in certain types of problems. The student completes an extensive critique of the interview session, including a written summary of client background and history of problem development. The instructor is present at the final videotape and later views the videotape while analyzing the student critique. The instructor meets with the student to provide evaluation of skill development during the interviewing segment of the course.

Videotapes are made available for the actors to view at the end of the course. Actors want to see their performance as a client. Final videotapes appeal to actors because they are produced professionally in the campus television studio. This experience serves as preparation and practice for the actors' career goals. In the past 3 years, actors' feedback to the instructor indicates this acting job is a positive experience and many want to participate the following year. Two actors began the client role in their second year of school and returned to this acting job until graduation. They listed it on their resume as paid acting experience. I invite acting students who have had experience with roles in school plays that are adaptable to the client role. The positive aspects of the experience go beyond the theatrical benefits. Acting students have reported learning about the counseling process, and several have said they were helped by being a client because they included their real problems in the role-play. Actors and students seem to benefit from the experience.

References

Boice, R., Andrasik, F., & Simmons, W. L. (1984). Teaching interviewing skills: A procedural account of measuring students' progress. *Teaching of Psychology, 11,* 110- 111.

Ivey, A. E. (1983). *International interviewing and counseling.* Monterey, CA: Brooks/Cole.

Oltmanns, T. F., Neale, J. M., & Davison, G. C. (1986). *Case studies in abnormal psychology* (2nd ed.). New York: Wiley.

Sommers-Flanagan, J., & Means, J. R. (1987). Thou shalt not ask questions: An approach to teaching interviewing skills. *Teaching of Psychology, 14,* 164-166.

Weiss, A. R. (1986). Teaching counseling and psychotherapy skills without access to a clinical population: The short interview method. *Teaching of Psychology, 13,* 145-147.

White, R. W., Riggs, M. M., & Gilbert, D. C. (1976). *Case workbook in personality.* Prospect Heights, IL: Waveland.

The Interviewing Team: An Exercise for Teaching Assessment and Conceptualization Skills

Bernard J. Balleweg
Lycoming College

The Interviewing Team *is an exercise for teaching students how to conduct assessment interviews and conceptualize client problems. The team consists of up to 10 students who take turns interviewing the instructor who role-plays a client. Each student is responsible for obtaining one type of assessment information (e.g., affective, somatic, cognitive, and behavioral symptoms). After each role-play segment, the instructor gives the student feedback and asks the team questions designed to develop hypotheses about the nature and etiology of the "client's" problems. The advantages of this approach to teaching conceptualization skills are discussed.*

Mental health professionals have developed a variety of training programs to teach interviewing skills to counselors (e.g., Carkhuff, 1987; Ivey, 1988; Okun, 1987).Such programs generally stress basic interviewing skills, such as empathic listening and effective questioning. A few training programs (e.g., Cormier & Cormier, 1985; Egan, 1986) go beyond these basic techniques and teach assessment and conceptualization skills. Assessment consists of gathering information about the key symptoms of a client's presenting problems; conceptualization involves integrating the information to develop hypotheses about the nature and etiology of the client's problem (Cormier & Cormier, 1985). Assessment and conceptualization are vital for treatment planning, and inadequate assessment has been identified as a major contributor to negative outcomes in psychotherapy (Hadley & Strupp, 1976).

Despite the importance of assessment and conceptualization, there are few methods for teaching these skills. Instead, articles on teaching techniques typically focus on more basic interviewing skills (e.g., France, 1984; Weiss, 1986). The absence of good teaching strategies is unfortunate because it is difficult to teach students how to interview effectively and to integrate the resulting information into meaningful conceptual frameworks. The instructor who tries to teach assessment and conceptualization skills through role-playing must overcome several problems. First, students are often overwhelmed with the number of variables they must assess; their anxiety may cause them to omit significant pieces of assessment information. Second, students have difficulty role-playing authentic clients (Weiss, 1986), which limits the quality of the learning experience for the "therapist." Finally, role-plays conducted in pairs or triads provide immediate feedback to only two or three students at a time, while others may be making similar mistakes.

To overcome these obstacles, I developed an exercise called the interviewing team that involves students working as a team and interviewing me as I role-play a client. The goals of the exercise are: (a) to develop assessment interviewing skills through authentic role-playing and immediate feedback, and (b) to teach students to use their knowledge of counseling theory and abnormal behavior to conceptualize client problems.

Preparation

Student Preparation

Before the interviewing team is assembled, the students attend lectures and complete reading assignments that cover the assessment and conceptualization process. Cormier and Cormier's (1985) multidimensional, cognitive-behavioral assessment model is used because students grasp it relatively quickly. The following dimensions of the client's presenting problem are studied: behavior, affect, cognitions, somatic functioning, contextual factors, interpersonal factors, and antecedents and consequences that might trigger or maintain the client's problems. After teaching students the Cormier and Cormier model, I role-play an entire assessment interview, using a student volunteer as a client, and discuss my case conceptualization.

Instructor Preparation

To enhance authenticity, I portray former clients from my practice, protecting confidentiality by altering all identifying information and combining features of several cases. Instructors who do not have access to a clinical population could role-play a client from a case study book (e.g., Oltmanns, Neale, & Davison, 1986) after securing the authors' permission.

Portrayals of serious depression are particularly useful for this exercise because depression frequently includes clear behavioral, somatic, cognitive, and affective symptoms. In addition, a wide variety of problems that frequently accompany or precipitate depression (e.g., substance abuse, illnesses, eating disorders, and personality disorders) are introduced to increase the complexity of the case. Before the exercise begins, students are given basic demographic data about the client and are informed that client information has been altered to protect confidentiality.

Implementation

Conducting Role-Play Segments

The 10 students who are selected as members of the interviewing team are told that they are to work together to interview the instructor who portrays a client. Their goal is to assess all relevant dimensions of the client's presenting problems and to develop a conceptualization that includes hypotheses about the etiology of the problems as well as tentative ideas regarding treatment strategies.

Each team member is then assigned one of the following tasks: (a) starting the interview; (b) assessing the affective, behavioral, somatic, cognitive, contextual, or relational problem dimensions; (c) identifying antecedents and consequences; (d) inquiring about prior attempts at problem resolution; and (e) determining the client's strengths and resources.

The first student begins the interview and proceeds for 5 to 10 min. The instructor then stops the interview, gives feedback about the student's interviewing technique, and encourages immediate feedback from the class. The instructor then asks the interviewer to share initial hypotheses about the nature, severity, and etiology of the client's presenting problems. For example, the instructor might ask the student to evaluate the intensity of the client's depression and to discuss how cognitive-behavioral theory could explain the origin of the depression. This type of questioning is a crucial part of the exercise because it challenges students to: (a) integrate initial information and impressions, (b) apply their knowledge of counseling theory and abnormal behavior, and (c) formulate hypotheses to guide subsequent inquiries. Although the person who is role-playing the therapist has the opportunity to answer these questions first, all members of the team are encouraged to offer their observations and hypotheses. This team effort reduces performance pressure on each individual and helps build class cohesion.

The sequence of interviewing, receiving feedback, and questioning is repeated for each of the 10 role-play segments. Team members are repeatedly challenged to revise preliminary hypotheses to accommodate new information.

Switching Therapists

The decision to switch from one therapist to another is partially dictated by time, because role-play segments must average 5 to 10 min in order to complete the interview within a 2-hr class period and still allow time between segments for feedback and discussion. To demonstrate how to obtain assessment information without disrupting the natural interview flow, I try to make transitions coincide with major shifts in content by the client.

On occasion, I make a transition to another therapist if the current therapist reaches an impasse and becomes anxious in searching for what to say next. Before the student's anxiety becomes counterproductive, I ask team members to recommend possible directions to proceed with the interview, and I encourage the student to try one of those directions. If the student quickly reaches another impasse, I shift to another student.

Concluding the Exercise

Throughout the exercise, students are encouraged to take notes on information relevant to their assessment area. When all role-play segments are completed, students are asked to review their notes and summarize the information obtained in their assessment area. The instructor helps the team discuss this information and use it to revise earlier hypotheses, identify areas that need further evaluation, and develop tentative treatment strategies.

Advantages and Disadvantages

The interviewing team exercise has several advantages as a method for teaching assessment and conceptualization skills: (a) it reduces student anxiety by dividing assessment responsibilities among team members, (b) it enhances the quality and authenticity of the role-play because the instructor role-plays the client, (c) it provides opportunities for immediate feedback, (d) it alerts the student about the necessity for reformulation and revision of hypotheses as more information is obtained, (e) it challenges students to apply their knowledge of psychological theory and psychopathology, (f) it helps build class cohesion, and (g) it provides students with the opportunity to observe and learn from each other.

Nevertheless, some drawbacks to the interviewing team approach need to be considered before it is implemented. This approach is difficult to use effectively in groups exceeding 10 students because larger groups lead to lengthy interviews, thus disengaging some members from the process. (A group with fewer students works well because the instructor can assign several tasks to one or more students.) Instructors of large classes can circumvent this problem by dividing the class into groups of 10 or fewer students and using specially trained students to play the role of the client and provide feedback as the interview unfolds. France (1984) successfully used peer trainers in an interviewing techniques course, and a similar process could be followed here. In addition, this exercise does not give individual students extensive practice in conducting assessment interviews and developing case conceptualizations. For additional practice, students can role-play full-length assessment interviews in pairs during subsequent class sessions or as homework assignments. Several students have told me that the interviewing team exercise significantly reduced their anxiety and gave them "a sense of direction" during later role-plays in pairs.

Applications

The interviewing team approach was developed for a senior-level, undergraduate, counseling techniques course and could be used in similar undergraduate courses on interviewing skills and counseling methods. At the undergraduate level, the goal of the exercise should be to introduce students to the assessment and conceptualization process. An introduction is important because it shows students that mental health professionals must combine interviewing techniques with knowledge of psychological theory and abnormal behavior to conceptualize and treat client problems. If undergraduates are not introduced to the conceptualization process, they may falsely assume that they are qualified to work with clients after acquiring basic interviewing skills. An introduction to the conceptualization process also does not quality undergraduates to work as professionals; consequently, they should be cautioned about the limitations of their expertise following training.

This exercise could be adapted for teaching assessment and conceptualization skills at the graduate level. For example, the instructor could require the team to include additional types of assessment information, such as life history data, a mental status exam, and a diagnosis. The instructor could also incorporate other theoretical perspectives. For example, within a psychoanalytic framework, students could be assigned various roles, such as noting characteristic defense mechanisms and identifying unconscious conflicts. The interviewing team offers the instructor a systematic approach to teaching assessment and conceptualization skills that maximizes class participation and immediate instructor feedback and can be used in graduate or undergraduate courses.

References

Carkhuff, R. R. (1987). *The art of helping VI*. Amherst, MA: Human Resources Development Press.

Cormier, W. H., & Cormier, L. S. (1985). *Interviewing skills for helpers: Fundamental skills and cognitive behavioral interventions*. Monterey, CA: Brooks/Cole.

Egan, G. (1986) . *The skilled helper: A systematic approach to effective helping*. Monterey, CA: Brooks/Cole.

France, K. (1984). Peer trainers in an interviewing techniques course. *Teaching of Psychology, 11,* 171-173.

Hadley, S. W., & Strupp, H. H. (1976). Contemporary views of negative effects in psychotherapy. *Archives of General Psychiatry, 33,* 1291-1302.

Ivey, A. E. (1988). *Intentional interviewing and counseling: Facilitating client development*. Pacific Grove, CA: Brooks/Cole.

Okun, B. F. (1987). *Effective helping: Interviewing and counseling techniques*. Monterey, CA: Brooks/Cole.

Oltmanns, T. F., Neale, J. M., & Davison, G. C. (1986). *Case studies in abnormal psychology*. New York: Wiley.

Weiss, A. R. (1986). Teaching counseling and psychotherapy skills without access to a clinical population: The short interview method. *Teaching of Psychology, 13,* 145-147.

Notes

1. An earlier version of this article was presented at the annual meeting of the American Psychological Association, New Orleans, LA, August 1989.
2. I thank Joseph Palladino and three anonymous reviewers for their comments on an earlier draft of this article.

Adjuncts to the Textbook for an Undergraduate Clinical Psychology Class

Janet R. Matthews
Creighton University

Introduction to clinical psychology is not an unusual undergraduate psychology course. However, only a few new texts are available (Garfield, 1974; Goldenberg, 1973; Hoch, 1971; Korchin, 1976; Phares, 1979; Sundberg, Tyler, & Taplin, 1973). Although these texts provide material on the theories and practice of clinical psychology, they do not typically include suggestions for experiential adjuncts. The value of such adjuncts is supported by theory and research.

Rogers (1969) stated that situations which produce involvement at both the feeling and intellectual levels lead to more pervasive and lasting learning consequences. Several articles have reported course projects requiring greater student involvement. Babad, Oppenheimer, and Katz (1978) found that it was difficult to integrate cognitiveintellectual learning and an affective component within a course in group dynamics, but that such an integration could be achieved through special projects. Hettich (1976) and Ware (1979) used the autobiography for different courses to increase student involvement. Riger (1978) employed a project requiring content analysis of the portrayal of men and women in the media as an adjunct to a psychology of women course. Howells (1978) increased student involvement in a course in environmental psychology by using a field project. Gardner (1976) described a class exercise exploring the question of the existence of mental illness. These reports indicate the need to evaluate the effectiveness of adjuncts in specific courses rather than to assume that there are adjuncts which are applicable for all classes.

Method. The subjects for this investigation were students enrolled in an upper division undergraduate course in clinical psychology. The course was an elective and the majority of students were psychology majors. Introductory psychology, abnormal psychology and three additional psychology hours were pre-requisites for this course, which was offered during the Spring term each year. Over a two year period, 64 students completed the course.

The adjuncts for the course were: films, exercises, and exposure to the professional literature. The instructor distributed the exercises throughout the semester.

Films. A large number of films exist for use in an undergraduate clinical psychology class, but time and budget limitations required selectivity. The final selection was limited to films illustrating therapy procedures. During the first year of the course, the "Gloria" interviews (Shostrom, 1965) were used. During the second year, a newer series of interviews with "Kathy" (Shostrom, 1978) were used.

Exercises. The instructor used the same three exercises in both years of the course. The first exercise, "introduction," involved pairing the students. The instructions stated that each pair was to carry on a conversation for 10 minutes. They were to ask whatever questions they wished in an attempt to gain sufficient information to be able to introduce that person to a stranger. The exercise was used to illustrate one method of getting members of a therapy group to become acquainted with each other.

The second exercise simulated an intake interview. The class was grouped in dyads. One member of each pair role-played a clinical psychologist and the other was in the role of the client. Each "client" was asked to come to class prepared to role play a behavior disorder learned in abnormal psychology. To prepare the students for this exercise, the instructor described the purpose of the initial intake interview in clinical practice, and also provided the students with a standard form for an initial clinical interview. She explained the reasons for the types of items included in the form and provided some appropriate questions for tapping psychotic thought processes.

The third exercise was called "spin the bottle." Students arranged their chairs in a circle. A deck of cards was prepared prior to class. Each card contained the description of an activity. Some of the activities required participants to engage in silly behavior while others were aimed at affect expression. Sample items include: "Recite a children's nursery rhyme;" "Describe the person in the group to whom you feel the least close without using that person's name"; and "Pretend you are 80 years old. Choose someone in the group as your 85-year-old companion and have a conversation with that person." One student spun a bottle placed in the center of the circle of chairs. The person toward whom the bottle pointed picked up the top card from the deck and followed the directions. Once the activity had been completed, that student then spun the bottle and the process was repeated.

Literature. Any student wishing to earn an "A" in the course was required to give a class report that consisted of a summary of an article from a clinically oriented journal. On the first day of class, the instructor provided a list of 13 such journals in our library. Other journals could be used by special permission. After summarizing the article, the student was required to respond to questions from the class and the instructor. In addition, each student was required to submit five written article abstracts, done in standard APA style. A sample abstract was provided on the first day of class.

The instructor administered an evaluation form during class near the end of the semester. A five point rating scale was used to evaluate the adjuncts. The steps ranged from "poor" (1) to "excellent" (5) with intermediate steps of "fair," "good," and "very good." Items comprising the evaluation form are shown as footnotes in Table 1. Open-ended questions were also included. They asked about those parts of the course the student would prefer to have replaced, would recommend for improvement, or would recommend remaining as presented. This form was completed anonymously.

Table 1
Percentage Responding to Each
Item by Scalar Units

Item	Scalar Unit					
	1	2	3	4	5	Med.
1	0	1.8	25.0	48.2	25.0	4
2	0	10.7	35.7	46.5	7.1	4
3	0	11.8	25.5	41.2	21.5	4
4	0	11.1	33.3	35.2	20.4	4
5	0	6.1	32.7	24.5	36.7	4
6	0	14.8	37.1	29.6	18.5	3
7	7.1	41.1	44.6	5.4	1.8	3
8	1.8	22.8	26.3	36.8	12.3	3

1. Overall, to what degree did the films enhance your knowledge of clinical psychology?
2. What is your usual reaction to films in the classroom?
3. How would you rate the "introduction" exercise?
4. What is your reaction to the simulated intake interview done in class?
5. What is your reaction to the "spin the bottle" exercise done in class?
6. If you gave an oral report, to what degree do you consider it to have been a learning experience?
7 To what degree was listening to the oral reports a learning experience?
8. To what degree was writing the abstracts a learning experience?

Results. A tabulation of the evaluations from 57 students attending class on the day data were collected revealed that all items had median ratings which were at or above the "good" category. There were some variations, however, across the types of adjuncts. In order to obtain a more complete picture of the students' pattern of responses, the percentage of the

sample responding at each scalar unit was considered. Table 1 presents these data for each item.

Items 1 and 2 provide a measure of student reaction to films. While students rated these specific films, overall, as "very good," such a rating is typical of their reaction to the use of films in the classroom. When scalar units 4 and 5 are considered jointly, the data indicate a slightly more favorable response to the psychotherapy films than is the typical reaction to films by these students. In the general comments section of the questionnaire, a number of the students added remarks indicating that they felt the films made the text material on therapy procedures considerably more clear to them. Others commented that the films had led to a type of class discussion which would have been impossible without the common starting point provided by the films. The range of responses within this category also adds support to the efficacy of using these films.

The exercises were specifically addressed with items 3, 4, and 5 of the evaluation. These exercises all received median ratings of "4." In the open comments section of the evaluation, some students indicated that it was difficult to conduct the interview. They stated that it made them more aware of the skill necessary for engaging in clinical work. Others indicated that this exercise made them more aware of their current level of competence, and it interested them in additional learning about the skills required for such work. A few students indicated discomfort with certain items from the spin the bottle exercise, and stated that they had been relieved when others in the class had been the ones faced with those items. Open comments did not tend to reflect on the introduction exercise except to suggest that it would be good to use it early in the term as a method of helping the students in the class become acquainted.

Exposure to the professional literature was tapped by items 6, 7, and 8 of the evaluation. The median rating for each of these three items was "3," indicating a less favorable response than to the two previous adjuncts. Of particular concern within this category was the response to item 7. More than 7% of the students assigned a rank of "1" to this item and over 41% gave it a rank of "2." These data indicate that students do not find listening to their peers to be a particularly good learning experience.

Discussion. The course adjuncts described in this article involve both cognitive and experiential levels of development. Cognitive development has been emphasized in the traditional form of undergraduate education, but a balance with the experiential is starting to be described in the literature.

The films are the least "active" of these adjuncts. One reason for their use is to provide visual input of material and maximize learning through the use of more than one sense modality. Another reason is to clarify procedures described in text and lecture. The proper introduction to the films is important. Setting the stage for discussion after the films leads to a different type of film viewing. A series of films, such as the interview films used here, provides continuity across a number of class periods. These films were shown during three consecutive classes. Since the class met for 90 minutes, the format was an introduction of the material for that particular day, viewing the interview, and discussion after the interview. The students were aware that the client would be interviewed by three different therapists and that they would be asked to compare the techniques used after the final interview was seen. Thus, even a passive act such as film watching can be made more active as a result of instructions.

The most highly experiential of the adjuncts were the exercises. The positive response of the students to the exercises may be partially a result of their novelty. They provide a change from the more typical classroom situation of note-taking. It is also possible that by taking a more active role in the learning process the impact of the material is greater, and thus is perceived as a more positive learning experience. The exercises, like the films, provide a common ground for discussion. The students can reflect, based on their text reading and lecture material, on how such exercises as "introduction" and "spin the bottle" might be used in a therapy setting. Such discussion is facilitated by active participation as contrasted to reading about such exercises.

Although the behavior of the interviewee in the simulated interview is no substitute for dealing with actual psychopathology, it does provide an initial exposure to the potential problems of dealing with psychologically disturbed individuals. Such exposure is of particular value to the student who wishes to pursue employment at the paraprofessional level. According to Urmer (Note 1), a major reason for the BA-level mental health worker being rejected for a potential position is the fear reaction often shown when first faced with a psychiatric patient. Gradual exposure of the undergraduate to psychopathological behavior through classroom simulation and field experience could prove especially valuable to those students who choose to seek BA-level mental health positions.

Some students find it difficult to "let go" and actively participate in exercises. This is particularly true of "spin the bottle." Care needs to be taken both in choosing the exercises and the types of items which are used within any given exercise to minimize discomfort while presenting a realistic picture of its use. Having the option of refusing a particular item within an exercise is helpful.

Within "exposure to the professional literature," there are both active and passive learning components. The passive role of listening to class reports was not rated highly by these students. A potential influence on this rating is that such reports can prove difficult to follow. With limited prior teaching experience, these students are often less than polished speakers. This factor may also have played a role in the ratings given to delivering a class report. Students who are accustomed to doing a good job and being near the top of the class may not feel comfortable when faced with a situation for which they do not feel they possess top skills. Their ability to see the advantage of practice in such skill development could have been a factor in keeping the rating of item 6 above that for item 7 (see Table 1). Although not seen as being as good a learning experience as films or exercises, the writing of abstracts was viewed as a reasonably positive learning experience. A more active method for considering the information from these articles could result in a more positive student rating of the adjunct.

Overall, the use of adjuncts to the text for this type of course is evaluated as a positive learning experience by the students. Some faculty have suggested the actual teaching of helping skills in an undergraduate clinical psychology course (Fling, Note 2). The adjuncts suggested in this article are intended to provide some exposure to the types of activities in which the clinical psychologist is engaged, without actually teaching specific skills. Such exposure may be used by the students in career decision-making, prior to commitment to actually learning the skills. The description provided is intended both as a suggestion to other academic clinical psychologists and as a call for others to share adjuncts which they have found to be effective in such a setting.

References

Babad, E. Y., Oppenheimer, B. T., & Katz, I. Teaching group dynamics in academic settings: Basic dilemmas and some tentative solutions. *Teaching of Psychology,* 1978, *5,* 122-127.

Gardner, J. M. The myth of mental illness game: Sick is just a four letter word. *Teaching of Psychology,* 1976, *3,* 141-143.

Garfield, S. L *Clinical psychology: The study of personality and behavior.* Chicago: Aldine, 1974.

Goldenberg, H. *Contemporary clinical psychology.* Monterey, CA: Brooks/Cole, 1973.

Hettich, P. The journal: An autobiographical approach to learning. *Teaching of Psychology,* 1976, *3,* 60-63.

Hoch, E L. *Experimental contributions to clinical psychology.* Belmont, CA: Brooks/Cole, 1971.

Howells, G. N. The field project as a tool for teaching environmental psychology. *Teaching of Psychology,* 1978, *5,* 195-198.

Korchin, S. J. *Modern clinical psychology: Principles of intervention in the clinic and community.* New York: Basic Books, 1976.

Phares, E. J. *Clinical psychology: Concepts, methods, and profession.* Homewood, IL: Dorsey, 1979.

Riger, S. A technique for teaching the psychology of women: Content analysis. *Teaching of Psychology,* 1978, *5,* 221-223.

Rogers, C. R. *Freedom to learn.* Columbus: Charles E. Merrill Publishing Co., 1969.

Shostrom, E. (Producer). *Three approaches to psychotherapy.* Orange, CA: Psychological Films, Inc., 1965. (Film)

Shostrom, E. (Producer). *Three approaches to psychotherapy II.* Orange, CA: Psychological Films, Inc., 1978. (Film)

Sundberg, N. D., Tyler, L. E., & Taplin, J. R. *Clinical psychology: Expanding horizons.* Englewood Cliffs, NJ: Prentice-Hall, 1973.

Ware, M. Use of the autobiography for personal development and as an investigative technique. *Transactions of the Nebraska Academy of Sciences,* 1979, 7, 183-186.

Notes

1. Urmer, A. H. *BA-level jobs in mental health facilities.* Paper presented at the meeting of the American Psychological Association. San Francisco, August 1977.
2. Fling, S. *Teaching and evaluating helping skills in an undergraduate clinical psychology course.* Paper presented at the meeting of the Southwestern Psychological Association, San Antonio, April 1979.

Teaching Counseling and Psychotherapy Skills Without Access to a Clinical Population: The Short Interview Method

Andrea R. Weiss
Drexel University

The method described is designed to teach verbal helping skills to students who do not have access to clinical populations. Open-ended interviews with "real" people are used as the primary training device; role-playing simulations and programmed instruction complement this experience.

Teaching helping and listening skills to psychology students is best accomplished by having them counsel with real people. However, in many educational settings, particularly those without doctoral training programs in counseling or clinical psychology that maintain their own clinics, clinical populations willing to be counseled are not available. Therefore, the counseling or psychotherapy instructor is forced to explore other alternatives for teaching basic helping skills. One alternative is to ask students to find their own counselees. When I first began to teach counseling psychology I resorted to this approach, which was productive for some students. These students managed to find strangers, or relative strangers, to counsel and did useful and helpful work with them. For example, students worked with friends of friends, or friends of relatives, or casual acquaintances from the dormitory or neighborhood. However, it was difficult for most stu-

dents to find people who were appropriate, that is, individuals over the age of 18 who were not friends or relatives of the counselor-in-training who wanted to talk for a limited period of time about an important but not serious personal problem with someone who had virtually no counseling experience.

An alternative for providing a counseling experience without using real clients is to have the students counsel each other in role-playing situations. These are often called *simulated counseling experiences.* (Allowing students to do "real" peer counseling with one another is not appropriate because group discussions of the counseling sessions would violate the principles of confidentiality and the welfare of the consumer.) These simulated counseling exercises have been useful training strategies, as they have enabled students to practice new skills in a supportive atmosphere and receive immediate feedback from classmates on their skill mastery. However, there is a general feeling of artificiality about these exercises, because they lend themselves best to practicing one helping skill at a time and because the counselees are usually playing the role of someone else or feeling some way that is not genuine at the moment.

A second alternative is to use a programmed instruction package, such as the one by Evans, Hearn, Uklemann, and Ivey (1984) in which students choose, from among several alternatives, a counselor comment or question that best represents a particular kind of interviewing skill or one that will be most facilitative to the depicted client. The Evans et al. (1984) book has much to offer. The programmed exercises allow the students more practice with each skill than they can get in any one real-life counseling session, the alternatives are excellent models of well-phrased therapeutic interventions, and the text includes discussion, which can be obtained immediately following the student's choice, of why each counselor intervention was appropriate or not for the given situation. However, there are limitations to programmed instruction as a substitute for an actual counseling experience. First, students are not required to generate their own comments or questions, but merely to recognize which of those already given is most appropriate. Second, it is not obvious that there is any transfer from this kind of experience to a real-life counseling or psychotherapy experience.

Procedure

After 4 years of teaching counseling and psychotherapy without regular access to clients for my students, I have developed an approach that incorporates both the role-playing technique and programmed instruction as complements to the primary clinical experience of conducting a series of short interviews. Specifically, as a homework assignment, students are asked to interview someone (anyone at all, and on tape) for not more than 5 or 10 min, in an attempt to answer an assigned open-ended question. Students accomplish this task by using the attending and listening skills they are practicing in classroom role-playing exercises and in their programmed instruction books. They are then required to transcribe the interviews completely and to label the microskills they have used according to the Ivey and Authier categories (Ivey & Simek-Downing, 1980). The transcription and labeling are crucial components of the assignment, as they permit the student and the teacher to do a microskill-based analysis of the effectiveness of the interview.

In a 10-week term the students are required to complete five of these interviews. At the beginning of the term, students receive a handout that includes the directions for doing and transcribing the five interviews. The handout also contains the five questions they will be asking and the due date for each assignment. Scheduling an interview question every 2 weeks has worked well. During the first week between assignments, I read and write comments on the most recently completed interview. The students then receive my feedback and have a full week to do their next interviews. Students are not permitted to turn in

the interviews in bulk. The third interview is recorded on videotape, and the class spends 2 to 4 hr (one or two class periods) watching these videotapes and providing feedback about each student's nonverbal and verbal interviewing behavior. For example, students are asked to comment on each other's posture, body position, and facial expressions, and each other's usage of the various attending and influencing skills. They observe that particular interviews seem richer than others, and are encouraged to try to understand why. Are certain helping skills facilitative, or is it the interviewer's flexibility in using different microskills?

The other four interviews are recorded on audiotape. We generally listen to portions of these interviews in class so that the students receive feedback and suggestions from their classmates in addition to the feedback they obtain on their written transcriptions of the interviews. The interview questions become progressively more challenging and/or personal as the term progresses, but all are selected with the primary goal of facilitating discussion that is stimulating, rich in personal meaning, and open-ended. In addition, because of my phenomenological/existential orientation I tend to assign questions that encourage the interviewees and interviewers to examine their values and their meaning constructs. The interview questions for undergraduate students are as follows:

Interview 1. How has the women's movement affected you?
Interview 2. If you won $1,000,000 in the lottery, what would you change about the way you live your life?
Interview 3. How might you be different if you were a male (female)?
Interview 4. How would you live your life differently if you knew you would live forever?
Interview 5. What role does adventure (or beauty, or friendship) play in your life?

Because our psychology graduate students are committed to the helping professions, their assigned questions include several that they may be likely to ask on practicum placements or in their jobs. Questions 4 and 5 have been included for this purpose. The interview questions for graduate students are as follows:

Interview 1. How has the threat of nuclear war affected your life?
Interview 2. How would you live your life differently if you knew you would live forever?
Interview 3. What role does friendship play in your life?
Interview 4. What are the things about yourself that you like most?
Interview 5. If you could relive any part of your life, what would you change?

The value of these interview assignments, in comparison with role-playing exercises or programmed instruction, lies in their closer approximation to a real-life counseling or psychotherapy experience. Students doing interviews are talking to people who are being themselves rather than playing roles, and they are forced to generate their own helpful questions and comments rather than rely on someone else's ideas. However, it is important to stress that interviews are not substitutes for role playing and programmed instruction experiences. During the early part of the term, when the students are learning the various attending and listening skills from lectures and their textbook, they also complete, as homework, the Evans et al. (1984) programmed instruction exercises illustrating these skills. In addition, we spend portions of many class periods practicing the microskills through role playing.

Students split up into pairs and take turns interviewing each other with the aid of a particular skill. For example, students who have taken the counselor role might be asked to spend 5 min using open questions to interview students who have taken the counselee role. Students who have taken the role of counselee will either adopt a psychological problem for the duration of the exercise or use a relatively minor personal problem that they feel comfortable sharing. When members of a pair have had a turn at each role, they repeat the exercise using closed questions. When that task has been completed, and student partners have given each other feedback on their performances as interviewers, the entire class discusses their experience with the two kinds of questions. During the next class period student pairs might practice using the skills of paraphrasing and directives, and compare effects of these approaches. This kind of focused practice is essential preparation for the outside-of-classroom interviewing assignments, because the students, in order to conduct productive interviews, need to know the relative advantages of the various skills.

An additional benefit of this interviewing approach is increased self-awareness for some students. Students are advised to prepare for their interviews by trying to answer the interview questions themselves. Because the questions are somewhat provocative, this preparatory exercise encourages self-examination and thinking about feelings, and in some students leads to expanded self-knowledge. Students have, for example, learned some things about their values, life goals, and personalities by trying to answer the question, "How would you live your life differently if you knew you would live forever?" Some have realized how important physical health and spending their lifetimes with family members are to them. Others have realized how important time pressure is in their accomplishments. It has occurred to them that without the pressure of finite deadlines they might drift through life and accomplish little. Struggling with the question, "How has the threat of nuclear war affected your life?," has led some students to realize more clearly that they were, in fact, being psychologically affected by this threat. The question, "How has the women's movement affected you?," has had some very interesting outcomes. Students too young to remember the heyday of the feminist movement often "rediscover" that change in sex role expectations has occurred and has affected their lives; and students interviewing students who are more chauvinistic in their outlook learn what it means to try to keep one's values of one's counseling work.

Students who have enrolled in one of the counseling courses are initially surprised to receive the interviewing assignments, some because it is more "hands-on" work than they have ever encountered in a course and others because they expected to do "real" counseling. Many also complain about the time-consuming transcription process. However, the undergraduate and graduate students almost universally evaluate these interviewing assignments as among their most useful learning experiences. The importance of detailed feedback from the instructor cannot be overemphasized. Although the microskills labeling does help the students to do a productive analysis of the effectiveness of their work, the instructor's comments add to their understanding and, perhaps of most importance, provide the positive reinforcement, encouragement, and goal setting necessary for continued progress.

References

Evans, D. R., Hearn, M. T., Uklemann, M. R., & Ivey, A. E. (1984). *Essential interviewing: A programmed approach to effective communication* (2nd ed.). Monterey, CA: Brooks/Cole.

Ivey, A. E., & Simek-Downing, L. (1980). *Counseling and psychotherapy: Skills, theories, and practice.* Englewood Cliffs, NJ: Prentice-Hall.

The Hypothesis-Testing Game: A Training Tool for the Graduate Interviewing Skills Course

Kathryn M. Rickard
Robert W. Titley
Colorado State University

This article describes an interviewing game used in a graduate level interviewing skills course. The goal of the game is to teach basic components of the interviewing process such as comfort with the interview, microcounseling skills, hypothesis generation, and hypothesis testing. The instructor plays the part of a client and is interviewed by two teams of students. Roles of students in the game and game procedure are explained. Favorable student ratings and positive feedback have been received.

Instructors of graduate-level introductory interviewing courses recognize a variety of training goals. Instilling subjective comfort with the interviewing process is an important elementary goal; fostering student's incorporation of basic microcounseling skills is another goal for many instructors (Ivey, Ivey, & Simec-Downing, 1987). Role playing and practice interviews provide excellent channels for training in these basic areas. However, according to the Ivey et al. "skills hierarchy" notion, higher level training goals include the development of the ability to conceptualize client problems and to use a hypothesis-generating and hypothesis-testing approach. These goals are more abstract than primary skills and, therefore, somewhat more difficult to present to the beginning graduate student. The assessment and rehearsal of skills at this level are also particularly problematic for another reason. Final grades or qualitative evaluations in interviewing courses taken early in training are often important criteria for evaluating performance and progress and for predicting subsequent success in the program. Because students are aware of such contingencies, they are often anxious and inhibited in their attempts to acquire skills and perform them, especially in the presence of instructors or supervisors.

This article describes a team game used in a graduatelevel interviewing course at Colorado State University. The game is designed to develop hypothesis-generation, hypothesis-testing, and conceptualization-building skills in what has proven to be a relatively nonthreatening atmosphere. The game, when used early in the course, can also serve to identify strengths and deficits in individual students. At the end of the course, it can be useful to help students measure their progress.

Guidelines and Rules for the Game

The instructor should introduce and explain the game in a way that fosters a comfortable, noncompetitive climate. An ideal number of players is 8 to 12 students. Materials needed include a stopwatch, two different colored strips of construction paper cut into 20 to 30 ticket-sized "markers," paper and pencil for each student, and preferably a long conference table so that players may sit on opposite sides of the table with timers and judges at either end.

The instructor role-plays a well conceptualized, hypothetical clinical case. Students interview the "client" in order to obtain information about the case and test the hypotheses generated as the game progresses. Diagnoses that have worked particularly well have been fairly standard and common ones such as personality disorders, phobias, depression, and adjustment disorders. Because the skills needed to deal with client resistance, avoidance, or passive aggressivity are not usually present at this stage, these characteristics should not be part of the instructor's client role.

Students volunteer to fulfill the following roles for the game: Team A members, Team B members, recording referees, and timing referees. Team A members (3 to 4 students) interview the client and record, in written format, hypotheses associated with questions asked of the client. They also challenge the questions asked by the opposing team. Team B members have identical responsibilities. Recording referees (1 or 2 students) act as judges and award points to the teams for questioning, hypothesis testing, appropriate challenges, and responses to challenges. They confer with the timing referees on their scoring of the teams and record the points accumulated. The timing referees (1 or 2 other students) also act as judges, but only in a consultation capacity to the recording referees; in cases of disagreement, the opinions of the recording referees are final. The primary duty of the timing referees is to monitor the information-gathering phases and interrupt the team members with a verbal command or electric buzzer when their allotted times are up.

Procedure

One and one half hours should be allotted for the game. Each team is allocated four 3-min segments for interviewing the client, with the teams alternating in sequence. During these 3-min segments, teams generate and evaluate hypotheses with the client. A total of 24 min of interviewing is conducted in this manner.

Students are told that the goals for interviewing are to gather information, use microcounseling skills when appropriate, follow up on relevant information, disregard irrelevant data, generate and test hypotheses, and maintain positive regard and rapport with the client. A student with a question or lead is encouraged to pursue and verbalize it at any time during the 3-min segment. Students are encouraged to make the introspective experience of dealing with clients more overt and explicit by using this deliberate, verbal form of evaluating the interviewing process. (Of course, such frequent interruptions during actual therapy would detract from the process.) There is no designated order or time limit for team members when interviewing. Members of the opposing team are encouraged to indicate a challenge by throwing markers onto the table at any time during the 3-min segment. Challenges are based on the challenger's belief that a crucial lead was bypassed, on the belief that a questioner is pursuing a "wrong track," or whenever there is a perceived problem with the interviewer's microcounseling skills.[1]

The timing referee records elapsed interview time prior to the challenge. When the challenge and response are completed, the referee restarts the game and indicates the amount of time remaining. Following each challenge and before interviewing resumes, the recording and timing referees confer and points are awarded. After the 3-min challenge segment, the opposing team is allowed a 3-min interview, and the game proceeds as just described.

---

[1]Information on procedure for referee's evaluations of challenges may be obtained by writing to Kathryn M. Rickard, Department of Psychology, Colorado State University, Fort Collins, CO 80523.

The Awarding of Points

Referees award points to teams as follows: After each segment of the game (each team's 3-min interview), the interviewing team evaluates the evidence for and against their hypotheses during a private team discussion. Then they present this evidence and their lines of reasoning, summarizing two hypotheses that the team believes might best be pursued during subsequent interviewing. Teams are now allowed to challenge or interact with one another during this period. Referees evaluate the interviewing team's presentation and award points on a 10-point scale. A score of 1 indicates the referee's impressions that: (a) the proposed hypotheses/questioning would lead nowhere; (b) the team is off target with its thinking and questioning; or (c) hypotheses (deemed relevant based on existing evidence) were disregarded during the interview or presentation phase. A score of 10 indicates superior team decision making in these areas.

When a challenger marker is thrown, 1 point is awarded to the challenging team in order to encourage active involvement. If the challenging team wins the challenge, 5 additional points are added. When the interviewing team is challenged and wins the challenge, 6 points are awarded to that team. In the spirit of encouraging risk taking, if the interviewing team is challenged and loses the challenge, no points are subtracted from the interviewing team's score. However, the challenging team receives 6 points for a successful challenge. The team that throws the most markers by the end of the game receives an additional 10 points. Again, this procedure encourages active participation during the game.

Following the 24 min of interviewing, referees total each team's points and announce the winner. An instructor made trophy or an inexpensive prize is awarded to the winning team. (See Figure 1 for a flow chart for the game.)

Evaluation and Discussion

Students consistently rate the game toward the favorable end of a scale ranging from *not very helpful* (1) to *extremely helpful* (5), with a recent mean rating of 4.93 (N = 17). Open-ended questions on evaluation forms elicited responses such as: "Not only was the game enjoyable, but it was lighthearted enough to allow us to develop and present our ongoing conceptualization of the case in a nonthreatening environment." Students have expressed no negative reactions to the game.

It appears that the game addresses and achieves a number of goals for the introductory interviewing course. Students benefit not only through direct and vicarious feedback, but through the group process of deciding which information may or may not be relevant to the case. An additional indirect benefit is the ice

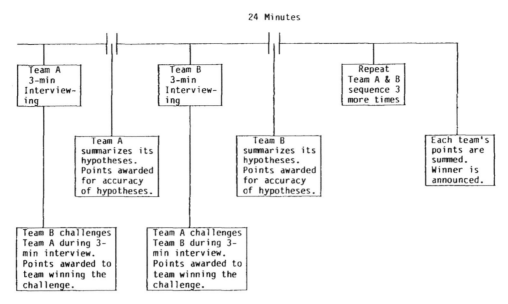

24 Minutes

Figure 1. Procedural flow chart for hypothesis–testing game.

breaking aspect of the game and subsequent disinhibition in students; even less vocal students participate.

Although this exercise does not provide a simulation of an actual clinical interview (e.g., multiple interviewers, possible interruption of interview flow), it appears to be an effective vehicle for introducing hypothesis-generating and decision-making techniques. This training tool should be used, of course, in conjunction with other training methods that compensate for these shortcomings and only as a part of a more comprehensive training format.

Reference

Ivey, A., Ivey, M., & Simec-Downing, L. (1987). *Counseling and psychotherapy.* Englewood Cliffs, NJ: Prentice-Hall.

Thou Shalt Not Ask Questions: An Approach to Teaching Interviewing Skills

John Sommers-Flanagan
John R. Means
University of Montana

This article describes four components of an approach used to teach interviewing skills to first-year graduate students. First students are told that they should not ask or answer questions during their first two interviews. Second, students evaluate, orally and in writing, their own behavior during the interview. Third, students are provided feedback from several sources regarding their interviewing skills and interpersonal styles. Fourth, effects of the interview on the subjects, and changes in their attitudes toward psychotherapy, are evaluated because subjects are acquired from an introductory psychology research pool.

Students enrolled in our Interviewing and Case History Techniques course are usually just beginning graduate school and have diverse backgrounds and experiences. Therefore, the first phase of the course consists of 2 weeks of teaching and learning. During this phase, students are oriented to the many categories of interviewer responses, depending on the goal of the interview or the interviewer's theoretical orientation, and are informed of the usual effects of each type of response on the interviewee. Students learn categories ranging from client-centered approaches (e.g., minimal nonverbal "encouragers" and reflection of content/feeling) to more directive responses (e.g., reassurance or advice). These categories are drawn from the work of Benjamin (1974) and Cormier and Cormier (1985). In addition, students are taught how to use questions and are required to complete several structured interviews toward the end of the course. For the most part, however, the four components of the course emphasized in this article occur during the 3 to 4 weeks following the teaching phase and before the students' experiences with structured interviewing.

The "No Questions Asked" Approach

The first component of the course is designed to help students become more client-centered and less directive in their initial interviews. They are required to complete 50-min interviews, record them using audio or video equipment, and present them to the class for feedback. The first two interviews must be completed without asking or answering any questions; the students rely exclusively on the less directive techniques of paraphrasing, reflection of feelings, and summary to "get their subject to talk." The purpose of having students rely on nondirective techniques during their first interviews is to assist them in developing good listening skills before learning more directive techniques. In this regard, Strupp and Binder (1984) stated: "Frequently underestimated is the degree to which the therapist's presence and empathic listening constitute the most powerful source of help and support one human being can provide another" (p. 41).

As the first interviews approach, the level of anxiety in class usually rises a bit, and a few students ask questions such as "What exactly is the goal of this first interview?" or "I'm not really sure what we're supposed to be focusing on?" We typically respond with "The goal of the interview is to listen and to communicate to your subject that you have listened, and no more than that" or "You are to focus on what your subject is saying and feeling." Other methods for decreasing students' anxiety include (a) giving them opportunities to practice the interviewing techniques during inclass role plays and (b) allowing them to view a videotape of the instructor conducting the type of interview that is required of them (i.e., a nondirective interview with an introductory psychology student volunteer). One of the most formidable obstacles to the development of good listening skills in these first-year graduate students is their tendency to believe that they need to "do" something for their clients. They are repeatedly assured that

the best thing they can do is listen and stay out of the way so that the client can talk more freely (Strupp & Binder, 1984). Clinicians of varied theoretical views have acknowledged the importance of good listening skills as a foundation on which more directive or interpretive techniques may be built (Cormier & Cormier, 1985; Goldfried & Davison, 1976; Strupp & Binder, 1984).

A final point about the first component of this course should also be mentioned. Students are informed that the use of questions in an interview is, contrary to popular belief, not an essential tool of the skilled interviewer (Benjamin, 1974). Sometimes when interviewers use questions during interviews, they do so because of their own needs or agendas (e.g., excessive reliance on questions may represent an interviewer's need for structure and control or a desire to focus on a specific topic, which may or may not be relevant to the client). This particular orientation is provided to help students explore how specific interventions may be manifestations of their own personal or professional needs. Thus, the first interviewing commandment for these students becomes "Thou shalt not ask questions." We assure them that there is a time and place for questions, but the first two required interviews are not the appropriate time or place.

Self-Reflection and Self-Correction

In the second component of the course, students evaluate their own work. They transcribe at least five interactions between themselves and their analogue clients and mention "improved" or "corrected" responses that might have been more effective. They are encouraged to develop several alternative responses and to speculate on how the analogue client might have responded to them. This process often produces the kind of self-reflection that may help beginning students become more effective interviewers. It also helps students gain some distance from their own work and thus become capable of a more objective evaluation of their interviews. For example, many students have reported that, in the process of listening to their interview and transcribing the interactions, they discovered that they could have improved their techniques in many areas. For students who have inadvertently asked questions or otherwise directed their subjects too explicitly, this process provides an opportunity to demonstrate that they have the knowledge necessary to conduct a good nondirective interview.

Feedback

The third component of the course involves extensive feedback from classroom peers, instructors, and analogue clients. In addition to the self-evaluation mentioned earlier, each student receives feedback from other members of the class. It is important to establish a strong level of trust within the group of students to enable them to accept and use the feedback with openness and comfort. The interviews are usually somewhat threatening for most students; therefore, we work on how to give supportive and corrective feedback primarily through instruction and modeling. For example, we recommend that students always try to give some form of positive feedback to individuals who are presenting their work to the class. In addition, the instructors openly acknowledge their own mistakes and weaknesses when presenting their material.

An additional unique aspect of the course is that each student gets copies of rating scales filled out by analogue clients whom they interviewed. These scales include a modified version of the semantic differential (Osgood, Suci, & Tannenbaum, 1957) and a combination of the client personal reaction form (Ashby, Ford, Guerney, & Guerney, 1957; Greenberg, 1969) and the helping relationship questionnaire (Luborsky, 1984). As a result, students learn the extent to which analogue clients perceived the interview as effective, warm, insightful, and positive. Although this aspect of the course often provides the most candid commentary, students are generally enthusiastic about such feedback.

Because students are likely to receive both positive and negative reviews of their performance from the analogue clients, we suggest three steps to facilitate this process. First, instructors should discuss the potential meaning of positive and negative responses from the analogue clients. For example, some clients report that the interview experience was helpful but negative or cold but effective. Discussing the possibility of such feedback can prepare students to cope with negative or inconsistent reviews of their performance. Second, it is often best if students are allowed to examine the feedback individually at first. Third, students should be encouraged to discuss the nature of their feedback with their peers in the classroom.

Obtaining Analogue Clients

It is often difficult or impossible to obtain a clinical population for beginning students to interview (Weiss, 1986). To alleviate the problem, we use subjects from the introductory psychology research pool as analogue clients. Obtaining subjects from the research pool requires several steps. First, approval of the university's human subjects review committee must be obtained. Second, subjects sign up to participate in a study that we call "interviewing experiences." Third, when students gather in a large group for the first screening session, they are informed of the requirements of the project. We emphasize that the interviewers are learning new skills, that the students will be asked to talk openly for about 50 min (preferably about issues of personal concern), and that their cooperation and feedback are highly valued to help the interviewers become more skilled. Fourth, all subjects are informed of the audiotape or videotape requirement and are asked to sign a release that permits graduate students in the interviewing course to have access to the tapes. Subjects are told that what they say to the interviewer will be confidential in the sense that only instructors and students from the interviewing course will have access to the tapes. Fifth, subjects are encouraged to relax, to enjoy the interview experience, and to view it as an opportunity to have someone listen closely to them for nearly an hour. Sixth, subjects' telephone numbers are obtained so that the interviewers may call them to schedule appointments. Finally, subjects are asked to return for a postinterview assessment meeting (from 1 to 2 weeks after their interview) to complete questionnaires that evaluate their reactions to the interview and receive credit for their participation. (Such activities could be completed immediately after the interview.)

From the outset, the faculty supervisor's telephone and office numbers are given to the subjects in case they have complaints about any aspect of their treatment. Not one of the more than 250 undergraduate students who have participated in this procedure has refused to participate or to sign the audio/video release. Moreover, we have yet to receive a formal or anonymous complaint about our procedure.

One note of caution may be helpful for others who use this procedure: Our research subjects have displayed emotional disturbances more frequently than we expected. Approximately 15% to 25% of the subjects who have been interviewed have reported symptoms of psychopathology such as depression, suicide ideation, anorexia, bulimia, alcohol/drug abuse, sexual abuse, generalized anxiety, and marital/interpersonal conflicts. Therefore, we provide interviewers with a list of referral sources ranging from a battered women's shelter to various clinics that offer psychological services. In addition, we present lectures on crisis management before the interviews begin. Graduate students also are told how to assist subjects in making appointments with local agencies.

There are several advantages of using the introductory psychology subject pool for obtaining analogue clients. First, it resolves our previous problem of a shortage of subject volunteers; therefore, graduate students may obtain analogue clinical experience. Second, various scales and questionnaires are now administered to analogue clients before and after they are interviewed. This research emphasis provides graduate students with important feedback about their impact on the subjects. In addition, the questionnaire information is gradually becoming a source of data concerning the effect of the interview experience on the subjects' attitudes toward psychology (e.g., how much more or less likely they would be to pursue psychotherapy, how positive they view psychology as a profession, etc.). Given the current interest in treatment-acceptability research and accountability in psychotherapy, such objective measures of the analogue clients' reactions to the interview are highly desirable (Strupp, Hadley, & Gomes-Schwartz, 1977). Third, introductory psychology students have an interview experience from which they can, to some extent, formulate more realistic attitudes toward psychotherapy and psychotherapists. In fact, a number of analogue clients usually request formal psychotherapy after their positive experience of being interviewed by a graduate student.

However, there are some distinct disadvantages of using introductory psychology students as analogue clients. For example, preinterview and postinterview sessions with students must be conducted by the instructor or a teaching assistant to administer the questionnaires, to orient the students about what to expect during the interviews, and to debrief them afterward. Scoring the scales and questionnaires is also time consuming. Nevertheless, we are more than satisfied with the benefits of this approach and recommend it to others.

References

Ashby, J., Ford, D., Guerney, B., & Guerney, L. (1957). Effects on clients of a reflective and a leading type of psychotherapy. *Psychological Monographs, 71*(24, Whole No. 453).

Benjamin, A. (1974). *The helping interview* (2nd ed.). Boston: Houghton Mifflin.

Cormier, W. H., & Cormier, L. S. (1985). *Interviewing strategies for helpers* (2nd ed.). Monterey, CA: Brooks/Cole.

Goldfried, M. R., & Davison, G. C. (1976). *Clinical behavior therapy.* New York: Holt, Rinehart & Winston.

Greenberg, R. P. (1969). Effects of presession information on perception of the therapist and receptivity to influence in a psychotherapy analogue. *Journal of Consulting and Clinical Psychology, 33,* 425-429.

Luborsky, L. (1984). *Principles of psychoanalytic psychotherapy: A manual of supportive/expressive treatment.* New York: Basic Books.

Osgood, C. E., Suci, G. J., & Tannenbaum, P. H. (1957). *The measurement of meaning.* Urbana: University of Illinois Press.

Strupp, H. H., & Binder, J. (1984). *Psychotherapy in a new key: A guide to time-limited dynamic psychotherapy.* New York: Basic Books.

Strupp, H. H., Hadley, S. W., & Gomes-Schwartz, B. (1977). *Psychotherapy for better or worse: An analysis of the problem of negative effects.* New York: Aronson.

Weiss, A. R. (1986). Teaching counseling and psychotherapy skills without access to a clinical population: The short interview method. *Teaching of Psychology, 13,* 145-147.

Note

The authors thank Joseph J. Palladino and three anonymous reviewers for their helpful comments on earlier drafts of this article.

The Use of Role-Playing in a Classroom Demonstration of Client-Centered Therapy

William R. Balch
Pennsylvania State University–Altoona

Of the dozen or more main topics covered in the typical course in introductory psychology, psychotherapy presents a unique problem for the instructor. On one hand, it is an area in which most students who enter the course seem particularly interested. On the other, the topic is essentially a clinical one. Therefore, it is difficult to convey the various therapeutic techniques and processes through textbooks or conventional classroom instruction. Many books do include sample dialogues between therapist and client (e.g., Wortman & Loftus, 1981; Morris, 1982; Smith, Sarason & Sarason, 1982). Moreover, there are a number of films which depict different types of therapy. However, I have found that putting on a live demonstration involving the students themselves is the most effective teaching tool in terms of the enthusiasm and class participation it generates.

In this demonstration four student volunteers play roles in front of the class, much in the manner of improvisatory theater. Client-centered therapy was chosen as the method to be illustrated, because its non-directive approach is well-suited for role-playing. One student plays the role of Pat, who is faced with several conflicts. Three other students play Pat's father, mother, and best friend. Each person discusses Pat's problems with Pat in a series of improvised two-way dialogues. In particular, each offers some directive advice to Pat, who remains confused and indecisive. Finally, a non-directive therapist talks to Pat using client-centered techniques (Rogers, 1965) to help clarify Pat's own feelings. This therapist can be played by the instructor. However, a counseling or clinical psychologist on the instructor's campus is a particularly ideal person to play the role.

A day or two before the demonstration, I recruit volunteers; and pass out a hand-out explaining the situation and roles to be enacted by the participants. I shall present the essential content of the scenario here in brief form.

Pat may be male or female. (From here on in "he" will be used in the general sense, meaning he or she). He is enrolled in a tough pre-medical program, but his grades are beginning to drop sharply. No longer sure he wants to be a doctor, Pat is considering acting on his long-standing interest in art and applying to a nearby school of art and design. The deadline for applications is drawing near. To add to his troubles, Pat has been having a problem with his girlfriend (or her boyfriend), Lee. Because Lee feels that Pat is selfishly preoccupied with his own concerns, she is threatening to break off with him unless he spends more time with her. Note that Lee serves as an off-stage presence, and does not appear as a role-player.

Pat's father is a struggling insurance salesman, who thinks that he could have been a doctor himself if he had applied himself a little more in school. He feels that Pat could make it through the pre-med program if he simply pulled himself together and worked a bit harder. Opposed to Pat's idea of going to art school, Pat's father is convinced that his son could be a fine doctor.

Pat's mother is a housewife who would also like to see him become a doctor. However, she may be a little more sympathetic than her husband to Pat's interest in art. She herself was told by her high school English teacher that she had a flair for writing. But rather than develop it, she married Pat's father at age 18. Her main concern about Pat is that she fears Lee will pressure him into an early marriage; the same mistake she feels she made.

Pat's best friend Jack (or Jackie) dropped out of high school, and is now working as a gas station attendant (or stock clerk, waiter, etc.). He is fed up with the middie-class values of education, hard work and suc-

cess. According to Jack, either medical or art school would be equally a waste of time for Pat. Pat should simply take`any old job, make enough to live on and get out of the rat race.

Pat's therapist uses client-centered techniques (unconditional positive regard, non-directiveness, clarification of feeling, restatement of content, etc.) to help Pat see what his own thoughts are. He avoids telling Pat what to do, even though Pat hopes the therapist has some answers for him.

During the demonstration, the *instructor* serves as more or less a stage manager. This function includes: introducing Pat; then ushering in and out, in turn, the father, mother, best friend and therapist; and providing any commentary deemed appropriate. Afterwards, the instructor should moderate an interactive discussion between the participants in the demonstration and the rest of the class.

To date, I have not quantitatively evaluated this demonstration. However, I believe that instructors who try it will find it has some benefits not always shared by the traditional methods of text, film or lecture. First, the role-playing scenario described above has been designed to be understandable and fairly familiar to college freshmen. Secondly, the student participants usually play their roles spontaneously, plausibly and creatively. In some classes, they even appear to become quite emotionally involved: particularly in the case of Pat's role. This feature of the demonstration raises the ethical problem of potential psychological risk. Though I've seen no evidence that any harmful aftereffects occur, the risk may be dealt with by a common sense screening of volunteers; and, by encouraging the participants to discuss afterwards their feelings during the demonstration. On the distinctly positive side, the involvement of the participants in their roles definitely seems to influence the rest of the class. Thus, the audience and role-players alike experience firsthand some of the emotional dynamics of a plausible therapy situation.

One particularly interesting set of phenomena I have noticed relates to behavioral changes in the student playing Pat. When talking to the client-centered therapist, Pat often speaks more softly and at a lower pitch than when talking to the more "directive" players. Usually Pat also engages in more eye contact with the therapist. Generally he or she gives the impression of being much more relaxed. This potentially measurable effect could serve as a discussion ice-breaker, or perhaps as the basis of some student projects.

References

Morris, C. G. *Psychology: An introduction* (4th ed). Englewood Cliffs, NJ: Prentice-Hall, 1982.

Rogers, C. R. *Client-centered therapy.* Boston: Houghton Mifflin, 1965.

Smith, R. E., Sarason, I. G., & Sarason, B. R. *Psychology: The frontiers of behavior.* New York: Harper and Row, 1982.

Wortman, C. B., & Loftus, E. F. *Psychology.* New York: Knopf, 1981.

Notes

1. The author wishes to thank Dr. Charles Kormanski, who has played the role of therapist in many demonstrations put on in my classes.
2. Copies of the class handout used for the demonstration are available from the author.

Synthesizing the Elements of Behavior Modification: A Classroom Simulation Game

Jerome D. Ulman
Ball State University

Even after students have learned the elements of behavior modification—measurement, intervention, evaluation, and maintenance—I find that they often experience difficulty seeing how the parts fit together into a systematic process of behavior change. To deal with this problem I use a classroom game that incorporates three instructional techniques: "synthesizing groups" to facilitate the acquisition of synthesizing skills (Bossley, 1978); team competition to encourage peer tutoring (DeVries & Edwards, 1973); and simulation games, a teaching device that has been reported to be effective for increasing student motivation and learning (Boocock & Schild, 1968). Implementation of the game involves no monetary cost, and the only preparation required is that students first acquire a basic understanding of the elements of behavior modification at a level typically found in introductory behavioral texts (e.g., Hall, 1974; 1975). The game is then conducted in three phases as follows:

Phase 1: Describe a problem. First, the game is introduced to the class by briefly explaining its purpose and describing the rules (see below). Second, the class is divided into small groups—four-to six-member groups seems to work best—and a leader is identified for each group. I do this randomly: the student having a Social Security number in which the last two digits form the lowest number (e.g., ". . . 12") is a group leader. The leader of each group then appoints a recording secretary Third, each group is assigned the task of describing a problem situation in an applied setting such as a classroom and instructed to include in the written description (a) the setting (time, place, and activity); (b) the relevant characteristics of the target person(s) exhibiting the problem; and (c) the problem behavior itself, which could be academic or social or both. The groups are advised to be as explicit and realistic as possible in creating their problem statements (i.e., to simulate an actual problem situation), but they are not required to provide precise definitions of the problem behavior—that comes later. After all the groups have finished writing their problem statements, they are instructed to give their written problem to another group. Then, in random order, the groups exchange problem statements.

Phase 2: Develop a solution. Each group is instructed to propose in writing a detailed intervention plan for the problem statement it received from one of the other groups. The plan must include (a) a precise definition of the problem behavior(s); (b) a description of the behavioral measurement system, including procedures for assessing inter-observer reliability; (c) an exact description of the procedures for modifying the behavior(s), not just the naming of a behavior modification technique such as "time out"; (d) specification of an appropriate behavior analysis research design; (e) a description of provisions for maintaining the desired behavioral change; and (f) a statement of and ethical justification for the expected outcome.

Phase 3: Evaluate proposed solutions. First, each group leader appoints a spokesperson to read to the

133

class the problem statement the group received and the group's proposed solution. Second, groups are instructed to evaluate each proposed solution (except their own, of course) by mean of a 5-point rating scale where "1" means "poor plan—not likely to get off the ground" and "5" means "excellent plan—almost sure to fly," with "2," "3," and "4" representing the intermediate range. The ground rules for ratings are that (a) technical adequacy and practicality that must both be taken into consideration, while weighing the plan against the scope and specificity of the problem the group was given; and (b) each group must agree on one, whole number rating score (2-3 min. per rating is usually sufficient for a group to reach consensus). Third, each group in turn is asked to state its assigned rating and to justify it, immediately after which the group being evaluated is given the opportunity to defend its plan. The instructor then asks the group that just gave the rating, "In light of Group X's comments, do you wish to change your rating or keep it the same?" and subsequently records on the chalkboard that group's final rating of Group X's plan. After a group has been rated by all of the other groups the instructor averages the ratings and writes the results on the chalkboard also. Finally, when all groups have presented their plans and have been rated by the other groups, the instructor states that the game has ended and announces the winning group.

Suggestions for Game Users. For the entire game to be completed, allow approximately one hour plus 15 additional minutes per group. I have found that Phases 1 and 2 can usually be completed in, respectively, 15-30 minutes and 30-45 minutes. Thus, with a class of about 25 students (5 groups) this activity will require 2-2.5 hrs. It is interesting to circulate around the room during the first two phases and listen to the surprising amount of verbalizations of behavior modification methodology the game generates in students. Also, by periodically checking on the progress each group is making and announcing aloud the moment when a group indicates it has completed the assigned task (in Phase 1, the problem statement; in Phase 2, the proposed solution), slower groups can be motivated to speed up their work. If the play of the game must span two class meetings, however, always collect the written work prior to dismissing the class.

While the game is in progress the instructor should discourage prolonged cross-talk among the groups, avoid offering advice or evaluative comments, and in general maintain a strictly neutral role. Although it is often instructive to discuss various issues that arise during the course of the game, such discussions should be postponed until after the winning group has been declared.

Based on my informal observations, the game seems to help students better conceptualize behavior modification as a systematic, step-by-step approach to effective problem solving (see D'Zurilla & Goldfried, 1971). It is obvious that the game generates verbal behavior in students which more closely approximates that of a behavioral psychologist, depending of course on the level of sophistication at which the elements of behavior modification were mastered prior to their playing the game. However, the need is apparent for empirical research to determine what contribution this classroom simulation game may make to student interest in and practical knowledge of the techniques and methodology of behavior modification.

References

Boocock, S. S., & Schild, E. O. *Simulation games in learning.* Beverly Hills, CA: Sage Publications, 1968.

Bossley, M. The synthesis group. *Teaching of Psychology,* 1978, *5,* 43-44 .

DeVries, D. L., & Edwards, K. J. Learning games and student teams: Their effects on classroom process. *American Educational Research Journal,* 1973, *10,* 307-318.

D'Zurilla, T. J., & Goldfried, M. R. Problem solving and behavior modification. *Journal of Abnormal Psychology,* 1971, *78,* 107126.

Hall, R. V. *Managing behavior, part 1: The measurement of behavior* (Rev. ed.) Lawrence, KS: H & H Enterprises, 1974.

Hall, R. V. *Managing behavior, part 2: Basic principles* (Rev. Ed.). Lawrence, KS: H & H Enterprises, 1975.

Teaching Adjunctive Coping Skills In a Personality Adjustment Course

Donald S. Meck
Robins USAF Hospital
John David Ball
Andrews USAF Hospital

The age-old educational debate regarding the value of experiential learning compared to more traditional classroom lecture methods has been broadened to include comparisons between educational programs emphasizing affective and cognitive objectives (Brown, 1971). Teaching practices generally reflect the prevalent attitude that experiential and content learning are both important, and Brown (1971) has argued in similar fashion for "confluent education" as a means of attending to both cognitive and affective growth for students. Controversy persists regarding the extent to which learning should be primarily either experiential or cognitive in nature, and except with elementary school aged children (Gordon, 1974; Bessell, 1973; Castillo, 1974), affective education has rarely been formalized.

This controversy is especially relevant when the course subject is personality adjustment. The opportunity for students to experience personal changes in their own adaptation to stress would seem to be a worthwhile course objective. On the other hand, an educational course that rewards students with academic credit also has an obligation to acquaint them with empirically based factual information and should be clearly differentiated from psychotherapy.

Seminars have been used to offer students the opportunity to explore and profit from personal emotional experiences related to course content. Modern clinical psychology, however, now offers another alternative via standardized coping skills programs which students may use with minimal supervision. These programs provide students in psychology the opportunity to experience their own emotional growth as an adjunct to traditional classroom instruction even in large lecture classes.

In a personality adjustment course at Texas A&M University, students participated in an experimental effort to introduce them to a formalized affective learning opportunity with systematic training in progressive relaxation. Since students had been typically encouraged to volunteer as subjects for research participation, the time they usually devoted to this activity was easily redirected toward their emotional growth by making the research project itself an investigation of the effects of the adjunct experiential learning opportunity. Thus, students were not asked to invest any more of their own energy and time than previous students of this course had given, and the instructor was not additionally burdened, even though he had added an important and relevant learning experience to the course.

The procedure was straightforward. Twenty students volunteered (10 males and 10 females) to participate in a commercially sold relaxation training program developed by Jack Turner and distributed by Cybersystems, Inc. This program was advertised in popular magazines and consisted of one cassette tape with recorded isometric relaxation exercises on one side and an autosuggestive relaxation induction procedure on the other. Printed rationale, instructions, illustrations and a chart accompanied the tape and provided the students with a comprehensive relaxation program. Participants were instructed to use this tape systematically for 17 days with the following recommended sequence: side 1 twice each day for five days, side 1 once each day and side 2 once each day for three days, side 2 twice each day for three days, side 2 once each day and self-induced relaxation (based on previously learned procedures) once each day for three days, and self-induced relaxation twice each day for three days. Ten volunteers (five males and five females) were randomly selected to use the program for the first seventeen day period (experimental group), and the remaining ten volunteers waited and served as controls. Both the experimental group and the control group were administered the Trait Anxiety Scale of the State-Trait Anxiety Inventory (Spielberger, Gorsuch, & Lushene, 1970) prior to and immediately after the seventeen day treatment program, to assess any changes in selfreported anxiety as a result of the program. The control group was then given the opportunity to use the same program in a second 17 day period.

The results of this investigation reflected the program's effectiveness. In a 2 X 2 (sex X treatment) factorial analysis of variance procedure using change scores on the Trait Anxiety Scale, the 10 subjects who had participated in the taped relaxation program showed an average reduction of 10 scale points on the Trait Anxiety Scale. The noted reduction differed significantly from the average increase of 2 scale points found in the control subjects ($F = 40.80$, $(1, 17)$ $p < .001$). There were no significant group differences in Trait Anxiety scores prior to program implementation, and no significant interaction was evident between treatment and sex.

The procedure reported here accomplished a number of objectives. First, students were offered an experiential learning opportunity that served to illustrate principles taught within the classroom regarding the relationship between psychological stresses and physiological responses. Secondly, the students' mode of adjusting to life stresses was improved as indicated by the significant reductions in anxiety proneness on trait anxiety as a function of their involvement in this psychology course. Third, students gained first hand experience in the manner in which psychology's scientific empirical methodology contri- butes to an understanding of personal adjustment. Fourth, a commercially packaged treatment program was empirically evaluated for its ability to yield results consistent with advertised claims of effectiveness. Finally, these objectives were all accomplished without appreciably increasing the time and energy that students and instructor usually invest in the course, and without diminishing the quantity or quality of content-focused reading and lecture material typically-presented.

The evaluation of the systematic relaxation training program was presented here as a specific suggestion for similar personality adjustment courses in other universities, and as an illustration of a procedure which might be employed in the teaching and evaluation of other packaged programs designed to enhance personal adjustment.

References

Bessel, H. *Methods in human development theory manual.* San Diego: Human Development Training Institute, 1973.

Brown, G. I. *Human teaching for human learning: an introduction to confluent education.* New York: Viking Press, 1971.

Castillo, G. A. *Left-handed teaching.* New York: Praeger Publishers, 1974.

Gordon, T. *T.E.T.: teacher effectiveness training.* New York: Peter H. Wyden, 1974.

Spielberger, C. D., Gorsuch, R. L., & Lushene, R. E. *Manual for the State-Trait Anxiety Inventory.* Palo Alto, CA: Consulting Psychologist Press, 1970.

A Simulated Mental Hospital as an Undergraduate Teaching Device

William L. Claiborn
and Raymond W. Lemberg
University of Maryland

In an educational setting, participation in simulation exercises is reportedly a more enjoyable and stimulating way of learning than conventional methods (Alger, in Guetzkow et al., 1963, pp. 152-154). Furthermore, simulation offers a means of experientially communicating divergent material in a context that allows the student to understand complex social roles and recognize relational patterns among the roles.

In clinical psychology graduate training, role playing has long been used to portray aspects of the client/therapist relationship. At least one mental institution has used simulation of a hospital ward to facilitate staff training (Orlando, 1973). In the present example, participation in a simulated mental hospital constituted a major portion of an undergraduate course at the University of Maryland entitled, "Introduction to Clinical Psychology."

The goals of the upper level course, in addition to teaching traditional material (such as: the roles of clinical psychologists, assessment, psychotherapy and the delivery of mental health services) included providing the students with accurate first hand information on the realities of potential career roles.

Method. In the fall of 1973, a class of over 70 students was introduced to the project, involving the creating, staffing and operation of a simulated mental hospital, in which each student would assume the role of a staff member or patient. A rough organizational sketch of the hospital structure was suggested (see Figure 1): several days were set aside later in the se-

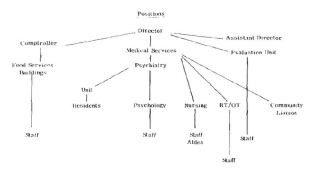

Figure 1. Tentative Hospital Structure

mester for the simulation and ten rooms (most equipped with video and sound recording equipment for observation and documentation) were reserved for the occasion.

The instructor and his teaching assistant, acting as the hospital's board of trustees, selected a hospital director on the basis of motivation and "role sophistication" from among several student applicants. She, in turn, hired people for the next level of hospital management. Subsequently, these individuals interviewed and hired their staffs. Within a few weeks the entire staff was constituted and began training and preparation for the simulation proper, including the development of: line budgets, menus, treatment plans, policies for admission and discharge, policies for payroll and personnel, and a bill of patient rights. Training of medical service staff involved role playing, visits to nearby mental institutions and didactic training provided by counseling center personnel and a health center psychiatrist. The hospital "points" budget for salaries (made salient by a direct relationship between points earned and final course grade) and cash budget for food and supplies were finally approved by the entire class community after a series of heated budget/taxation hearings.

The teaching assistant and a student "patient coordinator" created a list of hospital patients based upon statistical and demographic information on "typical" hospital composition which included ranges of age, pathology and prognosis. Students assuming patient roles set about to create case histories and learn complex symptom patterns. They researched symptomatology, listened to taped interviews of real patients, engaged in role playing rehearsals and visited local hospitals. Meanwhile, a community lawyer, "family members" and a social worker made plans for their roles in the simulation.

The Board of Trustees facilitated the development of the institution by continually asking for policy statements, progress reports and proposals from the administrative staff. Staff was encouraged to apply for grants to support innovative programs; these grant applications were then reviewed and funded, or rejected. The workload produced by reporting requirements forced hospital administrators to delegate responsibility; the lower level staff, in turn, was forced to learn its roles in great detail. Impressive studies of commitment laws and procedures, forms of psychotherapy, employee merit systems, halfway houses and other aspects of mental hospital operation were carried out by independently functioning students.

The actual simulation ran 56 hours over a period of two consecutive weekends, including one overnight. During the week prior to the simulation itself, most patients were processed through an intake procedure, although several were admitted at various, unexpected times throughout the simulation. Only one patient, after a lengthy series of court hearings, received a complete discharge, although a few others were discharged to an affiliated halfway house.

Results and Discussion. The most impressive outcome of the simulation experience lay in the development, over a two month period, of a self-perpetuating and evolving complex organization. Events seemed to unfold largely beyond anyone's immediate control, and the members of the staff responded to these developments in ways appropriate to their roles without imposed direction and supervision. As examples, faced with insufficient funds to support an adequate nursing staff, an enterprising "psychiatrist" went to psychology classes and to a neighboring community college to recruit volunteers to bolster the existing paid staff; litigious threats from the community lawyer were forever intruding upon hospital functioning, resulting in hearings and administration response; rumor of an impending rape and the threat of a magnesium fire impelled hospital staff into conference eventually leading to "beefed up" medication and a shakedown of patients' quarters. Despite the initial simple structure, the students became so involved in their roles that the simulation developed many of the features of a real life functioning hospital. Somewhat like the situation described by Kesay (1962) the nursing staff developed a certain indifference and disdain for the patients; nurses and other members of the medical staff responded in ways that showed that their primary satisfaction came from being with and relating among themselves. The volunteers made initial attempts to approach patients, but soon withdrew to talk to themselves or to sit and stare. The medical staff had meeting after meeting and seemingly endless paperwork. As a result, several patients were never seen by a therapist, while others received only cursory treatment.

Patients found it difficult to get into and stay in role. Faced with the ambiguity of a new situation and the powerlessness over one's daily routine, most patients felt the pressing need to communicate with one another in order to reduce the ambiguity and gain emotional support. But, for many, direct communication created self-imposed conflict as it served to take them out of role. Moreover, even open communication was unsettling, for many times it was difficult to know if one was communicating as a student or patient (since "patient behavior" would likely produce rejection and isolation when attributed to a fellow student). Some patients solved this problem by withdrawing, while others dealt with the stress by dropping their patient roles entirely. Exacerbating patient discomfort was the boredom and regimentation that marked the patient's day. In addition, many of the staff came to treat them, not as individuals, but as mental patients. One patient, who collapsed from a drug overdose, was left lying in the middle of the floor unattended until the medical staff completed their meeting.

In debriefing sessions conducted at the end of each simulation day it was revealed that many of the patients had suffered from somatic symptoms, including headaches, irritability and other signs of tension. A third of the patients expressed feelings of frustration, depression, powerlessness and helplessness.

Students surprised themselves by their level of involvement and learning. Although the course required many hours of work, most students found it stimulating and worthwhile. For many it was the first occasion in which they had actually taken personal responsibility for their own education. For most it was a new experience in taking on roles of authority and responsibility and as a result many students became more aware of their own competencies and limitations. The simulation seemed to provide an opportunity to sample many aspects, real and complex, of professional mental health roles and to examine experientially the "pressures" which produce stereotypic institutional behavior on the part of both patients and staff. Idealism succumbed to expediency and simulation to reality.

The simulation experience required surprisingly little outside intervention and support, hence its instructional cost was small; yet the personal benefits and lasting impressions seem to be great. The technique seems to have demonstrated its value in communicating the traditional areas of concern of clinical psychology as well as providing a pre-experience for students contemplating careers in mental health.

References

Guetzkow, H., Alger, C. F., Brody, R. A., Noel, R. C. & Snyder, R. C. *Simulation in international relations: Developments for research and teaching.* Englewood Cliffs, N. J.: Prentice-Hall, 1963.

Kesey, K. *One flew over the cuckoo's nest.* New York: The New American Library, Inc., 1962.

Orlando, N. J. The mock ward: A study in simulation. In O. Milton & R. Wahler (Eds.). *Behavior Disorders: Perspectives and Trends* (3rd Edition). Philadelphia: Lippincott, 1973.

2. USING COMPUTERS TO DEVELOP CLINICAL SKILLS

Teaching Psychological Defenses: An Interactive Computerized Program

Roger Bibace
David Marcus
Debra Thomason
E. Anne Litt
Clark University

An interactive computerized teaching program with which students learn to analyze behaviors as examples of psychological defense is described. Students are presented with a short paragraph describing a fictional situation in which a defensive behavior is enacted. These behaviors are analyzed in terms of actor-action-object propositions. The transformations in these three terms generate psychological defenses such as projection and reaction formation. Students' satisfaction with the program and their subsequent performance in identifying defense mechanisms indicated that it was useful for developing analytic skills.

Students can learn to analyze behaviors as examples of psychological defense through the use of an interactive computerized teaching program. Our review of the literature in this area revealed a paucity of material for teaching students to distinguish among various defense mechanisms.

Although it is important to acknowledge that there are theoretical differences and vagueness about the defenses, our intention is neither to introduce a new theory of the defense mechanisms, nor to endorse a particular theory as the "correct" one. For pedagogical purposes, we chose the approach developed by Suppes and Warren (1975). This conceptualization of defense was well suited for a computerized teaching program because, as an attempt to present a mathematical model of the defense mechanisms, it is a relatively clear and objective analytic system. Therefore, this approach can be easily adapted to a stepwise analysis of defensive behavior. Other theorists have presented formal models of. defense mechanisms (Holland, 1973), but these other algorithms were not as easily translated into computerized instruction. The Suppes and Warren approach is unique in that it articulates defensive behavior in terms of easily recognizable components.

Conceptual Framework

Central to Suppes and Warren's (1975) conceptualization of the defense mechanisms is the assumption that the contents of the unconscious consist of propositions that take the form of actor-action-object. This proposition takes the schematic form of Self + A + X, where A represents the action and X represents the object. A defense is a change in one or more of the three terms that make up the unconscious proposition in order for the proposition to become conscious. The defense mechanisms can then be generated by simply enumerating the various transformations that can be performed, singly and in combination, on each term in the proposition.

Suppes and Warren specified eight elementary transformations, thus generating eight basic defense mechanisms. The actor can be transformed from self as actor to other as actor (projection), and the propositional form that this takes is Other + A + X. The transformation from other as actor to self as actor (identification) is also possible. Suppes and Warren list four possible transformations of the action; for example, when an action is changed to its opposite, the defense is reaction formation (Self + Opp A + X). Finally, the object can be replaced with another object (displacement), and the propositional form this takes is Self + A + Y. A special case of this transformation occurs when the new object is the self (turning against the self), or Self + A + Self. Suppes and Warren also provided an exhaustive list of what they considered to be the remaining 36 defenses. For example, if the actor is transformed from self as actor to other as actor and the action is changed to its opposite, the defense would be a complex one, projection and reaction formation (Other + Opp A + X). Although the reification of some of these concepts is a potential danger in this approach, we found it useful for pedagogical purposes. In our program we used Suppes and Warren's tripartite representation of the defenses to have the learner analyze situations in which defensive behavior was exhibited and break them down into the three components: actor, action, and object. (Suppes and Warren should not be held responsible for our application of their framework. We are grateful for the contribution of their original ideas as presented in their article.)

Use of the Program

The program requires that the student first read a short paragraph describing a fictional situation in which a defensive behavior is enacted. The student is then asked a series of questions: Who is the actor? What is the action? Who or what is the object? Students are also provided with a glossary of the terms used in the program. Given the limited vocabulary of this program, the glossary aided students in choosing the proper synonym. If students answer any of these questions incorrectly, they are informed that the answer is incorrect and are given two more opportunities to respond. Unlike personalized system of instruction (PSI) books, a computer can inform students that their answer is wrong without immediately providing the correct response. After three attempts, the student is provided with the answer and proceeds to the next question. Following each question, the description of the situation is repeated along with a summary of the previous answers. Once the actor, action, and object are identified, the student is asked: Has the actor changed, and if so how? Has the action changed, and if so how? Has the object changed, and if so how? The correct answers to the last three questions combine to form the propositional statement of the defense. Finally, students are asked to name the defense represented by the propositional statement.

A total of 32 examples were used. After students successfully completed the first 16 examples, we assumed that they had internalized the analytic process by which the categorization was achieved. Therefore, students were given the opportunity to name the defense without having the computer go through the first seven questions. If the student incorrectly identified the defense, the program was designed to return to the seven preliminary questions.

The operation of the program may best be illustrated by a concrete example. What follows is extracted directly from the program:

> It was early in the morning and Mr. and Mrs. Johnson clearly were not getting along. Mr. Johnson dealt his parting blow as he was on his way out the door for work, leaving Mrs. Johnson no chance to vent her fury at his cutting remark. She muttered a few curses under her breath, and resigned herself to returning to the preparation of her kids' lunches. Moments later, while slicing vegetables, she cut right into her finger with the knife.

In this example, Mrs. Johnson (the actor) momentarily hates (the action) Mr. Johnson (the object). Neither the actor (Mrs. Johnson) nor the action (Mrs. Johnson's fury) have changed; however, the object is changed from Mr. Johnson to the self (". . . her fury at his cutting remark . . . she cut right into her finger with the knife."). The propositional form, in this case of turning against the self, would be Self + A + Self.

Table 1 outlines the defenses and their propositional forms that we used in this program.

Results and Evaluation

Although this program has proven useful in a number of different contexts (e.g., the training of residents in family medicine, clinical psychology graduate students, and advanced undergraduates), it was initially designed for an undergraduate course titled, Psychoanalytic Interpretation of Behavior. In this course stu-

Table 1. The Defenses and Their Propositional Forms

Mechanism	Number of Transformations	Propositional Form
Projection	1	Other + A + X
Identification	1	Self* + A + X[a]
Reaction formation	1	Self + Opp A + X
Intellectualization	1	Self + Intell A + X
Isolation	1	Self + Split A + X[b]
Repression	1	Self + Denial A (internal) + X[b]
Denial	1	Self + Denial A (external) + X[b]
Turning against the self	1	Self + A + Self
Displacement	1	Self + A + Y
Identification and reaction formation	2	Self* + Opp A + X
Projection and reaction formation	2	Other + Opp A + X
Projection and displacement	2	Other + A + Y
Reaction formation and displacement	2	Self + Opp A + Y
Intellectualization and displacement	2	Self + Intell A + Y
Projection, displacement, and reaction formation	3	Other + Opp A + Y

[a]self* = other as actor → self as actor.
[b]These are the modifications we introduced into Suppes and Warren's original list of the defenses.

dents were exposed to a traditional method of teaching defense mechanisms (cf. Brenner, 1955; Menninger, 1947) during lecture periods. In addition, students were required to attend two 3-hr discussion groups using the computerized teaching program, which was their only exposure to our adaptation of Suppes and Warren's (1975) formal model. Our evaluation of the teaching program included a comparison of students' ability to identify defense mechanisms on an exam using the two different approaches, as well as students' subjective comments on the program's merit.

Quantitative Analysis

It was not possible to measure the pedagogic value of the computer program because all of the students were exposed to both methods of analyzing defense mechanisms. However, we were able to assess the efficacy of the Suppes and Warren schema for identifying defenses by designing the midterm exam to permit a comparison of this method with the traditional approach. The exam included four essay questions that required students to identify the defense mechanisms described in a short vignette. Two of these questions dealt with an analysis using the traditional approach; the other two involved analysis using the Suppes and Warren model. The two questions involving the traditional approach required students to articulate the id, ego, and superego components of the behavior in identifying the defense mechanism. The two questions involving the Suppes and Warren model explicitly asked for each of the analytic steps (e.g., Who is the actor? What is the action?) which led to an identification of the defense. In order to get credit for naming the defense, students were required to follow the analytic sequence. Thus, students had to follow the Suppes and Warren schema in order for their responses to be scored as correct in our experimental design. No student introduced the traditional categories when analyzing these two examples.

A Wilcoxon matched-pairs signed-ranks test indicated that the number of correctly identified defenses was significantly greater when the Suppes and Warren model was utilized, T $(N = 52) = 276$, $p < .001$. It is possible that some students used the Suppes and Warren model on all four exam questions, but it is highly unlikely that they could have used the traditional approach to analyze the Suppes and Warren model questions. However, even the former possibility is counter indicated by the data. If students had only used the Suppes and Warren model, there should have been no difference between their performance on the two types of questions.

Qualitative Analysis

When students were asked to compare the traditional and computer methods, their responses were fairly consistent. Although two students believed that the traditional method was easier to understand, most students thought that the computer method was simpler and clearer. On the other hand, many students believed that the traditional method allowed for greater creativity and intuition, and for a holistic appraisal of the person's defensive behavior. A number of students commented that the two approaches were complementary; a combination of the computer and the traditional approach optimally facilitated the process of learning these interpretive methods. Furthermore, when students were asked whether the programmed instruction was useful enough to be continued, they unanimously agreed that it was.

Conclusion

From our analyses, it appears that our program is a useful pedagogical tool. The quantitative analysis indicated that the Suppes and Warren model is an effective way to teach students about psychological defense mechanisms. Further, students' qualitative responses favored the computer as a useful instructional tool: Students believed that the program aided their ability to identify defensive behaviors, and their belief was supported by the quantitative analyses performed. Students overwhelmingly favored the use of the program, despite the additional *6* hr of classwork it entailed. Given the ambiguity of traditional methods of analysis, communication about defense mechanisms may be facilitated by the use of this analytic method.

References

Brenner, C. (1955). *An elementary textbook of psychoanalysis.* New York: International Universities Press.

Holland, N. (1973). Defense, displacement and the ego's algebra. *The International Journal of Psychoanalysis, 54,* 247-257.

Menninger, K. (1947). *The human mind.* New York: Knopf.

Suppes, P., & Warren, H. (1975). On the generation and classification of defence mechanisms. *The International Journal of Psychoanalysis, 56,* 405-414.

Note

We thank Leonard Cirillo for his critical reading of the manuscript and Lisa Budzek for her help with the student evaluations.

Computer-Simulated Psychotherapy as an Aid in Teaching Clinical Psychology

John R. Suler
Rider College

Eliza, a widely known computer program that reacts to the user by simulating the responses of a psychotherapist, can be used as a teaching aid in undergraduate clinical psychology courses. Students' interaction with the program can enhance their understanding of interviewing and psychotherapy, the contrasts between clinical interactions controlled by humans and computers and the role computers may play in the mental health field. The methods for conducting the exercise, for integrating it into the course syllabus, and for evaluating its impact on students are discussed.

In the 1960s, researchers at the Massachusetts Institute of Technology pioneered the development of an interactive computer program, which simulates the actions of a psychotherapist, now widely known as Eliza. In reaction to the user's questions and statements, the program's responses imitate the therapeutic techniques of reflection, focusing, clarification, and open-ended inquiry. Although these programs were never intended to serve as "real" psychotherapy, they can be useful heuristic tools for understanding the psychotherapeutic process. I have used a version of Eliza adapted for IBM microcomputers as a teaching aid in an undergraduate clinical psychology course. Students' interaction with Eliza provides them with an intensive, individualized learning experience that can highlight important concepts about interviewing, psychotherapy, and clinical psychology. It can also enhance their understanding of the role computers may play in clinical activities.

Method of the Exercise

Instructions for the exercise and for operating the Eliza program are described in a handout and discussed in class. On their own time, students interact with Eliza for approximately 45 min. The instructions emphasize that during this time they honestly present a personal problem and persist in seeking help, despite any inadequacies or therapeutic mistakes they perceive in the program. After this period of seriously engaging Eliza in a therapeutic interaction, the students are instructed to "experiment" with the program, perhaps even "trick" it into responding with erroneous or nonsensical statements—and by doing so, gain insight into how the program works.

After the students completed the exercise, we discussed it in class and they prepared a paper in which they analyzed their interaction with Eliza. The following themes were emphasized: (a) their personal reactions to Eliza, including their perceptions of it as their "therapist," their thoughts and feelings about Eliza, whether or not they felt helped; (b) an evaluation of Eliza's therapeutic techniques and effectiveness, how the program seems to work, its strengths and weaknesses; (c) an analysis of the advantages and disadvantages of computers in psychoanalytic, behavioral, and humanistic therapies, and the types of problems and clients for which computers might be helpful; and (d) other possible applications in the field of mental health for computer programs that interact with clients.

Evaluation of the Exercise

After discussing the exercise and handing in their papers, one class (N = 19, 12 women, 7 men, M age = 21) answered a questionnaire consisting of rating scale items that assessed their reactions to the project. Their responses (see Table 1) indicated that the exercise had a substantial impact on them. A large majority agreed that the exercise was a valuable learning experience, and that it should be retained as part of the course. Ninety percent agreed that they better understood what is important for psychotherapy to be effective, and, in particular, what is important in the relationship between the therapist and client. These responses seemed to be related to the students' unanimous agreement that they had learned about the advantages and disadvantages of a computer conducting psychotherapy. In class and in their papers students covered important issues about human versus computerized therapy, such as (a) the role of empathy, warmth, identification, and "real" relationships in psychotherapy; (b) whether computers could be more ob-

Table 1. Percentage of Students Expressing Agreement and Disagreement With Questionnaire Items

Item	Agree	Cannot Say	Disagree
Was a valuable learning experience	80	10	10
Helped me with my problem	31	0	69
Learned something about myself	48	21	31
Future students should have this opportunity	95	5	0
Better understand what it would be like to be in therapy	43	14	43
Better understand what is important for therapy to be effective	90	5	5
Better understand what is important in client/therapist relationship	90	0	10
Learned about pros and cons of computerized psychotherapy	100	0	0
Better understand how computer programs are designed to interact with people	31	38	31
Learned about my own thoughts and feelings about psychotherapy	64	5	31
Better understand pros and cons of computerized psychoanalytic therapy	100	0	0
Better understand pros and cons of computerized behavior therapy	43	31	26
Better understand use of computers in mental health field	74	21	5

Note. N = 19. Agree = students responding "strongly agree" and "agree"; Disagree = students responding "strongly disagree" and "disagree."

jective and nonjudgmental; (c) whether fears about selfdisclosure, expressing emotions, and confidentiality would be greater with humans or computers; and (d) the cognitive and perceptual advantages of computers vis-à-vis humans, including breadth and efficiency of memory, language abilities, and access to visual and auditory information from the client.

The exercise was useful in highlighting important themes about the major theories of psychotherapy. The students unanimously agreed that they better understood the advantages and disadvantages of a computer conducting psychoanalytic therapy. We discussed such issues as the effectiveness of computers for creating the atmosphere of ambiguity and neutrality recommended by classical theory, transference reactions to computers, whether computers have countertransference, collecting data for interpretations, and computers as "selfobjects" in terms of contemporary theory. It was often necessary to clarify what computers nowadays can and cannot do, and to speculate about ire computers of the future. The students also contrasted computerized therapy with humanistic therapies that emphasize "authentic" relationships. Although we discussed re applications of computers in behavior therapy (their use behavioral assessments; shaping interpersonal, behavioral, and cognitive skills; conducting such procedures as systematic desensitization), not all students agreed that working with Eliza helped them better understand the role of computers in behavioral treatment. This result may have been due to the fact that Eliza takes an "insight" approach, or that we had not yet completed the section on behavior therapy in the course syllabus.

Nevertheless, most students did agree that they better understood how computers might be used in the mental wealth field. We discussed the cost-effectiveness of computers, their application according to different types of psychopathology; and their use for structured interviews, diagnostic assessments, and psychological testing. There was no consensus about whether they better understood how computer programs are designed to interact with people. This nay be attributed to the wide differences in the students' previous exposure to computer programming.

The students' personal reactions to Eliza varied greatly. They were divided on whether they thought working with Eliza gave them a sense of what it would be like to be in therapy and whether they learned anything about themselves. Ns compared to the students who agreed, twice as many disagreed that Eliza had helped them with their problem. In lass the students readily described their impressions of the)program's deficiencies as a psychotherapist. However, twice is many students agreed as disagreed that they had learned about their own personal thoughts and feelings about psychotherapy. Therefore, Eliza generally does not supply students with an accurate experiential understanding of what therapy is like; nor does it resolve their problems. It was not intended to. But it can be used as a stimulus to help them explore their thoughts and feelings about psychotherapy.

The results suggest that methods for improving the exercise may include: (a) providing guidelines that maximize each student's ability to apply previous knowledge of computers and computer programming; (b) including readings about computers in clinical activities; and (c) adding other interactive computer programs that illustrate methods in structured. interviewing, psychological testing, and behavioral treatments.

Software and Its Availability

There is a wide variety of software that may be used as teaching aids in clinical psychology courses. Programs that administer, score, and interpret psychological tests are available for standardized personality assessment inventories, including the Myers-Briggs Type Indicator, 16 Personality Factor Test, the Minnesota Multiphasic Personality Inventory, and the California Personality Inventory. Programs are also available for the Adjective Checklist and the Adaptive

Behavior Scale. For conducting structured clinical interviews, there is software for intake evaluations and mental status exams (which involve assessments of presenting complaint, symptoms, current situation, cognitive and emotional characteristics) and programs for taking a history of social, psychological, and developmental functioning (e.g., family relations, occupation, education, and social relationships). Software for assessing specific problem areas includes eating disorder inventories, health problem checklists, test anxiety scales, stress evaluations, and alcohol assessment. More general assessment programs include personal problem checklists that assess the number, type, and hierarchy of personal problems.

Catalogs that describe these programs are available from various psychological resource services including: The Psychological Corporation, San Antonio, TX; Publishers Test Service, Monterey, CA; Projected Learning Programs, Chico, CA; Western Psychological Services, Los Angeles; Consulting Psychologists Press, Palo Alto, CA; Psychological Assessment Resources, Odessa, FL; Multi-Health Systems, Lynbrook, NY.

The Eliza program is widely available from local user groups, and often can be found in the software packages of college and university mainframe systems. Eliza diskettes are also available from various computer resource services (e.g., Pan World International, North Brunswick, NJ; Projected Learning Programs, Chico, CA). Versions of Eliza seem to differ only in slight modifications of the breadth and variety of responses the program offers to the user's statements and questions. Versions sold by services that market Eliza as a computer "game" may include modifications of the program that detract from its potential as a serious educational exercise. For more information about the history and descendants of Eliza, as well as other information about computer applications in clinical psychology, see Schwartz (1984).

Reference

Schwartz, M. D. (Ed.). (1984). *Using computers in clinical practice: Psychotherapy and mental health applications.* New York: Haworth.

3. LEARNING ABOUT FAMILY DYNAMICS

The Family Environment Scale as an Instructional Aid for Studying the Family

J. Eugene Waters
Gordon Junior College

The author describes a method for theoretical and practical experience in understanding family relationships, personal growth, and structure.

In college socio-behavioral science courses, students seek answers to questions that are often very real to them—those which concern specific behaviors or problems of the students themselves. Sometimes the student presents clinical cases for resolution. Concerns about family relationships, problems with communication among family members, and questions about "family control and authority" are only a few of the points raised by students. Individuals often desire more information to aid them in understanding these familial problems. The purpose of this paper is to describe a supplemental instructional method for Marriage and Family courses. This technique addresses the students' request for concrete information about family communication and organization.

Moos' (1974) Family Environment Scale (FES) has been utilized in my Marriage and Family course to provide information to the students concerning interpersonal relationship patterns, organization structure, and personal growth aspects of their family. It was developed to assess the social climate of the family. Structurally, it consists of 90 true-false items which form 10 subscales. These subscales create a tripartite-dimensional conceptualization of the family environment: Relationship dimensions, Personal Growth dimensions, and System Maintenance dimensions. The statements are worded such that a "true" response indicates the presence or encouragement of a specific behavior within the family unit. "False" responses indicate that the respondent perceives the family as lacking a certain characteristic.

Listed below are the FES dimensions and the respective subscales, as defined by Moos (1974), with a sample for each item.

A. The Relationship dimension includes the following subscales:

(1) *Cohesion:* The extent to which family members are concerned and committed to the family and the degree to which family members are helpful and supportive of each other.
Example: Family members really help and support one another.

(2) *Expressiveness:* The extent to which family members are allowed and encouraged to act openly and to express their feelings directly.
Example: We say anything we want to around the home.

(3) *Conflict:* The extent to which the open expression of anger and aggression and generally conflictual interactions are characteristic of the family.
Example: Family members often criticize each other.

B. Personal Growth dimensions are reflected by the following:

(4) *Independence:* The extent to which family members are encouraged to be assertive, self-sufficient, to make their own decisions and to think things out for themselves.
Example: We think things out for ourselves in our family.

(5) *Achievement Orientation:* The extent to which different types of activities (i.e., school and work) are cast into an achievement oriented or competitive framework.
Example: We feel it is important to be the best at whatever you do.

(6) *Intellectual-Cultural Orientation:* The extent to which the family is concerned about political, social, intellectual and cultural activities.
Example: We talk about political and social problems.

(7) *Active Recreational Orientation:* The extent to which the family participates actively in various kinds of recreational and sporting activities.
Example: We often go to movies, sports events, camping, etc.

(8) *Moral-Religious Emphasis:* The extent to which the family actively discusses and emphasizes ethical and religious issues and values.
Example: Family members attend church, synagogue or Sunday School fairly often.

C. System Maintenance dimensions are measured by the following:

(9) *Organization:* Measures how important order and organization is in the family in terms of structuring the family activities, financial planning, and explicitness and clarity in regard to family rules and responsibilities.
Example: Activities in our family are pretty carefully planned.

(10) *Control:* Assesses the extent to which the family is organized in a hierarchical manner, the rigidity of family rules and procedures and the extent to which family members order each other around.
Example: There is one family member who makes most of the decisions.

Separate scores, ranging from zero to nine, are reported for each subscale. Higher subscale scores reflect a greater degree of emphasis on that characteristic of the family environment. Several forms of the FES exist: Form I measures the ideal or preferred family environment and Form R measures the real or present environment. The rationale for the development of the instrument and psychometric test construction data are reported elsewhere (Moos, 1974; 1975).

Prior to administering the scale, the instructor attempts to create an appropriate atmosphere for testing. The exercise is completely voluntary and tests are marked in such a manner to ensure anonymity of the students. Instruments may be completed in class or done as an out of class assignment. Form I is administered first. Normative data for the class are calculated by the instructor and distributed to the students as a handout. A class discussion follows in which students explore their preferred family environment and the reported class norms. Copies of the FES subscale descriptions are made available to the students to aid their discussion.

Form R is administered second. This scale assesses the present or real family environment as perceived by the respondent. Once again, normative data for the class are made available to the students. Furthermore, they are given information on national norms (see Moos, 1974). Thus, comparisons can be made among the individual student's family environment, the norms reported for the class, and the national data. Time is allocated to allow the students to discuss any issues that evolve from this aspect of the testing.

Finally, the instructor can provide the students with a written comparison of the real and preferred family environment. In providing this written analysis, the instructor is actually giving the students a "clinical" description of their families. The instructor can also give the students a profile of their perceptions of the family environment along the FES subscales. Figure 1 is a sample profile of a student's perception of the ideal and family environment.

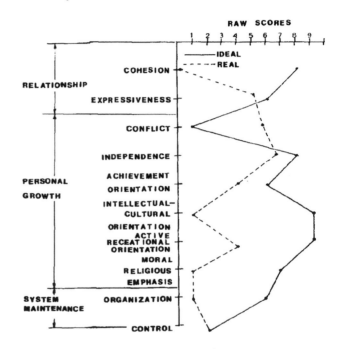

Figure 1. Sample FES profile of a student's perception of the ideal and real family environment.

As can be seen, extreme differences exist between the preferred and present family social climate on some of the characteristics. In this example, more cohesion, expressiveness, and less conflict in the family is desired. More emphasis within the family is preferred on all aspects of the Personal Growth dimensions (scales 4 - 8). In terms of System Maintenance, greater emphasis on family organization is desired, but the present level of control is considered adequate. The importance of this analysis can be seen in the systematic assessment of the differences between the desired and present environment in ten specific areas.

Some students have their entire family complete one or both instruments. Thus, more data are available to the student. Figure 2 is a profile of the present family environment for a family consisting of a mother, father, and two teenage sons. In this family, differ-

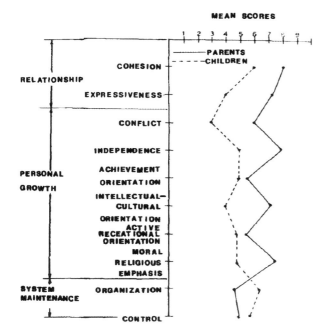

Figure 2. FES profile for parents' and children's perceptions of their present family environment.

ences exist between the parents' and children's perceptions of the family. Overall, the parents see the family as having somewhat more emphasis on the Relationship (scales 1 - 3) and the Personal Growth (scales 4 - 8) dimensions. The children disagree. Discrepancies also exist on the System Maintenance dimensions (scales 9 and 10), but in the opposite direction. Such a profile provides an interesting class discussion of parent-child relations on the three dimensions. Various issues, e.g., control, methods of family decision making, family meetings, and family intervention, can evolve from a class discussion of such a profile.

When an entire family completes Form R, the instructor can provide a "family incongruence score" concerning the family's agreement-disagreement on characteristics of the family's social setting (see Moos, 1974). For example, the four member family described above has a family incongruence score of 18.67 which converts to a standard score of 53. Incongruence within this family is slightly greater than the average of the families in the normative sample. Thus, classroom discussions may involve methods of family intervention to reduce the incongruence in a family.

As an educational aid, the Family Environment Scale provides practical and theoretical utility. The scale enables a student to study his or her family by means of a *systematic* assessment of the relationship patterns, personal growth dimensions, and organizational structure: After the student completes the instruments and the class has had an opportunity to raise questions and discuss the findings, the instructor may wish to discuss the clinical interpretations and research findings reported by Moos and Moos (1975).

For example, some dimensions (Cohesion, Expressiveness, and Independence) tend to decrease with family size, but others (Conflict, Control, and Moral-Religious Emphasis) tend to increase. Also, correlations between FES dimensions and drinking behavior have been reported (see Moos & Moos, 1975) as well as family environmental correlations of treatment success for alcoholics (Bromet & Moos, 1977).

Students have responded favorably to the exercise. Thus far, student evaluations of this instructional method have resulted in no negative responses. Students generally report that the exercise synthesizes information about their families, and they view the exercise as worthwhile. The willingness to participate and share information is an indication of the benefits derived from using the FES. In three recent classes (N's of 14, 18, and 19) in which the FES was used, no negative responses were received to several specific questions about the exercise. These questions addressed the academic and practical value of the exercise, the relevance of the information, the discrepancies, if any, between subjective feelings and the test results, and whether or not the exercise should be continued. Additional data on the usefulness of the scale will be gathered from future classes taught by this instructor, as well as from classes taught by colleagues .

Care should be taken in providing an appropriate, non-threatening situation for testing. As previously stated, participation should be voluntary. The instructor has an ethical obligation to insure anonymity, to fully describe the purpose of the scale and the exercise, to point out the limitations of standardized tests, to note the limited normative data presently available for the FES, and to explain the proper uses of the FES, or any test (e.g., the use of tests in conjunction with additional data). In situations such as those posed by teacher-student relationships, the instructor must be fully cognizant of the ethical and moral responsibilities involved in protecting the interests of the student and the family. Even when participation is voluntary, the instructor must take exceptional care because it may be difficult for students to believe fully that they will not be admonished for electing not to participate. Each instructor would need to address this issue in any type of nontraditional exercise involving students. Care should be taken to insure that students understand that participation by other family members is optional, and that they should not force family members to participate. A cover letter fully explaining the exercise and relevant details should accompany the materialssent home. In summary, the instructor has an obligation to protect the interests and well being of the participants. Also, the instructor may need to be prepared to assist students Who seek counseling after the scale confirms family problems. Depending upon the faculty member's training, orientation, and workload, he may wish to counsel the student (and perhaps the family) or make an appropriate referral.

Utilization of the FES can be time consuming. Numerous variables, e.g., faculty workload and class size, may preclude the detailed usage of the FES as outlined above. However, the scale can be used in some capacity to benefit students in college courses on the Family.

References

Bromet, E., & Moos, R. H. Environmental resources and the posttreatment functioning of alcoholic patients. *Journal of Health and Social Behavior,* 1977, *18*, 326-338.

Moos, R. H. *Combined preliminary manual: Family, work and group environment scales manual.* Palo Alto, California: Consulting Psychologists Press, 1974.

Moos, R. H. Assessment and impact of social climate. In P. McReynolds (Ed.), *Advancements in psychological assessment.* San Francisco: Josey-Bass, 1975.

Moos, R. H., & Moos, B. S. Families. In R. Moos (Ed.), *Evaluating correctional and community settings.* New York: Wiley-Interscience, 1975.

Training Undergraduates as Co-Leaders of Multifamily Counseling Groups

Judith Kuppersmith, Rima Blair and
Robert Slotnick
Richmond College, City University of New York

From a closely supervised pilot program, the authors describe a model for a field work/academic program beneficial to all of the participants.

In the winter of 1973 a probation officer from the Staten Island department of Probation approached the community psychology faculty at Richmond College for help with a problem. He wanted to create some form of group therapeutic treatment that would enable him to provide a meaningful service to an enormous caseload which included many young offenders whose parents had initiated PINS (People in Need of Supervision) petitions. As community psychologists in a college setting, we were especially interested in this problem because it provided us with an opportunity to create a training model using a treatment modality consistent with our theoretical orientation. We also could utilize our undergraduate population as providers of service through this treatment modality. Our theoretical approach is an integration of family process theory and developmental psychoanalytic ego psychology. From family process theory we use the differentiation of self formulations of Anonymous (1972), the structural model of Minuchin (1974) and Haley (1971), and the communication theory approach of Satir (1967). We succeeded in combining these approaches with the cognitive and ego function models of Bellak (1973), Jacobson (1964), and Erikson (1964). We felt that by integrating these major theoretical orientations we could provide the broadest educational benefit to students. It is from this vantage point that we approached problems of family breakdown and adolescent delinquency. We were especially interested in understanding individual and family functioning in relation to the broader societal context of community psychology.

As we developed our training model and plans for intervention, we chose to teach students to support areas of successful ego development and to foster positive mental health in the families they worked with. We felt it imperative to emphasize solving "real life" problems such as finding jobs for adolescents, and helping to build social networks for isolated single parent mothers. Students were also sensitized to recognize and deal with psychological problems, such as intervening to clarify dysfunctional communications between family members.

From this theoretical stance we analyzed the probation officer's proposal as having two components. One, a manpower problem, we felt we could help him with by training undergraduates as co-leaders of groups. The other problem was to develop a suitable treatment modality for these families in crisis. We knew that there was considerable evidence that undergraduates could undertake mental health roles successfully (Sanders, 1967; Cowen, 1967; Holzberg, Knapp & Turner, 1967; Persons, Clark, Persons, Kadish & Patterson, 1973; Poser, 1966; Freitag, Blechman, & Berck, 1973), but we had never read of a specialized training program for undergraduates preparing them to be co-leaders of multifamily groups working specifically within the court system. Consistent with our theoretical orientation, we chose the therapeutic modality of multifamily counseling groups (Leichter & Schulman, 1974) because we knew it to be a particularly effective treatment model for families experiencing a breakdown of parental control and family communication.

The multifamily group setting was useful for several reasons. Parents looking to the police and courts for rescue could experience competence by helping one another see their own children in a new light. Many of these families are isolated, rigid and/or missing a parent—these are indications that multifamily groups would be especially suitable. Adult-child relationships across family boundaries within the multifamily group potentially could develop, and, through understanding and empathy, lessen alienation between generations (Leichter & Schulman, 1974). We concluded that the existing psychological model of multifamily group counseling could provide a meaningful supplement to the handling of individual cases through the courts by probation officers.

Most Richmond College undergraduates come from Staten Island's working class ethnic communities; they are predominantly Italian and Irish Americans. The court cases we intended to work with came from these same communities. This meant that the selected undergraduate trainees would be familiar with the complex socio-economic and cultural family patterns which might have influenced parents who turn to the court. They would also be aware of the economic privations experienced by these families. Moreover, as long-term residents of Staten Island, the undergraduate trainees would have the knowledge and neighborhood contacts necessary to aid families in learning to deal with the community and with the organizational realities of the Island.

The three faculty members involved in the program developed a careful student selection process which will be described below. Then, with the help of the probation officer, we began planning the training sessions. We anticipated a 10 week training program for 16 undergraduates to be followed by 8 weeks of closely supervised experience in leading the multi-family counseling groups. (The undergraduate trainees received 6 college credits. As in any advanced college course, they were required to submit written work based on relevant readings in the psychological literature.

From the 16 students selected we chose two especially mature students who had already had considerable group work experience. They began at once to conduct a "pilot" group with the probation officer as well as also joining the 14 others in the complete training process. We did this because the Department of Probation had an immediate need and we had two students with a great deal of experience who were capable of leading groups. We also wanted these students to act as peer training models for the other students.

The faculty trainers made a careful evaluation after each training session and spent a great deal of time planning for the subsequent sessions. We kept a careful record of the curriculum as it developed. The next section of the paper describes the selection and training procedure in some detail in the hope that this will be helpful to those interested in undertaking a similar program.

Selection of Students. Faculty recruited students by describing the course in several advanced psychology classes, requesting interested students to sign up for an interview. We developed the following set of criteria in an attempt to elicit personality qualities and to account for actual life experience.

1. We asked students to describe ways in which studying psychology had influenced their relationship to their families and their communities.

2. We questioned them on their basic knowledge of psychology, especially as it pertained to social definitions of abnormality, treatment techniques they knew of and strategies of intervention in group conflict.

3. We questioned them on their knowledge and ability to negotiate the neighborhood and organizational realities of Staten Island (the community field setting for the course).

4. We reviewed their job and/or voluntary experience in helping roles.

5. We looked for such characteristics as maturity, warmth, flexibility, empathy, initiative, expressive ability, and the ability for self-reflection. Finally, all of the students were interviewed by the participating probation officer who had had no previous contact with them.

Training Procedures. The training sessions were designed to integrate the formal properties of didactic teaching with experiential learning. We feel we succeeded in enhancing the students' theoretical understanding by utilizing their emotional experiences while also focusing on their acquisition of particular clinical skills. We did this through the *Theme Focused Training Seminars.* At the beginning of each training session we announced the particular theme or topic to be covered. We then provided the students with a concrete, common, unifying group experience through an exercise, an observation, or a video demonstration, which gave them a vivid reference point for discussion of theoretical concepts related to the single theme chosen.

For each of the ten weeks of training, the 16 students were organized into two groups of eight students with two trainers (co-leader model) for each group. Thus they were members of a group which roughly resembled the ones they were being trained to lead. The following themes were covered, each one in a single training session:

1. Getting to know each other through the "Go-Around" technique.
2. Role Playing.
3. Group Dynamics and Non-Verbal Communication.
4. Verbal Communication Systems.
5. Observation of a Live Multi-Family Group.
6. Interventions for Improving Communication.
7. Simulation of Distressed and Well Families.
8. Leader Skills.
9. Co-Leader Skills.
10. The Family and the Identified Patient.

Each training session related the single theme to the particular problems of court referred clients. A brief description of the content of some of the sessions may help to clarify our training model.

In session two, role playing was used to help students break down stereotypes and to allow them to experience one another's point of view. Playing various familial and sex roles made students aware of the power and constraints of individual family members and helped them to conceptualize alternative role possibilities for family members. An added benefit was the students acquired role playing as a technique to be added to their skill repertoire.

By the middle of the ten week training period the undergraduates were expressing considerable anxiety about the prospect of running their own groups. We thought that this was an opportune time to have them observe an ongoing multifamily counseling group conducted by competent and accessible professionals. We took them to visit Bronx State Hospital where we had developed a consultative relationship with a multifamily therapy team. To the students' surprise they were able to intelligently participate in a post session

analysis of the group they observed. The Bronx State team became role models for the students, exemplifying cooperative co-leader relationships and a willingness to observe and criticize one another. Several weeks later in Training Session 7, the Bronx State team visited our training group and led a workshop in which they simulated problem families scapegoating the identified patient.

The Different Supervisory Models. The students began co-leading their own groups the week following the last training session. The multifamily counseling groups were established through referrals from the Department of Probation in the family court. A student serving as field coordinator for the project organized and scheduled the multifamily groups. Groups ranged from one large, extremely disorganized family, to four families within a single group. Once the groups were underway, our concern was directed toward providing necessary and appropriate supervision of the students. We felt that it was most helpful to employ varied and extremely thorough supervising techniques. This was necessary because of the relative inexperience of the students and our sense of responsibility to the families. These techniques will be distinguished from one another for reasons of presentation; however, they formed a coherent whole experienced by students as "continuous supervision." The techniques were the following:

1. Large group supervision.
2. Co-leader and peer supervision.
3. Continuous observation.
4. Tape recording and videotaping as supervision.

Large Group Supervision. All 16 students met for supervision one and one-half hours before the meeting with their actual multifamily groups. The supervision group generated energy and enthusiasm among the co-leaders, was particularly reinforcing when any difficulties arose, and generally helped to allay anxiety.

These supervisory sessions were attended by the faculty as well as the participating probation officer. Students could receive community and court information from the probation officer, whereas the three faculty members, differing in their personal and professional styles, provided diverse theoretical and technical information. Thus, students were exposed to various approaches and were free to seek out additional individual supervision.

Students were encouraged to discuss their training critically. Their comments tended to go through three stages. In stage 1, they began by overestimating what they had learned; stage 2 reflected the opposite, a marked underestimation. Finally, in stage 3, the students arrived at a fairly realistic evaluation of their training and skills. In stage 2, their most negative phase, students blamed all their difficulties or failures on the faculty and the "newness" of the course. Faculty encouraged immediate and direct ventilation of student anger so that they could continue to use their energies constructively with their family groups.

The decision not to become involved in lengthy interpretation of the students' feelings was based on reasoning similar to that which persuaded us to call our program counseling and not therapy. We were responding to certain realistic constraints: (a). That the co-leaders would be relatively inexperienced. (b). That the multifamily sessions were limited to 8 weeks. Therefore, students were taught to focus upon solving problems common to all members of the families and to open communications within and across families to encourage a supportive network of ties that could continue functioning outside of the multifamily sessions. This focus meant that co-leaders would not respond to or explore certain sensitive dynamic issues within families. It was felt that avoiding serious intrafamilial pathology would reduce the introduction of specific emotional and life history material. This material might have the effect of isolating the families from one another and would require therapeutic expertise of a level beyond the student's capabilities. Peer supervision was built into the training program by our focusing on the co-leader relationship as a support system and as a system of checks and balances.

Continuous Observation. The advantages of continuous observation as a form of in-service training were made clear to students and families alike. Students were encouraged to discuss their anxiety on being observed. On the whole there were few objections; the primary feeling seemed to be one of relief that faculty or experienced professionals would be around to help in case of difficulties. Midway through the course students complained if they were *not* observed.

Tape Recording and Videotaping Supervision. Co-leaders were encouraged to tape-record their sessions. They were told to listen to the tapes both alone and together and make "supervisory" comments to one another. Following the written consent of the families video tapes were made of four different multi-family groups. Families were invited to view the tapes either immediately following or during the actual group session or at another scheduled time.

The Technique of Posting. Posting consisted of an immediate review of what had occurred during the group session. The first fifteen minutes of the posting enabled the co-leaders to unwind and talk to one another about their session; the last fifteen minutes were opened to observer comments. The observation-posting techniques which were employed with families included: (a) families posting with the co-leaders and the observers and: (b) families observing the co-leaders and observers posting, immediately followed by joint discussion with the families taking the floor. These two techniques were increasingly success-

ful as the families became more engaged in their own group dynamics and as they learned about the purpose and process of the groups. They felt less of a separation between themselves and the co-leaders and observers and an increased sense of self-esteem.

Benefits of the Project. There were considerable benefits to all involved; the families, the students the community the Department of Probation and the College. We feel that pilot projects are an important and essential step to take before launching a new intervention with a large scale evaluation component. In short! we have found that pi lots are less costly« they iron out unforeseen problems test the feasibility of a curricular innovation} and provide a working basis for applying for additional funding.

Our pilot project was initiated in response to a pressing need . We did not want to sacrifice the opportunity to carry out this project just because in so short a time period we could not set up a formal evaluation based on empirical data. Instead, we developed an impressionistic and informal data base. Our informal evaluations include the following: videotaped sessions of the multifamily groups, student logs, verbatim interviews with families who participated, and the subjective appraisal of probation officers.

Benefits to Students. In February of 1975, we contacted the students who had participated in the program in the spring and summer of 1973. We asked them to describe the impact of their experience in the project on their career development. We were able to identify two areas in which the program was of direct benefit to students: (a) in their personal development and (b) through the acquisition of skills which enabled them to gain immediate employment in community mental health programs and/or helped them to gain admission to graduate schools.

Personal Development. Students were required to keep logs of their multifamily sessions. They unanimously wrote of their increased self-esteem and reported a more realistic understanding of their ego strengths and weaknesses.

There was some overlap of personal development with the development of skills related to career pursuits. Many of these students intended to become professionals in the helping services. This experience enabled them to define more accurately that professional role for themselves. A most significant aspect of this effect was how quickly the helping role was demystified. Several students reported they no longer felt that they could or should provide total solutions; they had begun to understand that the processes of change and/or development in people's lives was fairly slow, and they understood the meaning of "working through" interpersonal situations.

Even though our screening techniques enabled us to pick very suitable students for this project inevitably there were a few students whom we later felt should not be encouraged to work intensively with people. It was somewhat difficult to inform these students of our evaluations of their general ability but we felt it was our responsibility to do so. In so doing we were able to point out students' shortcomings honestly and early enough in their potential careers to encourage more appropriate and realistic career choices.

Skill Development. Students were required to conceptualize group and family dynamics in terms of theory. They realized that understanding these conceptualizations was essential to the timing and sequence of successful interventions.

Students were asked to share information about community resources with the families. In some cases students merely described the service and its location, but in other instances the students accompanied family members in order to provide mediation between service providers and the person in need of service. For instance family members often perceived any initial difficulty with agency personnel as insurmountable and they made a hasty retreats leaving an impression of disinterest. Students offered role modeling and support in seeking help from agencies, thus encouraging the family to persist in seeking the service.

Benefits to Families. On the impressionistic level the families appeared satisfied with the service since there was regular attendance and they expressed the desire for the project to continue.

The videotapes themselves provide more tangible evidence of family benefits. Over the duration of the project the tapes show evidence of greater communication between parents and children. A number of the children in getting part-time jobs (something we encouraged when appropriate) took significant steps toward establishing autonomy that was sanctioned by their parents.

Benefits to the College and the Community. The College benefited in several ways. It demonstrated to community agencies especially the Department of Probation, that the College was willing to make a commitment to provide training that was immediately useful to that agency and to the community. The Colleges being a small fairly new senior colleges was eager to establish itself as a resource institution within the community. The project required students to have some contact with a wide variety of social agencies and public programs.

Benefits to the Department of Probation. The project provided a much needed referral source for the Department of Probation. It also helped to lighten the heavy caseloads carried by the probation officers. Probation officers who referred their probationers reported that during the duration of the project probationers who ordinarily called them frequently asking for advice in family conflicts stopped doing so. Several probation officers observed the sessions and noted with surprise large differences in the demeanor of their probationers whom they had seen on a one to one basis and whom they now were seeing within the family context. Therefore] contact with the multifamily project gave probation officers a broader view of their clients. This project became an important source of skilled manpower for the Department of Probation. The Department of Probation eventually hired four undergraduates who had participated in the project.

Although this was a relatively small pilot project it has led to the development of two video training tapes which have application far beyond the scope of the project. In short this project is an excellent example of how a relatively short field training program can provide benefits to all those involved. Particularly at the teaching and training levels we feel that our model is an especially useful prototype for various community psychology and community mental health interventions.

References

Anonymous. Toward the differentiation of a self in one's own family. In J. L. Framo (Ed.). *Family interaction: A dialogue between family therapists and family researchers.* New York: Springer, 1972.

Bellak, L. *Twelve ego functions in schizophrenics, neurotics and normals: A systematic study.* New York: Wiley, 1973.

Cowen, E. L. Emergent approaches to mental health problems: An overview and directions for future work. In E. L. Cowen, E A. Gardner, & M. Zax (Eds.). *Emergent approaches to mental health problems.* New York: Appleton-Century-Crofts, 1967.

Erickson, E. H. *Childhood and society* (Rev. ed.). New York: Norton, 1964.

Freitag, G., Blechman, E., & Berck, P. College students as companion aides to newly-released psychiatric patients. In G. A. Specter & W. L. Claiborn (Eds.). *Crisis intervention.* New York: Behavioral Publications, 1973.

Haley, J. *Changing families: A family therapy reader.* New York: Grune & Stratton, 1971.

Holzberg, J D., Knapp, R. H., & Turner, J. L. College students as companions to the mentally ill. In E. L. Cowen, E. A. Gardner, & M. Zax (Eds.). *Emergent approaches to mental health problems.* New York: Appleton-Century-Crofts, 1967.

Jacobson, E. *Self and the object world.* New York: International University Press, 1964.

Leichter, E., & Schulman, G. L. *Multi-family group therapy: A multi-dimensional approach. Family Process,* 1974, *13*, 95-110.

Minuchin, S. *Families and family therapy.* Cambridge: Harvard University Press, 1974.

Persons, R. W., Clark, C., Persons, M, Kadish, M., &
Patterson, W. Training and employing undergraduates as therapists in a college counseling
service. *Professional Psychology,* 1973, *4,*
170-178.
Poser, E. G. The effect of therapist training on group
therapeutic outcome. *Journal of Consulting Psychology,* 1966, *30,* 283-289.
Sanders, *R.* New manpower for mental hospital service. In E. L. Cowen, E. A. Gardner, & M. Zax
(Eds.). *Emergent approaches to mental health
problems.* New York: Appleton-Century-Crofts,
1967.
Satir, V. *Conjoint family therapy.* Palo Alto, CA: Science and Behavior Books, 1967.

Notes

1. Judith Kuppersmith and Rima Blair are now at the
College of Staten Island, St. George Campus, and
Robert Slotnick is now at Creedmoor State Hospi-
tal.
2. The authors wish to express their appreciation to
Helen Brody, Larry Brown, and Carol Butler; and to
Ted Gross and Philip Vota of the Staten Island De-
partment of Probation.

An Interactive Problem-Solving Approach to the Teaching of a Marriage and Family Course

Louis E. Gardner
Creighton University

*This article describes a method for promoting stu-
dent interest and involvement in a marriage and family
course. The method supplements lectures with problem-solving sessions for small groups. The instructor
uses session outcomes to encourage critical evaluation
by the entire class. Students' positive reactions to the
course emphasize the complementarity of a traditional
scholarly approach and interactive personal involvement.*

Although an intrinsically interesting topic for most
college students, marriage and family, like any course,
can become dull when only a traditional lecture format
is used. Eshleman (1988) advised that textbooks for
marriage and family courses should not only include
data and theory, but they should also capture students'
interest. Although the criterion of interest can apply to
any course, it is easier to achieve in this area of study
because marriage is a typical developmental step for
many students during this time of their lives.

The method described in this article is an attempt
to apply these textbook criteria to produce worthwhile
and enjoyable learning experiences for the students.
During 4 years of teaching this course, I developed an
interactive problem solving approach to increase student interest and involvement in the course. I combined the lectures with weekly problem-solving
sessions that focused on real situations that individuals
may encounter in dating, courtship, or marriage as well
as on associated value questions. Students conducted
problem-solving sessions in small groups, followed by
interactions with the entire class and me at the end of
the period. During the class encounters, students and I
analyzed, critiqued, and evaluated problem solutions
and value issues in a discussion format. In this article,
I describe the methods used in the lectures, interactive
method, group sessions, and feedback sessions. In
addition, students' reactions to this approach to teaching are presented.

Lectures

I taught the course on a schedule in which two
thirds of the course time was used for traditional lectures. The subject matter of the course is consistent
with that in most textbooks on marriage and family. I
used a text by Cox (1987) because it provides excellent coverage and is student friendly. Having a comprehensive text that students easily understand
alleviated some of my anxiety about devoting lecture
time to the interactive approach.

Interactive Method

Small-group dynamics are a standard part of many college courses. However, because of the pedagogical success and favorable student reaction to the group dynamics in this course, I want to share my experiences with others.

Attendance at the problem-solving sessions is required. There were grade ramifications for absences without cause or for leaving the group session before the end of class. My insistence on attendance stems from my belief that the session experience is integral to the course and that there is no way to compensate for missing the experience. Also, I believe that the groups are not as effective with less than total attendance.

Each problem-solving group consisted of six students who remained in the same group throughout the semester. The only restriction to group composition was one of gender distribution. If there are not approximately equal numbers of men and women in each group, the method does not work well. For each problem-solving session, I designated one person in each group as the group leader and recorder. The leader was responsible for presenting the group with the instructor-prescribed problem or situation, keeping the discussion on target, and getting the group back to the classroom on time. After each session, the leader reported the group's solution to the entire class and submitted a one-page written report of that summary by the next class meeting. The leader received 5 credit points for successful completion of tasks. The schedule of group sessions was designed so that by the end of the semester everyone served twice as group leader.

Nature of Group Interactions

One of the major problems of using this method is finding places for students to work in small groups. I have found it too noisy and disruptive for five or six groups to hold a discussion in the same room. Therefore, it was necessary to find sites for their discussions. I have had a favorable experience allowing students to find their own meeting place (not too far from the classroom), letting me know where it is, and using the same place each week.

The procedure for the group sessions was always the same. I took roll, assigned leaders, handed a copy of the written problem to the leaders, and then had the groups retire to their respective meeting places. With the exception of unannounced visits, I left the group alone for 30 min to develop solutions or answers to that day's problem or question. Leaders were responsible for making sure that everyone returned to the classroom for the last 15 min of the period.

Four criteria were used to develop the problems or situations. First, the issue must deal with practical aspects of marriage and relationships. Second, the issue must relate to values concerning marriage and family. Third, the task must be amenable to concrete completion. Fourth, the task must relate to the material covered in lecture that week. The following situation was used during the week in which extramarital affairs were the topic of lecture.

Dale and Paula have been married for nearly 6 years. Dale gets involved with a woman he met at work, and they have a brief affair in which there is sexual intercourse. After ending the affair, Dale is plagued with remorse and guilt with a strong desire to confess everything to Paula.
List FIVE reasons why Dale should tell Paula and FIVE reasons why he should not tell her. After developing your lists, the group should attempt to reach a consensus regarding the question of whether Dale should or should not tell his wife about the affair.

Discussion of the contents of the two lists clearly involved value considerations concerning affairs, honesty, moral relativity, and the like. The problem was also practical for many people because it involves personal choice or advice that students may give in a role as friend or counselor. Finally, because the task consisted of creating specific lists and required a definitive answer to the question, a concrete solution could result.

The groups worked on the following assignment during the week when lectures focused on broken relationships:

You are counselor who has just received a call from a 25-year-old woman who is a college graduate pursuing a career in business management. Until 2 weeks ago, she was engaged to be married and planning the wedding for May of this year. Her fiancee abruptly broke off the engagement with the news that he had fallen in love with someone else and would be marrying her in May. Since getting this news, her life has become a shambles. She is in a state of depression, sometimes suicidal, unable to concentrate, disinterested in people, and feeling worthless and hopeless. Your group should list six suggestions for changing her behavior to help her fall out of love with this man.

The final example relates to the lecture on married sexuality and was presented to students in this way:

Someone once made the statement that men want a wife who is a virgin and a whore. Our perceptions of human sexuality often result from cultural expectations produced by this type of attitude. For today's assignment, I want each group to consider this perception of what men consider as desired sexual characteristics of a woman. Then, the men in the group should share their ideas about the perfect sexual partner; the women should do the same for the perfect sexual partner.

Because discussion time with the entire class was short, group leaders reported the result of group discussions by answering the question, presenting lists, and so forth. Students could respond to any issue in a critical or evaluative way. In most instances, however, I used the time to relate the group responses to past or future lectures or to relevant clinical or empirical data. If there was not enough time for all groups to report, we continued the reports in the next class. This strategy was less than ideal because student enthusiasm often dampened during the time interval.

After all of the reports and comments, I summarized the groups' reactions and synthesized them with information from the literature. For example, the exercise concerning the extramarital affair flows naturally into my description of the opposing viewpoints expressed in the clinical literature. This discussion leads to the revelation that there is no empirical evidence to support either position in this controversial area.

Students' Reactions

Students' responses to this method of teaching were overwhelmingly positive. This conclusion is based on informal comments, the way in which students participate in the class and in group activities, formal course evaluations, and course enrollment data. Formal evaluations consisted of five questions requiring a narrative reply concerning positive and negative aspects of the instructor's teaching style and the course format. Evaluations were completed by 233 students over a 3-year period.

The first two sources of evaluation are subject to instructor selection and bias. The formal course evaluations, however, support the conclusion about students' positive reactions to this method and their learning experiences. All students who completed evaluation forms reported positive reactions to the course in general. Among these respondents, 82% considered the interactive method as the most positive aspect of the course. The remaining 18% were not negative concerning this approach, but cited other facets of the course as the most positive. Some examples of these other facets include the instructor's humor, the text, films and tapes, and the professionalism demonstrated in the class.

At the risk of being selective, I quote the responses of three students concerning the course: "The groups really challenged me to look carefully at what I think and why I think that way—really helped me to understand myself better. " "Groups were a nice break from lecture and helped me to think about how course content applied to real-life situations." "Discussions were excellent. I loved our group and learned a lot." These three responses are representative of the student feedback, and they express the attainment of the instructor's objectives for the course.

Enrollment data provide an indirect measure of student response to a course. Each semester, this course has been the first psychology course to close out and one of the first in the college. Because large classes do not lend themselves to the use of the interactive method, the department restricts course enrollment to 40 students.

In summary, the interactive method has been highly successful, as judged by students and instructor. The students enjoy taking the class and seem to learn the material in a way that will be useful in the future. I enjoy teaching the class in this way, and the technique helps achieve the course objectives.

References

Cox, F. D. (1987). *Human intimacy: Marriage, the family, and its meaning* (4th ed.). New York: West.

Eshleman, J. R. (1988). *The family: An introduction* (5th ed.). Boston: Allyn & Bacon.

Notes

1. An earlier version of this article was presented at the Twelfth Annual National Institute on the Teaching of Psychology, St. Petersburg, FL, January 1990.
2. I thank Gary Leak and Mark Ware for their helpful comments.

4. INSTIGATING MISCELLANEOUS TECHNIQUES

Introducing Psychology Majors to Clinical Bias Through the Adjective Generation Technique

Gene F. Smith
Western Illinois University

In the exercise to be described, I used a technique devised by Allen and Potkay (1973) as a convenient method for summarizing student perceptions of a psychologist. The technique is the Adjective Generation Technique (AGT), and it involves having each subject generate five adjectives that describe a targeted stimulus person. Allen and Potkay (in press) have most often used the AGT as a method of self-description, but have used it as a method of other-description as well. In the present exercise, students were asked to describe a typical psychologist and a typical scientist via the AGT. It was assumed that the adjectives generated would reflect the "clinical bias" recently discussed by Korn and Lewandowski (1981). One result of the prevailing popular image of psychologists as clinicians is the disproportionate number of students who apply to clinical and counseling graduate programs. A second aspect of the bias, to be demonstrated with the current exercise, is the stereotypes students hold regarding psychologists and scientists.

The exercise was done during the first class meeting of an undergraduate General Experimental Psychology course. The eleven students who attended the initial class meeting were first asked to write on a piece of paper five traits or descriptive nouns which describe a typical scientist. Next they were asked to write down five traits or nouns which describe a typical psychologist. The exercise was valuable in two ways. First, when students were invited to present their adjectives to the class, it stimulated a lively discussion. Second, the exercise provided quantifiable evidence to support the hypothesis that there are systematic differences in student perceptions of scientists and psychologists.

With regard to the class discussion, the adjectives generated differed sufficiently so that it is "obvious" that students perceive psychologist and scientist differently. Among the words used to describe a psychologist were accepting, caring, observant, understanding, genuine, personable, and attentive. Among the words used to describe a scientist were methodical, analytical, resourceful, intelligent, and thorough. In the course of the discussion students reported that the adjectives they had generated described a psychologist in a clinical, interpersonal role, whereas the scientist was described in an experimental, laboratory role. That the students, all of whom were undergraduate majors in psychology, would reflect this clinical bias on the first day of General Experimental Psychology seems especially noteworthy; the bias must be strong, indeed, if it surfaces in such an inappropriate context! I concluded the first day of class by introducing to the students a bias of my own which would be heavily emphasized in the course, namely that scientist and psychologist are not different.

The second value of the exercise was that it provided quantifiable data by which to measure the extent of student stereotypes. Allen and Potkay (in press) have published a list of 2200 traits and descriptive nouns that people use in self and other-description. Their list contains normative ratings of favorability, anxiety, and masculinity/femininity for each of the 2200 descriptive terms. A rating, ranging from 0 to 600, is provided for each term on all three dimensions.

The descriptive terms used by the students were looked up in the Allen and Potkay list. The mean of the five adjectives on each dimension was determined for each student separately, and then the average rating was obtained across students. The mean favorability rating of 418.6 for psychologist was significantly more positive than the mean rating of 373.1 for scientist ($t = 2.60$; $df = 10$; $p < .05$). The mean masculinity/femininity rating of 281.2 for psychologist was significantly more feminine than the mean rating of 229.7 for scientist. ($t = 4.98$; $df = 10$; $p < .001$). The anxiety ratings of psychologist and scientist were not significantly different. These statistical analyses are not a necessary component of the exercise, although they do provide an objective demonstration of student stereotypes.

In sum, this is an exercise which can be easily used in any class setting. It awakens students to their conception of what a psychologist is and gives the instructor an opportunity to correct any misconceptions. Korn and Lewandowski (1981) advocate improved advisement to counteract the clinical bias prevalent among undergraduate psychology majors, and this exercise represents a convenient way to introduce the issue.

References

Allen, B. P., & Potkay, C. R. Variability of self-description on a day-to-day basis: Longitudinal use of the adjective generation technique. *Journal of Personality*, 1973, *41*, 638-652.

Allen, B. P., & Potkay, C. R. *Adjective Generation Technique (AGT): Research and applications*, New York: Irvington Press (in press).

Korn, J. H., & Lewandowski, M. E. The clinical bias in the career plans of undergraduates and its impact on students and the profession. *Teaching of Psychology*, 1981, *8*,149-152.

Therapy Evaluation: Using an Absurd Pseudotreatment to Demonstrate Research Issues

Richard J. Viken
Indiana University

The research presented in abnormal psychology, clinical psychology, and psychotherapy classes must compete for student attention with misinformation presented by the popular press and commercial interests. Abstract principles of research design rarely prevail in this competition. This article describes a classroom demonstration in which students apply abstract research concepts to a concrete analogue of therapy evaluation. Students rate their food consumption and mood before and after an absurd pseudotreatment. The data are used to demonstrate that absolutely useless treatments may initially appear to be highly effective and that careful attention to research design is necessary for appropriate therapy evaluation. Student evaluations indicate that this experience helps them understand and remember important issues in therapy outcome research.

Instructors of abnormal psychology, clinical psychology, and psychotherapy courses face a special problem in conveying course material. Research-based information must compete with inaccurate but skillfully packaged information from the media and from commercial interests that market fad treatments in the form of books, audiotapes, individual therapy, and various technologies. There are effective, validated techniques for behavior change (Garfield & Bergin, 1986), but students also face an array of unsubstantiated interventions that purport to be effective for depression, low self-esteem, procrastination, social anxiety, fatigue, smoking, and weight loss. Support for the efficacy of these approaches often comes from the testimony of developers, therapists, and former clients or from an appeal to common sense. Personal testimony and common sense do not provide a valid basis for therapy evaluation, and the efficacy of psychological interventions cannot be established without systematic research (Garfield & Bergin, 1986; McFall, in press; Smith, 1980).

Most textbooks for clinical courses include discussions of appropriate research strategies. In the face of a daily barrage of misinformation, however, the memorization of abstract principles of research design is unlikely to have a lasting impact on student judgment. It is important to find effective methods for conveying research information, because a class in abnormal psychology or psychotherapy is often our only opportunity to teach undergraduates how to be informed consumers in the psychological marketplace.

In most areas of psychology, abstract principles can be taught through laboratory demonstrations that provide concrete illustrations of basic psychological principles. However, it is difficult to construct demonstrations of critical thinking and research principles in clinical psychology, and only a few such techniques (e.g., Rabinowitz, 1989; Ward & Grasha, 1986) have been reported. This article describes a demonstration designed to provide students with a classroom experience in one important area of clinical psychology: therapy outcome evaluation.

The Demonstration

Students are informed that the class will engage in a demonstration of issues important in therapy evaluation. They are told that the demonstration will (a) be based on an absurd pseudotreatment invented by the instructor and pseudosymptoms that are really just normal variations in behavior, and (b) illustrate issues found in evaluation of real treatments for real problems.

Most instructors of clinical courses will already have discussed what students should do if they become concerned about symptoms or problems that are presented in the course. Although students have never reported concerns arising from this demonstration, please take this precaution. Students are free to participate or not, and they keep their own data, turning them in anonymously at the end of the demonstration. I have conducted this demonstration in four classes and have found that over 95% of the students participate.

On the first day of the demonstration, participating students make self-ratings of: (a) their mood in the last 24 hr. ranging from *happiest they have ever been* (100) to *saddest they have ever been* (1), with 50 representing *average mood;* and (b) their food consumption during the last 24 hr ranging from *most food ever consumed in 24 hours* (100) to *no food consumed* (1), with 50 representing *average food consumption.*

The treatment is administered in the next class period. I use a treatment that I call "Norwegian acupuncture" (a reference to my ethnic background), in which students press their left elbows with their right forefingers and solemnly repeat the words *Det er ikke gull alt som glimrer* (All that glitters is not gold). Instructors should modify the title and the treatment to enhance personal interest for themselves or their students. Any manifestly ridiculous treatment will do. To maintain the integrity of the "experimental design," there is no discussion at this point.

One week after the first ratings (a few days after the treatment), students rate their posttreatment food consumption and mood, recording them on the same paper used in the pretreatment ratings. I collect the anonymous food and mood ratings and select for analysis the pretreatment scores composing the bottom 10% of the mood ratings and the top and bottom 10% of the food ratings. These extreme pretreatment scores are paired with the posttreatment scores for the same people. Then, we have groups defined by the lowest pretreatment mood scores as well as the lowest and highest pretreatment food scores. A typical plot of the mean pretreatment and posttreatment scores for the three groups is presented in Figure 1.

The figure illustrates the substantial changes in food and mood ratings for these groups following treatment by Norwegian acupuncture. The sad people get happier, the overeaters eat less, and the undereaters eat more. In each of four classes, the changes from Time 1 to Time 2 in the low-mood, low-food, and high-food groups were statistically significant as judged by paired t tests. Absolute change scores for the group means have ranged from 14 to 30. Means and variances of the population (i.e., the class) generally did not differ significantly from Time 1 to Time 2, allowing evaluation of absolute change effects. On one

occasion, the population mean for mood was significantly higher at Time 2. Under these circumstances, the data can be mean corrected, allowing evaluation of regression effects relative to the Time 1 and Time 2 means.

In a class discussion, the Norwegian acupuncture treatment is evaluated using the standard criteria of effectiveness—generalizability, cost, side effects, acceptability to client, and ease of maintaining compliance. We establish that an effective treatment should

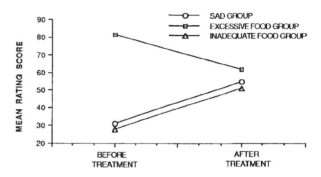

Figure 1. Change in mood and food ratings following treatment.

make sad people happier. It should make the people who are eating too much eat less and the people who are eating too little eat more. Using the figure, I demonstrate that my treatment is associated with all of these changes. Thus, we have a treatment that is effective, inexpensive, fast, has no negative side effects, and generalizes to at least two problem areas (in fact, to any symptom that varies week by week). It even has opposite but correct therapeutic effects for two extreme eating patterns. What do students make of these findings? Do they believe in this treatment? What could have gone wrong with our evaluation?

Students want to disprove Norwegian acupuncture because it is absurd and because they are certain that it could not have affected the class in the manner suggested by the figure. At this point, they begin to recall (or reinvent) standard research design issues. Hypotheses that are eventually rejected include placebo effects (it is important to use a very silly treatment), demand, maturation or other general trends, differential dropout, experimenter bias, and external events. The remaining possibility is a regression effect. Regression effects are a persistent source of errors in clinical judgment by researchers, practitioners, and consumers (Campbell & Stanley, 1963; Dawes, 1986; Kahneman & Tversky, 1973).

Avoiding any statistical treatment of the regression phenomenon, I point out that mood and food consumption fluctuate over time, and I draw a vaguely sinusoidal pattern on the board to illustrate. Students readily recognize that if they choose an extreme point, such as very sad mood, nearly all of the later points will be less extreme. The same fluctuations are characteristic of most of the symptoms for which people seek help from fad treatments. Because people are most likely to seek help when they are at a negative extreme, they will, on average, tend to feel better after the therapy. For this reason, absolutely useless treatments will often be judged to be beneficial by patients, therapists, and researchers using simple pre-post designs.

Students can now return to the abstract principles of research design that they learned in their text and use them to design a study (they usually choose a waiting list or placebo control) to prove that Norwegian acupuncture has no effect. The focus of the remaining discussion is on the reasons why common sense, pre-post designs, or testimony by therapists and patients are never sufficient to establish the efficacy of psychological interventions.

Evaluation

One month after the demonstration, students (N = 84) were asked to respond to the following statements on a scale ranging from *strongly agree* (1) to *strongly disagree* (5): (a) I learned more about the problems of therapy evaluation from the class demonstration than I did from reading about them or hearing a lecture about them (M = 1.3), and (b) I remember more about the problems of therapy evaluation from the class demonstration than I do from the readings or lectures (M = 1. 7). On the same scale, students were asked whether the class demonstration was useful (M = 1.8), enjoyable (M = 2. 0), interesting (M = 1. 9), or a waste of time (M = 4.3). More informally, the utility of the demonstration has been reflected in the fact that students often use this example in discussing the conclusions of

studies covered later in the semester. A few students also bring in examples of therapies described in the popular press for which regression effects or other confounds represent the most parsimonious explanation for therapeutic "success."

References

Campbell, D. T., & Stanley, J. C. (1963). *Experimental and quasi-experimental designs for research.* Chicago: Rand McNally.

Dawes, R. M. (1986). Representative thinking in clinical judgment. *Clinical Psychology Review, 6,* 425-441.

Garfield, S. L., & Bergin, A. E. (Eds.). (1986). *Handbook of psychotherapy and behavior change* (3rd ed.). New York: Wiley.

Kahneman, D., & Tversky, A. (1973). On the psychology of prediction. *Psychological Review, 80,* 237-251.

McFall, R. M. (in press). Manifesto for a science of clinical psychology. *The Clinical Psychologist.*

Rabinowitz, F. E. (1989). Creating the multiple personality: An experiential demonstration for an undergraduate abnormal psychology class. *Teaching of Psychology, 16,* 69-71.

Smith, M. L. (1980). Integrating studies of psychotherapy outcomes. *New Directions for Methodology of Social and Behavioral Science, 5,* 47-60.

Ward, R. A., & Grasha, A. F. (1986). Using astrology to teach research methods to introductory psychology students. *Teaching of Psychology, 13,* 143-145.

Teaching Psychological Issues in Context: A Library Exercise

Karl L. Schilling
Miami University

Having taught psychology for the past several years in a liberal arts college setting, one of my greatest disappointments and frustrations in teaching is the students' lack of an historical perspective—on themselves, psychology, and the world of ideas in general. My concern stems not so much from the students' lack of knowledge of historical facts but rather from their apparent inability to sense the importance of understanding the context of an idea (and of the thinker) in order to fully appreciate its meaning and impact.

The Problem. Many students seem to approach the writings of psychologists (both theoretical and empirical) as if the psychologists' ideas had sprung full blown from the head of Zeus. The concepts of a progressive flow of ideas in a culture and the building block process of science seem to be difficult notions for many students to grasp. Although students are able to learn a great deal from reading materials without this historical sense, they often develop a distorted picture of psychological writings by reading them as though they were written by their contemporaries. The students also miss the joy of understanding the intellectual struggles of authors as they work out responses to their mentors, their personal history, and their cultural context. For example, it is probably possible to understand Freudian concepts with little or no understanding of Victorian Vienna, Freud's personal history, and his medical training, but the greatness and the limitations of his work are more clearly understood when they are placed within these contexts.

The Course. In an attempt to address this concern, a course was designed which sought to provide this sense of historical context to the study of psychology without a direct focus on the history of the discipline. The primary goal, as listed on the course syllabus, was to help students to "appreciate the flow of ideas—the fact that ideas occur in a context, that important ideas come from somewhere and lead someplace; and to see the importance of understanding the role of cultural and professional context, the personal history and training of the writer and the spirit of contemporary times. " For this particular course, "Introduction to Clinical Psychology," three texts (Sundberg's *Assessment of Persons;* Allen's *Understanding Psychotherapy;* and Rappaport's *Community Psychology)* were chosen. These texts do not take a primarily historical perspective. (Although several historical texts exist, they usually relate facts, dates and personages, but the important concepts concerning the flow of ideas are frequently lost in the deluge of information. In addition, students generally find these books dry and tedious.) Therefore, it was necessary to provide another approach to this perspective. Because a secondary goal of the course was to increase the students' library skills, the two concerns were combined into several library exercises which sought not only to improve their library search strategies, but also to help them place issues and people in an historical context.

On the first day of class, students were given the assignment to find out as much information as they could about the authors of the three texts which were being used in the course. During the first class session, the students had used the instructor's vita to see how they might begin this detective game in seeking to discover the context of people and their ideas, the important shaping factors in their world view, and the limits of the vision which they present. At the end of the first class session, the students left to see what they could discover about the authors of their texts. The college librarian, using the same time limitations, undertook the same task.

The students and the college librarian arrived in class the next day to share their discoveries and their search strategies. There was a great deal of variation in the library skills of the students, but the sharing appears to have been an interesting way to help improve the search process of those students with less sophistication in this area.

Students and the librarian proceeded to share their discoveries and the source material in which they had found this information. This process exposed the students to a number of important library reference works. (Several students found material the librarian had not uncovered!) The class then made predictions as to the kind of material, interests and biases they would discover in each of the three books as they read them.

The second library exercise, which was spread throughout the term, involved working with several "classic" articles in the clinical psychology area. Each student selected one of these "classics" and developed an annotated bibliography utilizing at least ten of the references cited in the article. Then they used the Social Science Citation Index to find ten articles which cited the classic article. In their annotations, the students were asked to point out how the ideas in the references of the classic article might have influenced the development of the thinking of the author of that article and how that material was then utilized in the formation of the articles that cited the classic article. Through this exercise, the students gained a sense of the slow accumulation of information and refinement of ideas in the social sciences.

An Evaluation. These library exercises seemed to demonstrate a change in the approach that the students took to other material being covered in this course (and feedback from other instructors who had these same students in other classes suggested a similar "spill-over" effect). The students asked different questions and began to be concerned about the importance of being sensitive to the cultural context and the processes of science. Additionally, there is supporting anecdotal evidence that the course had an impact: During a Senior Thesis presentation by another student (who was not in the class), one of the students from the class began asking a series of contextual questions that suggested she had clearly understood our primary goal. Student evaluations, using a 1 -to-7 scale to rate the degree of achievement for the seven stated goals of the course, ranged from 5 to 7. I believe the library exercises allowed development of library skills (in a meaningful context) that in turn allowed the primary goal (appreciating the flow of ideas) of the course to be achieved for most of the students.

Note

Special thanks to Evan Farber, head librarian, Lily Library, Earlham College, Richmond, Indiana, for his assistance in the development of this approach.

Using Videotape Programs for Training Inmates in Peer Counseling Techniques

Gary O. George,
Federal Correctional Institution, Terminal Island
Ray E. Hosford,
University of California, Santa Barbara
C. Scott Moss
Federal Correctional Institution, Lompoc

Training was effective in improving skills and knowledge and for extending needed services to a large population.

Does the confinement to prison reduce subsequent crime? One hardly needs to read the professional literature to know the answer to this question. If it were so, then the prisons would serve society in the role originally intended for them. The high recidivism rates suggest that-confinement to prison is primarily custodial rather than rehabilitative. Indeed, incarceration may *promote* greater incidence of crime among most offenders than it does to reduce further criminal activity (cf. Hosford, George, Moss, & Urban 1975; Southerland & Cressey, 1970; Menninger, 1969). According to Southerland and Cressey, prisons cannot become rehabilitative agents of society—the role originally intended for them (cf. Commission on Attica, 1972)—as long as their staffs are trained to be guards rather than agents of change.

There is some evidence in the literature (cf. Hosford, et al., 1975; Gardner, 1972; Bednar, et al., 1970; Phillips, 1 968; Tyler & Brown, 1967) to indicate that various types of inservice training programs have resulted in significant changes in interpersonal functioning of correctional staff participants. These studies have been both descriptive and experimental assessments in which trained staff were compared with nontrained. A major problem, however, is that the staff members, whose job classifications may be designated as "correctional counselor," do not have time to put into practice their newly acquired counseling skills (custodial duties must take precedence over those which are rehabilitative in nature), thus, the newly acquired counseling skills of newly trained staff soon extinguish through lack of use and through the continual practice of interpersonal habits associated with being "policemen" as opposed to "counselors." In addition to the fact that correctional counselors often must serve in custodial rather than counseling roles, professional therapists such as counseling and clinical psychologists are few in number. Because of better working conditions and perceived status in other mental health settings, trained therapists are difficult to recruit for correctional positions. At the Lompoc correctional institution, for example, there are only one psychiatrist and two psychologists assigned to an institution of 1400 men. Because of the chronic shortage of staff, mental health personnel have been forced to explore a variety of ways other than traditional dyadic and group therapy for involving a larger percentage of inmates in counseling to help them learn more acceptable methods for solving their personal problems.

One source of change-agent manpower which corrections has in abundance, but which is seldom mentioned, is that of the inmates themselves. To date, few innovative programs have been developed in which the inmate has been viewed as a participant rather than recipient of the correctional process. For example, offenders have participated in a variety of research, counseling, and developmental programs for the past decade, particularly so in the sixties within the California State Prison systems (cf. NIMH, Note 1: Grant, Note 2; NIMH, Note 3). Within the federal system, only recently has corrections begun to evaluate the use of inmates as change-agents for other inmates (Kerish, 1975). These studies have demonstrated that peer counseling programs can be effective rehabilitative interventions in promoting a variety of positive attitude and behavioral changes among inmate participants. Kerish (1977), for example, found that newly incarcerated inmates who completed a peer counseling program subsequently received significantly more positive job performance and living unit behavior staff ratings than did similar inmates who volunteered but did not receive counseling. Further, the counseled inmates reported more positive self-images for themselves than did those in the control group.

The present study was designed to determine the effectiveness of a prepared training program presented primarily on videotape in which inmates were trained to serve as peer counselors for fellow inmates. The subjects, males confined to the Federal Penitentiary at McNeil Island, Washington, came from diverse educational and socioeconomic backgrounds and were incarcerated for a variety of federal crimes. The training was designed specifically to help these individuals learn the specific steps involved in helping other inmates learn how to more effectively use problem-solving methods in solving their own personal, social, and educational problems. A series of videotapes created from previous staff training (Hosford, et al., 1975) demonstrated by means of discussions and modeling specific ways in which counselors can help persons (a) define their problems in operational terms, (b) consider possible alternatives for solving those problems, (c) set goals which are meaningful and attainable, (d) conduct and record self-observational data, (e) determine and implement some specific kind of self-help intervention, and (f) evaluate the success of the various strategies implemented to solve the problem.

Procedures. A total of 15 inmates volunteered for the training. Of these, four were paroled before the training was complete, one was transferred to another institution, and one escaped from the facility. Thus, the total number of participants was nine. The training was carried out over a six-week period at three hours per session. It consisted of a series of ten one-hour videotapes edited from a staff training program conducted earlier at F.C.I., Lompoc (Hosford, et al., 1975).[5] After viewing a particular tape, the subjects were divided into triads for the purpose of practicing the specific skills demonstrated on the tape. They took turns rehearsing roles of client, counselor, and observer. The observer rated the counselor's performance and provided him with feed back on specific criteria using rating scales adapted from the Hosford-deVisser training program (Hosford & deVisser, 1974).

Assessments. Prior to and after termination of training, each participant was randomly assigned to counsel (while being Videotaped) one of two volunteerinmate "clients" who otherwise were not associated with the study. Each subject was given several kinds of fictitious data presented in writing about his "client," e.g., past criminal record, family relationships and educational information. The "clients" were similarly given written information regarding their "problem" and the "relevant background material" they were to portray. The inmate "clients" had been trained to ask specific questions and to demonstrate a variety of verbal and nonverbal behaviors indicative of being nonresponsive. The actual problems which the "clients" expressed included:

1. How do I get my wife to stay with me?

2. How do I handle my son whom I haven't seen much for nine years?
3. How do I handle my daughter and her *possible* sexual problems?
4. I am afraid of returning to my family after being gone for nine years.
5. How do I act at the Parole Commission?
6. I'm depressed and uptight most of the time but I don't want tranquilizers.
7. I'm losing my friends here and don't have any left on the outside.
8. I'm starting to get hassled by the officers about my attitude and lack of production in Industries.

The subjects were told that they were not being evaluated individually—which was true—but that the assessments would be used to evaluate the training program as a whole. Although no information was given to staff or recorded in any subject's institutional file, the inmates were free to mention their participation in the training to their unit supervisors if they so chose.

Subsequent to the termination of the study, the pre- and post-training videotapes of the subjects' "counseling sessions" were coded, randomized, and rated by a paid doctoral student in counseling psychology at the University of California, Santa Barbara, who otherwise was not associated with the study. The rater had no knowledge of whether a particular tape represented pre- or post-counseling or was even part of an experimental study. The Reinforcement Rating Scale and the Behavioral Counseling Training Rating Scale developed by Hosford and deVisser (1974) were used for this purpose.

Each subject's verbal and nonverbal response was rated contingent upon a "client's" emitting (a) an affective statement indicative of some personal concern and/or (b) a statement relative to some constructive action he could take to solve his problem.[6] Analysis of the data indicated the subjects demonstrated significantly more verbal and/or nonverbal reinforcements of their clients' behaviors after receiving training than they had performed prior to training, $t(16) = 3.41$, $p < .005$, two-tail.

Further, the inmates' interpersonal relationship skills, as measured by Behavioral Counseling Training Rating Scale, included significantly more positive counseling behaviors, e.g., establishing rapport with the clients with no apparent difficulties, helping clients successfully describe their problems in operational terms, etc., after training than before training, $t (16) = 3.45$, $p < .005$, two-tail.

To determine whether the inmates' knowledge about human behavioral counseling process increased as a result of the training, all subjects were administered a multiplechoice and short-answer written examination, both before and after training. The following questions are examples of those included in the questionnaire:

(1) Behavior that has been punished often reoccurs when:

    _____a. The punishing agent is no longer present.

    _____b. When no alternative behaviors are learned.

    _____c. When punishment is consistent.

    _____d. When punishment immediately follows the behavior

(2) List three behaviors which you can use to promote a good counseling relationship: (Space provided for answers.)

As with the videotapes, the pre- and post-training knowledge questionnaires were coded, combined, and scored randomly. The analyses for these data indicated that the subjects demonstrated a significantly greater amount of knowledge about counseling after training as compared with that before training, $t(16) = 7.5$, $p < .001$, two-tail.

Discussion. The fact that the training, for the most part, was conducted vicariously through the use of videotape is important not only in terms of its effectiveness, but also because of efficiency. The presentations demonstrate once again that knowledge and skills presented vicariously on videotape can substitute for a "live" training experience (Hosford, et al., 1975). This fact would appear to be extremely important for state, county, and federal correctional institutions which are always in short supply of mental health funds, even for necessary training to effect a change of security-minded officers into correctional counselors. In lieu of a basic alteration in staff attitudes, the huge numbers of inmates incarcerated in federal and state institutions represent a tremendous source of untapped manpower. The data in this study indicate that the inmate "counselors," as a result of training, can demonstrate significantly better performance on at least three behaviors associated with counseling— verbal and nonverbal following, overall counseling, and knowledge about counseling.

It is well-known that an inmate subculture emerges within the overall structure of any correctional facility. This subsystem has norms, patterns of behavior, and sources of reinforcement greatly different and often in conflict with that of the established institutional structure. The resulting division of the two subcultures often contradicts, conflicts, and impedes any therapeutic rehabilitative progress. By the use of selected peer inmates trained in basic counseling skills, other inmates might participate more fully in programs designed to help them acquire more effective personal, social, and vocational problem-solving skills, and as Kerish (1977) points out, they can do so without risking being alienated by other inmates for "copping out" to the system.

Ideally, of course, the same form of training should be given to both staff and selected inmates. Such a program was actually given for a year and a half (1969-71) under a prototype by Shapiro (1975) at this institution. The introduction of inmate and staff members led to some major innovations in group therapy; however, it was short-lived because of budgetary difficulties that terminated Shapiro's consultative efforts. This new format of using videotape training might not run into the same sort of problem that aborted that program.

References

Bednar, R. L., Zelerhart, P. F., Greathouse, L. & Wienberg, S. Operant conditioning principles in the treatment of learning and behavioral problems with delinquent boys. *Journal of Counseling Psychology,* 1970, *17,* 492-497.

Commission on Attica. *The official reports of the New York special commission on Attica.* New York: Bantam Books, 1972.

Gardner, J. M. Teacher behavior modification to non-professionals. *Journal of Applied Behavior Analysis,* 1972, *5,* 517-521.

Hosford, R. E. & deVisser, A. J. M. *Behavioral approaches to counseling: An introduction.* Washington, DC: APGA Press, 1974.

Hosford, R. E., George, G. O., Moss, C. S. & Urban, V. E. The effects of behavioral counseling training on correctional staff. *Teaching of Psychology,* 1975, *2,* 124-127.

Kerish, B. R. Peer counseling. In R. Hosford & C. S. Moss (Eds.), *The crumbling walls: Treatment and counseling of prisoners.* Urbana: University of Illinois Press, 1975.

Kerish, B. R. The effect of Peer Counseling in a correctional setting. Unpublished doctoral dissertation, University of California, Santa Barbara, 1977.

Menninger, K. *The crime of punishment.* New York: Viking Press, 1969.

Phillips, E. L. Achievement place: Token reinforcement procedures in a home-style rehabilitation setting for "predelinquent" boys. *Journal of Applied Behavioral Analysis, 1968, 1,* 213-223.

Shapiro, S. B. The group leadership training program at F. C. I., Lompoc. In R. Hosford & C. S. Moss (Eds.), *The crumbling walls: Treatment and counseling of prisoners.* Urbana: University of Illinois Press, 1975.

Southerland, E. H. & Cressey, D. R. *Criminology.* New York: Lippincott, 1970.

Tyler, V. O., & Brown, G. P. The use of swift, brief isolation as a group control device for institutional delinquents. *Behavior Research and Therapy,* 1967, *5,* 1-9.

Notes

1. N.I.M.H. *Experiment in culture expansion: The use of the products of a social problem in coping with the problem.* Proceedings of a conference held at

the California Rehabilitation Center, Norco, California, July 10-12, 1963.

2. Grant, D. J. New careers development in the change agent field. Paper presented at the 42nd meeting of the American Psychological Association, New York, March, 1965.

3. N.I.M.H. *The offender* as *a correctional manpower resource: A new approach to correctional research.* A collection of papers prepared by the California New Careers Development Project (1966), Sacramento: The Institute for the Study of Crime and Delinquency.

4. The proposal advocated in this paper does not necessarily represent the attitudes of the Federal Bureau of Prisons. No official support or endorsement is intended or should be inferred.

5. For a detailed description of the total training program see George, Gary. *An Evaluation of Two Behavioral Counseling Training Methods with Correctional Staff in a Federal Prison*, Doctoral dissertation, University of California, Santa Barbara, 1974.

6. Verbal and nonverbal reinforcements were combined because a near perfect correlation was found between the inmate counselors' use of positive verbal statements and that of head nods and smiles contingent upon specific client target behaviors.

Using a Group Workshop to Encourage Collaborative Learning in an Undergraduate Counseling Course

Gary S. Goldstein
University of New Hampshire at Manchester

This article summarizes a collaborative learning project for an upper level undergraduate counseling course. Groups of students designed and presented a workshop on a therapeutic intervention for a specific patient population. Each student also wrote a paper on an individually selected topic. Examples of students' workshops, reactions to and evaluations of the assignment, and grading procedures are described. The assignment provides a model for the kind of collaborative work students may encounter in advanced study.

Term paper assignments rarely encourage students to collaborate with each other. Instead, students usually write their papers individually and have little opportunity to share with each other what they have learned. Such assignments are quite different from the work of most psychologists, whose research and professional efforts are characterized by collaboration with and feedback from colleagues.

Some educators have recognized the importance of using collaborative assignments in the classroom. Magin (1982) used collaborative strategies successfully with engineering students, and Welds (1986) noted how her use of such strategies led to greater student self-direction in a semester-at-sea program. Dettmer (1986) argued that adult learners can make important contributions to collaborative assignments because of their extensive and varied backgrounds. Dunn and Toedter (1991) suggested that collaborative projects provide students with a model of peer review that they are likely to encounter in their professional lives. They also stated that such assignments sharpen students' awareness of the diversity of research interests and approaches in psychology as well as provide the opportunity for emotional support in the form of their peers' interest and understanding. In addition, collaborative assignments can nudge passive students out of their dependency on authority as the sole source of knowledge by combining individual research with peer teaching and learning. Working in a group can heighten students' sense of responsibility for their learning and expose them to a variety of perspectives on the topic at hand. Working on a group project throughout the semester can also help students critique their own work, allowing them to refine their writing in light of the feedback they receive from their peers.

Description of Assignment

For the past three semesters, I have used a collaborative learning project in my undergraduate, upper level counseling course. The students were all psychology majors, and about half were adult learners (i.e., 25 years or older, working part- or full-time, and supporting families). The central focus of the course was on the major schools of psychotherapy—classical and contemporary psychoanalytic, cognitive-behavioral, and humanistic approaches. The assignment asked students to choose a research topic that reflected a different focus, namely, working with specific patient populations. The project consisted of two parts: an individual research paper and a group workshop presented to the class. Although students worked on the projects as a group, each member was required to complete an individual paper based on a topic from his or her workshop. For example, one group's workshop examined the area of victimization; individual papers from that group focused on rape victims, battered spouses, sexually abused children, and battered homosexual couples.

Each time I taught the course, there were three or four groups comprised of four or five students each. Group formation was constrained by students finding other class members with a shared interest. I facilitated this process by using 45 min early in the semester to brainstorm ideas for workshop topics and to help students find commonalities among their interests. Although I never had a problem, the instructor should be prepared to create groups if students cannot.

Each group's task was to design and present a workshop that involved active participation by the class. Although some didactic presentation was allowed, workshop members were required to involve the class, using experiential exercises, role-playing, video, or personality inventories. The workshops lasted for 1 hr, with an additional 30 min for feedback and discussion from the class.

Students were responsible for arranging group meetings outside of class to develop workshops, discuss ideas for their papers, and read rough drafts of each other's papers. Groups also met twice during class for about 1 hr to allow for further planning. During these sessions, I met with the different groups to discuss their workshops. Each group then summarized in about 10 min its project for the class and received feedback from class members in a brainstorming session. Also, I met with each group for about 1 hr outside of class to discuss their ideas, and I met individually with students, as needed, to review their papers.

Examples of Workshops

The workshops generated spontaneous discussions and allowed the students to examine issues more personally than may have otherwise occurred. For example, in one workshop, students created videotapes of themselves role-playing suicidal patients, asked the class to respond to them, and then analyzed these responses. This workshop resulted in students confronting their fears about working with suicidal patients in a more personal way than would have likely occurred in a typical class discussion. Another group role-played

victimized patients in a therapy group. Class members then anonymously (through writing) shared their own experiences of victimization (sexual, physical, and emotional abuse) which the workshop leaders related to their earlier role-play. A third group asked the class to keep "eating diaries" and to reenact the typical dinner situation of their childhood. This group then integrated these data into a discussion of eating disorders. A fourth group asked the class to role-play a sixth-grade classroom in which members of the workshop group played the parts of children with different disorders (e.g., conduct disorder and attention deficit disorder).

Ethical and Practical Concerns

Ethical issues can arise as a result of giving this assignment because students often confront personally disturbing material. Several precautionary steps can be taken to minimize potential problems. First, it is important to create an atmosphere of trust in the class by designing several exercises that give students the opportunity to personalize the class content and to respond to each other with empathy and support. Second, students affected emotionally by a specific topic should have the opportunity to consider how they feel about openly participating in the workshop. If a student's discomfort level had appeared particularly high, I would have considered referring that student to an appropriate professional. Workshop summaries given during the brainstorming sessions gave students a good idea of what would be expected of them by the other groups. Third, I encouraged students to discuss with me any hesitation they had about participating in a workshop, both at the beginning of the semester and during brainstorming sessions, and emphasized that participation was not mandatory if they felt uncomfortable about it. In three semesters, no student has exercised this option. Quite the contrary, students opened up during the workshops and disclosed personal experiences, thus enriching the presentations.

The assignment is time consuming because the instructor may need to allow class time for group meetings and workshop presentations. Therefore, I would not use this assignment with more than five groups. The first time I gave the assignment students agreed to schedule brainstorming sessions and to present their workshops immediately after the 3-hr class; thus, time was not a major concern. We agreed on this meeting time by consensus after a discussion during the first class. Because the course met once a week at night, finding this common time was easy, and there were no scheduling conflicts with other classes. Some students, however, complained that the extra hour conflicted with family responsibilities. Therefore, in subsequent semesters, I added 1 hr per week (which we used about five times) to the course's meeting time, designated solely for workshop preparation and presentations. Faculty at my campus can add this extra time to their classes without increasing the number of credit hours for the course. However, students know when they register for the course that they will sometimes need to adjust their schedule around this extra hour, which provides a formal meeting time for all students in the class.

Group projects present the potential for some students not to share equally in the workload or for some students to dominate the process. Requiring an individual research paper can mitigate these problems. Also, each student's involvement can be monitored by meeting with the groups on a regular basis. I asked students to take responsibility for dealing with these possible problems by first trying to resolve the issue among themselves. If this approach did not lead to a successful resolution, the students were asked to involve me. The unequal sharing of work created some difficulty for one group, but I was not informed of it until after the semester ended. In the future, I will collect anonymous feedback throughout the semester so that I can intervene at the appropriate time.

Evaluating Student Performance

Twenty-five percent of the students' final course grade was based on their written paper, and 5% was based on participation in the group workshop. Students could earn one of two grades for the workshop—an A if they participated in its design and presentation or an F if they did not participate. Furthermore, not participating in the workshop carried the additional penalty of automatic failure on the written paper.[1] Essentially, then, students earned an A for the workshop by participating in its design and presentation. I did not grade the quality of the workshop. Thus, I did not use grades as an incentive for student performance on the workshop. Instead, I depended on the students' interest in the topic and commitment to the course, peer pressure, and my encouragement when meeting with each group. All students participated in the workshop, and grades on the papers ranged between B and A— slightly higher than what students receive on the assignment without the workshop. Although I believe this grading system was successful, it may not be appropriate for less motivated students in lower level courses with less general interest in counseling.

Student Feedback on the Assignment

Although students have voiced some objections to the workshops, their reactions have been mostly positive. The course has had a total enrollment of 51 stu-

dents during the past three semesters. Of these 51 students, 31 specifically mentioned the course project on end-of-semester anonymous course evaluations. Of these 31 students, 4 reported concern that the project required excessive work, 6 reported that the project produced scheduling problems, 3 reported difficulty working with other group members, 5 wished the project had counted more toward their final grade, and 23 reported positive feelings about the project. These numbers add up to more than 31 because some students wrote more than one comment. Sample responses included: "The workshop was most interesting as we had the opportunity to work collectively on a project"; "I felt the workshop was an effective example of learning group dynamics and management of therapeutic technique presented in class"; "I feel it was important to work with others and get their perspectives. I wish other classes required group collaborations"; and "I learned about the necessity of taking into consideration the different backgrounds, different priorities, and different points of views of others."

Students in one section of the course (n = 16) also rated items evaluating the project on a scale ranging from *strongly disagree* (1) to *strongly agree* (7). The items and their mean ratings were as follows:

"Working with my workshop group helped me learn about my topic" (M = 6.12).
"I found that listening to the other groups' workshop was a useful learning experience" (M = 6.5).
"Working on the group project was interesting" (M = 6.53).
"I would recommend using this group project again for the course" (M = 6.33).

Four of the 16 students wrote comments about the project on this instrument. Three students gave positive comments, and 1 reported that the project produced scheduling problems.

Overall, I concluded that the assignment was successful. I was impressed by the students' level of commitment and by the quality of their work. Workshop presentations were creative and generated exciting classroom discussions. Collegiality of the groups appeared to carry over into classroom discussion on a regular basis. Individual papers were, for the most part, outstanding and more original than typical term papers I have read. More important, the assignment provided a powerful collaborative model for the kind of work students may encounter in advanced study. It also added a unique dimension to the class by allowing students to personalize issues like suicide and abuse and enriched their learning by giving them perspective on how these issues relate to themselves and others.

---

[1] If students choose not to participate in a workshop, they will not suffer this penalty. Instead, they will be required to write the paper and outline their ideas for a workshop. Thirty percent of these students' final grades will be based on their paper.

References

Dettmer, P. (1986). Characteristics and needs of adult learners in gifted inservice and staff development. *Gifted Child Quarterly, 30,* 131-134.

Dunn, D. S., & Toedter, L. J. (1991). The collaborative honors project in psychology: Enhancing student and faculty development. *Teaching of Psychology, 18,* 178-180.

Magin, D. S. (1982). Collaborative peer learning in the laboratory. *Studies in Higher Education, 7,* 105-117.

Welds, K. (1986). Experiential education journal to develop self-direction and authority. *Innovative Higher Education, 10,* 128-133.

Note

I gratefully acknowledge the assistance of Charles L. Brewer and three anonymous reviewers for their comments on a draft of this article.

Participant Modeling as a Classroom Activity

Dolores Hughes
Iona College

Participant modeling was used to introduce students to this behavioral technique for reducing anxiety and avoidance behavior. An expert model and peer models performed appropriate approach responses when interacting with a red rat snake, Elaphe quttata. Using guided participation, students who had previously indicated they were afraid of snakes were encouraged to approach, touch, and hold the snake. Students' evaluations of this activity were highly favorable. Participant modeling provides an excellent introduction to behavior therapies and encourages students to think critically. This activity illustrates some of the difficulties encountered when evaluating the effectiveness of therapeutic techniques.

Participant modeling is a behavioral technique in which the therapist models approach and coping responses, encouraging and guiding the client to take a progressively active role in interacting with anxiety-provoking stimuli. Its major goals are the extinction of avoidance responses and the conditioning of appropriate approach responses. This technique has also been called *contact desensitization, demonstration plus participation,* and *guided participation* (Redd, Porterfield, & Andersen, 1979).

Many studies have demonstrated the effectiveness of participant modeling in the treatment of fears and phobias (e.g., Bandura, Adams, & Beyer, 1976; Bandura, Blanchard, & Ritter, 1969; Ritter, 1969). The classic study of modeling for this purpose used young adults whose fear of snakes was severe enough to restrict some of their everyday activities (Bandura et al., 1969). Although all subjects in three treatment groups showed improvement in comparison with a control group, the subjects who imitated the behavior of a live model with guided participation demonstrated the most improvement. Several subsequent studies have demonstrated that this type of participant modeling is the most effective method of reducing snake phobias (e.g., Bandura et al., 1976).

Bandura (1977) suggested that participant modeling is effective because it provides individuals with experiences that enhance their perceptions of self-efficacy. Efficacy expectations are governed by information from a variety of sources. The most reliable source of information derives from performance accomplishments. Because participant modeling requires these accomplishments, it is particularly effective for inducing behavioral, affective, and attitudinal changes (Bandura, Adams, Hardy, & Howells, 1980).

The following activity was designed to: (a) demonstrate participant modeling as a technique for reducing fear and avoidance of nonpoisonous snakes, (b) illustrate the concept of self-efficacy, (c) illustrate some of the problems encountered when evaluating the effectiveness of therapeutic techniques, (d) actively engage students in the learning process, and (e) encourage critical thinking.

Procedure

This activity was conducted in the context of a unit on behavior therapies in my Introductory Psychology course. Approximately 1 week before the activity, students completed a questionnaire about their fear of nonpoisonous snakes. I told them that an expert in wildlife biology, James Rod of the National Audubon Society, would be visiting class to help with this activity.

He began the activity with a brief lecture about the biology of snakes and their ecological importance. He answered several questions about snakes before uncovering an aquarium containing a red rat snake, *Elaphe quttata,* commonly known as a corn snake. He removed the snake and handled it with obvious competence and a complete lack of fear.

Students were invited to hold the snake, and some always did so. I then selected students, based on their scores on the fear questionnaire, who were moderately afraid. I requested, but did not insist, that they try to do some or all of the following steps in sequence as the expert held the snake: (a) approach the snake within a radius of 6 ft. (b) gradually approach the snake more and more closely, (c) lightly touch its tail, (d) lightly touch the middle of its body, (e) touch the middle of its body more firmly, and (e help the expert hold the snake. Then, students were asked to hold the snake by themselves.

Each of these steps was done slowly for each moderately afraid student with encouragement and reassurance from the expert, other students, and me. Students were asked to report what they were feeling as they went through these steps. Finally, I asked students who had scored high on the fear questionnaire if they were willing to do some or all of these steps, and some were always willing to try.

Students' Evaluations

Evaluations were obtained from 406 students in 14 sections of my Introductory Psychology course from 1976 to 1988. Class sizes ranged from approximately 20 to 40 students.

Using a 5-point scale, students were asked two questions: (a) How interesting was the activity? (1 = *not at all,* 5 = *extremely interesting*), and (b) How helpful was the activity for understanding the technique of participant modeling? (1 = *not at all,* 5 = *extremely helpful).* Combining all sections, the mean rating for interest was 4.33, and the mean rating for helpful was 4.21.

Discussion

The students' evaluations and comments were very favorable. Many students stayed after class to talk with the expert and touch or hold the snake. I am always struck by the combination of fear and fascination that students exhibit toward snakes.

Many students said they never believed they could touch or hold any snake. They seemed very proud that they were able to approach the snake and actually touch or hold it. Some students later reported that they had told their parents and friends about being able to touch or hold the snake. All of the students' comments were consistent with Bandura's (1984, 1986) concept of self-efficacy or sense of mastery, which has been emphasized as a component of all effective therapeutic techniques.

This activity is very interesting and helpful to students. It provides an excellent introduction to behavior therapies and introduces students to the difficulties involved in identifying the specific factors that are effective in therapeutic techniques. It also encourages students to think critically.

I ask students to think of the factors that were part of this activity. They usually report: (a) characteristics of the snake, such as size and color; (b) characteristics of the expert model and the peer models; (c) encouragement and reassurance from the expert model, other students, and me; (d) motivation to cooperate; and (e) participation in front of a classroom of peers. They understand that we did not isolate which factors may have been most strongly influencing behavior, and we did not use a control group. It is possible that all, some, one, or none of the factors were effective, and there may have been unidentified variables operating.

Students should realize that those who participated were probably not phobic. These students, therefore, were not representative of clients who enter treatment for phobias. This limitation leads to a discussion of the problem of treatment analogues (e.g., Bernstein & Paul, 1971; Borkovec & Nau, 1972). Much of our knowledge about the effectiveness of behavioral approaches for reducing anxiety derives from college students who volunteer for studies; they may not be typical of clients who share some specific problem.

Furthermore, we do not know if students' attitudes and behaviors will be permanently changed and will transfer to situations outside of the classroom. Some of the students who participated expressed doubts about touching a snake in other circumstances. These doubts lead to a discussion about the obstacles encountered in measuring the observable and permanent effects of any therapy.

I have always included an expert model as well as peer models, but the activity may be effective without the expert model. When modeling is used in the treatment of phobias, a distinction is often made between coping and mastery models. Coping models initially exhibit fearful performances and gradually become increasingly competent as modeling proceeds. Mastery models, in contrast, exhibit fearless performances from the beginning. Kazdin (1974) and Meichenbaum (1972) suggested that coping models may be more effective than mastery models. Coping models can, however, be ineffective. Geer and Turteltaub (1967), for example, found that models who demonstrated nonfearful behaviors toward snakes improved subjects' attitudes toward snakes. In contrast, fearful models did not produce attitudinal changes.

In my activity, some students served as coping models, and other students, who were not afraid of snakes, served as mastery models. If instructors prefer to include an expert model, and I do recommend using one, they may ask faculty or students in biology departments for help. Or they may check with pet stores, zoos, nature centers, and environmental organizations. Staff members of nature centers will probably help, because they want to educate people about wildlife.

The need to educate people about wildlife and help them overcome their fears of wildlife, especially snakes, was cogently addressed by Morgan & Gramann (1989). They successfully used a variety of behavioral techniques, including participant modeling, to help students change their attitudes toward snakes.

My experience suggests that people who are knowledgeable about snakes are eager to help others overcome their fears of snakes. They want people to appreciate that nonpoisonous snakes are harmless and ecologically important. I also discovered that some of my students have positive attitudes toward snakes before this activity.

This activity or modifications of it should be useful in courses such as abnormal psychology, behavior modification, learning, or research methods. It lends itself to a variety of modifications and applications that can engage students in the learning process. Students understand that participant modeling can be used in a variety of anxiety provoking situations. The concept of participant modeling and its broad applications are easy for students to understand and appreciate. Students find this activity interesting, helpful, and enjoyable.

References

Bandura, A. (1977). Self-efficacy: Toward a unifying theory of behavioral change. *Psychological Review, 84,* 191-215.

Bandura, A. (1984). Recycling misconceptions of perceived self-efficacy. *Cognitive Therapy and Research, 8,* 231-255.

Bandura, A. (1986) . *Social foundations of thought and action: A social cognitive theory.* Englewood Cliffs, NJ: Prentice-Hall.

Bandura, A., Adams, N. E., & Beyer, J. (1976). Cognitive processes mediating behavioral change. *Journal of Personality and Social Psychology, 35,* 125-139.

Bandura, A., Adams, N. E., Hardy, A. B., & Howells, G. N. (1980). Tests of the generality of self-efficacy theory. *Cognitive Therapy and Research, 4,* 39-66.

Bandura, A., Blanchard, E. B., & Ritter, B. (1969). Relative efficacy of desensitization and modeling approaches for inducing behavioral, affective, and attitudinal changes. *Journal of Personality and Social Psychology, 13,* 173-199.

Bernstein, D. A., & Paul, G. L. (1971). Some comments on therapy analogue research with small animal "phobias." *Journal of Behavior Therapy and Experimental Psychiatry, 2,* 225-237.

Borkovec, T. D., & Nau, S. D. (1972). Credibility of analogue therapy rationales. *Journal of Behavior Therapy and Experimental Psychiatry, 3,* 257-260.

Geer, J. H., & Turteltaub, A. (1967). Fear reduction following observation of a model. *Journal of Personality and Social Psychol*ogy, *6,* 327-331.

Kazdin, A. E. (1974). Covert modeling, model similarity, and reduction of avoidance behavior. *Behavior Therapy, 5,* 325-340.

Meichenbaum, D. H. (1972). Examination of model characteristics in reducing avoidance behavior. *Journal of Behavior Therapy and Experimental Psychiatry, 3,* 225-227.

Morgan, J. M., & Gramann, J. H. (1989). Predicting effectiveness of wildlife education programs: A study of students' attitudes and knowledge toward snakes. *Wildlife Society Bulletin, 17,* 501 -509.

Redd, W. H., Porterfield, A. L., & Andersen, B. L. (1979). *Behavior modification: Behavioral approaches to human problems.* New York: Random House.

Ritter, B. (1969). Treatment of acrophobia with contact desensitization. *Behavior Research and Therapy, 7,* 41-45.

Note

I thank my husband, James P. Rod, who is a wildlife biologist employed by the National Audubon Society, for generously volunteering to serve as my expert model.

The Effects of Behavioral Counseling Training on Correctional Staff

Ray E. Hosford, *University of California, Santa Barbara*
Gary O. George, *Federal Penitentiary, McNeil Island*
C. Scott Moss, *Federal Correctional Institution, Lompoc, California*
Victor E. Urban, *Federal Correctional Institution, Oxford, Wisconsin*

Methods used in graduate training of Counseling Psychologists are applicable to Correctional Staff, whether presented "live" or via videotape.

Although since 1870, the *raison d'être* of the American Penal System has been to rehabilitate society's criminals (Commission on Attica, 1972), correctional institutions have served primarily as custodial rather than rehabilitative agents of society. The reason that this situation exists, according to Southerland and Cressey (1970), is that prison staffs traditionally are encouraged to be guards rather than agents of change. They are given training in methods of control but little or no training in behavioral change procedures or even in interpersonal relationship skills, which would serve to promote the motivation inmates need for learning how to live successfully in society without resorting to criminal activity. A recent statement, however, by Frank Kenton, Warden, Federal Correctional Institution. Lompoc, California, indicates some progress is being made in this area. Kenton states:

We have come to recognize what I consider a most heartening development. that our correctional officers represent one of our richest sources in the institution for therapy and rehabilitation. . . Because they are with the inmates twenty-four hours a day, they are in the prime spot to counsel individuals who are trying to establish goals for themselves and to work out programs within the institution to achieve these goals. (Kenton, 1975).

Consistent with this policy, the Federal Correctional Institution, Lompoc, implemented and evaluated a series of in-service training programs designed to help staff members acquire the knowledge and skills necessary for being primarily rehabilitative rather than custodial agents of society's incarcerated individuals.

From a social learning point of view, if prisons are to change criminal behavior, correctional staff must have a working knowledge of how such deviant behavior is acquired, maintained and modified. Further, this knowledge must be implemented by those staff members having daily contact with the inmates if these individuals are to learn how to channel their personal, social, academic and vocational skills in more positive directions than those which resulted in their incarceration. Considerable evidence exists which demonstrates that individuals with problems of societal adjustment similar to those encountered by many inmates can and have been helped through intervention programs developed from the principles of social learning theory (cf. Bandura, 1969; 1973; Hosford & Moss, 1975).

A few studies have been reported in the literature in which the effects of training correctional staff personnel in behavioral change procedures have been explored, e.g., Tyler and Brown (1967); Bednar, et al., (1970); and Phillips (1968). However, Gardner (1972) was unique in providing a detailed description of his methods in training female attendants participating in an in-service program in a mental institution. Gardner's results suggest that the lectures and role-playing were effective in training the attendants in the theory and practice of behavioral counseling.

The present study was designed to determine the effects of two types of in-service training–live and videotape instruction—on the subsequent acquisition of knowledge and counseling skills of correctional staff assigned to work with incarcerated adult offenders. The study sought to assess the efficacy of these two types of training programs for helping subjects (a) gain specific knowledge and skills pertinent to behavioral counseling, (b) increase the extent to which they use verbal and nonverbal reinforcements during interviews with inmates, (c).use correctly the specific process steps involved in the behavioral counseling process, (d) improve their overall counseling skills, and (e) reduce the frequency of overt anxiety behaviors emitted during the counseling interviews.

Experimental Design

The subjects were federal prison staff members, i.e., case managers and correctional counselors (officers selected to work as institutional counselors) who volunteered to receive training in behavioral counseling techniques. Of the 17 volunteers, nine were randomly assigned to the "live" training sessions and eight to a "videotape" group which were trained three months later using the same lectures and discussions as those given in the first training sessions but presented on videotape rather than live. A professional counselor-educator conducted the training for the live group, and a staff member who was trained in the original sessions became the trainer for the videotape sessions.

The six, one-day, training sessions utilized a behavioral counseling training package developed by Hosford and de Visser (1974)[1] The subjects were divided into triads for the purpose of practicing the specific skills discussed and demonstrated during the first part of each training session. Each triad member took turns rehearsing the role of the counselor, client, and observer. The observer rated the counselor's performance on a rating scale specifically designed to measure the extent to which a participant demonstrated competency in the particular counseling procedure of concern.

After every session, each member turned in a videotape of his counseling performance. These tapes were rated each evening by the training staff and, on the following day, each participant was given written feedback indicating the three target skills most in need of improvement.

At the completion of the sessions, subjects who received' the live training and those in the videotape group, who first served as no-treatment controls, were randomly assigned to counsel one of four inmates who had been coached to ask specific questions and to demonstrate a variety of verbal and nonverbal behaviors indicative of hostility, shyness. etc. Videotapes were made of these sessions from which each member's performance from both groups was assessed for each of the skills that the training sought to promote.

Subsequent to the termination of the first part of the study. a series of ten, one-hour videotapes were edited from video recordings made of the lectures and discussions held during the live training sessions. These tapes subsequently served as the experimental treatment for members in the videotape group who had yet to be trained in the behavioral counseling techniques. Basically, the tapes utilized those presentations of the earliest training sessions which dealt with (a) basic concepts of behavioral counseling, e.g., how behavior is learned; (b) counseling steps involved in the behavioral change process, e.g., setting of goals, establishing base rates, etc.; (c) verbal and nonverbal skills involved in a reinforcing counselor-client relationship; and (d) instruction in specific behavioral counseling techniques, e.g., assertive training, self-as-a-model, etc.

Subjects in this videotape group practiced the same behaviors in triads as did those who received the live training. As in the first group, following the termination of training, subjects in the videotape group were randomly assigned to counsel one of the four volunteer inmates who served as "clients." As before, videotapes were made of these sessions which were rated at the same time as were those of the live training session and those of the pre-treatment videotape group.

Results

The treatment effects relative for both acquisition of knowledge and for the performance of specified counseling skills were measured by independent evaluations made by two raters who viewed the evaluation session videotapes. The two judges used the same rating scales included in the Hosford-de Visser training program which were previously employed during the training process. Each judge rated all tapes and each rated independently of the other. Interrater reliability coefficients on the four scales ranged from .90 to .98 (see Table 1).

Table 1
T-ratios Between the Live and Untrained (pre-video) Groups

Scale	Trained Mean	Untrained Mean	df	T	p	$r_{j_1 j_2}$
Behavioral Counseling Steps	13.67	8.56	16	3.82	.002	.95
Frequency of Reinforcement	15.11	8.13	16	2.17	.04	.98
Frequency of Anxiety Behaviors	37.44	41.81	16	0.54	.59	.98
Overall Evaluation of Counseling	27.56	17.50	16	2.21	.04	.90
Recall Questionnaire	75.00	41.38	16	10.29	.001	n/a

Because treatment effects for five dependent variables were measured, a multivariate analysis of variance (MANOVA) was computed so that relationships among these variables could be taken into consideration when determining the extent to which the experimental treatment affected the dependent variables as a whole. Using a computer program developed by Joreskog, van Thillo and Gruvoeus (1971), a chi square, significant at the .001 level, of 38.36 with five degrees of freedom was found. Standard t-ratios were then computed to determine the extent to which the two groups differed on Fe five criterion measures.

Live vs no Training. When compared to the videotape subjects, prior to their own training, those subjects given the live training sessions (a) recalled significantly more knowledge of behavioral counseling theory and practices ($p < .001$), (b) employed correctly in their counseling sessions more of the steps specific to the behavioral counseling process ($p < .002$), (c) used more reinforcements ($p < .04$), and (d) demonstrated better overall counseling skills ($p < .04$). No significant difference between the groups was found for frequency of overt anxiety behaviors ($p < .59$). (See Table 1.)

Live vs Videotape Training. To show the effectiveness of live vs videotape training, comparisons were made of both groups' performance on the five criterion variables. Because the data for the live presentation group already had been used for the first analysis and the fact that the pretraining data for the videotape group had been used as a base to assess the live training, assumptions needed for inferential statistical conclusions could not be satisfied. Therefore, clinical

analyses only were made for the purpose of developing further hypotheses. Thus, data for these comparisons are presented only in tern s of means (see Table 2).

The data in Table 2 suggest that the two treatments were equally effective on four of the five criterion variables. Only for the number of behavioral counseling steps used did those receiving live training demonstrate a significantly better score than did those in the videotape group. Although statements of inference are not possible, the hypothesis can be made that videotaped training programs should be equally effective in promoting desired counseling skills as is that presented in five training sessions. Thus, while initially heuristic, replication of this part of the present study is needed before any conclusions can be made relative to the effectiveness of training in behavioral counseling presented vicariously by videotape.

Discussion

When compared with staff who had volunteered but had not yet been trained in behavioral counseling techniques, those receiving training demonstrated significantly better performance on four of the five criterion variables that the training sought to promote: use of behavioral counseling steps, use of reinforcement, overall counseling skills and knowledge of behavioral counseling. No differences between the two groups were found for the number of overt anxiety behaviors, e.g., fidgeting exhibited during the evaluation counseling interview. This fact is interesting in that the training was specifically designed to promote the other four outcomes; nothing in the training per se was addressed to ways in which to modify overt anxiety behaviors.

The fact that the videotaped training sessions produced similar results to those achieved by the live training is particularly encouraging. It may well be possible to help large numbers Of correctional staff improve their interpersonal relationships and counseling skills by participating in in-service training programs in which specifically prepared videotape presentations provide the main training.

Table 2
Range of Scores and Group Post Test Means for Live and Videotape Training Groups

Scale	Range of Scores Live	Range of Scores Video	Mean Live (N=9)	Mean Video (N=8)
1. No. specific Behavioral Counseling steps used.	10-19	5-17	14	11
2. Frequency of Reinforcement	7-20	5-20	15	12
3. Frequency of Overt Anxiety Behaviors	10-65	12-70	37	40
4. Overall Counseling Skills Rating	9-47	8-40	28	24
5. Correct Items on Knowledge Test	65-88	45-87	75	74

References

Bandura, A. *Principles of behavior modification,* New York: Holt, Rinehart & Winston, 1969.

Bandura, A. *Aggression: A social learning process.* Englewood Cliffs, New Jersey: Prentice Hall, 1973.

Bednar, R. L., Zelerhart, P. F., Greathouse, L., & Weinberg, S. Operant conditioning principles in the treatment of learning and behavioral problems with delinquent boys. *Journal of Counseling Psychology,* 1970, *17,* 492-497.

Commission on Attica. *The official reports of the New York special commission on Attica.* New York: Bantam Books, 1972.

Gardner, J. M. Teaching behavior modification to non-professionals, *Journal of Applied Behavior Analysis,* 1972, *5,* 517-521.

Hosford, R. E., & de Visser, L. J. M. *Behavioral counseling: an introduction.* Washington, D.C.: A.P.G.A. Press, 1974.

Hosford, R. E., & Moss, C. S. *The crumbling walls: The treatment and counseling of the adult offender.* Urbana, Ill.: University of Illinois Press, 1975.

Jorsekog, K. G., van Thillo, M., & Gruvoeus, G. T. *ACOVSM: A general computer program for analysis of covariance structures including generalized MANOVA.* Princeton, New Jersey: Educational Testing Service, 1971.

Kenton, F. F. Prisons: Rehabilitative or custodial institutions. In R. E. Hosford & C. S. Moss (Eds.), *The crumbling walls: The treatment and counseling of the adult offender.* Urbana, Ill.: University of Illinois Press, 1975.

Phillips, E. L. Achievement place: Token reinforcement procedures in a home-style rehabilitation setting for "pre-delinquent" boys. *Journal of Applied Behavioral Analysis,* 1968, *1,* 213-223.

Tyler, V. O., Jr., & Brown, G. P. The use of swift, brief isolation as a group control device for institutional delinquents. *Behavior Research and Therapy,* 1967, *5,* 1-9.

Note

Both the manual, entitled *Behavioral Approaches to Counseling: An Introduction* and the films are available from the American Personnel Guidance Press Washington, D.C.

The Critical Incident as a Source of Structured Experiences for Group Therapy Courses

Henry Kaczkowski
University of Illinois

One of the basic problems in the preparation of group counselors is that of providing an instructional program that readily provides information about group counseling as well as experience in leading groups (Berman, 1975; Mayadas & Duehn, 1982). Typically, instructors require students to participate in some type of therapeutic group and use this experience as a basis for inculcating group leadership skills (Yalom, 1975; Halgin, 1982). Although studies have shown that students who have participated in a group counseling experience increase their ability to provide the core conditions in individual counseling (Gazda & Bonney, 1966; Woody, 1971; Eiben & Clark, 1973), the influence of a group counseling experience on counselor effectiveness has not been clearly demonstrated (McKinnon, 1969; Nye, 1972; Ohlsen, 1975; Yalom, 1975). Training programs developed by Carkhuff (1969), Ivey (1971), and Eagan (1975) may increase a trainee's ability to communicate more clearly and enhance his or her self-awareness level, but these factors in and of themselves do not necessarily lead to more effective counseling (Mahon & Altman, 1977).

Studies on the use of a therapeutic group experience as a medium for the development of group leadership skills have shown mixed results, primarily because of the role confusion (i.e. client vs student) experienced by the students (Burton, 1969; Yalom, 1975). Yalom believes that the best training approach is one that incorporates observations of actual group therapy with a discussion that features a review of the process and an analysis of student feelings and attitudes. Revich and Geertsma (1969) have proposed a training model that uses a videotape of desired therapist behavior as a means of helping students to translate therapy events into theoretical concepts and to show how therapist activities influence client behavior.

The Critical Incident Technique. The purpose of this paper is to discuss an experiential model of learning that I have been using for the past five years in a graduate counseling course as a medium for helping students develop group leadership skills. According to Jones and Pfeiffer (1975), the experiential model is a "cyclical learning process" whose "emphasis is on the *direct* experiences of the participant or learner as opposed to the *vicarious* experiences garnered through didactic approaches" (p. 3). The focus of the experiential model is the inductive rather than the deductive process because the students discover the principles of group leadership through participation in structured experiences rather than watching a videotape of exemplars of ideal leader responses (Jones & Pfeiffer, 1975). The procedure uses a videotape entitled *The Critical Incidents in Growth Groups* and is based on the work of Cohen and Smith (1976). Each of the 30 scenes examines a group thematic concern rather than a common group problem. After a scene is shown, the students are asked to write an intervention to the situation on a specially designed form. In the discussion that follows, the instructor .helps the students analyze their responses in terms of therapeutic impact and influence on group development. The videotape was produced as a class project.

Based on their experiences in training group therapy leaders, Cohen and Smith saw a need for developing a teaching mode that would confront students with actual group events that required a leader response. They used the critical incident technique described by Flanagan (1954) as a procedure for gathering significant group therapy events that required a leader's intervention. They combined the data obtained from therapists with the tenets of the critical incident technique to formulate a model for presenting in a systematic manner critical group events that would help students learn the principles of therapeutic intervention. Cohen and Smith (1976) described the critical incident in the following way:

> A critical incident is defined as a confrontation of a leader by one or more members, in which an explicit or implicit opinion, decision, or action is demanded of him. It may also be an observation, confrontation among members, an event taking place, or a period of silence in which an expectation or demand is being made of the leader. The essential property of a critical incident is that it is judged important enough for a group leader to consciously and explicitly consider to act in a specific way that is assumed to have an important impact on the group. (p. 114)

A critical incident is composed of four elements: a contextual framework, specific behaviors or interactions immediately preceding the choice point, surface and underlying issues that force the intervention, and implications of the interventions. In the videotape each of the 30 scenes depicted requires an intervention because the episode is construed to represent events leading to a choice point and some kind of leader action is required.

The following is a transcript of the first scene from the videotape:

NARRATOR: This is the first group session. The group climate is a mixture of awkwardness and anxiety, members being unsure of their direction and unfamiliar with one another. While a few dependency statements have been made by particularly anxious members, there has been little response. One member who appears somewhat more aggressive has apparently decided to initiate some action. . . .

DAVE: (in a loud, authoritative tone) Well, I think we should get to know something about ourselves. You know, go around, tell something about ourselves, who we are, where we're from, that kind of thing.

MEG: Good idea. Why don't you start?

DAVE: All right, My name's David. I manage a store here in town. I've been here 5 years, originally from Chicago. I like it down here, nice town.

MEG: Uh, my name is Meg and uh, I work at the Girl's Club as a recreation leader and uh, go to school part-time and I live in Savoy.

MARTY: My name is Marty and I work with the Housing Division for the University and I work with the Champaign Park District, too. And I'm single and available and all that. . . . (Group laughs.)

JUDY: My name is Judy and | just recently moved into town. I just decided to go back to school so I'm a student now.

JOHN: My name is John and I've taught clinical chemistry for George Washington University for 4 years and have been in Champaign about 2 years.

ARNETTA: My name is Arnetta and I've lived in Champaign for seven years and I'm married and have 3 boys.

CATHY: My name is Cathy. Uh, I'm a dance instructor over at the National Academy of Dance.

The student must identify the specific and underlying issues in the episode and relate their effects to the group process and to each individual member. The conclusion is used to select an intervention that addresses one or more of the issues inherent in the event. In the above episode, the issues could be a challenge to the leader's authority, member dissatisfaction, or improper leader structuring. The class discussion that follows each scene reveals student perceptions of the issues and range of interventions. It is not the instructor's task to judge what is right or wrong, but to point out the possible ramifications of perceptions and interventions.

In constructing the critical incident videotape i assumed, as did Cohen and Smith (1976), that group development is sequential in nature and that certain issues or themes will occur at certain specific points. Although there is some disagreement as to the precise nature of group development, the one suggested by Cohen and Smith has merit for it clearly delineates relationships among membership behavior, leader intervention, and therapeutic themes. By the end of the structured exercise, students begin to understand the complexities of group therapy and start to realize that leading a group is not the same as doing individual counseling.

Instrumentation. Prior to the use of the critical incident videotape, an inventory entitled Group Leadership Function Scale (GLFS) is administered to the students. This inventory is a modification of a scale developed by Conyne (1975) and consists of 28 statements of leadership functions that were derived from the research findings of Lieberman, Yalom, and Miles (1973). The GLFS is administered again at the conclusion of the structured experience. The following is a sample of items taken from the GLFS: As the facilitator of a personal growth group, I (1) challenge the behavior of others; (8) demonstrate or model desired behavior; (17) reflect feelings of group members; (20) repeat the content of messages in different words. Each statement is rated on a 7 point scale: 1 (very little) to 7 (very much). The items are grouped into 4 sub-scales: *Emotional Stimulation, Caring, Meaning, Attribution,* and *Executive Function.*

The *Intervention Guide Sheet (IGS)* on which the students record their interventions consists of two parts. The first section is used to write out the intervention to the scene. The second section consists of a list of 28 leadership behaviors, same as in the GLFS, which the student uses to classify written interventions. The student keeps track of these interventions and notes the distribution of them across the four major leadership functions (Lieberman, Yalom, & Miles, 1973). Students also compare their pre and postscores on the GLFS and the score derived from the IGS material. This comparison helps students understand that saying one thing and doing something else is part and parcel of life.

Birashk-Schnackel (1982) has shown that under experimental conditions, the critical incident technique videotape is a useful procedure for helping counseling students acquire group counseling skills. Among her findings were: (a) An analysis of pre-post GLFS scores showed a higher rating of *Caring* responses and a lower rating of *Executive Function* responses; (b) The discussion session that followed the initial viewing of a critical incident scene affected the responses made by the students to the immediate repeat viewing of the scene. Typically, the students made greater use of meaning attribution responses; (c) The trend in the general pattern of responses in the post-GLSF scores was in the direction of the effective group counselor profile reported by Lieberman, Yalom, and Miles (1973).

Modification. In the past two years I have added an additional structured experience. Students in this experiential exercise extemporaneously enact an episode based on one of the group themes from the Cohen and Smith model. The episode has no written script, but a scenario, based on the characteristics of the theme, is set up by the class and membership roles are allocated to those who volunteer to enact the episode. The behavior in the enactment is spontaneous and reflects a participant's own feelings and beliefs as they are affected by the characteristics of the theme. This type of role playing can last up to 10 minutes, so it gives the students a greater understanding of the complexities of group interaction than a critical incident scene does. A videotape playback can be used to critique the experience.

Because this structured experience relies on the creative nature of the students, the theme, when role played by another group of students, does not produce an identical interaction pattern. The lack of replication has value because it demonstrates to the students that, although it is possible to generalize about the group process, each group experience has its own characteristics. The apparent occurrence of random transactions within the role playing further demonstrates to the students that it is important for a group leader to "feel" the ebb and flow of group interactions rather than rely on theory as to what should be happening in the group and how to respond to it.

The underlying reason for the utility of these two structured experiences is the fact that they are based on observational learning. Bandura (1977) believes that "in observational learning of difficult concepts, abstract modeling is aided by providing concrete referents in conjunction with conceptual responses" (p. 41). The two structured experiences provide students with a model of group life and an array of interventions based on it. The format permits abstract modeling to take place, for during the role playing, students "extract common attributes exemplified" in the enactment and "formulate rules" for selecting appropriate leader interventions (Bandura, 1977, p. 41). I believe that structured experiences based on a model of group therapy can be used to train students in basic group leadership skills rapidly and safely. Although I have mainly used the Cohen and Smith model, I think that other models of group therapy can be used to generate structured experiences for a course on group counseling or therapy.

Those who are interested in obtaining a copy of the videotape, GLFS, and IGS can write to me for details.

References

Bandura, A. *Social learning theory.* Englewood Cliffs, NJ: Prentice-Hall, 1977.

Berman, A. Group psychotherapy training: Issues and models. *Small Group Behavior,* 1975, *6,* 325-344.

Birashk-Schnackel, M. *Influence of a critical incident techniques workshop on perceptions* of *group leadership behaviors.* Unpublished doctoral dissertation, University of Illinois, 1982.

Burton, A. (Ed.). *Encounter.* San Francisco: Jossey-Bass, 1969.

Carkhuff, R. *Helping and human relations* (Vol. 1). New York: Holt, Rinehart, and Winston, 1969.

Cohen, A. M., & Smith, R. D. *The critical incidents in growth groups: Theory and techniques.* San Diego, CA: Associates, 1976.

Conyne, R. K. Training components for group facilitators. In J. E. Jones & J. W. Pfeiffer (Eds.), *The 1975 annual handbook for group facilitators.* San Diego, CA: University Associates, 1975 (pp. 138-139).

Eagan, G. *The skilled helper: Model for systematic helping and interpersonal relating.* Monterey, CA: Brooks/Cole, 1975.

Eiben, R., & Clark, R. J. Impact of a participating group experience on counselors in training. *Small Group Behavior,* 1973, *4,* 486-495.

Flanagan, J. C. The critical incident technique. *Psychological Bulletin,* 1954, *51,* 327-358.

Gazda, G., & Bonney, W. Group counseling experience: Reaction by counselors. *Counselor Education and Supervision,* 1966, *5,* 205-211.

Halgin, R. P. Using an experiential group to teach a group therapy course. *Teaching of Psychology,* 1982, *9,* 188-189.

Ivey, A. *Microcounseling: Innovations in interview training.* Springfield, IL: Charles C Thomas, 1971.

Jones J., & Pfeiffer, J. Introduction to the structured experience section. In J. E. Jones & J. W. Pfeiffer (Eds.) *The 1975 annual handbook for group facilita-*tors. San Diego, CA: University Associates, *1975* (pp. 3-5).

Lieberman, M. A., Yalom, I. D., & Miles, M. B. *Encounter groups: First facts,* New York: Basic Books, 1973.

Mahon, B., & Altman, H. Skill training: Cautions and recommendations. *Counselor Education and Supervision,* 1977, *17,* 42-50.

Mayadas, N., & Duehn, R. Leadership skills in treatment groups. In E. K. Marshal & P. W. Kurtz (Eds.), *Interpersonal helping skills.* San Francisco: Jossey-Bass, 1982, (pp. 314-336).

McKinnon, D. W. Group counseling with student counselors. *Counselor Education and Supervision,* 1969, *8,* 195-200.

Nye, L. S. The development and implications of two pre-practicum approaches and evaluation of their effects upon counseling performance. *Dissertation Abstracts International,* 1972, *32,* 45-57.

Ohisen, M. M. Group leader preparation. *Counselor Education and Supervision,* 1975, *14,* 215-220.

Revich, R., & Geertsma, R. Observational media and psychotherapy training. *Journal of Nervous and Mental Disorders,* 1969, *148,* 310-327.

Woody, R. H. Self-understanding seminars: The effects of group psychotherapy in counselor training. *Counselor Education and Supervision,* 1971, *10,* 112-119.

Yalom, I . D. *The theory and practice of group psychotherapy.* New York: Basic Books, 1975.

Students as Case Writers

Dennis S. Klos
Williams College

How the-author teaches interviewing skills for a class project with a single sample and a multipurpose experience.

Allport's (1942) classic statement on the uses and limitations of personal documents as data for psychological analysis continues some thirty years later as the most extensive *rationale for research* using the single case study. Dukes' (1965) review of 246 studies where $N = 1$ concludes that single case studies represent a disproportionately high number of seminal or frequently cited articles and books. Both Allport and Dukes argue for the validity and uniqueness of case studies as sources of hypotheses for the study of individual differences. The different issue of how to teach with case studies is addressed by White (1974) and by Goethals and Klos (1976) in their case book introduction. The teaching suggestions by these authors apply to already published case material.

In contrast, this article summarizes a recent experience where students were given the option, as a course project, of *gathering* personal data for an original case study of one other person. A student has the academic task of designing a study, collecting interview data, writing a case narrative, and interpreting the case material in terms of two or more theories of development. In addition, a student has an opportunity for personal growth because the project includes soliciting the interviewee's evaluation of the interview and the case narrative and includes keeping a self-reflective journal at each stage of the project.

The Goals and Procedures of Case Writing. The final product of the case writing project is a three-part paper: the descriptive case narrative, a self-conscious assessment of the interview process and consequences, and an interpretation of the case narrative in terms of developmental theory. The case narrative constitutes data that represent the subjective self-report of the interviewee. Just as in any empirical study the data are kept separate from comments on method and from interpretation of the meaning of the data. The various procedures that lead up to the final product are discussed here along with the five general goals of the project.

1. The capacity to design an idiographic study that has relevance to developmental theory. The first step in a case writing project is the student's formulation of a series of interview questions that are clear, temporally organized, and representative of some point of view. The student takes an holistic-theoretical perspective and designs questions conducive to a psychoanalytic study, an interpersonal relations analysis, a phenomenological study—or some combination of two or more theoretical approaches which later can be contrasted.

2. An increased awareness of the ethical implications of case writing. Gathering personal data by interview can be done with benefit to both persons if certain "ground rules" are followed by the student. (a) Fifty-minute interviews on three or four different occasions are adequate opportunity to gather meaningful data. Interviews longer than one hour are tiring, are too long to reconstruct later, and often lead to the interviewee's expectation of interviewer self-disclosure. Interviewer self-disclosure should be postponed until all interviews are completed. (b) The purpose of the interview and the attitude of the interviewer should be one of *understanding,* not judgment. The interviewer strives to understand the subject from his or her own subjective point of view. (c) Confidentiality is the fundamental assumption both during and after the case writing. The student should not reveal any information

about the interviewee to anyone but the instructor. The interviewee should be encouraged to disguise all names during the interview process. (d) The interviewee should be given a straightforward explanation of the interview purpose and ground rules. The interviewee should be encouraged to hold to a minimum any discussion with friends about the interview process until completed. Interviews should be conducted within a day of each other so that there is continuity and quick resolution of the formal relationship. (e) The interviewer should communicate an openness to hearing but an aversion to prying; the interviewee must take responsibility for deciding on an acceptable level of self-disclosure. (f) The interviewee should be told that a copy of the descriptive case narrative will be shown to him/her to check its accuracy. (g) After seeing the case narrative the interviewee should be encouraged to evaluate frankly the interview process and personal consequences.

3. A greater capacity to understand another person's point of view. It is undesirable for a student to tape-record the interviews. Interviewing without notes forces the interviewer to listen and keep in mind what is important. Students are surprised at how much they remember when they reconstruct the interview in writing *immediately* after meeting with the subject Each separate interview produces 2-3 pages, double spaced, of case narrative. Capturing the interviewee's point of view also is enhanced by writing the case narrative in the first-person and using the subject's own words and style. After students are told that they will be reconstructing each interview in the first-person, they can be given some interviewing tips and some in-class experience to build confidence.

Instructors probably have different ideas about how to interview. I make the following suggestions to students: Encourage the interviewee to *describe* his personal experience and not to explain it; Focus on the present and recent past so that the data are fresh, remembered, and limited; Follow up on what the interviewee initiates and interrupt with a clarifying question when you do not understand what was said or were given too much information in a short time; Keep your attention focused on the subject's point of view, especially key words, phrases, and events that illustrate the individuality of the interviewee; Focus questions around a few important events and interpersonal relationships and pursue a thorough understanding of them—rather than gather a little understanding of numerous events and relationships; solicit feelings and fantasies, not just behavior; Periodically communicate your understanding by paraphrasing or summarizing.

Any type of role playing or videotaping followed by discussion is useful preparation for the actual interviewing. Another suggestion which helps students when recruiting a subject is: Choose someone of the same sex about whom you are curious, who is neither a friend nor a total stranger, and who seems relatively "normal." Most students find it easier to concentrate on the point of view of a same-sex subject, easier to approach someone who is a slight acquaintance, and easier to interview someone without obvious difficulties in living day-to-day.

4. *An increased awareness of the interviewer-interviewee relationship and of the effect of this personalistic research on both persons.* After the case narrative is written, the student gives a copy to the interviewee and asks: Would you comment on how well the case narrative represents your point of view as revealed to me in the interviews? Would you comment on the interview process itself and say how I could improve as an interviewer? Would you comment on whether these interviews have influenced your thoughts about yourself, other people, or psychological research? These questions follow from a philosophy of research that the subject should benefit from his participation and should be consulted for his opinion on the validity and personal effect of the research.

Personalistic research usually stimulates introspection in the researcher, and this natural tendency can be capitalized on by systematically recording the self-observations in a journal. This part of the case writing project culminates in a 4-5 page report on how the subject was recruited, the nature of the rapport over the course of interviewing, the interviewee's evaluation of the narrative and interview style and effect on him/her, and the interviewer's own evaluation of the effect of the project on himself/herself.

5. *An increased understanding of developmental theory and its application to actual case data.* The third part of the written case study is an 8-10 page interpretation of the developmental significance of the case data. The data are examined from two or more perspectives presented in the assigned course readings. This is an exercise in applying course concepts and then comparing the basic assumptions and explanatory strength and weakness of each perspective. The case interpretation is *not* shown to the interviewee because the student's interpretation is necessarily judgmental, is a non-professional psychological assessment, and is an academic exercise. If the course project has a growth-enhancing effect on the interviewee, this desirable but secondary purpose results from the *interview process* or the subsequent interaction between the two persons.

Evaluation of Students' Projects. Ideally a case narrative is data-rich, interesting, clear, specific, complex rather than caricatured, natural, and personal enough to evoke feelings in the reader. A skillful interviewer can redirect a vague or desultory interview and focus on the uniqueness of a person or on what is important to that person. The narrative is evaluated on the basis of how well the student formulated questions, pursued openings, and improved with experience.

A second consideration is how much the student learned from the interviewee's evaluation and from keeping a journal. When this part of the project is done

well the student addresses subtle and important patterns in the interviewer-interviewee relationship, maintains a balance between systematic data-gathering and personal learning, and keeps in touch with feelings, fantasies, defenses, and nuances of improvement as a researcher.

The third area of evaluation is the case interpretation. A good interpretation requires a thorough understanding of concepts, an identification of key data, and an organized presentation of conclusions that are clearly explained, linked to specific data, and based on multiple indications.

Evaluation of the Teaching Method. Students in two courses at different schools were given the option of doing a case writing project. At the conclusion they were asked to complete an anonymous questionnaire which asked for ratings of progress in eight skills (Table 1) and for frank, general comments about case writing as a learning method. There were no statistical differences between groups on any skills area, and ratings varied from "some progress" to "very much progress." Areas of greatest progress were *understanding another person's point of view*, *competent application of theory*, and *personal learning or benefit.*

Table 1
Case Writers' Evaluations of Their Progress

Project Goals	Mean Score for Each Goal[a]	
	Group 1[b]	Group 2[c]
Capacity to design a case study	2.5	2.9
Awareness of the ethics of case writing	2.7	3.0
Understanding another person's point of view	3.8	3.6
Skill at interviewing	3.0	3.3
Sensitivity to the interviewer-interviewee relationship	2.8	3.0
Personal learning or benefit	3.5	3.1
Thorough knowledge of theory	3.2	3.0
Competent application of theory	3.4	3.5

a. 0 = No progress; 1 = Slight progress; 2 = Some progress; 3 = quite a lot of progress; 4 = Very much progress.
b. *n* = 16 (of 22) Harvard University students in a section of a large course on Personality Theories who chose this option for a course project.
c. *n* = 12 (of 12) Williams College students in a senior seminar on Psychology of Youth who chose this option for a course project.

From the students' point of view the case writing project fulfilled the multipurpose task of data collection, theoretical interpretation, and personal learning. Comments in response to the open-ended question were consistent with these ratings.

An evaluation of this teaching technique would be incomplete without a survey of the views of the research subjects (Table 2). At both schools a student not associated with the course conducted a study of subjects' attitudes toward their participation in psychological research. Each interviewee was approached

Table 2
Research Subjects' Evaluations of Their Participation

Outcomes From Participation	Mean Score-This Study		Mean Score-Other Studies	
	Group 1[d]	Group 2[e]	Group 2[e]	Group 3[f]
(a) Learning about psychology[a]	2.3	1.8	1.8	2.0
(b) Personal learning or benefit[a]	3.3	3.3	1.2	1.7
(c) Stress during the study[a]	1.5	1.1	1.7	1.5
(d) Attitude toward psychological research[b]	2.8	3.0	2.3	2.0
(e) Recommend participation to a friend[c]	3.2	3.0	2.0	2.1

a. 0 = none; 1 = slight; 2 = some; 3 = quite a lot; 4 = very much.
b. 0 = negative; 1 = neutral; 2 = mildly positive; 3 = moderately positive; 4 = very positive.
c. 0 = would not recommend; 1 = would not encourage or discourage; 2 = mildly enthusiastic recommendation; 3 = moderately enthusiastic recommendation; 4 = very enthusiastic recommendation.
d. n = 19 interviewees who had not participated in another study.
e. n = 9 interviewees who had participated in another study.
f. n = 10 students not in this study who had participated in other studies.

two to four weeks after the completion of interviews and was asked by a "naive" student pollster (a) to say whether that person had participated in any studies during that academic year, (b) to describe what the study was about and (c) to evaluate participation in that study on five criteria. Nineteen interviewees reported participating only in this study (Group 1), whereas the remaining nine interviewees reported participating in other studies as well (Group 2). Students who had participated in more than one other study did separate ratings for each study, and then the average rating of other studies was computed. A third group of randomly selected students who had participated in other studies *and not* this one also was surveyed (Group 3).

There were no significant differences in attitude toward this study for Groups 1 and 2; participation in other studies did not influence attitude toward this study. And there were no significant differences between any groups in amount of *learning about psychology* or *stress during the study.* However, there were significant differences on the other three outcomes of participation. Interviewees who had participated in the case study only (Group 1) reported greater *personal learning or benefit (t = 4.8, df = 27, p < .001*; two-tailed, independent samples), a more favorable *attitude toward psychological research (t = 2.9, df = 27, p < .01)*, and a more enthusiastic *recommendation of research participation to a friend (t = 3.4, df = 27, p < .002)* than did subjects who had participated only in a social psychological experiment (Group *3).* And the subjects who had participated in both the case study and at least one other study (Group 2) reported greater *personal learning or benefit (t = 18.8, df = 8, p < .001*; two-tailed, correlated samples), a more favorable attitude toward *psychological research (t = 4.0, df = 8, p < .01)*, and a more enthusiastic *recommendation of research participation to a friend (t = 4.2, df = 8, p < .01)* after having participated in the case study. The

general conclusion is that being interviewed is experienced as beneficial by the subject. None of the twenty-eight interviewees reported being upset or disappointed by the participation.

Students who opt for case writing typical My work hard and do well; Project grades tend to be higher than examination grades. The instructor does more work than is required when an unsupervised term paper is assigned. Supervision after the first interview is crucial for insuring that the ground rules are being followed and for redirecting any inadequate interviewing. Probably it is unwise to supervise more than twenty case writing projects in one course. Because of students' motivation and involvement in the project, it is necessary to make somewhat extensive comments, written or oral, on the students' final products. Explanation of the criteria for grading and the actual grades requires greater than usual effort and tact. But it all seems worth it when most projects are interesting and educational for the instructor and when a few students mention their joy from personal insight or breakthrough in relating more meaningfully with another person. The case writing project is a multipurpose experience for students, subjects, and instructors.

References

Allport, G. W. *The use of personal documents in psychological science.* New York: Social Science Research Council, 1942.

Dukes, W. F. N = 1. *Psychological Bulletin,* 1965. *64,* 74-79.

Goethals, G. W., & Klos, D. S. *Experiencing youth: First-person accounts* (2nd ed.). Boston: Little, Brown, 1976.

White, R. W. Teaching personality through life histories. *Teaching of Psychology,* 1974, *1,* 69-71.

The Use of an Experiential Exercise to Teach About Assertiveness

Mitchell M. Handelsman
and Bobbin L. Friedlander
University of Colorado at Denver

Teaching people to be more assertive—to stand up for their rights and express their feelings without undue anxiety— is becoming an increasingly popular activity. The plethora of self-help books in the area (e.g., Alberti & Emmons, 1978; Fensterheim & Baer, 1975) is paralleled by a growing theoretical and empirical literature that presents the benefits of being assertive and the effectiveness of assertiveness training (e.g., Heimberg, Montgomery, Madsen, & Heimberg, 1977; Herson, Eisler, and Miller, 1973; Rimm & Masters, 1979). However, most people do not understand the concept of assertiveness and do not usually present themselves looking for improvement in that area (Rimm & Masters, 1979). Therefore, teaching about assertiveness may be a useful thing to do, and undergraduate courses in personal adjustment and introductory psychology lend themselves well to this activity.

A traditional method of teaching about assertiveness is to lecture, giving students a wealth of valuable information regarding the components of assertiveness, the relevant research, and the potential benefits of expressing feelings and saying no to unreasonable requests. Role-play exercises are sometimes included to better illustrate the important concepts.

Will the lecture method of teaching increase the likelihood that students will view assertiveness as important in their lives? Will it stimulate them to take advantage, if necessary, of the many assertiveness training opportunities available to them? We feel the answer is "no," Lecturing, even if stimulating or provocative, leaves it to students to make the concept of assertiveness relevant. Assertiveness remains an abstract idea, and students may tend to inflate their estimate of their own skills. For example, students might say to themselves, "I would *never* allow someone to butt in front of me in a movie line; I'm *very* assertive. Who needs training for that?"

In this article we shall describe the use of a potentially more effective approach to teaching about assertiveness. This method employed an experiential exercise; Students encountered a situation that presented them with the option of behaving assertively. Assertiveness concepts were *immediately* related to personal experience, thereby increasing the likelihood

that students would internalize the information, and so learn more effectively.

The Exercise. This exercise took place during the first of three fifty-minute class periods devoted to assertiveness. The professor (the first author) came into class, sat down at his desk and proceeded to write notes on a pad for the duration of the period. The goal was to provide a situation in which students' rights to an education were being violated, confronting the students with the option to intervene in their own best interests. Up until this class (which occurred two thirds of the way through the term) the professor had started every class period with relevant introductory comments. It was expected that students would rather quickly note the departure from normal procedure and ask the professor to begin class.

This situation was created in five different sections of a personal adjustment course during one academic year. A total of over one hundred students participated. Their reactions to the situation varied, but included virtually no active intervention. Many students remained in the classroom through the entire period; talking to friends, reading, or doing other work. Some students asked questions from time to time including, "Could you put the distribution from the last test on the board?" and, "Are you feeling okay today?" The professor did what was asked of him and responded to all questions. In four of the five classes one student (after approximately twenty minutes) meekly approached the front of the class to ask if anything was "going to go on" that day. When the professor stated that he didn't know, the student asked to leave and promptly departed. With the ice broken in this way, about half of the remaining people got up and left the room. Students continued to trickle out, but approximately 30% of the class remained at the end of the fifty minutes. Several comments were heard by the professor as he proceeded down the halls; students told their friends, "You wouldn't believe what happened in class today!" Several of the comments sounded angry or frustrated, and a few students questioned the mental health of the professor.

Only *one* student from all of the five classes asked the professor to start class. After about twenty minutes she came to the front and softly said, "Would you please teach us?" In another class three students returned and voiced their displeasure after everybody else had left. They noted that their time and money had been wasted, and questioned the professor's actions. These two responses (making a direct request and expressing feelings; Lazarus, 1973) were the *only* examples of assertive behavior exhibited by students.

Processing the Exercise. Students were asked to complete a questionnaire as they entered class the following day. This questionnaire contained items which probed students' reactions to the previous day's exercise. The questionnaire served as a tool in the important task of processing the exercise.

Processing the exercise serves three major purposes. First, it gives students a chance to air their feelings about the exercise and to learn about the feelings of others. Second, students practice the skill of introspection. Students learn to look more objectively at their own feelings and behaviors so they may more accurately assess the situation. Third, processing facilitates the students' understanding of assertiveness. For many of these students, the difference between situations which present them with assertive options and those which do not is often unclear. Similarly, the difference between assertive and non-assertive behaviors needs to be better defined. During the discussion of the questionnaire contents students began to become aware of their own relationship with the concepts involved with assertiveness.

The first part of the questionnaire dealt with students' feelings during the previous day's exercise. Of the 113 students who filled out questionnaires, 36 reported feeling angry or upset. Another 25 reported being confused, and 15 identified themselves as feeling tired or sick. Nine students said they were bored and the remaining students reported no feelings at all, or simply that they felt fine. Negative feelings were discussed as potential cues for assertive action, and several types of responses to those feelings were explored.

In the course of this discussion the difference between passive and assertive behavior began to emerge. Several students protested the fact that the professor did not start teaching; they were sure they had asked him to begin. When they were told what they had said, word for word, they began to understand the difference between what they had actually said and what they had hoped to communicate. Students came to realize that questions such as, "Are you going to do anything today?" are suggestive, but not direct and assertive. One student said that she had asked the professor to start teaching merely by entering the classroom. Discussion of this statement highlighted for her the difficulty involved in the interpretation of non-verbal behavior. It was pointed out that several students were perfectly content to work on other material or socialize with members of the class, and that

their behavior communicated that they did not want class to begin . Thus, *their* being in class did *not* communicate that they wanted the professor to begin.

The next question stimulated the most interesting discussion: "What *choices* did you have in the situation you were in?" Ninety-one students listed leaving class as one alternative, and 96 people listed staying in class: working, socializing, or just sitting. Four students reported no choice in the situation. Only 14 students listed assertive behavior; i.e., intervening directly with the professor. Of these, only one student actually carried out such behavior.

The analogy was made between students' options during the exercise and the experience of watching television. When people watch television, the only options they have are to watch or not to watch, the latter accomplished by changing the channel or turning the set off. The difference between attending class and watching television was discussed; the professor's presence during class was emphasized, as was the students' ability to deal with him directly.

Aware of the professor's presence, many students feared negative consequences, such as a reduced grade or the professor's disapproval, if they had asked him to teach the class. For example, one student pointed out, "You could have flunked us if we'd asked you to teach." The general tendency of people to feel intimidated by powerful others was discussed in light of this issue. Several students indicated that they "wanted to stay out of the professor's way," noting that they did not interrupt him because they felt he might have been doing something important. In respecting the professor's ostensible wish to be left alone, however, it was pointed out that the students had lost sight of the violation of their right to secure an education in return for their tuition. The students in each class were asked how long they would wait until the lack of teaching (which is traditionally equated with lecturing) would seem to them to be a "rip-off." This question highlighted the point that assertiveness is a matter of individual judgment, in which the rights and power of others are factors to be considered. For example, one student said that she had trouble saying "no" to salespeople because "they have a right to do their job." In the ensuing discussion, it became apparent to the students that salespeople do have the right to solicit business, but consumers have rights, such as the right to privacy and the right of free choice. In a similar sense it was pointed out that the professor has the right to his privacy but not at the expense of students' learning opportunities.

Many students equated assertiveness with "telling people what you really feel" in the sense of "giving them a piece of your mind. " At this point the difference between assertive and aggressive behavior was explored in terms of a balance between the rights of the individual and the rights of others.

It must be emphasized that students were not chastised because of their passivity during the exercise. Rather, they were encouraged to reflect upon their behavior and to view the exercise as a prototype situation in which they had more options than they initially imagined. It was in no way implied that those students who remained, or left, were not acting in what they perceived to be their best interests. It was pointed out, however, that students did not appear to accurately gauge *all* available behavioral options, and that this lack of accurate evaluation may have denied them access to more adaptive behaviors.

Some students did manage to find productive things to do. For instance, they used the class period to study for upcoming tests or to catch up on required reading. The students' lack of direct intervention in the exercise was not interpreted as a generalized lack of assertiveness. Students were told that assertiveness does not appear to be a stable personality trait (Gambril & Richey, 1975; Lawrence, 1970); therefore, their lack of action during the exercise is not predictive of their behavior in other situations.

Helping students make the distinction among passive, aggressive, and assertive responses was a major purpose of the exercise. In fact, the exploration of options may be more important than the actual performance of assertive behavior. Too much emphasis on doing the "right" thing in every assertive situation leads to what Rimm and Masters (1979) have termed assertive neurosis," wherein people feel they *must* behave assertively in all situations or else there is something wrong with them.

There is a great deal of individual discrimination involved in evaluating where and when to be assertive. Ideally, students should be able to learn to recognize the types of behaviors they are exhibiting and should be able to choose freely and knowledgeably their modes of response. This exercise allows students to perceive the reality that they do have choices, even in situations in which it appears that external constraints are compelling. It also gives them practice at considering alternative possibilities. We think that giving students the opportunity to employ the concepts discussed during class to their critical evaluation of the exercise facilitated their learning those concepts better than they would have through lecture.

Issues. Having quickly gotten the point of the exercise and the subsequent discussion, one student, whose sincerity was difficult to gauge, demanded that another class be added to the term since no "teaching" took place on the day of the exercise. It was explained to him that although there was no lecture, he had the opportunity to learn a great deal. Of course, how much learning took place is an empirical question. The classes did very well on those parts of the test which covered assertiveness, but it is not known if they did better than they would have with a more traditional method of instruction.

Although a controlled study would be relatively easy to design, implementing such a study as part of a course may present problems, because of the ethical responsibility of researchers to secure informed consent from participants. Telling students they will be exposed to alternative forms of learning may sensitize them to what's ahead and dilute the effectiveness of the exercise.

A related issue is whether it is ethical to "deceive" students by coming into class and doing Nothing." The answer seems to lie in the ends-justifies-the-means argument. Is education defined by the outcome (learning) or by the procedures employed? Is a professor doing his/her job if a lecture takes place but nobody remembers anything that was said? Conversely, is it a breach of contract to do "nothing," which subsequently leads to learning? Another issue is the use of "clinical" activities in educational settings. Is it ethical, no matter how much learning takes place, to foster unpleasant feelings such as frustration and anger?

It is important to find out if the benefit derived from the exercise presented here is enough to outweigh the potential discomfort which may be aroused by being "tricked." The skill of the professor will undoubtedly be important in lessening these ill effects. If the intent is well-communicated, the likelihood of adverse consequences is reduced. It must not be communicated that (a) students are guinea pigs, (b) the professor delights in deception, or (c) the intention is to highlight the *un*assertiveness of the students.

We believe that the welfare of students needs to be protected. We also believe that *not* to facilitate learning in the most effective way possible is unethical. Feelings are an integral part of the learning process (cf. Brown, 1971; Heath, 1971; Rogers, 1969) and some discomfort may be necessary. With proper sensitivity to students' discomfort. however, this type of exercise may be a powerful method for teaching this important concept.

References

Alberti, R. E., & Emmons, M. L. *Your perfect right: A guide to assertive behavior* (3rd ed.). San Luis Obispo, CA: Impact Press, 1978.

Brown, G. I. *Human teaching for human learning: An introduction to confluent education.* New York: Viking, 1971.

Fensterheim, H. W., & Baer, J. *Don't say* yes *when you want to say no.* New York: Dell, 1975.

Gambrill, E. D, & Richey, C. A. An assertion inventory for use in assessment and research. *Behavior Therapy,* 1975, *6*, 550-561.

Heath, D. H. *Humanizing schools: New directions, new decisions.* Rochelle Park, NJ: Hayden, 1971.

Heimberg, R. C., Montgomery, D., Madsen, C. H., Jr., & Heimberg, J. S. Assertion training: A review of the literature. *Behavior Therapy,* 1977, *8*, 953-971.

Hersen, M., Eisler, R. M., & Miller, P. M. Development of assertive responses: Clinical, measurement, and research considerations. *Behaviour Research and Therapy,* 1973, *11,* 505-521.

Lawrence, P. S. *The assessment and modification of assertive behavior.* Unpublished doctoral dissertation, Arizona State University, Tempe, 1970.

Lazarus, A. A. On assertive behavior: A brief note. *Behavior Therapy,* 1973, *4,* 697-699.

Rimm, D. C., & Masters, J. C. *Behavior therapy: Techniques and empirical findings* (2nd ed.). New York: Academic Press, 1979.

Rogers, C. R. *Freedom to learn.* Columbus, OH: Charles E. Merrill, 1969.

Notes

1. This paper was presented at the meeting of the Northern Rocky Mountain Educational Research Association, Jackson, Wyoming, October 1983.
2. The comments of Pam Kesson Craig and Jo Ann Basgall on the present article are gratefully acknowledged.

Earliest Recollections and Birth Order: Two Adlerian Exercises

Les Parrott
Seattle Pacific University

Two exercises demonstrate the potential influence of two Adlerian principles—earliest recollections and birth order—on personality. In one exercise, students record and study their earliest recollection. In another exercise, students discuss their position in their family constellation. Students rated both exercises highly; undergraduates valued the birth order exercise more, but graduate students valued the earliest recollections exercise more.

Adler holds an important place in psychology. He influenced neo-Freudians like Horney and Fromm as well as more modern theorists like Rogers and Ellis (Corsini & Wedding, 1989). Adler shifted the Freudian emphasis on the libido to the ego's striving for power and developed a personality model, a theory of psychopathology, the inferiority complex concept, and the foundation of a treatment method.

For Adler, individuals respond in ways that reflect neither genetic endowment nor social environment. Rather, persons are responsible and respond to their social field in adaptive, creative ways. Adler (1959) also contended that each individual strives toward an ideal that becomes apparent early in life and runs as a major theme throughout one's lifetime.

Surprisingly, Adler's influence often goes unnoticed. Ellenberger (1970) said "it would not be easy to find another author from which so much has been borrowed from all sides without acknowledgment than Adler" (p. 645). Wilder, in his introduction to *Essays in Individual Psychology* (Adler & Deutsch, 1959) wrote, "most observations and ideas of Alfred Adler have subtly and quietly permeated modern psychological thinking to such a degree that the proper question is not whether one is Adlerian but how much of an Adlerian one is" (p. xv).

Teaching Adler's principles can be challenging because of this apparent denial of his work (Ellenberger, 1970). The task, however, is further complicated by the basic misinformation about Adler's theory in many introductory textbooks. In a study of 12 basic propositions of individual psychology in introductory psychology textbooks, Silverman and Corsini (1984) concluded that Adler's work has been marred by either neglect or distortion.

Exercises that demonstrate Adler's principles should facilitate students' learning. Polyson (1983) found that students are more active in the learning process if personality theories are made relevant to their personal interests. Many studies support the advantages of active learning opportunities that allow students hands-on and "minds-on" experiences (e.g., Benjamin, 1991; Wittrock, 1984). The National Institute of Education's 1984 report, *Involvement in Learning: Realizing the Potential of American Higher Education,* identified active learning as the top priority in American higher education today. This article describes and evaluates two such exercises.

The Earliest Recollection Exercise

As homework, which takes 15 to 30 min. students write out their earliest memory. What they believe happened is important, not whether it actually did happen. I encourage students to describe the memory in detail and to draw a picture of it. To reduce potential socially desirable outcomes, I give no other instructions. For example, a student might invent a memory that is designed for a more desirable interpretation .

Later in class, I introduce Adler's concept of early recollections. Adler (1959) considered early recollections "the most trustworthy way of exploring personality" (p. 97) because they often encapsulate a person's life theme or script (i.e., fictional goals). Freud believed the past determines the future, whereas Adler believed that the present determines the past. In other words, it makes no difference whether the early event actually happened; a belief that an event happened will influence a person's present condition. Adler (1958) wrote:

> There are no "chance memories." Out of the incalculable number of impressions which meet an individual, he chooses to remember only those which he feels, however darkly, to have a bearing on his situation . . . so that he will meet the future with an already tested style of action. (p. 73)

Thus, if people live their lives believing that others are always trying to humiliate them, the memories they are likely to recall are interpreted as humiliating experiences. I also provide several examples from my life.

Next, students process their early recollections from an Adlerian perspective to discover what the early recollections say about their personalities. Students are asked to finish three sentences: (a) Men are . . ., (b) Women are . . .. and (c) Life is .... They are to complete these sentences with only the information they have from their early recollections. I say, "If all you knew about life was what is in your early recollection, how would you complete these sentences?" I then discuss how these sentences could represent the values students introjected into their personalities and the light these sentences shed on their life themes—what Adler called *life-style.* Students are encouraged to examine the emergence of these themes in their personalities, especially during periods of personal stress. Adler (1959) saw these patterns becoming especially manifested in moments of anxiety and crisis.

Next, students consider 10 questions to examine their early recollections in light of Adler's theory: (a) Who is present in your early recollection?—mom, dad, siblings, friends, strangers; (b) Who is not present?; (c) How are different people portrayed?—basic thoughts and feelings; (d) What is the world like?—friendly, hostile, cooperative, exciting; (e) What is your role or behavior?—helping, passive, sick, dependent; (f) What is the outcome of your behavior?—success, punishment; (g) What is your primary social attitude?—I or we; (h) What is your dominant emotion?—happy, worried, fearful, guilty, proud; (i) What is your primary motive?—to help, to gain attention, to exert power; and (j) What are the underlying themes, expressed as a single sentence?—for example, I need to rescue people. Some students may share their earliest recollections with classmates as part of a general discussion focusing on how earliest recollections seem to influence personality.

The Birth Order Exercise

This 20-min exercise examines the effects of birth order on personality. I introduce Adler's concept within the broader context of family influences on personality. Adler said that the most important influence on a person is one's mother. She "provides the greatest experience of love the child will ever have" (Adler, 1964, p. 130). One's father is theorized to be the second greatest influence on personality. The third influence comes from one's family constellation or birth order. Adlerian psychologists use this third influence as a diagnostic indicator and maintain that birth order contributes greatly to the formation of one's personality and to personality differences among siblings (Adler, 1958; Ansbacher & Ansbacher, 1956; Forer, 1977).

Adler pointed to many differences between the first born and the last born, between an only child and a child with many siblings, and so on. Adler (1959) commented that the first born "must share the attention of his mother and father with a rival. [First borns] feel deeply the arrival of another child; and their sense of deprivation [molds] their whole style of life" (p. 144). Because the happiest time of life was before the birth of the new child, oldest children often "are admirers of the past and pessimistic over the future" (p. 157).

Middle born children are raised in a world in which the mother divides her attention among the siblings. Middle borns are stimulated, or perhaps provoked, to match the older child's exploits. "He behaves as if he were in a race, as if someone were a step or two in front and he had to hurry to get ahead of him. He is under full steam all the time" (Adler, 1959, p. 148).

In a large family, each succeeding child "dethrones" the previously born one, but the youngest is never removed from the "most pampered" position. "A spoiled child can never be independent. He loses courage to succeed by his own effort" (Adler, 1959, p. 151). Because youngest children have many pace-setting models, they may be driven to desire success in everything. Because universal accomplishment is unlikely, they may be driven to discouragement (also see Adler, 1937).

Before I explain the details of specific birth orders, however, students form groups with others who are in their same birth position: first borns, middle borns, and last borns. Only borns can comprise a fourth group or join the first borns. One member in each group takes notes to record the process. First, persons in the group state their feelings about being in that birth order position. Next, students discuss three questions: (a) How would you be different in another position?, (b) How would you be different if you were the other sex in your same position?, and (c) How does your position continue to affect you today?

Next, the whole class discusses their experiences. I facilitate the discussion by asking students about their feelings toward the other positions, whether they now have a better understanding of their siblings' positions, and how birth order theory might influence their future parenting. Students usually find comfort in identifying with classmates of the same birth order and share similar feelings toward siblings in other positions. They also often express a new sense of empathy for their siblings. I follow this discussion with a brief lecture on the specific characteristics of the birth order positions.

Evaluation of the Exercises

I evaluated the effectiveness of these exercises in two undergraduate introductory counseling classes and two graduate introductory counseling classes. During each course, the two exercises were completed in the same class period, which lasted approximately 2 hr. At the beginning of the next class period, students completed an anonymous evaluation of the exercises, rating them on a scale ranging from *of no value* (1) to *extremely valuable* (10). Data from 3 undergraduates and 1 graduate student were discarded because of the absence of a response. Final sample sizes were 47 undergraduates and 38 graduate students.

Tests of mean differences indicated that undergraduates ($M = 8.4$) valued the birth order exercise significantly more than graduates ($M = 7.1$), $t(83) = 2.36$, $p < .05$. In contrast, graduates ($M = 8.2$) valued the earliest recollection exercise significantly more than did undergraduates ($M = 6.8$), $t(83) = 2.50$, $p < .05$).

Conclusion

These exercises demonstrate two major concepts important in counseling courses that cover Adlerian psychotherapy. Both exercises were rated highly; however, undergraduates rated the birth order exercise as more valuable than did graduates, and graduates valued the earliest recollection exercise more. A possible explanation for this difference is that graduate students could perceive the birth order concept as less sophisticated than early recollection theory. As one graduate student put it, "Birth order is just too simplistic. . . [early recollections] carry more substance." Undergraduates may favor birth order more because it seems to provide better defined categories and the early recollection exercise seems to require a less defensive examination of one's personal history.

In either case, students rated both exercises highly. Through an informal survey at the end of the course, I noticed an increase in the number of students who evaluate Adler's theory favorably in comparison to other counseling theories. These exercises may increase students' appreciation for Adler's theory, and according to Mellor (1987), personality theories that are evaluated as interesting and relevant are significantly associated with high recall. Whether or not my students evaluate Adler's theory positively, most of them view the two exercises worthwhile for actively demonstrating Adler's principles.

References

Adler, A. (1937). Position in family constellation influences life style. *International Journal of Individual Psychology, 3*, 211-227.

Adler, A. (1958). *What life should mean to you.* New York: Capricorn.

Adler, A. (1959). *The practice and theory of individual psychology.* Totowa, NJ: Littlefield Adams.

Adler, A. (1964). *Problems of neurosis.* New York: Harper & Row.

Adler, A., & Deutsch, D. (1959). *Essays in individual psychology.* New York: Grove.

Ansbacher, H. L., & Ansbacher, R. (Eds.). (1956). *The individual psychology of Alfred Adler.* New York: Basic Books.

Benjamin, L. T., Jr. (1991). Personalization and active learning in the large introductory psychology class. *Teaching of Psychology, 18*, 68-74.

Corsini, R. J., & Wedding, D. (1989). *Current psychotherapies* (4th ed.). Itasca, IL: Peacock.

Ellenberger, H. (1970). *The discovery of the unconscious: The history and evolution of dynamic psychiatry.* New York: Basic Books.

Forer, L. (1977). Bibliography of birth order literature in the '70s. *Journal of Individual Psychology, 33*, 122-141.

Mellor, S. (1987). Evaluation and perceived recall of personality theories by undergraduate students. *Perceptual and Motor Skills, 65*, 879-883.

National Institute of Education. (1984). *Involvement in learning: Realizing the potential of American higher education.* Washington, DC: U.S. Department of Education.

Polyson, J. A. (1983). Student essays about TV characters: A tool for understanding personality theories. *Teaching of Psychology, 10*, 103-105.

Silverman, N. N., & Corsini, R. J. (1984). Is it true what they say about Adler's individual psychology? *Teaching of Psychology, 11*, 188-189.

Wittrock, M. C. (1984). Learning as a generative process. *Educational Psychologist, 11*, 87-95.

Undergraduate Seminars: The Poster Session Solution

Douglas L. Chute
and Barry Bank
University of Toronto

We are still basking in the glow of that all too rare feeling of absolute success following a little pedagogical exercise. The poster-session really seems to be a good alternative to the undergraduate seminar.

The course happened to be in clinical psychopharmacology with an advanced undergraduate enrollment of about 30 students mostly majoring in Psychology or Neuroscience, but the technique would likely apply to any reasonably empirical area.

Quite frankly, our little project wasn't so much the product of striving for teaching excellence, but a fortuitous compromise caused by limitations of time. We just couldn't spend half of the course listening to nervous undergraduates awkwardly drone on in the usual seminar fashion. That's not to say, however, that we didn't believe students should master self-expression, an academic content area, and the techniques of formal scientific communication. Our simple idea was that a poster session, a now quite common medium of scientific communication, could satisfy our goals and save a little time (and tedium). During the course students had had to prepare a major review paper and it was suggested to them that their poster could present some aspect of this work with which they were already familiar. A few of our old "professional" posters from conventions gone by were put up as models. The format generally followed that of the APA divisions and the Society for Neuroscience (including a title, author, abstract, a few graphs or illustrations from the literature, conclusions and references).

The actual presentation session was in the evening and we allowed one half hour for each third of the class to be rotated as presenting authors and audience. We provided coffee and doughnuts with the idea of simulating a bit of "ersatz" convention environment. Our first surprise, however, was that students weren't role playing but seriously engaged in communicating their area of expertise to a most attentive audience. Every student had understood the requirement, and their posters were all sophisticated, appropriate and professional, many extraordinarily so. Being in fact somewhat general in content, we found we enjoyed ourselves more than is often the case at esoteric convention presentations.

The photograph illustrates the physical location of

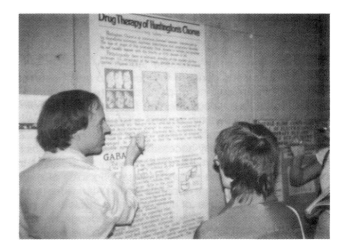

Figure 1. The Poster Session.

our session, a main hallway. This somewhat accidental arrangement had the advantage of making the session public. A number of our colleagues happened by with the fortunate result that for the first time some of them have discovered the nature of the content of this particular course that is required in the curriculum.

A factor that may have facilitated the animation and enthusiasm during the session was the comparative freedom from the spectre of evaluation. Students were told that only their posters, which were collected later, would be graded and not their actual presentation. However, it was understood that information from the poster sessions could appear on the essay style final examination.

We surveyed students during and after the session and comments were universally laudatory. Some students actually modified the scale to record a "6" (when 5 was the top provided). Not only did students feel they learned a great deal (mostly from preparation and presentation), but the sessions provided a social interaction. Presenters wore name tags and enjoyed the opportunity to "really meet" fellow students, a problem at an urban campus like ours. (We suspect, sadly, that the outrageously positive feedback we got may have been dependent, to some small extent, on this social factor).

The measure of success that we liked came from the final examination. The question asked was to summarize the content of a poster presentation (other than your own). In an examination where there was a good deal of choice this question was chosen by more than half the students. Trying of course to avoid bias in our grading, the average performance on this question was higher than on the remainder of the exam. We considered doing a Wilcoxin or something to "prove" this point but our enthusiasm is such that it would be a mistake to suggest our evaluation is objectively rigorous.

Skeptics might say we simply have a Hawthorne effect here. This may be true. We can draw no conclusion as to the cause, but we can assure the educator that the effect is most thoroughly satisfying.

SECTION IV:
SOCIAL

Focusing on Experimentation

Daniel Wann asked groups of students in an undergraduate social psychology class to select two interesting experiments and develop a dramatic script to describe the research. Students located the props necessary to implement the experiment and performed the play for the class. Students enjoyed the exercise and believed it enhanced their learning and interest in psychological research.

Neil Lutsky devised a research paradigm for use in undergraduate laboratory experiments in social psychology. Students compared the responses of control subjects on a survey question to those of experimental subjects who had been exposed to contrived responses of another person to the same question. This methodology allowed the students to extend the scope of their studies to topics such as social comparison, impression management and self-persuasion.

To demonstrate the social desirability bias in survey research, Randall Gordon administered a questionnaire to students to assess their oral hygiene practices. The method used to reduce subjects' response bias involved a manipulation of the questionnaire's instructions. Both instructions asked subjects to respond but not to sign their names. The modified instructions also contained information such as the assurance of anonymity, the need for accurate information, and the role of the subject as a contributor of valuable information. The results of the two forms of questionnaires differed as a function of instructions.

Illustrating Concepts in Social Perception and Social Cognition

Mark Costanzo and Dane Archer used The Interpersonal Perception Task, consisting of a videotape of 30 brief scenes, to illustrate the complexity of verbal and nonverbal cues. Viewers answered questions about the people in the videos by decoding the verbal and nonverbal cues in the scenes. Using this technique, the instructors highlighted the subtlety and complexity of communication cues, taught about specific cues to accuracy, demonstrate the relative importance of communication channels, and helped students understand the process of interpretation.

Joy Berrenberg demonstrated several impression formation principles by asking students to bring photographs of an acquaintance to class, having other students relate their first impressions of the persons in the photos, and assessing the accuracy of those impressions. The exercise gave students an opportunity to examine their own impression-formation processes. This activity can illustrate other processes such as the origins of implicit personality theories, person prototypes, and the accuracy of first impressions.

Mary Kite outlined three activities that demonstrated common perceptual errors described in the social psychological literature; the actor-observer effect, the false consensus bias, and priming effects. These activities produced reliable and robust results and demonstrated how cognitive shortcuts can result in inaccurate judgments.

Robin Lashley asked her students to complete a simple personality inventory about their instructor. The student responses served as discussion points that illustrated several social psychological concepts such as stereotypes, impression formation, actor-observer bias, and implicit personality theory.

Art Lyons varied his physical appearance on the first day of class in two different courses and asked students to rate him on several polar adjectives. He wore different clothing to alter his appearance (e.g., jacket and tie versus no jacket or tie). During the next class period he presented the results of the evaluations that showed strong differences in students' perceptions based on clothing. These differences helped the instructor introduce many social psychological concepts later in the course.

Dana Dunn asked students in a social psychology class to write down their strengths and weaknesses. The exercise generated a self-serving attributional bias, that is, students' selfdescriptions revealed a bias toward reporting positive attributes. The instructor used this bias to guide a discussion about motivational and cognitive processes in attribution.

Donelson Forsyth and Katherine Wibberly developed an effective demonstration of the self-reference effect, which occurs when individuals show superior memory for information that pertains to their self-schemas. Students evaluated whether or not each adjective in an orally presented list was self-descriptive. After a delay, they attempted to recall all the adjectives from the list. Memory for self-referent terms was superior to memory for terms that were not self-referent. The authors suggested that the exercise offered an effective demonstration of schematic processing under normal classroom conditions and confirmed predictions derived from depth-of-processing and schema-based memory models of social cognition.

Francis McAndrew asked students to grade exam papers of fictitious students. The patterns of responses on the "exams" reflected either an ascending or descending level of performance. Students expressed a significant primacy effect in the way they evaluated the intelligence and performance of the test taker. The exercise facilitated discussion of key issues related to experimental design and attribution theory.

Michael White and Debra Lilly presented Kelley's (1973) covariation attribution model by showing students videotaped behavior rather than the more traditional written descriptions. The videotape contained sets of sequentially presented behavioral situations that led students to analyze behavior using Kelley's model. Students easily made the appropriate attributions and applied them to everyday situations.

Teaching about Attitudes and Persuasion

David Carkenord and Joseph Bullington induced cognitive dissonance in students by pointing out inconsistencies between their behaviors and attitudes. The procedure assessed students attitudes on four issues (e.g., world hunger) after which they publicly proclaimed their adherence to the expressed attitudes. Students believed the experience enhanced their understanding of cognitive dissonance and provided self-insight.

Randall Gordon developed a demonstration to introduce the concept of stereotypes and their measurement. The demonstration relied on a diagnostic ratio measure of stereotypes developed in previous research. The author outlined the results of the demonstration along with suggestions for discussing several stereotype formation concepts.

In several classes, Melinda Jones projected slides of advertisements from current magazines and from magazines published in the 1950s. The classes analyzed the gender bias in the advertisements based on criteria from previous research. The advertisements showed significant gender stereotyping. This exercise is suitable for a variety of classes in addition to social psychology (e.g., psychology of women, introductory, or consumer psychology).

To help students identify major persuasion techniques employed in advertisements, Vivian Makosky used several activities that required students to locate and analyze prototypical examples. Students collected the advertisements according to four different variations developed by the author.

D. W. Rajecki asked students to rate the desirability of a snack that was progressively contaminated by contact with human residues (the instructor's coffee cup and a comb). Repeated measurements showed progressive contamination. The students' ratings revealed quick and statistically reliable shifts from accepting (liking) to rejecting (disliking) the snack. The author listed several courses that could benefit from this demonstration including research methods, learning and motivation.

Teaching about Aggression

To introduce the concept of aggression, Ludy Benjamin gave descriptions of several incidents (e.g., a spider eats a fly or a girl kicks a wastebasket) to students and asked them to determine if the incidents constituted aggression. The activity generated discussion about the definition of aggression and related issues of causation and control. It also provided a context for discussion about disagreements among psychologists on the operationalization of variables.

William Davidson gave his social psychology students a list of 12 aggression instigators and asked them to find scenes of violence in movies that illustrated the effects of these instigators. Students attempted to find a scene that included the maximum number of instigators. The student who found the scene with the most instigators received bonus points on the exam that covered aggression.

Dana Dunn's students read the 1932 "Why War?" correspondence between Albert Einstein and Sigmund Freud and composed letters responding to the letter. This assignment allowed students to explore several perspectives on the origins and functions of human aggression. The author described additional variations for the exercise.

David Rainey devised a simple method to demonstrate a gender difference in the acceptance of aggressive behavior during sport competition. Students read descriptions of behaviors from six sport competition situations and judged those behaviors as acceptable or unacceptable. Men endorsed significantly more aggressive acts than did women. The author examined several significant issues to guide classroom discussion.

Teaching Group Processes

George Goethals and Amy Demorest described an activity that reliably yielded risky shift responses from students in their social psychology classes. Students responded to items on the Choice Dilemma Questionnaire individually and in groups. Almost two-thirds of the group decisions represented shifts toward risk. The authors discussed ways to use the activity to promote understanding of the mechanisms underlying risky shifts.

Janet Larsen used two classroom demonstrations based on the prisoner's dilemma to illustrate elements of decision making. The demonstrations required minimal preparation and allowed the entire class to participate. In one demonstration, students asked for $1.00 or 10¢, with the proviso that, if more than 20% of the class asked for $1.00, no one got anything. The second demonstration involved students in an iterated prisoners dilemma game. The scores earned by students reflected their strategies to behave either cooperatively or competitively.

Blaine Peden and his colleagues gave students direct experience with the tensions that exist between outcomes based on individual versus collective decision-making. Based upon two different protocols, students chose to receive bonus points on their exams. One protocol required them to choose between one sure point or the possibility of a randomly determined zero to eight points; the second protocol required students to make a choice that was linked to the choices made by the entire class. The experience helped students learn more about psychology and scientific values; it also provided personal insight into their own decision-making strategies.

George Banziger developed a symposium on Middle East relations in which students played the roles of Israelis, Palestinians, and U.S. negotiators. After a lecture on the social psychology of international relations and problem-solving, students spent the next two class periods negotiating settlements to their conflicts. The author presented several suggestions for improving the activity.

Marianne Miserandino devised a classroom activity in which students surveyed peers' attitudes toward a target behavior and variations of it. Responses for each question were compiled and graphed. Results illustrated the group's approval and disapproval of the target behavior, the strength of the approval or disapproval, the ideal behavior, and the range of tolerable behavior. The activity increased students' understanding and appreciation of survey research and the power of a peer-group norm.

Teaching about Spatial Behavior

In an attempt to demonstrate the effects of crowding on the affective responses of students, George Banziger assessed students responses to the physical environment of the classroom under different crowding conditions. The activity showed that students' emotional reactions differed significantly in crowed versus uncrowded conditions.

Students in F. Richard Ferraro's introductory psychology class designed and implemented simple field experiments to test hypotheses about personal space violations. The exercise culminated in classroom presentations of the results and submission of APA style manuscripts describing the experimental procedures. Students believed the exercise was more valuable than lectures on the same topics.

In a demonstration of the regulatory nature of personal space, Bryan Gibson and his colleagues asked students to note the behavior of a partner who was asked to relate a personally intimate experience (e.g., describe your first kiss or most embarrassing moment). Although participants were not required to follow through on the instructions to relate the personal event, they displayed many behaviors that character-

ized attempts to regulate intimacy with their partner (e.g., lack of eye contact, and turning or moving away from the partner). The demonstration allowed students to see that personal space is one of several interacting nonverbal cues people use to regulate intimacy.

Instigating Miscellaneous Techniques

David Dodd deindividuated students by asking them to list the things they would do if assured that they would not be caught or held responsible for their actions. The majority of the responses fell into antisocial and nonnormative categories. The activity helped students understand the concept of deindividuation in a personally relevant manner. An interesting sidelight to this article was that the author found no response differences between prison and campus classes.

James Grosch and John Sparrow demonstrated lie detection, a topic that most students find fascinating, using an inexpensive, highly portable galvanic skin response monitor. The demonstration, which took only 10 min per subject, stimulated discussion about various methods used to detect deception. The authors concluded that students in a wide variety of courses such as perception, physiological, and industrial/organizational psychology could benefit from this exercise.

Don Osborn used the utopian novel *Erewhon* to illustrate a variety of social psychological concepts and to enhance the liberal arts value of his social psychology course. The novel afforded numerous examples of social psychological concepts such as attribution theory, interpersonal attraction, and the motivation for consistency between actions and attitudes. The author gave several helpful tips to instructors who might wish to adopt a similar strategy.

Jeffry Simpson developed a way to demonstrate the interaction between personality dispositions and a significant social behavior. Students completed and scored a self-monitoring scale and a dating survey. The instructor provided instructions for classifying the students (e.g., high vs. low self-monitors and exclusive vs. multiple daters). This results revealed that self-monitoring orientation was meaningfully related to commitment in dating relationships. Specifically, high self-monitors tended to adopt an uncommitted orientation to dating relationships, whereas low self-monitors tended to adopt a committed one.

Sara Snodgrass described several ways she facilitated students' writing in an introductory social psychology course. Students kept a journal, wrote analyses of published articles, implemented an observational study, and wrote a formal research report. The techniques described in this article can be applied to any course in psychology.

1. FOCUSING ON EXPERIMENTATION

Performing Experiments in Undergraduate Social Psychology Classes

Daniel L. Wann
Murray State University

Students in an undergraduate social psychology class selected two interesting experiments and developed a dramatic script to describe the research. Students located the necessary props and performed the play for the class. Student evaluations indicated that the exercise was informative and enjoyable.

Research has consistently demonstrated that learning is substantially facilitated by techniques that actively involve the students (Older, 1979). For example, Kixmiller, Wann, Grover, and Davis (1988) asked students to learn the details of a journal article in one of three ways. Some students simply read the article and studied its contents, others made a presentation about the article from a third-person point of view, and the rest made a presentation from a first-person viewpoint (i.e., students presented the article as if they were the experimenter). A later recognition test revealed that subjects in the first-person condition performed better than those in the third-person condition, who performed better than subjects who learned the material in a traditional manner.

Similar methods designed to increase student involvement have been popular in psychology courses. For example, students can play the roles of patients, volunteers, hospital staff, and therapists to simulate a mental hospital or clinical experience (Batch, 1983; Schofield & Klein, 1975). Toner (1978) asked students in an adolescent psychology class to write plays dealing with issues discussed in their textbook, and students in introductory psychology have role-played the various parts of a neuron (Hamilton & Knox, 1985). This article describes a role-playing technique that I used in a junior-level social psychology class. Comprehension of research and its methodology is vital to understanding social psychology. To facilitate such understanding, I required students to develop and perform dramatic plays covering research articles on social psychological phenomena.

Method

Undergraduate students (*N* = 25) in a junior-level social psychology class participated in this project. On the first day of class, students were informed that they would be required to perform two different psychological experiments. They were responsible for (a) acquiring a copy of the article, (b) using the article to write a script, and (c) developing the props necessary to perform the play. Instructions stressed accuracy and attention to detail, as these factors would weigh heavily in my grading of the exercise. For example, if the article stated that subjects were tested while facing a mirror, then students acting as subjects were to complete the materials in a similar setting. However, because research articles are not always explicit in describing the behaviors of experimenters and subjects, some poetic license was allowed. Students could ignore the gender of the participants and experimenters, unless it was vital to understanding the play (although it may be wise to inform students that gender can have dramatic effects that researchers are often unable to predict). Students would play the roles of experimenters, confederates, and subjects, and the plays were to be approximately 10 min long.

Students formed five groups of four to six individuals, and each group was given a reference list of 12 social psychological experiments. The list included classic studies, such as Milgram's (1963) research on obedience. I briefly described the focus and results of each experiment and indicated when each play would be performed. The groups then were allowed to discuss the research. Each group selected two experiments with the restrictions that its two plays could not be performed on the same day and that two groups could not select the same experiment.

At the end of the semester, students were asked to evaluate the exercise. The evaluation form contained items designed to assess students' impressions concerning the construction and performance of their own plays and their reactions to watching the performances of the other groups.

Results

Students' responses to the items assessing their reactions to performing the plays made it readily apparent that this exercise was informative and enjoyable. Eighty-eight percent of the students stated that the exercise was highly enjoyable, and 100% stated that the exercise should be used in other courses. In addition, 92% of the students perceived the exercise as an effective learning tool, and 88% said that it greatly increased their understanding of and interest in psychological research. Responses to items assessing students' attitudes toward viewing the plays also indicated the effectiveness of this technique. All students stated that they enjoyed watching the other plays, and 92% thought that viewing the plays greatly facilitated their understanding of and interest in the research. Finally, 96% reported that watching the other plays gave them a greater understanding of the various methodologies used in social psychological research.

Discussion

The evaluations suggest that this exercise was an interesting, enjoyable, and effective teaching technique. In fact, several students have asked other faculty members to use this exercise in other classes. This project can be altered to fit a wide variety of psychology courses. For example, plays dealing with experiments in animal learning (e.g., operant research or latent learning) could easily be written. Other courses that could effectively incorporate this exercise include developmental (e.g., attachment research) and cognitive psychology (e.g., memory research on eyewitness testimony).

Finally, instructors may wish to videotape the performances. Those that are especially effective in demonstrating the research could be shown to lower division courses, such as introductory psychology. Describing complicated research in a lecture is often difficult. Viewing a simulation of the research would probably increase understanding of and interest in psychological research.

References

Balch, W. R. (1983). The use of role-playing in a classroom demonstration of client-centered therapy. *Teaching of Psychology, 10,* 173-174.

Hamilton, S. B., & Knox, T. A. (1985). The colossal neuron: Acting out physiological psychology. *Teaching of Psychology, 12,* 153-156.

Kixmiller, J. S., Wann, D. L., Grover, C. A., & Davis, S. F. (1988). Effect of elaboration levels on content comprehension. *Bulletin of the Psychonomic Society, 26,* 32-33.

Milgram, S. (1963). Behavioral study of obedience. *Journal of Abnormal and Social Psychology, 67,* 371-378.

Older, J. (1979). Improving the introductory psychology course. *Teaching of Psychology, 6,* 75-77.

Schofield, L. J., Jr., & Klein, M. J. (1975). Simulation of the mental hospital experience. *Teaching of Psychology, 2,* 132-134.

Toner, I. J. (1978). A "dramatic" approach to the teaching of adolescent psychology. *Teaching of Psychology, 5,* 218-219.

Notes

1. Preparation of this article was supported by a Murray State University College of Humanistic Studies Innovative Approaches to Teaching Grant.
2. I thank Michael A. Hamlet for his assistance on this project and three anonymous reviewers for their insightful comments on an earlier draft of this article

A Scheme and Variations for Studies of Social Influence in an Experimental Social Psychology Laboratory

Neil Lutsky
Carleton College

This article describes a research paradigm for use in undergraduate laboratory experiments on social influence. The method is adapted from White (1975), who compared the responses of control subjects on a survey question to those of experimental subjects who were first exposed to the contrived responses of others to the same question. I review how students in an undergraduate social psychology laboratory use this method, demonstrate the reliability of the influence ef-

fect obtained, and discuss the educational value of this research paradigm.

How may undergraduates learn more about the significance and complexities of social influence? One means is to have students design and complete experimental studies based on a method that reliably demonstrates social influence. In this article, I review such a research paradigm for student experiments on social influence in a social psychology laboratory course.

The General Design of the Laboratory

The laboratory introduces the literatures, findings, logic, and methods of experimental social psychology by actively involving students in the planning, execution, and evaluation of research. The laboratory's approach is similar to Chamberlain's (1988). For each of four topics addressed (social influence, person perception, cognitive dissonance, and helping behavior), students discuss an assigned target article, identify factors that may have affected the research outcome reported in the article, generate possible explanations for the results, and consider how issues and ideas they have raised could be explored in research using a method similar to that presented in the target article. I guide this discussion and comment on why particular designs may be more or less tractable and meet or fail to meet the ethical standards that govern research at the college, but I allow the group rather free rein to settle on an issue of common interest and to design a related experiment.

During the remainder of the 3-hr laboratory session, the students draft the materials and specify the procedures for the study. I have obtained the prior approval of Carleton's Biosafety and Research Ethics Committee for the general study and ensure that the specific adaptation of the method falls within the bounds of what has been approved. After class, I prepare final instructions and research materials, which the students pick up and use to complete their data collection before a specified laboratory meeting. At that meeting, we analyze the project data and discuss results. Each student later submits a short research paper in APA format or poster for each project, and these are graded individually.

A Survey Paradigm for Experiments on Social Influence

The target article assigned for the laboratory on social influence is White (1975). White reported a series of field experiments on the effect of varying magnitudes of discrepancy between others' opinions and the subjects' likely private ones on subjects' public responses. He compared the uncontaminated survey responses of control subjects to the replies of experimental subjects responding to a survey question (e.g.,

"How many hours per week do you think you would be willing to donate to tutoring?") after others had apparently given their opinions. White designed the others' responses to differ from the subjects' presumed opinions in particular ways of interest (e.g., he varied the means and variabilities of the set of influence judgments) and documented substantial effects on stated opinions in all of the influence conditions he created.

Social psychologists have long used methods similar to White's (1975) to demonstrate social influence (e.g., Moore, 1921). All substitute what King and Ziegler (1975) called a "paper-stooge" for confederates in social influence research (e.g., Asch, 1955). (King & Ziegler actually proposed a paper-stooge version of the classic Asch experiment for laboratory courses.) The paper-stooge paradigm that White developed offers a particularly accessible and adaptable foundation for undergraduate work.

Using White's (1975) method, my class created two forms of a survey sheet containing identical instructions and 20 response lines. The instructions posed the following survey question: "How much should you be expected to spend on all of your textbooks for three courses during an average term at Carleton?" On half of the survey forms, all 20 response lines were blank; on the other half, 8 of the lines were filled in with handwritten names and with answers selected to be deviant from local norms (as previously determined in the laboratory). Members of the laboratory course each recruited a set number of potential respondents in the field and randomly assigned them to the experimental (social influence) or control survey conditions.

The results of two studies demonstrate that the paradigm produces robust influence effects. In one, 16 subjects exposed to paper-stooge textbook expense figures averaging $180.00 gave a mean response of $145.94. This differed significantly from the control (i.e., uninfluenced) mean response of $99.69, $t(30) = 3.59$, $p < .01$. In a second study, when 16 respondents were exposed to bogus responses averaging $80.00, their average response was $82.20. This differed significantly from the control result of $105.00 for this project, $t(54) = 3.01$, $p < .01$. Thus, socially influenced judgments obtained using these methods varied from uninfluenced ones in a high or low direction as a function of the locus of a social anchor.

Variations on a Scheme: Student Uses of the Social Influence Paradigm

My students have readily adapted White's (1975) basic paradigm to explore a variety of issues. A brief review of some examples illustrates the breadth of purposes that the basic paradigm can serve.

Several groups have explored the significance of the survey question, doubting that social influence would extend to more important matters. One group learned that the Financial Aid Office at the college was interested in student opinions on textbook expenses, which figured into students' financial aid packages. The class informed respondents that their opinions would be shared with the Financial Aid Office; opinions of subjects in the control group were shared with that office. Even with this indication of the importance of survey responses, respondents showed substantial social influence effects.

Another laboratory group developed a question with moral meaning. Their survey included a background statement providing arguments for and against euthanasia and asked respondents to indicate what chance of recovery, from 0% to 100%, they would recommend that a hypothetical patient's life support systems be discontinued. Social influence using an anchor mean of 50% resulted in a significantly looser recovery criterion of 35.9% compared to the mean uninfluenced response of 20.1%.

One laboratory section investigated the classic idea that influence is attenuated when the judgment to be given is more objectively grounded (Festinger, 1954). This class compared responses to the textbook expense opinion question to a factual version of that question: "How much did you spend on all of your textbooks for your three courses this term at Carleton?" The class documented massive social influence on the opinion question but no social influence on the factual one.

Students have read the posters prepared from previous social influence projects and have often built new designs on the findings and ideas of their peers. Some groups have explored possible accounts for influence effects, including the role of conformity pressure (Asch, 1955), social comparison (Festinger, 1954), self-persuasion (Petty & Cacioppo, 1981), peripheral persuasion (Petty & Cacioppo, 1981), impression management (Goffman, 1955), and project methodology. One class asked whether social influence was due to the social character of the frame of reference or to the cognitive anchor provided by the paper-stooges' responses (e.g., Tversky & Kahneman, 1974). To answer this, the class devised a cognitive anchor condition in which respondents indicated whether they should be expected to spend more or less than $180.00 on texts and then to specify how much more or less than $180.00 they should be expected to spend. Other subjects were exposed to a social anchor condition in which $180.00 equaled the paper-stooge mean. Although the mean response in the cognitive anchor condition was significantly different from the uninfluenced responses, the social anchor produced stronger effects.

Evaluation and Discussion

Student course evaluations indicate high satisfaction with the social influence laboratory. Students rated the value and interest of the four projects conducted in the laboratory using a scale ranging from *not at all* (1)

to *extremely* (7), and the rating of the social influence project ($M = 6.0$, $SD = .69$) exceeded that for the other three laboratories, which were also rated positively.

I believe students are impressed with the effects they reliably obtain with the social influence paradigm and with their own ability to develop and execute an informative experiment. The laboratory on social influence demonstrates how human behavior may be altered by the actions of others, a phenomenon of keen interest to students and of central import to the discipline (e.g., Allport, 1985; Paicheler, 1988; Turner, 1991). Moreover, White's (1975) paradigm for the study of social influence is one that students can easily understand and use. In addition, my students generally have little difficulty with the simple statistical analyses (usually t or F tests) the project requires. These potential challenges are of special concern to the many students in my laboratory who have not taken data analysis and methodology courses.

A primary virtue of White's (1975) paradigm is that it is so open to diverse applications. A student laboratory group could examine individual differences in influenceability (e.g., Rhodes & Wood, 1992) by assessing subject variables in the scheme presented. Another group could vary the subjects' perceived similarity to the members of the paperstooge reference group (e.g., Festinger, 1954). Other groups could construct appropriate paper-stooge manipulations to study magnitude of discrepancy effects (White, 1975) or the role of a dissenter on a group's social influence (e.g., Asch, 1955; Milgram, 1974). The paradigm is a rich and productive way to involve students as active and thoughtful researchers in social psychology. I highly recommend it.

References

Allport, G. W. (1985). The historical background of social psychology. In G. Lindzey & E. Aronson (Eds.), *The handbook of social psychology: Vol. 1. Theory and method* (pp. 1-46). New York: Random House.

Asch, S. E. (1955). Opinions and social pressure. *Scientific American, 193*, 31-35.

Chamberlain, K. (1988). Devising relevant and topical undergraduate laboratory projects: The core article approach. *Teaching of Psychology, 15*, 207-208.

Festinger, L. (1954). A theory of social comparison processes. *Human Relations, 7,* 117- 140.

Goffman, E. (1955). On face-work: An analysis of ritual elements in social interaction. *Psychiatry, 18*, 213-231.

King, M., & Ziegler, M. (1975). *Research projects in social psychology.* Monterey, CA: Brooks/Cole.

Milgram, S. (1974). *Obedience to authority: An experimental view.* New York: Harper & Row.

Moore, H. T. (1921). The comparative influence of majority and expert opinion. *American Journal of Psychology, 32,* 16-20.

Paicheler, G. (1988). *The psychology of social influence.* Cambridge, England: Cambridge University Press.

Petty, R. E., & Cacioppo, J. T. (1981). *Attitudes and persuasion: Classic and contemporary approaches.* Dubuque, IA: Brown.

Rhodes, N., & Wood, W. (1992). Self-esteem and intelligence affect influenceability: The mediating role of message reception. *Psychological Bulletin, 111,* 156-171.

Tversky, A., & Kahneman, D. (1974). Judgment under uncertainty: Heuristics and biases. *Science, 185,* 1124-1131.

Turner, J. C. (1991). *Social influence.* Pacific Grove, CA: Brooks/Cole.

White, G. M. (1975). Contextual determinants of opinion judgments. *Journal of Personality and Social Psychology, 32,* 1047-1054.

Notes

1. An earlier version of this article was presented at the annual meeting of the American Psychological Association, Washington, DC, August 1992.
2. I thank Ruth Ault for her perspicacious editorial assistance.

Social Desirability Bias: A Demonstration and Technique for Its Reduction

Randall A. Gordon
Western Carolina University

A demonstration of social desirability bias in survey research suitable for moderate to large class sizes is described. The method used to reduce subjects' response bias involved a manipulation of instructions on a questionnaire. The standard instruction format requested subjects to respond to three questions on dental hygiene behavior and not to sign their names on the questionnaires. The modified instructions included additional information regarding the anonymity of the subjects' responses, the need for accurate information, and the role of the subject as a contributor of valuable information. The results from the demonstration are reported and topics for classroom discussion are suggested.

The problems of overreporting socially desirable behaviors and underreporting socially undesirable behaviors have received wide attention in surveys of research literature (Cahalan, 1968; Hyman, 1944; Parry & Crossley, 1950). Many techniques have been developed to reduce this type of response bias on questionnaires, most of which involve modifying the manner in which the questions are asked (Sudman & Bradburn, 1982). Some techniques have involved reducing the degree to which the question is viewed as threatening by the respondent. For example, the overstatement of socially desirable behavior has been reduced by beginning a question with "Did you happen to . . .?" and by asking about behavior during a circumscribed time period as opposed to beginning the question with "Do you ever . . .?" (Bradburn & Sudman, 1979).

While pilot-testing a questionnaire to assess attitudes and behaviors regarding oral hygiene among college students, it became evident that the reported frequencies of behaviors such as dental checkups and tooth brushing were higher than the average for the general population (U.S. National Center for Health Statistics, 1974, 1979). These differences may have been partially due to increased awareness of the importance of dental hygiene, but they were large enough to suggest that some overreporting might have taken place. To examine the possibility that subjects were overreporting their frequency of dental hygiene behavior, a technique was devised that focused on highlighting the role of the respondent as a contributor of important information.

Before the questionnaire was administered, subjects were verbally given additional information concerning the purpose of the questions and the importance of honesty and accuracy in their self-reports. The confidentiality and anonymity of their responses were also emphasized, along with the important contribution that their responses would provide. Subjects who received these modified instructions reported substantially lower rates of dental checkups and other dental health care behavior than previous subjects who had only been informed of the anonymity of their responses.

The effect of the instructional manipulation led to the development of a simple classroom demonstration of social desirability bias in survey research. The demonstration reveals the effect of instructional sets on questionnaire responses and leads to discussion of possible reasons for underreporting and overreporting on questionnaires, in addition to other related issues in survey research (e.g., acquiescent response style and representativeness in sampling). The following is a description of a systematic assessment of the effect of such an appeal on reducing social desirability bias.

Method

Two forms of the questionnaire were developed; they were identical, except for the instructions. Both forms had the title "Dental Hygiene Behaviors" at the top, and the standard format included the following instructions:

Over the last several years, psychologists have started to work in conjunction with dentists in order to help improve this area of health care. We would appreciate your answering the following questions regarding dental hygiene behaviors. Please do not write your name on this sheet. Thank you for your participation.

The modified instructions read as follows:

Over the last several years, psychologists have started to work in conjunction with dentists in order to help improve this area of health care. One of the *most important* tasks in this area of research (behavioral dentistry) is to collect *accurate information* on the frequency of various dental hygiene behaviors. Therefore, we would appreciate your answering the following questions as *honestly* and *accurately* as possible. Please do not write your name on this sheet. We are not interested in individual responses, just the behaviors of people in general. Thank you for your participation.

Both forms of the questionnaire requested the respondent's age and sex and answers to the following questions:

1. Do you have regular dental checkups? If so, how often and why? If not, why not?
2. How often do you brush your teeth? Why?
3. Do you floss your teeth? If so, how often and why? If not, why not?

Forty-eight students (24 men and 24 women) enrolled in undergraduate courses in social psychology were randomly assigned to receive either the standard or modified form of the questionnaire. Students were given 15 min to complete the questionnaires. The forms were then returned facedown to the instructor. The purpose of the demonstration and a summary of

the results were presented to students during the following class meeting.

Results

Given the directional nature of the experimental hypothesis (that the modified instructions on the questionnaire would reduce the frequency of reported behaviors), all statistical tests were one-tailed. An assessment of the three major items revealed significant differences between the groups in the predicted direction.

Responses to the item "Do you have regular checkups?" were coded in the following manner: no = 0 and yes = 1. A significantly greater percentage of subjects who received the standard format responded affirmatively to this question (96%) than subjects who received the modified instructions (71%), $t(46) = 2.41$, $p < .01$. Subjects who received the standard instructions also reported brushing their teeth more times a day $(M = 2.63)$ than did the group that received the modified instructions $(M = 2.19)$, $t(46) = 1.92$, $p < .03$.

A difference approaching significance was found between the groups on the item that asked subjects if they floss their teeth. Responses were coded in the same manner used for the checkup question. The results revealed a trend in the predicted direction. Subjects who received the standard format answered affirmatively more often (79%) than subjects who received the modified format (58%), $t(46) = 1.56$, $p < .06$.

The results suggest that having regular dental checkups and brushing regularly may be considered to be more socially desirable behaviors than flossing one's teeth. Given the much smaller segment of the population that flosses regularly, subjects may have felt less pressure to overstate the frequency of this behavior. It should be noted that the majority of responses to the follow-up portion of the flossing question ("If not, why not?") produced responses that indicated a lack of knowledge regarding the purpose of flossing, the benefits, and the amount of time that it takes.

The degree to which random assignment produced experimental equivalence was partially assessed by examining the average age and sex ratios of respondents in the two groups. Random assignment produced groups with identical sex ratios (12 men and 12 women in each group) and relatively similar average ages: M (standard format) = 21.33 years and M (modified format) = 21.58 years.

Although the modified instructions significantly reduced the tendency to overreport socially desirable behavior, it is possible that these instructions did not alleviate the problem entirely. A comparison of the mean number of toothbrushings per day by the modified instruction group in this study $(M = 2.19)$ and the mean response to this question from a national health survey $(M = 1.60)$ revealed a relatively large difference (U.S. National Center for Health Statistics, 1974). As previously suggested, this finding may represent a real difference between the frequency of toothbrushing in the general population and among college students.

Discussion

To prepare material for lecture and discussion, additional information on the prevalence of social desirability bias and procedures that have been used to reduce it can be found in Sudman and Bradburn (1982). This book devoted a chapter to the problem of social desirability and described techniques for its reduction. A more recent review is provided by Nederhof (1985). This review was written from a self-presentational perspective that regards social desirability as the result of self- and other-deception. The article examined the relevant research literature and described seven methods that have been used to prevent or reduce social desirability bias.

The problem of social desirability remains as a source of error in much survey research, and this type of demonstration alerts students to this potential problem. To lead into a discussion of the results, students should first be told that there were two forms of the questionnaire that varied only in the content of the instructions. Some students may already be aware of this through discussion with classmates. Hypotheses regarding the purpose of the modified instructions should now be discussed. Students who participated in the demonstration were surprised to find out that the modified instructions could create the observed differences between groups.

After revealing the extent to which experimental equivalence has been attained, a discussion of possible reasons for the observed effect of the modified instructions can be conducted. This discussion might focus on whether students believe that social desirability bias on questionnaires is due to a desire to appear "good" to others or to oneself.

As Cahalan (1968) suggested, in a reevaluation of a major survey that examined social desirability, subjects may overreport socially desirable behaviors in order to protect their self-image. If a desire to appear good in one's own eyes is the cause of overreporting, then appearing socially desirable to others may be of little concern; a focus on anonymity may have a minimal effect on reducing such bias. It is possible that the manipulation used in the demonstration reduced the overreporting of behavior by focusing students on the contribution they were making to others (e.g., the scientific community), thereby reducing the need to appear "good" to themselves. It is clear that a variety of approaches must be used collectively in order to reduce this response bias to tolerable levels.

The use of dental hygiene behavior as the topic of the questionnaire was due to a personal interest in this form of behavior. The demonstration could easily be modified to focus on other forms of socially desirable behavior such as wearing seat belts or the amount of time spent studying. This type of demonstration could also be used in a variety of courses. It would be appropriate for classes in tests and measurement, research methodology, and other courses that focus on attitude measurement and survey research.

To summarize, the results support the hypothesis that more accurate responses can be obtained by stressing the following: the importance of the information being provided by subjects, the importance of honest and accurate self-reports, and the anonymity of subjects' responses. As a classroom demonstration, the exercise can be used to illustrate a potential source of bias in survey research. It may also be used to demonstrate the technique of random assignment and the relative degree of experimental equivalence that it provides.

References

Bradburn, N. M., & Sudman, S. (1979). *Improving interview method and questionnaire design: Response effects to threatening questions in survey research.* San Francisco, CA: Jossey-Bass.

Cahalan, D. (1968). Correlates of response accuracy in the Denver validity study. *Public Opinion Quarterly, 32*, 607-621.

Hyman, H. H. (1944). Do they tell the truth? *Public Opinion Quarterly, 8*, 557-559.

Nederhof, A. J. (1985). Methods of coping with social desirability bias: A review. *European Journal of Social Psychology, 15*, 263-280.

Parry, H. J., & Crossley, H. M. (1950). Validity of responses to survey questions. *Public Opinion Quarterly, 14*, 61-80

Sudman, S., & Bradburn, N. M. (1982). *Asking questions.* San Francisco, CA: Jossey-Bass.

U.S. National Center for Health Statistics. (1974). *Diet and dental health, a study of relationships: United States, 1971-1974* (Data from the National Health Survey, Series 11, No. 225). Washington, DC: Government Printing Office.

U.S. National Center for Health Statistics. (1979). *Dental visits volume and interval since last visit: United States, 1978-1979* (Data from the National Health Survey, Series 10, No. 138). Washington, DC: Government Printing Office.

Note

I thank two anonymous reviewers for their helpful comments and suggestions on an earlier version of this article.

2. ILLUSTRATING CONCEPTS IN SOCIAL PERCEPTION AND SOCIAL COGNITION

A Method for Teaching About Verbal and Nonverbal Communication

Mark Costanzo
Claremont McKenna College

Dane Archer
University of California, Santa Cruz

A method for teaching about verbal and nonverbal communication is described. The Interpersonal Perception Task (IPT) consists of a videotape of 30 brief scenes. Viewers answer interpretive questions by decoding the verbal and nonverbal cues in the scenes. Information is presented in all communication channels; several categories of interaction are represented; and for each scene, there is an objective criterion of accurate judgment. Instructional techniques using the IPT highlight the subtlety and complexity of communication cues, teach about specific cues to accuracy, demonstrate the relative importance of communication channels, and help students understand the process of interpretation.

The study of verbal and nonverbal communication has assumed a prominent role in psychology during the past 20 years (Knapp, 1978; Patterson, 1983). Nonverbal behavior discloses critical information about emotions and relationships (Hickson & Stacks, 1985). Even barely perceptible nonverbal behaviors can have interpretable meaning—for example, we can recognize a person's facial expressions of emotion from as little as a 1/24th-s exposure (Rosenthal, Hall, DiMatteo, Rogers, & Archer, 1979). Research on social intelligence shows that it is possible to interpret people's behavior, feelings, and relationships from something as simple as a photograph (Archer, 1980). Nonverbal cues are often more powerful and reliable than verbal cues (Archer & Akert, 1984).

Researchers are also investigating the process of interpretation—how we use nonverbal cues to form impressions and conclusions about others. Correct interpretation is a remarkable feat because, in any interaction, hundreds or thousands of verbal and nonverbal cues stream by us, vanishing in milliseconds. How do we discard most of these cues, seizing the few (e.g., a momentary facial expression, a vocal inflection) that tell us what another person means or is feelings The process of interpretation is one of the most impressive and least understood of human abilities.

Research attests to the importance of subtle expressive behaviors in how we communicate with others and in how we interpret their behavior. However, teaching about verbal and nonverbal behavior is a difficult challenge because the subtlety and complexity of verbal and nonverbal behavior are difficult to convey in lectures and readings. Students often come away with the impression that there is a simple codebook of nonverbal cues—that specific cues have invariant and unambiguous meanings.

This article describes instructional techniques that make use of the Interpersonal Perception Task (IPT). These techniques sensitize students to the variety and complexity of verbal and nonverbal cues, facilitate classroom discussion, and help students understand the process of interpreting these cues.

The IPT

The IPT consists of a videotape of 30 brief (20 s to 60 s) scenes. Every scene is paired with a multiple-choice question that has two or three options. The questions appear on the screen before each scene. Viewers are asked to reach a conclusion about the people who appear in the scene that follows. A 6-s blank interval on the videotape enables viewers to enter their responses on an answer sheet after each scene.

The design of the IPT is best conveyed by describing a few scenes. The first scene shows a woman and a man having a conversation with two 7-year-old children. The question corresponding to this scene is "Who is the child of the two adults?" A second scene shows a man first telling his true life story and then, after a pause, telling a completely fabricated version of his life story. The question posed is "Which is the lie, and which is the truths"

In the IPT, accuracy can always be verified against an external standard. In the examples just mentioned, one of the children is the child of the two adults, and one of the two versions of the man's life story is a lie.

For every scene, there is an objectively correct answer, which is verifiable and unambiguous.

The IPT has four other important design features:

1. Every scene contains a full communications repertoire, with information presented naturalistically in all channels (verbal, vocal paralanguage, and nonverbal behavior). Because natural streams of behavior are used, clues to correct interpretation can be found in a variety of channels.

2. All scenes contain spontaneous behavior and unscripted conversation. The 30 brief scenes were extracted from longer videotaped interactions.

3. A total of 54 different encoders (28 females and 26 males ranging in age from 18 months old to 67 years old) appear in the videotape. Each scene shows one to four people.

4. There is a coherent content focus. Viewers are asked to reach conclusions about five types of social interaction: status, kinship, intimacy, competition, and deception. There are six scenes for each of these areas.

The IPT challenges viewers to identify the right answer to each question by using the broad range of communication present in each scene (e.g., facial expressions, words, tones of voice, hesitations, eye movements, gestures, personal space, posture, and touching). The cues occur simultaneously in the scenes, just as they do in everyday life. The IPT has been shown to be both valid and reliable, and previous research indicates that performance on the task relates to social skills that are important in everyday life (Costanzo & Archer, 1989).

Instructional Uses of the IPT

Are People Just Guessing?

The simplest use focuses on audience accuracy for specific scenes or for the whole videotape. In making interpretations like those involved in the IPT, people may feel that they are choosing an answer at random. However, even when people feel they are guessing, they almost always reach correct conclusions at well above chance levels of accuracy. A quick test of whether people are "just guessing" is whether or not performance exceeds chance.

The multiple-choice format makes it possible to determine whether viewers are more accurate than chance would predict. After a portion of the IPT has been shown, the instructor can read aloud the correct answers while students score their own tests for accuracy. The instructor can ask for a show of hands of those who chose each answer. This show of hands illustrates dramatically that people are not choosing answers randomly but, instead, are systematically decoding the informative cues present in the scenes. Accuracy rates can also be used to identify scenes that are relatively easy or difficult.

Comparing Verbal and Nonverbal Cues

The IPT can be used to sensitize students to the varieties and importance of different communication channels. One way to approach this issue is to ask, "What cues found in nonverbal communication are unavailable in words alone?" A simple demonstration involves contrasting the usefulness of purely verbal information with the richer cues available in full-channel (verbal + nonverbal) communication. One way to do this is to compare the accuracy of students given only verbal transcripts of IPT scenes (written transcripts are included) with the accuracy of students shown the IPT videotape. Research indicates that the interpretability of words is overshadowed by the power of nonverbal cues (Archer & Akert, 1984). The group using verbal transcripts will be less accurate than the group with access to both verbal and nonverbal cues.

Alternatively, an entire class can be asked to determine the answers for several scenes using the transcript alone. Then, the same scenes can be shown using the full-channel videotape to see whether (and why) people would revise their original judgments.

Student Interpretations of Specific Cues

Another instructional technique involves focusing on viewer perceptions of potentially important cues. A good way to do this is to invite comments about why people chose a specific answer. The video can be stopped after a given scene to ask members of the audience two questions: "What do you think the correct answer is?," and "What specific cues led you to choose this answer?" This process is valuable and informative, because viewers will cite quite different cues, even if they agreed on the answer.

There is usually a high level of consistency across channels, and many different cues can lead a viewer to the correct interpretation (Archer, 1980). This tendency toward consistency usually produces a high level of redundancy across channels. The varied cues cited by viewers demonstrate that cues to correct interpretation are available in many channels simultaneously and that there are several paths to the correct answer.

Viewer perceptions provide a lively source of classroom participation because different people do not decode scenes in precisely the same way. The perceptions of people who chose an incorrect answer are also important because the cues that lead people astray will become apparent. Viewers who reach the correct judgment may have noticed these misleading cues, but assigned them less weight in their interpretation process. The IPT includes some illustrative viewer perceptions for each of the five scene types.

Silent Cues

Facial expressions, gestures, and other nonverbal behaviors usually occur along with words and act to change the perceived meaning of words. In many cases, however, nonverbal acts have independent meaning. It is easy to use the IPT to demonstrate the power of this "silent language." Scenes can be shown with the audio level on the TV monitor turned off. Students can use the cues they have available (e.g., facial behavior, gestures, eye contact, touching) to answer the questions.

This approach encourages viewers to focus exclusively on nonverbal behavior—for example, to determine if people are lying merely by watching (but not hearing) them. After students have tried answering the IPT questions using only visual cues, the scenes can be replayed with the audio. Do they change their answers? If so, what reasons do they give? Remind students that playing the videotape silently not only removes verbal cues, but also the important cues found in vocal paralanguage (e.g., pauses, tone of voice, and interruptions). This exercise also illustrates that verbal cues and vocal paralanguage are especially important for decoding some types of scenes (e.g., deception).

Subjective and Objective Accuracy

The process of interpreting verbal and nonverbal cues is only partly understood. However, it is clear that the processing of cues is not entirely conscious and that people have imperfect awareness of the cues they use (Smith, Archer, & Costanzo, in press). One way to encourage students to focus on process is to ask them to provide a confidence rating for each answer (e.g., a value between 0% to 100%). Students can also be asked to estimate the total number of items they answered correctly for some portion of the IPT. These subjective estimates can be compared to accuracy scores.

After a segment of the IPT has been shown, the instructor can announce the correct answers. If viewers are more accurate on the scenes they felt more confident about, it indicates that they were able to identify (and were consciously aware oft specific cues. If viewers were unexpectedly right (or unexpectedly wrong) on specific scenes, it may be that they were reaching interpretations without full awareness. Because the process of interpretation seems to rely on different types of cues (those we can articulate and those that we are not conscious of), both outcomes are possible.

This exercise sensitizes students to the tenuous relation between confidence and accuracy. Frequently, there is an overconfidence effect: People believe they scored higher than they actually scored, and most people think that they scored significantly better than average.

Using the IPT to Introduce Research Findings

The IPT is also useful for introducing important findings and current issues in the field of nonverbal behavior. For example, a substantial body of research indicates that women are somewhat more accurate than men at decoding nonverbal behavior (Hall, 1985). Research using the IPT supports this conclusion. Women may be better decoders because they detect more nonverbal cues or, perhaps, because they interpret what they detect differently. Before telling students about this gender difference, it is useful to ask them to indicate (by a show of hands) if they think men or women do better on tasks like the IPT. The introduction of this issue leads quite naturally to a discussion of differences in male and female socialization that may produce females' decoding advantage.

The IPT can also be used to prompt discussions of unresolved issues in the study of communication. An example is the question of whether there are "special" decoding abilities: Would police detectives be unusually skilled at decoding deception scenes? Would parents be more accurate than nonparents at identifying parent-child relationships in the kinship scenes? Would athletes be better able to spot winners and losers in the competition scenes? The answers are not yet clear, although research on the issue of special abilities is in progress.

Another set of unresolved issues concerns the role of cultural factors in verbal and nonverbal communication. For example, would interactions between status unequals be more formal (and, therefore, more easily decoded) if filmed in Japan? Would parent–child interactions be recognizable across cultural boundaries, or is there something uniquely American about the interactions depicted in the IPT? Assuming that the problem of verbal translation could be solved, would there still be a problem of nonverbal translation? Would a college student in China, Zaire, or Brazil have trouble decoding some scenes? The expressive behaviors present in the scenes are more complex than simple smiles or frowns (which may be universally recognizable), and it may help to be a cultural "insider" when trying to answer questions like those on the IPT.

Evaluation of the IPT as a Teaching Method

The pedagogical effectiveness of these exercises was evaluated in two social psychology classes. Theories and research findings on communication processes were summarized in both classes. One class (*n* = 34) received this information in traditional lecture format. The other class (*n* = 30) received the same information, but most of the material was presented via the exercises just described. Presentations to both groups included an outline of communication channels; examples of how different channels complement, reinforce, or contradict each other; and discussions of the readability of verbal and nonverbal cues.

Two weeks after the presentations, students in both groups took a midterm exam, which included the communication material. The exam contained three multiplechoice questions and one essay question on communication processes. Although the lecture group and the IPT group did not differ in the number of multiple-choice questions answered correctly (lecture group $M = 2.03$; IPT group $M = 2.33$), $t(62) = 1.48$, $p < .072$, one-tailed, the IPT group performed significantly better on the essay question (lecture group $M = 10.68$; IPT group $M = 12.07$), $t(62) = 2.83$, $p < .01$, one-tailed. The essay was scored using a grading scale on which 15 was equal to an A+ and 1 was equal to F-. The grader was blind to group membership. Finally, a global index of student interest and enjoyment was obtained by asking students to grade the overall quality of the presentations using the 15-point grading scale. The IPT group rated the presentation significantly higher than did the lecture group (lecture group $M = 12.35$; IPT group $M = 13.60$), $t(62) = 2.93$, $p < .01$.

These findings appear to indicate that use of the IPT offers advantages over the traditional lecture. Students gained a more sophisticated understanding of communication processes and rated the approach as preferable to a standard lecture. We also note a more qualitative, impressionistic finding: Use of the IPT produced greater student involvement and fuller, more wide-ranging discussions. The pattern of findings suggests that the IPT is an effective means of presenting complex material and promoting student involvement and participation.

A Cautionary Note: Feedback on Individual Performance

The IPT is designed for research and instructional uses. Although researchers sometimes communicate their findings to research participants, information about individual performance is usually not provided. In instructional settings, however, students are accustomed to being told how they scored on a particular task. We have found that students are usually eager to learn their IPT scores. A problem may arise if students interpret their score as an infallible indication of interpersonal sensitivity. It would be a disservice to allow students who obtain low scores to feel that they are poor judges of behavior. This negative feedback could outweigh the learning benefits of the IPT.

If people are told their overall scores, they should also be told that performance is probably influenced by several factors: motivation, practice, viewing conditions, fatigue, attention, and experience with similar tasks. It should also be pointed out that the IPT focuses on interpreting the behavior of unfamiliar others—it does not directly address the perception of one's intimates and acquaintances or other dimensions of social intelligence, such as judging motives or personality characteristics. Providing this information sug-

gests alternative explanations for poor performance and cautions students against drawing sweeping conclusions on the basis of their score.

The classroom exercises described here do not require giving students information about their total score. These exercises are designed to focus attention on the process of interpretation and the nature of verbal and nonverbal behavior, not the issue of individual accuracy. As a teaching device, the IPT highlights the subtlety and complexity of expressive behavior and promotes active learning by presenting social interaction in a vivid and involving manner.

References

Archer, D. (1980). How to expand your social intelligence quotient. New York: Evans & Co. (Dutton-Elsevier).

Archer, D., & Akert, R. M. (1984). Nonverbal factors in person perception. In M. Cook (Ed.), Issues in person perception (pp. 114-144). New York: Methuen.

Costanzo, M., & Archer, D. (1989). Interpreting the expressive behavior of others: The Interpersonal Perception Task. Journal of Nonverbal Behavior, 13, 225-245.

Hall, J. A. (1985). Nonverbal sex differences: Communication accuracy and expressive style. Baltimore: Johns Hopkins University Press.

Hickson, M. L., & Stacks, D. W. (1985). Nonverbal communication: Studies and applications. Dubuque, IA: Brown.

Knapp, M. L. (1978). Nonverbal communication in human interaction. New York: Holt, Rinehart & Winston.

Patterson, M. L. (1983). Nonverbal behavior: A functional perspective. New York: Springer-Verlag.

Rosenthal, R., Hall, J. A., DiMatteo, M. R., Rogers, P., & Archer, D. (1979). Sensitivity to nonverbal communication: A profile approach to the measurement of differential abilities. Baltimore: Johns Hopkins University Press.

Smith, H. J., Archer, D., & Costanzo, M. (in press). Just a hunch: Accuracy and awareness in person perception. Journal of Nonverbal Behavior.

Notes

1. The IPT is available from the University of California Media Extension Center, 2176 Shattuck Avenue, Berkeley, CA 94704. Telephone: (415) 642-0460. Rental price is $36.
2. Preparation of this article was supported by a Faculty Research Grant from Claremont McKenna College to Mark Costanzo.
3. We thank Joseph J. Palladino and three anonymous reviewers for their helpful comments on an earlier draft of this article.

A Classroom Exercise in Impression Formation

Joy L. Berrenberg
University of Colorado at Denver

This classroom exercise provides students with an opportunity to examine aspects of their own impression-formation processes. The data generated can be used to stimulate discussion about the origins of implicit personality theories, person prototypes, and the accuracy of first impressions.

The process of impression formation has been the focus of theory and research in social psychology for several decades. The topic is covered in a variety of courses, including introductory psychology, personality, social psychology, industrial/organizational psychology, and human relations. The exercise described in this article provides students with a vivid and concrete demonstration of their own impression-formation strategies.

Impression formation is concerned, in part, with the way in which we make initial judgments about others. Although these judgments are based on limited information, we depend on them to help shape expectations concerning subsequent social interactions (Levinger, 1983).

The process of forming first impressions is frequently introduced to students through a lecture on implicit personality theories (Bruner & Taguiri, 1954) and/or person prototypes (Cantor & Mischel, 1977). The central assumption of these positions is that people possess cognitive categories, which they use to judge and sort new acquaintances. More specifically, an implicit personality theory is thought to be a naive assumption that certain human characteristics are correlated. Thus, when we identify a particular trait in someone, we consult our personal theories for other characteristics that go along with that trait. For example, if a man is described as tall, we might assume that he is also dark and handsome.

In a similar vein, person prototypes consist of internal descriptions of standard types of people. We compare and match each new acquaintance to our prototypes. Once matched, we assume that the individual possesses all of the characteristics of the prototype. This process occurs frequently with first names. We meet a woman named Jane and feel an immediate fondness for her because we retrieve memories of our beloved Aunt Jane.

First impressions are usually formed without any direct evidence that the target person possesses the ascribed traits; thus, they are subject to considerable error (Norman, 1963). Such unverified impressions are relatively resistant to subsequent disconfirming evidence (Snyder, Tanke, & Berscheid, 1977).

Students frequently verbalize the unfairness of "judging a book by its cover." Clearly, many of them feel personally exempt from using impression-formation strategies. This exercise is an effective demonstration of the ubiquity of personal impression-formation strategies. It also generates data (e.g., an impression-agreement score) that can be used to stimulate class discussion.

Method

Part 1

Early in the course, students are asked to submit a clear, standard size photograph of someone 18 years or older whom they know fairly well. The only restriction is that the photo be in good taste (i.e., not lewd or bizarre in dress or pose). Students answer a series of questions about the person in their photograph to the best of their ability. There is a multitude of demographic and personality questions that can be used in this exercise. Some good ones include: (a) What is the person's occupation? (b) What is the person's favorite sport/hobby/activity? (c) What is the person's favorite type of music? (d) How shy/outgoing is the person on a scale of 1 to 10? (e) How liberal/conservative is the person on a scale from 1 to 10? (f) How warm/cold is the person on a scale from 1 to 10? Note that the potential for obtaining objective answers is decreased for questions that involve personality attributions. To maintain anonymity but allow for identification, students write their own birth date on the back of the photograph and on the completed questionnaire.

Part 2

Several weeks later, in conjunction with a lecture on impression formation, students are asked to form groups of four to six persons. Three or four photos (without matching answer sheets) are distributed to each group. It is important to establish that no one in a particular group is familiar with any of that group's photographs. Working individually at first, group members examine the photographs one at a time, form an impression, and then respond to the selected questions. It may be desirable to have students rate the confidence they have in their judgments. After completing this task, the groups discuss their answers. They are asked to assess the similarity of their impressions for each photograph by counting the number of same or similar answers on each question. In addition, they discuss and write down the cues (e.g., age, clothing, hairstyle) used in forming their own impressions. This phase of the exercise usually produces considerable enthusiasm as students share their implicit personality theories and person prototypes.

Part 3

After about 20 min, the groups are given the answer keys corresponding to their photographs. They compare their questionnaire responses to the answers provided by the acquaintance and assess their agreement by counting the number of matched or near-matched answers.

Results

The exercise generates several useful bits of data. First, a social consensus score can be computed by converting the group agreement scores into percentages. Typically, groups show low-to-moderate agreement (i.e., 20% to 30% of their responses are the same). Second, a rank-ordered list of cues used in impression formation can be obtained by counting the number of times a cue was used. Clothing is usually ranked first, followed by age, context/activity, facial attractiveness, and physical build. Finally, agreement scores can be derived by converting the number of corresponding answers to a percentage figure. In a recent demonstration with 58 introductory psychology students, 62% answered two or fewer questions correctly out of six questions.

Concluding Remarks

A class discussion follows the presentation of results; several topics can be covered. One topic focuses on the ease with which we form impressions of strangers and the confidence we feel in ascribing traits on the basis of limited information. Another possibility is to examine the social consensus figure and use it as a springboard for discussing the stereotypes and person prototypes that are shared by a culture.

The agreement data often provide students with direct evidence of the errors in their own judgment processes. The identification of these errors can lead to a discussion of why we continue to rely on our impression-formation strategies even when we know they can be incorrect.

Finally, the list of rank-ordered cues encourages students to examine their own implicit personality theories and person prototypes. Students can be encouraged to explain the origin of these structures in operant and classical conditioning terms.

This exercise has never failed to create interest and lively discussion. A recent course evaluation showed that 72% of the students (N = 58) found it to be an "extremely valuable" or "quite valuable" learning experience, 86% said that it was the "most enjoyable" or "one of the most enjoyable" class exercises they had ever done, and 80% recommended that it "definitely" be used in future classes.

The exercise can be modified to fit different situations. For example, the group component can be eliminated, with the entire exercise being completed on an individual basis. If there is concern about the ethics of using photographs without the subjects' written consent, it is possible to obtain photos and written consent from students in one class for use in other classes. An advantage of this latter approach is that it overcomes the limitation of relying on secondhand answers to the questions. In the former method, the personal information (particularly any personality attributions) provided by the acquaintance may itself be subject to impression-formation processes. Those desiring more rigor may control the amount of information provided in the photographs by asking for "head-only" or "full-body" poses.

Occasionally, the constraints of time or class size do not permit the collection of photographs from students. When this occurs, it is possible to use pictures from magazines or yearbooks. Although this format precludes the assessment of agreement, it does prompt a good general discussion of impression-formation processes. In sum, this exercise provides a concrete demonstration of our capacity for forming first impressions on the basis of limited information.

References

Bruner, J. S., & Taguiri, R. (1954). The perception of people. In G. Lindzey (Ed.), *Handbook of social psychology* (Vol. 2, pp. 634-654). Reading, MA: Addison-Wesley.

Cantor, N., & Mischel, W. (1977). Traits as prototypes: Effects on recognition memory. *Journal of Personality and Social Psychology, 35,* 38-48.

Levinger, G. (1983). Development and change. In H. H. Kelley, E. Berscheid, A. Christensen, J. H. Harvey, T. L. Huston, G. Levinger, E. McClintock, L. A. Peplau, & D. R. Peterson (Eds.), *Close relationships* (pp. 315-359). San Francisco: Freeman.

Norman, W. T. (1963). Toward an adequate taxonomy of personality attributes: Replicated factor structure in peer nomination personality ratings. *Journal of Abnormal and Social Psychology, 66*, 574-583.

Snyder, M., Tanke, E. D., & Berscheid, E. (1977). Social perception and interpersonal behavior: On the self-fulfilling nature of social stereotypes. *Journal of Personality and Social Psychology, 35*, 656-666.

Observer Biases in the Classroom

Mary E. Kite
Ball State University

This article outlines three activities that demonstrate common perceptual errors described in the social psychological literature: the actor-observer effect, the false consensus bias, and priming effects. These activities produce consistent results and demonstrate how cognitive shortcuts can result in inaccurate judgments. These simple demonstrations can also stimulate discussion of the bases of such miscalculations and their impact on everyday thinking.

Although humans are remarkably efficient information processors, efficiency and accuracy do not always go hand in hand. By rapidly interpreting their world, people can easily and inadvertently err. Myers (1990) labeled this process "illusory thinking" (p. 131) and suggested that such biases can have profound social consequences. Making people aware of such biases may decrease their vulnerability to these errors (Nisbett & Ross, 1980).

Studies of observer biases document the consistency with which we draw incorrect conclusions; however, sometimes the sheer number of such biases, as presented in textbooks, limits their impact on students. Other activities demonstrate perceptual biases, such as the primacy effect in social judgments (Lasswell, Ruch, Gorfein, & Warren, 1981; Watson, 1987a), the fundamental attribution error (Watson, 1987b), and the self-serving attributional bias (Dunn, 1989). This article describes other activities that illustrate the actor-observer effect, the false consensus bias, and priming effects. My goal is to show how efficient information processing can result in inaccurate perceptions—topics relevant to introductory, social, personality, and cognitive psychology courses.

The Actor-Observer Effect

Method

This demonstration is derived from Study 3 of Nisbett, Caputo, Legant, and Marecek (1973), which clearly demonstrated the actor-observer effect: People attribute their own behavior to situational factors and others' behavior to consistent traits. The activity takes about 15 min and introduces the topic of observer biases. Students use a list of 20 polar trait terms twice (see Table 1) . First, they rate a famous television personality (e.g., Dan Rather, Barbara Walters) by checking whether that person possesses a trait (or its polar opposite) or whether they believe the person's behavior depends on the situation. Second, they make the same ratings for themselves.

Students report the number of traits (or their opposites) and the number of "depends on the situation" responses checked for themselves and for the famous person. I record these responses in columns on the chalkboard and compute four mean scores. Although it is necessary to report only the mean number of traits, students grasp the concept more easily when presented with the means for the trait ratings and the means for the "depends on situation" ratings. The first pair of means highlights the belief that others' traits are more consistent than their own, whereas the second pair of means highlights the belief that their own traits ale more variable than others'. In lower level courses, I do not discuss how to analyze these means statistically; however, a *t* test comparing the students' self-ratings to their ratings of the television personality should reveal the expected significant differences.

Results and Discussion

Five social psychology classes produced results that consistently replicated those of Nisbett et al. (1973). Students from one class checked a mean of 16.4 consistent traits for Barbara Walters and a mean of 12.0 consistent traits for themselves. To reinforce the reliability of this bias, I report that Nisbett et al. (1973) found a mean of 15.1 traits checked for Walter Cronkite and a mean of 11.9 checked for myself. Nisbett et al.'s (1973) data for best friend ($M = 14.2$) and acquaintance ($M = 13.4$) show that the better one knows people, the more likely one is to believe that their behavior depends on the situation rather than their dispositions.

After the demonstration, at least one student notes that he or she did not engage in the actor-observer bias. I use this opportunity to discuss how mean scores apply to groups of people but do not necessarily predict every individual's behavior. This issue is, of course, relevant to most psychological research, and students who understand this distinction enhance their ability to focus on general patterns of results.

The False Consensus Bias

Method

The false consensus bias describes a tendency to overestimate the degree to which others share one's opinions, even extreme ones (e.g., Ross, Greene, & House, 1977). This effect can be demonstrated in less than 5 min. Ask the class to suggest an opinion topic (e.g., I like Madonna; George Bush is a good President) and then note their level of agreement with the statement on a scale ranging from *strongly disagree*

Table 1. Polar Trait Terms Used to Demonstrate the Actor-Observer Effect

Serious	Lighthearted
Subjective	Analytic
Future oriented	Present oriented
Energetic	Relaxed
Unassuming	Self-assertive
Lenient	Firm
Reserved	Emotionally expressive
Dignified	Casual
Realistic	Idealistic
Intense	Calm
Skeptical	Trusting
Quiet	Talkative
Cultivated	Natural
Sensitive	Tough-minded
Steady	Flexible
Self-sufficient	Sociable
Dominant	Submissive
Cautious	Bold
Uninhibited	Self-controlled
Conscientious	Happy-go-lucky

(1) to *strongly agree* (5). Then ask students to estimate the percentage of people in the class that share their opinion. Pigott and Leone (1990) suggested a similar procedure, using a yes-no format.

Results and Discussion

A show of hands provides the number of people selecting each response, and I record that number on the board. After I compute the percentage of students choosing each option, students indicate again by a show of hands whether they overestimated the number of people in agreement with them. In three social psychology classes, at least 60% of the students believed that others agree with them. Ross et al. (1977, Study 1) reported agreement rates ranging from 50% to 75%.

Mullen et al.'s (1985) meta-analytic study of the false consensus bias suggests possible topics for class discussion. First, this bias is quite general across reference groups (e.g., friends vs. college students in general) and issues (e.g., preferred type of bread or preferred presidential candidate). However, the strongest false consensus effects emerge with factual information or political expectations (e.g., outcome of presidential elections or future use of nuclear weapons), and the weakest effects occur with personal issues (e.g., donating blood or having difficulty making friends). Second, the effect may reflect people's tendency to overestimate the probability of events easily brought to mind (e.g., the availability heuristic; Tversky & Kahneman, 1973). Students are easily engaged in discussion of whether these ideas explain their tendency to exhibit this bias. Likewise, they typically recognize the social costs and benefits of a false consensus for both individuals and society. Finally, as Pigott and Leone (1990) suggested, students can debate whether having others agree with us makes our opinions "correct."

Priming Effects

Method

Activating, or priming, a category increases the likelihood that people will evaluate the stimulus person in those terms. Stated another way, recently used words or ideas influence the interpretation of new information (e. g., Bargh & Pietromonaco, 1982; Higgins, Rholes, & Jones, 1977). To demonstrate this effect, I have modified the "Donald" studies (Wyer & Srull, 1981). This activity requires some advance preparation and about 15 min from each of two class periods, but it also makes vivid a procedure and outcome that is difficult to visualize. The activity involves the unrelated experiment technique, wherein students

Table 2. List of Neutral, Hostile, and Kind Sentences for Priming Activity

Neutral	Hostile	Kind
walks dog he far	leg break arm his	child he helps friend
she clothes wears buys	hit boy dog she	girl buys gift boy
write you letter I	hate me I you	mother rocks him child
tall is man short	burns boy child girl	believe you me help
picture takes job she	kick chair she desk	house toy he builds
goes went out man	you bites dog boy	father fixes toy makes
slow he ran fast	me hurt you I	love him her you
job I do found	cat child you scratch	boy shares food eats
reads boy book you	man bird shoots boy	flowers picks she gives
map you read book	you beat I me	man cookies bakes bread
I watch him call	breaks glass he window	she makes friends has
I you bread eat	throws book he chair	man hugs child woman
rides fast drives she	you loud yell scream	hand package he holds
I call you me	kills he man bug	boy reads you book
women knew man boy	I you boy kick	cat girl pets dog

believe they are completing two studies together merely to save time (e.g., Durso & Mellgren, 1989). The first experiment purportedly examines how people build sentences. I distribute two sets of word groups on colored paper. One colored paper contains words that form "kind" sentences, whereas the other contains words that form "hostile" sentences; both word groups are intermixed with neutral word groups (see Table 2). The students' task is to construct three-word sentences from each series of four words.

While students complete the first task, I distribute the questionnaire for what they believe is the second study. Because I need to know whether students initially formed kind or hostile sentences, those with one color paper receive a questionnaire labeled A and those with the other color receive a questionnaire labeled B. This questionnaire is actually identical for both groups and contains an ambiguous story about "Donald" (see Table 3) followed by a series of questions about his characteristics: friendly, likable, kind, considerate, and thoughtful, assessed on scales ranging from *not at all* (1) to *very much* (7). Distributing the second questionnaire in this manner does not seem to arouse suspicion because it appears to save class time and students are busy constructing sentences. Students now complete the second experiment on person perception by reading the story and making anonymous evaluations of Donald. If priming is effective, students who created hostile sentences should rate Donald as less likable than students who created kind sentences.

Results

To save time, I collect the students' questionnaires and, before the next class, compute mean ratings for each question and for the sum of the five ratings. Before presenting the outcome during the next meeting, I return the questionnaires because students often forget what they completed. Although the results for two social psychology classes have not produced statistically significant differences, the means were in the predicted direction and serve to demonstrate the concept of priming. For one class, the hostility primed group reported a mean liking score of 2.5 and the kindness primed group reported a mean liking score of 2.9, with higher numbers indicating greater liking. Discussion focuses on the pervasiveness of priming effects (which are apparently not mediated by individual differences; Devine, 1989) and their implications for everyday life (e.g., advertising, watching violent movies, offering help in emergencies). Furthermore, I inform students that priming effects are more likely when additional time has passed between the activation of the category and the evaluation of the stimulus person (e.g., Higgins et al., 1977). The short time frame of this demonstration may explain why our effects are weaker than those in the published literature. Teachers might also note that priming studies are an excellent representation of the relation between social and cognitive psychology.

Table 3. Ambiguous Donald Story From Wyer and Srull (1981)

I ran into my old friend Donald the other day, and I decided to go over and visit him, since by coincidence we took our vacations at the same time. Soon after I arrived, a salesman knocked at the door, but Donald refused to let him enter. He also told me that he was refusing to pay his rent until the landlord repaints his apartment. We talked for awhile, had lunch, then went out for a ride. We used my car, since Donald's car had broken down that morning, and he told the garage mechanic that he would have to go somewhere else if he couldn't fix his car that same day. We went to the park for about an hour and then stopped at a hardware store. I was sort of preoccupied, but Donald bought some small gadget, and then I heard him demand his money back from the sales clerk. I couldn't find what I was looking for, so we left and walked a few blocks to another store. The Red Cross had set up a stand by the door and asked us to donate blood. Donald lied by saying he had diabetes and therefore could not give blood. It's funny that I hadn't noticed it before, but when we got to the store, we found that it had gone out of business. It was getting kind of late, so I took Donald to pick up his car and we agreed to meet again as soon as possible.

Discussion

These three activities illustrate how our beliefs and experiences influence our perceptions of others. Moreover, discussions of these activities can focus on the bases for such biases and their impact on everyday life. Students report that active participation helps them understand and remember these effects.

One discussion opportunity explores how efficient information processing sometimes has undesirable consequences, such as when the media capitalize on our perceptual biases to influence our preference for political candidates or a certain brand of toothpaste. Students might also consider whether prejudice is rooted in these biases. Does prejudice stem from our beliefs about the consistent traits of entire social groups? Is it perpetuated by our belief that everyone agrees with us about what those traits are? Does merely activating the social category influence our judgments of individual members of those social groups?

I have also used our views on the Soviet Union to explore how our perceptions can change but the process by which we draw those conclusions does not. We may, for example, have a more positive attitude toward the Soviets but still be likely to think their characteristics are consistent and that others share our beliefs.

Funder (1987) noted that perceptual errors are a "hot topic" (p. 75) and fun, as the number of teaching activities focused on such errors attests. These observations, however, preface a critical questioning of whether such perceptual processes represent mistakes with real-life consequences. Sophisticated students will find food for thought in Funder's criticisms and even beginners can consider whether judgments made in a laboratory setting have relevance to everyday social perception (see also Hogan, DeSoto, & Solano, 1977).

These activities are useful for units on person perception, and parallels can be drawn among the three kinds of biases. Any of the three activities, however, can stand alone and engender discussion about how human error affects our interpretation of others' characteristics and behavior.

References

Bargh, J. A., & Pietromonaco, P. (1982). Automatic information processing and social perception: The influence of trait information presented outside of conscious awareness on impression formation. *Journal of Personality and Social Psychology, 40,* 750-760.

Devine, P. G. (1989). Stereotypes and prejudice: Their automatic and controlled components. *Journal of Personality and Social Psychology, 56,* 5-18.

Dunn, D. S. (1989). Demonstrating a self-serving bias. *Teaching of Psychology, 16,* 21-22.

Durso, F. T., & Mellgren, R. L. (1989). *Thinking about research: Methods and tactics of the behavioral scientist.* St. Paul: West.

Funder, D. C. (1987). Errors and mistakes: Evaluating the accuracy of social judgment. *Psychological Bulletin, 101,* 75-90.

Higgins, E. T., Rholes, C. R., & Jones, C. R. (1977). Category accessibility and impression formation. *Journal of Experimental Social Psychology, 13,* 141-154.

Hogan, R., DeSoto, C. B., & Solano, C. (1977). Traits, tests, and personality research. *American Psychologist, 32,* 255-264.

Lasswell, M. E., Ruch, F. L., Gorfein, D. S., & Warren, N. (1981). Person perception. In L. T. Benjamin, Jr., & K. D. Lowman (Eds.), *Activities handbook for the teaching of psychology* (Vol.1, pp. 185-187). Washington, DC: American Psychological Association.

Mullen, B., Atkins, J. L., Champion, D. S., Edwards, C., Hardy, D., Story, J. E., & Vanderklok, M. (1985). The false consensus effect: A meta-analysis of 115 hypothesis tests. *Journal of Experimental Social Psychology, 21,* 262-283.

Myers, D. G. (1990). *Social psychology* (3rd ed.). New York: McGraw-Hill.

Nisbett, R. E., Caputo, C., Legant, P., & Marecek, J. (1973). Behavior as seen by the actor and as seen by the observer. *Journal of Personality and Social Psychology, 27,* 154-164.

Nisbett, R. E., & Ross, L. (1980). *Human inference: Strategies and shortcomings of social judgment.* Englewood Cliffs, NJ: PrenticeHall.

Pigott, M., & Leone, C. (1990*). Instructor's manual to accompany Brehm and Kassin's social psychology.* Boston: Houghton Mifflin.

Ross, L., Greene, D., & House, P. (1977). The "false consensus effect": An egocentric bias in social perception and attribution processes. *Journal of Experimental Social Psychology, 13,* 279-301.

Tversky, A., & Kahneman, D. (1973). Availability: A heuristic for judging frequency and probability. *Cognitive Psychology, 5,* 207-232.

Watson, D. L. (1987a). The primacy effect in social judgments. In V. P. Makosky, L. G. Whittemore, & A. M. Rogers (Eds.), *Activities handbook for the teaching of psychology* (Vol. 2, pp. 132-134). Washington, DC: American Psychological Association.

Watson, D. L. (1987b). The fundamental attribution error. In V. P. Makosky, L. G. Whittemore, & A. M. Rogers (Eds.), *Activities handbook* for *the teaching* of *psychology* (Vol. 2, pp. 135-137). Washington, DC: American Psychological Association.

Wyer, R. S., & Srull, T. K. (1981). Category accessibility: Some theoretical and empirical issues concerning the processing of social stimulus information. In E. T. Higgins, C. P. Herman, & M. P. Zanna (Eds.), *Social cognition: The Ontario symposium* (Vol. 1, pp. 161-196). Hillsdale, NJ: Lawrence Erlbaum Associates, Inc.

Note

I thank Saul Kassin who suggested replicating the Nisbett et al. (1973) experiment in the classroom and Bernard Whitley, .Jr. for comments on a draft of this article.

Using Students' Perceptions of Their Instructor to Illustrate Principles of Person Perception

Robin L. Lashley
Kent State University

This article describes a classroom exercise in which students respond to a simple personality inventory that assesses their perceptions of their instructor. The data thus generated are used to illustrate the basic cognitive processes by which individuals interpret the behavior of others, as well as numerous perceptual biases that often render such interpretations inaccurate.

The term *person perception is* used to refer to the various cognitive processes by which individuals interpret their own and others' behavior. This is an important topic in social psychology, and often receives coverage in adjustment, personality, applied, and introductory courses as well.

An effective technique for demonstrating the nature of person perception, and especially the many perceptual and memorial biases to which it is susceptible, is to have students respond to a simple personality inventory designed to assess their perceptions of their instructor. This exercise is most effective if used several weeks into the semester and shortly before the topic of person perception is introduced: long enough for students to have formed stable impressions of the instructor but not so long that they have too much information on which to base their judgments. The inventory consists of two sections. The first contains a number of multiple-choice questions that require the students to make judgments regarding the instructor's identifying characteristics (e.g., age and marital status), preferences (e.g., favorite kind of music, favorite color, ideal vacation, and hobbies), and background (e.g., number of siblings and state of origin). The second section contains a list of 20 personality traits (see Anderson, 1968, or a thesaurus) to which the student responds "yes" (this word describes my instructor), "no" (this word does not describe my instructor), or "it depends" (it depends on the situation my instructor is in).

To assure anonymity, students are instructed to make two copies of their ratings. They retain one copy; the other is collected and used to prepare a tabular summary, which is distributed when person perception is discussed in class. After sharing the "true" (i.e., self-perceived) answers, the instructor can use the data to illustrate numerous principles of person perception, including the following.

1. Agreements between the instructor's and the students' judgments serve as instances of successful person perception (Hastorf, Schneider, & Polefka, 1970). Many of these reflect inferences that are readily made by noting the instructor's physical appearance (e.g., a wedding ring to infer marital status and facial wrinkles to infer age), or consistent behavior (e.g., degree of eye contact both in and out of class to infer confidence and choice of clothing to infer favorite color).

2. Students' responses to Section 1 items often reveal strongly stereotyped thinking (Miller, 1982). College students have had ample experience to develop definite expectations about those who choose teaching as a profession. This "teacher stereotype" is strengthened each time they selectively note confirming instances and discount discrepant evidence. My students expect the typical teacher to be a married, conservative, introverted intellectual who prefers dark colors, sedentary hobbies, and structured vacations.

Other common stereotypes often surface as well. Many (often erroneous) judgments are made on the basis of the instructor's age, gender, and physical attractiveness.

3. The importance of first impressions (Asch, 1946) is easily demonstrated. In justifying their perceptions of the instructor, students often demonstrate greater use of events that occurred early in the semester. The students' impressions may have been determined even before the course began (i.e., by the instructor's "reputation" around campus). The instructor can point out how subsequent behavior may be selectively perceived and recalled to confirm the initial impression.

4. Responses to Section 2 items demonstrate the actor-observer difference in person perception. The actor (instructor) tends to explain his or her own behavior in terms of the situation; observers (students) tend to explain that same behavior in terms of the actor's dispositions hones & Nisbett, 1971). Therefore, the frequency of "it depends" responses by the instructor usually exceeds that of the students. The *fundamental attribution error,* the tendency for observers to underestimate situational factors and to overestimate dispositional factors when explaining an actor's behavior (Ross, 1977), can also be discussed. Students readily substantiate their "yes" or "no" responses with recalled instances of the instructor's classroom behavior, despite the fact that these observations are highly situationally constrained.

5. Any trait in Section 2 for which there is a discrepancy between the instructor's judgment and the majority of the students' judgment can be used to discuss the validity of self-perceptions versus others' perceptions. If the instructor's perception is more favorable than the students', a self-serving bias (Shavit & Shouval, 1980) may be operating. That is, the students may be focusing on behaviors that the instructor has discounted in an effort to maintain a positive self-concept.

6. Throughout the discussion, students will have discovered many of their own implicit beliefs about people and behavior: beliefs about which traits are correlated; beliefs about the causes of behavior; beliefs about traits that characterize persons of a particular age, gender, or occupation. In short, they will have become aware of the *implicit personality theories* (Schneider, 1973) by which they attempt to explain and predict instances of behavior.

Students generally enjoy this exercise and derive several benefits from it: They acquire a better understanding of person perception, they come to appreciate the relevance of this process to their own social interactions, and they get to know their instructor better in the process!

References

Anderson, N. H. (1968). Likableness of 555 personality trait words. *Journal of Personality and Social Psychology, 9,* 272-279.

Asch, S. E. (1946). Forming impressions of personality. *Journal of Abnormal and Social Psychology, 41,* 258-290.

Hastorf, A. H., Schneider, D. J., & Polefka, J. (1970). *Person perception.* Reading, MA: Addison-Wesley.

Jones, E. E., & Nisbett, R. E. (1971). *The actor and the observer: Divergent perceptions of the causes of behavior.* Morristown, NJ: General Learning Press.

Miller, A. G. (Ed.). (1982). *In the eye of the beholder: Contemporary issues in stereotyping.* New York: Praeger.

Ross, L. (1977). The intuitive psychologist and his shortcomings: Distortions in the attribution process. In L. Berkowitz (Ed.), *Advances in experimental social psychology* (Vol. 10, pp. 174-221). New York: Academic.

Schneider, D. J. (1973). Implicit personality theory: A review. *Psychological Bulletin, 79,* 294-309.

Shavit, H., & Shouval, R. (1980). Self-esteem and cognitive consistency effects on self-other evaluation. *Journal of Experimental Social Psychology, 16,* 417-425.

Notes

1. I thank Wayne Weiten and two anonymous reviewers for their helpful comments on an earlier draft of this article.

2. Portions of this article were presented at the Ninth Annual National Institute on the Teaching of Psychology sponsored by the University of Illinois at Urbana-Champaign at Clearwater Beach. FL, January 1987.

Introducing Students to Social Psychology Through Student-Generated First Impressions of the Professor

Art Lyons
Moravian College

Some faculty members teach two sections of Social Psychology during the same term. They may struggle with having to introduce new students to the subject matter, and themselves to the students. For the past two years, I have used a demonstration that has served these purposes. Specifically, I have varied my style of dress in the two different sections (wearing a coat and tie in one section, or condition, and removing them for the other), and have collected student-generated first impressions of the professor on 10 different trait dimensions (intelligent-stupid, conservative-liberal, etc.) using a semantic differential form. Discussion of the results provides one with a great opportunity to get active class participation, and to really set the stage for many of the concepts that will be dealt with more fully later in the course. Incidentally, it is fun to receive students' first impressions and it breaks down many of the role barriers between student and professor. The discussion can actually introduce the students to both content and methods of data collection that social psychologists commonly use.

In terms of course content, the following points can be addressed: Few students will predict that the coat and tie will make a difference in their perceptions. Yet the results indicate that the professor in the coat and tie is significantly more intelligent, attractive and open-minded than the professor in slacks and a collared shirt. Thus, the students experientially learn about the powerful influence the style of dress has on person perception. They also become conscious of how quickly and easily human beings form a cohesive impression of others. This is also an appropriate time to introduce students to the fundamental attribution era of minimizing the importance of the situational factors in influencing one's perception of the individual's personality traits. In other words, would they have perceived the professor in a similar fashion if they had not known his profession and had not been sitting in a college classroom? Students will often spontaneously begin to question the basis for their assessments at this point. Given the little variability in the data for each trait, were they in fact responding to a stereotype that they al l shared about what a young, bearded, male psychology professor ought to be like? How many other stereotypes about people do they have?

How do these influence their interaction with individuals? If one desires, the concept of selective perception can be introduced as an explanatory mechanism for why stereotypes are so difficult to challenge. In addition, the concept of experimenter expectancy, or the Rosenthal effect, tantalizes students with the realization that their expectations about the professor may, in fact, be a causal factor in producing those behaviors. How might the professor's stereotype of students shape their behavior?

At this point it is valuable to point out how much material has already been introduced that demonstrates the experimental method and the special challenges of applying it in social psychology areas. A good question to ask is: How could we be sure that it was the coat and tie that made a difference in person perception? The student response is usually a good common sense introduction into the concepts of good experimental control, the use of independent and dependent variables, the need for random sampling and random assignment to conditions, and what is necessary before one can infer causality. Students quickly note the value of collecting quantifiable measures of behavior in order to compare their data to the data that were collected in another section. They also begin to appreciate the need for statistics in order to determine which differences were meaningful and which may have simply been due to chance. It is also important to consider the ethical problems related to this whole demonstration. They have been deceived; the professor did not have their informed consent—was this ethical? How about in more serious research, given that approximately 40% of social psychological research does involve deception? If the course delves heavily into survey instrument construction, it is an ideal time to introduce such terms as halo effect, response sets, counter-balancing, and the influence of giving the socially desirable answer on a self-report measure.

Regardless of how far you decide to go with the demonstration, take the risk and try it. If you do not like the first impression feedback generated, you can always blame it on the strong stereotype that students harbor about college professors, and invite them to get to know the real you during the rest of the semester.

Demonstrating a Self-Serving Bias

Dana S. Dunn
Moravian College

A self-serving attributional bias is demonstrated in a classroom exercise. Students' self-descriptions reveal a bias toward reporting positive attributes, a result that allows for discussion of motivational and cognitive processes in attribution.

The presentation and discussion of particular attributional biases in introductory social psychology courses frequently engage student interest. Students readily recognize the overuse and abuse of dispositional attributions, for example, through the "fundamental attribution error" (L. Ross, 1977). I noticed, however, that self-serving attributional biases are not as readily recognized by students. As first time readers in social psychology, students seem to take note of their inferential failings when making attributions about others, but may be less likely to do so when making attributions about themselves. Self-serving or "hedonic" biases should be intrinsically interesting because they raise issues involving individual information processing as well as motivations to enhance self-esteem.

When attention is drawn to them, the differing roles for success and failure attributions seem obvious and familiar: Students accept personal credit for high scores on exams, for example, but are reluctant to accept responsibility for failing performances. Yet the recognition that such self-serving biases may extend beyond the internal-external dimension of success and failure often escapes students. My impression is that students frequently fail to consider other ways in which they seek to portray themselves in a favorable light. To broaden the understanding of self-serving attributions and to place them firmly in the realm of students' experience, I used a simple, in-class demonstration that both captures their interest and illustrates the impact of self-serving attributions.

I used two approaches. One method involves having students anonymously list what they consider to be their individual "strengths" and "weaknesses." I do not reveal the purpose of the exercise but, as I pass out a one-page questionnaire, I inform the students that the psychology of the self will be one of the topics discussed during the next class. The questionnaire simply asks students to first write down what they believe are their personal strengths and then list their weaknesses. I emphasize that anonymity must be maintained and remind students not to put their names on the questionnaires.

After collecting their lists, I promise to report the results in the next class. I tabulate the number of strengths and weaknesses, recording the mean for each category. Not surprisingly, students tend to report almost twice as many positive as negative attributes about themselves. In addition to eliciting a number of sheepish grins, the presentation of results usually prompts a discussion concerning the processes underlying self-serving biases. Do we tend to list more positive than negative self-descriptions due to some motivational bias such as self-esteem maintenance? Or, is our information processing the origin of the bias? Perhaps we recall more easily those situations in which we displayed positive rather than negative trays. Further, this differential recall may confirm existing expectations about ourselves; we simply spend more time thinking about our perceived positive attributes. The discussion allows me to introduce the egocentric bias (i.e., people overestimate their contributions to a jointly produced outcome, M. Ross & Sicoly, 1979). This may be another instance of differential recall influencing self-attribution.

In an alternative exercise, I have students verbalize their strengths and weaknesses during class. I write a heading for strengths on one half of a chalkboard and weaknesses on the other, while asking the class members to think about themselves in these terms. Student participation in this version of the exercise is voluntary; only those students who indicate a willingness to offer self-descriptions are called on. Instructors should be extremely cautious not to embarrass students by requiring them to participate in an exercise involving self-disclosure.

After students' responses are recorded on the chalkboard, I note that the number of strengths outweighs the weaknesses. Then, I turn exclusively to the weaknesses list, discussing each item individually. Usually, several (if not most) of the weaknesses show another example of self-enhancement. For example, "lazy" can be deemed a relatively negative trait, but descriptions like "too trusting," "workaholic," and "sensitive" still maintain some positive connotations.

Indeed, many of the weaknesses students offer resemble the negative-yet-still-positive traits they might use to describe themselves to a prospective employer during an interview. I point out that because these descriptions were collected in a public setting, some self-presentational concerns were probably operating. The discussion of self-presentational issues allows for a careful consideration of how presenting ourselves to observers may differ from the manner in which we reflect on our perceived self-images. A motivation toward modesty may have a role in the former situation; however, an informational bias better accounts for the latter situation. I discuss the aforementioned role of differential recall in emphasizing the positive rather than the negative aspects of our characters.

Regardless of which method I use, after considering the results in some detail, I try to guide class discussion toward the implications of self-serving biases. Are these biases adaptive or troublesome for our views of ourselves? When do they cease to aid us and, instead, become a potentially dysfunctional aspect of the attribution process? In response to these questions, students frequently raise the issue of individual differences, pointing out that extremes exist: Some people are truly narcissistic; others tend toward self-disparagement.

Students seem to enjoy this exercise because it makes discussing inferential bias and attribution theory more personal. It also presents a novel way of thinking about the self, one that offers some explanation for our tendency to see ourselves favorably. Comments of several students indicate that it is something of a revelation to discover that such self-reflection is susceptible to error and open to doubt.

Additional demonstrations of self-serving biases are included in Wood (1984). These exercises may lead students to scrutinize thoughts about themselves a bit more and to broaden their appreciation for potential bias in self-perception.

References

Ross, L. (1977). The intuitive psychologist and his shortcomings: Distortions in the attribution process. In L. Berkowitz (Ed.), *Advances in experimental social psychology* (Vol. 10, pp. 173-220). New York: Academic.

Ross, M., & Sicoly, F. (1979). Egocentric biases in availability and attribution. *Journal of Personality and Social Psychology, 37,* 322-336.

Wood, G. (1984). Research methodology: A decision-making perspective. In A. M. Rogers & C. J. Scheirer (Eds.), *The G. Stanley Hall lecture series* (Vol. 4, pp. 189-217). Washington, DC: American Psychological Association.

The Self-Reference Effect: Demonstrating Schematic Processing in the Classroom

Donelson R. Forsyth
Katherine Hsu Wibberly
Virginia Commonwealth University

The self-reference effect, *which occurs when individuals show superior memory for information that pertains to their selfschemas, was demonstrated in a classroom setting. Subjects first evaluated whether or not each adjective in an orally presented list was self-descriptive. After a 1–min delay, they attempted to recall all the adjectives from the list. As expected, memory for self-referent terms was superior to memory for terms that were not self-referent. The exercise offers a pedagogically effective way of demonstrating schematic processing under normal classroom conditions, and it also confirms predictions derived from* depth-of-processing and schema-based memory models of social cognition.

Schemas have emerged as central theoretical constructs in contemporary analyses of interpersonal perception. Drawing on studies of the reconstructive nature of memory, schema theory assumes that information about the social world is organized within a system of cognitive associations. These networks consist of memory nodes pertaining to specific schema-relevant concepts and pathways that link these nodes to one another (Kihlstrom et al., 1988).

Person schemas, for example, summarize one's intuitive understanding of other people, including their typical behaviors, traits, and goals. *Self-schemas* organize perceptions of one's own qualities, and *stereotypes* describe the typical characteristics of people in various social groups. *Event schemas,* or scripts, define and structure one's perceptions of social situations (Fiske & Taylor, 1991).

We could not encode, store, or retrieve social information if we did not possess schemas. Students, however, sometimes have difficulty recognizing the impact of schemas on social perception and cognition. Researchers have documented a number of schematic-processing effects, but these effects are often so subtle that relatively sensitive measures are required to detect them. Moreover, even though the effects of schematic processing are ubiquitous, individuals have no access to these cognitive processes; perceivers cannot monitor their use of schemas when encoding and retrieving information (Nisbett & Wilson, 1977). Behaviorally oriented students tend to question the need to posit these cognitive constructs.

Given the centrality of the schema concept in social and cognitive psychology and students' difficulties in grasping this complex construct, we developed a classroom demonstration of schema-based processing. The demonstration takes advantage of the self-reference effect: the tendency for individuals to show superior memory for information that pertains to their self-schemas. When individuals are asked to describe their political beliefs, those who possess well-defined self-schemas pertaining to politics can describe their beliefs in much more detail than individuals who are aschematic with regard to politics (Fiske, Lau, & Smith, 1990). People who adopt a feminine gender identity (feminine schematics) require less time when they are asked to rate their feminine attributes rather than their masculine attributes. Masculine schematics show the reverse tendency, and individuals who are aschematic on both masculinity and femininity respond with equal rapidity and confidence to both types of attributes (Markus, Crane, Bernstein, & Siladi, 1982). Also, when individuals are exposed to a long string of adjectives, they can recall more of the self-referent adjectives compared to the nonrelevant adjectives (Rogers, Kuiper, & Kirker, 1977).

We used an incidental memory procedure to demonstrate the self-reference effect. Students were asked to indicate which of a number of adjectives read aloud were self-descriptive. Next the students were, without previous warning, asked to recall as many of the adjectives as they could. Students then reviewed their list of recalled adjectives and indicated whether or not each recalled adjective had been previously rated as self-referent or nonreferent. The selfreference effect was demonstrated if the percentage of self-referent items recalled exceeded the percentage of nonreferent items recalled.

Method

Undergraduate (16 women and 14 men) and graduate (23 women and 5 men) students enrolled in Social Psychology participated in the study. At the beginning of the exercise, each participant numbered a blank sheet of paper from 1 to 20. The instructor, who was a man, then read a list of 18 adjectives aloud after telling the students to circle the number corresponding to the adjective if they felt it was selfdescriptive. If, for example, students thought that Item 6, "loyal, " described them, then they would circle the number 6 on their sheet of paper. The items were drawn from Tzuriel (1984) and included the following: forceful, quiet, generous, dominant, tender, loyal, independent, compassionate, adaptable, courageous, cheerful, secretive, principled, romantic, responsible, dynamic, forgiving, and careful.

When the self-rating task was completed, the instructor talked about miscellaneous class matters for 1 min. He then told the subjects to list, in any order, all of the adjectives they could remember. When students finished the incidental recall task, the instructor distributed the list of items. The students counted and recorded the total number of adjectives they circled during the self-rating task, the number of self-referent words recalled, and the number of nonreferent words recalled. Then they calculated the percentage of self-referent adjectives recalled and the percentage of nonreferent adjectives recalled. Percentages were used to take into account the varying number of self-referent words initially identified by subjects. If, for example, a subject felt that 12 of the 18 items were self-referent, then by chance alone his or her recall list would include more self-referent items. Evidence of self-reference, in this procedure, requires that the percentage of self-referent items recalled exceeds the percentage of nonreferent items recalled.

Results

Analysis of students' responses suggests that the demonstration effectively documented the self-reference effect. Subjects recalled only an average of 42.5% of the nonreferent words compared to 56.0% of the self-referent terms. A 2 X 2 (Sex X Type of Adjective [self-referent vs. nonreferent]) mixed analysis of variance yielded only a main effect for type of adjective, $F(1, 56) = 13.82, p < .001$.

Discussion

The procedures used in this demonstration, although rudimentary, are sufficiently sensitive to document the self-reference effect: Subjects' memory for self-referent items was superior to their memory for items that were not self-referent. The procedure is also a practical one. Because it does not require individual testing sessions or reaction time assessment, it can be used during class with a large group of students.

The demonstration also facilitates the analysis of several methodological and theoretical issues concerning schematic processing of information. Initially, students maintained that their incidental recall scores were shaped primarily by the vividness of the trait terms. Attention-getting trait terms, they contended, were better remembered than more pallid terms. The exercise, however, convincingly demonstrated to them the impact of their self-schemas because more memorable words were also more self-descriptive words. The discussion also proved useful in illustrating research design and data analysis. Some students, for example, failed to correct for initial frequencies of self-descriptive terms when they first explored the effect. Students often recalled more self-referent words than nonreferent words, but this difference cannot be interpreted until scores are adjusted to reflect the number of items initially selected as self-referent.

The demonstration also facilitated the analysis of depth-of-processing and schema-based memory models of social cognition (Klein, Loftus, & Burton, 1989). First, depth-ofprocessing theory maintains that self-referent information is processed at a deeper level than nonreferent information. If, for example, the students were asked "Does the word have more than two syllables?," they could respond without processing the word very deeply. Such shallow processing would not lead to particularly durable memories. In contrast, self-referent encoding requires much deeper processing (Klein & Kihlstrom, 1986). Second, schema theories suggest that the more elaborate the schema that will hold the incoming information, the better our ability to recall that information. Self-schemas may be the most complex and intricate associative networks in our memory system, so self-referent information is particularly memorable. Both of these theories could be demonstrated in the classroom by varying the initial question posed to subjects. Although some students could answer the question "Does the word describe you?," others could be asked "Does the word have more than two syllables" or "Does the word describe your psychology teacher?" (Bellezza, 1984).

Depending on interest, the exercise could also be used to explore the cognitive consequences of gender identity. Because the adjectives used fall into three categories—masculine, feminine, and neutral—students' self-ratings reflect their sex-role orientation. Masculine individuals, for example, should circle more of the items that reflect masculine qualities (e.g., dominant and independent), whereas feminine individuals should circle more of the items that reflect feminine qualities (e.g., tender and compassionate). Recall scores, too, can be reexamined to explore memory biases. Individuals who incorporated masculinity into their self-concepts should recall more masculine than feminine words, whereas feminine schematics should remember more feminine adjectives than masculine ones (Markus et al. 1982).

References

Bellezza, F. S. (1984). The self as a mnemonic device: The role of internal cues. *Journal of Personality and Social Psychology, 47,* 506-516.

Fiske, S. T., Lau, R. R., & Smith R. A. (1990). On the varieties and utilities of political expertise. *Social Cognition, 8,* 31-48.

Fiske, S. T., & Taylor, S. E. (1991). *Social cognition* (2nd ed.). New York: McGraw Hill.

Kihlstrom, J. F., Cantor, N., Albright, J. S., Chew, B. R., Klein S. B., & Niedenthal, P. M. (1988). Information processing and the study of the self. In L. Berkowitz (Ed.), *Advances in experimental social psychology* (Vol. 17, pp. 2-48). New York: Academic.

Klein, S. B., & Kihlstrom, J. F. (1986). Elaboration, organization, and the self-reference effect in memory. *Journal of Experimental Psychology: General, 115,* 26-38.

Klein, S. B., Loftus, J., & Burton, H. A. (1989). Two self-reference effects: The importance of distinguishing between self-descriptiveness judgments and autobiographical retrieval in self-referent encoding. *Journal of Personality and Social Psychology, 56,* 853-865.

Markus, H., Crane, M., Bernstein, S., & Siladi, M. (1982). Self-schemas and gender. *Journal of Personality and Social Psychology, 42,* 38-50.

Nisbett, R. E., & Wilson, T. D. (1977). Telling more than we can know: Verbal reports on mental processes. *Psychological Review, 84,* 231-259.

Rogers, T. B., Kuiper, N. A., & Kirker, W. S. (1977). Self-reference and the encoding of personal information. *Journal of Personality and Social Psychology, 35,* 677-688.

Tzuriel, D. (1984). Sex role typing and ego identity in Israeli, oriental, and western adolescents. *Journal of Personality and Social Psychology, 46,* 440-457.

A Classroom Demonstration of the Primacy Effect in the Attribution of Ability

Francis T. McAndrew
Knox College

The activity described in this paper gives students firsthand experience with the primacy effect that occurs when individuals make judgments about the ability of other people. The exercise serves as a springboard for discussion and as a useful vehicle for exploring some key issues related to experimental design as well as attribution theory.

One of the most active areas of research in social psychology today is the study of how individuals make judgments about the causes underlying the behavior of other people. This diverse area of investigation is loosely grouped under the label of "attribution theory." Given its current dominance in the field, most courses in social psychology and many introductory courses devote a large amount of time to exploring the various attribution theories and attributional phenomena that research has uncovered. As is the case with any psychological process, students gain a deeper appreciation of the dynamics of attribution if they are put in a situation where they see these processes at work in themselves and realize that what is being described is not simply some abstract textbook curiosity but something that they do every day. It can be especially valuable for students to become aware of some of the biases that seem to be built into the way they process information about other people.

A topic that is particularly well suited to classroom demonstrations of attributional processes is the question of how we make judgments about the ability of others. This question has advantages for the teacher. First, it is intrinsically interesting to students in that attributions based on performance in athletic events, job interviews, and the classroom ultimately come down to some conclusion about the stimulus person's "ability." Second, attributional situations relevant to ability can be full of very concrete, quantifiable information (such as the number of points scored on a test), allowing precise manipulation of the stimuli presented to the students.

One peculiar bias that commonly occurs when making attributions about ability is referred to as the "primacy effect." This phenomenon refers to the tendency for an observer's judgment to be influenced more strongly by the early information about a stimulus person than by information that comes later. A number of studies (e.g., Jones, Rock, Shaver, Goethals, & Ward, 1968; McAndrew, 1981; Newtson & Rindner, 1979) have demonstrated that subjects almost completely disregard late information when making judgments about the ability of others, as long as the task in question does not involve an ability that is thought to improve with practice (Larkin, D'Eredita, Dempsey, McClure, & Pepe, 1983). Newtson and Rindner (1979) proposed that the primacy effect occurs because individuals cease to process information effectively when they reach a point of subjectively sufficient information for making an attribution. For example, these studies have repeatedly found that a person who does well in the early stages of a problem-solving task is perceived as more intelligent than a person who does well in the later stages. In addition, the early achiever is judged as having performed better and is expected to perform better than the late achiever on subsequent tasks. All of these attributions occur even though the objectively measured performance of the two stimulus persons is exactly the same.

Because the primacy effect involves both the evaluation of others and the processing of information, it may be covered in courses on cognitive, social, industrial/organizational, or introductory psychology. A highly effective classroom demonstration of this primacy effect is based on a procedure developed by McAndrew (1981), and it can be made very flexible with some modifications suggested by Watson, deBortali-Tregerthan, and Frank (1984).

PROCEDURE

In the demonstration, students will correct the answer sheets from a multiple-choice test taken by two hypothetical students. The teacher must first decide whether a between-subjects or a within-subjects demonstration is more suitable. Using a between-subjects design, each student will correct only one answer sheet from one hypothetical student. In the within-subjects design, each student will receive two different answer sheets from two different hypothetical students. In either case, the teacher prepares two different sets of answer sheets. One set shows an "ascending" pattern of success whereby the hypothetical student begins by getting most of the questions wrong, but late in the test begins to improve. The "descending" pattern is the reverse of this; the student starts out doing well, after which performance deteriorates. If a between-subjects design is used, one half of the class receives the ascending pattern and the other half receives the descending pattern. In the within-subjects design, each student receives one copy of each pattern. The between-subjects design is more efficient for very large classes and can be used to demonstrate the process of random assignment and the logic behind comparing randomly assigned groups. On the other hand, Watson et al. (1984) have pointed out that the demonstration may be more meaningful if the students experience the primacy effect firsthand by serving as their own controls, and that dividing small classes in half can result in very small groups. For these reasons, the demonstration will be described hereafter as a within-subjects design, keeping in mind that it can easily be changed to a between-subjects procedure when circumstances call for it.

Materials

Each student will receive two multiple-choice answer sheets, one marked "Person #1" and the other marked "Person #2." Each answer sheet will appear to be a completed set of 30 items. Each item consists of five alternatives (lettered "a" through "e"), one of which is circled. Each answer sheet is followed by a second attached page containing the following three questions:

1. Out of the 30 problems, how many would you estimate that this student answered correctly?
2. If this person were to complete the test, taking the next set of 30 problems (the test has 60 problems), how many would you estimate that the person would get correct?
3. On the scale below, circle the "X" that best reflects your estimate of this student's general intelligence.

Unintelligent X X X X X X X X X Intelligent

Instructions to Students

The multiple-choice test should be described to students as the first 30 items of a 60-item test of mental ability. It will be more involving for the students if they believe that they are grading a *real* test taken by a *real* student. Details about the nature of the test questions, purpose of the test, and where the test takers were from can be added to make it more interesting and realistic without affecting the outcome of the

demonstration. The entire demonstration should be described as an attempt to find out how well people can form impressions about others based on nothing but a test performance.

Half of the class is assigned to correct Person #1's test first; the other half corrects Person #2's test. As the teacher reads through the list of "correct" responses, students put a check mark beside each wrong answer. As soon as the list of 30 items is finished, students complete the three questions on the second page of the questionnaire without referring back to the answer sheet. This procedure is then repeated for the second hypothetical student.

Answer Key

For the ascending pattern of success, the answers (in order) for the 30 items on the stimulus person's answer sheet should be: a, a, d, c, e, d, c, c, b, e, a, c, d, a, b, b, e, b, b, c, d, b, a, d, e, c, d, c, b, a. For the descending pattern, the answers should be: a, c, c, b, d, d, b, b, c, d, b, a, c, a, b, b, e, a, e, d, c, c, b, c, e, b, b, d, c, a. The "correct" answers read out loud by the teacher for the 30 items should be: a, c, c, b, a, d, b, b, a, e, a, a, c, a, a, a, e, b, b, d, c, a, a, d, e, a, d, c, b, a. Using these patterns, the number of "correct" answers will be 15 out of 30 (50%) for both the ascending and descending patterns of performance. The "ascending" stimulus person gets 5 correct answers on the first 15 items and 10 correct answers on the second 15. The "descending" person gets 10 correct out of the first 15 items and 5 correct on the second 15.

CONCLUDING REMARKS

Most students (experience suggests that 80% is not an unreasonable number to expect) will show a very strong primacy effect by estimating that the "descending" performer did significantly better than the "ascending" performer, by judging the intelligence of the descending performer as being higher, and by predicting that the descending performer will do better in the future. The effect is robust enough that a comparison of the group means using a *t* test will usually be significant, even with relatively small groups. However, it is usually easier for the teacher and more impressive for the students to note the high percentage of the class that fell prey to the primacy effect, and to put the raw data on the board so that differences in judgments made about the two stimulus persons are convincingly obvious. Many students will be so surprised to hear that the scores were the same in both cases that they will insist on counting the answers on the answer sheets to verify the fact. Discussing these results leads easily into a more general discussion of how we make judgments about others, the importance of first impressions, and other issues that are at the heart of attribution theory. The demonstration can be as useful as a springboard for discussion as it is for its purely didactic purpose. In addition, this exercise can be used to teach something about methodology rather than attribution theory; it is ideally suited to illustrate the trade-offs involved when deciding between within-subjects and between-subjects designs.

For example, in statistics and research methods classes students can be shown that the variability in each group can be (and should be!) the same even though the central tendencies are different, and that as group size increases, smaller differences between the means take on greater significance. It will also be clear that when deciding whether to use between-subjects or within-subjects designs, an experimenter will have to anticipate how the change in degrees of freedom will be balanced by other gains or losses in the experiment as a whole. The instructor might also point out that there are many different ways of interpreting any set of data. In this case, you may compare the mean scores from each stimulus person, examine the percentages of subjects giving higher ratings to one stimulus person versus the other, or simply compare the number of students who showed the primacy effect to the number who did not. Obviously, with a little ingenuity, many statistical/design issues can be introduced through this demonstration.

In summary, the exercise described here is easy, effective, and flexible; it is well suited for small dis-cussion-oriented classes as well as the large lecture hall.

References

Jones, E. E., Rock, L., Shaver, K. L., Goethals, G. R., & Ward, L. M. (1968). Pattern of performance and ability attribution: An unexpected primacy effect. *Journal of Personality and Social Psychology, 10,* 317-340.

Larkin, J., D'Eredita, T., Dempsey, S., McClure, J., & Pepe, M. (1983, April). *Hope for late bloomers: Another look at the primacy effect in ability attribution.* Paper presented at the meeting of the Eastern Psychological Association, Philadelphia, PA.

McAndrew, F. T. (1981). Pattern of performance and attributions of ability and gender. *Personality and Social Psychology Bulletin, 7,* 583-587.

Newtson, D., & Rindner, R. J. (1979). Variation in behavior perception and ability attribution. *Journal of Personality and Social Psychology, 37,* 1847-1858.

Watson, D. L., deBortali-Tregerthan, G., & Frank, J. (1984). *Instructor's manual to accompany "Social psychology: Science and application."* Glenview, IL: Scott, Foresman.

Teaching Attribution Theory With a Videotaped Illustration

Michael J. White
Debra L. Lilly
Ball State University

A videotaped illustration of Kelley's (1973) covariation attribution model is described. The videotape contains sets of sequentially presented behavioral situations that lead students to analyze information using Kelley's model. A description of one set of scenes illustrated on the videotape is provided. The cognitive implications of the use of videotaped illustrations to improve understanding of attributional concepts are noted. Informal observation suggests that the videotape illustration is highly effective. Students are easily able to make appropriate attributions using Kelley's model and to apply them to real-life situations.

Concept learning is an important teaching objective. Exclusive classroom focus on concepts, however, may create a sense of irrelevance and boredom in students. This is especially true if concepts are not tied to actual situations or otherwise illustrated. Apart from increasing student interest, vivid, real-life illustrations serve to define and emphasize meaningful relationships among concepts. And as meaning increases, so will retention (Anderson, 1985).

Social psychology's attribution theories embody an especially complex set of concepts. This loose collection of ideas attempts to explain how persons cognitively interpret (i.e., attribute) the cause, implications, and context of their own and others' behavior (e.g., Heider, 1958; Jones & Davis, 1965; Kelley, 1973;

Weiner, 1979). One strategy used to teach attribution theory encourages students' self-awareness of how they use attribution processes to explain the behavior of their friends and acquaintances (McAndrew, 1985). Although this approach is commendable, we have tried another. Specifically, a series of behavioral situations have been illustrated on an instructional videotape. Students who view the videotape are led systematically (indeed they are compelled) to arrive at attributions for the behavior shown on the tape. For several reasons, Kelley's (1973) covariation attribution model is the focus of these situations. The reasons are: (a) It is a highly complex theory or model, (b) students consistently have difficulty understanding its concepts, and (c) the nature of the theory lends itself to systematic visual representation.

The videotape was shot in our university's television production studio. The premise of the videotaped situations is taken from an example used by McArthur (1972) and involves persons at a dance. The question posed to viewers is, "Why did the woman have her feet stepped on by her partner?" Is it because she is clumsy, because her partner is clumsy, or because of some unique combination of events? These attributional questions force viewers to extract and analyze information presented using the analytical framework proposed by Kelley (1973). Three sets of scenes are presented on the tape. Only the first set of scenes is discussed in detail.

The tape begins with a graphic representation of Kelley's (1973) attribution cube, which illustrates the three referents available for social perceivers to observe. These referents include: (a) persons, (b) persons over time, and (c) entities (i.e., people with whom the referent persons interact or events in which the referent persons participate). The tape then continues with persons dancing at a "dance class. " The camera focuses on one couple. On four separate occasions, the viewer sees the male partner (Bob) step on the female partner's (Kim's) foot. A sentence appears on the screen: "Bob almost always steps on Kim's foot when they dance." This particular combination of events illustrates a condition of high consistency (i.e., Bob is consistent over time when interacting with Kim, the entity).

The next series of scenes appears. In them, Bob dances with Jane, Betty, and Michelle. He steps on no one's feet. The fourth scene shows Bob dancing with Kim. Bob trips over Kim's foot again. The sentence appears: "Bob almost never steps on anyone else's feet when they dance." This combination of events illustrates high distinctiveness (i.e., Bob reacts in a distinctive way to Kim, the entity).

Four more scenes follow. In the first three, Jim, George, and Alan dance with Kim. None of them trips over her foot. The fourth scene shows Bob stepping on Kim's foot again. This is emphasized with the sentence: "Hardly anyone else steps on Kim's feet when they dance." Low consensus has been illustrated; other persons do not interact with the entity, Kim, in the same fashion as Bob, the person of interest.

Finally, viewers are asked the question, "Why did Bob trip on Kim's feet?" They are given three possible answers: (a) Bob is clumsy (i. e., an attribution to a disposition of his), (b) Kim is clumsy (i.e., an attribution to an external cause from Bob's standpoint), and (c) it is due to some unique pattern of interaction between them (i.e., a joint explanation). Answer c is correct in this case. Viewers are also asked how certain they are concerning the cause. Under the conditions shown (i.e., high consistency, high distinctiveness, and low consensus), attributions are made with confidence according to Kelley's model. As noted earlier, 2 other combinations of 12 scenes each are shown in order to illustrate different combinations of behaviors and attributional possibilities.

It is also important for students to learn how persons deviate from Kelley's (1973) normative model. Accordingly, the tape is accompanied by a lecture and readings that describe the wide range of biases and errors in the attribution process (Fiske &Taylor, 1984; Lau & Russell, 1980; Storms, 1973). As Gayne (1966) suggested, these additional activities help the students to understand the principles underlying attribution processes.

Class discussion centers around the implications of the concepts, the operation of the concepts in the videotape, and the generalizations that students made to their own experiences. After the discussion, students are reminded that their attributions offer only possible explanations for the behaviors observed. Alternative perspectives, including those by Dweck and Licht (1980), Jones and Davis (1965), and Weiner (1982), are then introduced and discussed.

Informal observation suggests that this approach is highly effective. Students are animated while watching the videotape and easily draw the "appropriate" attributional conclusions. Their attention is directed to the ease and naturalness with which they make their attributions. By so doing, they experience one of the important premises of the theory: People are "naive scientists" who spontaneously use covariation in social information to make inferences about puzzling behaviors. Furthermore, the concepts of the theory are no longer abstract and removed, but are linked to their own thinking and perception.

References

Anderson, J. R. (1985). *Cognitive psychology and its implications.* New York: Freeman.

Dweck, C. S., & Licht, B. G. (1980). Learned helplessness and intellectual achievement. In J. Garber & M. E. P. Seligman (Eds.), *Human helplessness*: *Theory and applications* (pp. 197-221). New York: Academic.

Fiske, S. T., & Taylor, S. E. (1984). *Social cognition.* Reading, MA: Addison-Wesley.

Gayné, R. M. (1966). The learning of principles. In H. J. Klausmeier & C. W. Harns (Eds.), *Analysis of concept learning* (pp. 81-95). New York: Academic.

Heider, F. (1958). *The psychology of interpersonal relations.* New York: Wiley.

Jones, E. E., & Davis, K. E. (1965). From acts to dispositions: The attribution process in person perception. In L. Berkowitz (Ed.), *Advances in experimental social psychology* (Vol. 2, pp. 218-266). New York: Academic.

Kelley, H. H. (1973). The processes of causal attribution. *American Psychologist, 28,* 107-128.

Lau, R. R., & Russell, D. (1980). Attributions in sports pages. *Journal of Personality and Social Psychology, 39,* 29-38.

McAndrew, F. T. (1985). A classroom demonstration of the primacy effect in the attribution of ability. *Teaching of Psychology, 12,* 209-211.

McArthur, L. Z. (1972). The how and what of why: Some determinants and consequences of causal attribution. *Journal of Personality and Social Psychology, 22,* 171-193.

Storms, M. D. (1973). Videotape and the attribution process. Reviewing actors' and observers' point of view. *Journal of Personality and Social Psychology, 27,* 166-175.

Weiner, B. (1979). A theory of motivation for some classroom experience. *Journal of Educational Psychology, 71,* 3-25.

Weiner, B. (1982). The emotional consequences of causal attributions. In M. S. Clark & S. T. Fiske (Eds.), *Affect and cognition: The 17th annual Carnegie symposium on cognition* (pp. 185-209) . Hillsdale, NJ: Lawrence Erlbaum Associates, Inc.

Note

We thank Joe Pacino for his assistance in producing the videotape.

3. TEACHING ABOUT ATTITUDES AND PERSUASION

Bringing Cognitive Dissonance to the Classroom

David M. Carkenord
Joseph Bullington
Georgia Southern University

We describe a classroom procedure that induces cognitive dissonance in students by pointing out inconsistencies between their behaviors and attitudes. Given that experimental tests of the concept of dissonance can sometimes be difficult to explain, enabling students to experience dissonance may make the teaching task easier. In an assessment of the exercise, most students reported feeling some dissonance and positively evaluated its effectiveness.

The concept of cognitive dissonance (Festinger, 1957) is often difficult for instructors to explain and students to understand. Instructors in our department frequently express something akin to dread over an impending "cognitive dissonance" lecture.

Explanation of the concept often begins in a straightforward manner: If a person's thoughts and behaviors are inconsistent, the person is motivated to change attitudes or behaviors to reestablish consistency. After all, we do not want to appear to be hypocritical, either to ourselves or others. Students can generally follow the argument to this point. The problem begins when one then attempts to explain the experimental tests of cognitive dissonance theory, most notably Festinger and Carlsmith's (1959) classic study. In this study, a group of students completed a boring task and were later paid either $1 or $20 to tell a potential "subject" (actually a confederate) that the same task was really interesting. Subjects in each group, then, told the subject that the experiment was very interesting. On a later measure of their attitudes toward the task, subjects in the group that received $1 reported more favorable attitudes toward the boring task than subjects in the group that received $20. The $1 group, according to Festinger and Carlsmith, experienced more dissonance than the $20 group because $1 provided insufficient justification for their attitude-discrepant behavior (telling a person something they themselves did not believe).

In explaining this study to a class, we have noticed that the discussion typically gets bogged down over the notion of how dissonance, a psychological state, provides the motivation for a change in attitude. Many students fail to understand that it is the experience of dissonance that directly motivates the change in Festinger and Carlsmith's (1959) experiment, not the amount of money received (although the amount of money does induce the dissonance). It is as if students forget about the notion of dissonance and focus solely on the money variable. (Our students often state that subjects in the $20 condition should rate the task more favorably because they received more money!) We hypothesized that providing students with an opportunity to experience a state of dissonance resulting from discrepancies between their own attitudes and behaviors might better enable them to understand the concept of cognitive dissonance and, consequently, the subtleties of Festinger and Carlsmith's experimental manipulation. Thus, we developed a simple but effective in-class exercise that induces dissonance by comparing students' personal attitudes and behaviors on a number of social issues. Our findings suggest that a majority of students agree or strongly agree with a series of attitudinal statements, but only a minority perform behavior consistent with their reported attitudes.

Method

Materials

The stimulus material for the exercise consists of one double-sided page. Side 1 is titled "Attitude Survey" and contains four items to be rated on a 5-point scale ranging from *strongly disagree* (1) to *strongly agree* (5). The items are: (a) World hunger is a serious problem that needs attention, (b) Our country needs to address the growing number of homeless, (c) The right to vote is one of the most valuable rights of American citizens, and (d) Our government should spend less money on nuclear weapons and more on helping citizens better their lives. Instructions at the top of the page read, "Please indicate your attitudes on the four statements below."

Side 2 is titled "Behavioral Survey" and is headed with instructions reading, "Please indicate whether or not you perform the stated behavior on a regular basis." Below the instructions are four items corresponding to the attitudinal items on page 1: (a) Do you personally do anything to lessen world hunger (e.g., donate money or food or write your representative)?, (b) Do you personally do anything to help the homeless (e.g., volunteer at homeless shelter or donate money)?, (c) Did you vote in the last election for which you were eligible?, and (d) Do you personally convey your feelings to the government (e.g., write your representatives or participate in protests/marches)? Response options of "yes" and "no" are offered for each item.

Procedure

Prior to any discussion of cognitive dissonance, distribute copies of the handout to students with instructions to complete Side 1 (Attitude Survey) before Side 2 (Behavioral Survey). Then ask the class (by a show of hands) how many agreed or strongly agreed with attitudinal Item 1. Next, ask the students to turn to Side 2 and again raise their hands if they responded "yes" to the corresponding behavioral item. Repeat the process of comparing the attitudinal responses with the corresponding behavioral responses for the remaining three items. Most students will quickly get the point of the exercise.

A subsequent discussion of cognitive dissonance can begin with a simple question like, "How does it make you feel when these inconsistencies are pointed out to you?" Our students responded, "hypocritical," "guilty," or some related remarks. Further discussion can focus on formal definitions of cognitive dissonance and cognitive consonance, research studies on cognitive dissonance (e.g., Aronson & Mills, 1959; Festinger & Carlsmith, 1959), and dissonance reduction strategies.

For purposes of this article, we asked students to return their completed forms, but instructors would typically not need to collect the forms unless they plan to report the specific results to the class later. Table 1 displays the responses of 125 students; 53 were enrolled in two social psychology classes and 72 in two introductory psychology classes. These responses highlight the large discrepancies between students' attitudes and behaviors.

Only one student reported complete attitude-behavior consistency on all items. The remaining 124 students (99.2%) reported attitude-discrepant behavior on at least one of the four items. Twenty-nine students (23%) reported attitude-behavior inconsistencies on all four items. These findings demonstrate that the exercise highlighted inconsistencies in virtually all students in our sample.

Student Assessment

After the discussion, students evaluated their experiences on a 5-point scale ranging *from strongly disagree* (1) to *strongly agree* (5). For all four items, students' reactions were quite positive. They reported that (a) the exercise helped in understanding cog-

Table 1. Attitudinal and Behavioral Responses

Item and Course[a]	Attitudes (% Agree and Strongly Agree)	Behaviors (% Yes)
World hunger a problem		
Social	87	17
Introductory	90	7
Must address homeless problem		
Social	96	32
Introductory	95	33
Right to vote important		
Social	94	47
Introductory	85	40
Government should better people's lives		
Social	91	11
Introductory	88	3

[a]$n = 53$ for social, $n = 72$ for introductory.

nitive dissonance ($M = 4.5$), (b) they experienced dissonance ($M = 4.1$), (c) the exercise provided self-insight ($M = 4.0$), and (d) the exercise was a useful learning experience ($M = 4.3$).

Eight students also wrote comments, all of which were positive. One response was particularly interesting: "[The exercise] works well, even to the point where I 'fudged' on the second sheet [Behavioral Survey] to try to relieve some cognitive dissonance." Not surprisingly, this response was from the lone student who reported complete attitude-behavior consistency. Evidently, the exercise was especially effective for this individual.

Discussion

We believe the exercise is very useful for introducing and explaining the concept of cognitive dissonance, because virtually all students actually experience cognitive dissonance. Thus, students learn and understand the concept in direct relation to their own attitudes and behaviors. Later discussions of research on cognitive dissonance take on more meaning because students have recently experienced such a psychological state. Nevertheless, a number of related issues must be addressed.

First, some instructors may be concerned about the ethical nature of our exercise. Asking students to publicly admit to certain attitudes and behaviors may be considered too intrusive for a classroom demonstration. One strategy to avoid this problem would be to collect the completed surveys, shuffle them, and redistribute them to the class. At this point, proceed through the item-by-item comparisons, again by a show of hands. In this situation, students would be expressing the attitudes and opinions of anonymous fellow students. Although our data were not obtained in this manner, we believe such an approach would alleviate any ethical concerns while maintaining the overall usefulness of the exercise.

A second and related issue is whether the public admission of attitude-behavior inconsistencies may have induced the reported dissonance rather than (or in addition to) the inconsistencies themselves. Although this situation is possible, we believe students experienced dissonance before the public admission. We have no empirical data to support our belief, but our subjective appraisal of student responses during the exercise provides some evidence. As students completed Side 2 of the survey, extensive murmuring and mild laughter occurred. We interpret such activities as the behavioral manifestation of the students' dissonance resulting solely from completing the exercise instrument.

A final concern is whether the dissonance induced by our exercise ultimately results in any attitude or behavior changes, as predicted by cognitive dissonance theory. Such evidence, although interesting, would be difficult to obtain and is beyond the intended scope and purpose of our exercise. The goal of our procedure is to induce dissonance so that students can directly experience such a psychological state. The exercise is not intended as a test of cognitive dissonance theory or dissonance reduction strategies. Those topics could be addressed in the discussion following the exercise. Thus, although possible attitude or behavior changes resulting from our exercise would be an intriguing topic, lack of such information does not detract from the usefulness of the procedure. Future users of the exercise may want to devise a means to deal more extensively with this issue.

References

Aronson, E., & Mills, J. (1959). The effects of severity of initiation on liking for a group. *Journal of Abnormal and Social Psychology, 59*, 177-181.

Festinger, L. (1957). *A theory of cognitive dissonance.* Stanford, CA: Stanford University Press.

Festinger, L., & Carlsmith, J. M. (1959). Cognitive consequences of forced compliance. *Journal of Abnormal and Social Psychology, 58*, 203-210.

Note

We thank Bill McIntosh, Michael Zuschlag, and three anonymous reviewers for their helpful comments and suggestions on earlier drafts of this article.

Stereotype Measurement and the "Kernel of Truth" Hypothesis

Randall A. Gordon
Western Carolina University

A demonstration of stereotype measurement suitable for medium to large classes is described. The demonstration illustrates McCauley and Stitt's (1978) diagnostic ratio measure and examines the validity of the "kernel of truth" hypothesis. The exercise provides a starting point for a discussion of stereotypes and their measurement. The results of the demonstration are reported along with suggestions for discussion of a variety of concepts related to the diagnostic ratio measure and stereotype formation.

Katz and Braly's (1933) work is usually cited as one of the earliest examples of stereotype measurement. Replications of this classic study by Gilbert (1951) and Karlins, Coffman, and Walters (1969) revealed changes in the uniformity of racial stereotypes across time and a tendency for Americans to attribute more negative characteristics to themselves. However, the technique used to quantify social stereotypes in these studies has been criticized (Brown, 1986).

In the three studies just cited, Princeton University undergraduates were instructed to select from a large list of traits all descriptors that were typical of various ethnic groups (e.g., Germans, Japanese, and Jews). One problem with this technique is an incomplete understanding of how subjects interpreted the word *typical.* For example, was *typical* interpreted to mean that a trait could be found in all members of a specific group, 75% of the group or at least 50% of the group? More recent research by Brigham (1971, 1973) and McCauley and Stitt (1978) used different methods that shed light on how subjects from the Princeton studies may have interpreted "typical" traits.

This demonstration can be used to introduce stereotypes and to lead into a discussion on how they are formed and their relative degree of accuracy. Data from the demonstration illustrate advances in measurement, which can help students understand the cognitive basis of social stereotypes. The technique is appropriate for courses in general psychology, social psychology, attitude and survey research, or any other class that covers measurement. The demonstration, based on Experiment 3 from McCauley and Stitt (1978), also allows for an assessment of stereotype validity and the "kernel of truth" hypothesis (LeVine & Campbell, 1972). This hypothesis suggests that there is a kernel of truth in most stereotypes when they are obtained from people who have firsthand knowledge of the stereotyped group.

Method

This demonstration provides data on the validity of social stereotypes by comparing diagnostic ratios based on students' estimates of various measurable characteristics with criterion ratios (i.e., ratios calculated from objective data). According to McCauley and Stitt (1978), a diagnostic ratio is a quantitative measure of stereotyping "based on defining stereotypes as probabilistic predictions that distinguish the stereotyped group from others" (p. 929). The ratio is computed by obtaining estimates of the probability of a trait occurring among members of a specific group (e.g., the percentage of Germans who are efficient) and dividing this by the probability that the trait occurs among all people (e.g., the percentage of all people who are efficient).

Before conducting the demonstration, it is necessary to obtain data regarding the actual prevalence of various characteristics (e.g., having four or more children or completing high school) within specific populations (e. g., Black Americans, White Americans, or all Americans). With one exception, the data for the demonstration discussed herein were gathered from the *Statistical Abstract of the United States: 1986* (U.S. Bureau of the Census, 1986). The following reports Of percentages of characteristics were collected for Black Americans, White (nonHispanic) Americans, Hispanic Americans, and for all Americans: who completed high school, who received food stamps, who had four or more children, who had a female head of household, and who were unemployed in tire last month. Tile un-

employment information was based on data from September 1988 (Bureau of Labor Statistics, 1988).

Forty-seven students (42 White, 5 Black) from two undergraduate social psychology courses were asked to respond to the following instructions: "in the spaces provided, indicate the *percentage* of American people who have the traits or characteristics listed below. " The five items on each page of the questionnaire appeared as follows:

___completed high school (based on 1986 data)
___were unemployed last month (based on September 1988 data)
___received food stamps (based on 1986 data)
___had 4 or more children (based on 1986 data)
___had a female head of household (based on 1986 data)

Each student responded to the page regarding all American people and then responded to similar pages with the words *Black, White,* and *Hispanic* substituted for the word all at the top of the sheet. The order of completing the last three pages of the questionnaire was counterbalanced. Before they complete the questionnaire, it is important to inform students that the purpose of the demonstration is to examine the accuracy of their perceptions and that they should give their best estimates.

Results and Discussion

Results of the demonstration provide a method for assessing the accuracy of various stereotypes. To accomplish this, first calculate the diagnostic ratios (i.e., divide each subject's percentage estimate of a characteristic occurring within a specific group by the estimate for that same characteristic occurring among all Americans) and list the mean diagnostic ratios with the corresponding objective criterion ratios. The criterion and mean diagnostic ratios are listed in Table 1.

Consistent with results obtained by McCauley and Stitt (1978), the relative accuracy of the mean diagnostic ratios was striking. Ten of the 15 diagnostic ratios were significantly different from 1.0, all ts (46) > 2.04 and all ps < .05, two-tailed. However, of the 14

Table 1. Criterion and Mean Diagnostic Ratios for White, Black, and Hispanic Americans

Characteristic	White Americans		Black Americans		Hispanic Americans	
	Criterion Ratio	Diagnostic Ratio	Criterion Ratio	Diagnostic Ratio	Criterion Ratio	Diagnostic Ratio
Completed high school (1986)	1.02	1.06*	.83	.81*	.65	.70*
Unemployed (Sept. 1988)	.90	.89	2.03	1.87*	—a	1.92*
Received food stamps (1986)	.81	.68**	1.89	1.35**	1.47	1.11**
Had 4 or more children (1986)	.89	.93	2.19	1.94*	2.63	1.77**
Female head of household (1986)	.83	.89	1.43	1.45*	.89	.92

aUnemployment data were not available for this group.
*Significantly different from 1.00, p < .05, two-tailed; df = 46. **Significantly different from 1.00 and from criterion ratio, for both tests, p < .05, two-tailed; df = 46.

possible comparisons between criterion and mean diagnostic ratios, only 4 revealed significant differences, all ts (46) > 2.92 and all ps < .05, two-tailed. These results suggest that stereotypical perceptions should not automatically be characterized as gross overgeneralizations. In each case, the minority group diagnostic ratios were less extreme than the corresponding criterion ratios.

Presenting students' mean diagnostic ratios can start a discussion of techniques for measuring stereotypes. A good beginning point is Lippmann's (1922) discussion of stereotypes, their origins, and maintenance. The techniques used by Katz and Braly (1933), Brigham (1971), and McCauley and Stitt (1978) to measure stereotypes can be compared.

Students who have participated in this demonstration are usually surprised at the high level of accuracy among the group. An informal assessment showed that most students believed their participation in the demonstration and the classroom discussion helped them to understand the diagnostic ratio measure. Students also reported that comparing the three techniques helped them to understand the concept of stereotypes. Most students reacted favorably to the demonstration and felt that it should be included in future classes.

Although the data usually support, in part, the "kernel of truth" hypothesis, responses typically indicate less extreme stereotypes than the objective criterion ratio. A discussion of research pertaining to the "contact hypothesis" and its relation to stereotyping and intergroup conflict can be introduced at this point. Amir (1969) provided a good review of this literature. If the class is racially heterogeneous, a breakdown of the data by race of student can be used to make comparisons based on degree of familiarity and contact with members of a given race.

This type of outcome can also be used to introduce the topic of response biases (e.g., social desirability) that might influence stereotypes in general. It is important to remind students, however, that the instructions they received presented the task as one that focused on prediction and accuracy, not on attitudes or stereotype measurement. Data collected using this technique should be less likely to suffer from these response set problems (McCauley & Stitt, 1978).

Finally, the prescribed use of diagnostic ratios as individual measures of stereotypes should be mentioned. McCauley and Stitt (1978) introduced the diagnostic ratio as an individual and quantitative measure of stereotypes, not as a means of examining a stereotype held by a group of people. Unfortunately, they did not caution readers about the interpretation of mean diagnostic ratios.

Although most students will be impressed by how accurate their mean diagnostic ratios are, part of this accuracy is due to the "statisticized" nature of the group task. A statisticized group task involves averaging the products (estimates) of independent, noninteracting individuals. It is important to conclude the discussion of the demonstration with a description of "statisticized groups" (Stroop, 1932). One way to accomplish this is to select one of the classes' mean diagnostic ratios that was relatively accurate and list the corresponding distribution of individual diagnostic ratios. For example, the mean diagnostic ratio for Hispanic Americans having four or more children was 1.92. However, the distribution of these ratios ranged from .25 to 10. Students will see that what accounts for much of the accuracy is that overestimates and underestimates cancel each other out. Providing additional examples (e.g., guessing the temperature of the classroom or the number of jelly beans in a jar) should help students further understand the concepts of statisticized group tasks and random error.

I leave you with one final word of caution. Although the data collected in the demonstration are related to racial and ethnic stereotypes, they differ fundamentally from more traditional assessments of stereotypes that involve rating groups on personality characteristics (e.g., materialistic, industrious, or lazy). Accuracy found in the demonstration may be due, in part, to the transmission of relevant statistical information (e.g., unemployment figures) through the mass media. This type of transmission does not occur in quite the same manner for personality traits related to stereotypes.

References

Amir, Y. (1969). Contact hypothesis in ethnic relations. *Psychological Bulletin, 71*, 319-341.

Brigham, J. C. (1971). Ethnic stereotypes. *Psychological Bulletin, 76*, 15-38.

Brigham, J. C. (1973). Ethnic stereotypes and attitudes: A different mode of analysis. *Journal of Personality, 41*, 206-233.

Brown, R. (1986). *Social psychology the second edition.* New York: Free Press.

Bureau of Labor Statistics. (1988). *Employment and Earnings, 35*, 20.

Gilbert, G. M. (1951). Stereotype persistence and change among college students. *Journal of Abnormal and Social Psychology, 46*, 245-254.

Karlins, M., Coffman, T. L., & Walters, G. (1969) . On the fading of social stereotypes: Studies in three generations of college students. *Journal of Personality and Social Psychology, 13*, 1-16.

Katz, D., & Braly, K. W. (1933). Racial stereotypes of one hundred college students. *Journal of Abnormal and Social Psychology, 28*, 280-290.

LeVine, R. A., & Campbell, D. T. (1972). *Ethnocentrism.* New York: Wiley.

Lippmann, W. (1922). *Public opinion.* New York: Harcourt, Brace.

McCauley, C., & Stitt, C. L. (1978). An individual and quantitative measure of stereotypes. *Journal of Personality and Social Psychology, 36*, 929-940.

Stroop, J. R. (1932). Is the judgment of the group better than that of the average member of the group? *Journal of Experimental Psychology, 15,* 550-562.

U.S. Bureau of the Census. (1986). *Statistical abstract of the United States: 1986* (98th ed.). Washington, DC: U.S. Government Printing Office.

Note

I thank Bruce Henderson, Hal Herzog, and three anonymous reviewers for their helpful comments on an earlier draft of this article

Gender Stereotyping in Advertisements

Melinda Jones
University of Pittsburgh at Bradford

Students are not cognizant of gender stereotyping in mass media; consequently, they seldom realize the role of mass media in maintaining stereotypic beliefs. This demonstration, based on work by Goffman (1976), reveals extensive gender stereotyping in advertisements, provides an excellent introduction to the topic of gender roles, and encourages follow-up discussion.

Students are seldom aware of how gender stereotypes and expectations develop and are maintained. Messages about appropriate gender roles and behaviors permeate our language, school curriculum, working life, religion, and media (Basow, 1986). The effects of gender stereotypes can be seen on individuals and on society in general. On a personal level, evidence suggests that gender stereotypes affect peoples' self-esteem (Whitley, 1983) and psychological well-being (Whitley, 1984). On a societal level, gender stereotypes have contributed to gender bias in hiring decisions (Glick, Zion, & Nelson, 1988). Given these consequences, instructors may want to increase students' awareness of gender stereotypes and how cultural institutions foster gender distinctions. One effective technique to demonstrate the pervasiveness of gender stereotypes is to expose students to mass media, a ubiquitous source of gender stereotypes that both reflects and shapes society.

In an analysis of "gender advertisements," Goffman (1976) found numerous examples of subtle stereotyping in the portrayal of women and men. Five of these are: (a) function ranking (the tendency to depict men in executive roles and as more functional when collaborating with women), (b) relative size (the tendency to depict men as taller and larger than women, except

when women are clearly superior in social status), (c) ritualization of subordination (an overabundance of images of women lying on floors and beds or as objects of men's mock assaults), (d) the feminine touch (the tendency to show women cradling and caressing the surface of objects with their fingers), and (e) family (fathers depicted as physically distant from their families or as relating primarily to sons, and mothers depicted as relating primarily to daughters).

This article describes a demonstration that helps students realize that advertisements can communicate messages about gender roles. Using Goffman's framework to analyze selected advertisements leads students to think about advertisements in a novel way and to realize that advertisements not only sell products but also develop and maintain gender stereotypes.

Method

This demonstration requires the instructor to assemble a set of stimulus materials. My preference for stimulus materials is magazine advertisements displayed on slides because slides can be easily presented to large and small classes and the time of their exposure can be controlled. Finding advertisements that illustrate each of the five "genderisms" is not a difficult task. I have used advertisements taken from popular magazines (e.g., *Cosmopolitan, Glamour, Newsweek,* and *Vogue*), which promote a wide variety of products, including cigarettes, clothes, cologne, liquor, and soft drinks. Some of the selected advertisements depict more than one gender theme. Although not a requirement for the success of the demonstration, I intersperse the recent advertisements with some from the 1950s. This technique allows students to compare the portrayal of the sexes across different decades. To ensure that students do not perceive gender stereotypes when none are present, I also include advertisements that do not fit into Goffman's categories.

First, I introduce students to Goffman's work on advertisements by describing the five gender themes and displaying ads depicting each of these themes. Next, I inform students that they are to view a series of advertisements (20 slides) and instruct them to classify each ad according to Goffman's framework. Then, I remind students that some of the ads may not fit any of the gender themes and that some ads may depict more than one gender theme.

To assist with students' analyses of the advertisements, I provide an answer sheet numbered from 1 to 20, corresponding to each ad to be analyzed, with the names of the five gender themes placed beside each number. Students view each ad for approximately 15 s and respond by circling the "genderisms" they believe are depicted in the ad. After the slide presentation, students review the advertisements and contribute their perceptions of them. Then, I encourage students to use their imaginations to change the sex of the models and see whether the pictures still seem "natural." Usually the students' imaginary advertisements appear unnatural and somewhat silly to them, indicating that advertisements display men and women in roles consistent with our cultural beliefs. Class discussion focuses on the similarities and differences in the portrayal of men and women in today's advertisements and those of the 1950s. After reviewing the ads, I ask for a show of hands from those who correctly identified all the gender themes. Approximately 40% of the students successfully recognize the gender themes.

Results

Students are often amazed that they have not previously noticed the gender themes. Typical statements made during the discussion include: "It gave me a new and unique outlook into advertising"; "It made me realize some of the gender stereotyping I never considered before"; "I enjoyed looking at advertisements that I usually just take for granted"; "It was interesting to see how advertisers use gender."

Students (N = 67) in my recent introductory psychology course evaluated the slide presentation and ensuing discussion of gender stereotyping on several dimensions using scales ranging from *not at all* (1) to *extremely* (7). Students indicated that the demonstration was interesting *(M* = 5.92, *SD* = .65), informative *(M* = 5.74, *SD* = .88), and effective *(M* = 5.86, *SD* = .93) and recommended the use of the demonstration in future classes *(M* = 6.35, *SD* = .85). Students also judged the overall quality of the demonstration on a

scale ranging from *poor* (1) to *excellent* (5), and the outcome was very favorable (*M* = 4.36, *SD* = .65).

Discussion

This classroom exercise has many advantages for instructors. First, it is appropriate for use in a variety of courses, including introductory psychology, psychology of women, social psychology, and consumer psychology. Second, it introduces the topic of gender roles and gender stereotyping in a nonthreatening manner by using advertisements, a medium that is virtually impossible to ignore (Snyder & DeBono, 1985). Third, this demonstration facilitates discussion on a number of follow-up topics, such as how advertisements influence the viewer and whether advertisers are becoming more sensitive to the portrayal of women in advertisements (Ford, LaTour, & Lundstrom, 1991; Soley & Reid, 1988). Fourth, this discussion gives instructors an opportunity to address the role of imitation learning in acquiring sex-typed behavior in children (Bussey & Bandura, 1984) and to review research indicating that adults may be similarly affected by the content of advertisements (Geis, Brown, Jennings, & Porter, 1984). Finally, instructors may discuss other sources of gender role socialization, such as the educational curriculum and language.

From the students' perspective, this demonstration increases their knowledge of how advertisements communicate messages about gender roles. Student comments after the demonstration often reflect their surprise at the pervasiveness of gender stereotyping in the media and their observation that the media are powerful agents of sexist socialization. The issues surrounding gender stereotypes, particularly the personal implications, are often not carefully considered by college students. This demonstration provides an excellent vehicle for introducing the topic of gender and exploring students' beliefs about the sexes.

References

Basow, S. A. (1986). *Gender stereotypes: Traditions and alternatives.* Monterey, CA: Brooks/Cole.

Bussey, K., & Bandura, A. (1984). Influence of gender constancy and social power on sex-linked modeling. *Journal of Personality and Social Psychology, 47,* 1292-1302.

Ford, J. B., LaTour, M. S., & Lundstrom, W. J. (1991). Contemporary women's evaluation of female role portrayals in advertising. *Journal of Consumer Marketing, 8,* 15-28.

Geis, F., Brown, V., Jennings, J., & Porter, N. (1984). TV commercials as achievement scripts for women. *Sex Roles, 10,* 513-525.

Glick, P., Zion, C., & Nelson, C. (1988). What mediates sex discrimination in hiring decisions? *Journal of Personality and Social Psychology, 55,* 178-186.

Goffman, E. (1976). *Gender advertisements.* New York: Harper & Row.

Snyder, M., & DeBono, K. G. (1985). Appeals to image and claims about quality: Understanding the psychology of advertising. *Journal of Personality and Social Psychology, 49*, 586-597.

Soley, L., & Reid, L. (1988). Taking it off: Are models in magazine ads wearing less? *Journalism Quarterly, 65*, 960-966.

Whitley, B. E., Jr. (1983). Sex role orientation and self-esteem: A critical meta-analytic review. *Journal of Personality and Social Psychology, 44*, 765-778.

Whitley, B. E., Jr. (1984). Sex role orientation and psychological well-being: Two meta-analyses. *Sex Roles, 12,* 207-225.

Note

I gratefully acknowledge the helpful comments of Joseph J. Palladino, Jeff S. Topping, and three anonymous reviewers on a graft of this article

Identifying Major Techniques of Persuasion

Vivian Parker Makosky
St. Lawrence University

The purpose of this class exercise is to teach students how to identify the major persuasion techniques employed in advertisements such as: appeal to or creation of needs, use of loaded words or images, prestige or social suggestion.

Exposure to advertisements is a fact of everyday life. Vast amounts of money are spent on these attempts to control behavior, and there is at least some evidence that the persuasion techniques employed are successful. Surveys conducted by a market research firm indicate that we not only remember what advertisers tell us, we also believe it a lot of the time. In one survey, 82% could correctly name the product for "Please don't squeeze the . . . " (Charmin); 79% knew that "Plop, plop, fizz, fizz, oh what a relief it is" means AlkaSeltzer; 59% identified Coke for 'It's the real thing"; 57% knew that Morton Salt goes with "When it rains, it pours"; and 55% knew that you should "Give your cold to . . . " Contac (Feinsilber & Mead, 1980). These same authors report that in a second survey, the percentage of people who consider advertising claims to be "completely true" is surprisingly high.

Most discussions of persuasion in social and introductory psychology textbooks (e.g., Crider, Goethals, Kavanaugh, & Solomon, 1983) focus on such issues as: how credible, attractive, and similar to the target the communicator is; whether or not the communication is one-sided or two-sided; whether or not the target person is paying attention to the message, or has agreed to a similar request in the past. Advertising

uses additional techniques of persuasion, which are seldom presented, providing an opportunity for the instructor to present useful and interesting information without duplicating the text.

The purpose of this class exercise is to increase student awareness of common persuasion techniques used in advertising such as: (a) the appeal to or creation of needs, (b) social and prestige suggestion, (c) the use of emotionally loaded words and images. The instructor's presentation of these techniques draws on television commercials for illustrations, but the assignments to students use magazine advertisements because they can be brought to class more easily or attached to written reports.

THE APPEAL TO OR CREATION OF NEEDS

In this technique, the advertiser evokes a need and then represents the product (or recommends action) as a means of satisfying that need. The discussion of needs is structured with a modified version of the Maslow (1954) hierarchy of needs, including the following levels: physiological needs, safety and security needs, needs for belonging and love, self-esteem and status needs, cognitive needs, aesthetic needs, and self-actualization needs. It is easy to find TV commercials to illustrate appeals to physiological needs ("Aren't you hungry for Burger King now?"), safety and security ("Get a piece of the rock"), belongingness and love ("Brush your breath with Dentyne"), and self-esteem and status ("When E. F. Hutton speaks...").

Appeals to cognitive, aesthetic, and self-actualization needs are much less common. It would seem that those with advertising dollars to spend believe that some needs really are more basic than others, and are trying to reach as many people as possible. Information on targeting populations by advertising products on particular types of shows can be found in discussions of psychographics (Wells, 1975).

SOCIAL AND PRESTIGE SUGGESTION

The main point of this technique is that you should buy or do X because someone else does. With *social suggestion,* that someone else is everyone else. The Pepsi generation, Wrigley's Spearmint Gum, and virtually every other product that features lots of people, in different types of clothes and/or settings, often of different ages and races, is relying on social suggestion. With *prestige suggestion,* on the other hand, you should do or buy X because some famous or prestigious person says to do so. James Garner for Polaroid, Bill Cosby for Jello, Evonne Goolagong for Geritol, and all those famous names with unknown faces for American Express are examples of prestige suggestion.

LOADED WORDS AND IMAGES

This technique is the most subtle because it is not what is said so much as how it is said, or what you are seeing while it is being said. One example is the use of athletic, attractive people in the advertisements for snacks (e.g., jockeys, skiers, etc., who eat Snickers). Certain "buzzwords" fall into this category, including "natural" for beauty products and "light" for anything they want to sound dietetic. Often the best way to illustrate this technique is to talk about the product "image." For example, Anheuser-Busch has created completely different images for Michelob and Budweiser beers. Michelob has had a long series of advertisements emphasizing social situations, often with couples, and using such phrases as "weekends were made for Michelob" and, subsequently, "put a little weekend in your week" when the people were meeting after work. Budweiser, on the other hand, emphasizes achievement ("For all you do, this Bud's for you"), featuring Clydesdale horses and targeting an almost exclusively male population. Loaded words and images are used to enhance the impact of the message (as when beautiful people are associated with beauty products) and/or to suspend reason (as when cigarette advertisements feature the outdoor scenes and "fresh" taste).

Variations on this activity work well in introductory, social, personality, or motivation classes, or in discussions of the applications of psychology. The background discussion of the techniques is largely the same, regardless of the level of the class or the complexity of the rest of the assignment. Examination of actual advertisements makes it clear that they use more than one technique simultaneously, and the instructor may wish to modify the four variations suggested next in light of that fact.

VARIATION 1

Students bring to class the first five ads from an expensive magazine (e.g., *Vogue),* and the first five ads from a cheap magazine (e.g., *Family Circle).* Each collection of ads is referenced. Students are grouped in fives to analyze: the ads, the needs appealed to in the two types of ads, which type of suggestion was used, what words and images stood out, assumptions about the target populations of these magazines.

VARIATION 2

Students bring in the first five ads from a women's magazine and the first five ads from a men's magazine. The inclass activity proceeds as above.

VARIATION 3

Students bring in ads that appeal to them personally and ads that they think are a "turn off." In this case, the ads should be brought in before the lecture on techniques. In order to avoid potential embarrassment to individual students, the men's ads are pooled and the women's ads are pooled. The class discussion can then focus on the implied needs of college students, and whether the students believe the implications to be accurate. As always, the discussion should bring out the similarities/differences in the persuasion techniques in the two groups of ads.

VARIATION 4

Students bring in one ad appealing to each level in the needs hierarchy. The source of each ad is referenced. The small in-class groups discuss and then summarize the types of magazines the ads came from, and the products and images associated with each need level.

Students are very enthusiastic about this assignment and it is a good way to get discussion going. You should allow an entire class period for the discussion of ads, approximately half of the time for the small groups to reach their conclusions and half for each small group to report to the class at large.

If you want to make the same points, but do not wish to spend so much in-class time on it, each of these variations can be modified as out-of-class discussion assignments, with a brief report to the class at large. Alternatively, these can be writing assignments. In upper-level classes, frequency distributions in the various categories can be tabulated, along with calculations of reliability in coding ads, statistical significance of differences between two groups of ads, and so on. One of the advantages of this assignment is that it can be varied from term to term.

References

Crider, A. B., Goethals, R. D., Kavanaugh, R. D., & Solomon, P. R. (1983). *Psychology.* Glenview, IL: Scott, Foresman.

Feinsilber, M., & Mead, W. B. (1980). *American averages.* Garden City, NY: Doubleday.

Maslow, A. H. (1954). *Motivation and personality.* New York: Harper and Row.

Wells, W. D. (1975). Psychographics: A critical review. *Journal of Marketing Research, 12,* 196-213.

Note

For background material on advertising and persuasion, consult author for bibliographical list.

From Acceptance to Rejection: Food Contamination in the Classroom

D. W. Rajecki
Indiana University-Purdue University at Indianapolis

This demonstration allows students to experience and measure a shift from food acceptance to food rejection, based on the phenomenon of contamination sensitivity to disgusting substances. Students rate the desirability of a snack, which is then progressively contaminated by contact with human residues. Repeated measurements show progressive contamination: The students' ratings reveal quick and statistically reliable shifts from accepting (liking) to rejecting (disliking) the snack. This exercise generates meaningful data sets and is recommended for several courses.

This article describes an effective and efficient classroom demonstration of induced food rejection. The exercise is recommended for methodology and statistics courses in which students are required to generate and process data. It produces meaningful data sets that appeal to students because they are directly involved. The exercise could be advantageous in certain content courses. For example, in social psychology it could be used for an elaboration of attitude expression and change, and in learning or motivation courses it could provide insight into the formation of associations. Even introductory psychology students can gain from its demonstration of design and measurement principles.

The approach derives from the literature on contamination sensitivity to disgusting substances (Rozin & Fallon, 1987). Psychological contamination of otherwise acceptable food occurs in two ways: (a) trace contamination by contact with a disgusting substance (e.g., soup containing a human hair) and (b) associational contamination by contact with material associated with a disgusting substance (e.g., soup stirred with a clean fly swatter). My approach takes advantage of the power of trace contamination.

Materials

Relatively inexpensive materials proved sufficient to demonstrate trace contamination in class. First, I prepared a number of color slides of delectable foodstuffs, including several kinds of popular meats, finger foods, and pastries. The pictures were culled from direct mail catalogs and magazine ads. Other kinds of visual presentations would serve; the point of showing the pictures is to focus peoples' attention on food. Second, I made up color-coded decks of four index cards for the repeated measures to be taken.

Three additional items completed the materials list: (a) my coffee cup that was associated with and frequently used by me in prior meetings with the class, (b) my pocket comb, and (c) a small can (177 ml) of

V8 tomato juice cocktail. I picked V8 because I like it as a snack.

Rationale

The point of the tomato juice was to provide a vehicle for trace contamination; the cup and comb served as agents of pollution. Human residues—such as feces, urine, saliva, and mucus—are potent food contaminants. But even much subtler human traces can also be disgusting. For example, Rozin and Fallon (1981, p. 42) mentioned "the unpleasantness experienced by many on feeling the warmth of a seat used by another person." Based on this sort of insight, I expected that my cup would be a contaminant, and my comb even more so.

Procedure

To be effective, the contamination demonstration should be conducted without prior notification or warning. In the middle of a lecture, the decks of index cards were distributed. Scale responses and points used in the project were listed on the blackboard as follows: *like extremely much* (6), *like very much* (5), *like fairly much* (4), *like and dislike equally* (3), *dislike fairly much* (2), *dislike very much* (1), and *dislike extremely much* (0). Dawes and Smith (1985) described this instrument as a general rating scale. The scale and its potential applications were discussed until all students indicated that they understood how to use it. A color code was also drawn on the board to ensure that students would use the colored index cards in the proper sequence.

Apropos of nothing, I stated that it certainly would be agreeable if snacks were available during class. But what would we have? To help make a decision, the tantalizing food slides were shown. After the display, I explained that the idea was to rate one's desire to have a snack. I reminded the students of the food slides and asked them to refer to the scale points and values on the board. Using the designated first card, they were to express their desire for any snack they happened to have in mind by choosing a scale point that matched their desire. The students then recorded that scale point by writing down its particular scale value as an integer. (This first rating serves primarily as a warm-up or practice trial, and it is also useful as a manipulation check, as seen next.) When completed, the first cards were turned face down on the students' desks. Next, the small, unopened can of V8 was removed from hiding and was held aloft. The students then rated (on the second card) their desire to have the juice as a snack at the moment.

When the second rating was completed, I remarked that it is not very refined to drink out of a can. Looking around for an acceptable serving vessel, I spotted my own coffee mug, dumped out the liquid content (water), opened the can of V8, and poured the juice into the cup. This act presumably tainted the juice because of trace (and possibly associational) contamination with the residues in and on the cup. Holding the cup aloft, I inquired as to how much students desired that particular juice in that particular cup as a snack right now. The third card was used for this rating in the usual fashion.

When the third rating was completed, I said that I forgot to shake up the can of V8 to prepare it for drinking, but this oversight could be corrected. A small plastic comb was taken out of my pocket, and I ran it through my hair once or twice, inserted it into the juice in the cup, and stirred the liquid. With the soiled and contaminating comb jutting out, the cup was held aloft again. The students were asked how much they desired that particular juice in that particular cup containing that particular comb as a snack at the moment. The fourth card was used for this last measure. Each student then collected her or his cards in a package and bound them with a rubber band. The demonstration required less than 20 min.

Results

In a recent semester, I ran a class of 124 undergraduates (75 women and 49 men), through the demonstration. The impact of the slides was as expected; the average rating for "any snack" was 4.82 and 4.59 for men and women, respectively, which is a positive manipulation check. These means are not significantly different, $t < 1.00$, and gender did not affect any of the other tests reported here. Henceforth, gender, although taken into account in the appropriate analyses, will be dismissed from consideration.

The original plan was to use the whole class as a data base to test the effects of contaminating the V8. But, 77% of the men rated V8 per se between 3 and 0 on the scale and 70% of the women also rated it in this low range. Overall, 60% of the students initially rated the juice at 0 on the scale. This finding indicates that the scaling technique was sensitive to some students' aversion to V8, but people who are already at the lower levels—or at the floor—of a rating scale can hardly be expected to show much of a contamination effect. Accordingly, for this report, the data from individuals with initial V8 ratings of 3 or less were set aside. (This post hoc elimination of some subjects and retention of others may have biased the sample toward a certain kind of regression effect, but these concerns were relieved to an extent in a replication, as noted next.) To test the contamination hypothesis with this first class, I was left with a subsample of 33 people who had rated V8 per se at the 4-, 5-, or 6-point levels, and I cast their juice ratings in an analysis of variance (ANOVA). The average ratings by these students over the three V8 evaluations were: V8 alone = 4.67, V8 + cup = 2.30, and V8 + cup + comb = 0.21. The predicted contamination effect was very clear, and the repeated-measures statistical effect over the three ratings was significant, $F(2, 62) = 126.21$, $p < .01$.

Replication and Evaluation

The demonstration was replicated with refinements. In a meeting of 57 students from another class, I pretested—using the scale already described—a list of beverages that included apple juice, Coke, grape juice, milk, orange juice, Pepsi, R.C. Cola, 7-Up, V8, and water. Orange juice was the most popular beverage with an average pretest rating of 4.98. (Not surprisingly, by now, V8 had the lowest overall rating of 2.75.) It is noteworthy that 54 of the 57 students (95%) rated orange juice at the 4-, 5-, or 6-point levels.

At a subsequent meeting, I ran this second class through the contamination demonstration as described, this time using a small can of Donald Duck orange juice as the target. Based on data from all the students, the replication was a success. The average rating from the "any snack" manipulation check was 4.81. The mean ratings from the demonstration were: orange juice alone = 3.90, orange juice + cup = 1.27, and orange juice + cup + comb = 0.00, $F(2, 122) = 216.05$, $p < .01$. Of the 63 students who saw this demonstration, 62 (98%) showed some contamination shift over the three juice measures.

I obtained a short evaluation of the demonstration from this second section. After the purpose of the exercise was explained, a one-page questionnaire was distributed that stated: "As a teaching aid, the food slide and orange juice demonstration was. . . ." Judgments were expressed on four bipolar rating scales: dull-interesting, clear-unclear, unconvincing-convincing, and good-bad. Utilizing 10-point scales, the students' marks were scored from a low of 1 (negative pole) to a high of 10 (positive pole). The demonstration was fairly well received by the class; it was seen as interesting ($M = 8.84$), clear ($M = 9.71$), convincing ($M = 9.33$), and good ($M = 9.35$).

Discussion

To the extent that personal involvement is motivating in the mastery of subject matter, this trace contamination exercise has value. Students can be given the direct experience of feeling and expressing fairly strong evaluative reactions. The demonstration shows them that the scale can pick up the shift from acceptance to rejection of food, and that the ANOVA detects the effect. The technique has the advantage that large amounts of data from fairly complex designs can be generated quickly and inexpensively. The idea, of course, is that the students would be responsible for the data analysis.

This realistic exercise demonstrates some of the problems and anomalies that emerge in "real life" research. For example, the unexpected, partial floor effect for V8 ratings reported in the first demonstration illustrates the pitfalls of simply trusting one's assumptions in psychological research. The data from the replication also raise some questions. The orange juice mean of 3.90 was substantially lower than the overall pretest mean of 4.98. One explanation for this finding is that during the pretest, the students may have had their own, favorite type of orange juice in mind when they expressed their judgments, whereas in the demonstration itself, they had no choice but to rate a single commercial canned brand. So the two ratings differed. A more interesting possibility is that the instructor's contact with the unopened can was seen as a form of contamination of the juice. These propositions can be tested in the classroom with the technique described here.

References

Dawes, R. M., & Smith, T. L. (1985). Attitude and opinion measurement. In G. Lindsay & E. Aronson (Eds.), *Handbook of social psychology* (3rd ed., Vol. 1, pp. 509-566). New York: Random House.

Rozin, P., & Fallon, A. E. (1981). The acquisition of likes and dislikes for food. In J. Solms & R. L. Hall (Eds.), *Criteria of food acceptance: How man chooses what he eats* (pp. 35-48). Zurich, Switzerland: Foster-Verlag AG.

Rozin, P., & Fallon, A. E. (1987). A perspective on disgust. *Psychological Review, 94,* 23-41.

Note

I thank the students in my introductory psychology classes for their cooperation and assistance and the Methods and Techniques Editor and three anonymous reviewers for their helpful comments an earlier versions of this article.

4. TEACHING ABOUT AGGRESSION

Defining Aggression: An Exercise for Classroom Discussion

Ludy T. Benjamin, Jr.
Texas A&M University

This activity is designed to generate class discussion on the definition of aggression and related issues of causation and control. It exposes students to a large number of issues involved in defining aggression and helps them to understand the complexity of such a construct and thus the reasons why their classmates and psychologists are in disagreement about its meaning.

Aggression is a topic included in virtually every textbook on introductory psychology. Some books place aggression in the section on motivation and emotion while others cover it as part of social psychology. Most include it in reference to research on humans but discussion of some animal studies of aggression is also common. Treatment of related concepts such as violence, anger, frustration, and assertiveness are also common topics.

Whereas textbook coverage of aggression is almost guaranteed, a definition of the term is not. In a nonrandom sample of 10 introductory psychology books (selected from the author's bookcase), 5 provided an explicit definition of aggression but the others left the meaning embedded in a series of paragraphs and so required the reader to serve as lexicographer. Considering the complexity of the term *aggression,* it is not surprising that these authors might choose to avoid espousing a particular definition.

The exercise described in this paper uses aggression as an example of a typical construct in psychology, permeated with a host of subtle meanings and not so subtle disagreements that make it difficult to reach a consensual definition. One could use other constructs such as intelligence or self-esteem, but aggression was chosen because it generates considerable discussion among students. Anecdotal evidence for the fascination with this topic can be drawn from the prevalence of aggression as a theme in movies and television, the popularity of sports, and the interest many people show in reports of violent crime.

The activity described here can be used in a number of classes, including the course in introductory psychology and, in fact, anywhere you treat the topic of aggression. It should be used prior to any lecture on aggression and before the students have read their textbook coverage of the subject. This exercise works best in a class of 50 students or less, but by altering the data reporting procedures it can be used in much larger classes, although discussion obviously will suffer in large classes. The activity requires about 50 minutes but could be made shorter or longer depending on the preferences of the instructor. The instructor's role in this exercise is to serve as a tabulator of the data and as moderator of the discussion.

PROCEDURE

At the beginning of the class, give each student a copy of a questionnaire containing the 25 numbered statements shown in Table 1. Instruct the students to "read each statement and decide whether or not you believe the situation described is one of aggression." Wording of this instruction is critical so as not to bias the responses. Avoid using phrases like "aggressive act" or "aggressive behavior" because one of the issues to be discussed is whether some overt behavior needs to occur in aggression. Ask the students to circle the number of each statement that describes aggression. Tell them they should respond according to their own beliefs and not how they think they should respond or how they think most people would respond. Compliance with this request can be enhanced by telling the students not to put their names on the questionnaires. Indeed, there is no reason in this exercise to know how a particular person responded. You may want to have the students indicate their sex on the questionnaire if you would be interested in looking at potential sex differences in the definition of aggression. Such differences, if obtained, would undoubtedly add to the interest in the discussion.

Allow the students about 5 minutes to complete the questionnaire. Most, if not all, of the students will finish before that time, so you should be ready to proceed when the last person has finished. Collect the questionnaires, shuffle, and redistribute them to the class so that each student gets a copy. Most students will be given a questionnaire other than their own, but it is unimportant if they get their own copy back. This procedure allows students to report on the responses that may or may not be their own, thus eliminating a potential source of embarrassment.

Table 1. Aggression Questionnaire

1. A spider eats a fly.
2. Two wolves fight for the leadership of the pack.
3. A soldier shoots an enemy at the front line.
4. The warden of a prison executes a convicted criminal.
5. A juvenile gang attacks members of another gang.
6. Two men fight for a piece of bread.
7. A man viciously kicks a cat.
8. A man, while cleaning a window, knocks over a flowerpot which, in falling, injures a pedestrian.
9. A girl kicks a wastebasket.
10. Mr. X, a notorious gossip, speaks disparagingly of many people of his acquaintance.
11. A man mentally rehearses a murder he is about to commit.
12. An angry son purposely fails to write to his mother, who is expecting a letter and will be hurt if none arrives.
13. An enraged boy tries with all his might to inflict injury on his antagonist, a bigger boy, but is not successful in doing so. His efforts simply amuse the bigger boy.
14. A man daydreams of harming his antagonist, but has no hope of doing so.
15. A senator does not protest the escalation of bombing to which he is morally opposed.
16. A farmer beheads a chicken and prepares it for supper.
17. A hunter kills an animal and mounts it as a trophy.
18. A dog snarls at a mail carrier, but does not bite.
19. A physician gives a flu shot to a screaming child.
20. A boxer gives his opponent a bloody nose.
21. A Girl Scout tries to assist an elderly woman, but trips her by accident.
22. A bank robber is shot in the back while trying to escape.
23. A tennis player smashes his racket after missing a volley.
24. A person commits suicide.
25. A cat kills a mouse, parades around with it, and then discards it.

Record the data on the board by asking students for a show of hands on each numbered item, with hands being raised if the item is circled on the questionnaire they are holding. It is important to know the exact size of the class in this exercise to know when you have unanimity. For example, with a class size of 34, total agreement would come from a score of 34, in which case every student agreed that the item described aggression. A score of zero would mean that no one thought the item described aggression. Such unanimity is rare and typically occurs only on those items in which there seems to be no intent to harm. Tabulating the data on the chalkboard can be accom-

plished quickly, usually in less than 5 minutes, so that the bulk of the class time can be devoted to discussion.

CLASS DISCUSSION

Use the questionnaire results to get the students talking about how aggression is defined. You might begin with those items for which there is greatest agreement and proceed to those on which the class is evenly divided. Note that the 25 statements are quite diverse and are intended to span the gamut of issues relevant to consideration of aggression: harm to living versus nonliving things (9 and 23), accident versus intention (8 and 21), actual damage versus no physical damage (10, 13, and 18), self-defense (3, 13, and 14), duty or job responsibility (3, 4, 19, 20, and 22), predation and instinctual behavior (1, 2, and 25), survival (1, 6, and 16), acts involving animals other than humans (7, 16, 17, and 18), covert acts (11 and 14), inaction (12 and 15), self injury (24), and killing for sport (17 and 25).

Attempt to get students to make these points by grouping the related items in the discussion. For example, items 16 and 17 make an interesting comparison. The latter is more often viewed as aggressive, and a similar pattern emerges in items 1 and 25. In both pairs, students distinguish between killing for food and killing for sport. Many will argue that food-seeking justifies the act and would not label it aggression. Debate on these items and many others is typically lively and opposing viewpoints are common. Should alternate views not be forthcoming on some issues, the instructor may wish to play the role of devil's advocate.

If there is time, or in a separate lecture in the next class period, you can present some of the definitions of aggression proposed by psychologists. Consider the following examples:

1. "Behavior intended to hurt another person" (Freedman, 1982, p. 259).
2. "Any behavior whose intent is to inflict harm or injury on another living being" (McGee & Wilson, 1984, p. 503).
3. "Hostile or forceful action intended to dominate or violate" (Lefrancois, 1982, p. 596).
4. "Behavior that is intended to injure another person (physically or verbally) or to destroy property" (Atkinson, Atkinson, & Hilgard, 1983, p. 321).
5. "A response that delivers noxious stimuli to another organism" (Buss, 1961, p. 3).

The first four definitions require intent, but the last one does not. The first one limits aggression to humans, while the second and fifth broaden it to include all living organisms. But what about kicking wastebaskets and smashing tennis rackets? That could be considered aggressive under the fourth definition. All definitions talk about behaviors, actions, or responses but leave one unclear as to whether inaction can be aggressive or not. Providing these definitions to students helps them to understand that, like them, psychologists also have some difficulty in-agreeing on what does or does not constitute aggression.

Students in my class consistently have rated this activity high in terms of satisfaction and as an exercise in learning. Written comments indicate that a number of them believe that it serves to sharpen their critical thinking skills. A few miss the point and want to be told the "real" definition of aggression after the exercise is over, but that kind of reaction is quite rare.

ADDITIONAL SUGGESTIONS

You can use this exercise as a basis for discussion or as a lecture on the causes of aggression: Is aggression instinctual?; Is aggression a natural reaction to conditions such as frustration, conflict, and pain?; Is aggression learned, and if so, how and from what sources? This last question presents a good opportunity to discuss aggression in the media, particularly television, and what effect it may have on the behavior of viewers (see Liebert, Sprafkin, & Davidson, 1982).

Other topics of interest include: aggression in athletics, competitiveness versus aggressiveness, assertiveness versus aggressiveness, the positive role of aggression, violet crime, the relation of prejudice to aggression, and methods for the control of aggression.

References

Atkinson, R. L., Atkinson, R. C., & Hilgard, E. R. (1983). *Introduction to psychology* (8th ed.). New York: Harcourt, Brace, Jovanovich.

Buss, A. (1961). *The psychology of aggression.* New York: John Wiley.

Freedman, J. L. (1982). *Introductory psychology* (2nd ed.). Reading, MA: Addison-Wesley.

Johnson, R. N. (1972). *Aggression in man and animals.* Philadelphia: W. B. Saunders.

Kaufmann, H. (1970). *Aggression and altruism.* New York: Holt, Rinehart and Winston.

Krech, D., Crutchfield, R. S., Livson, N., Wilson, W. A., & Parducci, A. (1982). *Elements of psychology* (4th ed.). New York: Alfred A. Knopf.

Lefrancois, G. R. (1982). *Psychology* (2nd ed.). Belmont, CA: Wadsworth.

Liebert, R. M., Sprafkin, J. N., & Davidson, E. S. (1982). *The early window: Effects of television on children and youth* (2nd ed.). New York: Pergamon.

McGee, M. G., & Wilson, D. W. (1984). *Psychology: Science and application.* St. Paul, MN: West Publishing.

Note

The items in Table 1 were taken from Johnson (1972), Kaufmann (1970), and Krech, Crutchfield, Livson, Wilson, & Parducci (1982). Some of their items were modified for use in this questionnaire.

The Dirty Dozen: Classroom Demonstration of Twelve Instigators of Aggression

William B. Davidson
University of South Carolina-Aiken

A classroom exercise for demonstrating 12 instigators of aggression is described. Videotapes of scenes from movies that depicted aggression were brought to class by some students. All students in class then judged the scenes for the presence or absence of 12 instigators of aggression. Pedagogical benefits of the activity are discussed.

In my junior-level undergraduate social psychology class, I customarily require that students write a case study of a historical event, analyzing human behavior using the principles found in research on conformity, persuasion, self-justification, aggression, and attraction. Over several years, students have reported that this assignment is a very difficult one. Therefore, I developed several preparatory exercises to get them accustomed to seeing life through the "looking glass" of social-psychological principles. This article briefly describes one particularly effective exercise that trains students to identify 12 instigators of aggression in scenes from movies. Because the topic of aggression is covered in most undergraduate courses in social psychology, this "dirty dozen" exercise may be useful for other courses.

I spend about 2 weeks teaching aggression. On the first class day spent teaching this topic, I distribute a handout of the dirty dozen instigators of aggression (see Table 1) and discuss the meaning of each one. Then I announce the rules of a contest in which students are to find and submit scenes of violence in movies that have the largest number of instigators of aggression from the list of the dirty dozen. Students are limited to entering only one scene of no more than 5-min duration, and no student is required to enter the contest. Entering the contest is optional because some students do not have access to a VCR and rented movies. The incentive for entering the contest is that the student whose scene is judged to have the largest number of instigators receives one letter grade improvement on the test covering aggression, which counts 10% toward the course grade.

The contest is held during the first class period after the test on aggression, so students generally have about 2 weeks to rent movies in quest of an ideal scene. The contest is held after the test on aggression so that the judges, who are fellow students in the class, have sufficient expertise in the topic.

Students who enter the contest bring to class a videotape of their movie, wound to the selected scene ahead of time. I then show the scenes to all class members, who report the number of instigators they see in each scene by filling out a checklist of the dirty dozen. Contestants are allowed to introduce their scene to the class by providing the title of the movie and a brief background of the circumstances that led up to the scene; they are not allowed to discuss the dirty dozen or rate their own scene in the contest. The winning scene is determined by summing the instigators seen by the student-judges. Interestingly, the winning scene tends not to be the most violent one.

To provide an incentive for good judging during the class-room viewing of the scenes, I award the best judge a half letter grade increment on the aggression test. The judging award is slightly less than the award for the winning scene because entering the contest takes more work than judging. The best judge is the one whose ratings are closest to the class norm for each scene, which is determined by majority vote for each instigator. By using the class norm as an ideal profile against which to rate the judges, I assume that the norm is accurate. If consensus is any indication of

Table 1. Dirty Dozen Instigators of Aggression

1. Insult
2. Attack
3. Bad intentions of frustrator[a]
4. Unexpected interruption in progress toward goal[a]
5. Goal is near when progress toward it is thwarted[a]
6. Illegitimate or arbitrary blocking of progress toward goal[a]
7. Relative deprivation
8. Aggressive cues
9. Aggressive models
10. Deindividuation in aggressor
11. Dehumanization of victim(s)
12. Environmental factors
    a. Heat
    b. Noise
    c. Crowding

[a]Items 3-6 are types of frustration.

accuracy, then my assumption is justified because the judges' ratings are very similar.

Pedagogical Benefits

The primary purpose of the dirty dozen exercise is to sharpen students' ability to identify the social instigators of aggression. The exercise gives them instruction and practice in developing this ability. In the three semesters that I have used this assignment, the sections on aggression in the case study papers have been decisively better, indicating the salutary effect of the exercise. A secondary purpose of the exercise is to improve students' general ability to identify social-psychological determinants of attitudes, affects, and actions other than aggression. In other words, the abilities developed in the study of aggression should generalize to the study of other topics in the course, such as conformity, persuasion, self-justification, and attraction. This purpose cannot be directly evaluated because other training exercises are used in the course. However, many students have mentioned that the dirty dozen exercise helps them see the role of social influence in behaviors other than aggression.

In addition to its pedagocial benefits, the dirty dozen exercise generates a lot of interest. About one third of the students generally choose to enter a scene in the contest, and attendance on the contest day is typically very high, even in the classes before I introduce the incentive for judges to win an award. Instructors may adjust the exercise to fit their own needs and goals, but its pedagogical benefits should endure.

Perspectives on Human Aggression:
Writing to Einstein and Freud on "Why War?"

Dana S. Dunn
Moravian College

A letter writing exercise on the nature of human aggression is described. Students read the 1932 "Why War?" correspondence between Albert Einstein and Sigmund Freud (1932/1964) and then composed letters responding to it. Variations of the exercise are presented.

Referring to the only meeting he ever had with Albert Einstein, Sigmund Freud wrote to his disciple Ferenczi: "He understands as much about psychology as I do about physics, so we had a very pleasant talk" (Jones, 1957, p. 131). Freud later had much to say to Einstein about psychology, however, when they exchanged public letters on the origins of war and human aggression (Einstein & Freud, 1932/1964). The "Why War?" letters, organized by Einstein, were written at the behest of the International Institute of Intellectual Co-operation, a committee of the League of Nations. The letters are an ideal starting point for a discussion of aggression because they focus on the nature of large-scale conflicts among humans. In order to prompt a careful and critical examination of the arguments presented in these historic letters, I ask students to write a letter of response to Einstein and Freud.

The writing assignment serves three goals. First, the correspondence between Einstein and Freud contains an unusual mix of history, psychology, and personal opinion, allowing students to consider aggression in a broader scope than usual. Second, letter writing requires students to analyze and respond to arguments in a concise format. Finally, through writing letters, students can react to aggression as a psychological topic in a personal way. Before presenting the exercise, a brief overview of the letters' contents is appropriate.

Why War?

The first letter was Einstein's. It focused on whether humanity can be free from the threat of war. Early in the letter, he suggested that his usual objective approach to solving problems was limited when dealing with aggressive, human characteristics such as will,

feelings, and instinct. Yet he had little difficulty in pinpointing the causes of armed conflicts. Toward the end of the letter, Einstein faulted both "the political power-hunger" of governments and humanity's "lust for hatred and destruction" (Einstein & Freud 1932/1964, p. 201). He closed with an appeal to Freud for insights about how to eliminate armed conflicts.

Freud's reply was longer and more detailed, and it emphasized culture and instinct. He traced the origin of aggression to a general principle "that conflicts of interest between men are settled by the use of violence" (Einstein & Freud, 1932/1964, p. 204). In Freud's view, violence evolved from conflict among individuals and could only be thwarted by laws created by communities. But why do organized communities use violence to settle internal and external disputes? Freud held humanity's self-preserving (erotic) and destructive (death) instincts responsible and suggested that urges toward aggression were not easily eliminated. Freud closed by asking Einstein an important question: "Why do you and I and so many other people rebel so violently against war?" (p. 213). In answering for himself, Freud pointed to the process of civilization, both its benefits (e.g., intellect) and constraints (e.g., repression), as leading to pacifism. Freud neither recommended specific ways to promote pacifism nor commented on the likelihood that this philosophy would be successful.

Writing to Einstein and Freud

Instructions for the exercise are simple and straightforward. Students read the correspondence between Einstein and Freud (1932/1964) and then write a two-page letter responding to either or both of the authors. (It may seem unusual to write to both authors at once, but several students asked to do so because they felt that each letter merited comment.) Students are encouraged to agree or disagree with the authors and to comment on the perspectives on human aggression that each man offers. They may consider whether the content of either author's letter could be accurately described as optimistic or pessimistic about humanity's destiny. Are humans destined, for example, to wage war against one another due to avarice (nurture), to some unfortunate disposition (nature), or a combination of both?

Because students are encouraged to use their own creative ideas, strict guidelines (e.g., reliance on Freudian theory) are not required. I encourage students to be prepared to read their letters to the class so that they can discuss their responses in more detail. If students prefer not to read their letters aloud, they are not required to do so.

I used the exercise in two different classes. The first was an intensive January term course devoted to reading a variety of papers spanning Freud's long career (see Gay, 1989). Students wrote their letters toward the end of the term, which permitted them to incorporate as well as critique material gleaned from their in-depth experience with Freud's ideas. Poignantly, the exercise coincided with Operation Desert Storm. My students were quite upset by the war in the Middle East. They found the letter writing to be cathartic because it provided an opportunity to search for meaning in that conflict. The letters were very moving. They ranged from a portrayal of human aggression as innate but controllable to an acceptance of its inevitability.

I also used the exercise in a freshman core course that explored the theme of community in Western culture. In this context, an overview of Freud's ideas on dreams and the development of civilization served as background for the letters. Less familiarity with Freud's ideas did not decrease the exercise's impact on students. The exercise seems equally suitable for personality courses that cover Freud and for social psychology courses that include general theories of aggression.

Variations

One variation of the exercise I intend to try relies on freewriting (e.g., Belanoff, Elbow, & Fontaine, 1990). *Freewriting* involves writing continuously for a short time (usually 10 min or so) on any topic that comes to the writer's mind. For this variation of the exercise, I will use focused freewriting (Hinkle & Hinkle, 1990), in which uncensored comments are directed toward a chosen topic, such as the arguments found in the letters. Before attending class, students will read the Einstein and Freud (1932/1964) correspondence. When class starts, students will listen to a

brief review of the letters' main ideas and then freewrite for 10 min. Discussion of their letters will then proceed as usual. This approach to writing should encourage students to integrate the themes found in the letters with their own experience.

Another variation might have students extend the existing correspondence. After reading the two original letters, for example, students could impersonate Einstein by composing a third letter responding to Freud's views on culture and instinct. An additional letter written from Freud's point of view might consider his theories of aggression in light of historical events that have occurred in the last 60 years.

Although Freud was characteristically negative about the letters, at one point referring to them as "the tedious and sterile so-called discussion with Einstein" (Jones, 1957, p. 175), he was mistaken. The letters not only present the views of two intellectual giants, they can also serve as a fruitful starting point for discussing the nature of human conflict.

References

Belanoff, P., Elbow, P., & Fontaine, S. I. (Eds.). (1990). *Nothing begins with n: New investigations of freewriting.* Carbondale and Edwardsville, IL: Southern Illinois University Press.

Einstein, A., & Freud, S. (1964). Why war? In J. Strachey (Ed. and Trans.), *The standard edition of the complete psychological works of Sigmund Freud* (Vol. 22, pp. 197-215). London: Hogarth. (Original work published 1932)

Gay, P. (Ed). (1989). *The Freud reader.* New York: Norton.

Hinkle, S., & Hinkle, A. (1990). An experimental comparison of the effects of focused freewriting and other study strategies on lecture comprehension. *Teaching of Psychology, 17,* 31-35.

Jones, E. (1957). *The life and work of Sigmund Freud* (Vol. 3). New York: Basic Books.

Note

I thank Steve Gordy, Stacey Zaremba, and three anonymous reviewers for their comments on an earlier draft of this article.

A Gender Difference in Acceptance of Sport Aggression: A Classroom Activity

David W. Rainey
John Carroll University

Aggression is a common topic in sport psychology courses. Research has revealed a gender difference in the acceptance of aggressive behavior during sport competition. This article presents a classroom activity to demonstrate that difference. Participants were given descriptions of behaviors from six sport competition situations and were asked to judge those behaviors as acceptable or unacceptable. Males in three psychology classes endorsed significantly more aggressive acts than did females. A number of relevant discussion topics are suggested.

Sport psychology is a growing professional speciality and the focus of increasing scholarly interest. A number of professional journals, including the *International Journal of Sport Psychology,* the *Journal of Sport Psychology,* and the *Journal of Sport Behavior,* are devoted to research in this discipline. College and university courses in sport psychology are becoming more common. The current level of activity was demonstrated by a preconference workshop of the North American Society for Psychology of Sport and Physical Activity, entitled "The Teaching of Sport Psychology: Contemporary Course Options" (Landers, Singer, & Williams, 1985). Speakers described a wide variety of courses. Some are designed primarily for athletes and coaches, some are general elective courses for undergraduates, and others are seminars for graduate students.

A common topic in these courses is aggression in sport. Textbooks on sport psychology also reflect this interest (e.g., Silva & Weinberg, 1984; Cox, 1985, devote chapters to this issue). These authors define aggression, investigate its incidence in sport, examine the causes, development, and impact of aggression in sport, and review the emerging research.

The topic of aggression in sport generates considerable interest among students. Most students can recall incidents of aggression in their own competitive experience and infamous incidents in the history of collegiate and professional sport. However, students hold widely different views about what constitutes aggression, and about what is acceptable and unacceptable behavior in sport. Husman and Silva (1984)

proposed some guidelines for dealing with these issues. They define aggression as acting with the intent to physically or psychologically injure someone. They also distinguish between aggressive behavior and assertive behavior, with the latter defined as forceful, goal-directed behavior that neither violates the rules of the game nor intends harm to participants. Although they recognize the difficulty in establishing the intent of behavior, Husman and Silva concluded that aggressive behavior, so defined, has no place in sport (with the exceptions of boxing and karate).

The class activity presented here is a partial replication of a study that investigated students' attitudes about aggression in sport. Silva (1983) presented eight slides to 203 male and female athletes and nonathletes. Seven of the slides presented scenes of aggressive, rule-violating behavior, such as fighting in ice hockey, tripping in basketball, and spearing in football. Subjects were asked to rate the acceptability of the depicted behaviors on a 4-point scale ranging from *totally acceptable* (1) to *totally unacceptable* (4). Results indicated that males, on the average, rated the aggressive behaviors as acceptable and as significantly more acceptable than did females, who rated those behaviors as unacceptable on the average. Further, the acceptability ratings of male athletes increased as a function of the amount of contact in their sports, the number of years they played organized sports, and the level of organized sport attained. Conversely, female nonathletes were slightly more accepting of aggression in sport than female athletes who had participated in either contact or noncontact sports, at either the youth sport or high school level, or over a period of 1 to 10 years. Silva concluded that socialization in sport appears to legitimize aggressive behavior for males, but not for females. In fact, the sport socialization process may cause females to become less accepting of such behavior.

Teaching Technique

The following activity is based on Silva's (1983) study. It has been used with four classes, and data have been collected from three of those classes. It has been most effective when presented as an introduction to the unit on aggression in sport, without prior comment. In beginning the activity, the following instructions were read to each class: "You are going to receive descriptions of six situations or scenes involving sport competition. I want you to label the behavior in these situations as *acceptable* or *unacceptable,* based on your own ethical standards. Do not write your name on the paper, but do mark your paper M if you are male or F if you are female. Do you have any questions?" The six competition scenes are reproduced in Table 1.

Students are typically eager to discuss the six scenes when they hand in their responses, and athletes in each class have provided vivid descriptions of similar personal experiences. The ensuing discussion provides ample opportunity to introduce Husman and Silva's (1984) definitions of assertive behavior and aggression and to present their position against aggression in sport. This position usually generates considerable dissent, especially from male athletes. They often suggest that aggression, even as defined by Husman and Silva, is appropriate in sport. This debate has led regularly to discussion of such topics as the cathartic benefits of aggression in sport or, conversely, the negative effects of mod- eling such behavior for children. Further, male and female students frequently have marked differences of opinion, which provides the opportunity to present Silva's (1983) study and relate it to the class activity.

At this point in the activity, each class has analyzed its own data to compare them to Silva's (1983) results. First, the number of acceptable judgments by males and females was tabulated, and then the mean was calculated for each group and for the total sample. A *t* test was then conducted for these independent means. This analysis provided an opportunity for students in two of my advanced classes to apply their statistical skills. In each of the three classes where I have collected data, the results have confirmed Silva's findings that males are more accepting of aggression in sport, $t(63) = 6.05$, $p < .01$. Males have endorsed a mean of *2.8* aggressive behaviors, and females have endorsed a mean of 1.6 aggressive behaviors.

Following these calculations, discussion is focused on why males are so much more accepting of aggression in sports. A common student response has been that this gender difference occurs because males engage in more aggression, both in sport and other settings. Other students have suggested that, in adhering to socially acceptable stereotypes, males may overreport and/or females underreport the number of behaviors they actually find acceptable. A question that has proved to be very productive at this point in the activity is "What do you predict will happen to women's attitudes about aggression in sport as women become increasingly involved in sport?" Some female athletes have argued strongly that they will not succumb to what they perceive as inappropriate male attitudes.

Table 1. Sport Situations

1. A defensive back on the local football team has been repeatedly criticized by his father for not "punishing" receivers in his zone. He vows to satisfy his father. In the next game, he delivers as hard a "hit" as he can to a receiver who is in midair, flipping him, knocking him unconscious and out of the game. Is the defensive back's behavior acceptable or unacceptable?

2. A young woman tennis player has been beaten badly in the singles final. She is also in the doubles final and again facing her singles opponent, whom she thoroughly dislikes. She gets a weak and high return of serve at the net and smashes it at her opponent with obvious delight. Is this young woman's behavior acceptable or unacceptable?

3. An 8-year-old hockey player has been told by his coach that if he does not play more "physically," he will be benched. He is checked hard by an opposing defensive man and retaliates by "spearing" him with his hockey stick. Though he is penalized by the referee, he is cheered by his coach. Is this boy's behavior acceptable or unacceptable?

4. Two high school girls basketball teams meet in the regional finals. The only black player on the court is the star of one team. She is constantly heckled when she has the ball. This includes the organized use of racial slurs by the opposing team's cheering section. Is the behavior of these fans acceptable or unacceptable?

5. The Dodgers are playing the Giants. In the second inning the Dodgers' pitcher hits the Giants' first baseman because "the plate belongs to me." When the Dodgers' pitcher comes to bat the next inning, the Giants' pitcher purposefully hits him on his throwing arm. Is the behavior of the Giants' pitcher acceptable or unacceptable?

6. The coach of a women's volleyball team knows that the star of the opposing team has a very sore back. She instructs her players to "spike" every shot they can at the injured opponent, in an attempt to aggravate her injury and knock her out of the game. Is the coach's behavior acceptable or unacceptable?

Even if the results for a particular class should fail to reveal a gender difference, there are options for discussion. First, the class could consider why its results failed to replicate earlier findings, possibly by focusing on sample differences. A second point of departure is that all six of the sport situations in the activity contain behaviors that are unacceptable by Husman and Silva's (1984) definition. Thus, the discussion might consider why students in our culture consistently find about one third of the behaviors acceptable.

This activity does not exactly replicate Silva's (1983) study; however, it is a simplification that effectively represents the previous research and it promotes student inquiry. The activity is an effective stimulus for student involvement and generates discussion of such concepts as catharsis, social learning, limitations of self-report data, and the relationship between attitude and behavior. The three classes from which data were collected had an average of about 20 students, but the activity can be adequately presented to classes of 20 to 50 students in a 50-min class period. Further, though it was originally designed for a sport psychology course, it can be modified for use in other courses. It has already been presented to classes studying sex roles and violence and aggression, and it could be readily adapted for social psychology and even introductory psychology courses.

References

Cox, R. H. (1985). *Sport psychology: Concepts and applications.* Dubuque, IA: W. C. Brown.

Husman, B. F., & Silva, J. M. (1984). Aggression in sport: Definitional and theoretical considerations. In J. M. Silva & R. S. Weinberg (Eds.), *Psychological foundations of sport* (pp. 246-260). Champaign, IL: Human Kinetics Publishers.

Landers, D. M., Singer, R. N., & Williams, J. M. (Chairs). (1985, May). *The teaching of sport psychology: Contemporary course options.* Preconference workshop at the meeting of the North American Society for Psychology of Sport and Physical Activity, Gulf Park, MS.

Silva, J. M., (1983). The perceived legitimacy of role violating behavior in sport. *Journal of Sport Psychology, 5,* 438-448.

Silva, J. M., & Weinberg, R. S. (Eds.). (1984). *Psychological foundation of sport.* Champaign, IL: Human Kinetics Publishers.

5. TEACHING GROUP PROCESSES

The Risky Shift is a Sure Bet

George R. Goethals
and Amy P. Demorest
Williams College

For nearly twenty years students of social psychology have been interested in the phenomenon known as the risky shift. These students include both social psychologists themselves, who are still exploring and debating the causes of the shift (cf. Sanders & Baron, 1977; Burnstein & Vinokur, 1977), and undergraduates in social psychology courses who are learning about fundamental interpersonal processes. The risky shift, it will be recalled, is the phenomenon whereby individuals in a group make decisions which are riskier than the ones they make individually. It was discovered by James Stoner (1961) who showed specifically that when subjects in a group are asked to make a unanimous decision on an issue involving risk, their decision is riskier than the averaged the decisions they had made individually at an earlier time. This paper reports the results of a series of attempts over eight years to demonstrate the risky shift in social psychology classes as a way to elicit student involvement and interest in the course. These attempts have been highly successful.

Procedure. Risky shift demonstrations were attempted in eight classes varying in size from 28 to 68. In all but one case, these classes were composed of male and female undergraduates at Williams College. In the other case the students were enrolled in an adult education class and they represented men and women in the Williamstown area of various ages, occupations, and educational levels.

The ten items from Kogan and Wallach's (1964) Choice Dilemma Questionnaire II (CDQ) which had been found to reliably produce shifts to risk (Items 1-4 and 6-11) were used in the demonstrations. Each item describes a situation in which two alternative courses of action are available to an individual who must choose between them. One of the alternatives has a more desirable outcome than the other but it is also less likely to be successful. For example, in one choice dilemma the captain of a football team must choose between a play that would almost certainly work and produce a tie for his team and another play that is less likely to be successful but would produce a victory. For each dilemma subjects must choose the minimum odds of success they would demand before recommending that the risky course of action be taken. They must choose between probabilities of 1,3,5,7,and 9 out of ten or indicate that they would not select the risky course of action under any circumstances (scored as 11). The lower the minimum odds of success a person is willing to accept before attempting the risky course of action, the more risk that person is taking.

The demonstration is conducted as follows: At the end of the first meeting of the class students are asked to complete the ten CDQ items and are then dismissed. When they arrive for the next meeting they are divided into small groups and each group is given one CDQ item to discuss, and is asked to make a recommendation for that item. Typically, students are assigned to groups alphabetically to facilitate keeping track of which students are in what groups and to ensure some mix of students. In most cases there have been ten groups, each one discussing one of the ten problems, and group size has ranged from three to seven members. Our experience has been that group size makes little difference in producing the shift.

Following the usual instructions, the groups are asked to discuss the dilemma until they have reached a unanimous decision as to what odds to recommend to the person in the vignette. While the students are discussing the CDQ problems, the instructor calculates the average of the individuals' scores in each group for the item the group is working on. If any group finishes early they can be given another problem to discuss. Most groups can complete the task easily in fifteen minutes, and any group which cannot make a unanimous decision in that time is asked to decide by majority vote. After all groups have turned in their decision, the following date for each of the ten items are put on the blackboard: First, the overall class average for the item; second, the mean score of the individuals in the group discussing that item; and, finally, the group decision. Sometimes more than one group will have discussed a given problem and the data for both groups are recorded. Once these data are recorded the students in the class are asked to discuss them.

Table 1
Results of Risky Shift Demonstrations, 1971-1977

Year	Problem Number									
	1	2	3	4	6	7	8	9	10	11
1971	5.00-5	5.00-7**	6.00-7**	5.00-3*	5.00-1*	5.00-3*	6.20-5*	5.00-5	--	5.50-3*
1972	5.40-5	6.20-5*	--	3.80-1*	5.40-5	4.20-3*	5.00-3*	5.80-5	5.00-5	5.00-3*
1973[1]	4.33-3*	5.00-7**	9.00-7*	--	3.00-1*	7.28-5*	--	--	7.28-7	5.00-3*
1974	5.00-5	5.00-5	6.00-3*	4.00-5**	5.40-5	3.00-2*	7.00-7	8.00-5*	6.00-5*	3.50-1*
1975	4.50-4	7.00-7	8.60-3*	4.00-3*	7.50-7	2.50-3	6.20-5*	6.20-5*	4.00-3*	3.50-3
1976	7.00-7	8.50-9	5.00-5	5.33-3* 2.60-1*	4.67-3*	4.33-2* 4.33-3*	7.00-5*	5.33-7**	5.00-3*	4.70-3*
1977	4.00-3*	9.00-7* 9.00-7*	6.33-7	3.33-3	5.00-1* 8.33-7*	6.33-3* 4.00-1*	5.67-5 7.00-7	7.33-5*	5.00-5	4.20-3*

[1]Adult Education class.
*Risky shift
**Cautious shift
First values given are the means of the individuals; second values are group decisions.

Results The data for the first year's demonstration (1970) were not recorded. It was successful, however, so that plans were made to keep data thereafter. There were no significant differences between the results for undergraduates and adults, so the data for both groups were considered together. Table 1 presents the mean of the individual group members' individual scores and their group decision for each problem in the demonstrations conducted from 1971 to 1977. Shifts to risk or caution are indicated according to the following criterion: A group was considered to have shifted to risk or caution if its decision was riskier or more cautious than the closest available compromise position. Thus, for example, agroup whose average individual score was 5.8 was not considered to have shifted to risk if the group decision was 5 since 5 is the compromise choice closest to 5.8. However, if a group's average score was half-way between two choices it was considered to have shifted to caution if it chose the higher available choice and to have shifted to risk if it chose the lower available score. Thus a group whose average individual score was 6 was considered to have shown a risky shift if it chose 5 or below and a cautious shift if it chose 7 or above.

Using this criterion for shifts, among the total of 70 group decisions there were 41 shifts to risk (59%), 24 compromise or no-shift decisions (34%), and five shifts to caution (7%). It can be seen that the items which most reliably produced the shift in these demonstrations were number 7 (the chess player deciding whether to make a daring move), number 11 (the research physicist deciding between a challenging project and a more certain but less important one), and number 4 (the football captain deciding whether to attempt a risky play). The items least reliably producing a risky shift are numbers 1 and 2 (the engineer who could become an executive in a new firm and the accountant deciding on a heart operation).

Discussion The data above show that the shift to risk is a robust social psychological phenomenon that can be reliably demonstrated in a classroom setting. The students themselves are quick to recognize that it has occurred. When they are asked to comment on their own data on the board, several invariably point out that the odds recommended by the groups are lower on the whole, that is, riskier than the odds recommended individually prior to the discussion. Because the risky shift is inherently interesting and because the students are highly involved with data that they have generated themselves, it is easy to move directly into an animated discussion of choice shifts.

There are many facets of the history of the risky shift, its occurrence in real life decision-making groups, and its causes that students seem to enjoy discussing. Several specific topics can be mentioned: First, students are interested to learn that the risky shift was discovered more or less accidentally. It had been predicted that group discussions of the CDQ items would produce compromise decisions based on the average of individual scores or a slight shift toward cautiousness. Also, students are highly interested in knowing that the risky shift occurs with students who are risking painful physical side effects (Bem, Wallach, & Kogan, 1965) and with state trial judges at gambling establishments in Nevada (Blascovitch & Ginsburg, 1973). Accounts of decision making in government which seemed to have shown a risky shift elicit the most interest. One example is Arthur Schlesinger's (1965) account of the recommendations of President Kennedy's advisers regarding the Bay of Pigs invasion of Cuba in 1961.

Possible explanations for the shift can also be discussed. Experience has indicated that students are fairly adept at generating explanations and will quickly suggest the ideas that have been examined in risky shift research. These include the diffusion of responsibility in groups (Wallach, Kogan, & Bem 1964), the notion that group discussions will contain more risky arguments (Burnstein & Vinokur, 1975; Burnstein, Vinokur, & Trope, 1973),and the idea that risk is a cultural value (Brown, 1965; Baron & Roper, 1976). After demonstrating the phenomenon themselves and listing several competing explanations, students are usually eager to hear about the relevant research.

Other aspects of the data can also be discussed. One such topic of discussion may be why certain groups failed to shift to risk or why others showed a particularly large shift. Sex differences can also be discussed. Our experience shows only that women are initially more risky on some items and men on others. Usually the difference can be understood in terms of subjects being more cautious when they perceive the interests of their own sex to be involved. It can also be valuable to discuss how the data collected in class relate to particular explanations of the shift. For example, Jellison and Riskind (1970,1971) have proposed a social comparison of abilities explanation, which suggests that subjects would be more likely to shift on CDQ items where the ability of the protagonist can determine whether or not the risky course of action succeeds. This can be examined by deciding which items depend more on the individual's ability and which on external circumstances, and then considering the shifts for each type of item.

The risky shift is a simple and reliable classroom demonstration. It is also a valuable resource for class discussion. It can capture student interest at the beginning of the course and get it off to a good start. Whenever one conducts a classroom demonstration, particularly of a social psychological phenomenon, one goes out on a limb. The risky shift demonstration comes as close as any to being a sure bet .

References

Baron, R. S., & Roper, G. A reaffirmation of a social comparison view of choice shifts, averaging, and extremity effects in autokinetic situations. *Journal of Personality and Social Psychology,* 1976, *33,* 521-530.

Bem D. J., Wallach, M. A., & Kogan, N. Group decision-making under risk of aversive consequences. *Journal of Personality and Social Psychology,* 1965, *1,* 453-460.

Blascovitch, J., & Ginsburg, G. Blackjack and the risky shift. *Sociometry,* 1973, *36,* 42-55.

Brown, R. *Social psychology.* New York: Free Press of Glencoe, 1965.

Burnstein, E., & Vinokur, A. What a person thinks upon learning he has chosen differently from others: Nice evidence for the persuasive-arguments explanation of choice shifts. *Journal of Experimental Social Psychology,* 1975, *11,* 412-426.

Burnstein, E., & Vinokur, A. Persuasive argumentation and social comparison as determinants of attitude polarization. *Journal of Experimental Social Psychology,* 1977, *13,* 315-332.

Burnstein, E., Vinokur, A., & Trope, Y. Interpersonal comparison versus persuasive argumentation: A more direct test of alternative explanations for group induced shifts in individual choice. *Journal of Experimental Social Psychology,* 1973, *9,* 236-245.

Jellison, J. M., & Riskind, J. A social comparison of abilities interpretation of risk taking behavior. *Journal of Personality and Social Psychology,* 1970, *15,* 375-390.

Jellison, J. M., & Riskind, J. Attribution of risk to others as a function of their ability. *Journal of Personality and Social Psychology,* 1971, *20,* 413-415.

Kogan, N., & Wallach, M. A. *Risk taking: A study in cognition and personality.* New York: Holt, Rinehart and Winston, 1964.

Sanders, G. S., & Baron, R. S. Is social comparison irrelevant for producing choice shifts? *Journal of Experimental Social Psychology,* 1977, *13,* 303-314.

Schlesinger, A. *A thousand days: John F. Kennedy in the White House.* Boston: Houghton Mifflin, 1965.

Stoner, J. A. F. A comparison of individual and group decisions including risk. Unpublished master's thesis, School of Industrial Management, MIT, 1961.

Wallach, M. A., Kogan, N., & Bem D. J. Group influence on individual risk taking. *Journal of Abnormal and Social Psychology,* 1962, *65,* 75-86.

Prisoner's Dilemma as a Model for Understanding Decisions

Janet D. Larsen
John Carroll University

Two classroom demonstrations based on the prisoner's dilemma illustrate some elements of decision making. The demonstrations require minimal preparation and allow all members of the class to participate. In the first demonstrations, students ask for $1.00 or 10¢, with the condition that, if more than 20% of the class asks for $1.00, no one gets anything. In the second demonstration, pairs of students play a short matching game. The scores earned by students reflect whether they have played cooperatively or competitively.

When will people cooperate, and when will they decide to take advantage of others? Introductory and social psychology textbooks present the prisoner's dilemma (PD) as a framework for understanding the decisions people make when they have the choice of taking advantage of others or cooperating with them. It has been used to explain panic behavior in crowds (Gleitman, 1987) and the choices people make in labor union negotiations (Worchel & Cooper, 1983).

PD is best explained by a story about two men who are arrested on a minor charge and placed in separate rooms. Although the authorities believe that both men are guilty of a more serious crime, there is no proof of their guilt. The following options are explained to each man. He can continue to claim his innocence and, if his friend also continues to maintain his own innocence, they will both receive short sentences. The man can turn state's evidence and give the authorities the information they want. If he does, his friend will receive the maximum sentence but he will go free. However, the same options are offered to his friend. If his friend also confesses, both men will receive intermediate sentences. What will the men do?

It would be to the prisoners' mutual advantage for both to remain silent, but each takes a risk in doing so. Choosing to remain silent requires that the man be confident that his friend will not turn state's evidence. If he thinks his friend will confess, it is to his advantage to confess. Then, if his friend confesses, he assures himself of a lighter sentence; if his friend does not confess, the man will get off with no penalty .

This same analysis can be applied to the behavior of people when there is a fire in a theater. Common sense suggests that everyone has the best chance of escaping if people file out, taking turns to get through the door. However, we do not trust others to take turns. Like the prisoner, we make the exploitive choice and look out for ourselves first, because we expect others to act the same way. Rather than taking the chance of being pushed out of the way and burned to death, most people push ahead and many are hurt.

The following class activity allows students to experience the dilemma. If PD is discussed in your textbook, you may want to conduct this activity before students read that assignment; however, the demonstration is effective even if students have already read about PD.

Dollars, Dimes, or Doughnut Holes

Tell your class that you would like to give away some money, but only under certain conditions. Each student may ask for $1.00 or 10¢. You will give all of the students what they ask for if fewer than 20% of the students ask for $1.00. Ask students to write their choices on a slip of paper, along with their name or some identification code if they ask for $1.00. In addition, ask them to indicate the percentage of the class they expect to ask for $1.00. These choices should be made without consulting other members of the class, just as the prisoners made their decisions to confess or not confess without talking to each other.

Collect the slips, and read the choices. Sort the slips into $1.00 or 10¢ requests and, within each category, whether the person expects over or under 20% of the class to ask for $1.00. About half the students usually ask for $1.00. Some of the students in this group expect 20% or less of the class to make the same request (corresponding to the prisoner who decides to confess in the hope of going free). Most of those who ask for $1.00 expect a large proportion of the class to do the same. (These students correspond to the prisoner who confesses because he expects his friend to confess.) After students have had a real experience of choosing to exploit others or to trust that others will not take advantage of them, similar situations are easier to understand. The PD model can be applied to diverse situations such as: driving, where you must decide whether to get in line or stay in the lane that is about to end; infant inoculation, where parents must decide whether their child will receive a shot for diphtheria, pertussis, and tetanus and risk the rare but deadly reaction; and cheating on a test where, if everyone cheats, the curve will be raised and no one will benefit.

This activity can also be used to introduce the ideas in Hardin's (1968) article, "The Tragedy of the Commons." He argued that people behave selfishly in group situations because they expect others to make selfish choices. This analysis can be applied to problems such as trying to get manufacturers to stop polluting the environment or trying to get countries to limit fishing in international waters.

The Matching Game

PD can also provide the basis for understanding how people behave when they know they will relate to one another in the future. The iterated version of PD, or playing the game over and over with the same person, can serve as a model for understanding some of the features of labor union bargaining and international treaty negotiations.

Each student needs a coin for this game. Pairs of students play PD 20 times, indicating their choices by placing a coin on the desk heads up or tails up. If Player A and Player B choose heads, each gets 6 points. If both choose tails, both lose 6 points. However, if one chooses heads and the other chooses tails, the player choosing heads loses 8 points and the player choosing tails gets 8 points. Have students keep track of the number of points each person earns and report to the class the number of points earned by each player. When the pairs play cooperatively, both players have high scores. If one player chooses tails frequently, the other player usually does the same, and both end the game with low or even negative scores.

One of the factors that determines how people will play this game is how they define the goal. One way of viewing the goal of the game is to obtain the most points possible. In this case, players consistently make the cooperative play. As the 20th trial approaches, however, a player may succumb to the temptation to "defect" and earn a few more points than the other player. You should be aware of such defections because they may cause an emotional reaction on the part of the person who has been exploited. Many people define the goal as earning more points than their partner. In this case, both players will often choose tails and will have low scores, compared to people who have played cooperatively.

In the iterated version of PD, the way to get the highest score possible is to be consistently cooperative, but not a fool. Computer simulations have been used to test the success of various strategies for playing this version of the game (Campbell, 1985). The strategy that consistently led to the highest scores was a Tit for Tat strategy in which the player began by

making a cooperative choice and continued to be cooperative as long as the other player did not make the exploitive move. If the other player failed to cooperate, the Tit for Tat program began to follow the play of the opponent, continuing to copy what the opponent did on the last move. In this way, as soon as the other player signaled a willingness to cooperate by making the cooperative move, Tit for Tat responded by returning to cooperative play.

This iterated version of PD is similar to what occurs in labor union bargaining and in the negotiations of treaties between nations. One issue is whether the other party can be trusted to play the game cooperatively. The other issue is how the parties define the goal. For example, if labor and management define the situation as one in which there will be a winner and a loser, they will follow the equivalent of the "all tails" strategy. If they see the situation as one in which both parties can benefit, more cooperative strategies may be used. This model can also be applied to arms limitation talks, school rivalries, and dealing with unfriendly neighbors. By playing the game and discussing their strategies, students get a better view of the kinds of thinking that lead to different behaviors in situations where people have to deal with one another repeatedly.

Student reactions to these demonstrations are almost universally positive. A typical comment written by a student is, "At first I thought it was just a game, but I saw that it applied to many serious subjects in life." Students recognize different implications of the demonstration. For example, "If each would cooperate with each other, everyone would be better off. But because some wish to get ahead of others, we all get hurt"; "Being cooperative, one can get ahead"; and "People always want to get ahead, regardless of the other person." Both activities lead to lively discussions; they provide a model for helping students to understand some human behaviors that seem, at first glance, to be irrational.

References

Campbell, R. (1985). Background for the uninitiated. In R. Campbell & L. Sowden (Eds.), *Paradoxes of rationality and cooperation: Prisoner's dilemma and Newcomb's problem* (pp. 3-41). Vancouver, British Columbia, Canada: University of British Columbia Press.

Gleitman, H. (1987). *Basic psychology* (2nd ed.). New York: Norton

Hardin, G. (1968). The tragedy of the commons. *Science, 162*, 1243-1248.

Worchel, S., & Cooper, J. (1983). *Understanding social psychology* (3rd ed.). Homewood, IL: Dorsey.

Learning About Individual and Collective Decisions:
All for One and None for All

Blaine F. Peden
Allen H. Keniston
David T. Burke
University of Wisconsin-Eau Claire

Two hypothetical decision-making situations were transformed into an ecologically valid and personally meaningful activity to enhance introductory psychology students' understanding of the principles governing individual and collective decisions. This activity promotes knowledge of psychology, develops scientific values and skills, and stimulates personal development.

Teachers believe that classroom demonstrations promote students' awareness and understanding of psychological concepts and principles. Although students apparently enjoy and learn from these activities, they routinely deny the results and implications of demonstrations in which they (a) make predictable risk-averse and risk-prone choices, and (b) compete rather than cooperate. In both cases, students contend that they would behave differently in a "real" situation (Lutsky, 1987).

To enhance introductory psychology students' understanding of the principles governing individual and collective decisions, we combine two hypothetical decisions into an ecologically valid and personally meaningful demonstration. In this activity, students may earn bonus points by making "tough choices" after each of eight exams. *Tough Choice I* provides an analogue for the psychology of preferences (modeled after Problem 3 in Tversky & Kahneman, 1981) in which we expect students to make risk-averse choices. *Tough Choice 2* provides an analogue for cooperation and competition (modeled after the *Science84* Cooperation Experiment in Allman, 1984, 1985) in which we expect students to make risk-prone or uncooperative choices and to underestimate the number of classmates making uncooperative choices. Unlike participants in hypothetical one trial choice studies, our students repeatedly make the two tough choices with full knowledge about the consequences of their previous decisions (Silberberg, Murray, Christensen, & Asano, 1988).

Method

Subjects

This activity involved three classes of introductory psychology students from three different terms: summer 1988 (*n* = 36), spring 1989 (*n* = 117), and summer 1989 (*n* = 35).

Apparatus

A detachable questionnaire comprised the final page of a test. On Tough Choice 1, students selected either a certain outcome (1 bonus point) or an uncertain outcome (0 or 8 bonus points) and then explained their choice in a paragraph. A random-number generator determined whether an uncertain choice yielded 8, *p* = .125, or 0 bonus points, *p* = .875.

On Tough Choice 2, students requested either a smaller or a larger number of bonus points, wrote a paragraph that explained their choices, and estimated the percentage of their classmates asking for the larger number of points. The instructions clearly stated that: (a) if more than 20% of the class asked for the larger number, then no one would receive any bonus points; and (b) if no more than 20% of the class asked for the larger number of bonus points, then an individual would receive the requested number of points. In summer 1988 and spring 1989, the smaller number was 4 bonus points and the larger number was 20 bonus points, whereas in summer 1989 the numbers were 1 and 5 bonus points, respectively.

Procedure

Students completed the Tough Choices questionnaire after each of eight exams. We reported and discussed the results during the next class meeting.

Students' grades depended on a fixed percentage of the 500 to 600 points from tests and writing assignments. Bonus points from this and other activities contributed to an individual's point total.

We evaluated student opinion about this activity in the 1989 courses by distributing a 10-item debriefing questionnaire after the eighth exam. Students earned 1 bonus point by returning a completed form on the final day.

Results

Scores for the three classes were qualitatively similar in all cases and quantitatively similar in most cases. We computed grand means for quantitatively similar scores. Some students forfeited bonus points by withholding the questionnaire or by missing an exam. The high questionnaire return rates (95.5%), detailed explanations for choices, comments during discussions, and responses on the debriefing questionnaire confirmed that this activity was ecologically valid and personally meaningful to students.

Tough Choice 1

All three classes tended to make more frequent selections of 1 certain point over successive trials. The grand mean was 73.2%, and outcome somewhat lower than the one obtained for hypothetical choices (see Problem 3 in Tversky & Kahneman, 1981). Selections of the uncertain outcome produced 8 bonus points 11.8% of the time, a payoff ratio somewhat lower than the expected 12.5%. Although students earned from 0 to 21 bonus points on this problem, the grand mean was only 7.6 bonus points.

Tough Choice 2

Despite eight opportunities, all three classes failed to obtain any points on this problem. Over all trials, the percentage of students making the uncooperative choice averaged 49.2%, 36.9%, and 42.7% in the three courses, respectively. The grand mean of 40.4% was somewhat greater than the 34.9% of the participants who uncooperatively chose the larger of two sums of money in a hypothetical one-trial situation (Allman, 1984, 1985). The choices by students who selected either 4 or 20 points did not vary systematically from those made by students who selected either 1 or 5 points. Finally, students who earned a low grade in the course were more likely to select the uncertain outcome than were students who earned a high grade.

The choices by the summer 1988 class deserve special comment. A dramatic decrease in the percentage of students making the uncooperative choice on Trial 4 occurred after a discussion about the tragedy of the commons (Hardin, 1968) and social traps (Platt, 1973). After this discussion and before the fourth exam, a self-appointed and energetic champion of cooperation convinced fellow classmates to make their selections on the basis of a lottery. Seven lucky students were to ask for 20 points; all others were to re-

quest 4 bonus points. Despite warnings that complete cooperation was necessary for success, the endeavor failed because two students either deliberately "defected" or misunderstood the instructions. No similar effort to organize a cooperative venture occurred in the other two courses.

Students also estimated the percentage of classmates who would ask for the larger number of points. The estimate generally was less than the obtained percentage, especially on the initial trials. According to Allman (1985), two thirds of his 33,511 participants predicted that fewer than one fifth of them would choose the larger monetary sum. Moreover, this prediction was the same for those choosing either the smaller or larger monetary sum. Our results replicated this finding in that students' estimate of the number of students who ask for the larger number of bonus points was not related to their own choices. Allman's and our results contradict Dawes, McTavish, and Shaklee's (1977) finding that individuals making uncooperative choices in a commons dilemma situation expected more uncooperative choices than those making cooperative choices.

Table 1. Relative Frequency and Average For Student Responses

SD	Da	Ne	Ag	SA	M	Questionnaire Statements
1	7	27	46	22	3.8	I am very glad to have been involved in this activity.
9	29	42	20	3	2.8	This activity increased my interest in psychology.
34	38	11	17	3	2.2	I felt coerced or forced to participate in this activity.
23	48	23	8	1	2.2	It was not fair for our grade to be influenced by the points that we received for participating in this activity.
5	18	13	52	15	3.5	The purpose of this activity became clearer to me during our class discussions.
1	6	16	36	44	4.1	The offer of the instructors was genuine, and we really would have gotten the points on Tough Choice 2 if fewer than 20% of the class asked for 20 points.
4	21	21	50	7	3.3	Making and discussing these tough choices promoted my knowledge of psychology.
3	11	14	65	10	3.7	Making and discussing these tough choices promoted my development of scientific values and skills.
2	14	13	61	13	3.7	Making and discussing these tough choices promoted my personal development.
5	4	15	46	33	4.0	I recommend using this activity as part of this class in the future.

Note. SD = strongly disagree; Da = disagree; Ne = neither disagree nor agree; Ag = agree; SA = strongly agree.

Debriefing Questionnaire

Sixty-eight of the 101 students completing the course in spring 1989 and all 35 students in the summer 1989 course returned the debriefing questionnaire. Table 1 presents the question, the average rating, and the number of students strongly disagreeing, disagreeing, agreeing, strongly agreeing, or neither disagreeing nor agreeing with each statement. A score of 1.0 indicates strong disagreement; a score of 5.0 indicates strong agreement.

Approximately three fourths of the students gladly participated in this activity and did not feel coerced. Students indicating coercion commonly explained that they were always reminded to answer all the questions, detach the form, and submit it. This response suggests a misunderstanding about the meaning of coercion, an interpretation supportedfor Student Responses by the same students' comments that allowing these points to influence their course grade was fair.

Approximately two thirds of the students said that the discussions clarified the purpose of the activity; however, some indicated that the class never discussed the activity, and others asserted that the only purpose of the activity was to provide bonus points. Although some students said that this activity had nothing to do with psychology, the majority indicated that it promotes three course objectives. For example, over half indicated that making and discussing these tough choices enhanced their understanding of psychology. Approximately 70% agreed that making and discussing these choices promoted their development of scientific values and skills and stimulated their personal development. Finally, almost 80% of the students endorsed future use of this activity.

Discussion

Our "tale of two tough choices" is interesting; more important, the activity is easy to use and offers many instructional benefits. One or both questions can be included on multiple-choice tests. Evaluations by the instructors and students indicate that this activity promotes knowledge of psychology, develops scientific values and skills, and stimulates personal development.

Knowledge of Psychology

Unlike many easily performed and little remembered activities, this demonstration promotes knowledge of psychology. An instructor and students can analyze and interpret the choices and the outcomes within different domains of psychology, as the following examples illustrate.

Tough Choice 1 data plotted over trials resemble a learning curve and prompt a discussion about the role of experience in making decisions. Tough Choice 2 data raise questions about the control of behavior and an obvious failure of consequences to modify behavior. To the end of the course and sometimes beyond, students lament their inability to obtain points on Tough Choice 2, despite many discussions about the problem.

In a unit on social psychology, this activity illustrates the dilemma of cooperation and competition (Allman, 1984). We encourage students to cooperate on Tough Choice 2, but do not suggest techniques, such as publicly disclosing one's choice, having another complete and submit one's form, or forming cooperative subgroups (Dawes, 1980). Our experience indicates that several students in each class undermine these suggestions by saying that if they cannot have the larger number of points, then they do not care if anyone gets points. This assertion outrages others and produces lively discussion about issues of equity. Alternatively, G. D. Steinhauer (personal communication, November 7, 1989) modified the problem by requiring students to choose to protect or publicly disclose their individual choices. Under these conditions, 75% chose to publicly disclose their selections and only 8% asked for the larger number of bonus points.

Tenacious individuals who argue vehemently for one choice encourage discussion about how personality traits influence choices. Tough Choice 2 illustrates how difficult it is to predict behavior, a prominent concern in clinical psychology.

This activity shows how to plot data and helps students learn the distinction between observations and inferences. It challenges students' understanding about the concepts of probability. Paragraphs explaining choices typically reveal pathologies of statistical reasoning, such as the gambler's fallacy.

Finally, teachers can use this activity to illustrate that different sciences confront the same problem. The free-rider problem in economics, the irrationality of voting in political science, and the prisoner's dilemma in psychology all oppose group benefits with individual interests. In fact, a similar exercise produces comparable results in a shorter period of time, but involves a monetary cost to instructors (Bishop, 1986).

Scientific Values and Skills

This activity develops scientific values and skills. Students' inability to cooperate for mutual benefit forces them to evaluate their implicit personality theories, stimulates curiosity about behavior, and demonstrates the relation between theory and data: Theory guides observation, and results disconfirm or support theory.

Students use analytical and interpretive skills in their attempt to understand the results of Tough Choice 2. For example, some students note a correlation between trends toward cooperation and class optimism about possible bonus points. Many appear to extrapolate the trend, subsequently choose the larger number of bonus points, and guarantee another payoff of 0 points.

As the bonus point opportunities fall by the wayside, students better appreciate psychological theories about preference and cooperation in a meaningful situation. To further illustrate the value of theory and scientific skill inherent in accurate prediction, we frequently and confidently predict that the students will not obtain points on Tough Choice 2, even though our offer is genuine.

Scientific values include a concern for ethical teaching practices. Chute (1974) asked: How can we protect students as subjects when we develop and explore new instructional techniques? Our answer is three-fold: (a) Our students give implied informed consent by completing and submitting the questionnaire. The majority of students bolster this argument by indicating that they are not coerced to participate. (b) The potential harm from submitting the questionnaire and discussing the results in class is minimal or nonexistent. Students confirm this belief in two ways. They welcome participation in this activity (as did subjects in Milgram's, 1969, research), and they overwhelmingly endorse its use in the future. (c) The discussion section of this article illustrates that there is a favorable balance of risks to benefits for students. Moreover, the benefits accrue to present students rather than future students, which is an important concern for instructional innovations (Chute, 1974).

Another ethical question is whether grades should be influenced by bonus points from this activity (see Norcross, Horrocks, & Stevenson, 1989). Our defense is three-fold: (a) Our students (like Leak's, 1981) do not believe that it is unfair to obtain bonus points from this activity. (b) This activity is as legitimate a source of bonus points as any other because students learn much in their pursuit of them. (c) The few bonus points from this activity minimally influence students' grades. Perhaps a more pertinent concern is whether students obtain too few points for their efforts.

Personal Development

This activity promotes personal development because students confront their own troublesome and distasteful behavior (Lutsky, 1987). Our students demonstrate something akin to the Pollyanna effect in that the expected level greatly exceeds the observed level of cooperation. Some students eventually recognize and later publically admit that their own selfishness only hurts themselves and everyone else. Others indicate that the discussions help them understand and better accept opinions different from their own.

The results of Tough Choice 2 dramatically illustrate the tragedy of the commons (Hardin, 1968) and how difficult it is to overcome social fences despite an energetic superordinate authority's championing cooperation (Platt, 1973). In sum, this activity produces a compelling lesson against faith in the saving grace of attempts to induce individual sacrifices for the benefit of all. Our students find new wisdom in Pogo's moral that we have met the enemy and he is us (Kelly, 1972).

References

Allman, W. F. (1984, October). Nice guys finish first. *Science84,* pp. 24-32.

Allman, W. F. (1985, February). The *Science84* cooperation experiment: The results. *Science85, p.* 20.

Bishop, J. E. (1986, December *4).* 'All for one . . . one for all'? Don't bet on it. *The Wall Street Journal,* p. 7.

Chute, D. L. (1974) . Innovations in teaching: An ethical paradox . *Teaching of Psychology, 1, 85.*

Dawes, R. M. (*1980).* Social dilemmas. *Annual Review of Psychology, 31,* 169-193.

Dawes, R. M., McTavish, J., & Shaklee, H. *(1977).* Behavior, communication, and assumptions about other people's behavior in a commons dilemma situation. *Journal of Personality and Social Psychology, 35,* 1-11.

Hardin, G. *(1968).* The tragedy of the commons. *Science, 162,* 1243-1248.

Kelly, W. *(1972). Pogo: We have met the enemy and he is us.* New York: Simon & Schuster.

Leak, G. K. *(1981).* Student perception of coercion and value from participation in psychological research. *Teaching of Psychology, 8,* 147-149.

Lutsky, N. (1987) . Inducing academic suicide: A demonstration of social influence. In V. P. Makosky, L. G. Whittemore, & A. M. Rogers (Eds.), *Activities handbook for the teaching of psychology* (Vol. *2,* pp. 123-126). Washington, DC: American Psychological Association.

Milgram, S. (1969). *Obedience to authority.* New York: Harper & Row.

Norcross, J. C., Horrocks, L. J., & Stevenson, J. F. (1989). On barfights and gadflies: Attitudes and practices concerning extra credit in college courses. *Teaching of Psychology, 16,* 199-203.

Platt, J. (1973). Social traps. *American Psychologist, 28,* 641-651.

Silberberg, A., Murray, P., Christensen, J., & Asano, T. (1988). Choice in the repeated-gambles experiment. *Journal of the Experimental Analysis of Behavior, 50,* 187-195.

Tversky, A., & Kahneman, D. (1981). The framing of decisions and the psychology of choice. *Science, 211,* 453-458.

Notes

1. We thank Bernard Frank and Ken McIntire for helpful comments on this article. We also appreciate the comments and suggestions of editors Charles Brewer and Joseph Palladino and the

anonymous reviewers, especially the one who called our attention to the Bishop (1986) article.

2. The graphics were produced by the University of Wisconsin Eau Claire Media Development Center with support from the School of Graduate Studies and Office of University Research.

3. A preliminary report of these results was presented at the meeting of the Midwestern Psychological Association, Chicago, IL, May 4-6, 1989.

A Problem-Solving Workshop: The Middle East Comes to a Social Psychology Class

George Banziger
Marietta College

Social psychology is no stranger to the field of international relations. Social psychologists have elaborated on the conceptual and perceptual problems which underlie international conflict, such as the "diabolical-enemy image," (White, 1970) and the "mirror image" (Bronfenbrenner, 1961); they have also organized problem-solving workshops that employed some of the techniques of interpersonal communication common to sensitivity groups in order to generate solutions to problems, such as the border dispute in the Horn of Africa (Doob, 1970), the Turkish-Greek Cypriot conflict (Doob, 1974), and the Israeli-Palestinian conflict (Cohen, Kelman, Miller, & Smith, 1977). The latter issue seems to be one of the most complex, yet well known, international issues in the world and one that is constantly in the news due to its importance to U.S. foreign policy. This conflict between the security of Israel and Palestinian autonomy was chosen as the topic of a one-week symposium that was part of the requirements for an undergraduate social psychology course, taught at a small liberal arts college.

The Format. All 42 male and female students in the class were first given a handout describing the format of the symposium, the required readings, and student activities. The three 50-minute class periods for that week were allocated as follows: (a) the instructor lectured on the social psychology of international conflict, problem-solving workshops, and how they have been applied to international conflicts, and gave an overview of the history, geography, and politics of the Palestinian-Israeli conflict; at the end of the period students were assigned randomly to one of three roles—"Palestinian" students, "Israeli" students, and

U.S. "negotiators;" (b) the instructor briefly reviewed, with the help of another handout, the issue of Palestinian autonomy that was to be the focus of the symposium (it is with this issue that the 1979 Camp David accord left off) and divided the class into three equally sized groups which contained approximately the same number of "Palestinians," "Israelis," and "negotiators;" the students were encouraged to act out their assigned roles in a sincere, realistic, and informed fashion, and the first session of the workshop was begun; (c) the second session of the workshop was continued during the last class, and the three student groups were urged to reach some conclusion about the status of their negotiations and report to the entire class on the outcome.

Background Material. All the students were assigned two readings for the week. The first, the chapter on international relations from a social psychology textbook (Fisher, 1982), was common to all students; those assigned the role of Palestinians read a chapter on the history and politics of these people (Foreign Policy Association, 1982b); the "Israelis" read a background article from Congressional Quarterly (1981) about the history and politics of Israel in the larger context of the Middle East; and the U.S. negotiators read an article about the history of U.S.-Israeli relations (Foreign Policy Association, 1982a). The instructor read these and various other articles from the *Great Decisions* series published by the Foreign Policy Association and from the Congressional Quarterly materials on the Middle East. During the student-directed sessions of the symposium, the instructor acted as a resource person answering factual and policy questions in order to enhance in-role participation; he was assisted in this function by the President of the College, Dr. Sherrill Cleland, who is an expert and former consultant on the Middle East. Students were instructed to discuss the issue of Palestinian autonomy by talking to each other as individuals, by listening and reflecting others' feelings as is done in sensitivity groups, and trying to reach a decision; but more important, to behave in-role according to information they had read and heard.

Proposed Solutions. Two of the three groups reached agreements on the issue; the third group was on the verge of an agreement when the "Israelis" backed out. The first group agreed to recognize each other as *people* (although not yet as respective nations), to sign a mutual non-aggression pact, to keep the cities of Jerusalem, Bethlehem, and Ramallah as neutral sites, to provide for a withdrawal of Israeli troops from the West Bank over a six month period, to arrange a five-mile demilitarized zone between the border of Israel and the West Bank, and to provide for full Palestinian autonomy in the northern half of the West Bank; all of these would be gradually achieved by 1989. The second group reached similar, though not as elaborated, agreement that also involved an immediate non-aggression pact and a demilitarized zone, but also the eventual disbanding of the P.L.O., as it is presently constituted, and Palestinian autonomy in the Gaza strip and a portion of the West Bank.

Evaluation. The instructor gave some immediate feedback on the proposed solutions, remarking on the rapid progress in negotiation in such a short time as well as on the unrealistically high number of Israeli concessions shown in two of the groups. Each student submitted a short paper the following week in which he/she explained how one's own views on the Middle East situation had been modified, how social psychological techniques were used in the discussion, and how future symposia like this might be conducted. Grades for the symposium activity were based on the quality of oral participation and on the short paper. These papers indicated a high level of self-reported education about Palestinian autonomy specifically and about the Middle East in general and a tendency on the part of most participants to be more sympathetic to the Palestinian cause than the present U.S. foreign policy seems to be. Students also recommended that in the future more instruction on sensitivity groups be given; this could easily have been done by covering the chapter on this topic from the Aronson (1980) textbook that was used in the first part of the course. Other suggestions were: (a) more practice on listening skills be obtained before the symposium, perhaps using a simpler problem of an interpersonal nature; (b) the

negotiators should talk to the "Palestinians" and "Israelis" separately before the group discussion takes place; (c) the groups should be allowed (or required) to meet outside of class in order to have more time and fewer distractions; (d) the mediators should be disinterested social scientists rather than "representatives" of the American government, who may not be fully committed to reconciliation of these two groups. These student Suggestions are consistent with the impressions of the instructor.

Although no empirical data were gathered, reports from student papers, informal comments, and course evaluations indicated that this Middle East symposium was highly challenging and informative about the potential contribution of psychology to the resolution of international conflict. Copies of handouts describing the activity and the ground rules for the workshop are available from the author upon request.

References

Bronfenbrenner, U. The mirror image in Soviet-American relations: A social psychologist's report. *Journal of Social Issues,* 1961, *17,* 45-56.

Cohen, S. P., Kelman, H. C., Miller, F. D., & Smith, B. L. Evolving intergroup techniques for conflict resolution: An Israeli-Palestinian pilot workshop. *Journal of Social Issues,* 1977, *33,* 165-189.

Congressional Quarterly. Israel. In Congressional Quarterly (Ed.), *The Middle East* (Fifth Ed.). Washington, DC: Library of Congress, 1981, 127-134.

Doob, L. W. (Ed.). *Resolving conflict in Africa: The Fermeda Workshop.* New Haven, CT. Yale University Press, 1970.

Doob, L. W. *A Cyprus workshop: An exercise in intervention methodology. Journal of Social Psychology,* 1974, *94,* 161-178.

Fisher, R . J . *Social psychology: An applied approach.* New York: St. Martin's Press, 1982.

Foreign Policy Association. Israel and the U.S.: Friendship and discord. In Foreign Policy Association (Ed.), *Great Decisions.* New York: Foreign Policy Association, 1982, pp. 2,6,9,10-11.(a)

Foreign Policy Association. The Palestinians: History, politics, and conflict. In Foreign Policy Association (Ed.), *Great Decisions.* New York: Foreign Policy Association, 1982, 39-48.(b)

White, R. K. *Nobody wanted war: Misperception in Vietnam and other wars.* Garden City, NY: Doubleday, 1970.

Studying a Social Norm

Marianne Miserandino
University of Rochester

This article describes a classroom activity in which students identify and graphically represent a group's norm. Students take a survey of peers' attitudes toward a target behavior and variations of it. Mean responses for each question are computed and graphed. The resulting curve illustrates the group's approval and disapproval of the target behavior, the strength of this approval or disapproval, the ideal behavior, and the range of tolerable behavior. This activity helps students understand and appreciate survey research methods, the need for controlled research, and the power of a peer-group norm.

Group norms, the set of implicit or explicit rules established by a group to regulate the behavior of its members (Baron & Byrne, 1981), are studied in many psychology classes. The group's approval or disapproval of certain behaviors is implicit in the idea of norms. Groups may exert considerable pressure on members by making their approval or disapproval known to the deviant and thereby enforce a norm. In the activity described herein, students identify a group norm, take a survey of members' attitudes, graphically represent the group norm, and interpret the results. This project illustrates group norms and involves even beginning psychology students in doing and thinking about research.

This project is based on the return potential model that has been used to study a variety of norms, including authoritative behavior; job-related attitudes; behavior of mental patients; and the dancing, drinking, smoking, swearing, and church attendance of college students (Jackson, 1965). The group's opinion is graphed along the Taxis for each of the possible behaviors graphed on the x-axis. The curve drawn through these points is called the *return potential curve* and represents the group's opinion of what is accepted as normative behavior.

Class Activity

Survey

After a lecture on research methods, including experimental and quasi-experimental designs, my introduction to social psychology class investigated the amount of time undergraduates at Hobart and William Smith Colleges spend studying in a typical week. Students were instructed to take a survey on study behavior by interviewing five subjects:

> Find a volunteer stranger. Tell him or her this is a class project on people's attitudes toward studying and that it takes about five minutes of their time. Have the respondent answer to you privately. Do not have two respondents answer in front of each other. Be sure they haven't already done this for someone else in the class. Ask them the following questions and record their answers:

1. What year in school are you?
2. How many hours a week do you typically study?
3. What do you think about someone at this school who spends 1 hr per week doing classwork in a typical week? For each amount of studying time subjects are to indicate their attitude on a scale ranging from *highly disapprove (-4)* to *highly approve* (4), with 0 labeled *indifferent.*
4. What do you think about someone at this school who spends 3 hr per week doing classwork in a typical week?
5. What do you think about someone at this school who spends 5 hr per week doing classwork in a typical week?

Continue asking the subjects the same question but increase the target behavior by 2 hr. Stop after you reach 51 hr per week. When you have finished the questioning, thank the subject for his or her time. Repeat this procedure for all five subjects. Record subjects' responses on graph paper or coding paper. Remain neutral at all times. Do not act surprised or shocked at the answers people give you. You do not want your reaction to inadvertently influence the responses of your subjects. Respect your subjects' rights to confidentiality and anonymity.

Calculations

After data collection, students were instructed to calculate the average response to each question. (Remind students that a response of 0 is meaningful and should be included in the average.) Students then plot the return potential curve for their own data by graphing the average responses from the scale (on the Taxis) for each of the hours of study time asked in the questions (along the x-axis).

Interpretation

Finally, while studying their own samples and graphs, students answer the following questions and write a report on their findings:

1. The *ideal behavior* is that behavior for which the group expresses the highest approval. What is the ideal behavior of your sample?
2. The *range of tolerable behavior* includes those behaviors for which the group expresses approval, as illustrated by positive averages. What is the range of tolerable studying behavior in your sample? What is the range of intolerable behavior?
3. The *intensity of the norm is* how strongly people feel about the behavior—either positively or negatively. How intense does your sample feel about studying? On serious issues, people generally feel very strongly and the result is a steep curve peaking at either or both of the extremes (–4 or 4). On matters of personal taste, people often do not feel so strongly, as evidenced by a relatively flat curve with the highest and lowest points occurring at less than +2 or –2, respectively. What were the highest and the lowest averages in your sample? Did subjects feel more intensely positive or more intensely negative? What can you say about the intensity of the study norm in your sample ?
4. How does the ideal behavior, according to your sample, compare to the average amount of time your sample reports studying? Are they the same? Why or why not? Why do you think this occurs?
5. Do you see anything unusual on the graph? Are there any unusual or outlier subjects in your sample?

6. Recall that this survey was about the norm of studying on this campus. Based on the graph, comments your subjects may have made, and your knowledge of this school, how would you explain these results?
7. Describe one problem with this study, and discuss what you could do to solve, or to at least minimize, it.

These questions are challenging because each student's graph is different as a result of the small number of subjects in each sample. Therefore, students must make an interpretation that best fits their own results (see Figure 1 for examples of different student curves). Each student turns in a report, graph, and raw data for grading.

Class Discussion

In discussing these results, students are amazed by variations in reported study behavior and attitudes and by variations in the curves. They quickly realize that they cannot make accurate judgments based on only five subjects. (Depending on students' level and course content, you could discuss proper sample selection and size.) Suggest to them that combining all of the individual data can increase sample size and allow them to draw more accurate conclusions, but that this procedure would add a possible mediating factor by increasing the number of experimenters. Then display—on the chalkboard, overhead, or a prepared handout—what their combined data look like. To do this, I have students turn in the assignment on one day, and I grade their reports, collate their data, and present the results for the next class. To illustrate interpretation of the results, the return potential curves of the collated social psychology class's data are presented in Figure 2.

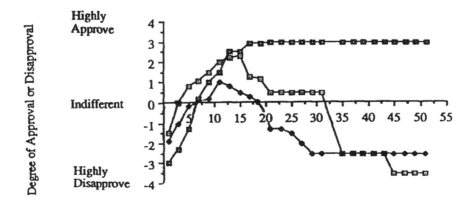

Figure 1. Sample curves from individual students' data collection. Each curve is based on the average responses of five subjects.

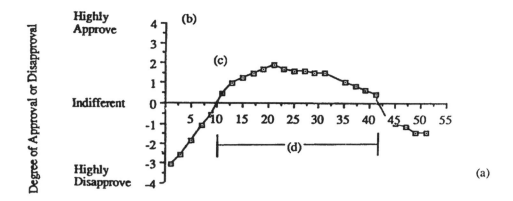

Figure 2. The return potential model of studying at Hobart and William Smith Colleges. (a) = the behavioral dimension—number of hours spent studying in a typical week; (b) = the evaluation dimension—approval or disapproval for each amount of time; (c) = the return potential curve; (d) = the range of tolerable studying behavior. Averages are based on the responses of 146 subjects collated from the data collected by 30 students.

As the graph illustrates, these students (N = 146) disapproved of studying 1 to 5 or 43 to 51 hr per week. Indifference was indicated toward those who study 7 to 13 hr or 33 to 43 hr, whereas approval was indicated toward those who study 15 to 31 hr. Although subjects were not asked their opinions for studying beyond 51 hr, the curve indicates that the group would continue to disapprove of studying this much, though not very strongly. Students reported that subjects were unwilling to indicate strong disapproval of a socially desirable behavior, such as studying. The average number of hours spent studying by this sample in a typical week was 17.86 (SD = 9.86) with a range of 2 to 60.

The range of tolerable behavior for hours spent studying in a typical week was 9 to 37 hr. In varying degrees, the group approved of all behavior within this range. The ideal behavior—the point at which the group expressed the highest approval—occurred for studying 21 hr per week, with a mean approval rating of 1.80. Surprisingly, this "ideal" behavior is viewed by the sample with only slight approval and is not generally put into practice; the mean studying time of this sample is less than the ideal (see Table 1 for reported studying times).

The intensity of the norm is indicated by the height of the curve above and below the point of indifference. Norms about matters of personal taste, such as dress, usually have low intensity and will show a relatively flat curve when graphed. When people are more concerned about the issue in question, the norms are generally more intense, as shown by higher peaks and lower valleys (Jackson, 1965). When it comes to studying, students on this campus do not have very strong feelings about the acceptability of various amounts of study time, as indicated by the wide range of tolerable behavior and by the strongest approval

being only 1.80 for studying 21 hr per week. The subjects felt more strongly about a person studying too little; they expressed the greatest disapproval of—2.93 for studying 1 hr per week. Similarly, the sample did not feel very strongly about the point at which a person studies too much. Indeed, the class reported that their subjects said it was people's prerogative to study as much as they wanted to or felt they needed to. Furthermore, many students reported that although subjects said that they personally would not spend so much time on their studies, many felt it was acceptable for others to do so.

Students spontaneously mentioned several sources of bias and mediating variables that could affect the results. Sources of bias include the location of the survey, time of the survey, subject selection, and attractiveness of the experimenter to the subject. Among the mediating variables mentioned by the class were a subject's major, year in school, gender, GPA, reasons for being in school, who pays tuition, and intellectual ability. Statistical analyses could be done to test some of these ideas.

Variations

Many variations of this demonstration are possible. One student suggested asking the questions in a random order so that subjects would not anticipate the questions or get bored. Another variation would be to compare the same norm in different groups (family vs. friends, fraternity/sorority members vs. nonmembers, friends vs. strangers) and discuss how the social pressures toward conformity change depending on the cohesiveness of the group. Other campus norms may elicit stronger approval or disapproval (e.g., drinking, dating, late-night noise, tuition increases, class length,

TV viewing, and clothing). Depending on the norm under investigation, smaller or larger increments of behavior may be more appropriate and would help reduce subjects' fatigue and/or boredom. Hence, the assignment can be designed to study whatever issue is most relevant to the class.

Evaluation and Conclusion

After collecting data, interpreting the results, and discussing the project as a class, students came to appreciate the need for experimentation and the problems of social desirability response bias, biased sampling, and limits in generalizing the results.

Overall, this demonstration effectively illustrates survey research methods and group norms in an enjoyable and engaging way. On a scale ranging from *not at all* (1) to *very much* (7), 29 students in the introductory social psychology class gave this demonstration a median rating of 6 for being "helpful in making me understand the group norm of studying at Hobart and William Smith Colleges," "helpful in making me understand group norms in general," and "helpful in making me understand survey research methods." For "enjoyable, fun" and "overall usefulness," the median

rating was 5. Students' comments, however, were the most revealing: "It was really interesting to do this study. I enjoyed listening to people's comments and seeing their reactions on [sic] studying," "It'll make me think a little more about surveys when I take them and when I give them," and "Active participation such as this exercise is more interesting and more significant to learning than simply reading about it."

The research experience enriches students' understanding, interpretation, and critiques of the experiments they learn about later in the course. This approach enables students to learn research skills, experience research, and gain insights about the power of a norm held by their own peer group.

References

Baron, R. A. & Byrne, D. (1987). *Social psychology: Understanding human interaction.* Boston: Allyn & Bacon.

Jackson, J. (1965). Structural characteristics of norms. In I. V. Steiner & M. Fishbein (Eds.), *Current studies in social psychology* (pp. 301-309). New York: Holt, Rinehart & Winston.

6. TEACHING ABOUT SPATIAL BEHAVIOR

Teaching About Crowding: Students as an Independent Variable

George Banziger
Marietta College

Research on crowding has come a long way since Calhoun's (1962) postulations on the "behavioral sink." The introductory psychology students however comes to this issue with some popular misconceptions about the causative effect of crowding and high density on negative behaviors in all species and is reinforced in this view by exposure to the Calhoun studies on rats. Yet studies done on other infrahuman species and other investigations done with humans (see Freedman] 1979) have demonstrated that the effects of crowding are more complicated than Calhoun's studies suggest. The purpose of the classroom exercise described here was to demonstrate the importance of situational and attributional cues in determining people's response to crowding. In summarizing studies of crowding done with many species Freedman (1979) concluded that the effects of high density depend on the situation and are not necessarily harmful. In reference to crowding in humans, Patterson (1978) has noted that the evaluation of the meaning of crowding (cognitive labeling) is critical in people's adjustment to such events and that such evaluations may show positive or negative affect. Other studies have indicated that the sex of the subject and degree of familiarity among subjects are important variables in determining the evaluation of a crowded environment (see Zlutnik & Altmans, 1972). It was assumed that students would appreciate a more sophisticated view of the psychology of crowding if they themselves were to experience high density under varying circumstances—that is, if the students were collectively involved as the independent variables.

Methods and Procedure. A brief five-question survey was given to a class of 43 male (*n* = 20) and female (*n* = 23) students of introductory psychology at Marietta College in the Spring Semester 1980. The students were asked to indicate first their sex and then on 10-point scales show how comfortable friendly happy, and satisfied they felt about the physical arrangement of the classroom. The classroom has 55 movable chairs a width of 21 feet and a length of 35 feet; the approximate distance between chairs is two feet. There were three conditions of physical arrangement: (1) the regular seating pattern with the usual spacing of seats which students voluntarily assumed—

measured on the first day of class; (2) the same seating pattern as (1), but pressed into half the spaces also measured on the first day of class; (3) the same as (2), but measured at the end of the semester. Presumably familiarity between students was greater at the end of the semester and affective reactions to crowding differed from those experienced earlier.

Results and Discussion. A 3 x 2 (Physical Arrangement by Sex) analysis of variance was computed four times using each question on affect as a dependent variable. Significant main effects of Physical Arrangement were obtained for Comfortable ($p<.01$), Satisfying ($p<.01$), and Happy ($p<.05$), but there were no main effects or interaction effects of Sex. Scheffé a posteriori comparisons indicated that the regular seating arrangement was judged to be significantly more comfortable ($p<.01$) and more satisfying ($p<.01$) than either of the crowded conditions and happier ($p<.01$) than the early crowded arrangement. Measures of crowding at the two different times in the semester were not significantly different on any of the a posteriori tests.

Although the instructor's intention in the class exercise was to demonstrate the complexity and possible interactive effects of crowding variables the results appeared to be fairly straightforward. Crowding, regardless of time of measurement and sex, seemed to produce more negative affect than normal seating arrangements in a classroom. The results were brought up in the class where the experiment was performed during a discussion on the psychology of crowding. Students and the instructor generated the following interpretations of the results: (a) there may have been some kind of reactance effect and, as a results negative affect in the high density conditions; that is, students might have experienced some restriction on their freedom by being told to squeeze into half the space of a normal classroom; (b) because the students were part of the independent variable, demand characteristics might have led them to respond in the way they did; some students indicated in the discussion that there was the expectation that psychologists will find negative effects Of crowding; (c) other manipulations and measures, such as perceived familiarity, taking a measurement of regular density at the end of the semester, measuring autonomic responses, performance measures, anticipated duration of the arrangement, or changes in the expectation about interaction, might have reflected some of the nuances of human crowding suggested in previous literature that were not shown in the present experiment.

This classroom experiment on crowding did not demonstrate the complexity of effects it was intended to show, but it did allow students to participate in an experiment both as subjects and as part of the independent variable. Subsequent class discussion indicated that this event brought additional insight into the subject matter of crowding, an understanding of experimental design, and an experience with which to provide helpful interpretations of experimental findings.

References

Calhoun, J. B. Population density and social pathology. *Scientific American*, 1962, *206,* 139-148.

Freedman, J. L. Reconciling apparent differences between the responses of humans and other animals to crowding. *Psychological Review*, 1979, *86,* 80-85.

Patterson, M. L. Arousal change and cognitive labeling: Pursuing the mediators of intimacy exchange. *Environmental Psychology and Nonverbal Behavior,* Fall, 1978, *3,* 17-22.

Zlutnik, S., & Altman, I. Crowding and human behavior. In J. Wohlwill & D. Carson (Eds.), *Environment and the social sciences: Perspectives and applications.* Washington, DC: American Psychological Association, 1972.

Field Experiments in Personal Space Invasion for Introductory Psychology

F. Richard Ferraro
University of Kansas

This article summarizes the use of field experiments designed to investigate personal space invasion. The experiments were designed and conducted by introductory psychology students and complemented classroom lectures. Student interest and enthusiasm were high throughout the experiments, which provided an understanding of personal space, personal space invasion, and the implications involved.

To supplement the typical introductory psychology lectures on personal space invasion, my students experienced this interesting topic firsthand. I had used class projects in previous semesters, but this effort was my first use of personal space invasion experiments.

This project coincided with the social psychology section of my course. My lecture discussed how behavior is influenced by other people (or groups of people) and what responses are elicited by others in certain situations (e.g., riding an elevator with a group of friends vs. riding the same elevator with a group of strangers). Because I emphasized the empirical aspect of psychology, a discussion arose in class concerning how experiments in personal space invasion could be conducted and what their practical value would be. This discussion led to my suggestion that the class members ($N = 80$), in groups of four to six, design and conduct their own personal space experiments, with a later class period being devoted to group presentations and discussion. In addition, each group was required to prepare an APA-style manuscript. During the next period, groups proposed their experiments to the class. This procedure helped to avoid overlap and to ensure that the research was feasible and ethical. All groups were encouraged to consult with me during the course of their projects, but few did so. I periodically inquired about each group's progress to be sure that all would finish in the allotted 2 weeks.

Locations for data collection included a library, an elevator, a cafeteria, a bus stop, and a dormitory lounge. The more ambitious groups performed experiments in several locations, although the majority remained at one site. The experiments were diverse. Some groups observed subjects unobtrusively (e.g., group members would sit in a parked car while taking notes). Other groups used confederates with one member recording subject reactions from a safe distance.

The popular choice for a dependent variable was the time taken by subjects to respond to the invasion of their *personal space*, operationally defined as the time from initial subject contact with an experimenter (or vice versa) until the subject left the testing area. One group used a questionnaire to inquire about personal space. This group diagramed a variety of personal space situations (e.g., a schematic of an elevator floor plan, varying the number of people in it) and asked subjects to place an X where they would stand if confronted with these situations.

Following data collection and analysis, groups made their presentations and submitted their manuscripts. Because no student had prior experience with formal statistics or APA style, great leniency was allowed in these areas (e.g., most groups used simple frequency tabulations).

Results generally conformed to previous findings (see Felipe & Sommer, 1966; Fisher & Byrne, 1975), but there were a few exceptions. Some students noted that people being observed often became interested in what the group members were doing. Such unexpected outcomes did not deter group enthusiasm, however, and added to class discussions concerning improved procedures for future experiments. Most group members were enthusiastic during all phases of their projects, with many expressing interest in future research opportunities in the psychology department, such as independent study and research assistantships.

All groups reported that the field experience was more valuable than lectures on the same topic. This information came from two sources. First, during data collection, many students said that their understanding was greatly increased by being the experimenter. Unfortunately, I was unable to compare performance on relevant examination questions between this semester and an earlier semester. Second, student evaluations at the end of the semester frequently noted that the nonlecture activities complemented a lecture or assignment on the same topic.

The hands-on experience highlighted problems associated with conducting research (e.g., time and effort expenditure) and reinforced the notion that research is not as easy as it is often portrayed to be in introductory texts. The students enjoyed their research experience, which provided opportunities for problem solving, critical thinking, cooperation, and collaborative learning. Such opportunities rarely occur in a large introductory psychology class.

References

Felipe, N. J., & Sommer, R. (1966). Invasion of personal space. *Social Problems, 14,* 206-214.

Fisher, J. D., & Byrne, D. (1975). Too close for comfort: Sex differences in response to invasions of personal space. *Journal of Personality and Social Psychology, 32,* 15-21.

Intimacy and Personal Space: A Classroom Demonstration

Bryan Gibson
Carleton College
Paul Harris
Carol Werner
University of Utah

The concept of personal space is intuitively straightforward for most students of psychology. However, some of the functions personal space serve in regulating intimacy among individuals are not so readily apparent. The demonstration described in this article allows students to see that personal space is one of a number of interacting nonverbal cues used by people to regulate intimacy, and it encourages discussion of these nonverbal mechanisms.

Research and theory on personal space has stressed the importance of personal space norms in regulating the intimacy of interpersonal interaction (Aiello & Thompson, 1980). In this regard, personal space norms can be seen as one of a number of inter-dependent nonverbal intimacy cues, including eye contact (Argyle & Dean, 1965), body orientation (Aiello, 1972), and topic intimacy (Baker & Shaw, 1980). This intimacy regulating function can be demonstrated to students through a straightforward activity that allows students to see how their personal space needs vary depending on the relative level of intimacy of other components of the interaction.

Procedure

Before any discussion of personal space, all students are asked to stand and choose a partner (preferably a person they do not know very well). Then they are asked to find space in the aisles or at the front of the classroom so that they can stand facing each other at a distance of about 8 ft. One student in each pair is then told to remain in a stationary position, and the other student is told to approach the partner. Students are asked to look toward the floor, and the approacher must then walk toward the stationary student until the approacher feels comfortable. Students are next instructed to look at each other; then the students who were stationary are asked to readjust their position by moving forward or backward until they feel comfortable. Finally, the students who were approached are asked to describe to their partners the appropriate steps necessary to use a condom properly. (Any intimate topic of conversation may be substituted here.) Other topics that have been used successfully include describing their first kiss, describing their most embarrassing experience, or imagining themselves in their underwear. At this point, there is typically a pause, and then students begin to look away from their partner, move back, turn their body, and/or laugh. After a few seconds, the instructor tells the class that they need not describe how to use a condom and that they can return to their seats.

Discussion

This activity demonstrates the important principle that personal space is one of several nonverbal mechanisms used to regulate intimacy. When students are instructed to look each other in the eye after one approaches the other, the most typical adjustment made by the person who was approached is to move back slightly. This movement shows that once eye contact is made, the interaction becomes more intimate, and adjustments in personal space are necessary to regain a comfortable state of interaction. Similarly, when students are asked to describe the proper use of a condom, a number of adjustments are made in the nonverbal cues used by students. They look away, reorient their body so as not to face their partner, or they move back even more. Each of these adjustments is designed to reduce the intimacy of the

interaction once the topic of conversation increases in intimacy.

While discussing the variety of behaviors students used to regulate intimacy, the instructor can also have students report their subjective experiences during the exercise. Most students will report that they felt uncomfortable or nervous when eye contact was established and when the topic of conversation became more personal; in fact, it is common to hear nervous giggling or laughter from students when these shifts in intimacy take place. Discussing these subjective experiences may help students relate at a personal level to the "discomfort" of intimacy shifts discussed in equilibrium models of intimacy (Argyle & Dean, 1965) and the increases in arousal postulated by arousal models of interpersonal intimacy (Patterson, 1976).

Discussion of these issues leads to a greater understanding of one of the purposes of personal space norms (i.e ., intimacy regulation), the behaviors associated with regulation, and the psychological processes that have been proposed as mediating this phenomenon. In addition, knowledge of the intimacy regulating function of personal space norms elicits discussion of interesting misunderstandings that may arise due to different personal space norms held by people of different cultures and by men and women. Hall (1966) first noted cultural differences in personal space use between what he called contact cultures (Latin American, Arab, and Mediterranean) and noncontact cultures (Northern European and North American). When people from contact cultures interact with people from noncontact cultures each may misinterpret the other on the basis of personal space use. The individual from the contact culture may view his or her noncontact culture acquaintance as distant and aloof, whereas the individual from the noncontact culture may see his or her opposite as overly assertive or intimate.

Similarly, men typically have greater personal space needs than do women (Patterson, 1977; Tennis & Dabbs, 1975). Thus, interactions between men and women also have the potential for misunderstanding on the basis of personal space use. A woman may feel that a man is uninterested in her because of his larger personal space needs, whereas a man may misinterpret the closer interaction distance of a woman to mean that she is attempting to increase intimacy when in fact she is simply interacting at a distance that is more comfortable for her. Discussions of these gender differences may lead to insights regarding misunderstandings that could occur between men and women in dating situations.

Evaluation

This demonstration has been received enthusiastically in courses from introductory psychology to social psychology and environmental psychology. Evaluations were collected in an introductory psychology class. Students were asked to rate the demonstration on a scale ranging from *not very useful* (1) to *very useful* (5). The class mean was 3.8 (*N* = 35), indicating a generally positive response to the demonstration. In addition, students were asked to make a recommendation regarding the use of this demonstration in future classes. Eighty percent thought that the demonstration should be used in the future, 20% responded "maybe," and no one suggested that the demonstration not be used in the future.

Results of this evaluation are particularly important, given the potentially embarrassing nature of this demonstration. To encourage a natural response from students, little information is given before the demonstration. This fact ensures that when the intimate topic is raised, students will respond with genuine surprise and without a measured consideration of their nonverbal behavior. Thus, it is encouraging to note that students rate this demonstration positively and support its continued use in the classroom.

Conclusion

Other teaching activities using personal space have successfully focused students on data collection and ethics in personal space research (Burzynski, 1990; Ferraro, 1990). However, these activities have focused on retreat as the only response to an invasion of personal space. In contrast, the demonstration described in this article makes students aware of the communicative nature of personal space and enhances discussion of how personal space differences may lead to misunderstandings across culture and gender. In addition, students gain insight into their own use of personal space—a process that is typically so highly ingrained that students have not recognized its communicative function.

References

Aiello, J. R. (1972). A test of equilibrium theory: Visual interaction in relation to orientation, and sex of partner. *Perceptual and Motor Skills, 49,* 85-86.

Aiello, J. R., & Thompson, D. E. (1980). When comparison fails: Mediating effects of sex and locus of control at extended interpersonal distances. *Basic and Applied Social Psychology, 1,* 65-82.

Argyle, M., & Dean, J. (1965). Eye-contact, distance and affiliation. *Sociometry, 28,* 289-304.

Baker, E., & Shaw, M. E. (1980). Reactions to interpersonal distance and topic intimacy A comparison of strangers and friends. *Journal of Nonverbal Behavior, 5,* 80-91.

Burzynski, P. R. (1990). The personal space violation demonstration. In V. P. Makosky, C. C. Sileo, L. G. Whittemore, C. P. Landry, & M. L. Skutley (Eds.), *Activities handbook for the teaching of psychology* (Vol. 3, pp. 136-137). Washington DC: American Psychological Association.

Ferraro, F. R. (1990). Field experiments in personal space invasion for introductory psychology. *Teaching of Psychology, 17,* 124

Hall, E. T. (1966). *The hidden dimension.* New York: Doubleday. Patterson, M. L. (1976). An arousal model of interpersonal intimacy. *Psychological Review, 83,* 235-245.

Patterson, M. L. (1977). Interpersonal distance, affect, and equilibrium theory. *Journal of Social Psychology, 101,* 205-214.

Tennis, G. H., & Dabbs, J. M. (1975). Sex, setting and personal space: First grade through college. *Sociometry, 38,* 385-394.

Note

We thank Sharon Akimoto and Neil Lutsky for their helpful comments on a draft of this article.

7. INSTIGATING MISCELLANEOUS TECHNIQUES

Robbers in the Classroom: A Deindividuation Exercise

David K.Dodd
Saint Mary College

A deindividuation demonstration, which I have developed and evaluated over the past 5 years, has yielded excellent results. The objective of the exercise is to illustrate deindividuation by asking students to imagine and anonymously report those behaviors in which they might engage if they were actually in such a deindividuated state. The idea for this demonstration is taken directly from Zimbardo (1979a), and is based more generally on Zimbardo's (1970) theory of deindividuation. Zimbardo defined deindividuation as "a complex process in which a series of social conditions lead to changes in perception of self and of other people," consequently "behavior that is normally restrained and inhibited is 'released' in violation of established norms of appropriateness" (1979b, p. 702). A major contributing factor to deindividuation, according to Zimbardo (1979b), is perceived anonymity, which psychologically protects individuals from being held responsible for their actions.

The primary purpose of this classroom demonstration is to illustrate the concept of deindividuation, and to reveal that even "normal, well-adjusted" college students are capable of highly inappropriate, antisocial behavior, given certain social and situational conditions. In the present study, 312 responses were generated from 229 undergraduate psychology students. Because 26 of the respondents were students in prison college programs, a secondary objective was to compare the responses of prisoners to nonprisoners in terms of the proportion and kinds of antisocial responses.

METHOD AND RESULTS

The deindividuation demonstration was used with 13 undergraduate psychology classes, including 11 general and 2 social psychology classes. Three classes (hereafter "prison") were conducted in maximum security prison settings: one of these classes was exclusively female and consisted of five respondents; the other two were exclusively male and consisted of 10 and 11 respondents. These students, all convicted of felonies, generally fell in the age range of 24-32, came from lower socioeconomic backgrounds, and were evenly divided between Caucasians and non-Caucasians. The remaining 203 respondents

(hereafter "campus") were enrolled in on-campus programs and were predominantly female, Caucasian, middle-class, and traditional college age (17-24).

The stimulus question for the demonstration was "If you could be totally invisible for 24 hours and were completely assured that you would not be detected, what would you do?" Because this instruction tended to yield many responses that were not humanly possible, such as "walk on the ocean" and "fly around at a party pinching people," the instruction was modified to, "If you could do anything humanly possible with complete assurance that you would not be detected or held responsible, what would you do?"

Students quickly recorded their responses and were asked to turn them in to the instructor, with no identifying information included. After receiving all the responses, the instructor outlined the basic premises of deindividuation theory and read the responses aloud to the class. The entire demonstration was usually completed in about 15 minutes.

In order to examine the deindividuation hypothesis, it was necessary to categorize and rate each response according to content and social desirability. After examining the data, the author established 11 content categories of responses: aggression, charity, academic dishonesty, crime, escapism, political activities, sexual behavior, social disruption, interpersonal spying and eavesdropping, travel, and a catch-all "other" category. To rate the social desirability of responses, the following terms and definitions were employed. *Prosocial* behavior was defined as intending to benefit others; *antisocial* behavior as injuring others or depriving them of their rights; *nonnormative* behavior as clearly violating social norms and practices, but without specifically helping or hurting others; and *neutral* behavior as meeting none of the above three definitions.

Three raters, blind to the specific deindividuation hypothesis and to the backgrounds of the individual respondents, independently categorized each response according to its content and rated its social desirability. A criterion of at least two-thirds agreement among the trio of raters was established, and this criterion was met for 97% of the responses for content and 98% for social desirability. Responses for which the criterion was not met were excluded from the relevant analyses.

Results revealed that 36% of the responses were antisocial, 19% nonnormative, 36% neutral, and only 9% prosocial. There was no significant difference between the social desirability of the responses of prison versus campus students, $\chi^2(3) = 3.67$, ns. Regarding response content, the most frequent responses were criminal acts (26%), sexual acts (11%), and spying behaviors (11%); here again, the prison and campus students did not differ significantly, $\chi^2(5) = 6.22$, ns. The most common single response was "rob a bank," which accounted for 15% of all responses, and jewel theft and counterfeiting were also popular responses under the "crime" category. Responses categorized as "sexual" were evenly divided among: sex with a famous person, stranger or casual acquaintance; sex with a lover; exhibitionism and public nudity; and voyeurism. Infrequent but notable responses from campus students included murder, rape, and political assassination.

DISCUSSION AND EVALUATION

This is a highly educational and entertaining demonstration. When the instructions for this demonstration are given, there is invariably an immediate reaction of excitement and anticipation of the results. Indeed, the results provoke much laughter and surprise at such "murderous thoughts," as one student put it.

Evaluation data were collected from 53 subjects representing three different campus classes. On a 7-point scale (7 = high value, 1 = little or no value), the demonstrations received mean ratings of 5.5 and 5.8 for educational and entertainment value, respectively. These high ratings are corroborated by written and spontaneous comments from students, who frequently describe the demonstration as "fascinating," "funny," and "hard to believe!"

In addition to illustrating the concept of deindividuation, this exercise can also be used to demonstrate the strengths and weaknesses of statistical prediction. After collecting the responses from a class, but before examining them, I can boldly predict the kinds of responses that have just been turned in based on analyses of previous data. For example, it is safe to predict that responses involving bank robbery, spying, and sexual behavior will be quite frequent. Academic cheating and vandalism, although infrequent, will usually draw at least one or two responses from even a small class. Likewise, charitable responses, also infrequent, appear to be reliable in content, and usually

include freeing hostages or solving international conflicts, alleviating social inequities such as poverty and hunger, and being kind to one's enemies.

Of course, I point out to my classes that my statistical predictions are based entirely on data obtained from previous demonstrations, and the issue of generalizing from one sample to another naturally arises. Furthermore, I emphasize that the data do not permit me (nor is it my intention) to predict the responses of individual students, and it is explained that this inability to predict the behavior of individuals is true of most social psychological research at this time.

Students are also impressed by the fact that no significant differences were found between my prison and campus students, regarding either the kinds of responses or the extent of their antisocial content In this respect, the deindividuation demonstration emphasizes the important role of situational conditions, such as perceived anonymity, rather than personal traits or characteristics, in antisocial behavior. Therefore, the demonstration can be effectively used in conjunction with lecture or discussion of such social psychological studies as Milgram's (1974) obedience studies or Zimbardo's Stanford prison study (Haney, Banks, & Zimbardo, 1973), both of which also emphasize the crucial role of situational determinants of antisocial behavior. Finally, whether or not my students fully appreciate the "moral of the story," that is, the educational value of the exercise, they quite obviously delight in observing the antisocial and nonnormative responses that are elicited from their own classmates!

References

Haney, C., Banks, C., & Zimbardo, P. (1973). Interpersonal dynamics in a simulated prison. *International Journal of Criminology and Penology, 1,* 69-97.

Milgram, S. (1974). *Obedience to authority.* New York: Harper & Row.

Zimbardo, P. G. (1970). The human choice: Individuation, reason and order versus deindividuation, impulse, and chaos. In W. J. Arnold & D. Levine (Eds.), *Nebraska symposium on motivation,* 1969 (pp. 237-307). Lincoln, NE: University of Nebraska Press.

Zimbardo, P. G. (1979a). *Instructor's resource book to accompany Psychology and Life (10th ed.).* Glenview, IL: Scott, Foresman.

Zimbardo, P. G. (1979b). *Psychology and life* (10th ed.). Glenview, IL: Scott, Foresman.

Detecting Deception: A Classroom Demonstration

James W. Grosch
Colgate University

John E. Sparrow
*State University of New York
College at Geneseo*

Lie detection, a topic that most students of psychology find fascinating, can be demonstrated using an inexpensive, highly portable galvanic skin response (GSR) monitor. This demonstration can be used to touch on the current controversy surrounding the use of physiological measures in detecting deception and is relevant to other topics, such as emotion, perception, and industrial/organizational psychology.

The attempt by behavioral scientists to detect when a person is lying has a long and varied history (see Ekman, 1985; Ekman & O'Sullivan, 1991). One of the most widely used instruments in lie detection is the polygraph, a device that simultaneously measures several physiological responses, including heart rate, respiration, and galvanic skin response (GSR). The GSR measures electrical resistance of the skin, which is affected by slight changes in moisture content. The polygraph's accuracy in detecting lies is controversial (e.g., Lykken, 1984; Raskin & Podlesny, 1979). Students can better appreciate this controversy when they view a classroom demonstration of lie detection and judge the process for themselves. Unfortunately, polygraphs are expensive and bulky, making it difficult, if not impractical, to bring them into the classroom.

The lie detection demonstration we developed uses an inexpensive GSR monitor. This technique can be carried out quickly and used in connection with many different topics, including physiological psychology, emotion, perception, and industrial/organizational psychology.

The GSR Monitor

We use an inexpensive, reliable GSR monitor described as a "biofeedback stress monitor" by its manufacturer, Micronta. This particular model has been updated to an electronically similar, although cosmetically different, model. The newer version works in the same fashion as the older model, al-though we have limited our review to the older prototype.

The device employs two metal finger electrodes held in place by velcro fasteners. These electrodes plug into the lightweight (185 g), palm-sized main unit that houses the electronic circuitry necessary for monitoring changes in the GSR. The electronics used on the main circuit board are modest, consisting of three capacitors, a potentiometer, four resistors, three transistors, and a small transformer. Mounted in the case's front is a 5-cm speaker that emits a tone whose pitch changes as skin resistance changes. The case also provides an earphone jack that bypasses the speaker for private listening. This jack can also be used to route the monitor's auditory output to an external amplifier for use with large audiences. We have tested this feature in large sections of introductory psychology and found it produced a tone easily audible throughout the classroom. The device is powered by a single 9-V battery; hence, the unit is completely self-contained, including the power source, and is easily transported.

Demonstrating Lie Detection

Our classroom demonstration involves a number selection procedure analogous to the Guilty Knowledge Technique (Lykken, 1981) used by professional polygraphers. We begin with a brief introduction of the polygraph and its use in lie detection, emphasizing that the GSR is only one of several measures that comprise the polygraph. After we describe the GSR monitor, the two electrodes of the GSR are attached to the middle and forefinger of a volunteer from the class. (We recommend cleaning the fingers with alcohol before attaching the electrodes to ensure a proper electrical contact.) To ensure a reliable reading, the subject's hand must be kept in a comfortable, stable position; the two electrodes should not touch.

While the instructor's back is turned, the subject selects one of five index cards, each of which has a number from 1 to 5 written on it; shows its number to the class; returns it to the deck; and shuffles the cards. At this point, the instructor turns around and adjusts the GSR so that its tone can be clearly heard by the class. The instructor then holds up each card so that the class and the subject can see it and asks, "Is this the number you chosen The subject is told to say "no" each time, resulting in a lie being told when the correct card is held up.

We recommend going through the deck at least twice, giving the class a chance to contrast the change in the GSR tone with each answer given. The instructor identifies the card that produces the largest GSR response as the target. This procedure takes approximately 10 min per subject and can be repeated several times with the same or new subjects.

We have used the GSR monitor in various sections of introductory psychology, research methodology, and industrial/organizational psychology. Across 16 occasions, the GSR monitor has produced accurate results 88% of the time.

Relevant Areas of Psychology

This demonstration can be used in many courses. For example, when discussing physiological psychology in the introductory course, we have used the GSR monitor to illustrate how the autonomic nervous system reacts to a situation involving arousal, such as that produced by telling a lie. In the area of emotion, changes in the GSR represent one of many sources of information that can be used to infer an emotional state (presumably guilt when one is telling a lie). The GSR can be compared with other sources (e.g., facial expressions) for accuracy and reliability. Sensation and perception students could profit from the demonstration if it is couched in terms of signal detection theory (Green & Swets, 1966). Here, hits, misses, correct rejections and false alarms could be described as plausible outcomes in a lie detection task. An important criticism of the polygraph is that although the percentage of hits may be high, so too are the number of false alarms, and innocent subjects may be falsely accused of lying (Lykken, 1984). Finally, lie detection is relevant to the field of industrial/organizational psychology because it has often served as a personnel screening device. A demonstration of the GSR monitor could be followed by a discussion of the problems that arise when a technique used in employment testing is not 100% accurate (see Sackett & Decker, 1979).

Ethical Issues Concerning Lie Detection

Whatever the context, students should understand that both the polygraph and the GSR monitor are far from foolproof and measure only physiological responses, not whether the subject is actually telling a lie. Indeed, it is this inference from a physiological response that makes the use of the GSR and the poly-

graph so controversial in detecting deception and so interesting in class.

In lecture, we stress that research on the polygraph presents a mixed picture of its overall accuracy. Some researchers (e.g., Raskin & Podlesny, 1979) have found polygraph accuracy as high as 90%, others (e.g., Lykken, 1979) have reported false alarms as often as 50% of the time. Factors that affect the accuracy of a polygraph test include the examiner's questioning technique, the subject's expectations, the severity of the lie being told, and the base rate of deception within the population (Ekman, 1985). Because the polygraph is less than perfectly accurate, ethical objections have been raised concerning its widespread use (e.g., Abeles, 1985; Alpher & Blanton, 1985), and about 25 states have banned its use in detecting deception. We present this information in class to emphasize that the GSR results must be interpreted cautiously. We want students to appreciate the complexity involved in lie detection and to realize that the accuracy of the device may vary with the situation and the subject.

An Experimental Assessment of the GSR Monitor

Although accuracy of the GSR monitor is fairly impressive (Raskin & Podlesny, 1979), a classroom setting may not be a fair test because the instructor may use cues other than the monitor's tone to detect deception. These cues, although often subtle, include the subject's facial expressions, the audience's reactions to the demonstration, and the subject's reactions to the monitor's auditory feedback. How accurate is the GSR monitor in light of these and other extraneous cues?

To address this question, we designed two laboratory experiments using the number-selection procedure mentioned earlier but with no audience present. In the first experiment, we tested the role played by facial cues in the context of auditory feedback. Twenty-eight introductory psychology students at Colgate University were randomly assigned to either a GSR/no facial cues condition in which they were seated behind a barrier, not visible to the experimenter, or a GSR/facial cues condition in which they were visible. In both conditions, the experimenter used the GSR monitor to help detect deception. Each subject also went through a no GSR/facial cues (or control) condition that consisted of the experimenter guessing the subject's selected number while the GSR monitor was turned off and while the subject was in full view of the experimenter. All three conditions consisted of three trials; a *trial* was defined as the experimenter guessing the selected number.

In the second experiment, we again looked at the role of facial cues but without the auditory feedback. We did this to make the GSR monitor more analogous to a standard polygraph that typically does not provide auditory feedback. To eliminate feedback to the subject, we routed the monitor's audio signal to an oscilloscope rather than the audio speaker. The experimenter made decisions based on changes in the waveform's pattern. Twenty seven introductory psychology students at the State University of New York-College at Geneseo were randomly assigned to the same three conditions as in the first study.

We analyzed the data using a modified Bonferroni test (Keppel, 1991) to control the familywise error rate for eight planned nondirectional comparisons. We determined the adjusted alpha level to be .044. As Figure 1 indicates, the auditory feedback was much more helpful than the visual feedback in detecting deception for both the GSR/facial cues and GSR/no facial cues conditions. Independent t tests revealed that these differences were statistically significant, $t(29) = 3.49$ for GSR/facial cues and $t(22) = 3.13$ for GSR/no facial cues, $ps < .01$. Thus, auditory feedback appears to make an important contribution to the device's overall accuracy. Although the GSR/facial cues condition produced slightly greater accuracy than the GSR/no facial cues condition for both auditory and visual feedback, these differences were not statistically significant ($p > .044$), as determined by independent t tests. Furthermore, for the control condition, in which only facial cues were available, accuracy was below chance performance for three of the four groups. This result suggests that facial cues alone contributed little, if anything, to accurate detection.

The GSR monitor itself provided fairly accurate information concerning deception. This was especially true for auditory feedback, in which both the GSR/facial cues and GSR/no facial cues conditions produced significantly greater accuracy than the control condition, $t(14) = 8.09$ for GSR/facial cues and $t(12) = 3.09$ for GSR/no facial cues, $ps < .01$, in paired

observation tests. For visual feedback, however, only the GSR/facial cues condition was significantly greater than the control, $t(15) = 3.22$, $p < .01$, in a paired observation test. Finally, note that the highest accuracy in any condition was 71%, which is substantially less than the 88% we found for the class. This difference suggests that other variables, such as the social influence produced by an audience watching a subject, are at work in a classroom setting and contribute to the accurate detection of deception.

Although many factors contribute to the GSR monitor's accuracy, our data show that, with auditory feedback, the device works well in classroom and laboratory settings. Even when the instructor fails to detect deception, the results can lead to a useful discussion of issues surrounding lie detection and the complexity of using physiological measures for inferring a psychological state.

References

Abeles, N. (1985). Proceedings of the American Psychological Association, 1985. *American Psychologist, 41,* 633-663.

Alpher, V. S., & Blanton, R. L. (1985). The accuracy of lie detection: Why lie tests based on the polygraph should not be admitted into evidence today. *Law and Psychology Review, 9,* 67-75.

Ekman, P. (1985). *Telling lies: Clues to deceit in the marketplace, politics, and marriage.* New York: Norton.

Ekman, P., & O'Sullivan, M. (1991). Who can catch a liar? *American Psychologist, 46,* 913-920.

Green, D. M., & Swets, J. A. (1966). *Signal detection theory and psychophysics.* New York: Wiley.

Keppel, G. (1991). *Design and analysis: A researcher's handbook* (2nd ed.). Englewood Cliffs, NJ: Prentice Hall.

Lykken, D. T. (1979). The detection of deception. *Psychological Bulletin, 86,* 47-53.

Lykken, D. T. (1981). *Tremor in the blood.* New York: McGraw-Hill.

Lykken, D. T. (1984). Detecting deception in 1984. *American Behavioral Scientist, 27,* 481-499.

Raskin, D. C., & Podlesny, J. A. (1979). Truth and deception: A reply to Lykken. *Psychological Bulletin, 86,* 54-59.

Sackett, P. R., & Decker, P. J. (1979). Detection of deception in the employment context: A review and critical analysis. *Personnel Psychology, 32,* 487-504.

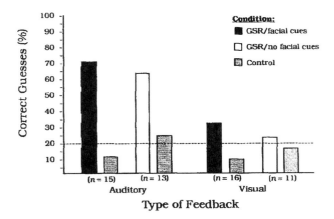

Figure 1. Percentage of correct experimenter guesses as a function of the type of feedback (auditory or visual) and the three different experimental conditions (GSR/facial cues, GSR/no facial cues, and control). The broken line indicates chance performance.

Note

We thank Rachel Andrews, Judith Brown, Sarah Duggan, and Sharon Feeney for assisting with data collection. We also thank Kathy Barsz and Ganie DeHart for their valuable comments on a draft of this article.

Samuel Butler's *Erewhon* as Social Psychology

Don R. Osborn
Bellarmine College

Samuel Butler's (1872/1983) utopian novel, Erewhon, was used in a social psychology class to demonstrate the universality of social psychological insights and to provide a literary dimension to the course. Erewhon provides numerous examples of five social psychological principles: (a) the relation of physical attractiveness to interpersonal attraction and judgments, (b) the human drive for interpersonal agreement, (c) the drive for congruence in values and behavior, (d) the importance of values in understanding actions, and (e) attribution theory. Student evaluations indicate that Erewhon can be successfully used as a supplementary reading to increase the liberal arts value of a social psychology course.

One of the challenges in teaching social psychology at a liberal arts college is finding a good supplementary reader to demonstrate that social psychology principles are also found in other disciplines. One of the best ways to connect psychology to a wider pattern of human experience is through literature (Grant, 1987). Gorman (1984) showed how the imaginative use of Vonnegut's (1975) *The Eden Express* enlivened an introductory psychology course. I similarly report the successful use of Samuel Butler's (1872/1983) novel *Erewhon*. It effectively illustrates at least five social psychological principles through the plot and interplay of characters.

In his afterword to the Signet edition, writer Kingley Amis called *Erewhon* "the first modern Utopian romance." It is played out in an imaginary land created by Samuel Butler as a basis for his attacks on "modern" life and thought. The protagonist, Higgs, is a sheep farmer in an unnamed British colony in 1868. He is the first outsider to traverse an impassable mountain range and discover Erewhon—a land populated by natives whose beliefs provide the basis for using this book in a social psychology course.

Five of the notable social psychological issues that *Erewhon* addresses are discussed here.

1. The importance of physical attractiveness in interpersonal attraction. The Erewhonians are described as robust and beautiful people, always glowing with good health and taking pride in their appearance. One's character is reflected by physical appearance to the extent that an Erewhonian may ask another more physically attractive friend to pose for his or her statue. One of the major factors in Higgs's positive reception and treatment by the Erewhonians was his superlative overall appearance and his rare light complexion. This theme anticipates the findings of classic interpersonal attraction research (e.g., Walster, Aronson, Abrahams, & Rottman, 1966), which demonstrated how judgments of others are influenced by physical attractiveness. Later, when Higgs falls into disfavor with the king, critical newspaper articles impugn his attractiveness on the grounds that a fair complexion is common in Higgs's homeland. This criticism anticipates Jellison and Zeisset's (1969) work, which confirms the rarity enhances attractiveness view. They found that an attractive feature has a greater positive effect on attractiveness judgments when it is rare than when it is common.

2. The human tendency to want others to agree with our ideas and values. Explicitly, this drive for interpersonal agreement occurs in various asides throughout the book as Higgs explains his behaviors and feelings. For example, as he is adjusting to the unusual Erewhonian view that treats crime as an illness, Higgs must accede to the government's desire for him to be the houseguest of a convicted embezzler. Higgs characterizes this situation as showing "a greater perversity of mental vision than I had been yet prepared for. And this made me wretched; for I cannot bear having much to do with people who think differently from myself" (Butler, 1872/1983, p. 93). The Erewhonians themselves hold "A man's business is to think as his neighbors do, for heaven help him if he thinks good what they count bad" (p. 189). These and other incidents provide excellent examples of the importance of similarity in several areas of social psychological research. Byrne (1971) showed that similarity is one of the most important determinants of interpersonal attraction. Concepts from balance theory (Heider, 1946) have been fruitful in understanding attitude organization and change.

3. The tendency to have our values and behaviors congruent. Use of the drive for logical-affective consistency in attitudes to modify attitudes and/or behavior

has been demonstrated by McGuire's (1981) work on the *Socratic effect*. McGuire showed that forcing people to logically justify the relation among their beliefs, attitudes, and behaviors can lead to change beyond the effect of a particular persuasive message. One of the historical developments in *Erewhon* was a political movement that outlawed meat eating. The citizens either had to become vegetarians or outlaws. The basis for the success of this Erewhonian movement was an application of the Socratic effect. The Socratic effect was used by first establishing the rights of animals as a philosophical value, thus causing Erewhon to go through a period of compulsory vegetarianism. Then this animal right-to-life viewpoint was extended to vegetables, and Erewhonians were logically (though temporarily) forced to live on a diet of rotten vegetables, without dairy products or eggs. This sequence shows, in a powerful and memorable way, how the need for cognitive and behavioral consistency can be used to change people's attitudes and behaviors.

4. The importance of values in understanding human action. The Fishbein model of attitudes fits nicely here (Fishbein & Ajzen, 1975). Fishbein posited that "normative beliefs" are elements in attitudes that are defined as our beliefs about what other people think we should do. The importance of others' evaluations was represented in Victorian times by Mrs. Grundy, a character in Morton's (1926) *Speed the Plough*. This character personified Victorian concepts of propriety and came to symbolize the powerful social controlling effect of conventional proprieties. Butler satirized this human tendency by anagramatically converting *Grundy* to a very popular god, *Ydgrun,* in Erewhon's polytheistic society. In addition to personifying and demonstrating Fishbein's concept of normative belief, the Ydgrunites (followers of Ydgrun) provide a fine example of Kohlberg's Level 3 moralizing. Kohlberg and Kramer (1969) identified six stages of moral development differentiated by the basis for judging an act moral. The Level 3 basis is the opinions of others.

In Erewhon, wealth is regarded as one of the best measures of social value, along with physical attractiveness. Rich people in Erewhon are so admired for their contributions to society that they are not taxed at all. This point is useful in discussing recent political belief systems. The reduction of tax rates for higher income Americans in the last major federal tax legislation shows this same positive attitude toward the rich in our society.

5. The importance of causal attributional schemas in determining our attitudes toward others, proper social behavior, and proper social policy. The Erewhonians deal with the problem of holding people responsible for their actions by maintaining that each person chose to be born. The Erewhonians believe there is a "World of the Unborn" wherein disembodied souls live; by choosing to be born, they become newborn babies. Newborn Erewhonians are required to sign a "Birth Formulae." This legal document asserts that they came into the world of their own free will, they imposed their existence on their unfortunate parents, and they take all responsibility for their lives on their own shoulders. This concept of preexistence seems initially quite odd to the typical student, but it is a view that is also Mormon dogma and characteristic of many New Age religious views (MacLaine, 1983). The similarity of these contemporary religious beliefs to the Erewhonian view provides a bridge for the students when discussing the implications of preexistence for attributional schemas.

The most fascinating attributional twist in Erewhon is that sick people are treated like criminals (fined and imprisoned), whereas criminals are treated like sick people (attended and cured by "straighteners" who prescribe floggings, bread and water diets, and other painful treatments). This reversal of our society's usual attributional schema and the implications of this reversal significantly add to the students' appreciation of the importance of attributional judgments in human behavior. The "Just World" hypothesis is exemplified by the Erewhonians because it is the basis for the law of the land. In the chapter, "Some Erewhonian Trials," the case of a man accused of having pulmonary consumption is discussed. This crime was punished by a life sentence of hard labor. As a general principle of Erewhonian justice, a judge lecturing a prisoner says, "You have suffered a great loss. Nature attaches a great penalty to such offenses, and human law must emphasise the decree of nature" (Butler, 1872/1983, p. 113).

These are the major points I found useful in enriching my class. The evaluation data reported in Table 1 show the success of this supplementary reader.

The data are combined from two semesters of classes: 19 students enrolled in fall 1986 and 18 in fall 1987. In the fall 1986 class, I assigned *Erewhon* as a supplementary text, included questions on the weekly quizzes, and pointed out some applications in lecture. I did not spend any significant class time on it. In fall 1987, I had small-group discussion sections every month of the semester. The students' task was to generate social psychological examples from *Erewhon.* Because there were no significant differences between classes in average ratings (except for Item 2G) the data were combined from both semesters in the table. The student evaluations suggest that *Erewhon* can be used successfully, even when the instructor does not spend class time on discussion groups.

For Item 2G, the fall 1986 class rating *(M* = 2.58) was significantly more positive toward this topic than the fall 1987 class *(M* = 3.44), *t*(35) = 2.18, *p* < .05. Although the reason for this difference is unclear, students in 1987 may have been more negative because they attended a campus event that strongly endorsed views opposed to Erewhonian beliefs. The Erewhonians make sharp distinctions between the

Table 1. Student Evaluation of Erewhon as a Supplementary Text

Item	M	SD
1. *Erewhon* added to the liberal arts value of the class[a]	2.89	.93
2. How valuable was *Erewhon* in demonstrating:[b]		
A. importance of physical attractiveness?	2.49	1.38
B. human tendency to want agreement with our own ideas and values?	2.30	.85
C. drive to have values and behavior congruent?	2.76	1.19
D. importance of values in understanding human actions?	2.65	1.11
E. overall importance of causal attributions?	2.46	.90
F. importance of attributions in the crime and illness issue?	2.33	1.07
G. attributions and the world of the unborn and the birth formulae?[c]	3.00	1.27

Note. $N = 37$.
[a]Item 1: The response scale ranged from *very strongly agree* (1) to *very strongly disagree* (7). [b]Item 2: The response scale ranged from *very valuable* (1) to *totally useless* (7). [c]For this item, ratings by the two classes were significantly different, $p < .05$.

value of different lives, whereas the "seamless garment" concept, discussed at the event, is a Catholic view that emphasizes the equal value of all human life.

There are many other relevant and fascinating issues in *Erewhon*. One student noted that the story supported the idea of social adaptability. Higgs easily and readily adapted to the strange Erewhonian belief system. Instead of missing a social engagement for illness, he knew to excuse himself with an expression such as "to have the socks," which is a way of saying the urge to shoplift was so great the missing guest had to stay home. This example fits the rule-role model (Goffman, 1959) of human behavior. This theory suggests that human actions should be interpreted as dramatic performances designed to produce certain effects in others. The example is also a good discussion starter on the "natural attitude" as elucidated by the phenomenologist Schutz (1932/1964), and ethnomethodologist Garfinkel (1967). This theory maintains that people are socialized to believe a culturally determined set of commonsense agreements concerning the nature of the world. The natural attitude is adopted when people accept these social conventions for reality and do not question their validity. For example, the natural attitude in the Middle Ages was that the earth is flat and the center of the universe. Sexism, racism, ageism, and speciesism are all current issues that provide good material for a discussion of the natural attitude.

Another major thematic example is Darwin's theory of evolution, which had a strong and profound personal impact on Butler (1812/1983). Five chapters deal with evolution as applied to organisms and machines. Within this topic, one organizing principle used by Butler is intelligence, which is shown to be a more complicated issue than the single-number-IQ people think. Discussions of Gardner's (1983) work would be enriched by Butler's arguments. In the chapter, "The Book of the Machines," Butler made some startlingly accurate predictions about the course of machine evolution, specifically his prediction of computer developments. His speculations on essential issues in judgments of adaptive behavior, personhood, and what is distinctively human are relevant to discussions of evolutionary theory, artificial intelligence, and cognitive psychology.

Psychology instructors looking for a different type of supplementary text could profit from reading *Erewhon*. It contains many incidents that can add a valuable literary dimension to general, developmental, social, and other psychology courses.

References

Butler, S. (1983). *Erewhon*. New York: Penguin Books. (Original work published 1872)

Byrne, D. (1971) . *The attraction paradigm*. New York: Academic.

Fishbein, M., & Ajzen, I. (1975). *Belief, attitude, intention, and behavior: An introduction to theory and research*. Reading, MA: Addison-Wesley.

Gardner, H. (1983). *Frames of mind*. New York: Basic Books.

Garfinkel, H. (1967). *Studies in ethnomethodology*. Englewood Cliffs, NJ: Prentice-Hall.

Goffman, E. (1959). *The presentation of self in everyday life*. Garden City, NY: Doubleday.

Gorman, M. E. (1984). Using *The Eden Express* to teach introductory psychology. *Teaching of Psychology, 11*, 39-40.

Grant, L. (1987). Psychology and literature: A survey of courses. *Teaching of Psychology, 14*, 86-88.

Heider, F. (1946). Attitudes and cognitive organization. *Journal of Psychology, 21,* 107-112.

Jellison, J., & Zeisset, P. (1969). Attraction as a function of the commonality and desirability of a trait shared with another. *Journal of Personality and Social Psychology, 11,* 115-120.

Kohlberg, L., & Kramer, R. (1969). Continuities and discontinuities in childhood and adult moral development. *Developmental Psychology, 12,* 93- 120.

MacLaine, S. (1983). *Out on a limb*. New York: Bantam Books.

McGuire, W. (1981) . The probabilogical model of cognitive structure and attitude change. In R. E. Petty, T. M. Ostrom, & T. C. Brock (Eds.), *Cognitive responses in persuasion* (pp. 291-308). Hillsdale, NJ: Lawrence Erlbaum Associates, Inc.

Morton, T. (1926). *Speed the plough*. London: Oxford University Press.

Schutz, A. (1964). The dimensions of the social world. In A. Brodersen (Ed.; T. Luckmann, Trans.), *Alfred Schutz: Collected papers II, Studies in social theory* (pp. 20-63). The Hague: Nijhoff. (Original work published 1932)

Vonnegur, M. (1975). *The Eden express*. New York: Bantam Books.

Walster (Hatfield), E., Aronson, V., Abrahams, D., & Rottman, L. (1966). Importance of physical attractiveness in dating behavior. *Journal of Personality and Social Psychology, 4,* 508-516.

Note

I thank Joseph Palladino and three anonymous reviewers for their helpful comments.

Self-Monitoring and Commitment to Dating Relationships: A Classroom Demonstration

Jeffry A. Simpson
Texas A&M University

Students are not always aware of the extent to which dispositions are associated with important aspects of social behavior. This classroom demonstration reveals how a certain disposition that students possess (self-monitoring orientation) is meaningfully related to a significant aspect of their lives (commitment in dating relationships). Specifically, this exercise demonstrates that individuals high in self-monitoring tend to adopt an uncommitted orientation to dating relationships, whereas those low in self-monitoring tend to adopt a committed one. The effectiveness of this demonstration and topics for further discussion are highlighted.

Individual differences can be strongly and systematically related to important aspects of social behavior. However, students are not always aware of and may underestimate the extent to which dispositions are associated with significant areas of their lives. One way to highlight the impact of dispositions on social behavior is to show students how a specific disposition they possess relates to an important aspect of their own social behavior. To introduce students to this topic, I use a classroom demonstration that reveals how a widely studied individual difference dimension (self-monitoring orientation) is meaningfully related to an important social behavior (commitment in dating relationships).

Self-monitoring orientation is assessed by an 18-item true/false inventory known as the Self-Monitoring Scale (Snyder, 1974; Snyder & Gangestad, 1986). The scale identifies persons whose behavior tends to be guided by what is socially appropriate in a given situation (high self-monitors) and persons whose behavior tends to be guided by their own attitudes, beliefs, and feelings, regardless of the situation at hand (low self-monitors). High self-monitors tend to endorse items such as, "In different situations and with different people, I often act like very different persons" and "I'm not always the person that I appear to be." Conversely, low self-monitors tend to endorse items such as, "I have trouble changing my behavior to suit different people and different situations" and "I can only argue for ideas that I already believe."

Because their social behavior tends to be guided by relatively stable factors, such as personal attitudes and feelings, low self-monitoring individuals should have stable relationships with persons toward whom they have strong, positive attitudes and feelings (e.g., dating partners). On the other hand, because their social behavior typically is guided by less stable, more transient external factors, such as concerns about social and situational appropriateness, high self-monitoring individuals should have less durable and rather short-term relationships with others. Relationship stability and permanence serve as indicators of commitment to relationships (Kelley, 1983); therefore, self-monitoring should be strongly associated with orientations individuals adopt toward commitment in dating relationships. In fact, high self-monitors typically do adopt an uncommitted orientation to dating relationships, whereas low self-monitors tend to adopt a committed one (Snyder & Simpson, 1984). To demonstrate this association, two studies reported by Snyder and Simpson can be replicated as part of the following classroom demonstration.

Table 1 Dating Survey

1. Are you currently dating someone *exclusively* (that is, one person and no one else)? (Check one.)

    Yes _____   No _____

2. If yes, how many *months* have you dated this person?

    _____

    (If you answer question No. 2, go to Question No. 5. If you did not, go to Question No. 3.)

3. If you are *not* dating one person exclusively at the present time, have you dated at least two different people in the past year? (Check one.)

    Yes _____   No _____

4. If yes, how many different persons have you dated in the past year? _____

5. If you are currently dating someone (whether exclusively or not), please write your current (or most steady) dating partner's initials on the first line below. Then write the initials of 3 opposite-sex friends on the lines that follow.

    Current partner _____

    Friend No. 1 _____

    Friend No. 2 _____

    Friend No. 3 _____

6. If you could *ideally* form a close, intimate dating relationship with either your current dating partner or Friend No. 1, whom would you choose? _____

7. If you could *ideally* form a close, intimate dating relationship with either your current dating partner or Friend No. 2, whom would you choose? _____

8. If you could *ideally* form a close, intimate dating relationship with either your current dating partner or Friend No. 3, whom would you choose? _____

Method

Students first complete the Self-Monitoring Scale. (The scale and its scoring instructions can be found in Snyder & Gangestad, 1986.) Students then respond to a Dating Survey attached to the Self-Monitoring Scale. The Dating Survey is presented in Table 1.

The survey assesses past dating behavior and willingness to change dating partners, both of which are components of commitment to relationships (Kelley, 1983). Students who answer "yes" to the first question on the survey (i.e., those who are dating one person exclusively) are referred to as *exclusive daters.* Students who answer "no" to the first question but "yes" to the third one (i.e., those who are not dating one person exclusively but who have dated at least two people in the past year) are referred to as *multiple daters.* Those who respond "no" to both questions because they are married or do not date cannot provide data for classroom analysis. However, only about 15% to 20% of undergraduates enrolled in daytime courses typically fall into this category. Although these students cannot provide data

Once students have completed the survey, they score their own Self-Monitoring Scale as the high self-monitoring response to each of the items is read out. The scale is keyed in a high self-monitoring direction. Students scoring above the median are classified as high self-monitors, and those scoring below the median are classified as low self-monitors. Students turn to Questions 6 through 8 on the Dating Survey to record the total number of items they selected a friend over the current partner as a preferred dating partner. They then pass all materials to the front of the room.

Results

One of the most desirable features of this exercise is that it allows students to see data generated and analyzed. I first focus on students' responses to Questions 2 and 4 on the Dating Survey, both of which deal with past dating behavior. I create four columns on the chalkboard, one for each of the four groups on which dating history data have been collected. They are: high self-monitoring—exclusive daters, high self-monitoring—multiple daters, low self-monitoring—exclusive daters, and low self-monitoring—multiple daters. The raw data are then written on the chalkboard.

Once the data have been reproduced, a student calculates the mean and variance for each of the four groups. I then compute two *t* statistics, one to test for differences in *the* number of months high and low self-monitoring—exclusive daters have dated the current partner, and one to test for differences in the number of different partners high and low self-monitoring—multiple daters have dated in the past year. Among exclusive daters, low self-monitoring students should report that they have dated their current partner for a significantly longer time than should high self-monitoring students. Among multiple daters, high self-monitoring students should indicate that they have dated a significantly larger number of different persons in the past year than should low self-monitoring students. These outcomes provide support for individual differences in commitment as revealed in past dating behavior.

Occasionally, these *t* tests may not reach significance because of small class sizes or the presence of extreme scores. Under these circumstances, the proportion of high and low self-monitoring students who classified themselves as exclusive and multiple daters can be calculated. I then compute two *z* statistics, one to test for differences in the proportion of high and low self-monitors who are dating someone exclusively, and one to test for differences in the proportion of high and low self-monitors who have dated multiple partners. A larger proportion of students classified as exclusive daters should be low, rather than high, self-monitors. Conversely, a larger proportion of students classified as multiple daters should be high, rather than low, self-monitors. These outcomes provide additional evidence for individual differences in commitment to dating relationships.

I next focus on the total number of friends students chose instead of the current partner as the preferred dating partner. I create two columns on the chalkboard, one for high and one for low self-monitoring students, and list the total number of friends chosen by each respondent. A student then calculates the mean and variance for each of the two groups and I compute a *t* statistic to test for differences in the number of friends chosen in place of the current dating partner by high and low self-monitoring students. High self-monitors should choose a significantly larger number of friends as preferred dating partners than should low self-monitors. This result provides support for individual differences in commitment as revealed in willingness to change dating partners.

When class sizes are small and/or extreme scores exist, I compute a *z* statistic to test for differences in the proportion of high and low self-monitors who express a preference for dating someone other than their current partner. A larger proportion of high, rather than low, self-monitors should express such a preference. This result provides further evidence for individual differences in commitment to dating relationships.

If time does not permit the instructor to analyze the data in class, the data can be analyzed outside of class and the results presented during the next class meeting. Depending on students' familiarity with statistical issues and the content of the course, the instructor may want to present the results in a series of graphs and/or use alternative test statistics (e.g., chi-squares) to analyze the data.

Discussion

This demonstration has several desirable features. First, it tends to replicate well. Second, it is suitable for use in a variety of courses, including personality, social, interpersonal relations, motivation, and human sexuality. Third, men and women do not differ in their responses to the Dating Survey. Fourth, it can be used in classes of 30 or more students. And fifth, students find the exercise interesting and educational.

Students (*N*=60) in one of my recent courses evaluated the demonstration on several dimensions. Using 7-point Likert-type scales ranging from *not at all* (1) to *extremely* (7), students indicated that the demonstration was interesting (*M* = 5.83, *SD* = .86), educational (*M* = 5.33, *SD* = .91), and effective relative to other classroom demonstrations they had participated in (*M* = 5.70, *SD* = .69). Moreover, 58 out of 60 stu-

dents (96.67%) recommended that the demonstration should be used in future courses.

This exercise provides the instructor with a number of follow-up discussion topics. First, it can be used to introduce and discuss additional theory and research on self-monitoring (see Snyder, 1979, 1987, for reviews of self-monitoring research). For example, to clarify why high and low self-monitoring students might adopt different orientations to commitment, the instructor can discuss how self-monitoring is systematically related to other important areas of behavior that might influence commitment (e.g., attitude-behavior consistency). Second, because the demonstration replicates previous work, it gives the instructor an opportunity to discuss the importance of replication in research. When the demonstration does not replicate, the instructor can discuss how sampling variability and extreme responses affect the replication process. Finally, the demonstration can result in a discussion of whether individual differences in commitment are likely to be stable over time and across the life span of whether they are likely to be transient states associated with only one stage of life (the college years).

References

Kelley, H. H. (1983). Love and commitment. In H. H. Kelley, E. Berscheid, A. Christensen, J. H. Harvey, T. L. Huston, G. Levinger, E. McClintock, L. A. Peplau, & D. R. Peterson (Eds.), *Close Relationships* (pp. 265-314). San Francisco: Freeman.

Snyder, M. (1974). The self-monitoring of expressive behavior. *Journal of Personality and Social Psychology, 30,* 526-537.

Snyder, M. (1979). Self-monitoring processes. In L. Berkowitz (Ed.), *Advances in experimental social psychology* (Vol. 12, pp. 85-128). New York: Academic.

Snyder, M. (1987). *Public appearances/private realities: The psychology of self-monitoring.* New York: Freeman.

Snyder, M., & Gangestad, S. (1986). On the nature of self-monitoring: Matters of assessment, matters of validity. *Journal of Personality and Social Psychology, 51,* 125-139.

Snyder, M., & Simpson, J. A. (1984). Self-monitoring and dating relationships. *Journal of Personality and Social Psychology, 47,* 1281-1291.

Writing as a Tool for Teaching Social Psychology

Sara E. Snodgrass
Skidmore College

The process of writing is a highly productive tool for learning the concepts and methods of social psychology. Writing, however, is most often used as an evaluative tool rather than as a teaching tool. This paper describes practical ways in which writing can be used in an introductory social psychology course to enhance the students' learning. Keeping a course log (a type of journal), writing analyses of published articles, doing an observational study, and writing a formal research report are among the ideas presented. The techniques described here can be applied to any course in psychology and are not uniquely applicable to social psychology.

In the typical psychology course, students write examinations and term papers in which writing is used almost exclusively as a tool for the evaluation of their learning. In recent years, the *process* of writing has been suggested as a useful tool, not just for evaluation, but also for learning (e.g., Emig, 1977; Flower, 1981; Irmscher, 1979). The process of writing can be used as a problem-solving tool and as a tool for producing creative and analytical thinking. In addition, Calhoun and Selby (1979) and Costin (1982) have expressed concern over the lack of basic communication and writing skills often found in college undergraduates. Boice (1982), Klugh (1983), Spiegel, Cameron, Evans, and Nodine (1980), among others, have addressed this issue by suggesting that the teaching of writing skills be incorporated into the regular psychology curriculum.

I have integrated writing into my introductory course in social psychology in several ways, primarily for the purpose of giving the students a tool for learning the material, secondarily for the purpose of helping them with their writing skills, and finally for the purpose of evaluation. Writing as a process is integrated into the Introductory Social Psychology course in several ways: (a) the students are required to keep a course log in which they write their reactions to the readings, class films, and demonstrations, ideas for papers and projects, and other "free" writing; (b) the students write two short analyses of journal articles, through which they learn how to find psychological literature in the library and learn ways to approach reading and analyzing journal articles; (c) each student plans and imple-

ments an observational study of some social psychological phenomenon. This project incorporates writing throughout the project's process.

COURSE LOG

The course log serves several different functions. First, it stimulates class discussions. Students are frequently asked to write in their logs for 5-10 minutes in class following a film or a class demonstration, freely writing their feelings about and reactions to what they have just experienced. The ensuing class discussion is always lively, with most students participating. The writing process provides each of them with something to contribute, and their own personal thoughts have already established an element of respect by being written. Spiegel et al. (1980) also report finding that students participate more readily in class discussions after writing for 5-10 minutes.

Second, the logs serve as a workbook as the students read the text. Many of the students choose to follow my suggestion to write out their thoughts about the textbook readings. This provides a means of summarizing the material, giving their own reactions, applying the content to their own lives, and is an excellent source for review for examinations. The first time I used the logs, I collected them and looked over them at the end of the semester to evaluate the technique (rather than to evaluate the students). I found that the students who made the best grades on tests were the ones who used the logs more extensively (taking notes from readings, writing anecdotes that came to mind as they read, etc.). Of course, I could not tell whether the use of the logs helped improve grades on tests, or if students who tend to do well on tests are also the students who will take more notes and do their assignments more conscientiously. Since that first time, I have not looked at the logs. I believe that the students are motivated to use them as they see fit without having to be "checked," and that checking them is likely to decrease their intrinsic motivation and their free expression.

Third, many class demonstrations incorporate writing in the logs. For example, when we study self-perception, we begin by writing 10 answers to the question "Who am I?" in the logs. When studying impression formation, the students describe their first impressions of someone they met at the beginning of the school year and then describe their current impressions, discussing why their impression may have changed. This is written in the logs, not to be turned in, but as "free" writing. When we discuss attitude change and persuasion, the students write what they would say to a good friend to persuade that person not to drive home from a party after heavy drinking. This stimulates discussion on styles of persuasion. Many other class activities incorporate writing in the logs. This procedure makes the material more relevant to their own lives and forces them to think about the material as they write. Hettich (1976, 1980) and Anderson (1982) also report success with the use of autobiographical journal entries as a means of processing class material.

Fourth, when we begin talking about final projects for the course, in which students are to observe unobtrusively some social behavior and collect data to analyze and report, they begin by brainstorming in their logs. The brainstorming is guided; they have to be taught how to brainstorm (i.e., I hand out a "Brainstorming Guide" with questions to guide them as they brainstorm in their logs). I found that after using this method of brainstorming in their logs, very few individual conferences were requested for help in choosing a topic for the projects.

The log is applicable to any content area and any size class. Perhaps in other content areas there are not such obvious assignments for the logs as the everyday social experiences that were used here, but to have the students write their understanding of some portion of a lecture that was particularly complex or particularly important would produce questions that might not surface without the writing process, and would also solidify the material in the students' minds. The use of class logs is one writing technique that is not limited to smaller classes. In fact, through writing in logs, the students in large classes are given the opportunity to react to the material and to express themselves even when class discussion is limited.

GRADED WRITING ASSIGNMENTS

The students are required to turn in five writing assignments throughout the semester; each of these assignments builds on the previous one. Each paper is returned with ample feedback about style, format, references, and citations, as well as content. This feedback is then used to improve the next paper. The first two assignments require students to analyze journal articles, learning to use psychological literature. The last three assignments comprise the final project, in which they design an unobtrusive observational study, collect data, and write a formal research report.

The primary purposes of these assignments are to give the students a tool with which to think about the class material and to teach them to use methods of

scientific inquiry. These assignments teach them to use the psychological literature to pursue their own interests and questions, and to experience the difference between systematic observation of social phenomena and the casual observations we make every day. In other words, students learn how scientific inquiry works and actually experience the process themselves. Cole (1982) addressed this issue when he wrote ". . . teaching the methods of psychology is more valuable to the student than the teaching of whatever psychologists 'know' about human behavior at a given point in time. . . . Content changes. It is the modes of inquiry that offer the surest road to the coping skills [necessary for career advancement in today's job market]" (p. 25).

Analyses of Journal Articles

The first assignment asks students to find and read one of five specified journal articles and to write a 5-page summary and analysis of the article. The assignment is completely described in a handout, giving them questions to consider as they analyze the article, what audience they should direct their writing toward, and the grading criteria. In addition, they are given guides for reading and summarizing journal articles.

The second assignment asks them to choose a topic from class, to find three articles in the library on the topic, and to write a 5-7 page paper summarizing the articles and analyzing their relevance to each other, their relevance to social psychology, and their relevance to life outside the laboratory. These assignments are used to teach the students about social psychological literature, where to find it, how to read it, how to research a specific topic, how to analyze it, and how to write in a psychological format (including citations and references). Again, a complete description of the assignment is handed out, including questions to consider while analyzing the articles, the audience they should direct their writing style toward, and grading criteria. In addition, I give them a guide to finding literature in psychology and a guide to doing references in psychology.

The last three assignments comprise the final project and are the (a) proposal, (b) introduction and methods, and (c) complete research report with abstract and references.

Final Project

This is the students' favorite part of the course. Each student chooses a social psychological phenomenon of interest and designs an unobtrusive observational study to examine the phenomenon. Students think of a hypothesis, research the literature, collect data, and write a formal research report in APA style. Writing is used throughout the project, beginning with brainstorming in the logs. Students turn in a short proposal in which they describe their idea, give a rationale for choosing it, and their initial ideas for how they might collect data. After the proposal is approved, they do a brief literature search on the topic and write a more formal paper, which is similar in format to the introduction and method sections of APA research articles. Feedback on this paper is used in improving their designs and methods of data collection and in improving the introduction and method sections for their final papers. The final project report is due at the end of the semester. This paper is written in formal APA style, including an abstract and references. Because the writing is done in steps, through the proposal and the literature review and methods, the final papers are much easier for the students to write, and the products they turn in are significantly better than when they are merely told to "write a term paper." Extensive handouts are prepared to lead the students through the project. They are given an overall description of the entire project, the brainstorming guide, a description of what I want in the proposal, a thorough description of the introduction and method sections with a step-by-step guide to preparing them, and a guide to the format of the completed report.

The students (predominantly sophomores) get very excited about this project, and course evaluations reveal that this is one of the best parts of the course in their opinions. They often comment that, even though the project is one of the most challenging things they have done, it did not seem so overwhelming a task as typical term papers or final projects because they were led through it step-by-step and were given feedback throughout. Also, the due dates of the three parts prevent them from leaving it all until the end of the semester.

From the teacher's viewpoint, I am extremely pleased with the improved quality of the final papers I receive now, as compared to when my assignment was to "write a term paper" or to "do a research project." The papers are much more carefully written, more reflective of their knowledge of social psychology, and more interesting to read. The students' grades on their final projects are much better as a result of feedback on smaller portions of them.

The graded assignments are also applicable to other areas of psychology. Obviously the analysis of published research articles is appropriate in all areas, but the final project can also be used in developmental psychology by having students collect data through observation of younger siblings or children in a nursery school; in cognition and perception by doing small experiments on roommates and friends; and, with a little creativity, in other areas as well.

SECOND THOUGHTS

Although I am firmly convinced that incorporating writing throughout the course as part of the process of learning is very successful, I admit that there are some negative aspects. The feedback on each assignment is tremendously time-consuming. In order for this to work as intended, each paper must have ample feedback about writing skills, style, content, format, and so on, so that the student can correct as many problems in the next paper as possible. Initially, creating all the guides and handouts took an inordinate amount of time, but I now know it was worth it. The papers I receive are much more interesting to read, are almost always the type of paper I intended, and are much better written, more thoughtful, and more reflective of students' understanding of social psychological concepts than before.

The first class in which I used these assignments had 30 students. I was exhausted at the end of the semester, but very satisfied with the class. The following semester I had 60 students enrolled in two sections of the class (apparently all the writing did not scare the students away). In an attempt at self-preservation, I decided to cut the number of writing assignments on which I had to give such detailed feedback by giving the students a grading option. Those who wanted an A for the course had to make an A average and do the final project with the three writing assignments to be turned in (proposal, introduction, and methods, which included journal article analysis, and final research report). Those who wanted a B had to make a B average or above and had to do a library paper (a slightly enlarged version of assignment #2 described above under "Analyses of Journal Articles"). Those satisfied with a C or less could get by with taking the three tests, and doing no writing other than test questions. My plan was that I would get only the best students doing the more extensive writing assignments. My plan failed. Initially, 78% of the students chose option A, to do the final project. After the proposal assignment, I encouraged several of them to take their topics and do library papers instead, and over time several more dropped the research project. I finished with 64% of the class doing the extensive writing assignments. Half of these students made B or C for the course and knew that they had no chance for an A, yet chose to do the project anyway. Apparently, students are not as prone to take the easy way out as we may have believed. I think that this failure of my plan to ease my workload provides strong evidence that using writing as a tool in the process of learning social psychology is appealing to students, and that the improved papers, test grades, and class participation are evidence that it works. However, the use of the graded assignments as described here would not be feasible for large classes (70+) without teaching assistants to help read and provide feedback on the papers. As is true of so many of the better methods of teaching, those that involve extensive feedback are dependent on a small to moderate student-teacher ratio.

Students learn much more about psychology by using these writing techniques. They are actively involved in the material, and writing forces them to think about it and to relate it to their own lives. Examinations are better because the students have actively worked with the material. They leave the course not only knowing much of the content of psychology, but feeling confident that they can use the psychological literature in the future, having great respect for research as a result of their own studies, knowing how to write a psychological paper, and having increased confidence in their own abilities to think analytically about psychological concepts.

References

Anderson, W. P. (1982). The use of journals in a human sexuality course. *Teaching of Psychology, 9*, 105-107.

Boice, R. (1982). Teaching of writing in psychology: A review of sources. *Teaching of Psychology, 9*, 143-147.

Calhoun, L. G., & Selby, J. W. (1979). Writing in psychology: A separate course? *Teaching of Psychology, 6*, 232.

Cole, D. L. (1982). Psychology as a liberating art. *Teaching of Psychology, 9*, 23-26.

Costin, F. (1982). Some thoughts on general education and the teaching of undergraduate psychology. *Teaching of Psychology, 9*, 26-28.

Emig, J. (1977, May). Writing as a mode of learning. *College Composition and Communication, 28*, 122-128.

Flower, L. (1981). *Problem-solving strategies for writing.* New York: Harcourt Brace Jovanovich.

Hettich, P. (1976). The journal: An autobiographical approach to learning. *Teaching of Psychology, 3*, 60-63.

Hettich, P. (1980). The journal revisited. *Teaching of Psychology, 7*, 105-106.

Irmscher, W. F. (1979, October). Writing as a way of learning and developing. *College Composition and Communication, 30*, 240-241.

Klugh, H. E. (1983). Writing and speaking skills can be taught in psychology classes. *Teaching of Psychology, 10*, 170-171.

Spiegel, T. A., Cameron, S. M., Evans, R., & Nodine, B. F. (1980). Integrating writing into the teaching of psychology: An alternative to Calhoun and Selby. *Teaching of Psychology, 7*, 242-243.

Notes

1. An extended version of this paper was presented at the annual convention of the American Psychological Association, August, 1984, Toronto, Ontario, Canada.
2. Copies of all assignments and guides are available from the author.

Table - Volume 3

Articles	Topics												
	1	2	3	4	5	6	7	8	9	10	11	12	13
Personality													
Emphasizing Writing Assignments													
Mueller									S	P	S	S	
Polyson	S									P	S		
Carlson	S									P	S		
Beers							S	S	S	P			S
Polyson	S									P			
Instigating Miscellaneous Techniques													
Embree							S	S	S	P			S
Logan										P			
Bauer & Wachowiak										P			
Einhorn										P			
Handelsman									S	P			S
Hess										P	S		
Carlson	S	S	S	S	S	S	S	S	S	P	S	S	S
Bear										P			
Davidson										P			
Benjamin	S									P			
Abnormal													
Teaching with Simulations													
Fernald	S									S	P	S	
Gardner											P	S	
Deffenbacher											P		
Gilliland	S										P	S	
Lambert & Lenthall											P	S	
Lyons, Bradley, & White											P		
Osberg	S										P		
Rabinowitz											P		
Schofield & Klein											P	S	
Using Field Experiences													
Scogin & Rickard											P		
White											P		
Teaching with Case-Studies													
Perkins											P	S	
Procidano										S	P	S	
Teaching about Suicide													
Domino											P	S	
Hubbard & McIntosh											P	S	
Instigating Miscellaneous Techniques													
Anderson											P		
Chrisler											P	S	
Keutzer,	S	S	S	S	S	S	S	S	S	S	P	S	S
LeUnes											P	S	
Fleming, Piedmont, & Hiam											P		

302

Clinical-Counseling													
Developing Skills Through Simulations and Role Playing Techniques													
Lane												P	
Balleweg												P	
Matthews												P	
Weiss												P	
Rickard & Titley												P	
Sommers-Flanagan & Means												P	
Balch												P	
Ulman												P	
Meck & Ball												P	
Claiborn & Lemberg												P	
Using Computers to Develop Clinical Skills													
Bibace, Marcus, Thomason, & Litt												P	
Suler												P	
Learning About Family Dynamics													
Waters												P	
Kuppersmith, Blair, & Slotnick												P	
Gardner												P	
Using Miscellaneous Techniques													
Smith	S											P	
Viken			S									P	
Schilling			S	S	S	S	S	S	S	S	S	P	S
George, Hosford, & Moss												P	
Goldstein												P	
Hughes	S										S	P	
Hosford, George, Moss, & Urban												P	
Kaczkowski												P	
Klos	S							S	S			P	
Handelsman & Friedlander												P	
Parrott										S		P	
Chute & Bank												P	
Social													
Focusing on Experimentation													
Wann			S										P
Lutsky			S										P
Gordon													P
Illustrating Concepts in Social Perception and Social Cognition													
Costanzo & Archer													P
Berrenberg	S												P
Kite	S												P
Lashley	S												P
Lyons													P
Dunn	S												P
Forsyth & Wibberly													P
McAndrew													P
White & Lilly													P

	1	2	3	4	5	6	7	8	9	10	11	12	13
Teaching about Attitudes and Persuasion													
Carkenord & Bullington													P
Gordon													P
Jones	S												P
Makosky													P
Rajecki													P
Teaching about Aggression													
Benjamin	S		S										P
Davidson													P
Dunn										S			P
Rainey	S												P
Teaching Group Processes													
Goethals & Demorest													P
Larsen													P
Peden, Keniston, & Burke													P
Banziger													P
Miserandino													P
Teaching about Spatial Behavior													
Banziger													P
Ferraro	S												P
Gibson, Harris, & Werner	S												P
Instigating Miscellaneous Techniques													
Dodd	S												P
Grosch & Sparrow													P
Osborn													P
Simpson	S									S			P
Snodgrass									S	S	S	S	P

1	Introductory	8	Cognition
2	Statistics	9	Developmental
3	Research Methods	10	Personality
4	History	11	Abnormal
5	Physiological-Comparative	12	Clinical-Counseling
6	Perception	13	Social
7	Learning		

P = Primary   S = Secondary

Appendix - Volume 3

Personality

Emphasizing Writing Assignments
Mueller, 1985, *12*, 74-78.
Polyson, 1983, *10*, 103-105.
Carlson, 1992, *19*, 153-155.
Beers, 1986, *13*, 75-77.
Polyson, 1985, *12*, 211-213.

Instigating Miscellaneous Techniques
Embree, 1986, *13*,78-80.
Logan, 1988, *15*, 103-104.
Bauer & Wachowiak, 1977, *4*, 190- 192.
Einhorn, 1985, *12*, 101-102.
Handelsman, 1985, *12*, 100-101.
Hess, 1976, *3*, 32-33.
Carlson, 1989, *16*, 82-84.
Bear, 1992, *19*, 174-175.
Davidson, 1979, *6*, 123-125.
Benjamin, 1983, *10*, 94-95.

Abnormal

Teaching with Simulations
Fernald, 1980, *7*, 46-47.
Gardner, 1976, *3*, 141-142.
Deffenbacher, 1990, *17*, 182-185.
Gilliland, 1982, *9*, 120-121.
Lambert & Lenthall, 1988, *15* 132-135.
Lyons, Bradley, & White, 1984, *11*, 41-42.
Osberg, 1992, *19*, 47-48.
Rabinowitz, 1989, *16*, 69-71.
Schofield & Klein, 1975, *2*, 132-134.

Using Field Experiences
Scogin & Rickard, 1987, *14*, 95-97.
White 1977, *4*, 200-202.

Teaching with Case-Studies
Perkins, 1991, *18*, 97-99.
Procidano, 1991, *18*, 164-167.

Teaching about Suicide
Domino, 1980, *7*, 239-240.
Hubbard & McIntosh, 1992, *19*, 163-166.

Instigating Miscellaneous Techniques
Anderson, 1992, *19*, 230-232.
Chrisler, 1992, *19*, 173-174.
Keutzer, 1993, *20*, 45-46.
LeUnes, 1984, *11*, 42-43.
Fleming, Piedmont, & Hiam, 1990, *17*, 185-187.

Clinical-Counseling

Developing Skills Through Simulations and Role Playing Techniques
Lane, 1988, *15*, 162-164.
Balleweg, 1990, *17*, 241-243.
Matthews, 1980, *7*, 47-50.
Weiss, 1986, *13*, 145-147.
Rickard & Titley, 1988, *15*, 139-141.
Sommers-Flanagan & Means, 1987,*14*, 164-166,
Batch, 1983, *10*, 173-174.
Ulman, 1980, *7*, 182-183.
Meck & Ball, 1979, *6*, 185-186.
Claiborn & Lemberg, 1974, *1*, 38-40.

Using Computers to Develop Clinical Skills
Bibace, Marcus, Thomason, & Litt, 1987, *14*, 35-37.
Suler, 1987, *14*,37-39.

Learning About Family Dynamics
Waters, 1979, *6*, 162-164.
Kuppersmith, Blair, & Slotnick, 1977, *4*, 3-6.
Gardner, 1991, *18*, 30-32.

Instigating Miscellaneous Techniques
Smith, 1982, *9*, 238-239.
Viken, 1992, *19*, 108-110.
Schilling, 1983, *10*, 57.
George, Hosford, & Moss, 1978, *5*, 205-207.
Goldstein, 1993, *20*, 108- 111
Hughes, 1990, *17*, 238-240.
Hosford, George, Moss, & Urban, 1975, *2*, 124-127.
Kaczkowski, 1984, *11*, 233-235.
Klos, 1976, *3*, 63-66.
Handelsman & Friedlander, 1984, *11*, 54-56.
Parrott, 1992, *19*, 40-42.
Chute & Bank, 1983, *10*, 99-100.

Social

Focusing on Experimentation
Wann, 1993, *20*, 235-236.
Lutsky, 1993, *20*, 105-107.
Gordon, 1987, *14*, 40-42.

Illustrating Concepts in Social Perception and Social Cognition
Costanzo & Archer, 1991, *18*, 223-226.
Berrenberg, 1987, *14*, 169-170.
Kite, 1991, *18*, 161-164.
Lashley, 1987, *14*, 179-180.
Lyons, 1981, *8*, 173-174.

Dunn, 1989, *16*, 21-22.
Forsyth & Wibberly, 1993, *20*, 237-238.
McAndrew, 1985, *12*, 209-211.
White & Lilly, 1989, *16*, 218-219.

Teaching about Attitudes and Persuasion
Carkenord & Burlington, 1993, *20*, 41-43.
Gordon, 1989, *16*, 209-211.
Jones, 1991, *18*, 231-233.
Makosky, 1985, *12*, 42-43.
Rajecki, 1989, *16*, 16-18.

Teaching about Aggression
Benjamin, 1985, *12*, 40-42.
Davidson, 1990, *17*, 252-253.
Dunn, 1992, *19*, 112-114.
Rainey, 1986, *13*, 138-140.

Teaching Group Processes
Goethals & Demorest, 1979, *6*, 177-179.
Larsen, 1987, *14*, 230-231.
Peden, Keniston, & Burke, 1990, *17*, 235-238.
Banziger, 1984, *11*, 36, 38.
Miserandino, 1992, *19*, 103-106.

Teaching about Spatial Behavior
Banziger, 1982, *9*, 241-242.
Ferraro, 1990, *17*, 124-125.
Gibson, Harris, & Werner, 1993, *20*, 180-181.

Instigating Miscellaneous Techniques
Dodd, 1985, *12*, 89-91.
Grosch & Sparrow, 1992, *19*, 166-168.
Osborn, 1990, *17*, 115-117.
Simpson, 1988, *15*, 31-33.
Snodgrass, 1985, *12*, 91-94.

Subject Index

A

Abnormal psychology
Case studies, 81–86
Field experiences, 73–78, 102–104
Preparing for the Final Exam, 101–102
Role playing, 49–50, 60–61, 64–67
Simulations (see also Abnormal—Role playing), 47–48, 51–60, 62–63, 67–69
Using Feature Films, 104–107
Writing Assignments, 97–100
Aggression, 249–257
Attitudes
Cognitive dissonance, 235–237
Persuasion, 242–246
Stereotyping, 237–242

C

Clinical and Counseling
Birth order, 190–192
Case Studies, 183–186
Clinical Bias, 163–164
Computer simulations, 141–146
Correctional settings, 168–171, 177–180
Family issues, 149–159
Role-playing, 123–133, 136–138
Simulations, 115–123, 133–136, 187–190
Treatment Simulations, 164–166, 174–176
Student Projects, 166–167, 171–174, 193–194
Using Video, 180–183

E

Experimenting in Social Psychology, 201–205